Readings in
Labour Economics

Readings in Labour Economics

EDITED READINGS WITH COMMENTARIES

BY

J. E. KING

OXFORD UNIVERSITY PRESS

1980

331
R 287

Oxford University Press, Walton Street, Oxford OX2 6DP

OXFORD LONDON GLASGOW
NEW YORK TORONTO MELBOURNE WELLINGTON
KUALA LUMPUR SINGAPORE JAKARTA HONG KONG TOKYO
DELHI BOMBAY CALCUTTA MADRAS KARACHI
NAIROBI DAR ES SALAAM CAPE TOWN

Published in the United States by
Oxford University Press, New York

British Library Cataloguing in Publication Data

Readings in labour economics.
    1. Labor supply – Addresses, essays, lectures
    I. King, John Edward
    331.1'2'08   HD5706   79-41096

    ISBN 0-19-877132-0
    ISBN 0-19-877133-9 Pbk

Typesetting by Anne M. Joshua, Oxford
and Printed in Great Britain by
Richard Clay (The Chaucer Press) Ltd,
Bungay, Suffolk

Foreword

Labour economics has always been disputed territory, a battle-field normally occupied by the massed ranks of the neoclassical armies, though never securely and always subject to attack. In selecting the readings in this volume, and the introductory notes, I have tried to convey something of the atmosphere of this guerilla warfare between orthodox theory and its critics.

Problems of individual labour supply form the subject of section 1, where the readings outline the essential features of human capital theory and indicate some of its limitations. The second section assumes a basic knowledge of the neoclassical analysis of labour demand, and concentrates instead on refinements to and difficulties with marginal productivity theory. Section 3 deals with the theory and practice of trade unionism, an area in which orthodox economists have (with good reason) felt ill at ease. Out of the interactions between workers, firms and unions, emerges the structure of earnings from employment, various dimensions of which are covered by the readings in the fourth section. Section 5 shifts the emphasis to a higher level of aggregation, focusing on such macroeconomic aspects of the labour market as inflation, unemployment, and the relative income shares of labour and property.

The perceptive reader will soon discover the boundaries between the five sections to be rather artificial. Thus the supply of (section 1) and demand for labour (section 2) are interdependent, most obviously where questions of effort and work incentives are concerned. Equally, it is unsatisfactory to discuss the economic impact of unions (in section 3) in abstraction from patterns of pay differentials (reserved to section 4) or from the theories of inflation and distribution (section 5). Evidently the subject-matter of labour economics does not lend itself to tidy classification. Nor are the controversies paraded in these readings easily resolved. Neoclassical economists and their critics come into conflict, and some blood is shed, but there is no decisive battle: no one ever wins (or loses). Genuinely peaceful co-existence, however, may be impossible; on this, as on all the other issues raised by these selections, readers will have to decide for themselves.

I am much indebted to John Corina for constant stimulation (especially with respect to section 1), and also to Andrew Schuller of Oxford University Press for his encouragement, understanding and remarkable patience.

Melbourne,   *J. E. King.*
July 1979.

Acknowledgements

Bibliographical details of each extract are given as footnotes. Permission is gratefully acknowledged from the following:

1.1 Columbia University Press
1.2 National Bureau for Economic Research
1.3 University of Chicago Press. Copyright © 1962 by University of Chicago Press
1.4 P. C. Langley, Longman Group Ltd. and the Editor
1.5 *Indian Economic Journal*
1.6 American Telephone and Telegraph Company
1.7 G. J. Stigler and The American Economic Association
2.1 W. Y. Oi and University of Chicago Press. © 1962 by University of Chicago Press
2.2 Lexington Books, D. C. Heath and Company, Copyright © 1971 by D. C. Heath and Company
2.3 The Rand Corporation and D. C. Heath and Company
2.4 Macmillan, London and Basingstoke and Basic Books, Inc., Publishers. © 1975 by Basic Books, Inc., Publishers
2.5 American Telephone and Telegraph Company and The Free Press.
3.1 Harvard University Press. Copyright © 1951, 1955 by the President and Fellows of Harvard College
3.2 P. D. Bradley
3.3 R. O. Hieser and The Economic Society of Australia and New Zealand
3.4 M. Bronfenbrenner and the *Southern Economic Journal*
3.5 C. Mulvey and J. I. Foster and *The Manchester School*
3.6 *British Journal of Industrial Relations*
4.1 National Bureau of Economic Research, Inc.
4.2 Lester C. Thurow. © 1972 by National Affairs, Inc.
4.3 Oxford University Press. © 1977 by Oxford University Press
4.4 National Bureau of Economic Research, Inc.
4.5 Michael Bradfield and The Regional Science Research Institute
4.6 The M.I.T. Press, Cambridge, Massachusetts.
4.7 M.C.B. Journals. © 1975 by M.C.B. Journals; all rights reserved.
4.8 H. M. Wachtel, C. Betsey and North Holland Publishing Company
4.9 A. G. King and *Southern Economic Journal*
4.10 Glen G. Cain and the American Economic Association
5.1 New York State School of Industrial and Labor Relations. © 1973 by New York State School of Industrial and Labor Relations
5.2 Macmillan, London and Basingstoke and W. W. Norton and Company Inc. Copyright © 1970 by W. W. Norton and Company Inc.
5.3 Heinemann Educational Books Ltd.
5.4 Longman Cheshire Pty Limited.
5.5 M. Friedman and University of Chicago Press. © 1966 by University of Chicago Press
5.6 *Economica*

5.7   D. Maki and Z. A. Spindler and Oxford University Press. © 1975 by Oxford University Press
5.8   P. B. Doeringer and M. J. Piore. © 1975 by National Affairs, Inc.
5.9   Macmillan, London and Basingstoke
5.10   *Kyklos Verlag*

Contents

1. The Worker

Introductory Note

THERE is a sense in which the scarcity of time is the essence of all economic problems. Certainly it is at the heart of labour economics, which concerns itself with the allocation and remuneration of time spent at work. This is a multi-dimensional question. There is evidently a geographical dimension, for people must choose the region and locality in which they will work. They must choose, too, a specific employer within their chosen locality: this is the work-place dimension. The occupational dimension of labour supply concerns the acquisition and use of skills at work, while the effort dimension requires a choice as to the intensity at which work is to be performed. Finally, and most familiarly, there is the quantitative dimension: how many hours of labour (if indeed any at all) are to be supplied?

The quantitative dimension lends itself most readily to formal analysis. Assume, like an earlier generation of economists, that an isolated individual is faced with just two demands on his (her) time, work (H) and leisure (L). Work is rewarded by wage income (Y), with which utility-yielding commodities can be bought, but it involves the sacrifice of leisure time, from which the individual also derives utility. This is a simple problem of maximization subject to constraints, of the type well known in consumer theory. The individual maximizes the utility function

$$U = U(Y,L) \tag{1}$$

subject to a *time constraint* requiring that all available time ($\bar{T}$) be spent either at work or at leisure:

$$\bar{T} = H + L \tag{2}$$

and an *expenditure constraint* limiting expenditure on commodities (in the absence of unearned income) to total earnings from work:

$$Y = wH \tag{3}$$

where w is the hourly wage rate. The two constraints may be combined[1] into a single *budget constraint*:

$$Y = w(\bar{T} - L). \tag{4}$$

The line $A\bar{T}$ in Figure 1.1 is one such constraint. It shows all the combinations of income and leisure open to the individual given the hourly wage rate (w). From the utility function, indifference curves such as I_1I_1 may be derived, showing the various combinations of income and leisure which yield equal levels of utility. Subject to the budget constraint, the individual moves to the highest available indifference curve, and is in equilibrium at P, spending $B\overline{T}$ hours daily at work (for a daily income of OC) and enjoying OB hours of leisure.

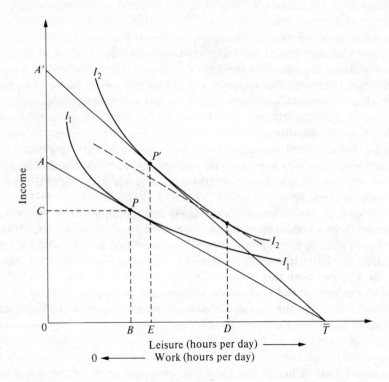

FIG. 1.1

More formally, to maximize (1) subject to (4) we form the Lagrangeian

$$U^* = U(Y,L) + \lambda[w(T-L) - Y] \qquad (5)$$

and set the partial derivatives equal to zero, obtaining, after manipulation, the first-order condition for a maximum:

$$w = \frac{\partial u}{\partial L} \Big/ \frac{\partial u}{\partial y}. \qquad (6)$$

This states that the real wage must equal the ratio of the marginal utilities of leisure and income. In terms of Figure 1.1, it means that the slope of the budget line $A\overline{T}$ must, in equilibrium, equal the slope of the indifference curve, as is the case at P.[2]

Clearly the wage rate is to be interpreted as the price of leisure in terms of income. If it increases there will be both income and substitution effects. A higher income can now be earned for any given number of working hours. On the safe assumption that leisure is not an inferior good, this will lead to a reduction in hours of work (that is, to an increase in hours of leisure). But the price of leisure has increased simultaneously, which will necessarily induce a reduction in leisure time (an increase in hours of work). The total or wage effect cannot be determined *a priori*, since it depends on whether the income effect outweighs the substitution effect, or vice versa. In Figure 1.1 the higher wage rate establishes the new budget line $A'\overline{T}$ and a new equilibrium position at P'. In this case the strong income effect (BD) has outweighed the relatively weak substitution effect (DE) to reduce hours of work (increase hours of leisure) by BE. In this case the individual's labour supply curve has a 'perverse' shape, sloping upwards from right to left. But this only illustrates one possibility. It is equally likely that the substitution effect outweighs the income effect, giving the 'normal' supply curve sloping upwards from left to right (see Vatter, 1961).

This simple analysis can be readily extended to allow for the receipt of unearned income, the payment of overtime premiums, and the phenomenon of multiple job-holding · or 'moonlighting'. It is also possible to examine the implications of restricting the worker's freedom to vary hours of work by employer-imposed standard working weeks (on all these issues see Perlman, 1969). Equally, it is a relatively simple matter to take into account the interdependence of the labour supply decisions of family members (see Cohen *et al.*, 1970). The most simple case is that of a two-adult nuclear family. An increase in the husband's wage rate will produce an income effect and a substitution effect on the husband's labour supply, which will take the form described above. But there will also be repercussions on the labour supply decisions of his wife. We would expect the wife to spend less time at work, both because there has been a *ceteris paribus* increase in household income, and because an hour of her husband's labour now earns more income than before (relatively to an hour of her own time). In other words, there is a 'cross-income effect' and a 'cross-substitution effect' on the wife's labour supply. Both effects induce her to spend less time at work, the first because the household as a whole will consume more leisure now that its income has increased, and the second because the husband will tend to substitute his better-paid labour time for that of his wife. An increase in the woman's relative wage rate will have analogous effects upon the labour supply behaviour of men, which suggests that equal pay legislation may have something to do with the progressive dissolution of traditional sex roles.

The labour supply decisions of any one family member, then, will depend on the wage rates available to all other household members. More fundamental changes must be made to the analysis if the traditional dichotomy between 'work' and 'leisure' is deemed inadequate. There are in fact *three* broad categories into which our use of time can be divided: market work, non-market work, and consumption. Market work is simply labour time sold to an employer for a wage. Non-market work takes place outside the sphere of market transactions when, for instance, time is spent in housework, child care, or 'do-it-yourself' activities. The third category, consumption time, serves to remind us that most leisure activities require the consumption of commodities, and that the consumption of commodities invariably requires the expenditure of time. In effect 'the human being is a multi-product firm' (Fisher, 1971, p. 7), a small factory in which inputs of time and commodities are combined to produce utility-yielding activities, whether these be clean houses and hot meals (as in the case of non-market work), or full stomachs and contented minds (consumption).

Reading 1.1 gives a brief sample of Linder's lively interpretation of the problems of time scarcity (a more indigestible version is that of Becker, 1965; see also Gronau, 1977). Note that Linder's two categories, 'culture time'and 'idleness', may be treated as subclasses of consumption time with, respectively, very low and zero 'goods-intensity' (that is, very low and zero inputs of commodities per unit of time). The logic of individual choice dictates, as Linder observes, that the marginal productivity of time be equal in every activity. The real wage rate — representing the marginal product of an hour spent in market work — has increased substantially over the last century. The marginal utility of consumption time has kept pace largely because it has become more goods-intensive, with more and more commodities consumed each hour. The increase in the marginal utility of time devoted to non-market work seems to have come about in two ways: a reduction in the amount of time spent in such activities as housework, and a technical revolution which has greatly increased its productivity. At all events, tranquillity is not among the fruits of economic growth; hence the paradox of the 'harried leisure class', frantically maximizing its utility but far from happy.

'Labour-saving' gadgets, which are really *time-saving* devices, play a prominent part in Mincer's classic analysis of the secular increase in the labour force participation rate of married women (Reading 1.2).[3] Mincer suggests that this phenomenon (which is international) is largely explained by the long-term increase in women's real wage rates. The simple own-substitution effect, favouring an increase in the supply of time to market work, has been reinforced by women's ability to substitute commodities for their time in non-market work, due to the invention of labour-saving applicances. Mincer's argument has not gone unchallenged. The empirical estimation of labour supply functions (with which a large part of his paper is concerned) comes up against an identification problem unless it can be assumed that the relevant demand functions are stable (Feldstein, 1968). It may be that the long-term increase in the participation rate of married women has come about more as a result of increased *demand* for female labour than of supply shifts like those analysed by Mincer (see Madden, 1972). This possibility raises the further question of the rationale for discrimination by employers (in this case between men and women), about which more will be said below (see Reading 2.3).

The non-market work activities discussed thus far have been of the type which yield utility now rather than in the future. When time is devoted to activities the benefits of which accrue in the future, a 'human investment' is being made, and 'human capital' is being accumulated. This may be thought of as a specific, and extremely important, form of non-market work. Time spent in education and formal training provides the most obvious example. Students' time could have been allocated to market work, to consumption, or to other forms of non-market work with immediate benefits. It is instead committed to the acquisition of knowledge which will enhance their utility in the future, most often by increasing their earning capacity in market work, but perhaps also by raising their productivity in non-market work (car maintenance courses) or even in consumption (amateur music classes).

The rational individual will acquire skills and abilities in such a way as to maximize total utility over his (her) lifetime, discounted at the appropriate rate. The implications of this statement are illustrated in Figure 1.2 (adapted from Thurow, 1970, p. 76). 'Present' and 'future' periods are assumed to be equal in length, but human investments can be made only in the former. If no such investments are made, consumption in both periods is the same, so that $OB = OC$ (here consumption is best regarded as a set of *activities*, involving both time and commodities). If some time is devoted to acquiring skills, present consumption is sacrificed in favour of higher consumption in the future. $BPP'E$ is the individual's inter-temporal budget constraint, the concave section $PP'E$ representing the (diminishing) returns to successive increments of investment in education or training. I_1I_1 and I_2I_2 are inter-temporal indifference curves, which show combinations of present and future consumption between which the individual is indifferent. The rational individual will choose that combination of present and future consumption which is represented by P', devoting AB to human investment which raises future consumption by CD. Here the marginal rate of substitution between present and future consumption (which equals the slope of I_2I_2) is equal to the marginal rate of return on human investment (which is equal to the slope of $PP'E$, that is, the marginal rate at which present consumption can be turned into future consumption).[4] If the individual is able to borrow in order to finance human investment, it is not difficult to show that in equilibrium the marginal rate of return on the investment must equal the rate of interest on the loan (see Thurow, 1970, who is rightly critical of the implicit assumption of a perfect market in such loans).

In addition to skills, the worker requires knowledge concerning the existence and nature of job opportunities. Unless, indeed, we are dealing with only the most general non-vocational education, these two requirements are interdependent. Why learn a skill unless one expects there to be a market for it? As a theory of occupational choice, then, human capital analysis must also serve as a theory about the acquisition of information.

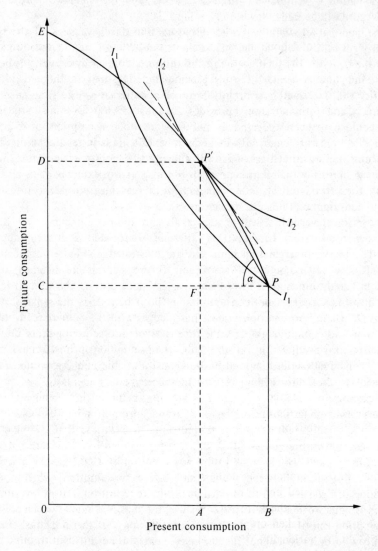

FIG. 1.2

At the simplest level, ignoring for convenience the occupational dimension, the worker needs to know the wage rates offered by different employers in the locality. Such information is rarely available without cost; not, at least, if time must be devoted to its pursuit, time which could have been spent in market or non-market work or in consumption. In Reading 1.3 Stigler argues that job search is a form of human investment to which time will be allocated until the expected marginal return from time spent in further search activities falls below its opportunity cost. Stigler's influential paper contains important implications for the analysis of wage differentials in local labour markets (see Readings 4.6 and 4.7) and for the theory of unemployment (see Readings 5.2, 5.7, and 5.8).

A wide range of labour market problems can be approached from a similar perspective. One is the theory of migration, to which human investment analysis was first applied by Sjaastad (1962). Moving home is a costly business, in terms of both time and money, and can be considered as rational behaviour only if it yields a return to the migrant. The most obvious form which might be taken by such a return is increased pay over his or her working life in the destination region. Such returns constitute part of the migrant's human capital, and Langley (Reading 1.4) finds that the pattern of inter-regional mobility in Britain can be explained in this way. Migration is found to be strongly influenced by the expected monetary returns to it (indicated by the level and variability of earnings in the origin and destination regions), and by its costs (as reflected in the distance to be travelled).

It is significant that Langley does not (indeed, cannot) claim his results as evidence that the marginal migrant is the individual for whom the (suitably discounted) costs and returns to migration are equal, as they would be if all migrants (and non-migrants) were strict utility maximizers. There are likely to be those who fail to move when they could substantially raise their earnings by so doing. Are they ignorant of the opportunities open to them, consciously placing a high value on old friends and familiar surroundings, or simply 'irrational'? We cannot say. Note, too, the considerable importance and profound ambiguity of Langley's 'migrant stock' variable, which captures *both* the availability of information to the potential migrant *and* the 'real' (non-pecuniary) income derived from contact with friends and relatives. Here are two of the weak spots in the neoclassical theory of labour supply: the failure of the concept of maximization under conditions of uncertainty, and the unsatisfactory treatment of non-pecuniary income. Both, it is clear, have implications far beyond the specific question of labour migration.

Linder himself grappled with the first problem (Linder, 1970, chapter 6). Information is needed before rational decisions can be made. Time is required to gather and assess the information. But time is valuable, so that decisions must *inevitably* be taken on the basis of incomplete information. Hence what Linder calls the 'rationality of irrationality': the greater the opportunity cost of time, the less rational it would be to take 'rational' decisions. He gives a trivial (but telling) example. How often these days do people bother to check their change? And who is the 'irrational' one: the customer who blithely accepts the risk of loss through being short-changed, or the one who squanders precious time counting the pennies when the chances of gaining anything thereby are so small? It is not at all clear, Linder suggests, what 'rationality' *means* under conditions of uncertainty.

In Reading 1.5 Rubin demonstrates, briefly but incisively, that this problem, writ large, renders indeterminate the whole theory of time allocation. Stigler

(Reading 1.3) claims to meet this objection, but in fact offers no solution. While postulating a probability-distribution of job offers as a substitute for knowledge of the full array of offers, he gives no indication as to how the probability-distribution itself might be known, nor, indeed, whether it would be sensible for an individual to attempt to discover it. In effect Stigler simply conflates *risk* and *uncertainty*, which evades the problem (see Shackle, 1955). The labour economists of the 1950s frequently concluded that most workers are inert, non-maximizing, non-participants in the labour market; having found a job they cling to it, seemingly oblivious of better opportunities elsewhere. Generally dismissed as inconsequential (see, for example, Rottenberg, 1956), these observations may perhaps be interpreted as evidence of the pervasiveness of uncertainty in the labour market, and of workers' intelligent — if not strictly 'rational' — reactions to it.

On the surface the second problem is less intractable. It is of special importance in the context of the inherent utility (disutility) of market (and non-market) work, a question which is entirely ignored in the elementary work-leisure model discussed earlier, but which presumably plays a significant part in determining the allocation of time between different uses. In principle the intrinsic pleasure or pain associated with different types of work can be incorporated into the model, at the cost only of an increase in complexity in the individual's utility function (Evans (1972) presents a simple version, and Becker (1965) a more general but also more cumbersome model). In practice the non-pecuniary elements in jobs, as in migration decisions, have proved almost impossible to quantify, and this has bedevilled all empirical studies of (for example) wage differentials and labour mobility within the local labour market (see Readings 4.6 and 4.7). Strictly speaking, competitive labour markets in which information is perfect and all workers behave rationally are not in equilibrium until 'net advantages' (pecuniary and non-pecuniary taken together) have been equalized in all jobs. As there is no way in which anyone might establish whether this is the case, discussion has wandered up either or both of two blind alleys. One is the assertion that equilibrium entails *wage* equalization, which is false but has testable implications. The other involves converting the statement that workers act rationally — that is, maximize utility — into a tautology, which renders any testing entirely irrelevant.

These are negative and destructive criticisms, albeit inescapable ones. On a more positive note, it can be suggested that orthodox theory has overlooked an entire dimension of labour supply in its neglect of work effort. Employers buy time, or the worker's availability for work; they do not buy work itself, or job performance. (As Marx puts it, the worker sells labour power, not labour.) Since no job is completely machine-paced, and intensive supervision is self-defeating, every worker enjoys some degree of discretion in the performance of his or her job. The worker thus supplies effort as well as time, and both are crucial to the determination of output. Leibenstein (Reading 1.6) regards his analysis of effort levels as a contribution to welfare economics and the theory of economic efficiency. It is, perhaps, even more relevant to labour economics. Once the traditional engineering relationship between work hours and output is denied, a vast new subject area (formerly the exclusive province of the organisation theorist) is opened to the labour economist. Stigler (Reading 1.7) is worried about the opening of such a Pandora's box, and is sitting hard on the lid. The reader will have to decide whether Stigler's treatment of work effort as merely a facet of 'technology' is a valuable insight or a characteristic Chicagoan evasion.

NOTES

1. But only on the assumption that work is 'neutral', that is, that it is intrinsically neither pleasant nor unpleasant; see Evans (1972).
2. Totally differentiating equation (1) we have

$$dU = \frac{\partial U}{\partial Y} \cdot dY + \frac{\partial U}{\partial L} \cdot dL.$$

Along any indifference curve $dU = O$, so that the slope of the indifference curve is

$$\frac{dY}{dL} = \frac{\partial U}{\partial L} \bigg/ \frac{\partial U}{\partial Y}$$

which is equal to the ratio of the marginal utilities of leisure and income.
3. For a more general discussion of the labour force participation decision, including the disputed question of cyclical fluctuations in participation rates, see Bowen and Finegan (1969) and Bowers (1975).
4. Note that the *average* rate of return to the investment is

$$\frac{CD - AB}{AB} = \frac{CD}{AB} - 1,$$

equal to

$$\frac{FP' - PF}{PF} = \frac{FP'}{PF} - 1, \text{ or } \tan \alpha.$$

REFERENCES

Becker, G. S. (1965) 'A Theory of the Allocation of Time', *Economic Journal*, 75, pp. 493–517.

Bowen, W. G. and Finegan, T. A. (1969) *The Economics of Labor Force Participation*, Princeton University Press.

Bowers, J. K. (1975) 'British Activity Rates: a survey of research', *Scottish Journal of Political Economy*, 22, pp. 57–90.

Cohen, M. S., Rea, S. A., and Lerman, R. I. (1970) *A Micro Model of Labor Supply*, Washington D.C., United States Department of Labor.

Evans, A. W. (1972) 'On the Theory of the Valuation and Allocation of Time', *Scottish Journal of Political Economy*, 19, pp. 1–17.

Feldstein, M. (1968) 'Estimating the Supply Curve of Working Hours', *Oxford Economic Papers*, 20, pp. 74–80.

Fisher, M. L. (1971) *The Economic Analysis of Labour*, London, Weidenfeld and Nicolson.

Gronau, R. (1977) 'Leisure, Home Production and Work: the theory of the allocation of time', *Journal of Political Economy*, 85, pp. 1099–1123.

Linder, S. B. (1970) *The Harried Leisure Class*, New York, Columbia University Press.

Madden, J. F. (1972) *The Economics of Sex Discrimination*, Durham, North Carolina, Duke University Press.

Perlman, R. (1969) *Labor Theory*, New York, Wiley.

Rottenberg, S. (1956) 'On Choice in Labor Markets', *Industrial and Labor Relations Review*, 9, pp. 183–99.

Shackle, G. L. S. (1955) *Uncertainty in Economics*, Cambridge University Press.

Sjaastad, L. A. (1962) 'The Costs and Returns of Human Migration', *Journal of Political Economy*, 70 (Supplement), pp. 80–93.

Thurow, L. C. (1970) *Investment in Human Capital*, Belmont, California, Wadsworth.

Vatter, H. G. (1961) 'On the Folklore of the Backward-Sloping Supply Curve', *Industrial and Labor Relations Review*, 14, pp. 578–86.

1.1 The Increasing Scarcity of Time*

> Good-by, Sir, excuse me, I haven't time.
> I'll come back, I can't wait, I haven't time.
> I must end this letter — I haven't time.
> I'd love to help you, but I haven't time
> I can't accept, having no time.
> I can't think, I can't read, I'm swamped, I haven't time
> I'd like to pray, but I haven't time.
>
> Michel Quoist[1]

THE PARADOXES OF AFFLUENCE

We had always expected one of the beneficent results of economic affluence to be a tranquil and harmonious manner of life, a life in Arcadia. What has happened is the exact opposite. The pace is quickening, and our lives in fact are becoming steadily more hectic. It used to be assumed that, as the general welfare increased, people would become successively less interested in further rises in income. And yet in practice a still higher economic growth rate has become the overriding goal of economic policy in the rich countries, and the goal also of our private efforts and attitudes. At the same time, much of our expenditure is no longer subject to any very careful consideration, as is clear from the successes noted by Madison Avenue. A growing proportion of the labor force is employed in the service sector, but in spite of this, our resources are in fact less well 'serviced' or maintained than ever. It is becoming increasingly difficult, for instance, for elderly people to obtain the special kind of service — care and attention — that they very much need. Our so-called service economy practices in reality a throw-away system at all levels, including the human level. We have long expressed hopes that the elimination of material cares would clear the way for a broad cultural advancement. In practice, not even those endowed with the necessary intellectual and emotional capacity have shown any propensity for immersing themselves in the cultivation of their minds and spirit. The tendency is rather the reverse.

*From S. B. Linder, *The Harried Leisure Class* (New York: Columbia University Press, 1970).

These are but a few examples of the surprising phenomena occurring in the rich countries. They seem paradoxical, as they fail to fit into the picture of affluence which we have painted. The cause of these and similar modern anomalies lies in a circumstance that has been entirely ignored, namely the increasing scarcity of time. The limited availability of time and the increasing claims made on it mean that our affluence is only *partial* and not total as we seem to believe. Our affluence takes only the form of access to *goods*. The idea of 'total affluence' is a logical fallacy.

TIME AS A SCARCE COMMODITY

In the natural sciences, the concept of time offers its particular mysteries. The ultimate implications of time, however, are a problem upon which we need not linger. It will be sufficient for our purposes to accept that there exists what we experience as a time dimension — a moving belt of time units which makes resources of time available to the individual as it passes. Time, unlike other economic resources, cannot be accumulated. We cannot build up a stock of time as we build up a stock of capital. As it passes, however, time puts into people's hands something that they can use. In economic terms, there exists a certain 'supply of time.'

But there is also a certain 'demand for time'. Time can be used by individuals in work, with a view to acquiring various goods. Time can also be used in consumption, i.e., the process in which goods are combined with time, in attempts to achieve the ultimate utility in the economic process — material and spiritual well-being. It is important to realize that consumption requires time just as does production. Such pleasures as a cup of coffee or a good stage play are not in fact pleasurable, unless we can devote time to enjoying them.

The scarcity of a commodity is determined by the supply in relation to the demand. Such a scarcity is normally reflected in the price. The demand for gold is high in relation to the supply, and gold, therefore, attracts a considerable price. The supply of sea water, on the other hand, is extremely great in relation to the demand, and sea water accordingly attracts no price at all. As regards the commodity in which we are interested, namely time, we have already noted that there is a certain supply and a certain demand. We can now add that the demand by individuals is usually sufficiently high in relation to the supply to make time a 'scarce commodity' in the economic sense. But if time is an economic utility in short supply, then it must be subject to the economic laws that prevail in the economist's universe. It must be distributed over its different sectors of use — different activities — in accordance with the general principles of economics.

When spending money, one presumably tries to balance one's expenditures in such a way as to obtain the best possible yield. This means that one will probably refrain from spending all one's assets on a single commodity. One will instead distribute one's expenditure over a variety of different goods and services.

The optimum situation will have been reached when it is impossible to increase satisfaction by reducing expenditure in one field and making a corresponding increase in another. A more technical description of this condition of equilibrium would be to say that the marginal utility of one dollar must be the same in all different sectors of expenditure.

In the same way, one tries to economize with one's time resources. They must be so distributed as to give an equal yield in all sectors of use. Otherwise, it would pay to transfer time from an activity with a low yield to one with a high yield and to continue to do this until equilibrium had been reached.

Some of my readers may object, perhaps, that this is a somewhat gross description of how people function. A moment's reflection, however, will reveal that if the reader should for this reason put down the book, such a reaction is in itself evidence that people actually try to allocate their time in order to achieve a maximum yield. Such a reader has the impression that it would be a waste of time to spend a couple of hours reading this essay and, therefore, decides to devote his time to some other, and he hopes better, pursuit.

THE INCREASING SCARCITY OF TIME

The yield on time spent working increases as the result of economic growth. Productivity per hour rises. This means that the time allocation which has represented equilibrium at our previous level of income is disrupted. The yield on time devoted to other activities must also be raised. We are aware that time in production becomes increasingly scarce with economic growth. What we will now claim in addition to this is that changes in the use of time will occur, so that the yield on time in all other activities is brought into parity with the yield on working time. In other words, economic growth entails a general increase in the scarcity of time.

The necessary increase in the yield of time in the nonwork activities can take place in many different ways. To some extent we try to achieve a change in attitudes of a kind that Walter Kerr points out in his book *The Decline of Pleasure*: 'We are all of us compelled to read for profit, party for contacts, lunch for contracts, bowl for unity, drive for mileage, gamble for charity, go out for the evening for the greater glory of the municipality, and stay home for the weekend to rebuild the house.'[2]

A more basic and radical method of raising the yield on time used in consumption is to increase the amount of consumer goods to be enjoyed per time unit. Just as working time becomes more productive when combined with more capital, so consumption time can give a higher yield when combined with more consumer goods. When this happens, the proportion between consumption goods and the time for consumption changes, so that the price of such time rises to the level of the price of time in production. Admittedly, no prices are openly quoted for time in consumption, but the individual will consciously or unconsciously apply in his actions and words what we can call a 'shadow price' to consumption time. This price will go up in step with the productivity of work time.

A critical reader may object that the increasing volume of consumer goods will not necessarily raise the demand for consumption time, but rather the reverse. Many consumer goods, it is claimed, save time. If a household increases its consumption by buying a washing machine, for instance, then the machine will not claim any additional time. It is true that there are many goods of this type. This must be borne in mind when deciding what to classify as 'consumer goods.' We normally mean all the goods bought by households. In the present study, however, we are considering a more limited category of goods. By 'consumption goods,' which is the term we shall be using from now on, we mean the definite end products that are combined with time in an attempt to create material or spiritual well-being. Washing machines belong to that category of goods which increases productivity in working life – in this case the work performed within households. We should not make any sharp distinction between activities within households and in production. Many of the former are by nature identical with work in production. Whether productivity rises at places of work within production proper, or in the household, it will have the same effects. The scarcity of time in working life as a whole has increased, and the yield from time in consumption must be increased to create an equilibrium between the yield on time in different sectors. This takes place by an increase in the volume of consumption goods per time unit in consumption.

As already observed, scarce commodities are distributed over different sectors of use in accordance with the principles of economics. Changes in the scarcity of different resources lead to changes in the distribution of resources. These changes, too, follow economic laws. The consequences of an increasing scarcity of time can, therefore, be studied with simple tools borrowed from the practice of economic analysis. [. . .]

It is indeed interesting to see how poorly incorporated free time is in economic theory. To give an example, one ambitious statistical study (by Gordon C. Winston) on the relationship between working time and level of income in different countries makes a distinction between the time used 'either on the earning of income (work), or on a host of alternative noneconomic activities (leisure).' To speak of nonworking time as a noneconomic use of time is symptomatic. The very term free time suggests a failure to realize that consumption time is a scarce commodity.[3]

That consumption is regarded as some sort of instantaneous act emerges most clearly from the fact that, when economists try to state the connection between the 'utility' of a certain commodity and the amount of that commodity available, they never take into account the time an individual has at his disposal to consume the commodity in question. In economic theory, the pleasure an individual can be expected to derive from a couple of theatre tickets is not taken to be dependent in any way on the time he can devote to playgoing. At most, economic writers take into account the time needed for consumption by pointing out that the utility of a product depends on the length of the time period within which it is to be enjoyed. 'Different levels of satisfaction are derived from consuming ten portions of ice cream within one hour and within one month.' This point made by J. M. Henderson and R. E. Quandt in their textbook is, however, by no means sufficient. It is not enough to know whether portions of ice cream are to be consumed within a month or within a year. It is far more important to know how much time within a given period can be specifically devoted to enjoying the commodity whose contribution to our material well-being we are studying. If one has no time during a whole week to drink coffee, then obviously even whole sacks full of coffee will give no yield that week. Similarly, a tennis player has no use for a new racket each year, if he never has the time to play. The utility of theatre tickets cannot be established without knowing whether or not the ticket holder has time to use them. What makes the difference is not so much the period of time during which a given quantity of the commodity is available, but rather the time that is available during this period to consume the commodity in question.[4]

Now that we have made these critical observations, we can note with satisfaction that a handful of economists has in recent years adopted a new position. Attention is beginning to be paid to the possibility that economic growth causes an increasing scarcity of time. The first, apparently, in this exclusive group was Roy Harrod, who published a short paper on this theme at the end of the fifties. However, no attention was paid to it by the profession and not even by its author either, since he has never followed up the ideas which he had presented. Harrod's thesis was that we may in time be faced with a consumption maximum, owing to an increasing scarcity of time, which is the result primarily of all the servicing and maintenance work required by consumption goods. It is Harrod's idea, puzzling at first sight, which originally triggered the thinking of the present study.[5]

Another economist who has allowed for the fact that consumption takes time and as a result reached interesting results is Jacob Mincer.[6] Only one economist, however, has attempted to formulate a general theory of time allocation. This is Gary Becker, whose work is presented in a paper published in 1965. The basic approach in this book and in Becker's paper are the same. Even though work on this book had reached a relatively late stage before Becker's paper became available, it has naturally been extremely valuable to be able to utilize Becker's line of thinking.[7] [. . .]

A FRAMEWORK FOR DISCUSSION

In the economic land of dreams that many see as the end result of a long process of growth, the inherent thrift of nature would be overcome. It is only by a sort of optical illusion that one can imagine this meanness on nature's part being eliminated in a material Utopia. In an economic heaven, the problem of time will be particularly pressing. We will find there an infinite volume of consumption goods, which pleasure-hungry angels will feverishly try to exploit during the limited time at their disposal per day. That one may in this heaven enjoy eternal life as a consumer fails to alter the situation. This can increase the total satisfaction derived over the course of centuries. What we are interested in, however, is the yield per time unit. To maximize this, time must be carefully stewarded by the servants of epicureanism.

To map the changes that economic growth will cause in the way we employ our time, it is convenient to classify time into different categories. Such a division of time into different areas of use could obviously be very detailed. Any minute classification, however, would be impractical. We will distinguish below between five different categories of time, each of which has been considered unequal from a philosophical point of view. Each of them is affected in different ways by economic growth.

The first category of time is working time or, more specifically, time spent working in specialized production. Such working time is of basic importance to the allocation of time. Like other activities, it claims time that could otherwise be spent in other ways. However, by its effect on the income level of the individual, it also influences the amount of time in demand for other activities. Work time is thus of twofold importance. It affects both the supply and the demand for time on other activities. As the level of productivity in working life changes, work time and the level of income send out impulses for the changes that can be made in allocation of time.

The second category we can call time for personal work. Personal work consists essentially of the production of what we customarily term services. The boundaries between the production of services and goods are elusive, but it is usually drawn. In the industrialized countries, the production of goods is almost entirely specialized. A large proportion of services is also the result of specialized production. We are left, even so, with a considerable number of services to produce on our own. Even the members of Thorstein Veblen's golden leisure class,[8] who by no means lacked the economic resources to buy services, were surely reduced to providing many services for themselves. The scope of personal work of the average earner in a highly industrialized country is surely considerably greater. Personal work can be subdivided into the maintenance of goods and of one's body (sleep, personal hygiene, etc.). We shall be interesting ourselves not only in the total time each individual devotes to personal work, but also to the average maintenance time devoted to consumption goods, i.e., the maintenance time per consumption good.

A third category is consumption time, i.e., the time, the existence of which we must be aware of, in order to see the use of time as an economic problem involving the allocation of limited resources. Just as with time for personal work, there is a correlation between increases in productivity and the demand for consumption time. Again in this case, we shall investigate the changes in consumption time per product.

The fourth component comprises time devoted to the cultivation of mind and spirit, i.e. the various exercises to which the optimistic believers in progress had thought we would devote our affluence. The difference between consumption time and what, for the sake of brevity, we may call culture time is that consumption goods play a central role for consumption time, but only an incidental role for culture time. For this reason, these two time components are affected in different ways by any productivity increase in working life. The distinction between these two components is of even greater importance in that they have been so differently judged in discussions relating to the aims of the economic process.[9]

Finally, we have a time component that is less specific in its nature. It is conceivable that people in the poor countries are subjected to free time in the strict sense of the word, i.e. time that is not utilized. Incomes are so low that people fail to obtain an economic level permitting anything except what we can call passivity during certain periods of the day. Such time can also occur in the rich countries during economic depressions. But even when economic circumstances are such that individuals are in a position to choose freely how they will distribute their time between work and other activities, there can still be what we can call "slacks" in the use of time. This finds expression in the pace at which time is used. If the scarcity of time is not particularly marked, people may find it reasonable to enjoy a relaxed life. We will call this fifth and last category of time idleness. [. . .]

NOTES

1. Michel Quoist, *Prayers of Life*, Logos Books, Gill and Son, Dublin and Melbourne, 1966, p. 76.
2. Walter Kerr, *The Decline of Pleasure*, Simon and Schuster, New York, 1965, p. 39.
3. Gordon C. Winston, 'An International Comparison of Income and Hours of Work,' *Review of Economics and Statistics*, February 1966, p. 28.
4. Many text books do not even bother to mention that the utility of a certain quantity of a product, say, a pound of coffee, depends upon the length of the period within which this quantity is to be consumed. See, however, Lloyd G. Reynolds, *Economics*, revised ed., Richard D. Irwin, Homewood, Ill., 1966, pp. 138–39; and J. M. Henderson and R. E. Quandt, *Microeconomic Theory*, International Student ed. McGraw-Hill and Kōgakusha, New York and Tokyo, 1958, p. 9. But perhaps other text book authors find this fact both self-evident and trivial.
5. Roy F. Harrod (unnamed paper) in Committee for Economic Development, *Problems of United States Economic Development*, Vol. I (mimeo), January 1958, pp. 207–13.
6. J. Mincer, 'Market Prices, Opportunity Costs, and Income Effects,' in *Measurement in Economics. Studies in Mathematical Economics and Econometrics in Memory of Yehuda Grunfeld*, Stanford University Press, Stanford, 1963.
7. Gary S. Becker, 'A Theory of the Allocation of Time,' *Economic Journal*, September 1965, pp. 493–517.
8. Thorstein Veblen, *The Theory of the Leisure Class*, Viking Press, New York, 1899.
9. The Ancient Greek concept of 'leisure' is discussed, e.g., by S. de Grazia, *Of Time*, Ch. I. For a treatment of what is the 'cultural' leisure problem in the U.S. and Soviet Union, see two papers by Paul Hollander, 'Leisure as An American and Soviet Value,' *Social Problems*, Fall 1966, pp. 179–88, and 'The Uses of Leisure,' *Survey – a Journal of Soviet and East European Studies*, July 1966, pp. 40–50.

1.2 Labour Force Participation of Married Women*

INTRODUCTORY: STATEMENT OF THE PROBLEM

On the assumption that leisure time is a normal good, the standard analysis of work-leisure choices implies a positive substitution effect and a negative income effect on the response of hours of work supplied to variations in the wage rate. An increase in the real wage rate makes leisure time more expensive and tends to elicit an increase in hours of work. However, for a given amount of hours worked, an increase in the wage rate constitutes an increase in income, which leads to an increase in purchases of various goods, including leisure time. Thus, on account of the income effect, hours of work tend to decrease. In which direction hours of work change on balance, given a change in the wage rate, cannot be determined *a priori*. It depends on the relative strengths of the income and substitution effects in the relevant range. The single assumption of a positive income elasticity of demand for leisure time is not sufficient to yield empirical implications on this matter.

An empirical generalization which fills this theoretical void is the 'backward-bending' supply curve of labor. This is the notion that on the average the income effect is stronger than the substitution effect, so that an increase in the wage rate normally results in a decreased amount (hours) of work offered by suppliers of labor. Extreme examples of such behavior have been repeatedly observed in underdeveloped countries. On the American scene, several kinds of empirical evidence apparently point to the same relationship:[1] the historically declining work week in industry; historically declining labor force participation rates of young and old males; an inverse relation between wages of adult males and labor force participation rates of females by cities in cross sections; an inverse relation between incomes of husbands and labor force participation of wives, by husbands' incomes, in budget studies. Similar phenomena have been reported from the experience of other modern economies.

The secular negative association between the length of the work week, participation rates of males, and rising real incomes is clearly consistent with the backward-bending supply curve.[2] Whether this is also true of cross-sectional data on males is a question which has as yet received little attention. Superficially, the cross-sectional behavior of females seems similarly capable of being rationalized in terms of a backward-bending supply response, or at least in terms of a positive income elasticity of demand for leisure. Such views, however, are immediately challenged by contradictory evidence in time series. One of the most striking phenomena in the history of the American labor force is the continuing secular increase in participation rates of females, particularly of married women, despite the growth in real income. Between 1890 and 1960 labor force rates of all females fourteen years old and over rose from about 18 per cent

*From Jacob Mincer, 'Labor Force Participation of Married Women: a study of labor supply', in National Bureau for Economic Research, *Aspects of Labor Economics* (Princeton: Princeton University Press, 1962).

to 36 per cent. In the same period rates of married women rose from 5 per cent to 30 per cent, while real income per worker tripled.[3]

The apparent contradiction between time series and cross sections has already stimulated a substantial amount of research. The investigation reported in this paper is yet another attempt to uncover the basic economic structure which is, in part, responsible for the observed relations.

The study starts from the recognition that the concepts of work, income, and substitution need clarification and elaboration before they can be applied to labor force choices of particular population groups, in this instance married women. The resulting analytical model, even though restricted to two basic economic factors, seems capable of explaining a variety of apparently diverse cross-sectional behavior patterns. It also, in principle, reconciles time series with cross-section behavior, though further elaboration is needed for a proper explanation of the former. The empirical focus of the paper is a reinterpretation of old cross-section materials, and an investigation of newly available data generated by the 1950 BLS Survey of Consumer Expenditures.

CONCEPTUAL FRAMEWORK

Work

The analysis of labor supply to the market by way of the theory of demand for leisure time viewed as a consumption good is strictly appropriate whenever leisure time and hours of work in the market in fact constitute an exhaustive dichotomy. This is, of course, never true even in the case of adult males. The logical complement to leisure time is work broadly construed, whether it includes remunerative production in the market or work that is currently 'not paid for.' The latter includes various forms of investment in oneself, and the production of goods and services for the home and the family. Educational activity is an essential and, indeed, the most important element in the productive life of young boys and girls. Work at home is still an activity to which women, on the average, devote the larger part of their married life. It is an exclusive occupation of many women, and of a vast majority when young children are present.

It is, therefore, not sufficient to analyze labor force behavior of married women in terms of the demand for leisure. A predicted change in hours of leisure may imply different changes in hours of work in the market depending on the effects of the causal factors on hours of work at home. Technically speaking, if we are to derive the market supply function in a residual fashion, not only the demand for hours of leisure but also the demand for hours of work at home must be taken into account. The latter is a demand for a productive service derived from the demand by the family for home goods and services. A full application of the theory of demand for a productive service to the home sector has implications for a variety of socioeconomic phenomena beyond the scope of this paper.

Family context

The analysis of market labor supply in terms of consumption theory carries a strong connotation about the appropriate decision-making unit. We take it as self-evident that in studying consumption behavior the family is the unit of analysis. Income is assumed to be pooled, and total family consumption is positively related to it. The distribution of consumption among family members depends on tastes. It is equally important to recognize that the decisions about the production of goods and services at home and about leisure are largely family decisions. The relevant income variable in the demand for home services and for leisure of any family member is total family income. A change in income of some family member will, in general, result in a changed consumption of leisure for the family as a whole. An increase in one individual's income may not result in a decrease in *his* hours of work, but in those of other family members. The total amount of work performed at home is, even more clearly, an outcome of family demand for home goods and for leisure, given the production function at home. However, unlike the general consumption case, the distribution of leisure, market work, and home work for each family member as well as among family members is determined not only by tastes and by biological or cultural specialization of functions, but by relative prices which are specific to individual members of the family. This is so, because earning powers in the market and marginal productivities in alternative pursuits differ among individual family members. Other things equal (including family income), an increase in the market wage rate for some family member makes both the consumption of leisure and the production of home services by that individual more costly to the family, and will as a matter of rational family decision encourage greater market labor input by him (her). Even the assumption of a backward-bending supply curve would not justify a prediction of a decrease in total hours of work *for the particular earner*, if wages of other family members are fixed.

Recognition of the family context of leisure and work choices, and of the home-market dichotomy within the world of work, is essential for any analysis of labor force behavior of married women, and perhaps quite important for the analysis of behavior of other family members, including male family heads. For the present purpose of constructing a simple model of labor force behavior of married women it will be sufficient to utilize these concepts only insofar as they help to select and elucidate a few empirically manageable variables to represent the major forces of income and substitution contained in the market supply function.

Work choices

Let us consider the relevant choices of married women as between leisure, work at home, and work in the market. Income is assumed to have a positive effect on the demand for leisure, hence a negative effect on total amount of work. With the relevant prices fixed, increased family income will decrease total hours of work. Since the income effect on the demand for home goods and services is not likely to be negative,[4] it might seem that the increased leisure means exclusively a decrease in hours of work in the market. Such a conclusion, however, would require a complete absence of substitutability between the wife and other (mechanical, or human) factors of production at home, as well as an absence of substitution in consumption between home goods and market-produced goods. Domestic servants, laborsaving appliances, and frozen foods contradict such assumptions. Substitutability is, of course, a matter of degree. It may be concluded therefore that, given the income elasticity of demand for home goods and for leisure, the extent to which income differentially affects hours of work in the two sectors depends on the ease with which substitution in home production or consumption can be carried out. The lesser the substitutability the weaker the negative income effect on hours of work at home, and the stronger the income effect on hours of work in the market.

Change in this degree of substitutability may have played a part in the historical development. At a given moment of time, the degree of substitutability is likely to differ depending on the content of home production. Thus substitutes for a mother's care of small children are much more difficult to come by than those for food preparation or for physical maintenance of the household. It is likely, therefore, that the same change in income will affect hours of market work of the mother more strongly when small children are present than at other times in the life-cycle.

While family income affects the total amount of work, the market wage rate affects the allocation of hours between leisure, the home, and the market. An increase in the real wage rate, given productivity in the home, is an increase in prices (alternative costs) of home production as well as of leisure in terms of prices of wage goods. To the extent of an existing substitution between home goods and wage goods such a change will lead to an increase in work supplied to the market. Again, the strength of the effect is a matter of the degree of substitution between wage goods and home production.

Temporal distribution of work

In a broad view, the quantity of labor supplied to the market by a wife is the fraction of her married life during which she participates in the labor force. Abstracting from the temporal distribution of labor force activities over a woman's life, this fraction could be translated into a probability of being in the labor force in a given period of time for an individual, hence into a labor force rate for a large group of women.

If leisure and work preferences, long-run family incomes, and earning power were the same for all women, the total amount of market work would, according to the theory, be the same for all women. Even if that were true, however, the *timing* of market activities during the working life may differ from one individual to another. The life cycle introduces changes in demands for and marginal costs of home work and leisure. Such changes are reflected in the relation between labor force rates and age of woman, presence, number and ages of children. There are life-cycle variations in family incomes and assets which may affect the timing of labor force participation, given a limited income horizon and a less than perfect capital market. Cyclical and random variations in wage rates, employment opportunities, income and employment of other family members, particularly of the head, are also likely to induce temporal variations in the allocation of time between home, market, and leisure. It is not surprising, therefore, that over short periods of observation, variation in labor force participation, or turnover, is the outstanding characteristic of labor force behavior of married women.

To the extent that the temporal distribution of labor force participation can be viewed as a consequence of 'transitory' variation in variables favoring particular timing, the distinction between 'permanent' and current levels of the independent variables becomes imperative in order to adapt our model to family surveys in which the period of observation is quite short.

AN ECONOMETRIC MODEL FOR CROSS-SECTIONS

'Permanent' levels of variables and area regressions

The simplest specification of a labor-market supply function of married women to which the theoretical considerations lead is:

$$m = \beta_p \cdot y + \gamma w + u \tag{1}$$

where m is the quantity of labor supplied to the market, y is a 'potential permanent level' of family income[5] computed at a zero rate of leisure and of home production, w is the wife's full-time market wage or market earning power, and u reflects other factors or 'tastes.' Since family income so computed is a sum of market earning powers of family members plus property income, we may write $y = x_p + w$, where x_p stands for the permanent level of income of the family which does not include earnings of the wife. For empirical convenience we shall identify x_p with income of the husband. This creates some inaccuracy, to the extent that contribution to family income of family members other than head and wife is important.

It is useful to rewrite equation 1 in terms of income of the husband since most data relate labor force behavior of wives to incomes of husbands. Indeed, the use of observed family income in empirical study of the supply relation would be inappropriate. Instead of serving as a determinant of labor force behavior, it already reflects such decisions.

Substituting for y into (1):

$$m = \beta_p(x_p + w) + \gamma w + u = \beta_p x_p + \alpha w + u \tag{2}$$

Since $\alpha = \beta_p + \gamma$, equation 1 can be estimated by means of equation 2.

In equation 1, parameter β_p represents the effect of 'permanent' family income on the wife's market labor input, keeping her market earning power constant; γ represents the effect of the wife's market earning power, keeping family income constant. The theoretical expectation is that $\beta_p < 0$ and $\gamma > 0$.

The statement of the hypothesis $\beta_p < 0$ in equation 2, when applied to cross sections is: Given a group of women with the same market earning power, and tastes for leisure assumed independent of husbands' earning power, there will be, on the average, a negative relation between husbands' income and hours of market work of wives.[6] This is so because, in this statement, a higher income of husband means a higher family income and, on the assumption that leisure is a normal good, this implies a lesser total amount of work of the wife, at home and in the market.

On the assumption that, in cross-sections, productivities of women in the market are unrelated to their productivities in the home, w measures the relative price of labor in the two sectors. In equation 1 γ is therefore a pure substitution effect, hence a positive number reflecting the attractive power of the wage rate in pulling women into the labor market. Parameter α in equation 2 is a relative price effect not compensated by a change in income. The question of its sign can be stated as follows: Given a group of women whose husbands have the same earning power, what is the effect of a difference in the female wage rate on hours of work on the market? Clearly, a higher wage rate will shift women from the home sector and from leisure to the market sector. However, since in this case family income increases as a result of the increase in the wives' earning power, *total* hours of work will tend to decrease. Whether hours of work in the market will increase or decrease depends on whether the job shift from home to market adds more hours of work to the market sector than is subtracted from it by a possibly increased consumption of leisure. Whether the net outcome is a positive or negative sign of α is, therefore, an empirical question. It is certainly incorrect to predict that the income effect of the wage rate on market work exceeds the substitution effect by analogy to the backward-bending supply curve. The two substitution effects involved in this comparison are quite different; the strength of substitution between wage goods and leisure time has no bearing on the strength of substitution between home production and wage goods. If anything, one would intuitively expect the latter to exceed the former. [. . .]

Adaptation of the model to analysis of family surveys

When labor force behavior (reported for a week or for the preceding year) of wives is related to current income of husbands in family surveys, the observed relation is a compound of two effects which it is important to distinguish: the responsiveness of labor force behavior (1) to husbands' long-run income positions, and (2) to current deviations of that income from its normal level.[7]

How the two factors, if distinct, may affect empirical results is easily discernible: Assume, for example, that, other things being equal, wives' market activities are geared to long-run or permanent income, and are not affected in quantity or in timing by current deviations from it. Compare two groups of families, standardized for other characteristics, and with the same observed distribution of husbands' incomes in each. If differences among incomes are purely transitory in one group, and of a lasting nature in the other, an inverse relation between income of husband and participation of wife will be observed in the second group, but not in the first. Exactly the opposite result is obtained if we assume that wives respond to transitory but not to permanent income. More generally, the observed negative relation will be steeper in the first group, if labor force behavior is more responsive to transitory than to permanent levels of income, and conversely if it is more responsive to permanent levels. Thus, survey observations may yield slopes of varying steepness in different bodies of data, depending on the differential responsiveness of labor force behavior to the two components of income, and on the extent to which the current income variation in the observed groups is 'made up' of the two components. [. . .]

The proper interpretation of survey data, therefore, requires a specification of transitory income (x_t) in addition to permanent income (x_p) which was included in equation 2. The model becomes:

$$m = \beta_p \cdot x_p + \beta_t \cdot x_t + \alpha \cdot w + u \tag{3}$$

Two avenues are open for empirical utilization of equation 3. One is an attempt to estimate the coefficients, particularly the new coefficient β_t. Another is the exploration of the implications of equation 3 for observable relations in various bodies of survey data. Both approaches are used. In both cases the major substantive interest is focused on the relative sizes of β_p and β_t, as well as on those of β_p and α.

Equation 3, if correct, points out two major reasons for the difficulties in understanding the usual cross-sectional findings.[8] No information is available on the extent to which current income represents long-run income. When labor force rates of wives are classified by characteristics of husbands, little or no information is given on characteristics of wives. Since the newly available data from the 1950 BLS Survey of Consumer Expenditures are less deficient in these respects, we turn first to them for an empirical anlysis.

BLS SURVEY OF CONSUMER EXPENDITURES

The more systematic testing of the analytical model (equation 3) and estimation of its parameters, particularly of β_t, the coefficient of transitory income, were made possible by cards especially prepared by the Bureau of Labor Statistics from its 1950 Survey of Consumer Expenditures. The cards contain information on economic and other characteristics of individual earners crossclassified by a number of such characteristics of the urban consumer units of which they are members. In what follows, employment status of wives is related to income and work experience of husbands, roughly standardized by age, education, and family type.

For the purpose of this study, the data were restricted to white husband-wife families, excluding units of which heads were self-employed or not gainfully occupied. The excluded population sub-groups are known to exhibit differential patterns of labor force behavior. Separate analyses and comparisons are therefore required. The resulting homogeneous sample contained 6,766 consumer units. It was stratified by age and education of head, as well as by presence or absence of young children in the younger age group.[9] The 12 strata so obtained (shown in Table 1.1) were in turn subdivided into units with heads working full time year-round, and heads not fully employed during the year. Whenever analytically convenient, these subgroups within strata were merged.

Table 1.1

Stratification and Sample Sizes of Husband-Wife Urban Consumer Units,
1950 Bureau of Labor Statistics Data

| Age of Head | Education of Head | | |
	Elementary (8 years or less)	High School (9–12 years)	College (13 years or more)
Less than 35, oldest child less than 16	139 75	747 216	283 119
Less than 35, no small children	55 15	258 59	45 43
35–54	851 287	1,308 280	618 139
55 and older	491 221	232 113	117 25

NOTE: Upper figures for each group refer to family units with heads working full time year-round. Lower figures refer to units with heads working less than a full year.

The first three columns in Table 1.2 provide information on average labor force responses of wives to empirical approximations of the permanent levels of the independent variables given by weekly earnings of fully employed heads and by weekly earnings of employed wives. The female labor force rates[10] (column 3) can be interpreted as such [a] response only within each of the four age-family type groups. Differences between groups are influenced by life-cycle phenomena.

Within each of the age-family type groups, except the first, average labor force behavior of wives is consistent with the findings in the area regression. That is, the positive effect of the female wage rate outweighs the negative effect of heads' income power. Indeed, the positive wage rate elasticity must be more than twice as large as the negative income elasticity since, moving from lower to higher education and income levels in each group, the percent increase in wives' weekly earnings is less than half the per cent increase in husbands' earnings. Over the life cycle as a whole, this excess of the wage rate elasticity over the income elasticity is not so great, since the young group with small children exhibits what

Table 1.2

Labor Force Rates of Wives of Fully Employed Heads, by Heads' Age,
Education, Income, and by Wives' Weekly Earnings

| | | | | Wives' Labor Force Rates[a] | |
| | | Heads'
Earnings
per Week | Wives'
Earnings
per Week | Average | When Head
Earned
$2,000–$3,000 |
Heads' *Age*	*Heads'* *Education*	(dollars) (1)	(2)	(per cent) (3)	(4)
Less than 35, oldest child less than 16	Elementary High school College	62.5 71.6 83.6	41.2 44.2 47.1	27 23 18	19 27 36
Less than 35, no small children	Elementary High school College	63.3 66.7 80.1	44.7 46.3 50.5	62 69 69	62[b] 65 83[b]
35–54	Elementary High school College	70.0 79.5 115.3	41.1 45.9 52.4	31 33 38	37 45 56
55 and older	Elementary High school College	65.8 85.6 122.5	38.6 41.1 58.1	16 20 23	21 38 38[b]

SOURCE: 1950 BLS data.
[a]Husbands employed full time year-round.
[b]Based on less than 20 observations.

seems to be a stronger negative income effect or a weaker positive wage rate effect, or both. The theoretical likelihood of such behaviour of units at the time when small children are present was discussed before.

Differences in labor force behavior between the age-family type groups are caused largely by life-cycle differences in family responsibilities. The low rates in the open-ended oldest age group probably reflect retirement age, as well as effects of larger property income and of greater contributions to family income by members other than head and wife. This is supported by the fact that the percentage difference between full-time earnings of heads and total family income increases after age 35 despite the declining labor force rates of wives.[11]

The last column of Table 1.2 suggests a response of labor force behavior to transitory components of income. At the same low current earnings of husbands ($2,000–3,000 in this illustration), labor force rates of wives increase with the heads' education, hence with their permanent income. The increase in rates is much more pronounced at the fixed income level than for the group averages. Clearly, the higher the education of the head, the larger the (negative) difference between the fixed current income figure and his expected or long-run income position. In other words, in column 4, negative income transitories increase as we move from lower to higher education levels of heads in each age-family type group. To sum it up, figures in column 3 reflect the fact that, in each age group, the discouraging effect of husbands' normal earning power is more than out-weighed by the positive effect of the female wage rate. The latter effect is augmented in column 4 by the negative transitory components of husbands' income exerting an additional push into the labor market.

More evidence on the influence of transitory components of family income on wives' labor force behavior is provided in Table 1.3. Rates for wives are higher when heads did not work a full year than when they did, in each of the 12 population groups except in the oldest with highest education level. The higher labor force rates in the second line for each group may have been expected in view of the lower annual earnings of heads. However, the differences between earnings within each group are of a quite different nature than those between groups. To the extent that the family units within each group have been made homogeneous by the stratification, income differences within them are of a transitory nature.

The extent to which the families within each group are homogeneous with respect to normal earnings of husbands can be inferred from the third line for each group. If the wage rate (weekly earning rate) were the same for the heads who were not fully employed as for those who were, the percentage 'loss' of time worked (weeks not employed) would account for, and would exactly equal, all of the 'decline' in the year's earnings. It is clear from Table 1.3 that (transitory) differences in weeks worked rather than (permanent) differences in wage rates account for the overwhelming part of the differences in the year's earnings between the 2 subgroups, particularly in the strata with elementary and high school education. In the college stratum, however, almost half of the drop is accounted for by permanent differences − the relative decline in earnings is almost twice as large as the relative decline in weeks worked. The heterogeneity of the group with respect to permanent income is not surprising; it lumps people with one year of college together with highly trained professionals.

Table 1.4 not only shows the existence of a negative labor force response to transitory income, but also suggests orders of magnitude of the elasticity. For each group ratios of percentage difference in labor force rates to percentage difference in earnings and to percentage difference in weeks worked provide rough alternative estimates of this elasticity. These estimates, shown in the last two columns of Table 1.4, generally exceed the estimate of the elasticity with respect to permanent income levels derived from the area regression [. . .] A more rigorous test for the hypothesis that the labor force response to transitory income is stronger than the response to permanent income is developed in a procedure (Table 1.4) which also yields numerical estimates of the elasticities.[12]

After merging the two employment groups, in each of the cells, a simple and a 2-variable regression of labor force rates of wives on the year's earnings of hus-bands and on weeks worked by him yielded the gross and partial slopes listed in Table 1.4. The slope (b_{mx}) of the gross regression of wives' labor force rates on earnings (column 1) combines the effects of permanent and of transitory income. The partial slope of the same relation ($b_{mx \cdot e}$ in column 2) keeps the

Table 1.3

Labor Force Rates of Wives, by Earnings and Employment of Heads

| | Education of Head | | | | | | | | |
| | Elementary | | | High school | | | College | | |
Age of Head	Heads' Earnings	Heads' Weeks[a]	Labor Force Rates of Wives	Heads' Earnings	Heads' Weeks[a]	Labor Force Rates of Wives	Heads' Earnings	Heads' Weeks[a]	Labor Force Rates of Wives
Less than 35, oldest child less than 16	$3,253	52	27%	$3,724	52	23%	$4,346	52	18%
	2,329	38	33	2,772	40	30	2,527	41	39
	−29	−27	+22	−26	−23	+30	−42	−21	+117
Less than 35, no small children	3,291	52	72	3,467	52	69	4,166	52	69
	2,407	38	66	2,385	39	73	1,902	32	88
	−27	−27	+6	−31	−25	+6	−54	−39	+28
35–54	3,636	52	31	4,135	52	33	5,996	52	38
	2,395	36	44	2,871	39	49	3,442	42	52
	−37	−31	+42	−30	−25	+48	−43	−20	+37
55 and older	3,420	52	16	4,450	52	20	6,370	52	23
	1,792	28	27	2,139	30	27	2,950	34	16
	−47	−44	+68	−52	−42	+35	−46	−35	−30

SOURCE: 1950 BLS data.

NOTE: Upper figures for each age-family group refer to heads who worked full time year-round; figures on second line refer to heads who worked part period or part time, or both; figures on third line for each group are the percentage difference between upper and lower lines.

aWeeks paid for.

Table 1.4

Gross and Partial Regression Coefficients of Labor Force Rates of Wives on Earnings and Weeks Worked by Head

Age of Head	Education	Slopes[a]			Elasticity estimates of:			Alternative Elasticity Estimates[b] of β_t	
		b_{mx} (1)	$b_{mx \cdot e}$ (2)	b_{mex} (3)	β_p (4)	$\beta_t - \beta_p$ (5)	β_t (6)	(7)	(8)
Less than 35, oldest child less than 16	Elementary	−0.132	+0.035	−0.327	+0.04	−0.61	−0.57	−0.79	−0.82
	High school	−0.604	−0.503	−0.347	−0.80	−0.75	−1.55	−1.19	−1.33
	College	−0.520	−0.423	−0.453	−1.02	−1.26	−2.28	−2.76	−5.60
Less than 35, no small children	Elementary	−0.460	−0.438	−0.071	−0.22	−0.05	−0.27	−0.24	−0.22
	High school	−0.246c	−0.188c	−0.210c	−0.09	−0.15	−0.24	−0.19	−0.24
	College	−0.624	−0.577	−0.190c	−0.35	−0.14	−0.49	−0.51	−0.77
35–54	Elementary	−0.623	−0.568	−0.124	−0.68	−0.20	−0.88	−1.14	−1.35
	High school	−0.511	−0.433	−0.535	−0.61	−0.81	−1.42	−1.61	−1.92
	College	−0.086	−0.338	+0.915	−0.54	+1.21	+0.67	−0.86	−1.85
55 and older	Elementary	−0.402	−0.346	−0.139	−0.73	−0.43	−1.16	−1.45	−1.50
	High school	−0.205	−0.254	+0.213	−0.56	+0.53	−0.03	−0.67	−0.83
	College	−0.092	−0.143	+0.326	−0.40	+0.71	+0.31	+0.66	+0.85

SOURCE: 1950 BLS data.

[a]b_{mx} = slope of regression of labor force rate (per cent) on earnings of head (thousands of dollars).

$b_{mx \cdot e}$ = slope of regression of labor force rate on earnings of head, keeping weeks worked constant.

b_{mex} = slope of regression of labor force rate on weeks worked, keeping earnings of head constant.

[b]Based on Table 1.3: Ratios of percentage difference in labor force rates to percentage difference in earnings (col. 7), and to percentage difference in weeks worked (col. 8).

[c]Not significantly different from zero, under a 5 per cent level.

number of weeks worked by the head constant. It, therefore, approximates the response to heads' normal earning power, rather than to their current income. Finally, $b_{me \cdot x}$ (in column 3) represents the response to weeks worked by heads, keeping their total earnings constant.

The sign of the slope $b_{me \cdot x}$ (column 3) provides a test for the difference between the strengths of the two income effects on labor force behavior of wives.

If the distinction between permanent and transitory income did not matter, a change in weeks worked by heads, with total earnings constant, would produce no labor force response. This hypothesis is rejected by the data. All slopes in column 3 are statistically significant, except those in the young group without small children. This exception is plausible: the stage in the life cycle represented by this group, namely the period between marriage and first child, is usually short, and during that time most of the wives are employed anyway; thus, there is very little scope for variations in timing of employment within that stage.

Now a decline in weeks, keeping total earnings constant, means a corresponding amount of increase in earning power, which is offset by a transitory loss of income of the same amount. The change in the permanent component of income is expected to bring about a *decrease* in labor force participation. The same change of the transitory component in the opposite direction is expected to stimulate an *increase* in market activities. The direction of the net outcome depends, therefore, on which income effect is stronger. Indeed, the negative sign of $b_{me \cdot x}$ provides evidence that the effect of transitory income outweighs the permanent income effect!

An estimate of the labor force response to transitory income (coefficient β_t in equation 3) is obtained as follows: The partial regression $b_{me \cdot x}$ measures the arithmetic difference in labor force rates of wives due to the equal (but of opposite sign) differences in permanent and in transitory components of income. Converting the arithmetic difference in labor force rates into a percentage difference (using rates of wives with fully employed husbands as base, column 3 in Table 1.2), and dividing it by the percentage difference in income, that is, by $(1/52 \times 100)$ we obtain the estimate of the difference $(\beta_t - \beta_p)$ in elasticity terms.[13] This estimate is shown in column 5 of Table 1.4.

The slope $b_{mx \cdot e}$ which serves as an approximation of the response to permanent income (β_p) is next converted into an elasticity at the mean by the usual procedure[14] using the averages in Table 1.3. The estimate is shown in column 4 of Table 1.4. The sum of column 4 and column 5 in Table 1.4 provides an estimate of the response elasticity to transitory income (β_t), which is shown in column 6. These estimates of transitory income elasticity in column 6 resemble the alternative estimates in columns 7 and 8, though they are somewhat smaller.

Looking at the sizes of parameter estimates in Table 1.4, we find perhaps most meaningful for purposes of comparisons with aggregates those in the modal population group (age 35-55, high school education). The estimate of the elasticity with respect to permanent income (β_p) in it is not very different from the corresponding estimate in the area regression [. . .]. The estimate of the transitory elasticity (β_t) is more than twice as large.

The estimates vary among population subgroups in a roughly systematic way: Response to permanent income is weaker the higher the educational level of heads 35 years of age and older. Responses to transitory income differ in a similar way. An opposite pattern is discernible in the young groups with small children. In the young but childless groups the magnitudes are either small or statistically unreliable.

It is difficult to say how much substance could be assigned to these differentials, given all the necessary qualifications — about the data and the estimating procedure. As previously mentioned, small income elasticities in the childless groups are theoretically plausible. But they may also be produced by the arithmetic of elasticities, since levels of participation are high in these groups. The weakening response to transitory income with rising education level in the groups with family heads over 35 years old is consistent with the hypothesis that the availability of assets obviates the need for offsetting temporary income change by means of labor input.

The differential extent to which transitory components in heads' incomes are offset by family labor input in the various population groups is shown in Table 1.5. In each stratum the regression slope of family income (before tax) on weeks worked by heads was divided by the regression slope of heads' earnings on weeks worked by them. This ratio measures the loss in family income relative to the loss in husbands' earnings due to one week's loss of employment. The

Table 1.5

*Estimates of Fraction of Negative Transitory Incomes of Heads,
Which is Offset by Family Labor Input*

Age	Education	b_{ye}[a]	b_{xe}[b]	$1 - \dfrac{b_{ye}}{b_{xe}}$
Less than 35,	Elementary	18.7	39.1	0.52
children	High school	27.4	51.2	0.47
under 16	College	33.2	60.5	0.45
Less than 35,	Elementary	15.4	43.8	0.69
no small	High school	23.1	47.1	0.51
children	College	32.4	60.1	0.46
35–55	Elementary	42.1	56.8	0.26
	High school	32.4	60.8	0.47
	College	46.7	75.1	0.38
Over 55	Elementary	40.6	54.6	0.25
	High school	45.1	54.1	0.17
	College	54.9	62.3	0.12

SOURCE: 1950 BLS data.

[a] b_{ye} = slope of regression of family income (dollars) on weeks worked by head.

[b] b_{xe} = slope of regression of heads' income (dollars) on weeks worked by head.

per cent by which the numerator is smaller than the denominator measures the extent to which a change in head's income was offset by an opposite change in income of other family members.[15]

The results in Table 1.5 show that the absorption of negative transitory components of heads' income declines with increasing education after age 35, and with advancing age in each education group. This absorption is, of course, a net effect of all earners, not just the wife, and is consistent with the hypothesis on alternatives to dissaving. [. . .]

IMPLICATIONS

Cross-sections and time series

If the orders of magnitude of the parameter estimates of equation 3 are roughly correct, there is no real contradiction between findings on labor force behavior of married women in cross-sections and in time series. The impression of a contradiction is due to the way cross-sections have been looked at, in terms of gross relations between income of husband and labor force participation of wife. Such gross comparisons yield results (slopes or elasticities) which are sensitive both to the existence of transitory components in income and to the covariation of wives' earning power with husbands' income. The transitory components accentuate the negative effect of income. In their absence, the cross-sectional negative relation would hardly be noticeable. If, in addition, the positive relation between husbands' and wives' income were stronger than is usually observed in cross-sections, a positive rather than negative relation would be found between labor force rates of wives and incomes of husbands, even at a point of time.

Thus, if equation 3 is projected onto time series, two facts intervene which convert the negative income relation in cross-sections into a positive secular relation: (1) short-run transitory components of income are not relevant to long-run developments, and (2) the female wage rate has risen over time at least as fast as the male rate [. . .]

NOTES

1. The pioneering works of research and interpretation in this area are well known. See: Paul H. Douglas, *The Theory of Wages*, Macmillan, 1934; John D. Durand, *The Labor Force in the U.S.*, Social Science Research Council, 1948; Clarence D. Long, *The Labor Force under Changing Income and Employment*, Princeton University Press for National Bureau of Economic Research, 1958.
2. For a rigorous statement, see H. Gregg Lewis, 'Hours of Work and Hours of Leisure,' *Proceedings of the Industrial Relations Research Association*, 1957.
3. Based on Long, *The Labor Force*, Table A-6; and *Employment and Earnings*, Bureau of Labor Statistics, 1960.
4. Fragmentary cross-sectional data on food preparation at home indicate a negligible income elasticity. The demand for other home goods and services (including care of children, and their number) may be more income elastic.

5. The definition of 'permanent' and 'transitory' components of income follows that stated by Friedman in his consumption theory. Permanent income is income in the long-run sense, measuring income status or normal income position. Transitory income is the difference between current and permanent income. See Milton Friedman, *A Theory of the Consumption Function*, Princeton for NBER, 1957.
6. To the extent that women with strong tastes for leisure tend to seek out rich husbands, the true income effect (keeping tastes fixed) is overestimated in cross-sections.
7. For present purposes, a similar distinction between current and 'permanent' levels of the female wage rate is not formally introduced. Short-run variations in it, or rather in employment opportunities, are largely a matter of industry differences among communities. We may assume that such differences are much less important in family surveys than in area comparisons.
8. Comprehensive summaries of census findings are provided by Gertrude Bancroft, *The American Labor Force, Its Growth and Changing Composition*, New York, Wiley, 1958, and by Long, *The Labor Force*.
9. Pre-school children are not important numerically in the older age groups. Unfortunately, time and budget considerations did not permit more detailed stratifications.
10. Strictly speaking, these are employment rates, that is, the proportion of wives who were employed at any time during the survey year. Labor force rates are, therefore, somewhat underestimated.
11. See Table III in the author's 'Labor Supply, Family Income, and Consumption', *Proceedings of the 1959 Annual Meeting of the American Economic Association, American Economic Review*, May 1960, p. 577.
12. The elasticity estimates are equivalent to estimates of regression coefficients of equation 3 stated in terms of logarithms of its variables. They are used for purposes of comparability. In the following discussion the same symbols are used for elasticities as for slopes, but the distinction is made explicit in the text.
13. $\frac{e}{m} \cdot b_{me \cdot x}$, where e is number of weeks worked by the heads, measures the percentage change in labor force rate per 1 per cent increase in weeks employed, keeping husbands' income constant. But a 1 per cent rise in e, as stated in the text implies a 1 per cent rise in transitory income x_t, *and* a 1 per cent decline in permanent income x_p. Hence: $\frac{e}{m} \cdot b_{me \cdot x}$, in elasticity terms.
14. Elasticity at the mean of y with respect to x is equal to the slope of the regression of y on x, multiplied by the ratio of the mean of x to the mean of y.
15. 'Loss' and 'change' are only figures of speech in a cross-section analysis.

1.3 Information In the Labour Market*

The young person entering the labor market for the first time has an immense number of potential employers, scarce as they may seem the first day. If he is an unskilled or a semi-skilled worker, the number of potential employers is strictly in the millions. Even if he has a specialized training, the number of potential employers will be in the thousands: the young Ph.D. in economics, for example, has scores of colleges and universities, dozens of governmental agencies, hundreds of business firms, and the Ford Foundation as potential employers. As the worker becomes older the number of potential employers may shrink more often than it grows, but the number will seldom fall to even a thousand.

*From George J. Stigler, 'Information in the Labor Market', *Journal of Political Economy*, Vol. 70 (Supplement), October 1962.

No worker, unless his degree of specialization is pathological, will ever be able to become informed on the prospective earnings which would be obtained from every one of these potential employers at any given time, let alone keep this information up to date. He faces the problem of how to acquire information on the wage rates, stability of employment, conditions of employment, and other determinants of job choice, and how to keep this information current. I shall concentrate attention on the determination of wage rates.

I. THE DISPERSION OF WAGE RATES

Even with strict homogeneity of commodities, we usually find some dispersion in the prices which are offered by sellers or buyers. Only if either buyers have complete knowledge of all sellers' offers, or all sellers have complete knowledge of all buyers' offers, will there be a single price. Complete knowledge, however, is seldom possessed, simply because it costs more to learn of alternative prices than (at the margin) this information yields.[1]

The labor markets display the same characteristics, but their analysis is much complicated by the lack of homogeneity of the workers (and, to a much lesser extent, of non-wage conditions of employment). In order to form some estimate of the nature of the 'pure' dispersion of wages due to imperfect knowledge, we shall begin with a very special class of college graduates.

A tolerably pure estimate of the dispersion of wage offers to homogeneous labor is provided by the contemporary offers to the same person. For forty-four graduates of the Graduate School of Business at the University of Chicago who received 144 offers (in 1960 and 1961) from corporations, the standard deviation of monthly rates was $43. The mean offer was $540.7, so the coefficient of variation was 7.9 per cent.[2]

Since this job market was completely localized in one office, and there is considerable intercommunication among the national companies whose representatives solicit prospective employees (and among prospective employees), this appears to be a conservative estimate of the gross dispersion for given quality. The fact that each student on average solicited only 2.25 offers works in the same direction. The differences in the attractiveness of non-wage elements of the various jobs, however, are impossible to discover.[3] On balance it appears that the true dispersion is substantially underestimated, and later evidence suggests that it may be much larger in less organized markets.

Unfortunately, distributions of offers to given individuals are not available for any large occupational group or any extended geographical market. One must deal with offers (or wage rates paid) by individual employers or groups of employers, and the dispersion of such offers may be either larger or smaller than the true distribution we desire. The dispersion of distributions of company average offers will be larger insofar as they reflect differences in quality of workers (or of jobs),[4] or cover several labor markets; the dispersion will be smaller insofar as intracompany dispersion is eliminated. In our sample of business graduates, the standard deviation of the average offers of companies is $40, compared with that of $43 for given students. Although no unique relationship between these dispersions can be assumed, we can and will assume that for similar labor markets they are reasonably well correlated.

The dispersion of wage offers in the small Chicago sample is approximately equal to that of the national sample of wage offers made each year by Frank Endicott.[5] The coefficients of variation of groups other than engineers range from 6.4 per cent to 9.1 per cent (Table 1.6); the corresponding figure for our sample was 7.3 per cent.

Table 1.6
*Monthly Hiring Rates of Large Corporations
for College Graduates, 1958-60*

Occupation	No. of Companies	1958	1959	1960
1. Mean Salaries				
Engineers	66	$472	$493	$515
Accountants	40	421	435	457
Salesmen	29	410	426	447
General business	41	403	416	431
2. Coefficient of Variation (per cent)				
Engineers	66	4.04	4.22	4.26
Accountants	40	6.45	6.93	6.42
Salesmen	29	8.78	8.18	9.11
General business	41	8.60	8.96	8.64

SOURCE: Endicott Survey worksheets. All companies here included reported in each of the three years.

If the expected period of employment exceeds one year (as it does), the worker must also make an estimate of future wage differences among employers. Endicott's data permit an estimate of the correlation of successive annual rates (Table 1.7). The correlations are high, and — what is more surprising — two of the four cases show no tendency to diminish when the time period is lengthened to two years. If the correlations were to remain high for long periods, the differences in wages would presumably reflect compensating differences in the non-wage terms of employment. But the normal pattern surely is one of declining correlation coefficients as the period is lengthened, if only as a Galton regression phenomenon.

Differences in initial wage rates would also be offset by different rates of increase in wages, so the present values of different jobs could still be equal. Endicott's survey for 1960 reported the average salary paid to college graduates after one year of service, and these salaries may be compared with those paid

Table 1.7

Correlation Coefficients of Salary Rates in 1958, 1959,
and 1960 for College Graduates

Occupation	No. of Companies	Correlation coefficient		
		1958 and 1959	1959 and 1960	1958 and 1960
Engineers	66	.660	.561	.577
Accountants	40	.723	.872	.720
Sales	29	.849	.885	.871
General business	41	.853	.891	.873

SOURCE: Same as Table 1.6.

initially. The relationship for accountants was

$$W_2 = 24.71 + 1.039W_1, \qquad (N = 67),$$
$$(.062)$$

where W_2 was the wage in 1960 and W_1 the wage in 1959; the relationship is close ($r = .900$). So far as these data go, they suggest that initial wage rates are a good predictor of wage rates in the following year.

These fragments illustrate rather than prove the existence of substantial dispersion in hiring rates for homogeneous labor. This dispersion cannot be measured precisely, but is of the order of magnitude of 5–10 per cent even in so well organized a market as that of college graduates at a single university.

II. THE PROBLEM OF INFORMATION

A worker will search for wage offers (and an employer will search for wage demands) until the expected marginal return equals the marginal cost of search. Under what conditions will this search eliminate all dispersion of wage rates for homogeneous labor?

The conditions are severe. It is not sufficient for demand and supply to have been stable indefinitely long, and hence 'the' equilibrium wage not to have changed for an indefinitely long period, in order to eliminate all dispersion. If workers were to change employment (perhaps because of improving skills) or employers were to change identity (because of the turnover of firms), it still would not pay to search enough to eliminate all dispersion. But if these changes were infrequent — say, once every three years or more — the dispersion of wage rates would be fairly small, although not negligible.[6] Changes in jobs due to changes in workers' tastes and abilities and employers' identities therefore set some minimum on the dispersion of wage rates. If the market has appreciable geographical extent, transportation costs of workers (and plants) add to this minimum dispersion.

The fluctuations of supply-and-demand conditions add a new a source of dispersion. The information of the worker (and employer) now becomes obsolete with time: there will be changes in the level of wages and in the relative wage rates of different employers (and workers) which call for additional search. The more rapidly 'the' equilibrium wage rate changes, the smaller the returns from search and hence the smaller the amount of search that will be undertaken – and the larger the resulting wage dispersion.

The subsequent analysis is devoted to an application of this approach to the costs and returns from search for various types of workers. The unavailability of a temporal sequence of closely spaced wage distributions makes it impossible to explore the effects of rates of change of equilibrium prices on the amount of dispersion.

The returns from search by workers

We shall begin our analysis of the returns from search by forming some estimate of the magnitude of the return as a function of the amount of search. To this end, let us assume that the wage offers by all possible employers are normally distributed.[7] Then the expected maximum wage offer (w_m) a man will encounter in n searches is approximately[8]

$$w_m = .65n^{.37}\sigma_w + \bar{w},$$

and the marginal wage rate increase from one additional search is

$$\frac{\partial w_n}{\partial n} = \frac{.24\sigma_w}{n^{.63}}$$

If $\sigma_w = \bar{w}/10$, the marginal wage rate gain from additional search is:

Search (n)	Marginal Wage Rate Gain
5	$.0087\,\bar{w}$
10	$.0056\,\bar{w}$
15	$.0044\,\bar{w}$
20	$.0036\,\bar{w}$

If the annual wage rate is $6,000, the marginal wage rate gain is therefore of the order of $20 to $50 in this range of search.

If the structure of employer wage offers were permanently fixed, and if the worker lived forever, the marginal income gain from additional search would be simply the capitalized value of the marginal *wage-rate* gain. If the structure were permanent and the duration of employment t_o years, the marginal *income*-gain would be the value of the corresponding annuity, namely,

$$\frac{\partial w_n}{\partial n} \frac{(1+i)^{t_o} - 1}{i(1+i)^{t_o}}$$

In this extreme case of a permanent wage structure, the order of magnitude of the marginal income gain from search is illustrated by the following table, where $\sigma_w = \bar{w}/10$ and $i = 6$ per cent.

Prospective years of employment	Amount of search	
	5 Employers	15 Employers
3	$.023\,\bar{w}$	$.012\,\bar{w}$
5	$.037\,\bar{w}$	$.018\,\bar{w}$
10	$.064\,\bar{w}$	$.032\,\bar{w}$

For the $6,000 salary level, these marginal income gains run from $66 (fifteen employers, three years) to $384 (five employers, ten years).

But these gains are exaggerated because there is not a perfect correlation between the wage offers of employers in successive time periods. The employers themselves do not know wage offers sufficiently well to preserve a perfect correlation even if they mysteriously wished it, and the appearance of new employers adds a further reason for continued search by the worker.

When the correlation of successive wage offers is positive but less than unity it will still pay the worker to search more intensively in the earlier periods because this search will have some value in subsequent periods. In a simple two-period model, the details of which are given in the appendix, the increased search in the first period due to correlation of wage rates will increase the expected maximum wage offer in the proportion $br^2/(1-b)$, or approximately $r^2/2$. If $r = .5$, the amount of search in period 1 will be increased by 20 per cent, with roughly a 12 per cent increase in salary.

It would be possible to analyze a variety of phenomena in the light of the correlation of successive wage offers. For example, the higher the correlation, the longer the expected tenure of a worker with a company, and therefore the lower the quit rate. Unfortunately there are no published data, so far as I know, which allow calculation of the correlations, although of course these data dwell in the worksheets of numerous wage surveys.

As a poor substitute, one can examine the average wage rates (measured by earnings per worker) on a geographical basis. The average earnings per worker in a state will be an index of wage rates in the given industry, and it will be a better index the more similar the occupational and wage structures of the industry in various states. A sample of such calculations is reported in Table 1.8.

Several features of these geographical patterns are noteworthy. The dispersion of earnings among states is much smaller in the recent period, and the decline occurred in twenty-one of twenty-five industries. The inference is that the national market has become more perfect, and the inference is commended by the fact that costs of movement have fallen substantially relative to wage rates over the period. The correlation coefficients reveal a slight decline on average, although they are based upon a seven-year interval in the later period (including

Table 1.8

Characteristics of Average Earnings in Selected Manufacturing Industries, 1904-9 and 1947-54 (Identical States)

Industry	No. of States	Correlation Coefficients		Average Coefficient of Variation (per cent)	
		1904 and 1909	1947 and 1954	1904 and 1909	1947 and 1954
Non-ferrous foundries	8	.895	.663	15.3	8.7
Motor vehicles and equipment	9	.349	.106	8.9	4.9
Structural clay products	23	.982	.938	29.4	19.3
Ship and boat building	9	.894	.703	17.6	10.6
Rubber products	8	.270	.672	8.1	6.4
Musical instruments and parts	7	.953	.460	25.7	8.7
Confectionery products	17	.819	.876	15.3	17.8
Beer and ale	12	.921	.834	15.4	10.8
Mattresses and bedsprings	9	.830	.906	22.0	22.9
Furniture and fixtures, excluding mattresses and bedsprings	33	.941	.912	26.2	17.0
Fertilizers	13	.905	.952	20.4	20.4
Meat products	29	.728	.922	18.5	15.8
Flour and meal	14	.935	.530	21.8	12.0
Bakery products	20	.952	.918	18.2	12.6
Bottled soft drinks	15	.954	.874	20.1	18.4
Manufactured ice	21	.926	.854	22.8	25.5
Woolen and worsted fabrics	8	.987	.844	17.6	8.7
Knitting mills	17	.955	.774	23.5	11.2
Paperboard containers	18	.906	.926	17.1	14.0
Printing and publishing	47	.912	.906	21.3	11.8
Drugs and medicines	13	.725	.924	16.2	14.0
Soap and related products	10	.950	.681	14.8	12.0
Paints and allied products	15	.742	.870	18.4	11.2
Leather tanning and finishing	9	.968	.906	19.0	13.8
Footwear (except rubber)	12	.932	.703	13.1	9.2
Average		.853	.786	18.7	13.5

a year of turbulent demobilization) as against a five-year interval in the earlier period.[9] The comparison timidly suggests that the difference in earnings increasingly represents differences in the quality of labor rather than in its compensation.

The most direct implication of the formal analysis is that the gains from search are larger the longer the prospective period of employment. When search is more extensive, however, the dispersion of maximum wage rates will be smaller — the lowest wage offers will more often be rejected for known better offers.[10] So the realized dispersion of wage rates should be smaller the longer the prospective period of employment. Several tests of this implication can be made.

Women generally expect to stay in the labor force a shorter period than men do, so among homogeneous groups of men and women we should expect that the latter have larger dispersions. The occupational wage surveys do reveal this expected difference.[11] The major difficulty in making extensive tests of this prediction is that the tabulated Census data on earnings (in 1940 and 1950) do not allow the removal of the effects of age (men have a much wider dispersion of ages) and of race (Negro women are a larger fraction of the female labour force than Negro men are of the male labor force).[12]

Similar comparisons can be made of younger and older workers. The coefficient of variation increases with age for engineers (see Table 1.5). The coefficient of variation of 1949 earnings of plumbers and pipefitters was 40.8 per cent; that of apprentices was 32.9 per cent.[13] The dispersion of salaries of

Table 1.9
Monthly Engineering Earnings, by Age, 1929

Age	Mean Monthly Earnings	Standard Deviation	Coefficient of Variation (per cent)
23	161.0	85.1*	52.9*
24–25	189.5	58.2	30.7
26–27	230.1	86.4	37.6
28–31	282.8	117.5	41.6
32–35	349.9	175.7	50.2
36–39	400.0	221.6	55.4
40–47	464.1	294.5	63.5
48–55	510.0	346.0	67.8
56–63	544.3	399.8	73.4
64 or more	487.6	356.3	73.1

SOURCE: A. Fraser, Jr., 'Employment and Earnings in the Engineering Profession, 1929 to 1934,' Bureau of Labor Statistics, Bull. No. 682, 233, Table 2.
*This class appears to be heterogeneous; two of the respondents had salaries 20 standard deviations above the mean.

college teachers is larger the higher the rank (and age) of the teacher.[14] A more powerful test would be provided by a comparison of wages of students in summer employment with young men of the same age who had permanently left school.

Our original estimate of the coefficient of variation of earnings in section 1 was of the order of 10 per cent. The differences cited above — for example, 60 per cent versus 30 per cent for engineers of fifty-five and twenty-five years of age — might suggest a much larger estimate of the effects of ignorance. These gross dispersions are due to at least three different components, however, only the first two of which involve information:

i. The dispersion of earnings of engineers increases with age because younger engineers make more extensive search than older engineers.
ii. The difference in ability of engineers becomes better known as they become older (and have worked longer for a given employer).[15]

iii. The older engineers have made different amounts of 'on-the-job' investment in training, which serves to increase their dispersion of abilities, a phenomenon discussed in Professor Mincer's paper.

The disentanglement of the second and third components of dispersion is especially difficult. We reach again the conclusion that the differences in quality of workers cast a deep shadow over all measures of pure dispersion due to differences in knowledge (or, for that matter, due to other forms of investment).

The effect of the absolute level of earnings, which may also enter into the determination of the gain from search, will be considered in the next section.

The costs of search

The larger the cost of search the less search will be undertaken by a worker at a given level of dispersion of employers' wage offers. These costs will vary systematically with various characteristics of occupations.

When prospective employers of a worker are readily identified – which is partly associated with how specialized a worker is – search for a job is more economical: one does not have to waste inquiries on wholly irrelevant possibilities. We should therefore expect the dispersion of actual wage rates to be less the more easily the employers are identified.

This prediction is supported by several analyses of earnings in the twenty metropolitan areas in 1950. Domestic servants have higher coefficients of variation than laundry operatives in nineteen of twenty areas (with means of 75.2 per cent and 54.0 per cent, respectively). The confirmation is less emphatic in the comparison of taxi drivers with truck drivers (the former have lower coefficients of variation in thirteen of twenty regions, but the means are virtually identical: 44.2 per cent and 45.7 per cent).[16]

The costs of search are also lower the higher the probability that a given, identified employer is taking on men. This would argue that in periods of expanding employment the dispersion of wages will be smaller. But unemployment among a class of workers also works in the opposite direction to reduce the cost of search. Within local markets the cost of search is primarily a cost in time, to be valued (at least approximately) by the mean wage rate, as a measure of the leisure value of time. But for the unemployed worker, this alternative cost of leisure is negligible. In the search in other labor markets, however, both transportation costs and foregone earnings must be incurred.[17]

The effects of the level of earnings on the amount of search are equally difficult to disentangle. If the absolute dispersion (σ_w) is proportional to the mean wage, the mean wage affects costs and returns from search proportionately, and there is no effect on the amount of search. On the other hand, it appears to have been the regular practice for employment agencies to charge a fee that is a higher percentage of larger initial salaries – the fee is progressive.[18] The simplest explanation would be that the expected duration of employment is greater the higher the initial wage rate. On the whole, this kind of evidence seems much more persuasive than that based on interoccupational comparisons.

The search for information may take forms other than direct solicitation: newspaper advertisements, employment agencies, employer search, and the myriad forms of pooling of information by workers. Some require little expenditure of time and — if used alone — would lead us to expect that the dispersion of wage rates should be equal in absolute terms (standard deviations, not coefficients of variation) for workers at different wage levels. Such information, however, is incomplete and limited, and if more is needed solicitation is eventually resorted to. The marginal cost of search may rise as search increases.

The private employment agencies offer a fertile field for investigation from this viewpoint. Their *raison d'être* is information, and they should have specialized in the occupations in which information is most difficult for the employer or worker to obtain. Their fees, indeed, would provide a direct estimate of the marginal cost of information in these occupations.

III. THE EMPLOYERS' SEARCH

There is direct search by employers, wholly comparable to that of workers, in certain industries. College teaching is an obvious example: the employer canvasses graduate schools, professional journals, and the like for potential employees and invites them in to be looked over. This kind of direct solicitation is most probable when the workers are highly specialized, of course.

The main reason for workers undertaking the burden of solicitation is that it is cheaper for them than for employers. When an employer has numerous employees the probability that a given employer needs additional workers is much greater than the probability that a given worker will accept a job offer. The identification problem is usually also less for a worker than for an employer — the fraction of wasted search will be much smaller for a steelworker than for a steel company. But where the number of employees per employer approaches unity (domestic service, vice-presidents in charge of marketing), the employer usually takes on some or all of the task of search.

The employers' search involves more than the identification of potential workers: they must be 'processed' to a degree set by the personnel practices, and there are training costs (including low productivity) for a time. Walter Oi estimates that the initial hiring and training cost per worker was (in 1951) about $382 for International Harvester, the cost rising rapidly with the level of skill.[19]

One way to reduce hiring costs is to pay higher relative wages. Not only is the quit rate of existing workers reduced by high wages, but on average, more obviously high-quality workers will accept offers. Wage rates and skilled search are substitutes for the employer: the more efficiently he detects workers of superior quality the less he need pay for such quality.

The small company has distinct advantages in the hiring process, so far as judging the quality of workers is concerned. The employer can directly observe the performance of the new worker and need not resort to expensive and uncertain rating practices to estimate the workers' performance. It is well known that wage rates are less in small plants than in large, and the difference reflects at least in part (and perhaps in whole) the lower costs to the small-scale employer of judging quality. A similar result obtains with respect to dispersion of wages: a sample of such data is given in Table 1.10. Men should in general enter smaller companies the greater their ability.

Table 1.10

Coefficients of Variation of Hourly Wage Rates of Male Employees in Selected Manufacturing Industries by Class of Worker

Industry and Employer	No. of Plants	Coefficient of Variation (per cent)		
		Skilled	Semiskilled	Unskilled
Radios:				
Two largest companies	2	12.8	16.7	13.8
Other companies	22	24.6	24.9	20.9
Soap:				
Large companies	13	15.1	16.8	17.2
Other companies	59	25.6	24.5	23.3
Explosives:				
Three largest companies	28	16.2	14.1	15.8
Other companies	23	19.8	17.4	19.5
Meatpacking:				
Four largest companies	59		20.4	
Small companies	182		28.1	

SOURCE: *Hourly Earnings of Employees in Large and Small Enterprises* ('Temporary National Economic Committee Monograph,' No. 14, 1948), pp. 21, 54, 59, 66, 70. The same pattern holds without exception for female employees. The meatpacking data refer to the northern wage district, and to all employees.

These last remarks represent in a sense a contradiction to the main argument of this paper. For previously I have accepted wage dispersion as a measure of ignorance but now take it as a measure of ability (less dispersion implies greater ignorance). The contradiction is only superficial because the problem of information on quality has been replacing that of information on price, and heterogeneity of quality has replaced homogeneity. Yet this shift poses again the central difficulty with which we began: the entanglement of quality and price variation in labor markets.

IV. INFORMATION AS CAPITAL

The information a man possesses on the labor market is capital: it was produced at the cost of search, and it yields a higher wage rate than on average would be received in its absence.

From the viewpoint of the individual worker, the capital value of his knowledge can be calculated by the usual method of valuing an asset; that is, discounting its future revenue. In section 1, above, we gave the marginal income gain from search as

$$\frac{\partial w_m}{\partial n} \frac{(1+i)^{t_o}-1}{i(1+i)^{t_o}}.$$

that is, the marginal wage rate gain times the present value of an annuity of duration t_o. The total income gained is the integral of this expression over the range of search, or

$$(w_m - \bar{w}) \frac{(1+i)^{t_o}-1}{i(1+i)^{t_o}}$$

This formula, as we observed, is an over-estimate to the extent that future wage rates paid by various employers are not perfectly correlated with present wage rates. Conversely, if the duration of work with one employer is t_o, there will be some value to the knowledge presently acquired, in the search for alternative employments after t_o. This offset will be larger the larger the correlation of wage offers over time.

The duration of given jobs varies systematically with age and skill. Gladys Palmer's study suggested an average duration of a job of about three years for men between the ages of twenty-five and thirty-four, rising to six years for men over sixty-five.[20] The turnover of jobs is higher among unskilled workers than among skilled workers. If the worker has a prospective job duration of three years, and the coefficient of variation of wage offers is 10 per cent, the capital value of his knowledge, by the above formula (with $i = .06$), would be

.32 $\bar{w}$ if 5 wage offers are found,

.47 $\bar{w}$ if 15 wage offers are found.

If such numbers are applied to the entire labor force, one gets an aggregate of private capital in laborer's information of the order of $100 billion.

The employer has a corresponding capital value of information: it is equal to the present value of the savings in wage rates for given quality of workers (or the superior quality of workers at given wage rates). The larger the amount of search by workers, the less will be the opportunity (or the greater the cost) for the employer to achieve a given saving in wage rates. The division of the investment in information between employers and workers will be determined by institutional characteristics of the market; where it is more economical for one party to acquire the information, the other party will make relatively small investments.

From the social viewpoint, the return from investment in information consists in a more efficient allocation of the labor force; the better informed the labor market, the closer each worker's (marginal) product is to its maximum at any given time. From this viewpoint, the function of information is to prevent less efficient employers from obtaining labor, and inefficient workers from obtaining the better jobs. In a regime of ignorance, Enrico Fermi would have been a gardener, Von Neumann a checkout clerk at a drug store.

The social capital is not necessarily equal to the sum of the private capitals. If most workers search intensively, employers who offer low wage rates will be unable to fill their jobs and will be forced either to close down or to raise wage rates — so if I enter the labor market and do not search, I nevertheless profit from others' knowledge of the market. This effect arises because of the existence of the economies of scale.

The amounts and kinds of information needed for the efficient allocation of labor, whether judged from the viewpoint of the laborer, the employer, or the community, extend far beyond the determination of wage rates. The kinds and amounts of skill men should acquire pose parallel informational problems, and so too do the non-monetary conditions of employment. The traditional litera-ture has not done these problems justice. It is doubtful that justice would be more closely approached by making exaggerated claims of the importance of the problem of information. There is no exaggeration however, in the suggestion that the analysis of the precise problems of information and of the methods an economy uses to deal with them appears to be a highly rewarding area for future research.

APPENDIX

Let n_1 and n_2 be the search in the two periods, λ the average cost of search. Then the 'profit' of a worker from search, neglecting interest, is

$$\pi = w_1 + w_2 - \lambda(n_1 + n_2),$$

where

$$w_1 = a n_1^b,$$
$$w_2 = a(n_2 + r^2 n_1)^b.$$

For a maximum,

$$\frac{\partial \pi}{\partial n_1} = abn_1^{b-1} + ab(n_2 + r^2 n_1)^{b-1} r^2 - \lambda = 0. \tag{1}$$

$$\frac{\partial \pi}{\partial n_2} = ab(n_2 + r^2 n_1)^{b-1} - \lambda = 0. \tag{2}$$

Equating values of λ,

$$n_2 = n_1 \{(1 - r^2)^{1/(1-b)} - r^2\}. \tag{3}$$

It follows from (3) that $n_2 = n_1$ when $r = 0$. It can be shown that if $r = 1$, $n_2 = 0,$[22] and

$$n_1 = \left(\frac{\lambda}{2ab}\right)^{1/(b-1)}$$

Search in period 1 makes a marginal wage contribution of

$$\frac{\partial w_2}{\partial w_1} = ab(n_2 + r^2 n_1)^{b-1} r^2$$

in period 2. The optimum amount of search in period 1, from equations (1) and (2), is

$$n_1 = \left(\frac{\lambda}{ab}\right)^{1/(b-1)} (1 - r^2)^{1/(b-1)}. \tag{4}$$

The wage rate in period 1 with a correlation of r exceeds that with no correlation in the proportion

$$\frac{a(\lambda/ab)^{b/(b-1)}(1 - r^2)^{b/(b-1)} - a(\lambda/ab)^{b/(b-1)}}{a(\lambda/ab)^{b/(b-1)}}$$

or by $(1 - r^2)^{b/(b-1)} - 1$, or approximately by $br^2/(1 - b)$.

NOTES

1. The argument is elaborated in my 'The Economics of Information,' *Journal of Political Economy*, June 1961.
2. There was no systematic or significant difference in the standard deviations for those who received 2, 3, 4, or 5 or more offers:

No. of Offers	No. of Students	Standard Deviation
2	17	$46
3	13	35
4	7	49
5 or more	7	43

The basic data were made available by courtesy of David Huntington of the Placement Bureau of the Graduate School of Business.
3. The extent to which initial wage rates are reliable indexes of subsequent wage rates is investigated below.
4. The variance of offers, within a given specialty, is usually much larger between than 'within' individuals who have received multiple offers.
5. We are indebted to Endicott for permission to examine the company reports for three years.
6. With a rectangular wage offer distribution between 0 and 1, the average maximum wage encountered in n searches is $n/(n + 1)$, so the expected marginal wage rate gain from $(n + 1)$ searches is

$$\frac{n + 1}{n + 2} - \frac{n}{n + 1} = \frac{1}{(n + 1)(n + 2)},$$

which, multiplied by the expected duration of employment, is the marginal income gain from search. If employment is expected to last m days, and the cost of search is k days, the amount of search will be given by

$$\frac{m}{(n + 1)(n + 2)} = \frac{kn}{n + 1},$$

or n is approximately $\sqrt{(m/k)}$, or (say) 25 with three years of expected employment, and $k = 1$. The coefficient of variation of wages is

$$\sqrt{\left(\frac{n}{(n + 1)^2(n + 2)}\right)} \frac{n + 1}{n} = \frac{1}{\sqrt{(n(n + 2))}} = \sqrt{\frac{k}{m}},$$

which would be 4 per cent in our example. This argument is an adaptation of that in 'The Economics of Information', *op. cit.*, p. 215.

7. The Chicago student wage offers are consistent with this assumption, and it seems intuitively more plausible than the rectangular distribution which was used (for algebraic convenience) in 'The Economics of Information' and in n. 6.

8. The expression is simply an approximation (for $3 < n < 20$) to the mean maximum observation from a normal population in random samples of size n; the precise values are given in W. J. Dixon and F. J. Massey, *Introduction to Statistical Analysis* (New York, 1957), p. 407.

9. The industries are also more homogeneous in the later period, and this serves to increase the correlation coefficients.

10. Or, more precisely, the distribution of maximum offers has a variance that decreases as the number of searches increases.

11. For example, hourly earnings of shipping packers in manufacturing in Chicago have the following characteristics:

	1952	1957
Males:		
Interquartile range	23.4¢	43.8¢
Median rate	144.2	182.0
Interquartile ratio (per cent)	16.2	24.1
Females:		
Interquartile range	28.4¢	45.8¢
Median rate	109.8	175.7
Interquartile ratio (per cent)	25.9	26.1

Source: Bureau of Labor Statistics, Bulls. 1105 and 1202–15.

With normally distributed variates, the interquartile ratio is 1.35 times the coefficient of variation.

12. A moderately extensive analysis was made of dispersions of income in 1949 in large cities for selected occupations, and an analysis was made of earnings in 1939 for waiters and waitresses. The 1949 data showed larger dispersions for women than for men; the 1939 data for the one occupation showed the opposite. The heterogeneity of age and race (and in 1940 the inclusion of self-employed workers) are such that I believe the results are wholly inconclusive. For the same reason, the consistently smaller *average* wages of women (which are predicted by the theory) are not supporting evidence.

13. On the other hand, the coefficients of variation for machinists and tool makers (30.1 per cent) and apprentices (29.7 per cent) were essentially identical. These are all United States data, influenced by extent of part-time work (which was much higher among apprentices than among machinists).

14. The interquartile ratios $[(Q_3 - Q_1)/Q_2]$ of academic salaries in 1959–60 were:

Rank	Per cent	
	Men	Women
Professor	33.0	31.8
Associate professor	23.3	26.2
Assistant professor	19.7	24.2
Instructor	19.3	21.7

These calculations are based upon National Education Association, Higher Education Series, Research Report, 1960–R3. See also my *Trends in Employment in the Service Industries* (New York: National Bureau of Economic Research, 1956), p. 128.

The smaller dispersion of salaries of women professors is found in every type of college and university reported. Women make up less than one-twelfth of the full professors and more than twice as large a fraction even of associate professors. The roles of ability and discrimination in producing this reversal of the basic pattern would be interesting to know.

15. This increased dispersion in earnings due to better recognition of differences in ability (the search for information on the quality of workers) is of course to be reckoned as a reduction in the dispersion of earnings of homogeneous workers.
16. These Census data are moderately more persuasive than those rejected earlier because differences due to race, part-time work, and age are smaller.
17. Hence the mean wage rates for given work should vary more among establishments in an extensive area than within a single labor market.
18. P. H. Douglas and A. Director, *The Problem of Unemployment* (1931), p. 267.
19. 'Labor as a Quasi-Fixed Factor of Production' (unpublished Ph.D. dissertation, University of Chicago, 1961).
20. *Labor Mobility in Six Cities* (New York, 1954), p. 53. The durations are biased downward for the younger men because not all were in the labor force for an entire decade.
21. If r approaches unity, equations (1) and (2) yield

$$\frac{ab}{n_1^{1-b}} = 0 \, ,$$

or n_1 becomes infinite, and by equation (2),

$$n_2 + r^2 n_1 = \left(\frac{\lambda}{ab}\right)^{1/(b-1)}$$

so n_2/n_1 approaches $-r^2$ as n_1 approaches infinity. Since n_2 has a minimum of zero, n_1 is fixed by (1) at the expression in the text.

1.4 The Theory of Migration*

[...]

The migration model specified here differs in a number of significant respects from those proposed by Hart and Jack. Rather than take a variant of the gravity or interactance hypothesis as our point of departure, a risk-theoretic human capital model of migration is developed. Such a formulation treats migration as an investment decision under uncertainty and focuses attention upon the expected return and associated variability of returns from migration as the crucial variables in the migratory decision. In introducing risk or uncertainty (where, in order to avoid unnecessary complications we treat the investment decision under uncertainty as though it were simply a case of risk) we are, in effect, proposing the human capital analog of the job opportunity differential hypothesis. However, unlike the traditional viewpoint, these two hypotheses — income differentials and job opportunity differentials — are conceived of as complements rather than substitutes.[1] In other words, in a regime of (at least) short run constancy in the structure of inter-regional earnings differentials, job opportunity differentials are of primary importance in the timing of migration decisions while earnings differentials (or the expected net return to migration) determine the direction of migration. Treating these two hypotheses as complementary — where wage differentials are a necessary but not a sufficient condition for movement — is a particularly fruitful line of enquiry in pointing to the fact that, in cross-section studies of migration, attention should be focused not upon the determinants of the volume of migration *per se*, but upon the

*From Paul C. Langley, 'The Spatial Allocation of Migrants in England and Wales: 1961–66', *Scottish Journal of Political Economy*, Vol. 21, November 1974.

determinants of the spatial pattern or reallocation of migrants by origin and destination region.

Other important differences between this study and those reported on by Hart and Jack should also be mentioned. First, we only consider the behaviour of male migrants, not total migrants, and, more significantly, male migrants disaggregated by age group. This follows from the requirement that in assessing the relative importance of particular explanatory variables, groups should be identified whose behaviour may be expected, on *a priori* grounds, to be homogeneous with respect to the variables under consideration. In consequence four age groups are identified: 15 to 19 years of age; 20 to 24 years; 25 to 44 years; and 45 to 64 years. More detailed age breakdowns, particularly for the younger migrant cohorts, were not possible given the format in which these data are published. In all cases the dependent variable, gross migration, is specified as an out-migration rate (M_{ij}/P_i) where i and j are origin and destination regions respectively, M is gross migration and P the population exposed to the risk of out-migration. For a full discussion of data sources and definitions adopted in the specification of the dependent variable the reader is referred to the appendix to this paper.

Second, particular attention is directed towards the interpretation that is to be placed upon the role of a distance variable in a gross migration model (in particular the possibility of non-linearities in the form of a distance function) and the effect of introducing a relatives and friends variable of the form proposed by Greenwood (1969); where relatives and friends in a potential destination region perform both an informational and real income function. A final point to note is that, in estimating our model on inter-standard region gross migration for the quinquennium preceding the 1966 census date, results may not be directly comparable to those of other studies which have focused upon one-year migration flows (e.g., Hart, 1970).

THE MIGRATION MODEL

The migration model proposed here, which is simply a special case of a more generalised mobility model, takes a human capital viewpoint of the traditional labour market adjustment mechanism. The treatment of migration as an investment decision is strictly neo-classical and is comparable to a number of recent developments in the theory of labour supply (e.g., Pencavel, 1970). It differs from the accepted human capital approach in one significant respect: an explicit introduction of risk as an element specified in the objective function faced by a potential migrant.[2] We assume (i) that the individual is a risk averter and (ii) that the individual has a unit period utility function[3] of the form

$$U = a - ce^{-b\delta}$$

where U is the utility from migration; a, b and c are parameters $c, b > 0, a \lessgtr 0$, and δ is the net return from migration in the period under consideration. The net return is a stochastic variable as there is uncertainty about both the costs and returns of migration (defined to include both monetary and psychic components). We assume that the probability distribution of returns, which may be taken as representing some measure of the degree of belief that a particular outcome will occur — which may itself be evaluated from observed actions or the migratory experience of other individuals or from the past migratory experience of the individual himself — is normally distributed:

$$\delta \sim N(\mu_\delta, \sigma_\delta^2)$$

The migrant is assumed to maximise the expected value of utility which, given the normality assumption, is

$$E(U) = a - c\left[\exp\left(-\frac{b}{2}\mu_\delta + \left(\frac{b}{2}\right)^2 \sigma_\delta^2\right)\right]$$

$$\max E(U) \leftrightarrow \max\left(\mu_\delta - \frac{b}{2}\sigma_\delta^2\right)$$

Following Farrar (1967) we can now specify the objective function which an individual is assumed to maximise as

$$Z = \mu_\delta - \frac{b}{2}\sigma_\delta^2$$

subject to the constraint that $\delta > 0$.

There are certain features of the objective function which should be clarified. In the first place it is only proposed as a theoretical framework — not as a particular functional form which is to be specified — for the analysis of mobility decisions. Second, in emphasising risk aversiveness (where b may be interpreted as a coefficient of risk aversion) it points to the fact that expected (net) returns and the variability of returns enter jointly into the utility function of the individual: an individual is faced with an opportunity set of potential alternative destinations (including the decision to remain where he is), each element of the set being described $(\mu_\delta, \sigma_\delta^2)$. Finally, in explicitly building up the maximising behaviour of an individual within a human capital framework, the objective function provides an approximation to the mean-variance or portfolio selection models characteristic of post-war developments in 'non-human' capital theory.

SPECIFICATION OF THE MODEL

In the specification of variables entering the objective function a crucial problem is the interpretation and estimation of risk. Risk, as defined above, clearly encompasses a variety of factors and should not be considered narrowly as simply the probability of having, obtaining or retaining a job in a given time interval. As our model is derived directly from the theory of occupational choice risk will encompass not only the variability of return specific to a given occupation but also the effect of general labour market factors upon the variability of return: short-time working, overtime and annual employment experience. As the influence of these factors will be captured by the distribution of annual returns characteristic of a region, an obvious candidate is some measure of the dispersion of income from employment: the standard deviation or coefficient of variation. The latter measure is to be preferred as it provides a measure of dispersion independent of the mean. We may argue therefore, as a first approximation, that the two objects of choice may be represented by expected earnings and the coefficient of variation of annual earnings. Unfortunately, compared to other countries, available earnings data for the standard regions of England and Wales leave a great deal to be desired. For the period 1961-66 the only source of regional earnings data is from the Inland Revenue sample of Schedule E returns (Inland Revenue, 1966). The deficiencies of these data are well known (Stark, 1972). Among the most significant are: (i) income is defined as income subject to tax; (ii) incomes below exemption limits are excluded; (iii) incomes reported, by class interval, correspond not to individuals but to income tax units; and (iv) omissions occur as a result of tax evasions, tax avoidance and erosion of surtax base. If these deficiencies are coupled with biases arising from choice of measure of dispersion (e.g., the standard deviation is biased towards dispersions at the upper end of a distribution) then it is clear that the resulting estimates may be misleading. Such was, in fact, found to be the case. From an examination of regional coefficients of variation of Schedule E income distributions, not only was there a significant positive correlation with the corresponding expected return estimate ($r = 0.43$) but also a positive and significant rank order correlation with female regional activity rates ($r' = 0.82$). In the latter case, the effect of regional differentials in female activity rates (given definition of income-tax units) is to increase the dispersion of returns more than in proportion to the expected returns. It may be argued, therefore, that observations as to a positive relationship between migration and coefficient of variation of Schedule E earnings is, in large part, indicative of differential female participation rates (see Table 1.11).

Two surrogate measures of a regional earnings dispersion variable were considered: (i) annual average unemployment rates 1961-65, and (ii) the expectation of remaining on the register of wholly unemployed on entry in weeks (Fowler, 1968).[4] Of these two surrogate measures the latter is to be preferred as it would appear to be a more sensitive barometer of regional differentials in annual labour force experience. In the case of the East Midland and London and South East regions, for example, while the annual average unemployment rate is the same (1.1 per cent), a person becoming unemployed in the East Midland region could expect to spend longer on the register of wholly unemployed than in London and the South East (Table 1.11). Regional differentials in the rate of turnover of the unemployed are therefore indicative of differentials in the incidence of annual employment experience which are not captured in an annual average unemployment rate — although the

Table 1.11

Standard Regions of England and Wales, Selected Economic Indicators 1965-66 and 1961-65

Standard region	Average earnings (£) 1965-66	Standard deviation earnings (£) 1965-66	Coefficient of variation earnings 1965-66	Female activity rate 1966	Annual average unemployment rate 1961-65	Expectation of remaining on unemployment register on entry (weeks) 1961-65
Northern	857.5	396.3	0.462	34.6	3.3	11.2
Yorkshire & Humberside	840.4	467.5	0.556	40.0	1.3	6.5
North Western	831.8	468.4	0.563	43.0	2.0	7.9
East Midland	895.3	431.0	0.481	39.6	1.1	8.0
West Midland	941.4	511.8	0.544	44.0	1.1	6.1
East Anglia	843.3	376.9	0.447	33.4	1.2*	6.1*
South East	974.0	574.9	0.590	44.0	1.1†	5.0†
South West	854.1	408.2	0.478	32.5	1.7	8.5
Wales	881.1	410.4	0.466	30.2	2.8	8.6

NOTE: *Eastern and Southern Region.   †London and South East Region

SOURCE: see appendix.

correlation between the two series is positive and significant ($r = 0.86$).

The next variable to be considered is distance — defined here as the highway mileage distance between the major regional population centres (not, unfortunately, population centres of gravity). Within a human capital framework, distance is introduced in order to capture some of the elements of the cost of migration: these costs are taken to include (i) transportation costs; (ii) other money costs of migration; (iii) the psychic costs of moving; and (iv) the difference in psychic income between sending and receiving areas. These cost elements are not encompassed in the specification of expected return and the associated variability of return as defined above. In addition, the introduction of a distance variable will also capture one aspect of the flow of labour market information. One would expect that, on *a priori* grounds, the density and content of an information flow would be inversely related to the distance over which a particular message has to travel. An observed negative relationship between the spatial reallocation of migrants may reflect, therefore, not simply the influence of cost factors (both monetary and psychic) but the attenuating effect of distance upon the quality and quantity of labour market information. If labour market information is sufficiently scarce, the spatial allocation of migrants will be determined by the spatial distribution of information.

Inter-regional labour market information flows may be classified as either general or particular in nature. General information flows merely give a summary picture of overall labour market conditions in a particular region; particular flows on the other hand provide information as to specific job openings and job opportunities. While it is true that migrants do move on the basis of low-content general information, such individuals are the exception rather than the rule. Recent evidence suggests (Nickson, 1969) that the majority of migrants who move for job orientated reasons do so on the basis of a particular job offer. Information as to specific job opportunities can arise in two ways: formally, through a firm advertising or contacting a local employment office, or informally, through its existing employees. Under competitive demand conditions there is no incentive for firms to incur the cost of distributing formal information, either locally or inter-regionally. Even if formal distribution of information is felt necessary, the market would have to deviate considerably from the competitive model to make recruiting at a distance worthwhile. Similarly, employment agencies are unlikely to recruit at a distance. Not only are unit administrative costs higher, but there may be an additional disincentive effect if the employment agency has to bear the cost, or could be charged part of the cost of moving the potential migrant.

Under competitive demand conditions, relatives and friends are expected to be the only group with an incentive to distribute informal, job specific information (Nelson, 1959). The existence of relatives and friends in a potential destination region may therefore be expected to increase the propensity of individuals to move to that region. Relatives and friends will also perform a real income function: not only do people prefer to live near relatives and friends (a 'taste' hypothesis; reduction in psychic cost of moving and a reduction in differences in psychic income between regions) but relatives and friends may fulfil a social security role in providing food and shelter to recent arrivals. Recognition of the possible informational and real income roles of relatives and friends has led a number of authors (e.g. Greenwood, 1969 and 1970) to introduce in single equation models of gross migration a migrant stock variable, number of persons living in j born in i ($MS_{j/i}$) to capture the distribution of relatives and friends in alternative potential destination regions. In introducing such a variable it is argued that since the distribution of relatives and friends is a function of past migration, it is a function of all variables which determined past migration. Thus, calculated regression coefficients between migration and given explanatory variables will tend to overstate the true direct relationship between these variables and current migration. This is because, in addition to their direct or current impact, these variables will affect the distribution of migrants indirectly through their past effect on the distribution of relatives and friends. Parameter estimates on most variables will therefore tend to obscure the true direct relationship between these variables and migration (Nelson, 1959; Greenwood, 1969).

While the general merits of this argument are recognised, a number of objections may be raised against the introduction of a migrant stock variable in the form proposed by Greenwood. The single most important objection is that the introduction of such a variable into a single equation gross migration model involves the implicit assumption that the migrant cohort in question is homogeneous with respect to its past migratory experience; specifically, that all migrants are new migrants as opposed to return or multiple migrants.[5] In other words, that the individuals concerned have no past migratory experience. If a migrant stock variable is to be introduced then an identification of migrants by past migratory experience or the lack of it is essential. If not, then some form of stock variable is required, amended to take account of the distribution of relatives and friends appropriate to the return and multiple migrant components. Unfortunately, given an almost complete lack of information as to the relative importance of new, return and multiple migrants in given uni-directional gross flows for the United Kingdom in addition to conceptual problems associated with the definition of the 'stock' appropriate to return and multiple migrants, it is not possible to suggest an appropriate variable. Fortunately, some preliminary investigations with respect to the role of a migrant stock variable for inter-provincial gross migration flows in Canada by the present author, where it is possible to isolate out the new migrant component in total gross flows, indicate that the impact of a relatives and friends variable of the form suggested by Greenwood is virtually identical for both total gross and new migrant flows. In consequence, there was felt to be some justification for the introduction of a stock variable for inter-standard region flows in England and Wales although disaggregation of migrants by past migratory experience was not possible.[6]

A further objection to the introduction of a stock variable of the form suggested by Greenwood is that there is no expectation that the density of given inter-regional information flows (number of messages per unit of time) will be a direct function of the size of migrant stock in the potential destination region. The density of any given information flow will be a function of (i) the number of relatives and friends who maintain contact with the 'home' region and (ii) the frequency of that contact. The probability that a given migrant will maintain contact with his home region may be assumed to be inversely related to his duration of residence in the non-home region. Given this assumption, the number of relatives and friends who might be expected to maintain contact will be a function of (i) the temporal pattern of past migration; (ii) the age structure of past migration; and (iii) mortality (including subsequent re-migration). The frequency of contact will be expected, *ceteris paribus*, to be an inverse function of the distance over which a message has to travel. In order to capture the density of information flows two procedures are hence necessary; first, a correction of the migration stock variable for the time pattern and demographic characteristics of past migration streams, and second, a correction for the expected frequency of messages per unit of time. In the absence of data which distinguish the temporal and demographic characteristics of past migration streams, we may approximate our migrant stock density variable by the distance (D_{ij}) between sending and receiving regions in the form $[MS_{j/i}]/D_{ij}$.

Turning to the real income function of relatives and friends, it follows from the arguments above that one cannot argue that the greater the migrant stock the greater the attraction of a region to a potential region to a migrant. The existence of relatives and friends with whom the individual has lost touch are unlikely to influence his migratory decision. Furthermore, for a potential migrant who has remained in contact 'taste' will be greater for those individuals with whom he has maintained a close association, i.e., with whom the frequency of contact is greatest. In short, rather than a simple migrant stock variable, a more appropriate specification of the real income effect will be identical to that for the density of information flows.

Given the four elements of our model — the expected return, the surrogate measure of the variability of return, distance and relatives and friends (definitions and data sources for these variables are given in detail in the appendix) — the model may be restated as follows:

$$M_{ij}^x = \phi(Y_i; Y_j; U_i; U_j; D_{ij}; MS_{j/i})$$

where M_{ij}^x is male gross migration from region i to region j in age group x;

Y_i, Y_j are expected income from employment (income tax units) in region i and j respectively;

U_i, U_j are the expectation (in weeks) of remaining on the unemployment register on entry in region i and j respectively;

D_{ij} is highway mileage distance between regional population centres i and j; and

$MS_{j/i}$ is migrant stock corrected for distance.

Expected signs on partial derivatives are:

(1) $\partial M_{ij}/\partial Y_i \gtreqless 0$ (4) $\partial M_{ij}/\partial U_j < 0$

(2) $\partial M_{ij}/\partial Y_j > 0$ (5) $\partial M_{ij}/\partial D_{ij} < 0$

(3) $\partial M_{ij}/\partial U_i \gtreqless 0$ (6) $\partial M_{ij}/\partial MS_{j/i} > 0$

Hypotheses (1) and (3) deserve some elaboration as we would normally expect to find a composite hypothesis that relates migration to the difference in expected return between destination and origin region $(Y_j - Y_i)$. This separation follows from the fact that there is no *a priori* expectation that the partial derivatives on income at origin and destination are equal but of opposite sign. The expectation of a negative sign on origin region income will be modified, as Vanderkamp argues (1970) through the influence of wealth and productivity effects. To the extent that average labour income in a region reflects average labour productivity, a low income region is more likely to be characterised by a lower quality labour force. Persons from low income regions will thus be expected to have a lower average income opportunity than persons from higher income regions moving to a given alternative region. It follows from this that average origin income will have a positive effect on migration. This positive effect will be reinforced via capital market imperfections and their effect upon the ability of individuals to finance a move. If wealth accumulation is a positive function of income then individuals with a high income level will be more able to finance a move. Once again, origin income may have a positive effect on migration. Similar arguments may be advanced in the case of hypothesis (3).

It is also to be noted that male migrants have been identified by age group; this follows from the requirement that groups be selected whose behaviour may be considered, on *a priori* grounds, to be homogeneous with respect to given explanatory variables. In the case of the distance variable, for example, given that age or duration of residence increases one's attachment to a community, we would expect to find that the attenuating effect of distance upon out-migration rates is a positive function of age. A similar expectation holds with respect to the sign and elasticity of migration with destination duration on the unemployment register (U_j).

A less obvious criterion for the disaggregation of migrant cohorts is past migratory experience or the lack of it. One of the basic objections to existing migration studies is the failure to recognise that migrants differ with respect to their past migratory experience. With one or two exceptions (Eldridge, 1965 and Vanderkamp, 1971) it has been assumed (implicitly) that the phenomenon of return and multiple migratory behaviour is of little relevance to the analysis of the determinants of gross migratory flows. Such an assumption is clearly unwarranted, given that recent empirical evidence analysed by the author indicates that new, return and multiple migrants differ significantly in their response to origin and destination characteristic variables and distance — at least in respect of inter-provincial gross migration in Canada. In the absence of data which permit the identification of migrants by past migratory experience there is little that can be done apart from recognising that any interpretation of estimated regression models is to be qualified accordingly.[7]

EMPIRICAL RESULTS

Before proceeding to a full specification and estimation of our model, it is of interest to consider the hypothesis that out-migration probabilities[8] are largely determined by average income from employment in sending and receiving regions and by the distance between them. Such an exercise is important for the following reasons: first, it provides a first approximation to our complete model on the assumption of risk neutral behaviour[9] and an absence of information constraints; second, it provides a basis for comparison with previous studies; and, third, it serves as a useful way of introducing the question of non-linearities in the migratory decision. Restricting our analysis to male migrants in the 15 to 64 age group, the ordinary least squares result for migration, income and distance is:

$$M_{ij}/P_i = -545.345 \quad -0.069Y_i \quad +0.709Y_j \quad -0.148D_{ij}$$
$$(-2.881) \quad (-0.500) \quad (5.704) \quad (-1.633)$$

$$\bar{R}^2 = 0.348$$

This result ('t' values in parentheses) clearly supports our expectations as to the role of destination income and, to a lesser extent, the attenuating effect of distance on migration probabilities. Even so, the overall significance of the equation is clearly less than satisfactory even for a cross-section model. In an attempt to improve the fit, it might be argued that the above specification is inappropriate in the sense that it ignores possible non-linearities in the migratory decision. This is of particular interest in the case of the distance variable. A number of authors have suggested that the migrant's view of remoteness may not be a simple linear one; nearby areas may be strongly differentiated while remote areas may be regarded as uniform. Hagerstrand (1957) has proposed that the psychological and economic view of distance be generalised within a logarithmic transformation of distance. Vanderkamp (1971) and Courchene (1970) suggest two alternative specifications of the income-distance hypothesis where the income variables are distance standardised and distance introduced in reciprocal form. Each of these alternative transformations was examined within the context of the simple income-distance model. It was found that a logarithmic-linear formulation gave the most satisfactory results and this form was in consequence adopted for the complete model.

In order to gauge the impact of introducing a migrant stock variable two sets of regression results are presented: (i) the model estimated without a migrant stock variable (table 1.12); and (ii) the complete model incorporating the migrant stock (Table 1.13). The results given in Table 1.12, omitting the migrant stock variable, give strong support to the hypotheses advanced as to the role of destination income, destination unemployment duration and distance in the allocation of out-migrants for the standard regions of England and Wales. Destination earned income and distance are consistently significant at the one per cent decision level and take the expected sign for all age groups. The attenuating effect of distance, elasticity of out-migration with respect to distance, is positively correlated with the age of migrant cohort, reaching a maximum for migrants in the 45 to 64 years group. The elasticity of migration with respect to destination income, on the other hand, is greatest for the age group 25 to 44 years and least for those aged 15 to 64 years. Interpretation of the age-specific impact of earned income is obscured, however, by the absence of age-specific earnings data for the standard regions. Destination unemployment duration is less significant as an explanatory variable − in the majority of cases only significant at the five per cent decision level, with a failure to meet even this criterion for migrants in the oldest age group.[10] The sign on U_j is, however, consistently negative, in support of the hypothesis advanced above with the disincentive effect of destination unemployment duration strongest for the age group 15 to 19 years, followed by a negative association with age for all other groups. Origin income and duration of unemployment are not significant at the five per cent level although, in the case of the latter variable, the sign is consistently positive. This result is not surprising given the arguments advanced above as to the off-setting impact of wealth and productivity effects. Following from this, it is to be noted that the absolute size of the regression coefficients on Y_i and U_i are less in all cases than the corresponding absolute size of coefficients on Y_j and U_j respectively.

Even though there is, separately, strong support for the hypotheses advanced above as to the role of destination region characteristics, the overall explanatory power of our model is low compared to the explanatory power of the models proposed by both Hart and Jack. This, in one sense, is not that surprising given the restricted nature of the model and the failure to incorporate job opportunity variables (for example, of the form suggested by Laber and Chase, 1971) or destination population size as suggested by Jack. While it would be possible to reformulate the model along these lines, it must be emphasised that the focus here is upon the role of selected destination–origin characteristic variables.

A major problem associated with the introduction of a migrant stock variable of the form proposed by Greenwood is the attendant possibility of introducing an unacceptable level of multicollinearity. Preliminary investigations revealed that not only was there a significant level of collinearity present in the non-migrant stock variant of our model (Glauber-Farrar chi-square statistic of 51.918 with 10 degrees of freedom) but that the introduction of the amended migrant

Table 1.12

England and Wales: Inter-regional Male Gross Migration 1961–66
Probability Distribution (M_{ij}/P_i) Regression Model

Migrant Age Group	Intercept	Y_i	Y_j	U_i	U_j	D_{ij}	$\bar{R}^2$
15 to 64 years	−32.613*	−0.160	5.748†	0.144	−0.760*	−0.504†	0.400
	(−1.875)	(−0.097)	(3.488)	(0.380)	(2.018)	(3.390)	
15 to 19 years	−27.753	0.006	4.912†	0.256	−1.283†	−0.459†	0.379
	(−1.400)	(0.004)	(2.614)	(0.598)	(−2.990)	(−2.707)	
20 to 24 years	−35.676	−0.072	6.234†	0.236	−0.987*	−0.546†	0.357
	(−1.656)	(−0.036)	(3.054)	(0.505)	(−2.117)	(−2.966)	
25 to 44 years	−29.813*	−0.593	5.809†	0.053	−0.719*	−0.473†	0.414
	(−1.802)	(−0.378)	(3.706)	(0.149)	(−2.007)	(−3.350)	
45 to 64 years	−37.576*	1.019	5.198†	0.292	−0.641	−0.602†	0.319
	(−1.886)	(0.540)	(2.753)	(0.676)	(−1.487)	(−3.537)	

NOTES: (1) 't' values in parentheses.
(2) As the dependent variable is scaled $(M_{ij}/P_i) \cdot 10^3$, the regression coefficients are to be interpreted as $(b \cdot 10^{-3})$.

*Coefficient is significant at 5% level.
†Coefficient is significant at 1% level.

Table 1.13

England and Wales: Inter-regional Male Gross Migration 1961–66 Probability Distribution
(M_{ij}/P_i) Regression Model (Including Migrant Stock Variable)

Migrant Age Group	Intercept	Y_i	Y_j	U_i	U_j	D_{ij}	$MS_{j/i}$	$\bar{R}^2$
15 to 64 years	−7.290 (−0.556)	−3.196† (−2.574)	2.802† (2.263)	0.099 (0.368)	−0.280 (−1.013)	−0.161 (−1.406)	0.522† (7.965)	0.692
15 to 19 years	−5.155 (−0.297)	−2.773 (−1.688)	2.214 (1.352)	0.216 (0.606)	−0.844* (−2.308)	−0.145 (−0.956)	0.478† (5.510)	0.570
20 to 24 years	−5.243 (−0.305)	−3.590* (−2.204)	2.820* (1.736)	0.185 (0.521)	−0.432 (−1.190)	−0.149 (−0.991)	0.605* (7.033)	0.629
25 to 44 years	−7.617 (−0.584)	−3.335† (−2.697)	3.149† (2.554)	0.013 (0.050)	−0.286 (−1.038)	−0.164 (−1.473)	0.472† (7.222)	0.670
45 to 64 years	−4.888 (−0.353)	−2.711* (−2.062)	1.578 (1.204)	0.237 (0.831)	−0.052 (−1.178)	−0.182 (−1.493)	0.641† (9.243)	0.701

NOTES: (1) 't' values in parentheses.
(2) As the dependent variable is scaled $(M_{ij}/P_i) \cdot 10^3$, the regression coefficients are to be interpreted as $(b \cdot 10^{-3})$.

*Coefficient is significant at 5% level.
†Coefficient is significant at 1% level.

stock variable ($MS_{j/i}/D_{ij}$) increased the significance of the degree of collinearity markedly (Glauber-Farrar chi-square statistic of 121.372 with 15 degrees of freedom). In comparison, the unamended form of migrant stock variable ($MS_{j/i}$) resulted in a much lower degree of collinearity (Glabuer-Farrar chi-square of 80.087). As the amended form of migrant stock variable added nothing to the additional explanatory power contributed by the unamended form, it was decided to substitute the latter form in all estimating equations.

The Nelson-Greenwood argument for the introduction of a migrant stock variable is that in the absence of such a variable, calculated regression coefficients between migration and selected explanatory variables will tend to overstate the 'true' direct relationship between these variables and the spatial distribution of out-migrants as these variables affect migration indirectly through their past effect on the distribution of relatives and friends. It follows that the introduction of a relatives and friends variable should result in a marked reduction in the absolute size of, at least, the coefficients on the destination characteristic variables (Y_j and U_j) and on the distance elasticity of migration. Inspection of the regression coefficients for the full model (Table 1.13) indicates that this is indeed the case; while the destination characteristic variables and distance retain their expected signs there is a marked reduction in the absolute size of the coefficients. In the case of distance the effect of introducing the migrant stock variable is to reduce the significance of the distance coefficient drastically with the net result that, for each age group, this variable fails to pass even the five per cent decision level test. Not only does this result suggest that distance entered into the determination of the spatial distribution of past migration but, as Greenwood (1970) argues, to the extent that the migrant stock variable picks up the effects of non-economic factors for which distance is a proxy and hence allows the distance elasticity to reflect more clearly the effects associated with the economic factors, this indicates that the simple money costs of moving are not of themselves a crucial obstacle to the migratory decision.

Although the direct effect of destination income from employment on current migration is still significant for total male migrants and for migrants in the age groups 20 to 24 and 25 to 44 years, the overall significance of this variable is less than when the effects of income on past migration are taken into account.[11] A similar conclusion holds with respect to the role of destination unemployment duration, although the direct effect of this variable is only significant at the five per cent decision level for migrants in the age group 15 to 19 years. Given the historical constancy in England and Wales in the structure of inter-regional earnings and unemployment experience differentials, these conclusions are not too surprising.

While it is recognised that the bulk of the explanatory power in the full model is to be attributed to the migrant stock variable, the empirical results point to the fact that destination income and duration of unemployment have significant indirect, if not direct, effects on the spatial allocation of migrants. Highway mileage distance, on the other hand, if it is interpreted narrowly as reflecting the variable costs of migration is relatively unimportant. The crucial factor in the allocation of migrants is, it is suggested, the informational and real income role of relatives and friends.[12]

CONCLUSIONS

It has been recognised for some time that past migration influences current migration through the informational and real income role of relatives and friends. The introduction of a migrant stock variable into a relatively crudely specified risk-theoretic model of migration confirms that not only do relatives and friends play a significant role but that destination region characteristic variables also contribute significantly, both directly and indirectly, to locational choice. Even though the results of this investigation compare favourably with those reported on by other authors, migration studies for the United Kingdom are still in their infancy. One important limitation, the failure to identify migrants by past migratory experience, has been spelt out in some detail. There are many others. In such a poor data regime it is in fact surprising that our results are as useful as they are. Quite clearly, considerably more work needs to be done before we can hope to come to grips with the analysis of the determinants of inter-regional mobility for this country. [. . .]

NOTES

1. The traditional view is that, at least in the short run, they are substitutes (Reynolds, 1951). While the neo-classical model of the labour market would relate mobility to the price of labour in one employment relative to another, a view emerged following upon findings of the National War Labor Board in the United States that the price system operates sluggishly in the labour market. If the price of labour adjusts only slowly and inefficiently to disequilibrium, adjustment is thrown onto the quantity of labour. Mobility is thus related to the availability of jobs. A corollary of this is that, if wage differentials are not to emerge, quantity adjustment must be rapid. This is, in fact, not the case. It is for this reason that a complementary view is proposed, i.e. equilibrium is achieved via both price and quantity adjustments in the short run.
2. One of the major criticisms of the theory of human capital or the theory of occupational choice is its implicit assumption of risk neutrality. It is only recently that an attempt to explicitly take account of risk, along the lines of this model, has been formulated (Weiss, 1972). Such a neglect is all the more surprising given the comments of Friedman and Savage (1948) in their analysis of choices involving risk.
3. The time dimension is implicit rather than explicit as we are only concerned here with expository convenience.
4. It is to be noted that the reciprocal of the expectation for a stationary register is equal to the rate of turnover of the register (Fowler, 1968, p. 6).
5. Return migrants may be defined as individuals who, in some sense, are returning to their 'home' region; multiple migrants as those who have migrated at least once before and who, in their next move, do not return 'home'.
6. It would be a relatively easy task to produce such tabulations given that both the 1966 and 1971 census of England and Wales permit the identification of usual place of residence at two different points in time (one year and five years) before the census date.

7. Vanderkamp (1971) demonstrates that the existence of return migration (in a data regime which does not permit the identification of a return migration component) implies either a reduced form estimating equation – which eliminates the simultaneity created by return migration linking migration flows in opposite directions – or the introduction of an estimate of average return migration as an explanatory variable. In the absence of data which would permit the estimation of average return migration for England and Wales, it would be possible to develop a reduced form estimating equation. There are, unfortunately, problems associated with the specification of such a reduced form. First, Vanderkamp's arguments are developed for a regime in which multiple migration is absent. Once the existence of return migration is recognised it is not obvious how this group could be incorporated. Second, as argued above, the concept of a migrant stock variable is not applicable with respect to return and multiple migrants. Introduction of a migrant stock variable of the form suggested above into a reduced form would impart a degree of bias which would render difficult the interpretation of reduced form parameters.

8. This form of migration rate (M_{ij}/P_i), where P_i is the population exposed to the risk of out-migration is preferred to a gravity based rate ($M_{ij}/P_i.P_j$) as this latter form implies a number of assumptions as to the underlying pattern of gross flows. Preliminary tests were also carried out to determine whether or not a distributional migration rate was more appropriate (i.e., $M_{ij}/\sum_i M_{ij}$). While the distributional form performed marginally better, there was no real benefit to be derived from using it. For any one destination region, of course, an out-migration rate is a linear transformation of the distributional measure.

9. Recognising that uncertainty may enter via the distance variable.

10. The model was also estimated substituting annual average male unemployment 1961–65 for the duration of unemployment variable. In all cases this variable performed less well than unemployment duration.

11. It is to be noted that the impact of origin income from employment, in the full model, has in the majority of age groups a significant negative (direct) effect on out-migration.

12. It might be argued that the migrant stock variable is in fact picking up the effect of destination population size, which might crudely be interpreted as some measure of job opportunities. A model which incorporated a destination population size variable in place of the migrant stock variable did not perform as well. The zero order correlation between migrant stock and population size was estimated to be, for 1961, equal to 0.56 (significant at the 5 per cent level).

REFERENCES

Courchene, T. J. (1970). Interprovincial Migration and Economic Adjustment. *Canadian Journal of Economics.*

Department of Employment (1971). Regional Female Employment Activity Rates, 1966–70. *Gazette*, October 1971.

Dodd, S. C. (1950). The Interactance Hypothesis. *American Sociological Review.*

Eldridge, H. T. (1965). Primary, Secondary and Return Migration in the United States, 1955-60. *Demography.*

Farrar, D. E. (1967). *The Investment Decision Under Uncertainty.* Markham.

Friedman, M. and Savage, L. J. (1952). The Utility Analysis of Choices Involving Risk. In *Readings in Price Theory.* Irwin.

Fowler, R. F. (1968). *Duration of Unemployment on the Register of the Wholly Unemployed.* Central Statistical Office, Studies in Official Statistics, No. 1, H.M.S.O.

Greenwood, M. J. (1969). An Analysis of the Determinants of Geographic Labor Mobility in the United States. *Review of Economics and Statistics.*

Greenwood, M. J. (1970). Lagged Response in the Decision to Migrate. *Journal of Regional Science.*

Hagerstrand, T. (1957). Migration and Area: survey of a sample of Swedish migration fields and hypothetical considerations of their genesis. *Land Studies in Geography, Series B, Human Geography.*

Hamilton, C. H. (1965). Practical and Mathematical Considerations in the Formulation and Selection of Migration Rates. *Demography.*

Hart, R. A. (1970). A Model of Inter-Regional Migration in England and Wales. *Regional Studies.*

Hart, R. A. (1972). The Economic Influences on Internal Labour Force Migration. *Scottish Journal of Political Economy.*

Inland Revenue (1966). Report of the Commissioners of HM's Inland Revenue, Annual Income Survey 1965–66. Cmnd. 3508.

Isard, W. (1960). *Methods of Reginal Analysis: an introduction to regional science.* New York.

Jack, A. B. (1971). Inter-Regional Migration in Great Britain: some cross-sectional evidence. *Scottish Journal of Political Economy.*

Laber, G. and Chase, R. W. (1971). Interprovincial Migration in Canada as a Human Capital Decision. *Journal of Political Economy.*

Nelson, P. (1959). Migration, Real Income and Information. *Journal of Regional Science.*

Nickson, M. (1969). *Geographic Mobility in Canada: October 1964 to October 1965.* Special Labour Force Studies, No. 4. Ottawa.

Oliver, F. (1964). Inter-Regional Migration and Employment, 1951–61. *Journal of the Royal Statistical Society*, Series A.

Pencavel, J. (1970). *An Analysis of the Quit Rate in American Manufacturing Industry.* Princeton.

Reynolds, L. G. (1951). *The Structure of Labor Markets.* Harper.

Stark, T. (1972). *The Distribution of Personal Income in the United Kingdom, 1949–1963.* Cambridge.

Vanderkamp, J. (1970). *Toward a Theory of Labour Mobility.* Discussion Paper No. 47, Department of Economics, University of British Columbia.

Vanderkamp, J. (1971). Migration Flows and their Determinants, and the Effects of Return Migration. *Journal of Political Economy.*

Weiss, Y. (1972). The Risk Element in Occupational and Educational Choices. *Journal of Political Economy.*

1.5 A Paradox Regarding the Use of Time*

1. THE PROBLEM

In his well known article, Becker[1] introduces time to be spent in consuming into the decision set of the consumer. However, he does not consider all of the implications of introducing the time constraint. In particular, he does not consider the effect of spending time in making a decision. We will show that when this element is included, indeterminacies appear in the solution.

We will use the simplest of Becker's models, that in which per hour earnings are constant. We will also ignore the non-wage part of income. Finally, we will use Becker's equations in one of their intermediate forms. These simplifications do not affect our results; they merely make our point clearer.

The goal of the consumer is to maximize

$$U = U(x_1, \ldots, x_m; T_1, \ldots, T_m) \text{ (Becker's equation 4, p. 495)} \quad (1)$$

*From Paul H. Rubin, 'A Paradox Regarding the Use of Time', *Indian Economic Journal*, Vol. 20, January–March 1973.

Subject to

$$\Sigma x_i p_i + \Sigma T_i \bar{w} = T\bar{w} \text{ (Becker's equation 9, p. 497)} \qquad (2)$$

where x_i is a market good used in the production of commodity Z_i

   T_i is the time used in production of Z_i $[Z_i = f_i(x_i, T_i)]$

   P_i is the price of x_i

   $\bar{w}$ is the market wage

   T is total time available.

First order conditions are:

$$Ux_i = \lambda p_i \qquad (3)$$

$$UT_i = \lambda \bar{w} \qquad (4)$$

$$\Sigma x_i p_i + \Sigma T_i \bar{w} = T\bar{w} \qquad (5)$$

We have $2m + 1$ equations and $2m + 1$ unknowns (the x, T_i and λ). It appears that we have a determinate solution.

This is not so. In particular, consider the time which the consumer must spend in actually solving the problem. Presumably, the solution to the problem of how to spend his time and money is one of the goods which the consumer is buying, say, Z_m. Then surely we are through: we have solved for T_m already.

However, our indeterminacy has appeared. The consumer must spend time in solving the problem before he knows how much time to spend. It is possible that, e.g., the optimal value of T_m is ½ hour and he has spent 1 hour in solving the problem. Clearly, this is not an optimal solution; and just as clearly, there is nothing in the problem to prevent this from happening. It is just as likely that he will have spent less time than the optimum in solving the problem; in this case he will not spend his resources optimally. It will only be by coincidence that he will have spent just as much time in solving the problem as the optimum. (This is not a cost of information problem in the usual sense; we can assume that he knows exactly $\partial U / \partial T_m$ i.e., the effect on his utility function of spending more time in reaching a decision. None the less the problem remains.)

One apparent way out of the dilemma is to introduce another variable into the system, $Z_{m+1} = f_{m+1}(x_{m+1}, T_{m+1})$. Z_{m+1} can be defined as a solution to the problem, 'How much time should I spend in solving the problem of allocating my time?' Clearly, this will not work, for there is nothing to guarantee an optimal value for T_{m+1}. We can continually add new variables, but ultimately we will reach an impasse. The problem cannot be solved.

This does not mean, of course, that decisions cannot be made; obviously, such decisions *are* made. What it does imply is that such decisions cannot be made optimally, except by coincidence; there is always some misallocation in consumer decision making resulting from consideration of time spent in decision making.

II. EXTENSIONS

We have demonstrated an indeterminacy in consumer theory. The same problem will arise in producer theory when we begin to consider the problem of allocating the time of management. A manager must spend time in deciding how to spend his time; again, it will be only by coincidence that he will spend the right amount of time in making this decision. (Alternatively, we may say that a manager should allocate his time so that the marginal product is the same in all directions; but he will not know his marginal product until he solves for it, and by then it is too late.) In fact, it may well be that the misallocation in this area is more significant than the misallocation which arises in the behaviour of the consumer. It has been ignored in the literature because of the implicit assumption of instantaneous calculation.

Baumol and Quandt, in their discussion of rules of thumb, argue that such rules may be '. . . among the more efficient pieces of equipment of optimal decision making' because in many cases '. . . no more than an approximate solution may be justified.'[2] Our argument is stronger than this; rules of thumb in many cases are one way of avoiding the insoluble problem we have discussed; a rule of thumb may be used because an 'optimal' solution is impossible, not merely expensive.

This argument may also be related to Leibenstein's concept of X-efficiency. While the costs of necessary inefficiency are probably less than the costs of X-inefficiency in Leibenstein's examples,[3] they are part of the costs of X-inefficiency. That is, it may be impossible for a firm to reach what an outside observer would consider an optimum because of the decision making problem regarding time discussed in this paper.

Friedman has pointed out several examples of fundamental indeterminacies:[4] 'The interaction between the observer and the process observed' in both the physical and social sciences: the Heisenberg uncertainty principle; Godel's theorem in logic, which asserts the impossibility of a complete axiomatization of mathematics.[5] What we have attempted to show here is that similar indeterminacy appears if we include *all* inputs in the attempt at rational decision making.

NOTES

1. Gary Becker, 'A Theory of the Allocation of Time', *Economic Journal*, September, 1965.
2. William J. Baumol and Richard E. Quandt, 'Rules of Thumb and Optimally Imperfect Decisions', *American Economic Review*, March, 1964, p. 23.
3. Harvey Leibenstein, 'Allocative Efficiency vs. "X-Efficiency" ', *American Economic Review*, June, 1966.
4. Milton Friedman, 'The Methodology of Positive Economics', from *Essays in Positive Economics*, reprinted in Breit and Hochman, eds., *Readings in Microeconomics*, Holt, Rinehart, and Winston, 1968, p. 24, n. 4.
5. Ernest Nagel and James R. Newman. *Godel's Proof*, London, 1958.

1.6 Effort and X-efficiency*

1. INTRODUCTION

In conventional micro-theory firms are assumed to minimize costs irrespective of the market structure or economic environment in which they operate. The aim of this paper is to sketch a theory of the organization of the firm, and its relation to its environment, under which firms do *not* minimize costs. In other words, according to our theory identical purchasable inputs at identical prices and equal access to knowledge of the state of the art will normally lead to a wide variety of outputs under different organizational circumstances. In order to pursue this aim we shall sketch a framework of analysis that looks at the firm from an unconventional viewpoint. The main element emphasized is that similar individuals will supply different amounts of effort, where effort is a multidimensional variable, under different organizational and environmental circumstances. While the proposition that firms do not minimize costs is the main vehicle around which the sequence of ideas sketched in this paper is organized, it will turn out that there are a number of other interesting implications that flow from the theory. For example, some firms will not introduce improvements when it is profitable to do so. Finally, we shall argue that changes in the environment in which a firm finds itself will result in different costs per unit of output.

In order to follow the structure of the argument it may be helpful if we indicate briefly the various interrelated components of the theory to be sketched. (1) Initially we substitute for the conventional assumption of maximizing or optimizing behavior by economic agents a different set of psychological postulates which attempt to capture some components of an individual's personality, as well as other elements which determine the supply of effort. (2) We assume employment contracts which separate, within limits, the purchase of labor time and the supply of effort. (3) Once an individual becomes a firm member, we argue that he or she has to interpret his job. This essentially involves choosing what we shall call an 'effort position,' out of a possible set of such positions, and we determine in various circumstances the supply of effort for this portion of his firm's activities. We shall attempt to show that, in general, the individual will not choose an optimal job interpretation (or effort position) either from his viewpoint, or from the viewpoint of the interests of the firm. (4) Once individuals are established in their effort positions, they respond to a flow of signals, some of which initially come from outside the organization, others of which originate within the organization. (5) The nature of these responses, and the organizational contexts in which they are made, determine the supply of effort.

A basic part of the paper deals with some structural elements of the

*From Harvey Leibenstein, 'Aspects of the X-efficiency Theory of the Firm', *Bell Journal of Economics*, Vol. 6, Autumn 1975.

organization, and with how these elements influence the flow of signals intended to spur effort, as well as the flow of signals which result from, and form part of, the incentive structure of the organization. Finally, we shall consider briefly the relation between the environment in which the firm is embedded and the effort flow that is influenced by this environment. Thus, in essence we shall look at the firm as an entity in which human beings are organized to supply effort, usually with the aid of equipment and other materials, rather than look at the firm as an entity which makes price and quantity decisions on the basis of the demand functions it faces, the production techniques available to the firm, and the cost functions internal to the firm.

A basic difference between the theory to be sketched and the conventional theory is that in our theory, the basic micro unit is the individual rather than the firm. Hence, individual motivations, and interactions between individuals, turn out to be critical aspects of the analysis. The ideas to be presented have to some degree been presented elsewhere in connection with what the author has referred to as X-efficiency. [. . .]

A word on the meaning of X-inefficiency.[1]   X-inefficiency is contrasted with allocative efficiency.[2] Inputs or factors of production may be allocated to the *'right'* decision units. However, there is no need to presume that the decision and performance units involved *must* decide and actually use inputs as effectively as possible. We refer to the difference between maximal effectiveness of utilization and actual utilization as the degree of X-inefficiency. The basic X-efficiency hypothesis is that neither individuals, nor firms, nor industries are so productive as they can be.

I have argued elsewhere that, in primarily market economies, X-inefficiency is frequently much more important as a social cost than is allocative efficiency. While some of the empirical literature[3] suggests these hypotheses, it is of interest to see whether we can formulate a reasonable vision of human behavior within the organizational context of the firm and the industry out of which various degrees of X-inefficiency emerge as a result.

2. NEW PSYCHOLOGICAL POSTULATES: SELECTIVE 'RATIONALITY'

Since our analysis depends on a model in which the basic decision-making entities are individuals, it may be useful to indicate the psychological assumptions that form the basis of individual behavior — assumptions which are in contrast to the principle of maximizing (or optimizing) behavior of conventional micro-theory, and differ from Simon's principle of satisficing.[4] We use the overall concept of selective rationality to designate a set of psychological postulates which suggests that individuals behave neither 'fully rationally,' nor 'irrationally,' but choose some degree of rationality *as this term is used by economists.*[5] Although individuals come in a variety of psychological types, we try to designate an essential element of behavior behind this variety by assuming that in general individuals behave on the one hand (a) *as they like to,* and on the other hand, (b) *as they feel they must*. In other words, they strike a compromise between (a) the way they would like to behave if they had no sense of 'obligation' and/or are *not* subject to any constraining influences, and (b) the 'pressures' they feel because of their sense of obligation. Of course, the extent of the compromise will differ for different individuals. [. . .]

3. THE FIRM MEMBERSHIP RELATIONS, INERT AREAS, AND EFFORT POSITIONS

In this section we present a compact review of X-efficiency theory to the extent necessary for this paper.[6] To start with we visualize the firm as an entity composed of individuals who (1) have to interpret their membership relation to the firm, or their job, (2) recognize their relation to various groups within the firm, (3) function within a complete or partial hierarchical structure, and (4) respond to articulation of firm aims *to some degree*. We also assume that individuals are paid on a time basis (per week or per month, etc.) rather than by results.[7] Now a basic consideration is that the firm membership (or employment)[8] contract is incomplete and vague. Therefore, there are significant elements of choice open to individuals — *everyone associated with a firm has to interpret his or her job.*

An individual comes to a firm with certain vague notions of how to carry out his prospective job. He receives certain vague hints or incomplete information as to what, roughly, he is expected to do. As a result of experience and trial and error he discovers additional behavioral options. But to indicate how an individual determines his job interpretation we have to specify how he or she uses knowledge that the individual may gather during his interactions with others. The visualization of the process of knowledge acquisition and use sketched below will be presumed to hold throughout the paper. We bypass the problem of uncertainty. In its place, we posit what might be called a principle of temporarily sufficient knowlege. Although individuals make decisions in the face of intrinsic uncertainty, they may find it convenient to use even less knowledge than is available. Consider the following hypothetical situation. Suppose an 'encyclopedia' of twenty volumes contains the knowledge to make decisions with certainty; i.e., a complete catalogue of the external world's reactions to every option. Now assume that four volumes are destroyed and many decisions face some uncertainty. Suppose further that the sixteen other volumes are dismembered page by page and placed in a library in more or less random fashion. Decision-makers gather information in order to discover the responses to various options, but obviously such information gathering involves a cost. At some point they find they can make decisions which they believe will yield a positive reward. They then face two options. They can gather more information and undergo the utility cost involved or they can decide to stop the process. At some point they stop the process at approximately the point at which they feel that the utility cost of gathering more information is greater than the anticipated utility gain.

We are now in a position to indicate the meaning of a job interpretation. It is a process by which a firm member or employee selects a subset, from a set of possible *activity-pace-quality-time* bundles (to be referred to as *APQT* bundles or *effort points*). I.e., he must choose among alternative activities (A), the pace (P) at which he will carry out these activities, the quality (Q) of these activities, and the time (T) he will spend on each activity, and their sequence. Each *effort point* is associated with (1) *a productivity value* (contribution to value of output) which may or may not be known, and (2) *a utility value* for effort to the one putting forth the effort, including the utility of income from firm membership.

There are usually a variety of constraints on a person's choice determined by interdependent, interpersonal relations. In some analytical contexts, it helps to divide the activity part of the *APQT* bundles into those that involve other people (to be designated by A') and those that do not (designated by A''). Thus, people choose one or more $A'A''PQT$ bundles. The A' choices involve interpersonal relations and provide the contexts in which some individuals have influence on, or impose constraints on, a set of effort bundles available to others.

We distinguish between an effort point and an effort position. Individuals will normally not interpret their membership roles in rigid and precise terms. What is really chosen in interpreting one's job is an effort *position* − i.e., *a set of effort points*, or a neighborhood of effort points adjacent to each other, within which the individual is willing to extend his effort depending on circumstances. One reason for emphasizing the contrast between effort positions and effort points is the nature of the signals received by an employee (e.g., a verbal request, a written request, an order, a complaint, etc.) indicating varying *demands* for effort. Such signals, as usually interpreted, when heeded, trigger what the individual believes to be the appropriate effort response or one that he likes to give.[9] Aspects of the work context which could not be anticipated may be viewed by some individuals as signals to change effort, including the reduction of effort. However, we should *not* assume that individuals associate equal utility to all points in their effort positions.[10] [. . .]

Another aspect of the determination of the effort position is what we might refer to as the economy of habitual modes of behavior. In other words, there is a utility cost to seeking new modes of behavior, and hence, it is likely that most personalities will determine a satisfactorily *habitual* way of handling their jobs. Such habitual patterns may be connected psychologically with what we might refer to as 'ego entrenchment.' That is, the person will experience discomfort, or what is the same thing, some degree of disutility, if his habitual mode of handling the job is challenged in some way or another. We shall see later that this becomes an important element in making adjustments between the effort positions of different individuals.

A critical element in our theory is the concept of *inert areas*. The fact that there is a utility cost in a shift from one position to another implies that there is an area within the utility cost bounds such that movements from one position to another within these bounds will not take place. Opportunities for change which do not lead to a gain in utility (or to the avoidance of a loss of utility) greater than the cost of the shift will not be entertained. The inert area idea is related to human inertia. It depends, among other things, on some of the following considerations: the magnitude of the insensitivity area, the utility costs of decision-making, and habitual position preference — i.e., the gradual habituation of doing things in a certain way, etc. In some contexts, it may be especially useful to distinguish two separate components: (1) the utility cost of moving *away* from the present position — i.e., 'packing up' costs, so to speak, and (2) the utility cost of getting set up and 'settling in,' into the new position.

We can visualize a set of points where the utility cost of shifting from any one point within the set to any other *within* or *outside* that set is greater than the utility gained. Such a set of points is an 'inert effort area.'[11] By the means already described an individual will choose a subset of the effort points from what he believes to be a known and allowable choice set in order to determine his effort position. While the utility derived from effort will differ for different personalities, in the interest of simplicity we limit ourselves to what is likely to be a representative case. The utility from effort is the sum of the utility from income derived from the job and the satisfaction obtained from effort. A plausible assumption for a representative individual is that he prefers some effort to no effort, but beyond some point effort becomes less pleasurable, and as a result, the total utility from effort declines. However, there is likely to be a relatively flat section close to the utility peak since it is assumed that average individuals are relatively insensitive to small variations in effort.[12]

Before proceeding further to discuss the relation between effort positions and inert areas we have to consider the constraining influences that others in the firm will have on the individual, which in turn will influence the individual's utility from alternative effort positions. We distinguish three categories of constraining influences. (1) *Traditional constraints*: these represent those constraining influences that derive from history and tradition. Certain effort points will not be chosen because 'it has never been done that way' *traditionally*. Some traditions may be functional while others may be *arbitrary* in the sense that they have outlived the context in which they were functional, or they were imposed arbitrarily as a consequence of the power positions of some individuals. (2) *Vertical constraints*: these involve an asymmetry in the direction of influence. Examples abound in formal hierarchical systems in which superiors convey orders, transmit communications, or other 'signals' to subordinates. (3) *Horizontal constraints*: essentially these are the interpersonal influence relations among peers, some of which are taken into account in choosing effort points. All constraining or influence relations may be functional or *arbitrary* and dysfunctional.

The work-role choice confronts an individual with potential utilities and pressures that influence his *effort-utility* (*EU*) relations. These are the utilities ascribed to (1) good relations with superiors, (2) good relations with subordinates,

(3) good relations with peers, and (4) the value of conflict avoidance or roles outside of work. Given the possible collisions with other people's roles and with the person's own roles (outside work), it would seem at first blush that the pressures inherent in conflict, in view of their number, are likely to be very large. But serious role conflicts are cushioned or avoided by two basic factors: (a) the inert areas that surround not only one's own effort choices but also those of others, (b) the trade-off between role choice and informal group rewards such as approval, disapproval, etc., which influences both one's utility level and the nature of the adjusted effort-utility relation.

What rules in specific cases depend on personality characteristics? The pressures discussed so far are pressures *for* performance. These probably narrow the inert areas, but shift it towards the right. Pressures from peers (horizontal pressures) frequently are pressures *against* excessive performance and generally work in the opposite direction. [. . .]

NOTES

1. For further readings on our concept of X-efficiency the reader is directed to [6, 7, 8]. Since some of our ideas about the nature of X-efficiency have evolved since then, they will be reported briefly in a later section. This is especially true of the concept of 'effort positions.' Also, in some cases where our notions overlap with those of others, but where their nature or use is not identical, an attempt will be made to indicate the distinctions involved at the point where the ideas are initially introduced.

2. See Liebenstein [6]. While there is an overlap between our concept of X-inefficiency and the concept of 'slack' as used by both Williamson [19], and others [5], the concepts are not the same. According to Cyert and March [5], p. 36, 'Slack consists in payments to members of the coalition in excess of what is required to maintain the organization.' In our formulation, X-inefficiency is not uniquely connected to 'payments of a coalition,' but is related to the many motivational facets both within and outside the firm that determine the *effort* responses of individuals, as well as with the psychological assumptions expounded in Section 2.

3. Ibid. See also Bergsman [3], Shelton [13], and Shen [14].

4. See Simon [15, 16].

5. We have in mind here the frequent equating of rationality with maximization or optimization. It is our impression that even among economists usage is not always consistent. In an important sense there is nothing really irrational about behavior in accordance with the psychological postulates we assume. On a related issue, see Baumol's interesting discussion in [2].

6. To some extent the concepts presented here differ somewhat from those presented in earlier writings since they represent a gradual evolution of ideas. For a more comprehensive and detailed treatment of some of these ideas, see [7, 8]. Note, we use the terms 'firm membership relation,' and 'employment relation' or 'job' interchangeably.

7. For some groups within a firm it may be appropriate to consider the utility of the job as a function of the present value of the discounted income stream expected during the tenure of the job, and the utility from the job interpretation itself. In circumstances where the income stream depends on a career, part of the pressure will depend on the probabilities of promotion at various points in the career.

8. This is a somewhat broader concept than the 'employment relation' developed by Simon and Williamson. For a detailed exposition and analysis of the 'employment relation' see Williamson [20]. Also, see Simon [15].

9. We do not exclude the possibility that some effort positions may contain only a single

effort point. Also, there may be work contexts where individuals are given a certain task which they perform day in and day out, and in which there is little evidence that they respond to any flow of signals. However, even in such instances emergencies arise – equipment may break, some piece of material may appear defective, etc.

10. The reader should not assume that there is necessarily an effort-leisure trade-off involved in the choice of an effort position. Low levels of effort do not imply necessarily higher levels of leisure. Usually, leisure that is valued is 'non-job leisure' – i.e., more time away from the job. With respect to 'job leisure,' we must keep in mind that increased levels of effort may also be associated with increases in utility. There are many instances where people find that a shift in an effort point involves that they work a little harder and yet they get more satisfaction out of the change. There are other instances under which having 'time on one's hands' is irksome. In other words, we assume that there exist effort choices which involve more effort and more utility than some less effortful options.

11. Formally we should distinguish 'internal inert areas,' which are sets of points *within* which any move from one point to another involves a greater utility cost than utility gain, from a proper inert area, which is a set of points for which any movement from a point in the set to any believed allowable point inside or *outside* the set involve a utility loss from moving greater than the utility gain.

12. For a detailed discussion of utility effort function for different personality types, see Leibenstein [6].

REFERENCES

1. Baumol, W. J. *Welfare Economics and the Theory of the State*. Cambridge: Harvard University Press, 1965, p. 135.
2. Baumol, W. J. and Stewart, M. 'On the Behavioral Theory of the Firm,' in Marris and Wood, eds., *The Corporate Economy*, Cambridge: Harvard University Press, 1971, pp. 118–141.
3. Bergsman, J. 'Commercial Policy, Allocative and "X-Efficiency",' *Quarterly Journal of Economics*, Vol. 88, No. 3 (August 1974).
4. Cohen, K. J. and Cyert, R. M. *Theory of the Firm: Resource Allocation in a Market Economy*, Englewood Cliffs, N.J.: Prentice-Hall, Inc., 1965.
5. Cyert, R. M. and March, J. G. *A Behavioral Theory of the Firm.* Englewood Cliffs, N.J.: Prentice-Hall, Inc., 1963.
6. Leibenstein, H. 'Allocative Efficiency vs. "X-Efficiency".' *The American Economic Review*, Vol. 56 (June 1966).
7. Leibenstein, H. 'Competition and X-Efficiency: Reply,' *Journal of Political Economy*, Vol. 81, No. 3 (May/June 1973).
8. Leibenstein, H. 'Organizational or Frictional Equilibria, X-Efficiency, and the Rate of Innovation,' *Quarterly Journal of Economics*, Vol. 83 (November 1969).
9. March, J. G. and Simon, H. A. *Organizations*. New York: John Wiley and Sons, Inc., 1958.
10. Marglin, S. 'The Social Rate of Discount and the Optimal Rate of Investment.' *Quarterly Journal of Economics* (1963).
11. Nelson, R. R. and Winter, S. G. 'Toward an Evolutionary Theory of Economic Capabilities.' *The American Economic Review*. Vol. 63, No. 2 (May 1973), pp. 440–9.
12. Sen, A. K. 'Isolation, Assurance and the Social Rate of Discount.' *Quarterly Journal of Economics* (1967).
13. Shelton, J. P. 'Allocative Efficiency vs. X-Efficiency – Comment.' *The American Economic Review*, Vol. 57, No. 5 (December 1967), pp. 1252–8.
14. Shin, T. Y. 'Technology Diffusion, Substitution, and X-Efficiency.' *Econometrica*, Vol. 41, No. 2 (1973), pp. 263–84.
15. Simon, H. A. *Models of Man*. New York: John Wiley and Sons, Inc., 1957.
16. Simon, H. A. 'New Developments in the Theory of the Firm,' *The American Economic Review*, Vol. 52, No. 2 (May 1962), pp. 1–15.

17. Spence, A. *Market Signaling: Informational Transfer in Hiring and Related Screening Processes*. Cambridge: Harvard University Press, 1974.
18. Williamson, O. E. *Corporate Control and Business Behavior*. Englewood Cliffs, N.J.: Prentice-Hall, Inc., 1970.
19. Williamson, O. E. *The Economics of Discretionary Behavior: Managerial Objectives in a Theory of the Firm*. Chicago: Markham Publishing Co., 1967.
20. Williamson, O. E. *Markets and Hierarchies*. Chapter 4. New York: Free Press, 1975.
21. Williamson, O. E. 'Markets and Hierarchies: Some Elementary Considerations.' *The American Economic Review*, Vol. 63, No. 2 (May 1973).
22. Winter, S. G. 'Satisficing, Selection, and the Innovating Remnants.' *Quarterly Journal of Economics*, Vol. 85, No. 2 (May 1971).

1.7 X-efficiency Challenged*

Harvey Leibenstein called attention in an influential article (1966) to a source of economic inefficiency which was given the awful name of X-[in]efficiency. He cited studies in which misallocations of resources due to monopoly or tariffs had trifling social costs, whereas simple failure to attain the production frontier apparently led to social losses of a vastly greater magnitude. I propose to argue that this type of inefficiency can usefully be assimilated into the traditional theory of allocative inefficiency.

It is a question (to be discussed below) whether one ascribes failures to reach the ultimate limits of output from given inputs in any state of technology to inadequacy of knowledge alone, or adds also inadequate 'motivation.' Leibenstein (1966) separates the two:

It is obvious that not every change in technique implies a change in knowledge. The knowledge may have been there already, and a change in circumstances induced the change in technique. In addition, knowledge may not be used to capacity just as capital or labor may be underutilized. More important, a good deal of our knowledge is vague. [pp. 404–5]

He ascribes increases in X-efficiency to (1) increases in motivational efficiency — workers are stimulated by incentive pay, or management by competition or other adversities; and (2) improvements in the inefficient markets for knowledge. I shall first deny the propriety of treating changes in motivation as a source of changes in output, and then proceed to the question of knowledge.

I. MOTIVATIONAL LOSSES

Leibenstein (1973) has emphasized that X-inefficiency arises largely from losses of output due to motivational deficiencies of resource owners:

[F]or the same set of human inputs purchased and the same knowledge of production techniques available to the firm, a variety of output results are possible. If individuals can choose, to some degree, the APQT bundles [choice of Activity, Pace, Quality of work, Time spent] they like, they are unlikely to choose a set of bundles that will maximize the value of output. [p. 768]

*From George J. Stigler, 'The Xistence of X-Efficiency', *American Economic Review*, Vol. 66, March 1976.

If management seeks to impose output-maximizing *APQT* bundles on the workers, indeed, these assignments of tasks would likely be '. . . less efficient than those that individuals would choose themselves under an acceptable set of [managerial] restraints' (p. 769).

In this case, and in every motivational case, the question is: what is output? Surely no person ever seeks to maximize the output of any one thing: even the single proprietor, unassisted by hired labor, does not seek to maximize the output of corn: he seeks to maximize utility, and surely other products including leisure and health as well as corn enter into his utility function. When more of one goal is achieved at the cost of less of another goal, the increase in output due to (say) increased effort is not an increase in 'efficiency'; it is a *change* in output.

The concept of motivational efficiency seems to extend also to the task of getting a 'predetermined output' from hired factors (see Leibenstein, 1966, pp. 408, 412). There are important and pervasive problems in all contracts between people, in seeking the fulfillment of the reciprocal contractual promises, and substantial resources are necessary to enforce the agreements (see Armen Alchian and Harold Demsetz). Both the avoidance of unpleasant tasks and the enforcement activity designed to curtail this avoidance can be carried on to the utility-maximizing degree and generate no inefficiency in producing utility. Output and utility would be larger if resources were not necessary to the enforcement of contracts, but output and utility would also be larger if water boiled at 180°F or a day had 25 hours. New techniques of contract enforcement may be as productive as other improvements of technology.

Thus X-inefficiency attributed to motivational factors characterizes as inefficiency either the existence and pursuit of other desired outputs or the expenditure of resources required for the optimal enforcement of contracts. This tunnel vision of output seems entirely unrewarding: it imposes one person's goal upon other persons who have never accepted that goal. There is no waste in this sort of X-inefficiency: waste is a foregone product that could be acquired for less than its cost.

Leibenstein achieves much of the importance of motivation in X-efficiency by that ancient and powerful scientific technique, definition. When he copiously illustrates that 'changes in incentives will change productivity per man' (1966, p. 401), he is assigning motivation an independent role whereas ordinary economic language would classify the methods of remuneration of employees as a part of the state of technology. Again, when an Egyptian petroleum refinery becomes more 'efficient' with a change of management, we are told that 'It is quite possible that had the motivation existed in sufficient strength, this change could have taken place earlier' (1966, p. 398). Potential motivation could indeed rewrite all history: if only the Romans had tried hard enough, surely they could have discovered America. (Thus motivation can be invoked to explain every unperformed task that is physically possible, no matter how unrewarding.) We may sympathize with Leibenstein's desire to associate his X-efficiency with economic behavior, but this shotgun marriage is not fertile.

II. THE STATE OF TECHNOLOGY

The near-universal tradition in modern economic theory is to postulate a maximum possible output from given quantities of productive inputs — this is *the* production function — and to assert that each firm operates on this production frontier as a simple corollary of profit or utility maximization. The merit of this conventional tradition is also its demerit: it eliminates the problem of the choice of technology.

Alfred Marshall followed an entirely different approach, and it is remarkable that he had virtually no followers. He proposed to characterize production possibilities by the *average* outputs obtained from given inputs, and in particular labelled the user of this average relationship the Representative Firm:

We shall have to analyse carefully the normal cost of producing a commodity, relatively to a given aggregate volume of production; and for this purpose we shall have to study *the expenses of a representative producer* for that aggregate volume. On the one hand we shall not want to select some new producer just struggling into business, who works under many disadvantages, and has to be content for a time with little or no profits, but who is satisfied with the fact that he is establishing a connection and taking the first steps towards building up a successful business; nor on the other hand shall we want to take a firm which by exceptionally long-sustained ability and good fortune has got together a vast business, and huge well-ordered workshops that give it a superiority over almost all its rivals. But our representative firm must be one which has had a fairly long life, and fair success, which is managed with normal ability, and which has normal access to the economies, external and internal, which belong to that aggregate volume of production; account being taken of the class of goods produced, the conditions of marketing them and the economic environment generally. [p. 317, and Bk. IV, ch. 13]

Marshall suggested two causes of variation among firms in costs of a given output: the age of the firm (which he emphasized), and variations in entrepreneurial capacity. Strictly speaking, the latter element (the departure from 'normal ability') is inappropriate: differences in quality of an input do not lead to differences in outputs from given inputs.

The reason Marshall's approach was not adopted by the science is lucidly presented in the leading attack that was made on the representative firm by Lionel Robbins. In a once-famous essay, Robbins argued persuasively that when costs of firms differed because of quality of entrepreneurs (or other inputs), the differences in productivity would be reflected in differences in profits (or other input prices). Just as differences in efficiency of workers are reflected in their wages, so differences in entrepreneurial skills (including the choice of technology) will be reflected in their 'profits.' He states:

There is no more need for us to assume a representative firm or representative producer, than there is for us to assume a representative piece of land, a representative machine, or a representative worker. [p. 393]

Robbins was of course correct: the Representative Firm is not needed to reconcile the existence of differences among entrepreneurs with the existence of stable competitive equilibrium.

What one may lament, however, is the failure of Robbins and Leibenstein, and all of us in between, to recognize the problem of determining which technologies will be used by each firm (and, for that matter, each person). The choice is fundamentally a matter of investment in knowledge: the costs and returns of acquiring various kinds and amounts of technological information vary systematically with various characteristics of a firm: its size, the age of its present capital assets, the experience of its managers, the prospects of the trade. No attention has been paid by economists to the analysis of the optimal amount of technological knowledge that a firm should possess. Leibenstein deserves credit for reviving this Marshallian question, but his attention to X-inefficiency as the explanation is an act of concealment: it simply postulates the differences in technology among firms which should be explained.

III. THE INTERPRETATION OF OUTPUT DIFFERENCES

We observe two farmers with reasonably homogeneous land and equipment, who nevertheless obtain substantially different amounts of corn. We measure this corn output over some period of time to reduce the effects of stochastic variation (i.e., unenumerated inputs such as weather). The observed variation is due, perhaps, to differences in knowledge, including the knowledge of technology or the knowledge of how far to carry the application of each productive factor. The farmers will differ in the cost of learning new things or the expected returns from new knowledge — one may be planning to leave agriculture shortly shortly — so they 'rationally' devote different amounts of resources to acquiring knowledge. Or one is simply more intelligent than the other, and learns more quickly or thinks more precisely (for example, makes fewer mistakes in arithmetic).

The effects of these variations in output are all attributed to specific inputs, and in the present case chiefly to the differences in entrepreneurial capacity. In neoclassical economics, the producer is always at a production frontier, but his frontier may be above or below that of other producers. The procedure allocates the foregone product to some factor, so in turn the owner of that factor will be incited to allocate it correctly.

Leibenstein does not attempt to understand the allocation of 'inefficient' resources, and hence does not see the necessity for attributing his X-inefficiency to specific inputs. Just as automobile accidents are palpable inefficiencies to many people so X-inefficiency is a palpable inefficiency to Leibenstein. But accidents and 'inefficiencies' are associated with returns as well as costs, and a useful theory must take both sides of their roles into account.

Indeed, Leibenstein's apparatus does not allow him to analyze effectively concrete economic problems. Consider his argument that monopoly is less efficient than competition. To reach this result, he must assume that (1) monopolists do not maximize profits, and (2) competitors are driven closer to 'the' minimum costs by the entry of new rivals, some of whom are efficient, by a Darwinian process. The first assumption is an abandonment of formal theory, and one which we shall naturally refuse to accept until we are given a better theory. It 'solves' the question of the effect of monopoly on efficiency without argument or evidence. The latter assumption of competitive selection coolly ignores the problem of general equilibrium (where do the driven out entrepreneurs go?, and where do the efficient entrepreneurs come from?), and fails to demonstrate (or even to argue) that inflows and outflows of entrepreneurs of various qualities will converge on a high-efficiency equilibrium in each competitive industry.

Earlier I defined waste as the situation in which foregone products could be obtained for less than they cost. Waste can arise *ex post* because *ex ante* plans rested upon erroneous predictions. This type of waste is unavoidable, although its magnitude is subject to control. Waste can also arise in the absence of uncertainty if the economic agent is not engaged in maximizing behavior. Unless one is prepared to take the mighty methodological leap into the unknown that a non-maximizing theory requires, waste is not a useful economic concept. Waste is error within the framework of modern economic analysis, and it will not become a useful concept until we have a theory of error.

REFERENCES

Alchian, A. A. and Demsetz, H., 'Production, Information Costs, and Economic Organization,' *Amer. Econ. Rev.*, Dec. 1972, *62*, 777–95.
Leibenstein, H., 'Allocative Efficiency vs. "X-Efficiency",' *Amer. Econ. Rev.*, June 1966, *56*, 392–415.
Leibenstein, H., 'Competition and X-Efficiency: Reply," *J. Polit. Econ.*, May/June 1973, *81*, 765–77.
Marshall, A., *Principles of Economics*, 8th edn., London 1948, 317.
Robbins, L., 'The Representative Firm,' *Econ. J.*, Sept. 1928, *38*, 387–404.

2. The Firm

Introductory Note

THE simple neoclassical theory of the firm's demand for labour is a relatively straightforward exercise in the implications of profit maximization. In the product market, equilibrium requires that marginal cost equals marginal revenue. Similarly, with respect to its inputs, the firm must set the additional revenue derived from the employment of an extra unit equal to the increase in cost which results. In other words, it is a necessary condition for profit maximization that the net marginal revenue productivity of labour (MRP for short) be equal to the marginal cost of labour (MCL). If this rule were not obeyed, it would be possible for the firm to increase its profits by changing the amount of labour it employs.

Matters are not quite as simple as this suggests. Like the analysis of labour supply, the theory of the demand for labour must be multi-dimensional. The employer buys labour services, a package with three component parts: the number of workers employed, the number of hours per worker performed in any given period, and the intensity of work (or the amount of effort extracted). Simplicity of exposition demands that, for much of this section, we assume that both hours per worker and effort levels are constant, only the number of workers remaining to be determined.

A rigorous and extremely thorough treatment of this question is provided by Ferguson (1969). Some of the more important points can be brought out in a more impressionistic way. The firm's MCL can be derived immediately from its labour supply curve

$$L = L(w) \tag{1}$$

which relates the quantity of labour supplied to the firm (L) to the wage rate (w). The MCL is defined as the change in the firm's total wage bill ($w \cdot L$) as employment changes:

$$\text{MCL} = \frac{d}{dL}(w \cdot L) = w + \frac{dw}{dL} \cdot L. \tag{2}$$

The shape taken by the MCL curve depends entirely on the shape of the labour supply curve. If the firm is a perfect competitor in the market for its labour, able to buy as much as labour as it wishes without affecting the wage rate (and therefore facing a perfectly elastic labour supply curve), then $dw/dL = 0$, and

MCL is equal to the wage. If the firm has any degree of monopsony power, being unable to increase its labour force indefinitely at a given wage, its labour supply curve will be upward-sloping, dw/dL will be positive, and MCL will exceed the wage. The recruitment of additional labour will be possible only if the firm offers a higher wage, which, we assume, must be paid to the existing labour force as well as to the new recruits (that is, we rule out the possibility of wage discrimination between individuals by the firm). There is very little empirical evidence about the shape of firms' labour supply curves, despite considerable theoretical speculation.

The net marginal revenue productivity of labour (MRP) is defined as the change in the firm's total revenue (R) after subtracting for changes in other costs, resulting from the employment of an additional unit of labour. Total revenue is, of course, the product of price and quantity, where

$$p = f(q) \tag{3}$$

is the firm's product demand function, and

$$q = f(K,L) \tag{4}$$

is the production function facing the (single-product) firm, relating its output to the quantities of capital (K) and labour employed. It can be shown without too much difficulty[1] that

$$\text{MRP} = \frac{\partial}{\partial L}(p \cdot q) = \frac{\partial q}{\partial L}\left(p + \frac{dp}{dq} \cdot q\right). \tag{5}$$

Here $\partial q/\partial L$ is the marginal physical product of labour (MPP), derived directly from the production function. The bracketed term is the firm's marginal revenue (MR), obtained from the product demand curve. The MRP, then, is the product of MPP and MR.

There is a related concept which is often confused with the MRP. This is the value of the marginal product (VMP), which is defined as MPP multiplied by *price*. It is clear from equation (5) that the VMP will equal MRP *only* when the product price equals MR, that is, when the firm is a perfect competitor in the market for its product. In general MRP will be less than VMP, since (given a downward-sloping product demand curve) MR is less than price.

The four possible combinations of product and labour market conditions are represented in Figure 2.1, where (for simplicity) we disregard the existence of distinct types of non-perfect competition. It is only in the *special case* where the firm is a perfect competitor in *both* markets that the wage will equal the VMP. Generally the wage will be less than VMP. Moreover, in the absence of perfect competition in the labour market, the wage will also be below the MRP.

For a firm which possesses no monopsony power, the MRP function constitutes its labour demand schedule, that is, the function relating the quantity of labour employed to the wage rate imposed upon the firm by the perfectly competitive labour market in which it operates. Such a firm will almost certainly

	Perfect Competition in the Labour Market	Non-Perfect Competition in the Labour Market
Perfect Competition in the Product Market	$MRP = VMP$ $w = MCL$ $\therefore\ w = VMP$	$MRP = VMP$ $w < MCL$ $\therefore\ w < VMP$
Non-Perfect Competition in the Product Market	$MRP < VMP$ $w = MCL$ $\therefore\ w < VMP$	$MRP < VMP$ $w < MCL$ $\therefore\ w < VMP$

FIG. 2.1

employ less labour as the wage rate increases. This will be the case for two reasons. First, and according to the law of variable proportions ('law of diminishing returns'), MPP will eventually decline as labour input increases. Second, marginal revenue will certainly not increase as more labour is employed (and a larger output thrown on to the product market); unless the firm faces a perfectly elastic product demand curve, it will decline. This point, which is fundamental to much of neoclassical labour economics, may be put rather differently. A *ceteris paribus* increase in the wage rate will reduce equilibrium employment because it induces two kinds of substitution: in production, as relatively cheaper capital replaces relatively more expensive labour, and in consumption, as purchasers switch to relatively cheaper commodities. Even if substitution in production is impossible (owing the existence of rigidly fixed technical coefficients of production), substitution in consumption will generally ensure that the firm's labour demand curve is downward-sloping.

If the firm is a monopsonist, there are complications. Such a firm cannot be said to have a labour demand curve, in the sense of a function establishing a one-for-one relationship between the wage rate and the equilibrium quantity of labour employed. This is so because a change in the elasticity of labour supply will alter the MCL associated with each wage rate, thereby changing the equilibrium employment level with an unchanged wage.[2] Surprisingly, Rees (1973, p. 76) seems to have been the first to make this clear, and to draw the (in retrospect) obvious parallel with the well-known proposition that the product market monopolist has no supply curve.

The practical importance of this conclusion is uncertain, as there is no reason to suppose, *a priori*, that the forces which produce shifts in labour supply curves either do or do not affect their elasticities at each wage rate. One extreme but interesting case involves the creation of perfectly competitive conditions (of a sort) in monopsonistic markets. Consider, for example, the impact of a statutory (or union-imposed) minimum wage, which has the effect of rendering perfectly elastic a section of the firm's labour supply curve. This permits a simultaneous increase in both the wage rate and employment. In Figure 2.2 the firm is initially

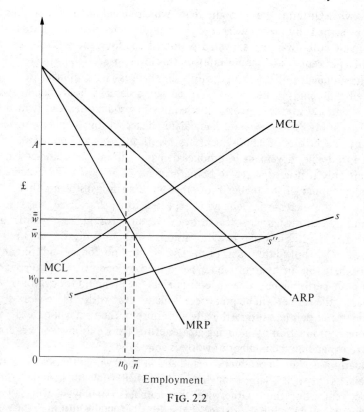

Employment

FIG. 2.2

in equilibrium with a wage of w_0 and employment n_0, earning excess profits of Aw_0 per unit of labour employed. When a minimum wage of $\bar{w}$ is imposed its supply curve shifts from ss' to $\bar{w}s''s'$, as it can pay no less than $\bar{w}$, at which wage rate it can (up to ss'') obtain as much labour as it wishes. This results in an *increase* in the equilibrium level of employment, to $\bar{n}$. The minimum wage could be set as high as $\bar{\bar{w}}$ without any reduction in employment. Of course, once the minimum wage has been established, any further increase must lower employment.

Up to now it has been assumed that the employment relationship is a purely impersonal one, and that adjustments to the level of employment are instantaneous. As Oi (Reading 2.1) demonstrates, neither assumption is tenable once allowance is made for the existence of fixed labour costs, of which training expenses are generally the most important. To the extent that such costs are borne by the firm rather than the worker, they represent an investment by the firm in the worker. Like investments in physical capital, this human investment will be undertaken only if it is expected to be profitable. It is only when labour is a purely variable cost that the firm will maximize profits by equating marginal revenue productivity and marginal labour cost. In general MRP must *exceed*

MCL by what Oi terms the 'periodic rent', which he defines as 'the surplus that must be earned by each worker in order to amortize the initial fixed employment costs over the expected period of employment realizing a rate of return of r per cent [the discount rate] on this investment' (Oi, p. 122).

One consequence of this is that short-run changes in the number of workers employed will tend to be rather muffled. In a casual labour market, where labour is entirely a variable cost, fluctuations in product demand (which lead to changes in MRP) will generate immediate changes in the numbers employed. When the fixed costs of employment are significant, this will no longer be the case. A favourable movement in product demand will induce an increase in employment only if it is expected to be permanent, or at least to be sustained for a period long enough to render profitable the human investments that will be required. If the increase in demand is expected to be short-lived, the firm will rely upon its existing labour force, through overtime working or attempts to call forth greater effort. The other two dimensions of labour demand briefly referred to above now come into their own. The firm is no longer indifferent, for example, between an hour of labour performed by one of its existing workers and an hour performed by a new recruit; unless the premium for overtime working is large, the former will be preferred. Equally, even with a piece-work system which increases earnings proportionally with output, the firm will have an incentive to raise production by inducing greater effort from existing workers in preference to expanding the number of workers employed.

Similarly a decline in product demand and in MRP will in the short-run result in dismissals only if it is large enough to reduce MRP below MCL, wiping out the periodic rent altogether. Otherwise the numbers employed will fall only gradually, through 'natural wastage',[3] the bulk of the adjustment in output coming about through reductions in hours worked per worker (via cuts in overtime, and short-time working), and perhaps also through a slackening in effort standards. At the macroeconomic level this helps to explain why unemployment is a 'lazy indicator', reflecting changes in aggregate demand only after a considerable time-lag. It also accounts, in part, for the perverse pro-cyclical fluctuations in aggregate labour productivity (see Taylor, 1974). As Oi observes, it indicates reasons for the higher average level and greater volatility of unemployment among less-skilled workers. The fixed costs of employing such workers are relatively low, so that they are the first to be dismissed in a recession and the last to be recalled by their employers.

Further implications of fixity are developed by Doeringer and Piore in Reading 2.2. An obvious feature of human capital is that — outside slavery — its ownership is vested in the worker even if it has been financed by the firm. The worker is free to leave the firm, even though a quit will render the firm's investment in the worker totally worthless. It follows that employers will be unlikely to finance *general* training, thereby producing skills which can be used in other concerns, since (unless the labour market is highly imperfect) competition between prospective employers is likely to increase wages and reduce periodic rents towards zero. The firm will finance *specific* training, creating skills which are useless in other enterprises, but only if it expects the newly-trained worker to remain in its employ for long enough to amortize the investment and provide a satisfactory rate of return.[4] Accordingly a firm which finances training has a direct interest in reducing labour turnover. The institutional manifestation of this concern is the set of rules which constitutes the internal labour market, shielding the worker against competition from outside the firm and protecting the firm from the losses occasioned by high rates of turnover. The essence of the internal labour market is the provision of incentives for job stability, the most important of which are security of tenure, seniority payments, and opportunities for internal promotion. The result is a fragmentation of the labour market – a 'Balkanisation' as Kerr expresses it in Reading 4.6 – which (as intended) significantly impedes labour mobility,[5] and greatly complicates the analysis of wage differentials.

On this interpretation the internal labour market represents a thoroughly rational cost-minimizing, and therefore profit-maximizing, strategy. What if the firm does not in fact attempt to maximize profits, but has alternative goals? It has often been suggested that the interests of managers of large corporations differ from those of the owners, and that 'managerial utility' has supplanted profit as the firm's maximand (Williamson, 1964). It should be noted that this will affect its labour market behaviour only if the size or rates of pay of its labour force enter into the managers' utility function(s). There are in any case cogent arguments against placing great significance upon any conflict of interest between owners and managers (Nichols, 1969). No such conflict is supposed by Arrow's discussion of one form of non-profit motivation, that of racial prejudice (Reading 2.3). Arrow's premiss is that white employers (be they owners, or managers, or both) incur disutility from the proximity of black employees. Their distaste for blacks influences their behaviour by inducing them to employ blacks only at wage rates lower than those paid to white workers with comparable skills. Racial discrimination, it appears, can be explained in terms of the operation of an atomistically competitive labour market, without resorting to monopsonistic market imperfections, and certainly without recourse to such factors as social stratification and class power which are favoured by radical economists (Reich, 1971).[6]

Arrow recognizes the weakness of his own argument: it provides no evident reason why discrimination should not be competed away. Unless diseconomies of scale are implausibly large, no employer of whites will long survive competition from non-prejudiced firms using cheaper black labour. The racists will be bought out or driven into bankruptcy. This process might be delayed by the labour fixity considerations emphasized by Arrow, but not for more than one generation (the time taken to train a new, cheap, black labour force). Racially prejudiced employers cannot indefinitely persist in paying lower wages to black workers than to (equally productive) whites. They can simply refuse to hire any black workers, operating all-white establishments and leaving their non-prejudiced competitors to employ the blacks. But this gives rise only to the racial *segregation* of employment, not to long-run *wage differentials* between the races; and such differentials have persisted for generations. Arrow's unease is reflected towards the end of Reading 2.3 in his reluctant concession to radicalism. *Faute de mieux*, Arrow is forced to accept the possibility that only an explanation in terms of class co-operation among white employers, prejudiced and unprejudiced alike, may be adequate, 'though it is contrary to the tradition of economics' (p. 133). We shall see in the next section that a rather similar form of 'irrationality' — or, rather, non-individualistic behaviour — must be attributed to workers if any sense is to be made of trade unions.

Objections of a different kind are raised by Lester Thurow in Reading 2.4. Thurow argues that the level of applicability of marginalist theory has never been adequately defined. Is a worker's marginal product defined at a single point in time, for example, or (as Oi's argument might suggest) over his or her working life? Workers are frequently paid in groups, like the grades established by job evaluation procedures, and within the groups individual differences in productivity do not give rise to differences in earnings. Is this phenomenon consistent with, or evidence against, a marginalist theory of wages? It is unclear, he suggests, how economies and diseconomies of scale can be accounted for. If they exist, the sum of marginal productivity payments must either exceed or fall below total output, and the resulting problems have no obvious solution. Other open questions concern the indeterminacy of prices (and hence of marginal revenue products, and hence of wages) in oligopoly, and the treatment of disequilibrium in general. The apparent elegance and precision of marginal productivity theory, Thurow believes, is largely spurious. 'Fortunately or unfortunately, each reader is going to have to construct his or her own marginal productivity theory. Many of the necessary judgements have not been examined in the literature of economics, and others are subject to little, if any, consensus . . . As long as marginal productivity is left as a general amorphous theory, it can neither be used nor criticized' (p. 148). Thurow's personal conclusion, amplified in Reading 4.2 below, is that orthodox theory is of relatively little use in explaining the over-all distribution of labour income.

Even at the level of the individual firm, its empirical value has often been questioned. Lester (1946) claimed that most firms were not in fact cost-minimizers, as proved by their ability to achieve *ceteris paribus* reductions in costs in the face of unexpected economic adversity. Machlup's (1946) celebrated reply could deal with this element in Lester's case only by converting the theory into an (irrefutable) tautology.[7] Reynolds and Gregory (1965) came to conclusions very similar to Lester's from their study of successive increases in minimum wages in Puerto Rico. In short, there is much evidence that firms do not, in general, operate on their MRP curves, but employ more labour, or pay higher wage rates, than would in principle be necessary to produce any given level of output. It is probably true that part of this apparent 'X-inefficiency' represents the hoarding of labour in which fixed investments have been made, and is therefore entirely consistent with cost-minimization (see Reading 2.1). But it must be doubted whether this is the whole story. We saw in the previous section that under conditions of imperfect information the definition of rational behaviour is problematical. Uncertainty affects the firm no less than the worker, and may lead to the adoption of *satisfactory* rather than ideal solutions in both cases (see Reading 1.5 and, more generally, Cyert and March, 1963).

A rather difficult explanation is hinted at by Williamson in Reading 2.5. This reading suggests that the operation of internal labour markets is indeed consistent with cost-minimization, but it does so from a very individual view-point.[8] Williamson's argument is as follows. Many skills are 'idiosyncratic', that is, are not merely specific to the firm but also to some degree unique to the individual worker who has acquired them. This allows the worker to behave 'opportunistically', for example by shirking on the job and concealing from the employer that his or her effort level could be much higher. Williamson defines opportunism as 'self-seeking with guile' and argues that it can best be overcome through the combination of incentives and disincentives offered by the internal labour market. While this is an interesting contribution to the microeconomic analysis of industrial conflict – an unduly neglected area – it does not go far enough. In particular, Williamson ignores the possibility that internal labour markets and their rules and procedures may *themselves* be subject to opportunistic manipulation by workers. To the extent that this occurs, costs will not be minimized, and what may be termed the fundamental theorem of the neo-classical analysis of labour demand – 'higher wages means lower employment' – need no longer apply. A more general conclusion might be that the effort dimension to labour demand remains very much an enigma.

NOTES

1. By the product rule,

$$\frac{\partial}{\partial L}(p \cdot q) = q\frac{\partial p}{\partial L} + p\frac{\partial q}{\partial L}.$$

Equations (3) and (4) show that p is a function of q, while q is a function of L. Using the function-of-a-function rule, we can write

$$\frac{\partial p}{\partial L} = \frac{dp}{dq} \cdot \frac{\partial q}{\partial L},$$

so that

$$\frac{\partial}{\partial L}(p \cdot q) = q\frac{dp}{dq} \cdot \frac{\partial q}{\partial L} + p\frac{\partial q}{\partial L} = \frac{\partial q}{\partial L}\left(p + \frac{dp}{dq} \cdot q\right).$$

2. The elasticity of labour supply is defined as

$$n_L = \frac{dL}{dw} \cdot \frac{w}{L},$$

so that

$$\frac{1}{n_L} = \frac{dw}{dL} \cdot \frac{L}{w} \quad \text{and} \quad \frac{dw}{dL} \cdot L = \frac{w}{n_L}.$$

Hence

$$MCL = w + \frac{w}{n_L} = w\left(1 + \frac{1}{n_L}\right).$$

If elasticity changes, each wage rate is now associated with a different MCL from that prevailing before.

3. That is, quits, retirements, and deaths. Of course, in the long run the firm may close down altogether.
4. The *worker* too may be willing to finance specific training, depending on its expected effect on his (her) wage rate and the anticipated stability of employment in the firm concerned.
5. It does so partly through raising job search costs by increasing the amount of information that the worker requires; but only partly, because even a worker with perfect information has less incentive to change employers if such a move involves the loss of seniority and the devaluation of firm-specific skills.
6. For a detailed survey of theories of discrimination, see Marshall (1974). The model seems to have much less to offer to the analysis of sex discrimination (see Madden, 1972).
7. Lester has been accused of a gross methodological error, in that he attacked neoclassical analysis because of the lack of realism of its assumptions rather than challenging the truth of its predictions (see, for example, Friedman, 1953). On this point, at least, Lester had his orthodox critics hoisted neatly by their own petard.
8. Williamson argues that Doeringer and Piore deny that internal labour markets are cost-minimizing devices; this does not appear to be warranted.

REFERENCES

Cyert, R. M. and March, J. G. (1963) *A Behavioral Theory of the Firm*, Englewood Cliffs, N.J., Prentice-Hall.
Ferguson, C. E. (1969) *The Neoclassical Theory of Production and Distribution*, Cambridge University Press.
Friedman, M. (1953) 'The Methodology of Positive Economics', pp. 1–43 of his *Essays in Positive Economics*, University of Chicago Press.
Lester, R.A. (1946) 'Shortcomings of Marginal Analysis for Wage Employment Problems', *American Economic Review*, 36, pp. 63–82.
Machlup, F. (1946) 'Marginal Analysis and Empirical Research', *Amercian Economic Review*, 36, pp. 519–54.
Madden, J. F. (1972) *The Economics of Sex Discrimination*, Duke University Press.
Marshall, R. (1974) 'The Economics of Racial Discrimination: a survey', *Journal of Economic Literature*, 12, pp. 849–71.
Nichols, T. (1969) *Ownership, Control and Ideology*, London, Allen and Unwin.
Rees, A. (1973) *The Economics of Work and Pay*, New York, Harper and Row.
Reich, M. (1971) 'The Economics of Racism', pp. 107–13 of D. M. Gordon (ed.), *Problems in Political Economy: an urban perspective*, Lexington, Mass., D. C. Heath.
Reynolds, L. G. and Gregory, P. (1965) *Wages, Productivity and Industrialisation in Puerto Rico*, Homewood, Ill., Irwin.
Taylor, T. (1974) *Unemployment and Wage Inflation*, Harlow, Longman.
Williamson, O. E. (1964) *The Economics of Discretionary Behavior: managerial objectives in a theory of the firm*, Englewood Cliffs, N.J., Prentice-Hall.

2.1 Labour as a Quasi-Fixed Factor*

The cyclical behavior of labor markets reveals a number of puzzling features for which there are no truly satisfying explanations. Included among these are (1) occupational differences in the stability of employment and earnings, (2) the uneven incidence of unemployment, (3) the persistence of differential labor turnover rates, and (4) discriminatory hiring and firing policies. I believe that the major impediment to rational explanations for these phenomena lies in the classical treatment of labor as a purely variable factor.

In this paper I propose a short-run theory of employment which rests on the premise that labor is a quasi-fixed factor. The fixed employment costs arise from investments by firms in hiring and training activities. The theory of labor as a quasi-fixed factor is developed in Part I. In Part II, the implications of this theory are subjected to various empirical tests. Finally, Part III turns to an examination of alternative theories and an extension of my theory to a theory of occupational wage differentials.

The concept of labor as a quasi-fixed factor is, in my opinion, the relevant one for a short-run theory of employment. Its implications are amenable to empirical verification and are, in the main, borne out by the available evidence. Thus my theory provides a unified explanation for various aspects of the cyclical functioning of labor markets.

I. A SHORT-RUN THEORY OF EMPLOYMENT

According to the theory presented here cyclical changes in employment are explained by differential shifts in factor demands and supplies. The first two sections develop a theory of factor demands assuming rigid wage rates. In the next two sections this assumption is relaxed, allowing for variations in factor supplies.

A. *Nature of the classical short-run adjustment process*

In the classical short-run model certain paths of adjustment are barred to the firm. These barriers usually postulate the presence of fixed factors, short-run changes in output being effected by varying only the remaining factors.

Changes in the amount demanded of any factor are composed of two parts: (*a*) response to changes in the rate of output − the scale effect − and (*b*) response to variations in relative factor prices − the substitution effect. With an assumption of rigid wage rates, the substitution effects may be neglected and attention focused on the scale effects.

Consider a firm faced by a decline in product demand. The adjustment process involves a reduction in output accompanied by a decline in the demand for each variable factor. There is no reason to expect that the demands for all

*From Walter Y. Oi, 'Labor as a Quasi-Fixed Factor', *Journal of Political Economy*, Vol. 70, December 1962.

variable factors will be decreased by the same proportion. The reduced demands for variable factors led to an increase in the relative employment of fixed factors. In a sense, the firm now employs too much of the fixed factors and would, therefore, try to substitute fixed factors for variable factors. Consequently, those variable factors that tend to be most substitutable for, or least complementary with, the fixed factors will experience the greatest relative declines in demand due to any given decrease in product demand. The converse holds for an increase in product demand. Thus the variable factors that are most substitutable with the fixed factors will exhibit the greatest relative shifts in factor demands.

B. *Demand for a quasi-fixed factor of production*

A quasi-fixed factor is defined as one whose total employment cost is partially variable and partially fixed. In the classical short-run model all factors are classified as either variable or fixed. In the classical short-run model all factors are classified as either varible or fixed. Each factor may, however, possess a different degree of fixity along some continuum rather than lie at one extreme or the other.

From a firm's viewpoint labor is surely a quasi-fixed factor. The largest part of total labor costs is the variable-wages bill representing payments for a flow of productive services. In addition the firm ordinarily incurs certain fixed employment costs in hiring a specific stock of workers. These fixed employment costs constitute an investment by the firm in its labor force. As such, they introduce an element of capital in the use of labor. Decisions regarding the labor input can no longer be based solely on the current relation between wages and marginal value products but must also take cognizance of the future course of these quantities. The theoretical implications of labor's fixity will be analyzed before turning to the empirical magnitude of these fixed costs.

For analytic purposes fixed employment costs can be separated into two categories called, for convenience, hiring and training costs. Hiring costs are defined as those costs that have no effect on a worker's productivity and include outlays for recruiting, for processing pay-roll records, and for supplements such as unemployment compensation. These costs are closely related to the number of new workers and only indirectly related to the flow of labor's services. Training expenses, on the other hand, are investments in the human agent, specifically designed to improve a worker's productivity. The effect of training on productivity could be summarized by a production function showing the increment to a worker's marginal value product in the tth period, ΔM_t, due to an investment in training of K dollars per worker.[1]

$$\Delta M_t = g(K). \tag{1}$$

The total discounted cost, C, of hiring an additional worker is the sum of the present value of expected wage payments, the hiring cost, H, and training expense, K.

$$C = \sum_{t=0}^{T} W_t(1 + r)^{-t} + H + K, \tag{2}$$

where W_t is the expected wage in the tth period, r denotes the rate at which future costs are discounted, and T denotes the expected period of employment. The total discounted revenue, Y, generated by the additional worker is similarly defined as the present value of his expected marginal value products that, in each period, consist of his marginal product without training, M_t, and the increment due to his training, ΔM_t.

$$Y = \sum_{t=0}^{T} (M_t + \Delta M_t)(1 + r)^{-t}. \tag{3}$$

Profits will be maximized when the total discounted cost of an additional worker is just equal to the total discounted revenue.

$$H + K = \sum_{t=0}^{T} (M_t + \Delta M_t - W_t)(1 + r)^{-t}. \tag{4}$$

Equation (4) yields the first implication. In equilibrium a worker's total marginal product, $M_t + \Delta M_t$, must exceed the wage rate, W_t, so long as the firm incurs any fixed employment costs. Even under perfect competition wages would be equated to marginal value products if and only if labor is a completely variable factor.

At this point, a digression on the firm's investment in training is in order. The net value of training to the firm is simply the present value of the expected increment in marginal value product, ΔM_t, due to training.

$$V = \sum_{t=0}^{T} \Delta M_t(1 + r)^{-t}. \tag{5}$$

An investment in training will prove profitable if the net value to the firm, V, exceeds the training expense, K. Conceptually training may be categorized as either general or specific. Specific training is defined as that which increases a worker's productivity to a particular firm without affecting his productivity in alternative employments. The time required to adapt workers to the firm's particular production processes, or to its accounting and marketing processes, exemplifies specific training. General training, on the other hand, is defined as that which increases a worker's productivity in several competing employments, as, for example, the training of workers to operate computers or to read railroad tariffs.

Rational behavior implies that the bulk of a firm's investment in training must be devoted to specific training. If training were completely general, all returns would accrue to the worker and none to the firm. Upon completion of general training, the worker would find that his marginal productivity to several firms had been increased. He could now demand a higher wage, either from a competing firm or from his present employer. In either case, the net value of the training to the firm would be reduced to zero. Indeed, a firm could capture these returns only if there were impediments to competition such as imperfect knowledge or binding labor contracts. Thus, no rational firm would underwrite completely general training.[2] If, however, training is specific to a firm, then the worker's alternative marginal product remains unaffected. In this latter case, the firm could weigh the expected returns from this investment against the training cost. To simplify the analysis, I shall assume that the firm bears all specific training costs. As will be shown in section D below, the implications of the theory are not seriously affected by relaxing this assumption.

Returning to the equilibrium condition, it is clear that some expectations model must be formulated since the variables refer to future quantities. Suppose that the firm formulates the following single-valued expectations:

$$W_t = W^*, M_t = M^*, \Delta M_t = \Delta M^* \qquad \text{(for all } t = 0, 1, 2, \ldots T).\tag{6}$$

Substituting these expected values into equation (4), the equilibrium condition reduces to

$$M^* + \Delta M^* = W^* + \frac{H+K}{\displaystyle\sum_{t=0}^{T}(1+r)^{-t}}.\tag{7}$$

The concept of a periodic rent, R, may be defined as

$$R = \frac{H+K}{\displaystyle\sum_{t=0}^{T}(1+r)^{-t}}.\tag{8}$$

The periodic rent represents the fixed employment costs during each period. It is the surplus that must be earned by each worker in order to amortize the initial fixed employment costs over the expected period of employment, realizing a rate of return of r per cent on this investment. Thus, the equilibrium condition may be rewritten as

$$M^* + \Delta M^* = W^* + R.\tag{9}$$

In equilibrium, the total expected marginal value product must exceed the expected wage rate by the amount of the periodic rent. The degree of fixity, f, of a factor will be defined as the ratio of the periodic rent, R, to the total employment cost, $W^* + R$. A value of zero corresponds to a completely variable factor while the degree of fixity, f, of a completely fixed factor is designated by a value of unity.

The periodic rent drives a wedge between the wage rate and the marginal value product, the relative magnitude of the wedge being measured by the degree of fixity. In the short run, any fixed employment costs associated with the acquisition of a labor force in prior periods are sunk costs; as such they should not affect a firm's short-run decisions.

Suppose that the firm is initially in a position of long-run equilibrium; that is, the equilibrium condition, equation (9), is satisfied by every factor or grade of labor. For a competitive firm, a decline in product demand is equivalent to a fall in product price, P^*.[3] The relevant comparison for short-run profit maximization is that between total expected marginal value product and the expected wage rate, representing the variable component of the total employment cost. Thus the short-run equilibrium condition applicable to cyclical declines in product demands becomes

$$M^* + \Delta M^* = W^*. \tag{10}$$

The employment of a quasi-fixed factor will only be reduced when $M^* + \Delta M^*$ falls below W^*.

For a completely variable factor, the long- and short-run equilibrium conditions, (9) and (10), are equivalent. Any decline in P^* will reduce the demand for a variable factor; with falling employment, the variable factor's marginal physical product will be increased until the equilibrium conditions are again satisfied. The decline in P^* may not be sufficient, however, to warrant a reduction in the demand for some other factor with a higher degree of fixity. In fact, there is, for each quasi-fixed factor, a critical price at which the firm will reduce its demand for that factor. Furthermore, the critical price, in relation to the long-run equilibrium price, will be lower for factors with higher degrees of fixity. Thus, a given decline in P^* may induce a reduction in demand for factors with low degrees of fixity without affecting the demand for factors with higher degrees of fixity. Consider next, the case of an increase in P^*. Beginning at an initial position of long-run equilibrium, there is no reason to expect differential shifts in demand for factors with varying degrees of fixity. Alternatively, in the initial position, the firm may have adjusted to a prior decline in P^*. Specifically, assume that the short-run equilibrium condition, (10), is satisfied by each quasi-fixed factor. The demand for a factor will be increased if its total marginal product, $M^* + \Delta M^*$, exceeds its total expected employment cost, $W^* + R$. In this latter case, the argument is completely analogous to that for a decline in P^*. Each quasi-fixed factor again has its unique critical price at which the demand for it will be increased; these critical prices will be higher for factors with greater degrees of fixity. Thus, a given increase in P^* leads to greater relative shifts in demand for the factors with the lower degrees of fixity.

Up to now, changes in P^* have been treated as if they were known with certainty. The introduction of uncertainty about future product prices reinforces the argument. Suppose that a firm makes appropriate adjustments in factor employments in response to an increase in P^*. If the subsequent increase in actual product prices is less than the expected increase, the firm will be obliged to reduce employment. The readjustment due to an error in forecasting product demand necessarily shortens the expected period of employment, thereby increasing the magnitude of the *ex post* periodic rent.[4] The costs of these readjustments are greater for factors with higher degrees of fixity since the periodic rent comprises a larger share of the total employment costs for these factors. Conversely, consider the case where a reduction in the quantity employed of some factor is greater than that warranted by the subsequent decline in actual prices. The readjustment in this case involves the re-employment of that factor, with additional outlays for hiring and training. One might argue that the firm will simply recall those workers who were previously laid off, thereby avoiding the hiring and training expenses. The Bureau of Labour Statistics data on accessions for the period 1953–58 reveal that only 39 per cent of total accessions in the manufacturing sector were recalls. Even in this case, readjustments are costlier for factors with higher degrees of fixity since the firm cannot be assured that workers who were laid off will be available for recall. If a readjustment in factor employments is required by the subsequent course of actual prices, it will be preferable to make these readjustments in the employment of factors with low degrees of fixity. Such a policy will tend to minimize the costs of readjustments (reversals) in factor employments due to discrepancies between actual and expected product prices.[5]

In summary, certain fixed employment costs are associated with the employment of labor. Firms may invest in hiring – to acquire particular workers – or in specific training to improve labor's productivity. The periodic rent, representing the amortization of these fixed employment costs, drives a wedge between the marginal value product and the wage rate. The relative magnitude of this wedge, measured by the degree of fixity, differs among occupations or grades of labor. In a sense, the periodic rent forms a buffer absorbing short-run variations in a factor's marginal value product. Thus, short-run changes in product demands lead to differential shifts in factor demands, depending on the degree of fixity. Factors with lower degrees of fixity will experience relatively greater shifts in demand as the result of any given short-run change in product demand.

C. *Short-run factor supplies*

In the preceding sections all factor supplies were assumed to be infinitely elastic at fixed market wage rates. This assumption is surely reasonable for a single competitive firm. The supply curve of labor as a whole or of certain skill categories may, however, be less than infinitely elastic or may shift over time. This section deals with the effect of variations in short-run factor supplies on relative factor employments.

Consider the extreme case in which all factor supplies have zero elasticity and markets adjust rapidly. In a downswing, the demand for labor shifts to the left, the percentage shift being smaller for factors with higher degrees of fixity. The downward shifts in demand lead to reductions in wage rates only; factor employments are determined exogenously by the assumed supply conditions. The relative decline in wage rates will be smaller for factors with higher degrees of fixity. This case is, however, inconsistent with the emergence of involuntary unemployment and may be dismissed as unrealistic.

Granted the existence of involuntary unemployment in cyclical downswings, the relevance of the concept of a market supply curve becomes highly questionable. If all factor demands have the same wage-rate elasticity, and if all wages fall by the same proportion, the ultimate decline in the employment of high fixity labor will still be less than the decline in the employment of labor with lower degrees of fixity. On the other hand, if the elasticity of demand and/ or the relative fall in wages are greater for labor with lower degrees of fixity, there is a tendency in the opposite direction. This could offset or perhaps even reverse the differential shifts in employment predicted by the fixed-cost hypothesis.

With the exception of the 1929–33 recession, the available evidence suggests a widening of occupational wage differentials in the downswing and a narrowing in the upswing.[6] Even in the 1929–33 recession, the data are consistent with a hypothesis that there was no change in the occupational wage structure. As will be shown in Part II, the wage rate of an occupation is highly correlated with its degree of fixity. Thus, over a cycle, the high-wage occupations with greater degrees of fixity exhibit smaller relative changes in wage rates. Finally, I suspect that the high-wage, skilled jobs tend to be most complementary with the fixed factor, capital. *Ceteris paribus*, greater complementarity with the fixed factor implies a lower elasticity of demand. The evidence thus indicates smaller relative changes in wage rates and lower elasticities of demand for factors with higher degrees of fixity. The observed short-run variations in factor supplies therefore predict differential shifts in employment contrary to those implied by the fixed-cost hypothesis.

D. *Specificity of labor to a firm*

The provision of specific training alters the labor input. Labor no longer represents an anonymous variable factor but rather a differentiated stream of services from certain workers who have received specific training. These workers are, in a sense, specific to the firm.

In section B, I tacitly assumed that each factor received a wage equal to its marginal productivity in alternative employments. Since a worker's alternative marginal product is unaffected by specific training, competitive wages should not affect the expected period of employment. Examination of equation (5), however, shows that the net value of specific training is increased by an extension of the expected period of employment. Consequently, it behoves a firm to initiate practices that tend to minimize the turnover of specifically trained workers.

Policies aimed at this goal are exemplified by pension and profit-sharing plans, provision of better working conditions, promotion from within, and payment of wage premiums. Under some profit-sharing plans, workers forfeit all benefits unless they remain with the firm for a specified period of time. Firms may also adopt discriminatory hiring policies, hiring only those workers who possess characteristics associated with long employment tenure.

A wage policy of paying premiums to specifically trained workers may prove mutually profitable for both workers and firm. Consider the analysis of section B where the incidence of all training expenses falls on the firm, with workers bearing none of the costs. In this case, a wage premium is clearly profitable for the worker and should encourage longer periods of employment. From the firm's viewpoint, the payment of a wage premium affects total employment costs in two opposing ways. First, the wage premium increases the present value of expected wage payments. Second, if the wage premium induces longer employment tenure, the initial fixed employment costs can be amortized over a larger number of periods, thereby reducing the periodic rent. Such a wage policy would be profitable for the firm if the following inequality holds:

$$\frac{\Delta W}{W} \leqslant \left(\frac{R}{W}\right) \frac{\sum\limits_{t=T+1}^{T+k} (1+r)^{-t}}{\sum\limits_{t=0}^{T+k} (1+r)^{-t}}. \tag{11}$$

The equality in (11) indicates the maximum relative wage premium, $\Delta W/W$, consistent with an induced increase in the period of employment of k periods. For a given increment of k periods the maximum relative wage premium will be larger for factors with higher degrees of fixity or with lower initial expected periods of employment. If the equality in (11) applies, the added wage costs would just offset the savings to the firm from longer expected periods of employment. If, however, the inequality holds for some factor, that factor does not satisfy the full equilibrium condition given by (9). The expected total marginal product will exceed the expected total employment cost. Hence the firm has an incentive to invest further in specific training. The firm may also choose to pay even higher wage premiums if by doing so it induces an even greater extension in the expected period of employment.

Suppose that a share of the training cost is borne by the worker. During the training period a worker might accept a wage below his alternative marginal product; the difference represents his investment in specific training. The firm could compensate the worker for his investment by promising him a wage premium upon completion of the specific training. If the present value of his expected wage premiums exceeds his share of the training cost, the arrangement would be acceptable to a rational worker. Consider the extreme case in which all specific training costs are paid by the worker.[7] The worker clearly prefers to remain with the firm since his marginal product and wages in the specific firm are higher than his alternative marginal product. In this case, however, all labor costs become variable to the firm, and the firm has no motive for retaining these workers during a cyclical downswing.

A sensible policy is to have both parties share the specific training expense. If both workers and firm have made investments in specific training, both can gan from longer expected periods of employment. The specifically trained worker could receive a wage above his alternative marginal product but below his total marginal product to the firm.[8] At the same time, the firm could lower its total employment cost by amortizing the fixed employment costs over a longer period of time. Short-run variations in factor supplies would tend to be smaller for workers who had invested in specific training. Thus the payment of wage premiums and the sharing of the specific training costs promote even greater stability of employment for specifically trained workers.

To sum up, the specificity of labor to a firm favors the establishment of policies to lengthen expected periods of employment. To achieve lower labor turnover, a firm might adopt a policy by which workers were required to share specific training expenses and were rewarded by subsequent wage premiums. Under such a policy, both workers and firm would benefit from lower labor turnover. Finally, the gains from lower labor turnover are greater for factors with higher degrees of fixity. Thus a higher degree of fixity leads not only to greater stability of employment in terms of numbers or man-hours employed but also to lower labor turnover rates.

II. TESTS OF THE THEORY

A. *Wage rate as index of degree of fixity*

A direct test of the theory would require estimates of the degree of fixity for different grades of labor. Since such data are not readily available,[9] an auxiliary variable that is closely correlated with the degree of fixity must be employed as a proxy. The use of an occupation's wage rate as the proxy seems justifiable and derives support from the empirical evidence presented in this section.

A study undertaken by the International Harvester Company (hereinafter referred to as 'IH') in 1951 estimated fixed employment costs for three job categories.[10] The total fixed cost associated with an annual labor turnover of 28,623 workers was $15.9 million, or roughly 5.4 per cent of total wage payments. The component cost items were placed in three categories. The IH estimates of the amount invested in each new worker are presented in the first four columns of Table 2.1; my revised estimates appear in the last column.

Hiring costs comprised less than 5 per cent of total fixed costs. They include the costs of terminating, laying off, and recalling since each worker has a positive probability of passing through each stage during his prospective tenure with the firm. The IH study weighted each cost by its relative frequency.

Table 2.1
Amount of Money Invested per New Employee,
International Harvester Company, 1951

Costs	Common Labor	Two-Year Progressive Student	Four-Year Apprentice	IH Average	Revised IH Average
Hiring costs:					
Recruiting	$ 4.33	$ 86.38		$ 5.48	$ 5.48
Hiring	13.23	29.08	$ 28.89	13.23	13.19
Orientation	1.56	1.56	1.56	1.56	1.56
Terminating	3.77	3.77	3.77	3.77	3.77
Laying off	1.21	1.21	1.21	1.21	1.21
Recalling	1.30	1.30	1.30	1.30	1.30
Total	25.40	123.30	36.73	26.55	26.51
Training costs:					
Training	9.08	11,850.00	18,503.00	238.40	151.36
Tools and materials			164.76	41.19	41.19
Unfilled requisitions	14.92			83.12	24.66
Intrawork transfers	3.50			94.14	64.49
Total	27.50	11,850.00	18,667.76	456.85	281.70
Unemployment compensation	73.52	73.52	73.52	73.52	73.52
Total fixed employment cost	126.42	12,046.82	18,778.01	556.92	381.73

SOURCE: International Harvester Company, *op. cit.*

Training cost is by far the major fixed employment cost. Two items under this heading require further explanation. 'Unfilled requisitions' refers to the implicit cost of lost output, resulting from the lag between the separation and subsequent replacement of a worker.[11] In the IH study the hourly cost of lost productive time was the gross profits per man-hour of $1.84. I have revised the estimate by assuming that standby, overtime labor is used to recoup any lost productive time; the result is a substantial reduction in this cost item. 'Intrawork transfers' represents additional training expenses due to transfers of old workers to new jobs within the plant.

Finally, the cost of unemployment compensation represents the difference between the firm's actual contributions and the minimum legal contributions for unemployment compensation.[12] Higher labor turnover will, in general, increase a firm's actual contributions.[13] The difference between the actual and minimum legal contributions resembles hiring costs and is therefore included in fixed employment costs.

Each component of total fixed costs appears to rise either at the same rate as the wage rate of a job or faster. The data in Table 2.1 suggest that the ratio of total fixed employment costs to wage rate increases as one moves to higher wage jobs. If the IH estimates of Table 2.1 are coupled with some assumptions about wage rates and expected periods of employment, it is possible to estimate degrees of fixity for two overlapping groups of workers. Thus, degrees of fixity of 0.073 and 0.041 were obtained for 'All employees' and 'Common laborers.'[14] The high-wage, highly skilled jobs appear to be associated with higher degrees of fixity. In the subsequent empirical tests I shall assume that an occupation's wage rate serves as an index of the degree of fixity.

B. *Cyclical behavior of employment by occupation*

During cyclical changes in aggregate employment different rates of change in employment are observed for different occupations even within the same firm. This phenomenon is the subject of the first empirical test of the theory.

The basic proposition of Part I may be stated as follows: those factors with the highest degrees of fixity and the lowest degrees of substitutability with the fixed factor will experience the smallest relative changes in employment due to any given change in product demand. For the empirical test occupational wage differentials are assumed to reflect differences in the degree of fixity. The hypothesis submitted to a test is: 'there is no relation between wage rates and the observed rates of change in employment.' The alternative hypothesis is that the high-wage occupations will experience smaller rates of change in employment.

The contingency table was chosen as the experimental design for testing the hypothesis. The contingency table tests for the independence of two variables of classification. The χ^2 statistic is the criterion for the acceptance or rejection of the null hypothesis. The occupations in a firm are first divided into two equal groups according to the wage rate of the occupation. The same occupations are again separated, by reference to the observed rates of change in employment over a fixed time interval, into equal groups. All occupations thus fall into the cells of a contingency table where the cells identify groups of occupations with different wages and percentage changes in employment. The marginal totals, which are fixed in advance, determine the number of occupations in each cell to be expected if in fact the null hypothesis is true. The major advantages of the contingency table over alternative test procedures[15] include the following:

1. No assumptions are required about the joint probability distribution of the two variables of classification.
2. The design is fairly insensitive to extreme values. Since the wage rate is an imperfect index, the possibility of a few extreme observations must be acknowledged.

Data for this test were taken from the BLS industry wage structure studies. Each study presents data on employment, hours, and earnings, classified by occupation, sex, state, and industry, for a single year. Since two adjacent studies are needed, attention was focused on the period 1928-31. For each of four industries a sample of states was selected. The states included in the sample reported roughly the same number of establishments covered in the two adjacent surveys. The states were also grouped by geographic region.[16] For each state, the occupations were classified as high wage or low wage, depending on whether an occupation's wage rate was above or below the median wage rate for all occupations. The occupations were then reclassified by the observed percentage change in employment into two equal groups. Employment, in this context, refers to the number of employees; the alternative concept of man-hours yielded virtually identical results. The two-way divisions fix the marginal totals which, in turn, determine the expected numbers of occupations under the null hypothesis.

The contingency tables for four industries are presented in Tables 2.2 and 2.3, where the numbers in parentheses denote the expected numbers under the null hypothesis.[17] For furniture and men's clothing, the χ^2 statistic indicates that the null hypothesis can be rejected at a 5 per cent level of significance.

Table 2.2

No. of Occupations in Selected Industries, Classified by Wage Group and Per Cent Change in Employment*

Wage Group	Per cent Change in Employment (No. of Employees)			χ^2 Statistic†
	Below Median	Above Median	Total	
Furniture:				
High wage	40 (29.26)	18 (28.74)	58	16.345 (3.841)
Low wage	17 (27.74)	38 (27.26)	55	
All wages	57	56	113	
Foundries:				
High wage	20 (18)	16 (18)	36	0.889 (3.841)
Low wage	16 (18)	20 (18)	36	
All wages	36	36	72	
Men's clothing:				
High wage	13 (9.76)	7 (10.24)	20	4.102 (3.841)
Low wage	7 (10.24)	14 (10.76)	21	
All wages	20	21	41	

*Source of the data and detailed breakdown by states are shown in my thesis, Appendix C, C-5, C-6, and C-7.
†Numbers in parentheses denote the 5 per cent critical values.

The χ^2 statistic is significant at only a 10 per cent level for lumber mills. Finally, the data for foundries are consistent with the null hypothesis. The discrepancies between actual and expected numbers of occupations in the cells of the contingency tables conform to the pattern anticipated by the fixed-cost hypothesis. Given these systematic discrepancies,[18] the additive nature of χ^2 permits a test for the aggregate of all four industries. For the four industries combined, the null hypothesis can be rejected at a 1 per cent level. Thus, the evidence from the BLS studies refutes the null hypothesis, and the alternative can be accepted.

Table 2.3

*No. of Occupations in the Lumber Industry Classified by Wage Group
and Per Cent Change in Employment, 1928–30**

Wage Group	Per Cent Change in Employment			Total	χ^2 Statistic†
	Lowest 3d	Middle 3d	Top 3d		
No. of employees (ΔE):					
High wage	14	17	11	42	6.999
	(13.57)	(14.86)	(13.57)		(9.488)
Middle wage	19	15	12	46	
	(14.86)	(16.28)	(14.86)		
Low wage	9	14	19	42	
	(13.57)	(14.86)	(13.57)		
All wages	42	46	42	130	

*Source of data and breakdown by states are shown in my thesis, Appendix C, Table C-8.
†Numbers in parentheses denote the 5 per cent critical values.

The wage rate of an occupation is associated with its percentage change in employment. Low-wage occupations, corresponding to low degrees of fixity, do experience relatively greater changes in employment.

C. *Employment of non-production workers*

Non-production workers in manufacturing industries are more highly paid[18] and tend to be more specific to the firm than their production worker counterparts. Thus, according to the fixed-cost hypothesis, non-production workers should exhibit greater employment stability.

Consider a simple model in which the desired rate of employment in the tth year, E_t^*, is a linear function of the rate of output, X_t. That is, the desired demand for some factor is solely a function of the scale effect, ignoring all substitution effects.

$$E_t^* = a + bX_t. \tag{12}$$

Suppose the actual change in employment from the preceding period is some proportion, k, of the desired change.

$$E_t - E_{t-1} = k(E_t^* - E_{t-1}). \tag{13}$$

Substitution in (13) by the expression for E_t^* in (12) yields the following reduced form, containing only observable quantities:

$$E_t = ak + bkX_t + (1 - k)E_{t-1}. \tag{14}$$

The parameter, k, may be interpreted as a short-run coefficient of adjustment. Higher values of k imply faster short-run adjustments. Indeed, a value of unity means that actual and desired rates of employment always coincide. If non-production workers are truly specific to the firm, they should exhibit a smaller k relative to production workers.

The slope parameters of the reduced form, equation (14), were estimated by least squares using annual data for the 'All Manufacturing' sector. The analysis was confined to the prewar period, 1920–39, because of a strong secular trend in employment of non-production workers during the postwar period[20] that destroyed the validity of the demand relation. Output, X_t, was measured by the Federal Reserve Board's Index of Indsutrial Production. The least-squares estimates are given by equations (15) and (16), where N_t and P_t, respectively, designate non-production and production worker employment.

$$N_t = ak + .0132X_t + .5611N_{t-1} \qquad (15)$$
$$\quad\;\; (.0024) \quad\; (.1100)$$

$(R^2 = .7793)$.

$$P_t = AK + .0722X_t + .3318P_{t-1} \qquad (16)$$
$$\quad\;\; (.0146) \quad\; (.1340)$$

$(R^2 = .7219)$.

The short-run coefficient of adjustment for non-production workers is 0.44 while that for production workers is 0.67; the difference is statistically significant at the 10 per cent level. Furthermore, an examination of seasonally adjusted monthly employment data for the postwar period reveals lags in the turning points of non-production worker employment. The turning points in non-production worker employment for the 'All manufacturing' sector lagged from two to six months behind the turning points in production worker employment. The smaller short-run coefficient of adjustment and the lags in turning points are entirely consistent with the higher degree of fixity of non-production workers.

D. *Differential unemployment and the fixed-cost hypothesis*

Involuntary unemployment is never uniformly distributed among all workers. The fixed-cost hypothesis may help to explain some of these differences. Fixed employment costs constitute an investment by the firm in its labor force. A firm faced by a cyclical decline in product demand could protect this investment by following a discriminatory layoff policy.

To the extent that labor is a quasi-fixed factor, each new hire, whether an addition or a replacement, entails an investment outlay by the firm for hiring and training. Suppose that a firm is obliged to reduce the rate of employment of some factor. At any point in time each firm observes a distribution of its workers according to their expected periods of employment. The average employment tenure of the workers who remain employed can be lengthened by laying off the workers with the shortest expected periods of employment. Such a discriminatory layoff policy tends to reduce the voluntary quit rate facing the firm. The policy tends to lower total fixed employment costs by minimizing the number of future new hires that would be required to replace old workers who might voluntarily quit in subsequent periods. Thus, an implication of the fixed-cost hypothesis is that the incidence of unemployment should be highest for those workers with the shortest expected periods of employment. Since a worker's prospective employment tenure cannot be known with certainty and since labor contracts are rarely binding on employees, the firm can never exercise complete control over the expected period of employment. Furthermore, seniority rights or other union practices may prevent a firm from following a discriminatory layoff policy.

Certain personal characteristics such as age, sex, and marital status are allegedly associated with employment tenure. Middle-aged workers would, in general, be expected to have longer expected periods of employment than either very young or very old workers; this expectation has been corroborated by a study of labor turnover in Swedish factories.[21] At the same time, married males with spouse present tend to be less mobile and should exhibit longer employment tenures than either single males or males who are divorced, widowed, or separated.

Unemployment rates classified by race, age, sex, and marital status are presented in Table 2.4 for the census year 1950.[22] For both races, and in almost all age groups, married persons with spouse present revealed the lowest unemployment rates. The only exception for males was in the '14–17' age group, while single women had lower unemployment rates in two cases. The observed differentials in male unemployment rates thus conform to the pattern implied by differences in expected periods of employment.

The distribution by age of unemployment rates is roughly the same, except for level, for each race-marital status group of the male labor force; similar patterns are evident in data for other years. Unemployment rates fall over the range from fourteen to thirty-five years of age even when marital status is held constant. Beyond thirty-five years of age increasing age is associated with higher unemployment rates although the trend is reversed in the oldest age group ('65 and over'). The problems inherent in defining the labor force for older workers make the interpretation of their unemployment rates particularly difficult. Hauser speculates that this reversal in the age pattern might be attributable to a withdrawal of older workers from the labor force when they become unemployed.[23] A logical implication of the withdrawal hypothesis is that the labor-force participation rate of older workers will be negatively correlated with cyclical changes in employment. The latter implication is not supported by data presented in a study by Long.[25] I cannot explain this contradiction, but the data indicate, in the main, higher unemployment rates for younger and older workers than for middle-aged workers.

The sex differentials in unemployment rates cannot be explained by differences in expected periods of employment. The volatility of femlae labor-force participation rates suggests that unemployment rates are not the appropriate

Table 2.4
Unemployment Rates by Color, Age, Sex, and Marital Status, 1950

Sex and Age	White			Non-White		
	Single	Married, Spouse Present	Other	Single	Married, Spouse Present	Other
Male:						
14 and over	9.4	3.1	8.7	12.1	5.7	11.2
14–17	10.6	7.8	4.4	9.5	*	*
18–19	11.2	6.3	17.1	14.1	8.6	18.7
20–24	9.9	4.5	12.0	14.1	7.2	15.8
25–29	8.4	3.1	10.2	12.5	6.8	13.9
30–34	7.6	2.5	8.8	11.2	5.8	11.4
35–44	7.9	2.6	9.0	9.9	5.1	11.3
45–54	8.5	3.0	9.0	10.5	5.2	10.0
55–64	9.5	3.7	8.8	10.3	6.0	10.3
65–74	8.3	4.3	6.7	7.0	5.7	8.9
75 and over	3.1	2.8	3.8	*	2.7	6.5
Female:						
14 and over	4.7	3.2	5.6	10.7	6.6	8.1
14–17	12.6	13.9	16.1	13.8	18.7	*
18–19	6.9	6.6	17.5	15.8	12.0	22.8
20–24	4.3	4.0	9.5	12.3	10.1	15.0
25–29	3.5	3.5	7.1	8.8	7.8	11.8
30–34	3.4	3.3	6.5	6.0	6.5	9.5
35–44	2.8	2.7	5.6	6.5	5.7	6.6
45–54	2.3	2.8	5.0	5.5	5.0	6.4
55–64	3.0	2.8	5.0	4.7	4.6	5.5
65–74	3.1	2.3	3.9	6.9	7.8	4.9
75 and over	3.0	2.8	2.8	*	*	3.3

*Base less than 3,000.
Source: Hauser, *op. cit.*, pp. 256–7.

variable. Furthermore, the evidence that there are differences in employment tenure by sex is not at all convincing.[25] Finally, the occupational differentials in unemployment rates are also consistent with the implications of the fixed-cost hypothesis.

E. *Additional evidence*

The analysis of subsection ID implies that labor of higher degrees of fixity should enjoy lower labor turnover rates. Manufacturing industries vary widely in the skill composition of their labor forces. The high-wage industries typically employ larger proportions of skilled workers with higher degrees of fixity. Low labor turnover rates should, therefore, be observed for high-wage industries. Other factors that affect labor turnover rates were held constant by a multi-variate regression model that cannot be fully reported here. Based on annual data for sixty-four manufacturing industries from 1951 to 1958, the regression model revealed a partial correlation between an industry's average quit rate and its wage rate of −0.497, a value that is significantly different from zero at the 1 per cent level. A turnover rate, defined as the lower of the total accessions and total separations rates, provides a measure of average replacement demand. Using this latter variable, the partial correlation drops to −0.195, which is significant at the 10 per cent level. Thus, an industry's wage rate, which presumably reflects the average degree of fixity of the labor force, is related to its labor turnover rate. The low-wage industries that employ workers with lower degrees of fixity do experience higher labor turnover rates.[26]

The differential shifts in factor demands over a cycle imply greater inequality of wage incomes during periods of low employment. In a recession the demand for labor with high wages and high degrees of fixity falls by a smaller percentage than that for labor in the low-wage occupations. The greater decline of employment in the low-wage occupations implies larger relative declines in wage incomes in these occupations than in the high-wage occupations. The changes in the distribution of wage incomes during the recession of 1929–33, discovered by Mendershausen,[27] indicated an increase in the dispersion of wage incomes as unemployment increased. The pattern held despite the fact that hourly wage differentials failed to widen in this recession.

III. ALTERNATIVE HYPOTHESES

In this paper certain aspects of the cyclical behavior of labor markets have been explained by the fixed-cost hypothesis. What are the alternative hypotheses that offer explanations for the same phenomena? The theory that changes in factor employments are due to variations in relative wage rates was considered in sub-section IC. This theory was dismissed because it implied changes in factor employments that were contrary to the observed changes.

Another theory is contained in the Reder model.[28] Although Reder's theory is primarily addressed to occupational wage differentials, it implies systematic changes in factor employments. According to Reder, firms adjust to a downswing by raising hiring standards. As a result the average quality of workers in each skill category is improved. The higher standards displace some workers from each skill category. Some of the displaced workers in the higher skill categories are downgraded to lower skill jobs, creating even further displacement of workers in these lower skill categories. The successive bumping effect sifts down through the skill hierarchy of jobs and results in relatively greater unemployment in the low-skill categories. In the upswing, firms adjust by relaxing hiring standards and upgrading workers to higher skill jobs. It is never explicitly stated, but Reder seems to assume that all factor demands shift proportionally. If this interpretation of Reder is correct, there is nothing in his theory that implies differential shifts in employment. The theory is, however, consistent with the emergence of differential unemployment rates since unemployed workers would be classified by their previous occupational status.

There are two possible ways in which differential shifts in employment could be deduced from Reder's theory. First, workers in high-skill jobs could perform the tasks of low-skill jobs while retaining their old job titles. This would appear to be highly unlikely. A second possibility is that hiring standards for high-skill jobs are advanced less than those for low-skill jobs. The elusive nature of hiring standards makes it difficult to test the latter possibility.

As a theory of the cyclical behavior of occupational wage differentials, Reder's theory has an intuitive appeal.[29] If the theory were stated formally, I believe that its basic behavioral relation could be put as follows: the relative rate of change in the wage rate of an occupation, $\Delta W/W$, is proportional to the relative excess demand for or supply of that grade of labor. Algebraically, it may be written:

$$\frac{\Delta W}{W} = k\left(\frac{D-S}{S}\right). \tag{17}$$

where k is a constant and D and S denote the amounts demanded and supplied of some grade of labor.

In the Reder model the cyclical adjustments involving the upgrading and downgrading of workers generate differential shifts in S for different occupations. In a downswing, the downgrading of workers creates larger excess supplies (in absolute values) in the lower skill jobs. If the same k applies for all occupations — and this must be assumed — the differences in excess supply imply relatively larger declines in the wage rates of low-skill jobs. The fixed-cost hypothesis would also predict a widening of occupational wage differentials in a downswing and a narrowing in the upswing if the behavioral relation (17) holds. Unlike the Reder model, the fixed-cost hypothesis involves differential shifts in D. The advantage of the latter explanation over Reder's theory is that it can simultaneously explain the cyclical behavior of occupational wage differentials and of relative factor employments.

IV. CONCLUDING REMARKS

The central theme of this paper has been the treatment of labor as a quasi-fixed factor. This concept of labor was suggested by J. M. Clark, who dealt primarily with the social cost of unemployment.[30] The theory of the demand for a quasi-fixed factor generated implications regarding the short-run behavior of labor markets. Differences in the degree of fixity for different occupations imply (1) differential short-run shifts in employment, (2) differences in labor turnover rates, (3) emergence of differential unemployment rates in the cycle, and (4) cyclical variations in relative wage rates. The implications of the fixed-cost hypothesis are, in the main, borne out by the data examined.

The theory of labor as a quasi-fixed factor may also help to explain other phenomena. It is sometimes argued that a firm will maintain its labor force even though the wage rate exceeds the current marginal value product. If the labor has a high degree of fixity, it is to the firm's advantage to maintain its labor force rather than to risk high replacement demands in future periods. Fixed employment costs could also account for a range of indeterminacy in wages frequently mentioned in the literature.[31] In the short run, the specificity of labor to a firm places an upper limit on the wage rate equal to labor's total marginal product; the lower limit is determined by labor's alternative marginal product. Under collective bargaining a short-run wage rate could be set and maintained anywhere within this range.

The classical treatment of labor as a completely variable factor may be adequate for a long-run analysis. To explain the short-run behavior of labor markets, I believe that labor should be viewed as a quasi-fixed factor of production.

NOTES

1. The training activity typically entails direct money outlays as well as numerous implicit costs such as the allocation of old workers to teaching skills and rejection of unqualified workers during the training period.
2. That a firm offers general training to its employees does not necessarily imply that the firm underwrites the general training expense. The worker may bear the training cost by accepting a lower wage than that which he could obtain in some alternative employment.
3. The term, $M^* + \Delta M^*$, in eq. (9) denotes the expected marginal value product. For a competitive firm, this is simply the expected product price, P^*, times the expected marginal physical product, $X^* + \Delta X^*$.
4. A reduction in the expected period of employment, T, increases the periodic rent, R, since the initial fixed employment cost of $H + K$ dollars must be amortized over a smaller number of periods. From equation (8), the elasticity of R with respect to T is found to be negative, independent of $H + K$, and less than one in absolute value.
5. The case where the readjustment involves no reversal in the direction of change in factory employments has not been discussed. This is the case where an increase (or decrease) in employment is less than that warranted by the actual price change. There is no *a priori* reason why this type of error should lead to differential costs for factors with different degrees of fixity.
6. Phillip W. Bell, 'Cyclical Variations and Trends in Occupational Wage Differentials in American Industries Since 1914,' *Review of Economics and Statistics*, XXXIII, No. 4 (November, 1954), 329–37.
7. Firms and workers may differ in their evaluation of expected periods of employment and pertinent discount rates. As a result, the optimum investment per worker in specific training may differ depending on the incidence of these training costs.
8. Where training is specific to a firm the situation closely resembles one of bilateral monopoly. From the firm's viewpoint, the specifically trained worker is differentiated from other workers. At the same time, the worker finds that his value to his present employer is higher than his value to some competing employer. I wish to thank Professor Rees for pointing out this analogue.
9. The necessary data include (1) the initial fixed employment cost, $H + K$, (2) the discount rate, r, (3) the expected period of employment, T, and (4) the expected wage rate, W^*.
10. International Harvester Company, 'The Costs of Labor Turnover' (mimeographed), 1951.
11. Supplementary data in the IH study showed an average lag between separation and replacement of 39.1 hours. The lag was longer for jobs with higher skill requirements.
12. Actual unemployment compensation tax rates differ widely among firms, across states,

and over time. For a discussion of these differences the reader is referred to R. A. Lester, 'Financing Unemployment Compensation,' *Industrial and Labor Relations Review*, XIV, No. 1 (October, 1960), 52–67.

13. An exception to this generalization arises if all separated workers immediately obtain new jobs. This is, however, rarely the case.

14. In arriving at these estimates I assumed expected periods of employment of 24 and 12 months for 'All employees' and 'Common labor.' The discount rate was fixed at 1 per cent per month; variations of ±0.5 per cent had very little effect on the degree of fixity. Finally, the IH study reported average hourly earnings for 'All employees' of $1.952 in 1951. This figure was converted to a monthly wage and applied to 'All employees.' For 'Common labor' I arbitrarily fixed an hourly wage of $1.50.

15. Two alternative test procedures are (1) a least-squares regression between the wage rate and the percentage change in employment, and (2) a Student's 't' test for the difference in mean percentage changes in employment for two groups of occupations classified by wage rates. The contingency table design resembles a non-parametric correlation technique known as tetrachoric r. This latter technique is described in W. J. Dixon and F. J. Masey, *Introduction to Statistical Analysis* (New York: McGraw-Hill Book Co., 1951), p. 235.

16. In these studies the BLS attempted wherever possible to cover the same establishments as those covered in the preceding study of the same industry. Hence, inclusion of only those states showing approximate equality in the number of establishments covered tends to minimize errors arising from a shifting establishment composition within states. Geographic grouping was incorporated to minimize differential shifts in product demands.

17. The procedure was slightly altered for lumber mills. The larger number of occupations in this industry permitted a three-way division.

18. The contingency table design can only uncover an association between two variables of classification. The direction of this association is only discernible from an examination of discrepancies between actual and expected numbers.

19. Data from the 1954 Census of Manufactures indicate that the average annual earnings of non-production workers always exceeded those of production workers. The ratio of the earnings of non-production to those of production workers ranged from a low of 1.47 in chemicals to a high of 2.11 in textile mill products.

20. In the prewar period, the ratio of non-production to production workers exhibited no secular trend. From 1947 to 1958, virtually all the increase in manufacturing employment is attributable to the growth in non-production worker employment. For a discussion of these trends the reader is referred to United States Bureau of Labor Statistics, 'Non-production Workers in Factories, 1919–56,' *Monthly Labor Review*, LXXX, No. 4 (April, 1957), 435–40.

21. Magnus Hedberg, 'Labor Turnover, the Flow of Personnel through the Factory' (Stockholm: Swedish Council for Personnel Administration). (Mimeographed.)

22. This table is reproduced from Phillip M. Hauser's article with his kind permission. The reader is referred to 'Differential Unemployment and Characteristics of the Unemployed in the United States, 1940–1954,' *The Measurement and Behavior of Unemployment* (Princeton, N.J.: Princeton University Press, 1957), pp. 243–80.

23. Ibid., p. 251.

24. Clarence D. Long, *The Labor Force under Changing Income and Employment* (Princeton, N.J.: Princeton University Press, 1958), pp. 323–25, Table B-2.

25. The BLS turnover data by sex for two-digit manufacturing industries reveal slightly higher turnover rates for females. Hauser finds (p. 244) that females in a previous state of employment are less vulnerable to unemployment than males. This same stability of employment of female workers was also found in the Philadelphia study; see United States Department of Labor, Bureau of Labor Statistics, *The Social and Economic Character of Unemployment in Philadelphia* (Bulletin No. 520, April, 1929).

26. There is, of course, an identification problem. For example, high wage rates that result from union bargaining may reduce turnover rates. Although this difficulty is recognized, the results still appear to verify the implication of the fixed-cost hypothesis.

27. Horst Mendershausen, *Changes in Income Distribution during the Great Depression*

('Studies in Income and Wealth,' Vol. VII [New York: National Bureau of Economic Research, 1946]), 69-70.
28. M. W. Reder, 'The Theory of Occupational Wage Differentials,' *American Economic Review*, XLV, No. 5 (December, 1955), 833-52, see esp. pp. 833-40.
29. Reynolds agrees with Reder's explanation of the cyclical behavior of occupational wage differentials; see L. G. Reynolds and C. B. Taft, *The Evolution of Wage Structure* (New Haven, Conn.: Yale University Press, 1956), p. 364.
30. *Studies in the Economics of Overhead Costs* (Chicago: University of Chicago Press, 1923), pp. 357-85.
31. Reynolds and Taft, *op. cit.*, p. 1.
32. The range of indeterminacy will be wider for factors (grades of labor) with higher degrees of fixity. This range is, however, a short-run phenomenon. The firm would not continue to invest in specific training unless it could recoup the benefits.

2.2 The Internal Labour Market*
[...]

The central concept around which this volume is organized is that of the *internal labor market*, an administrative unit, such as a manufacturing plant, within which the pricing and allocation of labor is governed by a set of administrative rules and procedures.[1] The internal labor market, governed by administrative rules, is to be distinguished from the *external labor market* of conventional economic theory where pricing, allocating, and training decisions are controlled directly by economic variables. These two markets are interconnected, however, and movement between them occurs at certain job classifications which constitute *ports of entry and exit* to and from the internal labor market.[2] The remainder of the jobs within the internal market are filled by the promotion or transfer of workers who have already gained entry. Consequently, these jobs are shielded from the *direct* influences of competitive forces in the external market.

The rules governing internal labor allocation and pricing accord certain rights and privileges to the internal labor force which are not available to workers in the external labor market. The internal labor force, for example, has exclusive rights to jobs filled internally, and continuity of employment, even at entry ports, is protected from direct competition by workers in the external labor market. The phenomenon of internal labor markets is thus closely akin to the problems which other authors have identified as 'industrial feudalism,' 'the balkanization of labor markets,' and 'property rights' in a job.[3]

The scope and structure of internal labor markets varies considerably among industries and occupations. The production and maintenance units of a steel plant with their limited entry ports and lengthy promotion lines, the garment factory with its many entry ports, the military services, and the exclusive hiring hall in the building trades — each constitutes a type of internal market. However, because the research upon which this volume is based focused primarily upon blue-collar employment in manufacturing, the concepts and applications presented have particular relevance for this sector. [...]

*From Peter B. Doeringer and Michael J. Piore, *Internal Labor Markets and Manpower Analysis* (Lexington, Mass.: Lexington Books, D. C. Heath, 1971).

[. . .] Internal labor markets appear to be generated by a series of factors not envisioned in conventional economic theory: (1) skill specificity, (2) on-the-job training, and (3) customary law. These factors are defined and developed in the first section of the chapter. In the second section, they are combined with the economic forces recognized in conventional theory to develop an explanation of how internal markets arise and evolve over time. The analysis of this section abstracts from the behavior of managerial and trade union organizations and from actual historical events. These institutional and historical complexities are introduced in the third and fourth sections respectively. The final section of the chapter summarizes the discussion.

THE MAJOR FACTORS GENERATING INTERNAL LABOR MARKETS

Skill Specificity

The terms 'specific training' and 'general training' have been made current in the vocabulary of modern economics by Gary S. Becker. In Becker's terms, completely specific training is defined as 'training that has no effect on the productivity of trainees that would be useful in other firms.'[4] Completely general training increases the marginal productivity of trainees by exactly the same amount in the firms providing the training as in other firms.'[5]

In the present volume, *specific* and *general* are used in a somewhat different sense. Here they fundamentally relate to *skill* and to the frequency with which various skills can be utilized within different internal labor markets. A completely specific skill is unique to a single job classification in a single enterprise; a completely general skill is requisite for every job in every enterprise. The terms *specific* and *general* may also be applied to training, as in Becker's usage. Training is more or less specific according to the type of skill which it provides.

Skill specificity has two effects important in the generation of the internal labor market: (1) it increases the proportion of training costs borne by the employer, as opposed to the trainee, and (2) it increases the absolute level of such costs. As skills become more specific, it becomes increasingly difficult for the worker to utilize elsewhere the enterprise-specific training he receives. This reduces the incentive for him to invest in such training, while simultaneously increasing the incentive for the employer to make the investment.[6] Skill specificity tends to increase the absolute cost of training (regardless of who provides it) because the less prevalent a skill in the labor market, the less frequently training for that skill is provided, and economies of scale in training cannot be realized.[7] Both of these effects encourage the employer to seek to reduce labor turnover.

Training is not the only labor cost affected by skill specificity. Recruitment and screening costs are influenced in much the same way. The reduction in turnover which skill specificity encourages increases the employer's willingness to accept these costs. Similarly, the absolute costs of recruitment and screening are reduced by economies of scale and standardization. Broad-scale advertising campaigns and standardized testing procedures, for example, can be used to find and certify workers with skills which are in frequent demand, but these techniques are unsuitable for recruiting and screening workers with less common skills. These scale effects are further encouraged by specificity because it increases the amount of such activities in which individual employers engage.

Although, in the generation and operation of the internal labor market, it is the specificity of skills and training that is the key, it is not always the focus of managerial decisions. Such decisions often center instead upon *the job* or *the technology*, and the requisite skills appear to be derived incidentally from these decisions. Because the job and technology are so often the focal point of the decisions determining skill, it is useful to define and apply the terms 'specific' and 'general' to these concepts as well.

Job specificity   The specificity of a job, as that term is used here, is defined by its skill content. Jobs utilize a set of skills, and each of the skills in the set may be more or less specific. A completely specific job is one which utilizes only specific skills; a completely general job is one all of whose skills are general.[8]

Almost every job involves some specific skills. Even the simplest custodial tasks are facilitated by familiarity with the physical environment specific to the workplace in which they are performed. The apparently routine operation of standard machines can be importantly aided by familiarity with a particular piece of operating equipment. Even mass-produced machines have individual operating characteristics which can markedly affect work performance. In some cases workers are able to anticipate trouble and diagnose its source by subtle changes in the sound or smell of the equipment. Moreover, performance in some production and most managerial jobs involves a team element, and a critical skill is the ability to operate effectively with the given members of the team. This ability is dependent upon the interaction of the personalities of the members, and the individual's work 'skills' are specific in the sense that skills necessary to work on one team are never quite the same as those required on another.[9] There are no true examples of a completely general skill. In an industrial economy, however, generally transferable skills are approximated by basic literacy, by the ability to communicate, and by a commitment to industrial work rules.[10]

Technology specificity   Closely related to job specificity is the specificity of a technology, where technology refers to the entire set of tasks which comprises a work process. A technology, like jobs, utilizes skills of varying degrees of specificity. Technology does not impart specificity to skills so much through the motions of the tasks which it requires as through the speed and accuracy with which they are executed. In most manufacturing enterprises, for example, speed and accuracy of work are considered the critical determinants of labor cost. Both are heavily dependent upon the peculiarities of particular pieces of equipment, the type of materials, the particular product, the length of production runs, and the environment in which that product is being produced.

For example, the production of a pair of shoes requires some skilled operators and some skilled equipment repairmen. Similar operating and repair skills are utilized in many labor markets, and it is generally possible to engage new employees as machine operators. But operators familiar with the idiosyncracies of the particular pieces of equipment can produce much faster and are also able to anticipate machine breakdown, thereby minimizing equipment downtime. Downtime is further reduced when the repair crew is also familiar with the equipment so that the trouble can be quickly diagnosed and repaired. These skills are highly specific in character.

In one way or another every piece of equipment is unique, and every technology involves *some* skills which are specific in the above sense. But specificity can rise above this irreducible minimum, and, while its level is influenced by a number of variables beyond managerial control, discussion with managers and engineers suggests that they can exercise some discretionary restraint.

A general principle appears to govern many technologies: the greater the variety of tasks a machine is built to perform, the less efficient it tends to be in the performance of any one of them. Since production departments are under continued pressure to minimize costs, the operation of this principle results in the tendency for technology to become increasingly enterprise specific over time. Line supervision, and sometimes operatives and maintenance crews as well, are forever modifying equipment in order to improve its efficiency. Such changes accumulate quickly and can produce considerable movement toward specificity.

Countervailing pressure against specificity is generated by the savings in fixed capital costs and fixed labor costs associated with standardized equipment which can utilize widely available skills. Economies of scale in production generally make standardized equipment cheaper than custom-made machinery. The availability of standardized parts reduces repair and maintenance costs and the need for spare-parts inventories. Standardized equipment also tends to reduce the cost of adjusting to changes in the composition of demand.

Specific technologies are also less apt to be described formally in blueprints, operating instructions, or repair manuals for several reasons. First, technologies often become specific through a long series of minor changes in initially standard equipment, each of which is too trivial to warrant recording. Second, many of the factors which make machinery and jobs idiosyncratic, such as the sounds and smells of equipment, are extremely difficult to describe. Finally, there are fixed costs for developing and maintaining detailed written instructions and designs. If this investment cannot be spread over many pieces of equipment, it is less likely to be undertaken. When not formally recorded, the technology exists only in day-to-day operations, and the skills required tend to be the unique possession of the internal labor force. This in turn further enhances the importance of the internal labor force as a stable and self-perpetuating body and thus fosters rigidity in the rules governing internal training.

On-the-Job Training[11]

The second factor critical in the development of internal labor markets is the process of on-the-job training. In the past, economists have tended to ignore this phenomenon altogether. Economic theory, when it has considered training at all, has assumed that it occurs in a formal educational institution which is implicitly treated as a part of a separate educational industry. There has been a recent upsurge of interest in on-the-job training, but analysts have viewed such training primarily as a shift in the locus of the educational process and in the distribution of training costs.[12] Very little attention has been paid to the training *process* and its effect upon the establishment in which it occurs. It is the process, however, which is important in understanding internal labor markets and which is examined in this section.

By far the largest proportion of blue-collar job skills is acquired on the job.[13] Such training appears relatively less important for white-collar professional and managerial jobs where formal education attainment requirements tend to dwarf skills previously acquired on the job.[14] But, even for these positions, formal education is often used more as a screening device for selecting people with certain aptitudes and social backgrounds. On-the-job training then provides either the larger proportion of skills actually utilized in the performance of work or is a prerequisite for the successful utilization of formal education.[15]

For blue-collar manufacturing jobs, the hallmark of on-the-job training is its informality. The process is variously described as 'osmosis,' 'exposure,' 'experience,' or 'working one's way up through promotion.' Very often on-the-job training is not recognized as a distinct process at all; it is simply assumed that a worker who has 'been around' for a while will know how to do certain things. For relatively simple operating jobs, new workers are typically given a brief job demonstration. They then begin to produce on their own, receiving occasional help from foremen or neighboring operators. On more complex jobs, particularly those involving maintenance or repair, the novice may serve as an assistant to an experienced employee. In other cases, training takes place along a promotion ladder in which work on the lower-level jobs develops the skills required for the higher level. Workers may also learn other jobs by observing their neighbors and by practicing on, or 'playing around with,' equipment during lunch hours and other production breaks. Learning often occurs by observing neighboring workers. Sometimes even the trainee is not conscious of the learning process. Thus, even when the jobs within a department are not skill-related, the ability to perform them is correlated with the length of time the worker has 'been around.'

The informality of on-the-job training makes it difficult to identify the precise nature of the process, but the following elements appear to be involved. First, training typically occurs in the process of production, partly through trial and error. It is the production process that disciplines the learning process and provides indications of success and failure. Both monetary and psychological rewards and penalties stimulate the mastering of the skills.

Second, when instruction of one kind or another is required, it is usually provided by a supervisor, by the incumbent worker, or by workers on neighboring jobs. The experienced workman deliberately demonstrates new tasks to a subordinate; or the subordinate may, after brief instruction, fill in for his superior during temporary absences. In all cases, the 'instructor' generally continues to discharge his productive responsibilities. The participants in the training process therefore assume dual roles: one in the production process, as supervisors or subordinates, the other in the learning process, as instructors or students.

Third, the very process of on-the-job training tends to blur the distinction between jobs. In many respects, on-the-job training might best be described as one of a rolling readjustment of tasks between experienced and inexperienced workmen. The experienced workman begins by assigning novices the simpler parts of the jobs which he originally performed. He then gradually assigns more complicated tasks connected with teaching and supervision. As the workman shifts more complex tasks to the trainee, he also reduces his supervisory and teaching efforts, and reabsorbs some of the simpler tasks to allow the trainee time to master the complex work. Somewhat the same thing occurs when on-the-job training occurs through temporary assignments of trainees to the job of the experienced workman. The novice performs the routine aspects of the work, and the more complex tasks are either performed by a superior or are postponed until the experienced man returns.

In all of these cases, the formal distinction between one job classification and another is maintained. Work assignments are referred to as temporary or permanent, and different wage rates are attached to the jobs. But the wage rates and the job definitions tend to be somewhat arbitrary. They are artificial distinctions, imposed upon a situation where one job merges into another and where the skills acquired and the tasks performed are continually changing in subtle ways. For example, screw machine operators may normally perform set up and minor maintenance tasks on four or five machines. When a 'green hand' is hired, the skilled operator may assume set-up and maintenance responsibilities for seven or eight machines. The trainee will observe the operation of these machines, and keep the tool bit clean and oiled. Gradually the trainee will absorb the more complex tasks and operate more machines until he is weaned from his reliance upon the experienced worker, except for an occasional problem.

Sometimes training in manufacturing plants is described as 'formal.' But, in many cases, this involves little more than a systemization of informal procedures which leave the underlying nature of the training process unchanged. For example, vestibule training, which is usually called formal, often involves the development of a separate production facility where the slower pace of new workers does not interfere with the opeation of experienced personnel. Another example is maintenance apprenticeship programs occasionally offered in manufacturing plants. These programs are described as formal, but the classroom portion is secondary to training on the job. The formal dimension of on-the-job training often involves little more than a systematic rotation of the trainee through enough job classifications to ensure exposure to the full complement of tasks which craftsmen are expected to perform. Similar managerial arrangements are utilized for training college graduates entering large corporations and for medical interns.

The prevalence of on-the-job training appears to be associated with several different factors. These factors, because they determine when the training occurs and also because they may influence other aspects of the work environment, are worthy of note. First, for certain jobs there is no alternative to training on the job. These jobs exist only as work performed and cannot be duplicated in the classroom. Incumbent employees have difficulty describing or demonstrating the skills they possess, except in a production context. In some cases they also have a strong incentive to hide what they do from management who might use this knowledge to extract greater output from them or to correct a loose incentive rate. Hence, managers find it impossible to develop a formal curriculum which might be taught in classrooms and must rely, by default, upon a teaching technique in which skills are directly transmitted from the job incumbent to his replacement.

Because so much of the learning process is automatic and dependent upon the individual's curiosity about what goes on around him, as well as his desire to master a job for its extrinsic and intrinsic rewards, it tends to seem 'natural' in the eyes of both management and workers. Such training also seems costless, and thus little attention is paid to the training process. Moreover, managers can often capitalize on the 'natural' learning process by breaking technological processes into jobs and arranging the physical proximity of workers in order to increase the amount of automatic learning which occurs. One example of this is the promotion unit: each job in the progression line develops skills requisite for the succeeding job and draws upon the skills required in the job below it.

It should be emphasized, however, that not all on-the-job training is in fact free. The process frequently involves waste of material, machine damage, reduction in product quality, and sacrifices in the productivity of both the trainee (whose attention is diverted from his current job to that of a neighbor or superior) and the instructor who becomes preoccupied with training and supervising his subordinates. These costs are difficult in practice to separate from the costs of production, but virutally all managers are aware that they exist.[16]

Some of the resources absorbed by the training process, moreover, might otherwise be wasted. Such is the case when the novice learns by playing around with idle equipment during a production break, when scrap material is used to demonstrate a new technique, or when the instruction is provided during lulls in the production process when workers would otherwise be resting. Frequently the best learning situation coincides with the most efficient staffing arrangements. Subordinates, for instance, often learn by filling in during the temporary absence of their superiors. The subordinate might not perform the job as efficiently as the experienced workman, but the arrangement may still be less expensive than the alternative of having redundant experienced replacements available to substitute for skilled workers during unexpected absences.

On-the-job training may be more economical than formal instruction in several other respects as well. Because on-the-job training is derived from the content of the job itself, it is confined only to those skills required for the job and involves no excess training. Since much of the training takes place through demonstration rather than verbal communication, persons incapable of teaching in the classroom can serve as instructors. When the number of trainees required at any given time is small, and the training period short, the economies of scale provided by classroom instruction cannot be obtained. The cost of on-the-job training is further reduced by the output produced by a trainee which is unavailable when training is conducted outside the plant.

Even when more costly, on-the-job training has certain advantages over classroom instruction. Instruction of the job is individual and can be tailored to the learning capabilities and idiosyncracies of each trainee. Moreover, the relevance of the instruction is immediately apparent, which tends to make the trainee more attentive. Vestibule training, which is occasionally used for blue-collar jobs in manufacturing, represents a compromise between on-the-job training and classroom training. Such programs only partly prepare a worker for job performance despite attempts to simulate work conditions.

As should be apparent from the preceding analysis, on-the-job training is closely related to skill specificity. Specificity tends to promote this type of training by reducing the number of people learning a particular skill at a given time. By precluding large-scale, standardized training, formal instruction is discouraged. Moreover, to the extent that skill specificity leads to unrecorded knowledge, it necessitates the process of direct skill transmission from incumbent to successor in the process of production – the essence of on-the-job training.

The relationship between skill specificity and on-the-job training, however, runs in both directions. The narrowness of this training, which makes for economies, makes the skills which it produces highly specific to the context in which they were acquired. Reliance upon on-the-job training also encourages the mutation of technology in the direction of increasing specificity. Skills change with time as they are transferred from one worker to the next. Since instruction does not depend upon formal records or the use of skill developed by formal classes, there is little incentive to maintain standard jobs. Operators and repair crews are allowed latitude to modify equipment on their own, and innovations are frequently introduced by engineers and supervisors without written record.

Custom

Custom is the third of the major factors important to an understanding of internal labor markets. Its role in economic activity has only occasionally been recognized by economists, most frequently in discussions of wage relationships. But it is generally used as a residual explanation: one which is used as a catchall to account for events which cannot otherwise be explained.[17] Economists have not attempted to define the concept of custom precisely or to explain when it is generated and how it might be changed.[18]

Custom at the workplace is an unwritten set of rules based largely upon past practice or precedent. These rules can govern any aspect of the work relationship from discipline to compensation. Work customs appear to be the outgrowth of employment stability within internal labor markets. Such stability, as will be seen from the following discussion, is of value to both the employer and the work force, and one of the factors producing internal labor markets is the desire to effectuate stability. When employment is stable, the same workers come into regular and repeated contact with each other. The result is the formation of social groups or communities within the internal labor market. Communities of this type — in a workplace or any other social setting — tend to generate a set of unwritten rules governing the actions of their members and the relationship between members and outsiders. Eventually, these rules assume an ethical or quasi-ethical aura. Adherence to these rules tends to be viewed as a matter of right and wrong, and the community acts to retaliate against behavior which is at variance with them. It is to such rules that the term 'custom,' as it is used in this volume, applies. The generation of custom in the internal labor market closely resembles the development of customary law in medieval Europe, and both appear to be the product of the psychological behavior of groups.[19] Indeed, the feudal manor, to which medieval custom has reference, can be viewed as a self-contained internal labor market.

The existence of customary law at the workplace is indicated by the 'ethical' phrases which appear in the language of industrial relations: 'just cause for discharge,' 'equal pay for equal work,' 'a fair day's pay for a fair day's work,' and so forth. At each workplace, the vague terms 'just,' 'fair,' and 'equal' are given meaning largely by past practice and precedent. Workers who violate the code are subject to discipline, either by supervision or by their co-workers. For example, fighting or drinking at work may result in discharge or suspension by management; exceeding output norms which the internal work force has determined as 'fair' may result in verbal abuse by the work group, or, in the extreme, being 'sent to coventry' or being subject to sabotage or physical harm.

Customary law is of special interest in the analysis of internal labor markets both because of the stabilizing influence which it imparts to the rules of the workplace and because the rules governing the pricing and allocation of labor within the market are particularly subject to the influence of custom. These rules become constrained and less responsive to market forces, thereby explaining much of the apparent rigidity of internal wage and allocative structures.

[. . .]

NOTES

1. John T. Dunlop, 'Job Vacancy Measures and Economic Analysis,' *The Measurement and Interpretation of Job Vacancies: A Conference Report*, National Bureau of Economic Research (New York: Columbia University Press, 1966).
2. See Clark Kerr, 'The Balkanization of Labor Markets.' in E. Wight Bakke, *et al., Labor Mobility and Economic Opportunity* (Cambridge, Mass.: Technology-Press of MIT, 1954), pp. 92–100. [See Reading 4.6 – Ed.]
3. Arthur M. Ross, 'Do We Have a New Industrial Feudalism?' *American Economic Review*, vol. XLVIII, no. 5, December 1958, pp. 914–915, and Frederick Meyers, *Ownership of Jobs: A Comparative Study*, Institute of Industrial Relations, Monograph Series (Los Angeles: University of California Press, 1964), p. 11.
4. Gary S. Becker, *Human Capital: A Theoretical and Empirical Analysis, with Special Reference to Education* (New York: Columbia University Press, 1964), p. 18.
5. Ibid.
6. These results can be stated formally as follows: employers and employees will invest in training so long as the expected return is greater than the expected cost. For the employee, the expected return is equal to the difference between the income on the job to which the investment permits him to aspire and his income in his current job *weighted by the probability that he will obtain the job to which he aspires*. This probability is a decreasing function of specificity. The employer's expected return is equal to the difference in the productivity of the trained worker, and the productivity of the untrained worker corrected for any differences in wage rates which result from the training and *weighted by the probability that the worker will remain on the job*. This probability is also an increasing function of specificity.
7. The effect of training scale upon absolute training costs may, however, be diminished if the specific skills are widely utilized in the internal market of the employer providing the training.
8. The reference of the term 'specificity' to skill even when applied to a job, is important. It implies that a job could be unique to an enterprise, in the sense that the set of the skills which it utilized was not required elsewhere, and yet each skill in the set might be quite general. Such a job would *not* be enterprise specific.
    A second source of confusion surrounding the concept of job specificity is derived from the instability in the definition of jobs in most enterprises. As will be seen subsequently in the discussion of on-the-job training, the skills and duties associated with a given job vary systematically as part of the internal allocative process, and this, plus the wide variation among enterprises in jobs with similar titles, makes the concept of the job a difficult and elusive one to work with. The concept is, none the less, necessary for an understanding of some phenomena. An employer, for example, may be induced to finance the training of the general skills required by a job because he knows that the specific training which the job also requires will minimize turnover.
9. Edith T. Penrose, *The Theory of the Growth of the Firm* (New York: Wiley and Sons, 1959) and Robin Marris, *A Managerial Theory of Capitalism* (New York: Free Press of Glencoe, 1964).
10. See Clark Kerr *et al., Industrialism and Industrial Man* (Cambridge, Mass.: Harvard University Press, 1960).
11. Much of the material in this subsection appeared initially in Michael J. Piore, 'On-the-Job Training and Adjustment to Technological Change,' *The Journal of Human Resources*, vol. III, no. 4 (Fall 1968), pp. 435–449; and Peter B. Doeringer and Michael J. Piore, 'Labor Market Adjustment and Internal Training,' *Proceedings of the Eighteenth Annual Meeting*, Industrial Relations Research Association, New York, December 1965, pp. 250–263.
12. See, for example, R. S. Eckaus, 'Economic Criteria for Education and Training,' *Review of Economics and Statistics*, May 1964, pp. 181–190; Kenneth J. Arrow, 'The Economic Implications of Learning by Doing,' *The Review of Economic Studies*, June 1962, pp. 155–173; Jacob Mincer, 'On-the-Job Training: Costs, Returns, and Implications,' *Journal of Political Economy Supplement*, vol. LXX, no. 5, part 2

(October 1962), pp. 50–79; and Walter Y. Oi, 'Labor as a Quasi-Fixed Factor,' *Journal of Political Economy*, vol. LXX, no. 6 (December 1962), pp. 538–555. [See Reading 2.1 – Ed.]

13. See U.S. Department of Labor, 'Formal Occupational Training of Adult Workers,' *Manpower/Automation Research Monograph No. 2*, December 1964, Table 11, pp. 43–45. See also U.S. Department of Health, Education, and Welfare, Office of Juvenile Delinquency and Youth Development, *Getting Hired, Getting Trained* (Washington, D.C.: U.S. Government Printing Office, 1965); National Manpower Council, *A Policy for Skilled Manpower* (New York: Columbia University Press, 1954), pp. 208–233; and Department of Labour, Canada, *Acquisition of Skills*, Research Program on the Training of Skilled Manpower, Report 4 (Ottawa: Queen's Printer and Controller of Stationery, 1960). George Strauss's study indicates that the training of construction craftsmen is often equally informal; see 'Apprenticeship: An Evaluation of the Need' in Arthur M. Ross (ed.), *Employment Policy and Labor Market* (Berkeley: University of California Press, 1965).

14. Ibid.

15. See Lester C. Thurow, 'The Occupational Distribution of the Returns of Education and Experiences for Whites and Negroes,' in *Federal Programs for the Development of the Human Resources*, papers submitted to the Subcommittee on Economic Progress of the Joint Economic Committee, U.S. Congress (Washington, D.C.: Government Printing Office, 1968); vol. I, pp. 267–284.

16. The presence of such costs does not necessarily deter on-the-job training. Given the automatic character of the learning process, it may be impossible to prevent these costs. Where training alternatives exist, they may be even more costly to operate.

17. See, for example, J. R. Hicks, *The Theory of Wages* (London: Macmillan Co., 1963), especially pp. 316–319, and J. S. Mill, *Principles of Political Economy* (New York: Longmans, Green, and Co., 1926), pp. 242–248. More recent examples can be found in Lloyd G. Reynolds, *Labor Markets and Labor Relations* (Englewood Cliffs, N.J.; Prentice-Hall, 1968), p. 509; and George W. Taylor and Frank C. Pierson (eds)., *New Concepts in Wage Determination* (New York: McGraw-Hill Co., 1957), pp. 117–172.

18. Considerably more work has been done in this area by sociologists, legal historians, and psychologists. This section draws heavily upon articles by Edwin Sapir and Charles S. Lambinger in *The Encyclopedia of Social Sciences* (New York: Macmillan Co., 1931), vol. IV, pp. 658–667, and Marc Bloch, *Feudal Society*, L. A. Manyon (trans.) (Chicago: University of Chicago Press, 1964), vol. I, pp. 113–120. The connection between legal behavior and economic behavior is suggested by Justice Douglas in the Supreme Court's opinion in *United Steelworkers of America vs. Warrior and Gulf Navigation Co.*, 363 U.S. 574 (1960).

19. See Bloch, *op. cit.*

2.3 Discrimination in the Labour Market*

SOME MODELS OF RACIAL DISCRIMINATION IN THE LABOR MARKET

The real subject of this chapter is economic theory itself or, more precisely, the use and meaning of neoclassical price theory in application to the allocation of resources and the distribution of income in the real world. More specifically, these are some reflections that have grown out of attempts to analyze the differentials in income between blacks and whites in the United States with the tools of economic theory. The phenomenon of income differentials is, after all, an economic phenomenon, however much it may be linked with other social

*From Kenneth J. Arrow, 'Models of Job Discrimination', in A. Pascal (ed.), *Racial Discrimination in Economic Life* (Lexington, Mass.: Lexington Books, D. C. Heath, 1972).

dimensions. There is no reason to impose the burden of a full explanation upon economic theory, but it should provide insight into the links between the social, cultural, and individual facts on the one hand and the economic facts on the other just as the theory of production is supposed to provide a link between the facts of technology and the uses and rewards of factors.

My discussion will therefore be a programmatic and methodological one rather than a confident analysis. My intention is to present the deficiencies of neoclassical analysis, as brought out by the attempt to use it as a tool for the analysis of racial discrimination in the economic sphere, and by so doing to suggest the areas in which further research may be more fruitful.

To avoid misunderstanding, let me make clear my general attitude toward the fruitfulness and value of marginal analysis. On one hand, I believe its clarifying value in social thought is great. Especially when dealing with problems central to economics, the difference in approach between trained economists and others, however able, is enormous. The importance of the search for possible alternatives, the value of consistency in different contexts as a guide to judgment, and, above all, the appreciation that the workings of institutions may be such that the outcomes are very different from the intentions of the agents are among the lessons of economic theory. So long as scarcity is an issue and social organizations for coping with it are complex, these principles and their logical elaboration and empirical implementation will be important. Though this is not the place for an elaborate defense, I reject, on both logical and historical grounds, the widespread suspicion that neoclassical economics is simply an apology for the *status quo*.

On the other hand, everyone knows that neoclassical economics is seriously deficient in two directions: (1) its implications, though often exemplified in the real world, are also often falsified (mass unemployment and failures in economic development are the most conspicuous examples); and (2) the implications of neoclassical economics are frequently very weak. Consequently, neoclassical economics says nothing about important economic phenomena. Thus, a highly disaggregated Walrasian model implies a distribution of income; but it would be difficult indeed to say if the observed facts are or are not compatible with the model.

Let us turn to the case at hand. Today, mean earnings of blacks in the United States are about 65 percent of those of whites. This ratio has varied over time; it is certainly cyclical, being higher in prosperity than in recession, and seems to show a very slow upward trend, though one cannot be sure. The tight labor markets of World War II brought a sharp rise of about ten percentage points; the ratio remained near that level until the slackening of employment in the 1950s, after which there was a decline until about 1963 (*Economic Report of the President*, 1970: 200, Table C-20). The present higher levels may be due to the change in political climate, through fair unemployment laws and through changes in attitudes by economic agents, employers, unions, and individual employees, or again it may simply be due to a high demand for labor. We really do not know.

There are differences in unemployment rates partly because of the concentration of blacks in occupations with high-employment rates, but a good part of the difference remains even after correction for the occupational distribution (Gilman, 1965). Nevertheless, the differential unemployment rates are not a major explanation for black-white income differentials. If the unemployment rates were equalized, the earnings differentials would be reduced by only a few percentage points. The bulk of the difference is accounted for by differences in wage rates, partly because blacks are concentrated in low-income occupations and partly because they receive lower wages even within given occupations, at least as conventionally classified. In what follows, I will therefore speak of racial discrimination in the labor market as being evidenced only through wage differentials.

What would a disciple of Marshall and Walras have to say by way of economic analysis? The most obvious explanation goes back to Cairnes' noncompeting groups; that is, it concerns the supply. For one reason or another, it can be argued, the marginal productivity of black labor is lower than that of white on the average. Some supply factors indisputably exist. The educational level of blacks in the labor force is lower, and we know from many studies that earnings are correlated with educational level. (As an aside, I am not persuaded that differences of earnings with educational level are entirely due to increases in productivity, but that is a different story.) The educational gap is being rapidly reduced; indeed, there is only about a six-month difference in the median numbers of years of education between the races among those leaving school today. But of course this change has not yet had time to have much effect on the comparative average educational levels of the entire labor force. It is also undoubtedly true that the quality of education received by blacks is inferior, though understanding of this fact is not easy to come by. Age distribution is another supply factor; blacks are on the average younger, and, up to a certain point, age is a positive factor in earnings. Less well-known supply factors also have their role. More black families are headed by women. Black families are somewhat larger, and it is apparently a well-established fact that individuals with many siblings earn less.

Various authors have made corrections to the income differential based on these factors (Duncan, 1969: 98 and 106; Tables 4.3 and 4.4). The analysis is indeed reminiscent of sources of growth. The studies tend to show that these factors will, taken together, account for one-half or more of the observed income differential, but there remains at least 40 percent unexplained. No doubt failure to explain is not the same as proof of nonexplanation. There may easily be other supply factors overlooked or not easily quantifiable; motivational differences due to cultural variation and especially the heritage of slavery have often been cited by popular writers and by some social scientists, though the evidence is less than compelling. Thus, for instance, it is frequently held that blacks have, because of cultural and historical conditioning, a stronger tendency to discount the future and, because of this, a lower propensity to make investments in themselves. It may indeed be true that they make less personal commitment with a view toward later reward, and I will return to this point later, but I doubt that this behavior is due to a basic difference in attitude towards the future. If it were, it should also be reflected in lower propensities to save; but in fact repeated studies have shown that at any given income level blacks save, if anything, a higher proportion of their income than whites (Friedman, 1957: 70–85 and references).

Since it appears that supply considerations can explain only part of the black-white income differential, it is advisable to turn to the demand side, which is, in any case, what I am primarily interested in. There are some obvious positive reasons for expecting the demand for black labor to differ from that for white labor of the same productivity. For one thing, we have other evidence that on the average whites act as if they dislike association with blacks. Residential segregation is an obvious and well-documented example. No explanation exists, other than the desire of whites to avoid blacks. The only possible alternative hypothesis would be segregation by economic status, but comparison between blacks and whites of equal income shows conclusively that blacks are far more segregated (Taeuber and Taeuber, 1965; Pascal, 1967). Also, at least in the recent past, discrimination in some labor markets, particularly those where unions controlled entry, has been completely overt.

Another positive reason for arguing that a racial discrimination exists in the demand for labor is that the measured income differentials are greater at higher educational levels. For example, among males aged 35 to 44 in the northern United States in 1959, the ratio of mean nonwhite to mean white income was 79 percent for those with elementary school education, 70 percent for those with high school education, and only 59 percent for those with college education. Indeed, the mean income of nonwhite college graduates is or was, as of 1959, no greater than that of white high school dropouts (Miller, 1966: 140, Table VI-3). (Incidentally, my shift in reference from 'blacks' to 'nonwhites' has no deep significance. The Census figures I have just been quoting give only the white-non-white breakdown, but in fact blacks constitute the overwhelming majority of nonwhites in the United States.) Since the successive stages of schooling select those most in tune with the needs of the dominant culture in all aspects, including the economic, it is hard to give any explanation for these figures based on supply considerations. It is most reasonable to explain them on the hypothesis of a racial discrimination in demand that is more intense for higher economic positions, the jobs into which the more educated ordinarily go.

From now on I will speak of black and white as being interchangeable in production, at least within given skill levels, so as to emphasize the demand determinants of wage differentials. The relevant theoretical literature is surprisingly small in view of the importance of the subject and the great attention it has received by the public. The main study is that of Gary Becker (1957) some thirteen years ago; still earlier, Edgeworth (1922) had written on some aspects of wage discrimination according to sex. The possible channels by which discriminatory attitudes come to affect wages are well stated by Becker, but what might be termed the general equilibrium aspects are largely ignored; that is, the effects of wage differentials on the stimulation of compensating behavior are slighted, and, as will be seen, these create a crucial dilemma for an appreciation of the value of economic theory.

The most natural starting point for analysis is to look at the proximate determinant of the demand for labor, the employer's decisions. If we assume away productivity differences between black and white employees, the simplest explanation of the existence of wage differences is the taste of the employer. Formally, we might suppose that the employer acts so as to maximize a utility function that depends not only on profits but also on the numbers of white and black employees. Presumably, other variables being held constant, the employer has a negative marginal utility for black labor. A positive marginal utility for white labor might also be expected, if only in some sense to offset and dilute the black labor. A specific version of this hypothesis would be that the employer's utility depends only on the ratio of black to white workers and is independent of the scale of operations of the firm.

Under these circumstances, the employer will hire white workers up to a point somewhat beyond where their marginal productivity equals their wage, since he is also rewarded through their positive marginal utility. Similarly, he will stop hiring black laborers at a point somewhat before the point that equates their marginal productivity to their wage. Under the assumption that the two kinds of workers are perfect substitutes in production, the marginal productivities of the two kinds of workers are equal. Their common value depends only on the total number of workers of both races hired. It follows, then, that equilibrium is possible only when the wages of white workers are above the marginal product of labor and the wages of black workers below. To be precise, white wages will exceed marginal product by the marginal rate of substitution between white workers and profits, the rate being computed at the white-black ratio in the labour force. A similar statement holds for black wages.

Under this model, it is clear that black workers incur a definite loss, as compared with the competitive level in the absence of discrimination. On the other hand, white workers are likely gainers relative to the nondiscriminatory level. It can be shown that aggregate output is unaffected if all employers discriminate equally; otherwise there may be some efficiency loss in total output. Whether employers gain or lose in the aggregate is a quantitative question about which *a priori* theory gives no definite answer in general. However, in the special case where it is assumed that an employer's utility depends only on the ratio of the two kinds of workers, the employer neither gains nor loses, as compared with a non-discriminatory situation.

Once we start applying utility analysis to racially discriminatory behavior, we may extend it to other members of the productive team. In those cases where the entry of workers into jobs is controlled directly by unions, as in the building trades, discriminatory attitudes by fellow workers become decisive. The results are more apt to be total or partial exclusion rather than wage differentials. I am more interested in pressures that work through the market, however.

Consider white workers who supply services complementary to those of another class of workers, for example, white foremen working with a floor force of mixed race. If the foremen dislike working with blacks, they may offer their services at a higher wage to those firms with higher proportions of black workers. That is, given the choice of working for different firms with different proportions of black workers and different wages, they will choose according to some utility function that represents the trade-off between wages and the number of white and black workers. The firm's offers of employment to foremen will then have two dimensions, the wages and the proportion of blacks in the floor force. But this in turn means that the firm will have a different demand for black laborers than for white, even if they are perfect substitutes in production and even if the employer himself has no discriminatory feelings.

It should be understood that the wage differentiation for foremen according to the proportion of black floor workers may in practice appear in a disguised form. The cost to the employer of increasing the number of blacks may be measured not in statistically observed higher wages for his foremen but in lower morale, lower productivity, or simply lower quality of personnel.

If, parallel to our earlier assumption about the utility functions of employers, we assume that the discriminatory tastes of foremen are determined by the *ratio* of blacks to whites under them rather than by the amounts, it can be shown that in equilibrium the black workers lose, the white floor workers gain an equal amount, and neither the foremen nor the employers gain or lose money income.

I have spoken thus far of foremen and floor workers, but obviously the analysis applies to any two complementary forms of labor. A particularly interesting possibility is discrimination by lower-level workers against supervisors. That is, the costs of hiring labor may be higher if they have to work for black supervisors. Indeed, it may be expected that the effects of discrimination of this type are greater than the reverse, and this for two reasons. First, the resentment against working under a supervisor belonging to a despised group may be more intense than the simple dislike of having them close by. Indeed, sufficiently superior social status can certainly completely compensate for nearness, as in the master–servant relation. Second, effects of discrimination by lower echelons against higher may be greater than the reverse simply because there are so many more of the former. Thus, even if the wage compensation needed to work with blacks is the same in two situations, lower working with higher and vice versa, the cost to the employer is much greater in one case than the other.

I find this last observation especially interesting, because it explains why more highly educated blacks are more heavily discriminated against. They would expect to go into the higher-level jobs where the discrimination may be greater.

Parenthetically, let me say that I have omitted still another taste element in the explanation of discrimination, namely, discrimination by customers. If whites dislike associating with blacks in any capacity, they may in particular dislike dealing with them when purchasing goods. Several interesting questions arise here, particularly with regard to the exact social nature of the buyer–seller relation in different contexts, but in any case this aspect is irrelevant to the more normal situation in which those who make the goods do not meet buyers face to face.

At a certain level, then, we have a coherent and by no means implausible account of the economic implications of racial discrimination. In the grossest sense, it accounts for the known facts. For example, the fact that discrimination against blacks increases with the level of education implies that the rate of return to the investment in human capital is lower for blacks than for whites, explaining in turn why the proportion of blacks in college is lower than that of whites.

Still, I do not think this is satisfactory. To begin with, we can be troubled by the lack of specificity in the hypotheses being advanced. This is, of course, a defect common to all utility explanations of economic behavior. The theory does not give any quantitative clues. A marginal productivity theory of demand for labor, true or false, asserts a highly specific relation between the production function and the demand for labor, each of which is observable under ideal conditions. A utility theory in and of itself asserts much vaguer connections, usually of a qualitative nature and frequently not even that. To take a parallel case, we know that as *per capita* incomes increase, the proportions in which different commodities are purchased alters. This generalization about behavior is, in fact, of the greatest importance from the practical point of view. It can only be explained by invoking the nature of tastes, in technical language the nonhomotheticity of the indifference surfaces. Have we explained anything? I do not want to get involved in the meaning of explanation as an epistemological concept, but it is fair to say that the explanation in terms of tastes is not useless. If we add the assumption that the tastes of individuals are similar, at least in a statistical sense, then we may be able to make inferences from the history of demand patterns in one country to that of another. Similarly, in the case of racial discrimination, we may be able to infer from the behavior of employees of one type to those of another on the hypothesis that their tastes are similar.

The hypotheses of the theory lack specificity in a second sense. They invoke a dislike of association with blacks, but as I have already suggested, the dislike may depend upon the nature of the association. Physical proximity is probably significant only because of its implications for status and for feelings of superiority and of fear. The slave owner and his overseer felt no reluctance to work with an all-black labor force. Railroad and airline porters tend to be blacks. Still the matter is not just one of status; detailed studies show wage differences even in narrowly specified low-level occupations, though these differences are much smaller than the average in the economy. No doubt the general concept of association with blacks has to be broken down into several dimensions. But the fact that utility analysis leads to such more detailed questioning is, in my view, an evidence of its fruitfulness.

The excessive generality of utility hypotheses about economic behavior is, then, a drawback, but one that seems intrinsic in the nature of the case. There is a second objection to this and other utility explanations that I will discuss more briefly; namely, that we offer no explanation of racial discrimination but simply refer the problem to an unanalyzed realm. We all remember Molière's intellectual who explained that opium produces sleep because it contains a great deal of the dormitive principle. Yet in a sense, all scientific explanation involves the same process of musical chairs; all we ask is that the explanatory principles have some degree of generality and parsimony. In the context of racial discrimination, however, one may worry that this advice is too cheap. Explaining an economic phenomenon such as the impact of attitudes, taken as given, on the workings of the economic system is legitimate enough; but what if those attitudes are themselves the result of economic behavior? Specifically, and in more emotional language, what if racial discrimination and the tastes that underlie it are tools of economic exploitation?

I have mentioned two possible difficulties with accepting utility explanations. A third, which I wish to emphasize most strongly, is of a very different nature and has different implications. The question can be raised whether the economic system does not have other forces that counteract the tendency toward wage discrimination. Sherlock Holmes, a man much concerned with the formulation of hypotheses for the explanation of empirical behavior, once asked about the barking of a dog at night. The local police inspector, mystified as usual, noted that the dog had not barked at night. Holmes dryly noted that his silence was precisely the problem.

Have we some dog whose silence should be remarked? Yes; those vast forces of greed and aggressiveness that we are assured and assure students are the main-springs of economic activity in a private enterprise economy; not the best but the strongest motives of humanity, as Marshall had said. For some employers, the trade-off between discrimination and profits is less than for others. There need be no assumption of higher morality; if interpersonal comparisons are admitted, it might simply be that some employers are greedier than others. Presumably, they will take advantage of the gap between black and white wages by demanding the black labor. In the long run, the less discriminatory will either drive the more discriminatory out of business or, if not, will cause the wage difference to fall. If we suppose that there are some actual or potential employers who do not discriminate at all, then the wage difference should, in the long run, fall to zero. The discriminating employers may possibly continue to operate, but they will employ only white labor.

This kind of argument is not unfamiliar in other fields of application. As soon as utility-maximizing behavior is introduced into the productive side of the economy, the question arises of its relation to profit-maximization and particularly to the role of competition. The theory of the firm, particularly under imperfect competition, has found a considerable, if fitful place for tastes. Hicks (1935) noted that a monopolist might prefer a quiet life to maximum profits. Herbert

Simon (1959) and his students, especially Oliver Williamson (1967), have suggested that entrepreneurs might seek to maximize a utility function in which other variables entered besides profits: the emoluments of the higher officers and the sheer size of the firm, as well as avoidance of decision making. Marris (1964) has taken up a dynamic version of the size theory; his entrepreneurs have tastes for growth as well as profits.

There has also been a countervailing current of opinion that argues, in effect, that the utility functions of entrepreneurs do not matter. Competition will force firms to maximize profits, since otherwise they will not survive. Even under imperfect competition, profit maximizers will find it profitable to take over firms from utility maximizers. I should note here that from the viewpoint of formal analysis, this case is not as different as might appear from the first; it still presupposes a considerable amount of competition in the capital market.

The prevailing opinion seems to be that the question of utility maximization can be raised only under conditions of imperfect competition. Those who defend the importance of tastes for size and growth usually are first concerned to argue that the firm has potential access to monopoly profits, and it is these that might be dissipated in seeking after nonpecuniary goals.

Upon reflection, I believe the relevant distinctions are wrongly drawn. Even under perfect competition, if I have a taste for size and derive pleasure from it, I might perfectly well accept a rate of return below the competitive level in order to indulge my tastes. Indeed, all the statistical evidence I know of suggests that self-employed businessmen in general are accepting less than a competitive rate of return (or alternatively less than their competitive wage) for such pleasures. A perfectly competitive equilibrium is compatible with utility maximization by entrepreneurs; of course, the price they have to pay for their tastes will depend on the tastes of others in the market, but they are not driven out as sharply as might be supposed.

I want to argue, however, that the hypothesis of competitive elimination might have more force in the case of racial discrimination. More generally, I would suggests, rather tentatively, that this hypothesis might be more likely to hold when the nonpecuniary variables have negative marginal utilities than when they have positive ones. The reason is simple enough: the employer can always avoid the negative utilities and still achieve a competitive rate of return by simply becoming a pure capitalist, a stockholder.

Before going into more details and qualifications, let me again draw an analogy, this time with the spread of innovations. In explaining a failure to introduce an innovation, historians frequently invoke a conservative spirit on the part of the entrepreneurs in question; for example, Landes (1969) in comparing English and French attitudes toward innovation at the end of the eighteenth century. Theorists find themselves puzzled. No doubt it is possible for French entrepreneurs to have, on the average, a utility function that has a negative weight for innovation. But if even a few entrepreneurs for some eccentric reason lack this distaste, they will introduce the innovation and the forces of competition will force the others to follow suit, at the peril of elimination. These competitive tendencies operate through the capital market as well as the product market, of course; new capital will flow to the successful innovators.

No doubt this argument has to be modified in the case where monopoly profits are earned. It will pay the firm to remain in business and indulge its distaste for innovation or for hiring blacks. But the fundamental point is that the competitive pressures, to the extent, that they are decisive, work toward the elimination of racial differences in income, under the usual assumptions of economic theory.

Thus, after building up a more or less reasonable mechanism that gives a rationale for linking economic discrimination with other social attitudes, I now argue that if the logic of the competitive system is accepted, discrimination should still be undermined in the long run. This forces us to reconsider the meaning of long-run competition, which I do below. I must also call to your attention that the negative discussion has so far only concerned discrimination by employers. I must also ask whether discrimination by other employees is also eroded over time. This raises some other questions of a more technical nature.

A model in which white employers and employees were motivated by a dislike of association with blacks as well as more narrowly economic motives would give a satisfactory qualitative account of observed racial discrimination in wages but, at least as far as employers are concerned, it is hard to understand how discriminatory behavior could persist in the long run in the face of competitive pressures. Several assumptions have been made, implicitly or explicitly, and perhaps should be restated here: constant returns to scale in the long run, a sufficiently wide spectrum of tastes toward discrimination and in particular a sufficient number of actual or potential nondiscriminating employers, and an adequate freedom of entry. The last condition, let me stress, is consistent with a certain amount of imperfect competition. If there is enough entry by nondiscriminating entrepreneurs to absorb the entire black labor force and some more, then wages would be equalized, but the surviving discriminating firms would now be completely segregated. Obviously, the degree of freedom of entry necessary to eliminate racial wage differentials depends upon the proportion of blacks in the labor force. But, in the United States, the black workers constitute some fifteen percent of the labor force; if employer discrimination were the sole cause of wage differences, it is hard to believe that competitive forces are inadequate to eliminate racial wage differentials.

What then of employee discrimination? Let me take up a case not touched on explicitly before. Because of its extreme nature, it lends itself to simple analysis. I refer to discrimination by white employees who are perfect substitutes for blacks. The discussion itself is due to Becker, but I want to draw attention to its wider implications.

Suppose for a simple model that there is only one kind of utility function expressing a trade-off between wages and the proportion of white workers in the labor force of the firm. Any employer can purchase black labor at a fixed price, but for white labor he must choose some point on an indifference curve between wages and the white proportion. A little reflection makes it obvious that if the wages required by whites for an all-white labor force are lower than black wages, total segregation for whites is optimum for the firm, while in the contrary case an all-black labor force is cheapest. We are, of course, still assuming equal productivity for the two races. At a general equilibrium with full employment of both types of labor, some firms must be segregated in one direction and some in the other. It would never pay a firm to have a mixed labor force, since they would have to raise the wages of their white workers above the level for the all-white option. The firms would also have to find the two types of segregation equally profitable; otherwise, they would all switch to one or the other. This requires that wages paid to whites in the all-white firms equal that paid to blacks in the all-black firms. There would be again no wage differentials.

The relation of this result to the possibility of discrimination by complementary types of labor will be discussed shortly, but the model and the kinds of processes of which it is symbolic deserve some attention. Obviously, we are concerned that we have drawn an implication — no wage differentials — that is contrary to observation. We also have drawn another implication — segregation — that is very much a fact. Indeed, some 70 percent of the small firms in Chicago have no black workers at all, although about 14 percent of the Chicago labor force is black. The evidence is that even in large firms blacks tend to be separated by department and by occupation (Baron and Hymer, 1968: 262–63: U.S. Department of Labor, 1969:44, Table 12). Thus, the pure theory turns up with tantalizing results, partly clearly false, partly yielding unusual insights.

The analysis just used, simple as it is, is not typical of economic theory. We tend to infer that conflicting forces will balance somewhere in the middle. Here, on the contrary, it is of the essence that firms prefer extreme alternatives to compromises. In technical language, we have a failure of convexity. The situation is similar to, though not identical with, a famous crux of economic theory, the relation between increasing returns and competitive equilibrium. Here too under competitive conditions the firms will either shut down completely or go to some high level of activity, possibly too high to be compatible with resource limitations.

The recognition of nonconvexities and their importance in economic life is hardly new; we all recall the central role that Adam Smith gave to division of labor and its relation to the size of the market. Indeed, Smith's ideas of specialization among individuals, firms, and even nations are exactly analogous in formal structure to the occurrence of racial segregation in production. But it has proved very difficult to incorporate nonconvexities in systematic general theories. Marx, for example, talks a good deal about concentration of ownership of capital, based on what we would call increasing returns; but his models of simple and expanded reproduction display perfectly orthodox constancy of returns. In the last 20 years, the increasing formalization of economic theory has made more prominent than ever the role of the convexity assumptions that literary economists have always used freely. There is now a growing body of literature, however, starting with Farrell's paper of 1959, that is seriously attempting to wrestle with the relaxation of convexity hypotheses. At least this much seems to be possible to assert: if the nonconvexities are small on the scale of the entire economy, then something like a competitive equilibrium is still possible. But the structure of that equilibrium may be different from what would obtain under convexity. There will be a tendency toward specialization, in the present context toward segregation. Though price levels may not be so much different than they would be in a comparable convex world, the distribution of individuals among occupations and of output among products may display much more concentration on widely separate positions.

Let me return to the problem at hand. The vision of firms rushing from one kind of segregation to another in response to small wage changes is troublesome, and I will come back to that point. Meanwhile, let us ask if the analysis of discriminatory feelings by perfect substitutes has any lessons for discrimination by complementary types of labor. I think the answer is clearly yes, if we suppose that there are black workers available at both higher and lower levels, for then the employer can exploit any racial wage differentials by hiring a labor force that is black at all levels. If the proportions of the different skills in the black labor force are different from those desired, the resulting equilibrium will not necessarily equate wages at each level, but there will be a tendency to equate wages on the average. It is possible, for example, that black foremen, presumably scarce, will be paid more than their white counterparts because they are willing to work with a black floor force, which is cheaper to the employer.

We thus see that the structure of tastes that seems adequate to give a short-period explanation does not seem to resist the operations of competitive pressures in the long run. One might search for other and more stable explanatory structures, but I know of none that have been proposed or that seem at all credible. Instead, I propose that we look more closely at the long-run adjustment processes. In particular, as I have already suggested, when dealing with nonconvexities, the adjustment processes may have to be very rapid indeed. You must recall that in these circumstances marginal adjustments are punished, not rewarded. If the firm is to gain by a change, it has to go all the way. Intuitively, we are not surprised that a firm will hesitate to scrap its entire labor force and replace it with another. The problem is to give an acceptable formalization of this intuition.

In several different contexts, there has been a recognition that adjustment, even when convexity is not an issue, is costly in itself. Edith Penrose (1959) and Robin Marris (1964) have made costs of growth an intrinsic part of the dynamic theory of the firm. By this I mean that, if a firm grows in size and capital, the cost to the firm is the accumulation of capital plus an additional term that depends on the rate at which the firm grows. The latter can be explained in several different ways. One is that the organization of the firm has to alter with its size and there is a cost to acquiring new channels of communication and control within the firm. Another is that the firm needs to expand its markets; but a customer, once acquired, will remain one cheaply, so that the cost is that of acquiring the customer and therefore is determined by the rate of growth. Note that in both cases we are really saying that some kind of intangible capital goods is acquired − either communication channels within the firm or goodwill among customers − and these capital goods are costly.

The same principle − that capital costs of an unconventional kind play an important role in economic behavior and decisions − has been applied to the study of labor turnover, a problem more closely connected with ours. Operations researchers, in trying to draw up plans for the hiring of personnel, have incorporated in their models a fixed cost of hiring an individual. Sometimes it is also held that cost is attached to firing as well. These costs are partly in administration, partly in training. Even in the case of workers who have already been generally trained in the kind of work to be done, learning the ways of the paticular firm is a necessity. This approach, it has been argued by some, has important general economic implications; it implies that firms should not adjust their labor force very rapidly to cyclical shifts in demand, since they may incur both hiring and firing costs if they do − costs that are avoided if the worker is retained during slack periods. This hypothesis provides some explanation for the well-known fact that the average productivity of labor falls in slack periods. Workers are being held in employment even though they contribute little to output to avoid the costs of rehiring them in the expected future boom. I do not myself know whether this explanation is in fact adequate but merely note that it is seriously considered.

I suggest that a similar consideration explains why the adjustments that would wipe out racial wage differentials do not occur or at least are greatly retarded. We have only to assume that the employer makes an investment, let us call it a *personnel investment*, every time a worker is hired. He makes this investment with the expectation of making a competitive return on it; if he himself has no racial feelings, the wage rate in full equilibrium will equal the marginal product of labor less the return on the personnel investment. Let us consider the simplest of the above models, that of discrimination by fellow employees who are perfect substitutes. If the firm starts with an all-white labor force, it will not find it profitable to fire that force, in which its personnel capital has already been sunk, and hire an all-black force in which a new investment has to be made simply because black wages are now slightly less than white wages. Of course, if the wage difference is large enough, it does pay to make the shift.

Obviously, in a situation where costs arise in the process of change, history matters a good deal. A full dynamic analysis appears to be very difficult, but some insight can be obtained by study of a very special case. Suppose that initially the labor force is devoid of blacks. Then some enter; at the same time an additional entry of whites occurs, and some new equilibrium emerges. Under the kinds of assumptions we have been making, a change, if it occurs at all, must be an extreme change, but three kinds of extremes, or corner maxima now exist. The typical firm may remain segregated white though possibly adding more white workers, it may switch entirely to a segregated black state, or it may find it best to keep its present white working force while adding black workers. In the last case, of course, it will have to increase the wages of the white workers to compensate for their feelings of dislike, but may still find it profitable to do so because replacing the existing white workers by blacks means a personnel investment. If we stick closely to the model with all of its artificial conditions, we note that only the all-white firms are absorbing the additional supply of white workers, so there must be some of those in the new equilibrium situation. On the other hand, there must be some firms that are all black or else some integrated firms whose new workers are black in order to absorb the new black workers. It can be concluded in either case, however, that a wage difference between black and white workers will always remain in this model. Furthermore, there will be some segregated white firms. Whether the remaining firms will be segregated black or integrated will depend on the degree of discriminatory feeling by white workers against mixing with blacks.

I have not worked out the corresponding analysis for the case that has several types of workers with different degrees of discriminatory feelings against racial mixtures in the complementary types. Nevertheless, one easily surmises that similar conditions will prevail.

The generalization that may be hazarded on the basis of the discussion thus far can be stated as follows: if we start from a position where black workers enter an essentially all-white world, the social feelings of racialism by employers and by employees, both of the same and of complementary types, will lead to a difference in wages. The forces of competition and the tendency to profit-maximization operate to mitigate these differences. The basic fact of a personnel investment, however, prevents these counteracting tendencies from working with full force. In the end, we remain with wage differences coupled with tendencies to segregation.

This concludes what may be thought of as the central model. I cannot help but feel that still other factors exist. I have two suggestions to make, both of a very tentative nature. The first is that what I have referred to as the discriminator tastes of the employer might in fact be better described as a problem in perception. That is, employers discriminate against blacks because they believe them to be inferior workers. Notice that in this view the physical prominence of skin color is highly significant. As an employer, I might have all sorts of views about the relative productivities of different kinds of workers. Determining what kind of a worker he is may be a costly operation in information gathering; even if I hold my beliefs strongly, it may not, in many circumstances, be worthwhile in my calculations to screen employees according to them. Skin color is a cheap source of information, however, and may therefore be used. In the United States today, I believe it fair to say that school diplomas are being widely used by employers for exactly that reason; it is believed that schooling has something to do with productivity, and asking for a diploma is an inexpensive operation.

The structure of this argument and the range of its applicability need to be carefully considered. It only applies if the employer incurs some personnel investment cost. Presumably after a worker is hired, his performance is or can easily be made to be a matter of known fact. If there were no personnel investment, the employer would hire everyone who applied and simply fire those unqualified. But presumably any testing operation, even a trial period, is some form of personnel investment.

The second assumption is that the qualities of the individual are not known to the employer beforehand. The most interesting case of that kind is one in which the worker must make some investment in himself but one which the employer can never be sure of. I am thinking here not of the conventional types of education or experience, which are easily observable, but more subtle types the employer cannot observe directly: the habits of action and thought that favor good performance in skilled jobs, steadiness, punctuality, responsiveness, and initiative. A worker who has made the requisite investment will be said to be *qualified*.

The inefficiency that arises here because employers do not know the qualifications of workers as well as the workers do, is the same in principle as that caused by 'adverse selection' in insurance. The insured may represent different degrees of riskiness, and each may have some perception of his own degree, but in many cases the insurance companies have much poorer ability to differentiate. If the insurance companies set rates corresponding to average riskiness, the less risky will eliminate or curtail their purchase of insurance, so that the actual experience of the company will be less favorable than the mean in the population. The rates will have to be raised further, thereby eliminating still more of the favorable risks; either the given type of insurance will eventually be eliminated altogether, or an equilibrium will be reached that is inefficient relative to one in which different premiums are charged to those of different riskiness.

We have two primary elements in this model: the employer's investment of personnel capital will be wasted if the employee turns out not to have made his investment; and the employer cannot know beforehand whether or not the employee is qualified. The employer does know the race of the individual, however, and he holds some subjective beliefs about the respective probabilities that white and black workers are qualified. It is of course immediately obvious that if the subjective probability in the mind of an employer that a white worker is qualified is higher than that a black worker is qualified, there will have to be a wage difference if the employer is to hire any blacks at all.

The effects of this model are similar to those based on tastes, but the causes are different. We would still want to know why the subjective probabilities are different. The simplest explanation is prejudice, in the literal sense of that term, that is, a judgment about abilities made in advance of the evidence and not altered by it. Of course, the persistence of prejudice really should not be left unexplained. One possible explanation is to be found in theories of psychological equilibrium, such as Festinger's (1957) theory of cognitive dissonance. If an individual acts in a discriminatory fashion, he would, according to this theory, tend to have beliefs that justify his actions. Indeed, precisely the fact that discriminatory behavior is in conflict with an important segment of our ethical beliefs will, according to this theory, intensify the willingness to entertain cognitive beliefs that will supply a socially acceptable justification for this conduct.

Another model of this type is more narrowly economic. Suppose that employers do not misperceive, that they know correctly the proportions of black and white workers who are qualified. Suppose also that the acquisition of human capital in the form of qualifications by workers is costly and that they face an imperfect capital market in any effort to finance this acquisition. Then the actual proportion of whites who are qualified is a function of white wages and similarly with blacks. I assume here, as always, that blacks and whites are essentially identical, so these two functional relations are the same.

Clearly, a nondiscriminatory set of wages that will be an equilibrium is possible, but it is also possible that this equilibrium may not be stable. Suppose, to begin with, that the proportion of qualified whites is slightly higher than that of blacks. Then white wages will be higher. In response to this differential, there will be an incentive for whites to increase their qualifications relative to blacks, thereby accentuating the initial discrepancy.

This verbal argument is not conclusive, and the formal discussion is more complex. The stability of the nondiscriminatory equilibrium, however, depends on quantitative values of the parameters; that is, on the supply functions for qualified labor and on the personnel investments needed by the firms.

Since personnel investments are greater at higher levels, this model of personnel investment and uncertainty about qualifications also helps to explain the increasing discrimination against blacks in higher-level jobs. Indeed, the motive for developing the observed model was to explain the observation that much discrimination occurred in the form of a disproportionate representation of blacks in lower-wage occupations, analogous in many ways to the dual economies characteristic of underdeveloped countries. The analogy has been suggested by some who have made detailed studies of local labor markets; for example, Baron and Hymer (1968) for Chicago, and Doeringer and his students (Feldman, Gordon, and Reich, 1969) and Piore with reference to Boston. Without going into detailed discussion of the somewhat variant viewpoints, the common view is that blacks are largely, though not exclusively, confined to marginal jobs marked by low wages, low promotion possibilities, and instability of employment. The instability, incidentally, is in large part voluntary; it is interpreted as a rational response to limited opportunity, which both increases the value and decreases the cost of search.

In particular, both research groups feel that coexistence of segregation and discrimination is in some sense an equilibrium condition, that no employer or employee will find it individually profitable to depart from the existing situation. Within conventional deterministic models, it is hard to formalize this possibility, as indeed is true in dual economy models for underdeveloped countries; why does not competition from the victims of discrimination reduce wages in the preferred occupations and permit them to enter?

The foregoing model is designed to suggest a mechanism in terms of which partial occupational segregation is nevertheless an equilibrium condition. In view of its desperately oversimplified character, it is perhaps best thought of as a metaphor.

Finally, a comment on the question of group interests. It is certainly a common view that in some sense racial discrimination is a device by which the whites in the aggregate gain at the expense of the blacks. Hence, the whole problem is to be interpreted as an exploitative relation. A stable relation exists here; the values inherent in discrimination uphold a structure that is profitable to those holding those values.

On purely methodological grounds, I do not think such a view can be denied, provided it works, though it is contrary to the tradition of economics. Economic explanations for discrimination or other phenomena tend to run in individualistic terms, and the models presented earlier are no exception. Economists ask what motivates an employer or an individual worker. They tend not to accept as an explanation a statement that employers as a class would gain by discrimination, for they ask what would prevent an individual employer from refusing to discriminate if he prefers and thereby profit. Economists do indeed recognize group interests if they appear in legal form, as in tariffs, licensing, or legally enforced segregation. The distinction between the legal structure and other social pressures, however, is hardly a sharp dichotomy. If perceived group interests can lead to legislation, they can also lead to other social pressures.

I think something can be said for views of this kind, but their mechanism needs careful exploration. We must really ask who benefits, and how are the exploitative agreements carried out? In particular, how are the competitive pressures that would undermine them held in check? The exploitation of the blacks can work only if the tendency of individual employers to buy the cheapest labor is somehow suppressed. Recall the great difficulty that producers of rubber and of coffee have had in their efforts to create a mutually beneficial monopoly.

Obviously, from the preceding analysis, the whites certainly gain by discrimination. I must add, though, that it seems very difficult to construct a model in which employers gain in any obvious way; the gains to the whites appear to accrue to white workers primarily. This fact, if it is one, already creates difficulties for the group interest hypothesis; after all, the employers are the most direct possible agents of exploitation, and it would be better for the theory if they were beneficiaries.

In any case, we are not to imagine conspiracies in which 170 million white Americans put their heads together. The process of communciation by which the white race agrees on means to further its collective interests must operate unconsciously through its value-forming and allocating social institutions. The argument would have to be that the discriminatory tastes as given up to this point are themselves the mechanism by which discrimination profitable to the whites is carried out. These discriminatory values must be internalized and felt to be genuine by those holding them. It was an obligation of conscience for Huckleberry Finn to turn over the runaway slave, Jim, to the authorities for return to his master, and he resolved to do so for inner peace. Finally, Huck could not return his friend to such misery, but he well knew that his failure was only another proof of his fundamental depravity and that anyone with a stake in society would return a runaway slave rather than suffer the disutility of a failure to carry out his social duty. The process by which these discriminatory values are formed and transmitted is certainly complex and lengthy in time, and we may easily suppose that the exploitation that results is far from optimum for the exploiters.

Notice that the question at issue is not whether racist utility functions are socially conditioned. We accept that the tastes for material goods are affected by the surrounding culture; and how much more so tastes about status relations. The crucial question, to my mind still an open one, is whether the acceptance and preservation of racial attitudes are in some way related to their profitability to the group. One might hypothesize some sort of Darwinian process for utility functions in which those economically profitable for the group have a greater chance of survival. All this is at the moment merely speculative, at best a suggestion for research.

One further point should be made here. I do not see how the process of racial discrimination can begin in the economic sphere or out of purely economic motives. It always pays any group with enough power to discriminate against some other, but redheads or blue-eyed individuals do not seem to suffer much. Since color is seized on as a basis for discrimination, there must be an extra-economic origin, although it is not precluded that its economic profitability reinforces the discrimination once started.[1]

I have chosen a topic on which many of us feel the greatest moral outrage and have analyzed it most dispassionately. Neither the moral indignation nor the cool analysis is misplaced: their juxtaposition is one of those paradoxes inherent in the nature of human society of which only the naive are ignorant. Our mastery of ourselves as social beings needs all the reinforcement it can get from study of ourselves in all contexts. Indeed, in the absence of analysis from a self-imposed and sometimes painful distance, our moral feelings can lead us to actions whose effects are the opposite of those intended. This is not intended to imply that social action must wait on adequate analysis. Inaction may be, and in this case surely is, as dangerous as any likely alternative. Indeed, social action may be indispensable to increasing our knowledge when the consequences are subjected to adequate study. But a firm commitment to ends must not preclude a tentative, questioning attitude to particular means of achieving them.

NOTE

1. Hodge and Hodge advanced the hypothesis that, other things being equal, wages in an ocupation were lower the greater the number of blacks and suggested this might make social barriers to entry of blacks a rational procedure and a possible cause of prejudice. (Their interpretation of the empirical evidence is far from conclusive, but that is another question.) In reply, Taeuber, Taeuber, and Cain argued that it would pay the members of any occupation to bar any group of people; the selection of blacks as the target could be explained only on noneconomic grounds. (See Robert W. and Patricia Hodge, 'Occupational Assimilation as a Competitive Process,' *American Journal of Sociology* 71 (1965): 249–85; Alma F. Taeuber, Karl E. Taeuber, and Glen G. Cain, 'Occupational Assimilation as a Competitive Process: A Reanalysis,' *American Journal of Sociology* 72 (1966): 273–85. There seems to be considerable confusion in this controversy. An individual has many interests, and for each interest he may find a different set of other individuals who share them. Why certain kinds of groups perceive themselves as having common interests and not others is a question on which economics does not seem likely to throw much light. But *given* group identification, it is not so unreasonable that the members of the group will work together to promote group interests, even though it would pay any individual to depart from them.

REFERENCES

Baron, H. M. and Hymer, B. 'The Negroes in the Chicago Labor Market.' In J. Jacobsen, ed., *The Negro and the American Labor Movement*. Garden City, N.Y.: Anchor Books. 1968.

Becker, Gary S. *The Economics of Discrimination*. Chicago: University of Chicago Press, 1957.

Duncan, Otis Dudley. 'Inheritance of Poverty or Inheritance of Race?' In Daniel P. Moynihan, ed., *On Understanding Poverty*. New York: Basic Books, 1969.

Economic Report of the President. Washington, D.C.: U.S. Government Printing Office, February 1970.

Edgeworth, F. Y. 'Equal Pay to Men and Women for Equal Work.' *Economic Journal* 31 (1922): 431–57.

Farrell, M. J. 'The Convexity Assumption in the Theory of Competitive Markets.' *Journal of Political Economy* 67 (1959).

Feldman, P. H., Gordon, D. M., and Reich, M. in P. Doeringer, ed. 'Low-income Markets and Urban Manpower Programs: A Critical Assessment.' Discussion Paper no. 66. Harvard Institute of Economic Research, 1969.

Festinger, Leo. *A Theory of Cognitive Dissonance*. Palo Alto, Calif.: Stanford University Press, 1957.

Friedman, Milton. *A Theory of the Consumption Function*. Princeton, N.J.: National Bureau of Economic Research, 1957.

Gilman, Harry J. 'Economic Discrimination and Unemployment.' *American Economic Review* 55 (1965): 1077–95.

Hicks, J. R. 'Annual Survey of Economic Theory: The Theory of Monopoly.' *Econometrica* 3 (1935): 1–20.

Hodge, Robert W. and Patricia Hodge. 'Occupational Assimilation as a Competitive Process.' *American Journal of Sociology* 71, no. 3 (November 1965), 249–85.

Landes, David. *The Unbound Prometheus*. Cambridge: Cambridge University Press, 1969.

Marris, Robin. *The Economic Theory of 'Managerial' Capitalism*. New York: The Free Press of Glencoe, 1964.

Miller, Herman P. *Income Distribution in the United States*. Washington, D.C.: U.S. Bureau of the Census, 1966.

Pascal, Anthony H. *The Economics of Housing Segregation*, RM-5510-RC. Santa Monica, Calif.: The Rand Corporation, November 1967.

Penrose, Edith. *The Theory of the Growth of the Firm*. Oxford: Oxford University Press, 1959.

Simon, Herbert, 'Theories of Decision-making in Economics and Behavioral Science.' *American Economic Review* 49 (1959): 253–83.

Taeuber, Alma F., Taeuber, Karl E., and Cain, Glen C.,'Occupational Assimilation as a Competitive Process: A Reanalysis.' *American Journal of Sociology* 72, no. 3 (November 1966): 273–85.

Taeuber, Alma F. and Taeuber, Karl E. *Negroes in Cities: Residential Segregation and Neighborhood Change.* Chicago: Aldine, 1965.

U.S. Department of Labor. *Handbook of Labor Statistics*, Bulletin no. 163. Washington, D.C., 1969.

Williamson, Oliver E. *The Economic Theory of 'Managerial' Capitalism.* Chicago: Markham, 1967.

2.4 A Do-It-Yourself Guide to Marginal productivity*

[. . .]

If marginal productivity is to be used as a functional theory of distribution, it is necessary to make a series of judgments as to what is meant by the marginal-productivity theory of distribution. Once these determinations are made, it then becomes possible to test the theory against actual data to see whether the theory does or does not explain what occurs.

The purpose of this appendix is to outline the judgments that anyone would have to make if they were to actually apply the marginal-productivity theory of distribution. Each person can make these determinations for himself or herself, construct his or her own version of marginal productivity, and then see whether their versions explain the actual distribution of economic prizes better than the theories outlined in this book.

LEVEL OF APPLICABILITY

Marginal-productivity factor payments could exist on a number of levels. Depending upon the level at which the theory holds, different types of evidence would be relevant to proving or disproving the hypothesis.

In its most rigorous form, marginal productivity states that each individual factor of production is paid his, her, or its marginal product at each instant of time. From this position there exists a continuum of possibilities where individual factors are paid their marginal products but only over longer and longer periods of time. At the other end of this continuum, factors are paid their marginal products, but only over the course of their entire lifetimes.

QUESTION: *What is the time period over which marginal products are paid?*

The importance of this question can be seen in seniority wage payments. Seniority wage schedules are not evidence contrary to the lifetime marginal-productivity hypothesis, but they are evidence contrary to the instantaneous marginal-productivity hypothesis.

Instead of being a theory of individual-factor payments, marginal productivity can be interpreted as a theory of group-factor payments. Individuals

*From Lester C. Thurow, *Generating Inequality, Mechanisms of Distributions in the Economy*, Appendix A (Basingstoke: Macmillan 1976).

are not paid their marginal products, but groups are paid their average marginal products. Skill differences provide the most obvious groupings. Plumbers, for example, are not judged on the basis of their individual productivity, but are instead paid in accordance with the average marginal productivity of plumbers as a group. Individual plumbers who are below average will be paid more than their marginal productivity would warrant, whereas plumbers who are above average will be paid less than their marginal productivity would warrant.

QUESTION: *Are groups of individuals paid their marginal products?*

If groups are paid their marginal products, common wages for large groups of individuals is not evidence contrary to marginal productivity even if there are productivity differences among the members of the group. If individuals are supposed to be paid their marginal products, it is damaging evidence.

If the group interpretation of marginal productivity is used, a set of subsidiary questions must be answered. What grouping theory determines which individuals will be lumped together and paid a common wage? Does the economy generate large groups of heterogeneous skills or small groups of homogeneous skills? Obviously, as the groups grow smaller and smaller the skill group theory of marginal productivity gradually approaches the individual theory of marginal productivity.

QUESTION: *What is the theory that determines whether marginal-productivity groups are large or small, heterogeneous or homogeneous?*

Skill groups are not the only dimension upon which a group theory of marginal productivity could be constructed. Other possible groupings exist along industrial rather than skill lines. In this interpretation the relevant group is not the skill class to which an individual factor belongs, but the industrial group in which the individual factor is employed. Factors of production employed in the automobile industry, for example, are paid in accordance with the average marginal productivity of factors of production in automobiles. The same individual factor employed in textiles would be paid less because that factor is playing on a less productive team, but both factors are being paid in accordance with industrial marginal productivity.

QUESTION: *Do groups exist along skill or industrial lines?*

If marginal productivity exists along industrial lines, different skill-factor payments across industries are not evidence against marginal productivity; if marginal productivity exists along skill lines, however, different factor payments across industries are contrary evidence.

Once again there is a subsidiary question of how industrial groupings are formed and the level on which they apply. Do they exist at the level of the plant, the firm, or the industry? Whatever the level of applicability, what causes these particular groups rather than some other particular groups to come about?

With industrial marginal productivity it is also necessary to subscribe to some subsidiary theory of distribution. The whole industrial team may be paid in accordance with its average marginal product. But what determines wage differences among different members of the same team? What is the theory of distribution that applies within the industrial group?

Another possible grouping exists across geographic areas. In this variant the geographic region in which the factor is employed is relevant to determining its marginal product. Does marginal productivity hold at the level of the world, the nation, the state, the city, or at even more narrowly circumscribed geographic regions? Clearly, the problem is to determine the geographic extent of the market for factors of production. If the market is less than worldwide, what are the explanations for geographically circumscribed markets for factors of production?

QUESTION: *What is the geographic area over which marginal productivity applies?*

If the area is the nation, geographic wage differences within the nation constitute evidence that is contrary to the theory, but if marginal productivity exists only within local areas, interarea wage differentials are obviously easy to explain.

In its most aggregate form the marginal-productivity theory of distribution simply means that an average unit of capital is paid in accordance with the average marginal productivity of capital and that an average laborer is paid in accordance with the average marginal product of labor. Individual units of capital and labor may not be paid their marginal products, but the pluses and minuses cancel out.

QUESTION: *What is the level of aggregation at which capital and labor are paid their marginal products?*

As this particular variant of marginal productivity clearly indicates, the more aggregate the theory, the more necessary it is to have some subsidiary theory of distribution to explain how differences are distributed within group earnings. As marginal-productivity theories become more and more aggregate, they come closer and closer to a tautology. At the most aggregate level, factors in general must be paid in accordance with the productivity of factors in general. Factors produce the GNP and factors receive the GNP. At this level marginal productivity exists by definition if economies or diseconomies of scale do not exist (see below).

Subsidiary distribution theories are necessary in every variant except the strict interpretation in which every individual factor is paid his marginal product at every instant of time. If factors are paid lifetime marginal products, what determines the distribution of payments over a lifetime? If factors are paid in accordance with average group-skill marginal products, how are individuals assigned to groups? If factors are paid in accordance with industrial marginal products, how are intragroup earnings differences determined? If factors are paid in accordance with regional marginal products, what determines the geographic extent of the market for factors of production? If marginal productivity exists at the level of capital and labor aggregations, how are intragroup payment differences explained?

Obviously, it is also possible to argue that marginal-productivity factor payments are some combination of these different variants of marginal productivity. A factor's payments depends upon its own productivity, its skill's productivity, its industry's productivity, its region's productivity, and the productivity of the factor class to which it belongs. In this case it is necessary to determine the weights of the different components and then explain why these particular weights come about.

THE PROBLEM OF ECONOMIES AND DISECONOMIES OF SCALE

If either economies or diseconomies of scale exist within an economy, factors of production *cannot* be paid in accordance with the marginal-productivity theory of distribution. With economies of scale, marginal products exceed average products and paying marginal products would more than exhaust total output. There simply is not enough output to pay each factor its marginal product since the last factor adds more to output than the first factor. Similarly, if diseconomies of scale exist, average products exceed marginal products and paying marginal products leaves an unclaimed residual. Output is left over since the last factor adds less to output than the first factor. Technically, marginal productivity is only applicable when there are constant returns to scale.

If there are increasing or decreasing returns to scale, the marginal-productivity theory of distribution does not say what should be done about the positive or negative residuals. Who is to be paid less than his marginal product; who is to be paid more than his marginal product? There are no answers within the marginal-productivity theory. What is the answer?

Whether economies or diseconomies of scale are or are not a problem depends upon the level at which marginal productivity is to be applied. If marginal productivity means paying marginal products to capital and labor, then the only question is whether there are economies or diseconomies of scale at the level of the entire economy. If marginal productivity applies at the level of the individual, the skill, the industry, or the region, the problem exists if there are economies or diseconomies of scale at the appropriate level. Although the U.S. economy seems to exhibit constant returns to scale as a whole, there are many industries with economies or diseconomies of scale.

QUESTION: *What theory of distribution exists when marginal productivity cannot be applied because of economies or diseconomies of scale?*

THE IMPACTS OF MARKET IMPERFECTIONS

Since marginal productivity flows from perfect competition, it is necessary to specify how different real-world imperfections influence it. Are the imperfections so large and important that they require major modifications in the marginal-productivity theory of distribution, or do they only cause minor deviations?

Monopoly and Monopsony

If monopolies or monopsonies exist, there are monopoly profits that must be allocated to those that control them and subtracted from those that are controlled by them. The monopolist receives more than his equilibrium marginal revenue product, and the factors controlled by the monopoly receive less than their equilibrium marginal revenue product.

In the case of a product market monopoly, the monopolist sets its price at the point where the marginal cost curve (supply curve) crosses the marginal revenue curve rather than the demand curve. Less output is sold at a higher price. The result is a variety of real income changes from those dictated by marginal productivity. Monopoly profits exist and are allocated to the owners of the monopoly. Since less output is produced and sold at higher prices, real incomes fall for the consumers who purchase the monopolized goods. With less output being produced, the derived demand curves for factors of production shift inward, lowering equilibrium factor prices. Relative factor prices are also affected since the supply curves for different factors of products do not have identical elasticities and since the industry may not use the economy's average mix of land, labor, and capital.

Assume, for example, that the monopolized industry has a higher than average capital-labor ratio and that supply curves for capital and labor have similar elasticities. With cuts in output the derived demand curves for both capital and labor fall, but the curve for capital falls more than that for labor. The result is a greater reduction in the price of capital than in the price of labor, with consequent income distribution effects.

Any student of micro-economics can quickly work out the income changes that occur under different assumptions about the characteristics of the product market monopoly and the changes that would occur in the case of a monopsony in the product market, a monopoly in the factor markets, or a monopsony in the factor markets. The changes are predictable, but the distribution of real incomes that emerges in these cases is not a marginal-productivity distribution of economic resources.

QUESTION: *To what degree does the economy fit the competitive model and to what degree does it fit the monopoly model? The actual economy is a mixture, but what are the relevant proportions?*

To apply marginal productivity it is necessary to specify the extent to which the distribution of economic prizes is a marginal-productivity distribution and the extent to which the distribution of economic prizes reflects monopolies.

Although there is a perfectly adequate theory of monopoly income determination, the real world is marked more by oligopolies than pure monopolies. The literature on oligopolies does not contain a well worked-out theory of distribution but generally depends upon a complicated unspecified bargaining process in which there is a range of possible outcomes. In the long run an oligopoly will never rationally charge more than a monopolist in the same position, and it will never charge less than a competitive firm. But within this range what is the relevant theory of distribution?

Monopoly profits also have an impact on the distribution of income long after the actual monopolies have disappeared. To the extent that they have made someone permanently wealthy, they influence the structure of demand in all later periods. With different demand curves different equilibrium marginal products emerge.

Time lags and disequilibrium

How fast do markets reach equilibrium? Do they reach equilibrium quickly or only after a long period of time? Consider the problem posed by a sudden expansion of the derived demand curve for medical doctors as the result of Medicaid or Medicare. There is a long-run equilibrium supply curve of medical doctors that depends upon the rate of return on a medical education, but there is also a short-term disequilibrium supply curve that may be much more inelastic. Over time, the economy's supply curve gradually shifts from this short-run disequilibrium supply curve to the more elastic long-run equilibrium supply curve. But in the interval before the long-run equilibrium is attained, there are short-run disequilibrium quasi-rents. These quasi-rents are necessary to efficiently allocate a limited supply of doctors, but they are payments over and above what would be necessary to guarantee the appropriate long-run supply of doctors.

Disequilibrium conditions are apt to be even more prevalent than those implied by the time lags necessary to get from one set of equilibrium conditions to another. If the basic factors that determine equilibrium are changing rapidly in relationship to the time necessary to achieve equilibrium, the economy may never be in equilibrium — even if it is always rapidly heading toward equilibrium. Equilibrium marginal products are never being paid, and quasi-rents play an important role in determining the distribution of income at all points in time.

In this case both the short-run and long-run distributions of factor payments are marginal-productivity distributions, but the short-run distribution is a disequilibrium marginal-productivity distribution, whereas the long-run distribution is an equilibrium marginal-productivity distribution.

QUESTION: *To what extent is the actual distribution of economic prizes a long-run equilibrium distribution and to what extent is it a short-run disequilibrium distribution? Rate of return on different investments must be equal in the first case but can be unequal in the second case.*

Quasi-rents are important not only because they influence the current distribution of income but also because they influence and alter the economy's equilibrium conditions. Whenever quasi-rents exist, they influence demands and hence the derived demand curves for factors of production. As a result of the induced alteration in demands, the economy's equilibrium conditions change. Disequilibrium quasi-rents do not disappear. Through their long-run impact on demand, they have a long-run impact on the economy even if the economy should ultimately attain an equilibrium position. An economy with a history of quasi-rents will have a different equilibrium position than an economy without such a history.

What this means is that comparative statics — the analysis of two periods of equilibrium without regard to the disequilibrium conditions in between — is fundamentally in error. The disequilibrium quasi-rents incurred in moving between two equilibrium positions will alter the final equilibrium. The disequilibrium path can never be ignored. It always make a difference. The distribution of economic prizes will be different with and without periods of disequilibrium. QUESTION: *To what extent is the current distribution of economic prizes determined by past disequilibriums and to what extent is it determined by current disequilibriums?*

Knowledge and ignorance

The marginal-productivity theory of distribution depends heavily on the existence of perfect, low-cost, widely dispersed knowledge. To reach a marginal-productivity distribution of factor payments in either the short run or the long run, each buyer and seller in both the product markets and the factor markets must know where he can find the best price. Knowledge is never perfect in the sense of having perfect foresight of future conditions. Here, the problem has not only to do with a lack of knowledge but with the distribution of existing knowledge.

Some informational differences spring from the competence of individual buyers and sellers in different markets, but much of it springs from the costs of acquiring the relevant information. In some markets information is simply expensive to acquire. The expected costs in terms of both time and money may exceed the expected value of the information to be acquired. In this case the market can be perfect in the sense that each individual is acquiring the optimum (costs-benefits) amount of information, yet very imperfect in the sense that all of the relevant information is not at hand and the market is not in equilibrium.

Either ignorance or high-cost information will lead to a system in which identical factors of production are not paid identical amounts and in which the same goods and services cost different amounts. The market is reacting perfectly to what the players know, but the outcome is not a marginal-productivity outcome. The individual lucky enough to be at the right place at the right time will sell at above-equilibrium prices, and the individual unlucky enough to be at the wrong place at the wrong time will sell at below-equilibrium prices with obvious consequences for the distribution of income.

QUESTION: *To what extent does the level and distribution of ignorance cause deviations from the marginal-productivity distribution that would be expected in the case of perfect knowledge?*

Once again the question is not the existence of ignorance and high-cost information, but the extent to which the ultimate distribution of economic prizes is determined by the distribution of information and luck rather than the distribution of marginal products.

Constraints and imperfections imposed by government

All economies work within a framework of rules and regulations laid down by society and enforced by government. This framework provides a set of constraints within which marginal productivity operates. If governments enforce private property rights, a different set of economic prizes will emerge than if governments do not enforce private property rights. Imagine the resources that each individual would need to be devoted to property defense if society did not attempt to enforce and inculcate a respect for private property. The distribution of real earnings and wealth would surely be substantially different.

Similarly, programs like truth in lending or advertising all serve to influence the demand for goods, services, and factors of production. Demand with subliminal advertising might be quite different from demands without subliminal advertising. The distribution of income that emerges within a framework of governmental regulations is still a marginal-productivity distribution, but the outcome of the process can be quite different depending upon what framework is in effect.

One of the basic changes in the U.S. framework was the abolition of slavery. Private property rights in other human beings were abolished. This meant that it was not possible for one person to appropriate the factor earnings of another, but it also had consequences for human-capital investment. Since an individual could sell himself into slavery or servitude, lending institutions could not obtain mortgages on human-capital investments as they could on physical investments. As a result, private human-capital loans were extremely rare before recent government programs to guarantee these loans. These loans could be defaulted, and the lending institutions had nothing that they could claim as theirs.

With limited human-capital loans, such investments must be self-financed. Each individual invests to the point at which his investments earn a rate of return equal to his rate of time preference. If his rate of time preference exceeds the market interest rate, he does not make the investments that perfect capital markets would indicate. The result is a different distribution of income than what would occur if individuals could mortgage themselves.

The examples are endless, but the basic point is that marginal productivity works within a framework that is prescribed by governmental regulations. The shape of the frame helps define the nature of the picture within the frame. But once again the question is to what extent.

QUESTION: *Which, if any, government actions cause major changes in the distribution of factor payments? Do governments, for example, pay their employees in accordance with the dictates of marginal productivity?*

Governments are not under the profit maximization dictates of the private economy, but cost-benefit maximization would lead to the same need to have maginal-productivity wage payments to insure efficiency.

THE MAXIMIZATION HYPOTHESIS

The marginal-productivity theory of distribution depends upon an underlying assumption of maximization. Everyone in the economy is trying to maximize his or her money income. Analytically, it is possible to apply the maximization calculus of economies in either money or utility terms, but to be a valid explanation of money prizes, individuals must maximize their money prizes and not their utility prizes. Questions about money maximization arise with respect to both capital and labor, but they are most acute in the labor area.

When discussing work-leisure choices, economists quickly slip from money-income maximization postulates to utility or psychic-income maximization postulates. (As the social sciences are becoming less utilitarian and more Freudian, the jargon is gradually shifting from utility to psychic income, but the two refer to exactly the same phenomenon.) The shift is natural since a laborer must personally accompany his labor or human capital, whereas he does not need to accompany his physical capital. Since he must be personally present, he is interested in a range of nonmoney benefits that may spring from work. Some jobs are dirty; some jobs are clean. Some jobs provide prestige and power; some jobs do not. Some jobs provide enjoyable working conditions and friends; some jobs do not. The possibilities of being interested in nonmonetary factors are endless and real. An individual might, for example, be perfectly willing to be an absentee slum landlord or to loan money to a slum landlord yet be unwilling to manage or live in a slum apartment house. In the first two instances, he does not need to enter the slum in question; in the latter two cases, he must work or live there.

As a result, we quite naturally swing into talking about psychic-income maximization when we start talking about job choices. The problem springs from the fact that an individual who is a psychic-income maximizer is not a monetary-income maximizer. He maximizes a combination of money earnings plus nonmonetary benefits and costs. He works on a psychic-earnings supply curve rather than on a money-earnings supply curve.

When nonmonetary factors enter the maximization process, the distribution of total income (psychic benefits and costs plus monetary earnings) is a marginal-productivity distribution but the distribution of money earnings is not a marginal-productivity distribution. The money results are conditioned by a whole set of psychic benefits and costs. These psychic benefits and costs can easily dominate the distribution of money income and lead to a distribution of money income that does not resemble the distribution of total income (monetary plus psychic). To explain the distribution of money incomes, it would be necessary to know the distribution of the factors that create psychic incomes as well as the workings of the marginal-productivity mechanism. Each person's nonmonetary psychic income would be subtracted from his marginal product to obtain his money earnings.

Suppose, for example, that we were dealing with a job with substantial net nonmonetary benefits. Because of these benefits, the actual supply curve of labor falls to the right of the supply curve that would exist if the job provided nothing but money earnings. This leads to a lower monetary wage than would have existed if the psychic-income benefits had not existed. Ramifications also occur in other markets. The labor supplies to other industries decrease since more labor is now used in the industry or job with positive net nonmonetary benefits. Thus, the distribution of monetary prizes − the prize distribution that we measure and seek to explain − could be very different depending upon the extent and distribution of nonmonetary psychic-income benefits.

QUESTION: *To what extent do psychic-income benefits and costs alter the actual distribution of monetary prizes? Are they so large or distributed in such a manner as to noticeably alter the distribution of monetary rewards? Alternatively, is the marginal-productivity theory of distribution meant to apply in monetary space or in utility space? If marginal productivity applies only in utility space, then there is a need to have a subsidiary theory to explain the distribution of nonmonetary rewards before it is possible to explain the distribution of monetary rewards.*

In the capital area, maximization disputes revolve around the extent to which firms (capitalists?) are long- or short-run profit maximizers and the extent to which they are growth maximizers rather than profit maximizers. The first has to do with the quantity of quasi-rents that exist in the system at any one moment. A long-run profit maximizer may not set prices at the short-run disequilibrium level even if these prices could be charged and collected. The second has to do with the extent to which firms are willing to accept below-equilibrium rates of return on capital in order to promote more growth than would occur if they insisted on market rates of return. In this case the distribution of factor payments is still a marginal-productivity distribution, but it is a disequilibrium as opposed to equilibrium distribution. The problem, as before, is that to actually use the marginal-productivity theory of distribution to explain economic prizes, it is necessary to specify the extent to which these two situations occur.

THE INITIAL CONDITIONS

In addition to specifying the mechanism of marginal productivity itself, it is necessary to specify the initial conditions from which the mechanism starts if actual distributions of economic prizes are to be explained. These conditions can be treated as exogenous events that do not need to be explained by economic theories − they simply need to be determined − or they can be treated as economic phenomena that need an explanation in any systematic theory of income and wealth determination.

The initial distributions of wealth and earnings

Two neglected but important initial conditions have a large impact on the actual distributions of earnings and wealth that will be produced in competitive markets. These are the *initial* distributions of earnings and wealth. They have a double-barreled impact on the distribution of economic rewards, since they represent both the initial distribution of potential purchasing power and the initial distribution of ownership claims.

The initial distribution of purchasing power is critical, since it determines each individual's demand curves for goods and services and hence the derived demand curves for factors of production. As the distribution of purchasing power shifts, derived demand curves shift and different equilibrium marginal-revenue products emerge in the factor markets. Two economies with identical wealth and earnings, but different distributions of purchasing power, will generate different distributions of earnings and wealth.

The distribution of ownership claims is important since it determines to whom the marginal revenue products will be paid. Altering the distribution of ownership rights (human or physical) leads to different distributions of income, since marginal revenue products are paid to the owners of factors of production. An economy in which all factors of production are owned by one person will have a very different distribution of income than an economy in which all factors of production are equally owned even if the equilibrium marginal revenue products are identical in the two economies.

As a consequence, the competitive distribution of earnings and wealth is a function of the initial distribution of earnings and wealth. Neither the immediate distribution of earnings and wealth nor the latter distributions of earnings or wealth is independent of the starting conditions. The distributions generated in the economy do not necessarily replicate the initial conditions of the economy, but they are always dependent upon these initial conditions. Different initial distributions of wealth and purchasing power will generate different historical sequences of income as the economy moves along. These might become more or less unequal as time passes, but they are not independent of the initial conditions. The economy does not move toward the same outcome regardless of its starting point.

The process can be easily visualized if the economy is thought of in terms of discrete rounds of purchases, production, and generation of incomes. The distribution of incomes at the end of the first round may differ from the initial conditions and will in turn lead to yet a new distribution of income at the end of the second round, but the income in each round depends upon the initial starting point. The economy always achieves 'equilibrium,' but the actual equilibrium depends upon where the economy starts. As a result, actual distributions of earnings and wealth are partly dependent upon the functioning of marginal productivity and partly dependent upon the initial conditions. Since marginal productivity does not explain the initial conditions, an explanation must be found for these conditions if one is to have a complete theory of distribution.

The distribution of knowledge

The spectrum of technical knowledge is an important determinant of the distribution of income since it ultimately influences both the level and variance in incomes. The marginal physical productivity of any factor of production depends upon the state of technical knowledge. Profit-maximizing economic substitutions can only occur within the economic space created by the spectrum of technical knowledge. To take the extreme case, if the world were in fact an input-output world with fixed coefficients, technology would completely determine the distribution of income with no room for any economic substitutions of one factor for another. Although the world is probably not a rigid input-output world, it also is not a world characterized by complete knowledge and unlimited technical substitutions.

Technology and changes in technology thus join the initial distributions of wealth and purchasing power as exogenous factors that impinge on the distribution of income even if marginal productivity is fully operational. The relevant question becomes one of the range within which marginal productivity and economic substitutions can take place. Is it a wide range or a narrow range? Depending upon the answer to this question, marginal productivity becomes more or less important vis-à-vis technology as an explanation of the actual distribution of income.

Exogenous ingredients in factor supplies

There are also a variety of exogenous factors that affect the distribution of earnings and wealth from the factor supply side of the market. Factor supply curves are to some extent created by economic incentives and factor payments, and they are to some extent exogenously given. To the extent that they are exogenously given, these factors will have an independent influence on the final equilibrium marginal products and on the distribution of economic prizes.

The basic problem is most easily seen in the case of land. To a great extent the supply curve for land is exogenously given. Land either exists or it does not exist; it is not supplied in the economic sense of that term. Economic incentives are not necessary to bring it into existence and cannot in fact bring it into existence. The price of land simply serves to allocate the exogenously given supply efficiently. (Remember, however, that land is not a synonym for space. Space is augmentable, using labor and capital in conjunction with land — high-rise buildings, draining the sea, etc.) As a result, that part of income that is composed of land rents will be heavily dependent upon the exogenous supply of land.

A similar problem exists in the human-capital area, where the supply of human capital is to some extent dependent upon the exogenously given supplies of unaugmentable human skills (natural talent). In this case the distribution of economic prizes contains human rents as well as land rents. As before, the importance of these human rents depends partly upon the exogenously given supplies. To explain the distribution of earnings, it is necessary to know the extent of these supplies as well as the mechanism of marginal productivity.

Stochastic versus deterministic

Regardless of which variant of marginal productivity is being applied, there is still a problem of whether the model is supposed to be a deterministic model or a stochastic model. In the first case the model determines *ex post* factor payments, and in the second case it only determines *ex ante* factor payments. *Ex post* factor payments are composed of an expected *ex ante* payment plus or minus some random disturbance term.

QUESTION: *Is the marginal-productivity model a deterministic model or a scholastic model? If the marginal-productivity model is a stochastic and not a deterministic model, then there is a problem of determining the stochastic process that augments marginal productivity. What is it?*

CONCLUSIONS

Although it would be possible to go on at greater length examining the judgments that must be made if marginal productivity is to be used to explain actual distributions of earnings and wealth, the previous question illustrates the kinds of specifications that must occur. Fortunately or unfortunately, each reader is going to have to construct his or her own marginal-productivity model. Many of the necessary judgments have not been examined in the literature of economics, and others are subject to little, if any, consensus.

I urge the reader to make a serious effort to spell out his own version of maginal-productivity theory since only then is it possible to think about the relative merits of different alternatives. As long as marginal productivity is left as a general amorphous theory, it can neither be used nor criticized. Technically, it is not a theory of distribution until it has been spelled out in sufficient detail to be testable. [. . .]

2.5 The Internal Labour Market: an Alternative Interpretation*
[. . .]

This chapter is concerned with the implications of an extreme form of non-homogeneity — namely, job idiosyncrasy — for understanding the employment relation. Although it refers largely to production workers, the argument can be extended, with appropriate modifications, to cover nonproduction workers as well. The purpose is to better assess the employment relation in circumstances where workers *acquire*, during the course of their employment, significant job-specific skills and related task-specific knowledge.[1] What Hayek referred to as knowledge of 'particular circumstances of time and place' (1945, p. 521) and

*From Oliver E. Williamson, *Markets and Hierarchies: analysis and antitrust implications* (New York: The Free Press 1977).

what was referred to as first-mover advantages (Section 3.2 of Chapter 2)* thus play a prominent role in the analysis.

The principal labor economics studies on which I rely are Becker's work on human capital (1962), the internal labor market literature (especially Doeringer and Piore (1971)), and discussions of collective bargaining by labor law specialists (principally Cox (1958)). This chapter is not, however, mainly a synthesis. I examine the transactional attributes of alternative contracting modes in a more detailed way than previous treatments and interpret the employment relation in an intertemporal systems context. Also, whereas much of the internal labor market literature emphasizes noneconomic considerations, I interpret evolving institutional practices with respect to idiosyncratic production tasks principally in efficiency terms.

This is not to suggest, however, that extra-economic considerations are thought to be unimportant. To the contrary, the proposition advanced in Chapter 2* that supplying a satisfying exchange relation is part of the economic problem, broadly construed, has special relevance where an employment relation is involved. Indeed, some of the ways in which internal labor markets bear on this proposition are developed in Section 4.3, below.* But placing primary reliance on atmosphere to explain internal labor markets poses the following dilemma: assuming that the same considerations of contractual satisfaction with respect to the nature of the exchange relationship applies to production jobs of all kinds, how is the coexistence of structured (internal) and structureless (recurrent spot) labor markets to be explained? By contrast, rationalizing the absence of structure, where jobs are fungible, and the conscious creation of structure, for idiosyncratic jobs, is relatively straightforward if an efficiency orientation is adopted. Accordingly, the argument runs throughout principally in efficiency terms.

Four alternative labor contracting modes are examined. Two of these, recurrent spot contracting and contingent claims contracting, rely entirely on market-mediated transactions. The other two modes involve a mixture of market-mediated exchange and hierarchy (internal organization). What is commonly referred to as the 'authority relation' and the internal labor market mode are of this second kind. These several alternative contracting modes are assessed in cost-economizing terms, where costs include both production and transaction cost elements. Considering that the focus throughout is on contracting, transaction costs naturally receive primary attention.

My purposes, briefly, are as follows:

1. To demonstrate that the interesting problems of labor organization involve the study of transactions and contracting and, except in a rather special idiosyncratic sense, do not turn mainly on technology.
2. To isolate and assess the idiosyncratic job features which characterize

[*Not reprinted here – Ed.]

internal labor markets with the help of the organizational failures framework.

3. To set out the transactional detail that would attend complex contingent claims contracting in idiosyncratic job circumstances, thereby to disclose why such contracts are prohibitively costly or infeasible.

4. To demonstrate that sequential spot contracting is unsuited to the idiosyncratic tasks in question, whence Alchian and Demsetz' (1972) discussion of the employment relation requires qualification.

5. To examine the authority relation and indicate the limitations associated with Simon's (1957) evaluation of alternative contracting modes.

6. To develop the transactional rationale for internal labor markets (in terms mainly of economizing on bounded rationality and attenuating opportunism) where jobs are idiosyncratic in nontrivial degree. [. . .]

Doeringer and Piore describe idiosyncratic tasks in the following way (1971, pp. 15-16):

Almost every job involves some specific skills. Even the simplest custodial tasks are facilitated by familiarity with the physical environment specific to the workplace in which they are being performed. The apparently routine operation of standard machines can be importantly aided by familiarity with the particular piece of operating equipment. . . . In some cases workers are able to anticipate trouble and diagnose its source by subtle changes in the sound or smell of the equipment. Moreover, performance in some production or managerial jobs involves a team element, and a critical skill is the ability to operate effectively with the given members of the team. This ability is dependent upon the interaction skills of the personalities of the members, and the individual's work 'skills' are specific in the sense that skills necessary to work on one team are never quite the same as those required on another.

More generally, task idiosyncracies can arise in at least four ways: (1) equipment idiosyncracies, due to incompletely standardized, albeit common, equipment, the unique characteristics of which become known through experience; (2) process idiosyncracies, which are fashioned or 'adopted' by the worker and his associates in specific operating contexts; (3) informal team accommodations, attributable to mutual adaptation among parties engaged in recurrent contact but which are upset, to the possible detriment of group performance, when the membership is altered; and (4) communication idiosyncracies with respect to information channels and codes that are of value only within the firm. Because 'technology is [partly] unwritten and that part of the specificity derives from improvements which the work force itself introduces, workers are in a position to perfect their monopoly over the knowledge of the technology should there be an incentive to do so' (Doeringer and Piore, 1971, p. 84).

Training for idiosyncratic jobs ordinarily takes place in an on-the-job context. Classroom training is unsuitable both because the unique attributes associated with particular operations, machines, the work group, and, more generally, the atmosphere of the workplace may be impossible to duplicate in the classroom, and because job incumbents, who are in possession of the requisite skills and knowledge with which the new recruit or candidate must become familiar, may be unable to describe, demonstrate, or otherwise impart this information except in an operational context (Doeringer and Piore, 1971, p. 20). Teaching-by-doing thus facilitates the learning-by-doing process. Where such uniqueness and teaching attributes are at all important, specific exposure in the workplace at some stage becomes essential. Outsiders who lack specific experience can thus achieve parity with insiders only by being hired and incurring the necessary start-up costs.

The success of on-the-job training is plainly conditional on the information disclosure attitudes of incumbent employees. Both individually and as a group, incumbents are in possession of a valuable resource (knowledge) and can be expected to fully and candidly reveal it only in exchange for value. The way the employment relation is structured turns out to be important in this connection. The danger is that incumbent employees will hoard information to their personal advantage and engage in a series of bilateral monopolistic exchanges with the management — to the detriment of both the firm and other employees as well.

An additional feature of these tasks not described above but nevertheless important to an understanding of the contractual problems associated with the employment relation is that the activity in question is subject to periodic disturbance by environmental changes. Shifts in demand due to changes in the prices of complements or substitutes or to changes in consumer incomes or tastes occur; relative factor price changes appear; and technological changes of both product design and production technique types take place. Successive adaptations to changes of each of these kinds is typically needed if efficient production performance is to be realized. In addition, life cycle changes in the work force occur which occasion turnover, upgrading, and continuous training. The tasks in question are thus to be regarded in moving equilibrium terms. Put differently, they are not tasks for which a once-for-all adaptation by workers is sufficient, thereafter to remain unchanged.

The production tasks that are of transactional interest in this chapter are ones that are either themselves rather complex or are embedded in a complex set of technological and organizational circumstances. Furthermore, successive adaptations are required to realize efficiency in the face of changing internal and environmental events. A nontrivial degree of uncertainty/complexity may thus be said to characterize the tasks. Training for such tasks occurs in an on-the-job context because of the impossibility, or great cost, of disclosing job nuances in a classroom situation. The relevant job details simply cannot be identified, accurately described, and effectively communicated in a classroom context on account of information processing limitations of both originators (teachers) and receivers (trainees). Sometimes, indeed, the requisite language will not even exist. The pairing of bounded rationality with an uncertainty/complexity condition thus gives rise to the job-specific training situation. *Teaching-by-doing and learning-by-doing both economize on bounded rationality in these idiosyn-cratic job circumstances.*[2]

Specialized skills and knowledge accrue to individuals and small groups as a result of their specific training and experience. But while such skills and informa-tion accrue naturally, they can be disclosed strategically — in an incomplete or distorted fashion — if the affected parties should choose to. Whether this will obtain depends on the structure of the bargaining relationship. Where job in-cumbents acquire nontrivial first-mover advantages over outsiders, and, in addi-tion, are opportunistically inclined, what was once a large-numbers bidding situation, at the time original job assignments were made, is converted into a small-numbers bargaining situation if adaptations to unplanned (and perhaps unforeseeable) internal and market changes are subsequently proposed. The reasons for and consequences of this shift from a large-numbers bargaining rela-tionship at the outset to bilateral bargaining subsequently are further developed below.

Four types of individualistic contracting modes can be distinguished: (1) contract now for the specific performance of x in the future; (2) contract now for the delivery of x_i contingent on event e_i obtaining in the future; (3) wait until the future materializes and contract for the appropriate (specific) x at the time; and (4) contract now for the right to select a specific x from within an admissable set X, the determination of the particular x to be deferred until the future. [. . .]

The upshot is that none of the above contracting schemes has acceptable properties for tasks of the idiosyncratic variety. Contingent claims contracting (Meade, 1971, Chap. 10) fails principally because of bounded rationality. Spot market contracting (Alchian and Demetz, 1972, p. 777) is impaired by first-mover advantages and problems of opportunism. The authority relation (Simon, 1957, pp. 183–195) is excessively vague and, ultimately, is confronted with the same types of problems as is spot market contracting. Faced with this result, the question of alternative contracting schemes naturally arises. Can more effective schemes be designed? Do more efficient contracting modes exist?

The analysis here is restricted to the latter of these questions, which is answered in the affirmative. Although it cannot be said that internal labor market structures are optimally efficient with respect to idiosyncratic tasks, it is nevertheless significant that their efficiency properties have been little noted or understated by predominantly non-neoclassical interpretations of these markets in the past.

My assessment of the efficiency implications of internal labor market struc-tures is in three parts. The occasion for and purposes of collective organization are sketched first. The salient structural attributes of internal labor markets are then described and the efficiency implications of each, expressed in terms of the language of the organizational failures framework, is indicated. Several caveats, including a brief discussion of atmosphere, follow.

To observe that the pursuit of perceived individual interests can sometimes lead to defective collective outcomes is scarcely novel. Schelling has treated the issue extensively in the context of the 'ecology of micromotives' (1971). The individual in each of his examples is both small in relation to the system – and thus his behavior, by itself, has no decisive influence on the system – and is unable to appropriate the collective gains that would obtain were he voluntarily to forego individual self-interest seeking. Schelling then observes that the remedy involves collective action. An enforceable social contract which imposes a co-operative solution on the system is needed (1971, p. 69).

Although it is common to think of collective action as action by the state, this is plainly too narrow. As Arrow (1969, p. 62) and Schelling (1971, p. 68) emphasize, both private collective action (of which the firm, with its hierarchical controls, is an example) and norms of socialization are also devices for realizing cooperative solutions. The internal labor market is usefully interpreted in this same spirit.

Although it is in the interest of each worker, bargaining individually or as a part of a small team, to acquire and exploit monopoly positions, it is plainly not in the interest of the *system* that employees should behave in this way. Opportunistic bargaining not only in itself absorbs real resources, but efficient adaptations are delayed and possibly foregone altogether. Accordingly, what this suggests is that the employment relation be transformed in such a way that systems concerns are made more fully to prevail and the following objectives are realized: (1) bargaining costs are much lower; (2) the internal wage structure is rationalized in terms of objective task characteristics; (3) consummate rather than perfunctory cooperation is encouraged; and (4) investments of idiosyncratic types, which constitute a potential source of monopoly, are undertaken without risk of exploitation. For the reasons and in the ways developed below, internal labor markets can have, and some do have, the requisite properties to satisfy this prescription.[3]

A leading difficulty with individual contracting schemes where jobs are idiosyncratic is that workers are strategically situated to bargain opportunistically. The internal labor market achieves a fundamental transformation by shifting to a system where wage rates are attached mainly to jobs rather than to workers. Not only is individual wage bargaining thereby discouraged, but it may even be legally foreclosed (Summers, 1969, p. 531). Once wages are expressly removed from individual bargaining, there is really no occasion for the worker to haggle over the incremental gains that are realized when adaptations of degree are proposed by the management. The incentives to behave opportunistically, which infect individual bargaining schemes, are correspondingly attenuated.

Moreover, not only are affirmative incentives lacking, but there are disincentives, of group disciplinary and promotion ladder types, which augur against resistance to authority on matters that come within the range customarily covered by the authority relation.[4] Promotion ladder issues are taken up in conjunction with the discussion of ports of entry [. . .] below; consider, therefore, group disciplinary effects.

In this connection Barnard observes (1962, p. 169):

Since the efficiency of organization is affected by the degree to which individuals assent to orders, denying the authority of an organization communication is a threat to the interests of all individuals who derive a net advantage from their connection with the organization, unless the orders are unacceptable to them also. Accordingly, at any given time there is among most of the contributors an active personal interest in the maintenance of the authority of all orders which to them are within the zone of indifference. The maintenance of this interest is largely a function of informal organization.

The application of group pressures thus combines with promotional incentives to facilitate adaptations in the small [group].[5] Even individuals who have exhausted their promotional prospects can thereby be induced to comply. System interests are made more fully to prevail. This concern with viability possibly explains the position taken in labor law that orders which are ambiguous with respect to, and perhaps even exceed, the scope of authority, are to be fulfilled first and disputed later (Summers, 1969, pp. 538, 573).

Internal labor market agreements are commonly reached through collective bargaining. Cox observes in this connection that the collective bargaining agreement should be understood as an instrument of government as well as an instrument of exchange. 'The collective agreement governs complex, many-sided relations between large numbers of people in a going concern for very substantial periods of time' (1958, p. 22). Provision for unforeseeable contingencies is made by writing the contract in general and flexible terms and supplying the parties with a special arbitration machinery. 'One simply cannot spell out every detail of life in an industrial establishment, or even of that portion which both management and labor agree is a matter of mutual concern' (Cox, 1958, p. 23). Such contractual incompleteness is an implicit concession to bounded rationality. Rather than attempt to anticipate all bridges that might conceivably be faced, which is impossibly ambitious and excessively costly, bridges are crossed as they appear.

However attractive, in bounded rationality respects, adaptive, sequential decision-making is, admitting gaps into the contract also poses hazards. Where parties are not indifferent with respect to the manner in which gaps are to be filled, fractious bargaining or litigation commonly results. It is for the purpose of forestalling the worst outcomes of this kind that the special arbitration apparatus is devised.

Important differences between commercial and labor arbitration are to be noted in this connection. For one thing, '. . . the commercial arbitrator finds facts — did the cloth meet the sample — while the labor arbitrator necessarily pours meaning into the general phrases and interstices of a document' (Cox, 1958, p. 23). In addition, the idiosyncratic practices of the firm and its employees also constitute 'shop law' and, to the labor arbitrator, are essential background for purposes of understanding a collective agreement and interpreting its intent (Cox, 1958, p. 24).

In the language of the organizational failures framework, the creation of such a special arbitration apparatus serves to overcome information impactedness because the arbitrator is able to explore the facts in greater depth and with greater sensitivity to idiosyncratic attributes of the enterprise than could normal judicial proceedings. Furthermore, once it becomes recognized that the arbitrator is able to apprise himself of the facts in a discerning and low cost way, opportunistic misrepresentations of the data are discouraged as well.

Also of interest in relation to the above is the matter of who is entitled to activate the arbitration machinery when an individual dispute arises. Cox takes the position that (1958, p. 24)[6]

. . . giving the union control over all claims arising under the collective agreement comports so much better with the functional nature of a collective bargaining agreement . . . Allowing an individual to carry a claim to arbitration whenever he is dissatisfied with the adjustment worked out by the company and the union . . . discourages the kind of day-to-day cooperation between company and union which is normally the mark of sound industrial relations — a relationship in which grievances are treated as problems to be solved and contracts are only guideposts in a dynamic human relationship. When . . . the individual's claim endangers group interests, the union's function is to resolve the competition by reaching an accommodation or striking a balance.

The practice described by Cox of giving the union control over arbitration claims plainly permits group interests, whence the concern for system viability, to supercede individual interests, thereby curbing small numbers opportunism.

Acceding to authority on matters that fall within the zone of acceptance[7] merely requires that employees respond in a minimally acceptable, even perfunctory way. This may be sufficient for tasks that are reasonably well-structured. In such circumstances, the zeal with which an instruction is discharged may have little effect on the outcome. As indicated, however, consummate cooperation is valued for the tasks of interest here. But how is cooperation of this more extensive sort to be realized?

A simple answer is to reward cooperative behavior by awarding incentive payments on a transaction-specific basis. The employment relation would then revert to a series of haggling encounters over the nature of the *quid pro quo*, however, and would hardly be distinguishable from a sequential spot contract. Moreover, such payments would plainly violate the nonindividualistic wage bargaining attributes of internal labor markets described [. . .] above.

The internal promotion practices in internal labor markets are of special interest in this connection. Access to higher-level positions on internal promotion ladders are not open to all comers on an unrestricted basis. Rather, as part of the internal incentive system, higher-level positions (of the prescribed kinds)[8] are filled by promotion from within wherever this is feasible. This practice, particularly, if it is followed by other enterprises to which the workers might otherwise turn for upgrading opportunities, ties the interests of the workers to the firm in a continuing way.[9] Given these ties, the worker looks to internal promotion as the principal means of improving his position.

The practice of restricting entry to lower-level jobs and promoting from within has interesting experience-rating implications. It permits firms to protect themselves against low productivity types, who might otherwise successfully represent themselves to be high productivity applicants, by bringing employees in at low-level positions and then upgrading them as experience warrants. Furthermore, employees who may have been incorrectly upgraded but later have been 'found out,' and hence barred from additional internal promotions, are unable to move to a new organization without penalty.[10] Were unpenalized lateral moves possible, workers might, considering the problems of accurately transmitting productivity valuations between firms, be able to disguise their true productivity attributes from their new employers long enough to achieve some additional promotions. Restricting access to low-level positions serves to protect the firm against exploitation by opportunistic types who would, if they could, change jobs strategically for the purpose of compounding evaluation errors between successive independent organizations.

Were it, however, that markets could perform equally well these experience-rating functions, the port of entry restrictions described would be unnecessary. The (comparative) limitations of markets in experience-rating respects, which were referred to in Chapter 2,* warrant elaboration. The principal impediment to effective interfirm experience-rating is one of communication.[11] By comparison with the firm, markets lack a rich and common rating language. The language problem is particularly severe where the judgments to be made are highly subjective. The advantages of hierarchy in these circumstances are especially great if those persons who are the most familiar with a worker's characteristics, usually his immediate supervisor, also do the experience-rating. The need to rationalize subjective assessments that are confidently held but, by reason of bounded rationality, difficult to articulate is reduced. Put differently, interfirm experience-rating is impeded in information impactedness respects.

Reliance on internal promotion has affirmative incentive properties because workers can anticipate that differential talent and degrees of co-operativeness will be rewarded. Consequently, although the attachment of wages to jobs rather than to individuals may result in an imperfect correspondence between wages and marginal productivity at ports of entry, productivity differentials will be recognized over a time and a more perfect correspondence can be expected for higher-level assignments in the internal labor market job hierarchy. [. . .]

[*Not reprinted here – Ed.]

NOTES

1. As will be apparent, the employment relation is not an isolated case of idiosyncratic exchange conditions. The vertical integration problem turns in no small degree on these same considerations (see the discussion of Stigler's treatment of vertical integration in Section 3.3 of Chapter 1 as well as the more general discussion in Chapter 5, especially Section 4). [Not reprinted here – Ed.]

2. Doing-while-learning also contributes to the output of the firm. Classroom training is typically at a disadvantage in this respect.

3. Commons' discussion with Sidney Hillman concerning the transformation of membership attitudes among the Amalgamated Clothing Workers illustrates some of the system attributes of collective agreements (1970, p. 130):

   > Ten years after World War 1, I asked Sidney Hillman . . . why his members were less revolutionary than they had been when I knew them twenty-five years before in the sweatshop. . . . Hillman replied. 'They know now that they are citizens of the industry. They know that they must make the corporation a success on account of their own jobs.' They were citizens because they had an arbitration system which gave them security against arbitrary foremen. They had an unemployment system by agreement with the firm which gave them security of earnings. This is an illustration of the meaning of part-whole relations.

4. Authority relation is used here in the qualified short-run sense suggested in our discussion of Simon in Section 3.3 above. [Not reprinted here – Ed.]

5. Of course, informal organization does not operate exclusively in the context of a collectivized wage bargain. Autonomous bargainers, however, are ordinarily expected to behave in autonomous ways. The extent to which group powers serve as a check on challenges to authority is accordingly much weaker where the individual bargaining mode prevails (March and Simon, 1958, pp. 59, 66). By contrast, the individual in the collectivized system who refuses to accede to orders on matters that fall within the customarily defined zone of acceptance is apt to be regarded as cantankerous or malevolent, since there is no private pecuniary gain to be appropriated, and will be ostracized by his peers.

6. I am informed that his practice is changing and offer three comments in this regard. First, institutional change does not always promote efficiency outcomes; backward steps will sometimes occur – possibly because the efficiency implications are not understood. Second, relegating control to the union on whether a grievance is to be submitted to arbitration can sometimes lead to capricious results. Disfavored workers can be unfairly disadvantaged by those who control the union decision-making machinery. Some form of appeal may therefore be a necessary corrective. Third, that workers are given rights to bring grievances on their own motion does not imply that this will happen frequently. Grievances that fail to secure the support of peers are unlikely to be brought unless they represent egregious conditions on which the grievant feels confidently he will prevail. The bringing of trivial grievances not only elicits the the resentment of peers but impairs the grievant's standing when more serious matters are posed.

7. The zone of acceptance is discussed in the quotation from Barnard, p. 154 above.

8. For a discussion, see Doeringer and Piore (1971, pp. 42–47).

9. Since access to idiosyncratic types of jobs is limited by requiring new employees to accept lower-level jobs at the bottom of promotion ladders, individuals can usually not shift laterally between firms without cost: 'Employees in nonentry jobs in one enterprise often have access only to entry-level jobs in other enterprises. The latter will often pay less than those which the employees currently hold' (Doeringer and Piore, 1971, p. 78).

10. Agents seeking transfer may have gotten ahead in an organization by error. Experience-rating, after all, is a statistical inference process and is vulnerable to 'Type II' error. When a mistake has been discovered and additional promotions are not forthcoming, the agent might seek transfer in the hope that he can successfully disguise his true characteristics in the new organization and thereby secure further promotions.

Alternatively, the agent may have been promoted correctly, but changed his work attitudes subsequently — in which case further promotion is denied. Again, he might seek transfer in the hope of securing additional promotion in an organization that, because of the difficulty of interfirm communication about agent characteristics, is less able to ascertain his true characteristics initially.
11. Interfirm experience-rating may also suffer in veracity respects, since firms may choose deliberately to mislead rivals. The major impediment, however, is one of communication.

REFERENCES

Alchian, A. A. and Demsetz. H. (1972) 'Production, Information Costs, and Economic Organisation', *American Economic Review*, 62, December, pp. 777–95.

Arrow, K. J. (1969) 'The Organisation of Economic Activity', in *The Analysis and Evaluation of Public Expenditure: the PPB system*, Joint Economic Committee, 91st Congress, First Session, pp. 59–73.

Barnard, C. I. (1962) *The Functions of the Executive*, second edition, Cambridge, Mass., Harvard University Press.

Becker, G. S. (1962) 'Investment in Human Capital: a theoretical analysis', *Journal of Political Economy*, 70, Supplement, October, pp. 9–44.

Commons, John R. (1970) *The Economics of Collective Action*, Madison, University of Wisconsin Press.

Cox, A. (1958) 'The Legal Nature of Collective Bargaining Agreements', *Michigan Law Review*, 57, November, pp. 1–36.

Doeringer, P. and Piore, M. (1971) *Internal Labor Markets and Manpower Analysis*, Lexington, Mass., D. C. Heath.

Hayek, F. (1945) 'The Use of Knowledge in Society', *American Economic Review*, 35, September, pp. 519–30.

March, J. G. and Simon, H. A. (1958) *Organisations*, New York, Wiley.

Meade, J. E. (1971) *The Controlled Economy*, London, Allen and Unwin.

Schelling, T. C. (1971) 'On the Ecology of Micromotives', *The Public Interest*, 25, Fall, pp. 61–98.

Simon, H. A. (1957) *Models of Man*, New York, Wiley.

Summers, C. (1969) 'Collective Agreements and the Law of Contracts', *Yale Law Journal*, 78, March, pp. 527–75.

3. The Union

LATE in 1976 the majority of respondents in an opinion poll named Mr Jack Jones, then general secretary of the Transport and General Workers Union, as the most powerful man in Britain. It is a safe assumption that none of the authors represented in this section would go that far. None the less the sources, extent, and consequences of trade union economic power[1] have always attracted considerable analytical attention, out of all proportion (or so some would argue) to the real significance of the issue. Not that very much has been achieved. 'The literature on the incidence of collective bargaining', wrote Martin Bronfenbrenner twenty years ago, 'is not one of which we can be proud as professional economists' (Reading 3.4, p. 202). At the theoretical level this verdict would command substantial support today, while the ensuing two decades of empirical research have failed to produce anything more concrete than continuing disagreement, often of a very basic kind. The readings provide, or so it is hoped, some impression of the main area of controversy and interest. They can certainly do no more.

Mancur Olson (Reading 3.1) asks a very fundamental question: exactly why do workers join unions, pay subscriptions, and occasionally incur the much greater sacrifices entailed by striking? The obvious answer, he argues — that the benefits outweigh the costs — is false. In an earlier chapter of his book (not reprinted here), Olson draws a parallel between union gains and the monopoly profits shared by the members of a cartel. Collectively, cartel members benefit from an agreement to restrict the output of the industry, and the consequent rise in the price of the product. Individually, any single firm will find it more profitable to ignore the agreement than to limit its own output in accordance with the rules of the cartel. Unless the number of firms involved is very small, a defection by any one of them will not significantly affect the (common) price they are able to charge, and the defector will be able to reap the benefits of the others' output restriction without incurring the costs. Monopoly profits, Olson suggests, are a form of public good, like clean air and whales. Uninhibited individual maximization leads to the collapse of cartels, pollutes the atmosphere, and hunts the world's largest mammals to the verge of extinction.

Olson's point is that most of the benefits of trade unionism are also public goods, since the higher wages and improved working conditions produced (so it is supposed) by union intervention are generally available to members and non-members alike. It follows that no rational worker, maximizing his or her utility subject only to the usual budget constraints, will ever willingly accept any share of the cost of union activities, since the benefits will accrue anyway.[2] Unions began life as very small bodies, under circumstances in which individual withdrawals would affect the collective benefits, and where voluntary affiliation might well have been a rational decision. Today free rides are costless, so why pay? Large modern unions avoid collapse, so Olson believes, only through compulsion (the closed shop, ostracism of non-members), or — less importantly — through the provision of 'selective benefits' (for example, legal representation in accident cases) which are supplied only to union members and therefore take on the characteristics of private rather than public goods.

This argument can be supported by a mass of evidence. Coercion has always played a part in the maintenance of union solidarity, from the solemn oaths which martyred the Tolpuddle farmworkers in 1834 to the highly formalized modern closed shop agreement. The attractions of the free ride are reflected in widespread apathy among union members concerning the affairs of their unions. Participation increases, as Olson would predict, at the workplace level, where the numbers involved are often small enough for the individual's voice to 'count for something'. But not *all* union members require compulsion; many pay their subscriptions, and some hold office, gladly, even enthusiastically, though the union would not disintegrate in their absence (the only reason, according to Olson, for voluntary membership). Nor is the closed shop merely a form of industrial terrorism. It derives its strength from, and could not be sustained without, the deeply-felt sentiment that free riding is *wrong*, and the belief that one is morally obliged to share in the costs of trade unionism so long as one enjoys the benefits, even if — perhaps especially if — one is not actually compelled to do so (McCarthy, 1964).

Unwittingly, Olson has produced a *reductio ad absurdum*: his argument demonstrates quite brutally that if people really did behave like completely amoral, individual utility maximizers, then trade unions (and most other forms of organized social life) would be quite impossible (see also Hirsch, 1977).[3] The implications of their existence are far-reaching, though little explored. 'If, in fact, individuals could be predicted to choose among "public" alternatives on the basis of group rather than an individual interest, we could discard much of the theory of public goods and of welfare economics . . . and utility functions of the standard variety simply would not exist' (Buchanan, 1968, pp. 146–7).

Given that unions exist, under what conditions will they prosper? Lewis (Reading 3.2) and Hieser (Reading 3.3) approach this question from a partial equilibrium framework, while Bronfenbrenner (Reading 3.4) bravely attempts a more general overview. Lewis's distinction between 'competitive' and 'monopolistic' unionism provides a useful starting-point. If all labour and product markets were perfectly competitive, product prices would tend towards equality with marginal costs, and firms would earn only normal profits. Unions could achieve nothing, at the expense either of employers or of customers, that would not have resulted from atomistic competition between their members. Unless employers somehow derive satisfaction from the unionization of their workers,[4] any benefits derived from collective bargaining — improved working conditions, feelings of equity and due process — would have to be paid for by a *reduction* in the wage rate below what it would have been in the absence of the union. Strange though all this may sound, it does point to one important conclusion. Unions will be able to increase the earnings of their members only if they can somehow inhibit the normal operation of competitive market forces.

One source of monopoly power is the ability to limit the size of the potential labour force, for example by enforcing apprenticeship requirements while at the same time limiting the number of approved trainees. If this is deemed to be the only foundation upon which 'monopolistic unionism' might be based, then economic power is clearly going to be the province of a small minority of entrenched craft unions, and will be negligible elsewhere (as is concluded by Friedman, 1951). This, though, is an unnecessarily sweeping conclusion. Strikes, actual, threatened, or feared, constitute the main buttress of union 'bargaining strength', as indeed they have for two centuries. A strike enables the union to inflict losses upon the employer, in the form of the profits which are forgone when production ceases. The profit-maximizing firm will avoid these losses by meeting the union's demands, unless the losses which result from concession are expected to be even greater. The union, for its part, will employ the strike weapon only if it expects the fruits of victory to exceed the costs (which consist largely of the wages forgone by its members) of the battle.

This insight, simple but profound, guides Hieser in his ingenious attempt to solve an age-old problem. The relationship between employer and union can be seen as one of bilateral monopoly, where the sole buyer of a particular type of labour (the firm) faces the only seller (the union, acting on behalf of its members). Generations of economists, confronting this relationship, have concluded that the outcome of wage bargaining under bilateral monopoly must be regarded as indeterminate. Upper and lower limits may be established, but very little could be said as to where between these limits the negotiated wage rate would fall, except that it would depend on the 'bargaining power' of the parties. And this, it was clear, was largely tautological.

Hieser suggests a way out of this impasse. Each party to the negotiations must decide whether to concede or to fight. Its decision will depend on the expected balance of gains and losses. Where these are equal, it will be indifferent as to whether a strike occurs. Hieser shows that there is one wage rate at which *both* parties are indifferent as between conflict and agreement. Here 'pressure and counter-pressure from both sides will cease' (p. 193), and a settlement will be reached. Under certain simplifying assumptions[5] this can be calculated precisely: it is that wage rate corresponding to an elasticity of labour demand of minus 5/3. This is the fully determinate outcome of the bargaining process.

This is, alas, a little too good to be true. It was suggested in the previous section that the firm may not operate on its marginal revenue function at all, and one does not need to be wildly imaginative to realize that unions may be a source of X-inefficiency. At the extreme, a really powerful union may be able to squeeze the last drop of excess profit from the firm (making the relevant constraint the curve DD', not DR, in Hieser's Figure 3.4). It is possible, as Lewis indicates, that some of the union's gains may be taken in non-pecuniary form, for example, through a relaxation in the pace of work. Current concern with 'overmanning' — 'featherbedding' is the more eloquent North American term — may be relevant in this context (see Weinstein, 1965).

The model can probably be adjusted without too much difficulty to allow for these objections, but there are other, and more fundamental, criticisms. The determinacy of Hieser's solution is heavily dependent on the availability of information to the parties, who are assumed to calculate their respective gains and losses from the same data. Both firm and union, that is, are supposed to know the shape and position of the firm's marginal revenue productivity function. This raises a host of problems. It is not simply that the function is prone to frequent shifts, and that information about it will be scarce and costly, though all this is true (Ross, 1948). Doubts have been expressed as to whether the function may be objectively known even in principle, since according to one celebrated interpretation it is inevitably no more than a series of 'subjective estimates, guesses and hunches' (Machlup, 1946, p. 522). And even if the function is known to the firm, it is by no means clear why this knowledge should be imparted to the union. On the contrary, the employer has every reason to lie, bluff, cheat, and deceive, for these strategems will encourage its opponent to take a more pessimistic view of its prospects and settle for less than it might otherwise have taken.

It may be objected to this that the long-term relationship between employers and union would be damaged by such manoeuvres, as indeed it might, but such long-term considerations play no part whatever in Hieser's model. Dishonesty, of course, need not be confined to the employer. The union, too, will have a material interest in concealing its true 'indifference function' from its opponent, and for identical reasons. Equally it may call strikes to demonstrate to the employer just what its preferences are (or are supposed to be). 'One of the chief difficulties of the basic-indeterminacy school', Hieser argues (p. 183), 'is that in the real world the general experience is, in fact, achievement of comparatively stable, determinate positions'. Deadlocks and disputes are uncommon enough to have news value, while agreements are not. But in terms of Hieser's model conflict should not occur at all: strikes are essentially *mistakes*, and the threat or fear of strikes cannot affect the outcome of negotiations. The conclusion appears inescapable that the bargaining process is too complex, and too fraught with uncertainties of all kinds, to be cast successfully in Hieser's restrictive mould. Once taken out of it, indeterminacy reappears in all but name (see Johnston, 1972).

Perhaps we can learn more about the economic power of trade unions from a more empirical study of the manifestations of their influence, for which

Bronfenbrenner (Reading 3.4) supplies a useful framework. He regards collective bargaining as a tax, and attempts to assess its incidence. Who pays, he asks, for the benefits (pecuniary and non-pecuniary) that unions provide for their members? Figure 3.1 (for which Bronfenbrenner bears no responsibility) illustrates the wide range of answers which may be given to the question. The left-hand branch of the 'tree' drawn there indicates the possibility that no one pays.

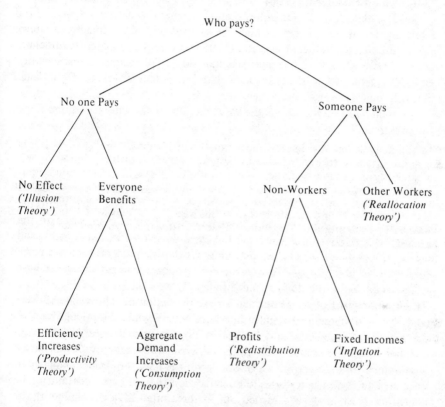

FIG. 3.1 The Incidence of Collective Bargaining

This will be so if the apparent benefits are in fact illusory, that is, if unions are unable to achieve anything that would not otherwise have occurred through the automatic workings of the competitive market. It will also be so if everyone gains from union presence. This may occur if persistent union pressure upon management forces increased efficiency (the 'productivity' theory), or if wage increases generate higher aggregate demand and increased output (the 'consumption' theory).

Otherwise there must be losers. The various candidates are illustrated in the right-hand branch of the 'tree'. The tax-payers, to continue with Bronfenbrenner's analogy, may be the recipients of non-wage income, either directly through a reduction in the share of profits in national income (the 'redistribution' theory), or indirectly through the erosion of the real value of fixed incomes (the 'inflation' theory). They may, finally, consist of non-union workers, who find their real wages reduced as the earnings of union members increase (the 'reallocation' theory). This comes about as follows. Union members in well-organized firms or industries obtain higher wages, and employment in these firms or industries declines. Displaced workers from this 'union sector' compete for jobs in the residual 'non-union sector', driving down wages there. On this interpretation trade unionism is innately self-centred and sectionalist, whatever its protestations to the contrary. Rees (1963) provides a graphical treatment of this analysis, while Johnson and Mieszkowski (1970) supply a mathematical exposition from which they conclude that this outcome is more likely than a redistribution from profits to wages.

Bronfenbrenner's verdict on the evidence, up to the late 1950s, took up a full paragraph.

In summary, then, my eclectic theory of the incidence of collective bargaining is an inflationary theory for an easy-money prosperity, or for a depression with a carelessly expansionary fiscal policy, an illusion theory once inflation is under way, and a reallocation theory under most other circumstances. A redistributionist strain underlies the entire process, but on a scale too small to produce significant consumption effects or otherwise to influence the course of prosperity or depression. The illusion theory also warns us usefully at all times against exaggerating the quantitative significance of the other patterns of incidence. The evidence for and against the productivity theory still awaits detailed examination (p. 269)

It is impossible to be more concise today. As we shall see in section 5, the inflation and consumption theories are markedly less fashionable than they were (and the illusion theory possibly slightly more so), while the present hiatus in the analysis of income distribution makes any judgement concerning the redistribution theory extremely difficult. The productivity theory is still largely unexamined (but see above p. 84). Studies of the impact of trade unions on the wage structure, which test only the reallocation theory, have been much more numerous. Most have been carried out in the United States, including the encyclopaedic work of Lewis (1963) which concluded that unions had raised the relative wages of union members by no more than 10 per cent, except in deep depression when the effect was rather greater. According to Lewis, union power, if not quite illusory, could easily be exaggerated.

More recent North American studies have produced a wide range of estimates, many of them much larger than Lewis's, but it was not until 1974 that the first comparable exercise appeared for Britain (Pencavel, 1974). Mulvey and Foster (Reading 3.5) provide a worthy example of what is now a rapidly-expanding literature. Their estimate is that British unions have raised the earnings of their members, relatively to those of non-union workers in comparable occupations, by between 22 per cent and 36 per cent. By using the degree of coverage of collective agreements as a proxy for union power, rather than the proportion of the labour force in membership, Mulvey and Foster largely overcome the problem of spillover of union wage gains to non-members which bedevilled earlier research.[6] Their estimates are, nevertheless, likely to prove controversial, not least because of the necessarily rather crude measures of human capital endowments employed, and their failure to include establishment variables in their occupational earnings functions (see below pp. 000-00).

In Reading 3.6 Metcalf surveys a number of related studies, all of which report a significant relative wage effect for British unions. He, too, stresses the difficulties of controlling for variations in the quality of the labour force. Rather more is involved here than attempts to measure the level of skill. High-wage employers of union labour may obtain compensation through lower turnover rates, or a 'more rigorous industrial relations regime' (p. 229), which raises the intriguing possibility that union members — contrary to popular folklore — may work *harder* than non-unionists!

Metcalf observes that these estimates of the impact of unions on the wage structure 'do not rely on any model of "union power". They are obtained solely by manipulating an identity and estimating a regression of earnings on unionisation and other variables. The *reason* union members/covered earn more than similar people who are not members/covered has not been investigated in these studies' (p. 224). Perhaps the reason has something to do with the bargaining considerations discussed earlier, in which the ability to inflict (or threaten to inflict) losses upon employers plays a crucial role. It is not unreasonable, on the face of it, to assume that employers will be more frightened of a numerically strong union than of one which has failed to recruit a large proportion of the relevant labour force. But there are serious problems in this connection, as we have seen. Much depends on the employer's perception of the union threat, and it is not clear that this can be satisfactorily captured in any numerical ratio. It is also likely that unions will hold some power in reserve, through inertia, corruption, or simply as a precaution against emergencies (Reder, 1959). This is just one reason for suspecting that *changes* in the union membership ratio — sometimes taken as a proxy for changes in union power — may be a misleading indicator of unions' influence over the rate of wage inflation (see Purdy and Zis (1974) for a thorough discussion)

One final conclusion is in order. Even conclusive evidence as to the extent of the union relative wage effect would have only weak and indirect implications for the other dimensions about which Bronfenbrenner speculates. At least in principle, relative wage gains are consistent with stable prices, a constant share of profits, and unchanged levels of aggregate productivity and aggregate demand. This is not to say that unions do not in fact exercise any influence over these variables, only that we do not know what this influence might be.

NOTES

1. Economic power is defined here in the narrow sense, as the ability (actual or potential) to influence wages, conditions of work and other aspects of the employment relationship, but excluding indirect effects produced by political pressure exerted by unions on the state (and vice versa). Equally, political conflict within unions – as, for example, between officials and ordinary members – is for simplicity ignored.
2. This conclusion is not affected by the possibility, recognized by Olson, that the individual's utility function is dominated by a wholly selfless concern for the well-being of others. A rational altruist seeks to do good; if the good in question will occur irrespective of his or her efforts, inactivity is the only sensible policy!
3. Later in the book Olson takes issue with Marx, and other sociologists, by asserting that no rational individual can ever act out of class-consciousness, so that the driving force of world history must lie elsewhere.
4. It is quite possible that unionization is profitable for the firm if it improves labour discipline and encourages higher effort levels; see Reading 2.5 above, and more generally on the 'incorporation' of unions, Hyman (1971).
5. Both sides discount the future at the same rate, and are influenced only by monetary magnitudes.
6. The union rate' is often paid to non-unionists, either to retain their services or to guard against their joining the union themselves (the latter being known as the 'threat effect' of union activity). Such spillovers render a direct comparison of 'union' and 'non-union' wages a very misleading indicator of the economic impact of unions.

REFERENCES

Buchanan, J. M. (1968) *The Demand and Supply of Public Goods*. Chicago, Rand McNally.
Cross, J. G. (1969) *The Economics of Bargaining*. New York, Basic Books.
Friedman, M. (1951) 'Some Comments on the Significance of Labor Unions for Economic Policy', in D. McCord Wright (ed.), *The Impact of the Union*, New York, Kelley.
Hirsch, F. (1977) *Social Limits to Growth*. London, Routledge.
Hyman, R. (1971) *Marxism and the Sociology of Trade Unions*, London, Pluto Press.
Johnson, H. G. and Mieszkowski, P. (1970) 'The Effects of Unionisation on the Distribution of Income: a general equilibrium approach', *Quarterly Journal of Economics*, 84, pp. 539–61.
Johnston, J. (1972) 'A Model of Wage Determination Under Bilateral Monopoly', *Economic Journal*, 82, pp. 837–52.
Lewis, H. G. (1963) *Unionism and Relative Wages in the United States*, University of Chicago Press.
Machlup, F. (1946) 'Marginal Analysis and Empirical Research', *American Economic Review*, 36, pp. 519–54.
McCarthy, W. E. J. (1964) *The Closed Shop in Britain*, Oxford, Blackwell.
Pencavel, J. H. (1974) 'Relative Wages and Trade Unions in the United Kingdom', *Economica*, 41, pp. 194–210.
Purdy, D. L. and Zis, G. (1974) 'On the Concept and Measurement of Trade Union Militancy', pp. 38–60 of D. Laidler and D. Purdy (eds.), *Inflation and Labour Markets*, Manchester University Press.
Reder, M. W. (1959) 'Job Scarcity and the Nature of Union Power', *Industrial and Labor Relations Review*, 13, pp. 349–62.
Rees, A. (1963) 'The Effects of Unions on Resource Allocation', *Journal of Law and Economics*, 6, pp. 69–78.
Ross, A. M. (1948) *Trade Union Wage Policy* Berkeley, California University Press.
Weinstein, P. A. (ed.) (1965) *Featherbedding and Technical Change*, Boston, D. C. Heath.

3.1 Coercion in Labour Unions*

[...]

In this age of big business and big labor, most labor unions are large organizations. But it was not always so. The first labor unions were small, local organizations, and they remained small and local for some time. The American labor movement began as a series of small unions with local interests, each independent of the others. (This incidentally was also true in Great Britain.[1]) The development of viable national unions in the United States took over half a century after local unions had emerged; and, even after national unions had been established, it was some time before they superseded the local unions as the main manifestation of labor's strength. Many of the earlier national unions, such as the Knights of Labor, failed. It was not only true that local unions were formed well before national unions; it was also significant that these first unions emerged, not in the larger factories, but in the smaller workplaces, so that the early unions were not nearly as large as some modern union locals. Unions are naturally supposed to have the greatest function to perform in the large factory, where there can be no personal relationships between employer and employee, and it is in such factories that many of the powerful unions are found today. Yet the early unions sprang up, not in the factories being spawned by the industrial revolution, but mainly in the building trades, in printing, in shoemaking, and in other industries characterized by small-scale production. The vast factories of the steel industry, the automobile industry, and the like were among the last workplaces organized. The usual explanation is that skilled workers are supposed to be the most amenable to organization and they were perhaps more common in smaller firms. But this explanation at best cannot be the whole story, for the coal-mining industry has been dominated by unskilled workers, and yet the small-scale firms of this industry were organized long before the great industrial giants.[2]

There may be many different factors that help to account for this historical pattern of labor-union growth, but that pattern may be explained at least partly by the fact that small groups can better provide themselves with collective goods than large groups. The higher wages, shorter hours, and better working conditions that unions demand are collective goods to the workers. The sacrifices required to create and maintain an effective union are moreover quite considerable, for a continuing organization must be supported, and the strike that is the union's major weapon requires that each worker normally forego his entire income until the employer comes to terms. Small unions may have a further advantage over larger unions stemming from the fact that they can be meaningful social and recreational units, and thus also offer noncollective social benefits that attract members. The social aspect seems to have been significant in a number of the earliest unions.[3] For these reasons it may be significant that in

*From Mancur Olson Jr., *The Logic of Collective Action* (Cambridge, Mass.: Harvard University Press, 1965).

their earlier days, when the faced the resistance of inertia and an especially hostile environment, unions began as small and independent local units and remained so for some time.

Once a local union exists, there are, however, several forces that may drive it to organize all of its craft or industry, or to federate with other local unions in the same craft or industry. Market forces work against any organization that operates only in a part of a market. Employers often will not be able to survive if they pay higher wages than competing firms. Thus an existing union often has an interest in seeing that all firms in any given market are forced to pay union wage scales. When only part of an industry or skill group is organized, employers also have a ready source of strikebreakers. In addition, workers with a given skill who migrate from one community to another have an interest in belonging to a national union that gives them access to employment in each new community. Finally, the political strength of a large union is obviously greater than that of a small one. The incentives to federate local unions and organize unorganized firms increase considerably as improvements in transportation and communication enlarge the market.[4]

The attempts to create large, national unions are accordingly understandable. But how can the success of some of these attempts to provide collective goods to large, latent groups be explained? By far the most important single factor enabling large, national unions to survive was that membership in those unions, and support of the strikes they called, was to a great degree compulsory.

The 'union shop,' the closed shop,' and other such instruments for making union membership compulsory are not, as some suppose, modern inventions. About sixty years ago Sidney and Beatrice Webb pointed out that the closed shop was even then a venerable institution in England. In words that fit contemporary America quite as well, they attacked the 'strange delusion in the journalistic mind that this compulsory trade unionism . . . is a modern device.' Compulsory union membership was something any student of trade union annals knows to be . . . coeval with trade unionism itself,' they said. 'The trade clubs of handicraftsmen in the eighteenth century would have scouted the idea of allowing any man to work at their trade who is not a member of the club . . . It is, in fact, as impossible for a non-unionist plater or rivetter to get work in a Tyneside shipyard, as it is for him to take a house in Newcastle without paying the rates [property taxes]. This silent and unseen, but absolutely complete compulsion, is the ideal of every Trade Union.'[5] Compulsory unionism has retained its 'silent and unseen' character in Britain to the present, and the 'right-to-work' question is hardly a live issue there.[6]

In the early years of the American labor movement, too, the closed shop was enforced whenever possible by the labor unions, though the specific contractual union-shop guarantees that now are typical did not normally exist then. For example, in 1667 in New York City the carters, predecessors of the teamsters, apparently obtained a closed shop.[7] And in 1805 the constitution of the New York Cordwainers (shoemakers) declared that no member could work for anyone who had any cordwainers in his employ who were not members of the union.[8] In printing the closed shop was fully developed by 1840.[9] 'If all the available evidence is summed up,' says one student of the question, 'it may be said that practically every trade union prior to the civil war was in favor of excluding non-members from employment.'[10]

In sum, compulsory unionism, far from being a modern innovation, goes back to the earliest days of organized labor, and existed even in the small, pre-national unions. Compulsory membership cannot, however, explain the creation or emergence of the first, small local unions, as it can account for the viability of the later, larger, national unions that the local unions ultimately created. Compulsory membership implies some instrument or organization to *make* membership compulsory, that is, to enforce the rule that nonunion members may not work in a given workplace. It is not possible for unorganized workers to create a *large* union, even if they are aware of the need for coercion, since they have to organize first in order to have an organization that will enforce the union-shop policy. But it is possible for a small union to emerge without compulsion, and then, if it so decides, to ensure its survival and increase its strength by making membership compulsory. Once a union exists, it may be able to expand in size, or combine with other unions, in order to represent large groups of workers, if it has compulsory membership. The early use of coercion in labor unions is not therefore in any way inconsistent with the hypothesis that unionism had to begin with small groups in small-scale firms.

In view of the importance of compulsory membership, and the fact that strikebreakers are *legally* free to cross picket lines and make any strike ineffective, it should not be surprising that violence has had a prominent place in the history of labor relations, especially in periods when there were attempts to create or expand large, national unions.[11] This violence has involved employers with mercenary gangs as well as workers. (Jay Gould boasted: 'I can hire one half of the working class to kill the other half.'[12]) As Daniel Bell points out, 'Beginning with the railroad strikes of 1877 . . . almost every major strike for the next forty years was attended by an outbreak of violence.' This he ascribes to the 'Social Darwinism' in American thought, which accounted for an 'integrated value system' that 'sanctioned industry's resistance to unionism.'[13] No doubt fanatical ideologues among employers and their friends accounted for some violence, but since the more radical *political* movements did not usually occasion similar amounts of violence, this must not have been the ultimate cause. The conservative or 'business unionism' philosophy typical of American labor unions was no doubt less offensive to conservative ideologues than communism, socialism, or anarchism; yet it seems to have led to much more violence. The correct explanation surely centers around the need for coercion implicit in attempts to provide collective goods to large groups. If some workers in a particular firm go out on strike, the supply function for labor tends to shift to the left; so for those who continue working, or for outside strikebreakers, wages will if anything be higher than they were before. By contrast, for the duration of the conflict the strikers get nothing. Thus all the economic incentives affecting *individuals* are on the side of those workers who do not respect the picket lines. Should it be surprising, then, that coercion should be applied to keep individual workers from succumbing to the temptation to work during the strike? And that antiunion employers should also use violence?

Violence is apparently the greatest when unions first try to organize a firm.[14] If the employer's forces win the early tests of strength, the union is apt to disappear and peace will be re-established. If the union wins, the hazards of 'scabbing' will likewise be evident and workers will soon make it a habit not to cross picket lines, thereby bringing a period of peaceful collective bargaining.

Compulsory membership and picket lines are therefore of the essence of unionism. As Henry George put it: 'Labor associations can do nothing to raise wages but by force; it may be force applied passively, or force applied actively, or force held in reserve, but it must be force; they *must* coerce or hold the power to coerce employers; they *must* coerce those among their members disposed to straggle; they *must* do their best to get into their hands the whole field of labor they seek to occupy and to force other workingmen either to join them or to starve. Those who tell you of trades unions bent on raising wages by moral suasion alone are like those who would tell you of tigers who live on oranges.'[15] The argument that collective bargaining implies coercion need not be used to attack unions. It can equally well be used to contend, as some students of the labor movement have contended, that when the majority of the workers in a particular bargaining unit vote to go out on strike, all of the workers in that unit should be barred by *law* from flouting the majority decision by attempting to continue working.[16] This would leave compulsion to the police and prevent mob violence.

In addition to compulsory membership, picket lines, and violence, some unions have also had selective incentives of a positive kind: they have offered noncollective benefits to those who join the union, and denied these benefits to any who do not. In certain special cases these noncollective goods have been important. Some large labor unions have offered various forms of insurance to those who join the union. Significantly, the first large, national union to prove viable in Great Britain was the Amalgamated Society of Engineers, established in 1851, which offered a wide range of noncollective benefits. As G. D. H. Cole explained:

The Amalgamated Society of Engineers is commonly acclaimed as a 'New Model' in Trade Union organization . . . it became the model for a whole series of 'Amalgamated' Societies formed during the next twenty years.

The essential basis of the 'New Model' was a close combination of trade and friendly activities. The A.S.E. provided for all its members a wide range of benefits, ranging from dispute and unemployment benefit to sickness and super-annuation·benefit . . . In short, it was a Trade Union and a Friendly Society almost in equal measure.[17]

The railroad brotherhoods in the United States have at times also attracted members by providing insurance benefits to those who joined the union. In the early days of the railroad unions accident rates were high and many insurance companies did not sell insurance to railroad workers. Thus the fraternal insurance benefits of the railroad brotherhoods offered potential members a considerable incentive for joining. In its early years the conductors' union went so far as to emphasize its insurance program to the virtual exclusion of all else.[18]

There were periods, however, when the insurance programs of some of the railroad unions lost money. Then they had to rely mainly on the seniority rule to hold membership. Union members were guaranteed seniority rights in the unions' contracts with the railroad companies, but nonunion workers had to depend on the goodwill of the railroad companies for any rights of seniority. It is significant that the railroad unions were for certain periods the only major national unions without some form of compulsory membership. The newspaper of the Brotherhood of Locomotive Engineers put it this way: 'The closed shop in the industries bears the same relation to the shop craft unions as the senior rule does to the train service brotherhoods. They are the backbone of both and if either are broken down they are no longer effective for collective bargaining. In fact, it would be impossible to maintain an organization today without them.[19]

It seems difficult to find more than a few examples of large unions that have supported themselves primarily by providing noncollective benefits, such as insurance or seniority privileges. On the other hand, most unions do provide something in the way of noncollective benefits, such as insurance, welfare benefits, and seniority rights.[20] A few unions help their members find employment. More important, almost every union handles members' grievances against the employer; that is, it attempts to protect each member against too much (or too little) overtime, against a disproportionate share of the most unpleasant work, against arbitrary foremen, and the like. While unions may process grievances for nonunion members as well, partly to impress them with the usefulness of the union, the nonmember is no doubt aware that his grievance against management may some day be the last to be acted upon if he persists indefinitely in staying out of the union.[21]

Finally, many national unions draw some strength from federation, that is from the fact that their members belong to small union locals, and thus at one stage have the advantages of the small group. The small groups, in turn, can be held in the national union through noncollective benefits provided to the locals by the national union. The national may provide a staff of experts upon which the local unions may draw, and may offer the locals what might perhaps be called 'strike insurance' in the form of a centrally administered strike fund. The national may also provide a noncollective benefit to some members directly by arranging for members of a local union who migrate to another community to get access to employment and membership in the local branch of the union in the new community.

With the growth of large-scale industry and the penetration of unions into large manufacturing enterprises in recent times, the small local that was once a major source of strength is becoming less important. Now many union members belong to locals with over a thousand members — to locals so large they are no longer small groups. Moreover the national unions are taking over the functions that union locals once performed.[22] Ordinarily no union local with thousands, or perhaps even hundreds, of members can be an effective social unit. A detailed empirical study of some modern union locals had this finding:

A few unions try to provide a full recreational program for their members as well as protection at work. However, the locals we observed found it impractical to compete with the established social activities in the community. To be sure, a picnic for the entire family in the summer and a dance in the winter will be successful, particularly if the local itself foots a large part of the bill. In fact it was not unusual to observe a union appropriating 10 per cent of its treasury for a social affair 'so that the members will feel they're getting something for their dues.' Parties for the children at Christmas are also popular, but this was the extent of such social activities.[23]

Thus it appears that in many unions (though certainly not all) in the present day, not much strength can be gained from constituent small groups, since even the local units are sometimes large, and with the growth of the average local a union may also not be able to support itself any longer by providing social benefits.

Probably also the growth of social security and unemployment insurance, sponsored by government, and the proliferation of private insurance companies have made union insurance schemes much less useful for attracting members than they once were. This sort of selective incentive could in any case be provided only in unions with very good business judgment, and it seems that only a few American unions have survived by this means. The noncollective benefits provided through union action on individual members' grievances have also been limited in recent decades by the legal requirement that a union must fairly represent all workers in a given group whether or not they belong to the union. In return for the right to 'exclusive jurisdiction' a union is legally required to represent every worker within its jurisdiction.[24] Though it is presumably impossible to ensure that the nonmember's grievances get represented with as much vigor as the member's grievances, this legal requirement must nonetheless reduce the incentive to join a union in order to get action on grievances.

In short, most unions can no longer draw a great deal of strength from small groups, and a union's noncollective benefits cannot usually be sufficient to bring in very many members. Smallness and noncollective benefits can probably now explain only the exceptional union. In most cases it is compulsory membership and coercive picket lines that are the source of the union's membership. Compulsory membership is now the general rule. In recent years roughly 95 per cent of the unionized workers have been covered by various types of 'union security' (or sometimes dues check-off) schemes that normally make it impossible, or at least in practice exceedingly difficult, for a worker to avoid being a member of the union under whose jurisdiction he falls.[25] There are admittedly 'right-to-work' laws in a number of states (almost all of them nonindustrial states) but these laws are seldom enforced.[26]

This general reliance on compulsory membership should be expected, for labor unions are typically large organizations that strive for benefits for large or latent groups. A labor union works primarily to get higher wages, better working conditions, legislation favorable to workers, and the like; these things by their very nature ordinarily cannot be withheld from any particular worker in the group represented by the union. Unions are for '*collective* bargaining,' not individual bargaining. It follows that most of the achievements of a union, even if they were more impressive than the staunchest unionist claims, could offer the rational worker no incentive to join; his individual efforts would not have a noticeable effect on the outcome, and whether he supported the union or not he would still get the benefits of its achievements. [. . .]

NOTES

1. G. D. H. Cole, *A Short History of the British Working Class Movement, 1789-1947*, new edn. (London: George Allen & Unwin, 1948) pp. 35-43.
2. See Lloyd Ulman, *The Rise of the National Trade Union* (Cambridge, Mass.: Harvard University Press, 1955); Robert Ozanne, 'The Labor History and Labor Theory of John R. Commons: An Evaluation in the Light of Recent Trends and Criticism,' in *Labor, Management, and Social Policy*, ed. Gerald G. Somers (Madison: University of Wisconsin Press, 1963), pp. 25-46; Norman J. Ware, *The Labor Movement in the United States, 1860-95* (New York: D. Appleton, 1929); Richard A. Lester, *Economics of Labor*, 2nd edn. (New York: Macmillan, 1964), pp. 55-116.
3. Foster Rhea Dulles, *Labor in America: A History* (New York: Thomas Y. Crowell, 1949), p. 23. G. D. H. Cole points out that the early English unions often met in inns or pubs, which suggests a significant social aspect. See his *Working Class Movements*, pp. 35 and 174.
4. Ulman, *passim*; Lloyd G. Reynolds, *Labor Economics and Labor Relations*, 3rd edn. (Englewood Cliffs, N.J.: Prentice-Hall, 1959), pp. 140-2.
5. Sidney and Beatrice Webb, *Industrial Democracy* (London: Longmans, Green, 1902), pp. 214-15. John Head has called my attention to the fact that some of the English classical economists, presumably observing the difficulties of early English trade unions, recognized that unions needed compulsion, or at least powerful social sanctions, to perform their functions. See John Stuart Mill, *Principles of Political Economy*, Book V, ·chap. xi, section 12, and Henry Sidgwick, *The Principles of Political Economy* (London: Macmillan, 1883), pp. 355-360.
6. Allan Flanders, 'Great Britain,' in *Comparative Labor Movements* ed. Walter Galenson (New York: Prentice-Hall, 1952), pp. 24-26; W. E. J. McCarthy, *The Closed Shop in Britain* (Oxford: Basil Blackwell, 1964).
7. Jerome Toner, *The Closed Shop* (Washington, D.C.: American Council on Public Affairs, 1942), pp. 1-93, and esp. p. 60. Toner points out that the medieval guilds were essentially closed shops. The closed-shop practices of labor unions developed independently, however.
8. Ibid., p. 64.
9. F. T. Stockton, *The Closed Shop in American Trade Unions*, Johns Hopkins University, Studies in Historical and Political Science, series 29, no. 3 (Baltimore: Johns Hopkins Press, 1911), p. 23. See also John R. Commons and Associates, *History of Labour in the United States* (New York: Macmillan, 1946) I, 598.
10. Stockton, p. 68. For a different view about the prevalence of compulsory membership in the history of American unionism, see Philip D. Bradley, 'Freedom of the Individual

under Collectivized Labor Arrangements,' in *The Public Stake in Union Power* ed. Philip D. Bradley (Charlottesville: University of Virginia Press, 1959), pp. 153–6. But Bradley's curious, polemical essay shows such an unthinking bias against the closed shop, and such confused arguments, that there is no reason to give his conclusion any weight.

11. 'The threat of potential violence and intimidation through the device of the picket line are powerful factors – so powerful, in fact, that nowadays a firm rarely attempts any operations at all if a strike has been called, although it would be within its legal rights to do so. For all practical purposes the alternative of making a bargain with anyone other than the union has been removed.' Quotation from Edward H. Chamberlin, 'Can Union Power be Curbed?' *Atlantic Monthly* (June 1959), p. 49. See also Robert V. Bruce, *1877: Year of Violence* (Indianapolis: Bobbs-Merrill, 1959); Stewart H. Holbrook, *The Rocky Mountain Revolution* (New York: Henry Holt, 1956). For a vigorous polemic that includes lurid and interesting accounts of the bloodiest strikes, as seen from the far left, see Louis Adamic, *Dynamite: The Story of Class Violence in America*, rev. edn. (New York: Viking Press, 1934).

12. Herbert Harris, *American Labor* (New Haven, Conn.: Yale University Press, 1939), p. 228.

13. Daniel Bell, *The End of Ideology* (Glencoe, Ill.: Free Press, 1960), pp. 195–7. In *Atchison, T. & S. F. Ry. v. Gee*, 139 Fed. 584 (C.C.S.D Iowa, 1905), the court stated: 'There is and can be no such thing as peaceful picketing, any more than there can be chaste vulgarity, or peaceful mobbing, or lawful lynching. When men want to converse or persuade, they do not organize a picket line.' This is an extreme view – the Supreme Court has since legalized peaceful picketing – but one that has an element of truth in it, especially for the days before labor legislation allowed unions to organize a factory merely by winning a representation election. See also Georges Sorel, *Reflections on Violence*, trans. T. E. Hulme (New York: B. W. Huebsch, n.d.), esp. pp. 43 and 289.

14. Bell, pp. 195–7.

15. Henry George, *The Conditions of Labor: An Open Letter to Pope Leo XIII* (New York: United States Book Co., 1891), p. 86.

16. See Neil W. Chamberlain, 'The Problem of Union Security,' *Proceedings of the Academy of Political Science*, XXVI (May 1954), 1–7, which was also published by the Academy of Political Science as a booklet edited by Dumas Malone and entitled *The Right to Work*.

17. Cole, *Working Class Movement*, p. 173.

18. Toner, pp. 93–114. See also J. Douglas Brown, 'The History and Problems of Collective Bargaining by Railway Maintenance of Way Employees,' unpub. diss., Princeton University, 1927, pp. 36–8, 69–70, 222.

19. T. P. Whelan, 'The Open Shop Crusade,' *Locomotive Engineers' Journal* LVI (1922), p. 44.

20. *The House of Labor*, ed. J. B. S. Hardman and Maurice F. Neufeld (New York: Prentice-Hall, 1951) pp. 276–319.

21. Leonard R. Sayles and George Strauss, *The Local Union* (New York: Harper, 1953), pp. 27–80; George Rose, 'The Processing of Grievances,' *Virginia Labor Review* XXXVIII (April 1952), 285–314; Labor and Industrial Relations Center, Michigan State University, *The Grievance Process* (1956). For quotations from conversations with union members who felt that nonmembers' 'gripes' or grievances 'won't have any backing,' see Joel Seidman, Jack London, and Bernard Karsh, 'Why Workers Join Unions,' *Annals of the American Academy of Political and Social Science* CCLXXIV (March 1951), 83, and also McCarthy (note 6, above), p. 93.

22. Albert Rees, *The Economics of Trade Unions* (Chicago: University of Chicago Press, 1962), pp. 4–7; Reynolds (note 4, above), pp. 40–3.

23. Sayles and Strauss, p. 11.

24. For an interesting explanation of this requirement see N. W. Chamberlain, 'Problem of Union Security,' and also Summer H. Slichter, *The Challenge of Industrial Relations* (Ithaca, N.Y.: Cornell University Press, 1947), pp. 8–14.

25. Orme W. Phelps, *Union Security* (Los Angeles: Institute of Industrial Relations, University of California, 1953) p. 50; Toner, p. 91; Philip D. Bradley in *Public Stake*

in Union Power, pp. 143 ff., and the same author's *Involuntary Participation in Union-ism* (Washington, D.C.: American Enterprise Association, Inc., 1956); Reynolds, p. 202; E. Wight Bakke, Clark Kerr, and Charles W. Anrod, *Unions, Management, and the Public*, 2nd edn. (New York: Harcourt, Brace, & World, 1960), pp. 56–111. On the great degree of compulsion existing even when there is no closed or union shop, see Seidman, London, and Karsh. 'Why Workers Join Unions,' pp. 75–84, especially the sections entitled 'Joining Despite Opposition,' 'Dues Inspection Line,' and 'Forcing Nonmembers to Join.'
26. Richard A. Lester, *As Unions Mature* (Princeton, N.J.: Princeton University Press, 1958), p. 145.

3.2 Monopoly and Competitive Unionism*
[. . .]

The first half of this chapter applies competitive theory to unionism; the second half, monopoly theory. In this sense the first half of the chapter may be said to contain a theory of the 'competitive union'; the second half, a theory of the 'monopoly union.' The competitive union and the monopoly union, how-ever, are ideal types used for purposes of analysis rather than mutually exclusive descriptive categories for the classification of real unions. Throughout the chapter I use these analytical constructs to classify the *data* of unionism, not *unions*.

Let me illustrate. Competitive unionism, as we shall see, produces no real wage effects; monopoly unionism, on the other hand, does produce such effects though in particular cases they may be imperceptible. Now suppose that one of the implications of competitive unionism is that union dues will be equal to zero, while the corresponding implication of monopoly unionism is that union dues will tend to be greater, the greater a union's impact on real wages. Theory thus would point to union dues as likely to be a useful indicator of relative real wage effects of unionism.

In view of the common assertion that the purpose of unionism is 'to take competition out of the supply side of the labor market,' it may seem strange to think of unionism as conceivably having some aspects that may be quite com-patible with competitive theory. Students of industrial relations tell us, however, that unionism often provides a set of rules and procedures for employee-employer relations (a 'system of industrial jurisprudence'), opportunities for social relations among employees, a way of life for the worker at his place of work, that are substitutes for those offered in non-union employments. We have never viewed 'labor relations' in non-union plants as something which by its very nature was incompatible with competitive theory. In the same way we need not view 'collective bargaining' as having no aspects consistent with competitive theory.

*From H. Gregg Lewis, 'Competitive and Monopoly Unionism', in Philip D. Bradley (ed.), *The Public Stake in Union Power* (Charlottesville: University of Virginia Press, 1959).

In order to isolate the effects of competitive unionism, assume that unions have no monopoly power. In other words, treat unionism simply as a technique by which a distinct set of non-pecuniary aspects of employment, a substitute for the set in non-union firms, is produced in a competitive labor market. To begin with I shall use a simple model that makes the assumptions that:

1. Unionism produces non-pecuniary conditions of employment — call them 'collective bargaining' — the same in kind and amount from one union employment to another and the absence of unionism produces conditions — call them 'individual bargaining' — homogenous in the same sense from one non-union employment to another. For both employers and employees there are only two 'industries': union which produces collective bargaining and non-union which produces individual bargaining.

2. Collective bargaining costs the same to produce in real terms as individual bargaining and neither enters the production functions for other outputs produced by union and non-union firms.

3. Employees sell labor services that are perfect substitutes for each other; each employee supplies a fixed quantity of labor services, the same for all employees; and each employer demands a fixed quantity of labor services, the same for all employers.

The problem is to find the relative *money* wage which will compensate employees and employers for any net non-pecuniary advantages or disadvantages of collective bargaining relative to individual bargaining and the distribution of employment between union and non-union firms. This problem is essentially the same as one treated by Gary S. Becker in his *The Economics of Discrimination*[1] and I refer you to Becker's work for a full statement of the framework for analyzing non-pecuniary aspects of labor markets.

Consider first the relative supply of labor to the union industry. Let k measure an individual employee's relative tastes for collective bargaining in the following manner:

If W is the market ratio of money wages in union firms to money wages in non-union firms, the individual employee will act as though the market *real* wage ratio were kW, where k is a positive number that is larger, the greater the employee's preference for collective bargaining relative to individual bargaining.

The employee will supply his labor services to the industry with the larger real wage; thus he will supply his labor to the union industry only if kW is not less than unity — that is, only if W is not less than $1/k$. Thus $1/k$ is his minimum relative money supply price of labor to the union industry.

Employees to some extent will have different tastes for collective bargaining. Thus for some, probably few, the minimum supply price will be substantially less than unity, say 0.9 or less. These individuals will be willing to sacrifice money wages ten per cent or more higher in non-union firms than in union in order to enjoy collective bargaining. There will be others, also few, whose minimum supply prices may be quite high, 1.1 or more, who would have to be paid wages in union firms ten per cent or more higher than in non-union firms to compensate them for their relative distaste for collective bargaining.

The market relative supply curve of labor to union firms is now easily constructed. Calculate the fraction s(W) of all employees whose 1/k is less than or equal to any specified relative money wage, W. This fraction is the relative supply of labor to union firms at the wage W. If tastes differ, s(W) will be greater, the greater is W. The curve SS in the diagram below shows for each W, the corresponding fraction s(W) of labor services supplied to union firms. It is thus the relative supply curve of labor to the union industry.

The relative demand curve for labor in the union industry can be developed in much the same way. Let k_e measure an employer's tastes for collective bargaining relative to individual bargaining as follows:

He acts as though the real wage cost 'per hour' of union labor relative to non-union labor is $k_e W$ where k_e is a positive number that is *smaller* (not *larger*, as for employees) the greater his preference for collective bargaining relative to individual bargaining.

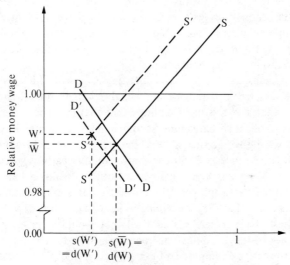

Ratio of union employment to total employment

FIG. 3.2

He will choose to demand union labor — that is, to be a union employer, only if the real wage cost of union labor does not exceed that of non-union labor; that is, he will demand union labor only if $k_e W$ does not exceed unity. Thus $1/k_e$ is his maximum relative money demand price for union labor. The maximum demand prices for some employers, surely a small fraction, may be quite high, 1.1 or more. These employers are willing to buy union labor services even though it may cost them ten per cent (or more) more than non-union labor because they very much prefer collective bargaining relative to individual bargaining. There will be other employers whose maximum demand prices for union labor will be quite low, 0.9 or less. These will choose to be union employers only if they are compensated for their relative distaste for collective bargaining by a money wage for union labor that is ten per cent or more below that of non-union labor.

The fraction of employers, $d(W)$, whose maximum demand prices, $1/k_e$, exceed a specified relative money wage, W, is the relative demand for union labor at the relative wage W. If employers' tastes differ, the relative quantity of labor demanded, $d(W)$, falls as the relative money wage, W, rises. The relative demand curve for labor in the union industry is the curve DD in Fig. 3.2.

Market equilibrium is at the point of intersection of the relative demand curve and the relative supply curve. The equilibrium value of W is $\overline{W}$, with the fraction $s(\overline{W}) = d(\overline{W})$ of employees and employers in the Union industry.

The difference $(1 - \overline{W})$ is the 'equalizing differential' in money wages. If this differential is positive, it measures the percentage excess of non-union over union money wages; if it is negative, its numerical value measures the percentage excess of union money wages over non-union. Whatever its value, it is the differential in money wages that compensates employees and employers at the margin for any net non-pecuniary advantages or disadvantages of collective bargaining relative to individual bargaining.

Is a $\overline{W}$ as large as, say, 1.05 – an equalizing excess of union over non-union money wages as large as five per cent – likely? I think not. It should be clear from Fig. 3.2 that a $\overline{W}$ this high implies either that (a) at least half of the employees dislike collective bargaining so much relative to individual bargaining that they are willing to sacrifice at least five per cent of the income they could earn in union firms (at least $150 per year at union yearly wages of $3,000) in order to avoid being employed in the collective bargaining industry, or that (b) at least half of the employers like collective bargaining so much relative to individual bargaining that they are willing to incur wage costs as union employers that are at least five per cent higher than they would incur as non-union employers. Neither of these implications seems plausible to me as a general characterization of the tastes of employees or employers in the United States.

Similarly a $\overline{W}$ as low as 0.95 – an equalizing excess of non-union over union money wages as high as five per cent – implies either that (a) at least half of the employees like collective bargaining so much relative to individual bargaining that they are willing to sacrifice at least five per cent of the money income they could earn in non-union employments in order to enjoy collective bargaining or (b) that at least half of the employers dislike competitive – not monopoly – unionism so much that they are willing to incur wage costs at least five per cent higher as non-union firms than as union in order to avoid collective bargaining. These also seem to me to be implausible general characterizations of the tastes of employers and employees. On the other hand, it seems quite possible to me that $\overline{W}$ might be one or two per cent below unity, and this seems more reasonable to me than any figure above unity. [. . .]

Private monopolizing may be thought of as a trade, employing both labor and other resources, in which the practitioners — the residual income recipients — earn income by driving the demand price for a commodity or productive service above its supply price. Thus a successful labor monopolist will cause the demand price of labor — the wage rate — to rise along the demand curve for the labor 'covered' by the monopoly to a level above that of a competitive unionism. This is the direct relative wage impact of the labor monopoly. Since the demand curve for labor covered by a successful monopolist will be negatively inclined, the rise in the wage rate will cause employment in the covered field to fall below its competitive level. This is the direct relative employment effect of the monopoly.

The rise in the wage rate for covered labor also will cause the demand schedules for substitutes of the covered labor to rise and those for complements to fall. Therefore, 'employment' of substitutes will tend to rise, of complements to fall. These are the indirect employment effects. If the supply schedules of the substitutes and complements are infinitely elastic, there will be no changes in their prices, but if the supply schedules are positively inclined, prices of substitutes will rise, prices of complements will fall. These are the indirect relative price effects.

Will there be any tendency for the direct relative wage effects of the same monopolist at different times or among different monopolists at the same time to be correlated with the direct and indirect relative employment effects? In one important sense the answer is surely 'yes,' for *un*successful monopolists will cause neither wage nor employment effects. But what about the correlation for successful monopolists?

Refer to Fig. 3.3. The curve DD is the demand curve, MR the corresponding marginal revenue curve, and pS the supply curve of labor in the covered area. In the absence of monopoly the wage rate would be Op and employment would be Ox. If monopolizing were a costless activity to the monopolist, he would drive the wage rate to Op′ and employment to Ox′. For some problems it does no harm to assume that monopolizing is costless. But for others, including some discussed in this chapter, it is essential to assume that monopolizing is an expensive business in which the costs of driving the wage rate above Op may in some cases increase rapidly as the wage rate increases.

The curve AP in Fig. 3.3 is the sum of the supply price, Op, and the costs of monopolizing per unit of employment; the curve NP is the corresponding marginal cost curve. The monopolist will maximize his net receipts by driving the wage rate to Op_m, employment thus to Ox_m, the employment level at which his marginal costs equal his marginal receipts.[2] The monopolist's net revenue is $GF \times Ox_m$.[...]

Where does the union fit into this scheme? For purposes of analysis I make two alternative extreme assumptions about the residual income recipients of monopoly unionism. Consider first the 'boss-dominated' union, one that behaves as though the residual income recipients of the monopoly gains were the union 'bosses.' Employees in the field covered by the monopoly, though they may be

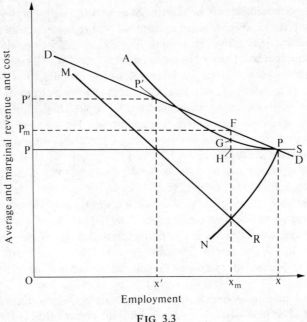

FIG 3.3

'members' of the union, are simply hired hands who are paid competitive wages by the bosses for the monopolizing services such as striking and picketing they perform. Ideally, in such a union there would be a check-off of union 'dues' for all covered employees amounting (per unit of employment) to GF plus the fraction of HG that is not 'wages' paid to covered employees for services performed for the union. Given such a check-off, the closed shop and similar arrangements would be superfluous. A complete check-off may be more costly, however, than to require that all covered employees be members of the union and to collect the dues directly from the members. Thus the closed shop and like devices are simply substitutes for the check-off in the boss-dominated union. In either case, the device for rationing employment in the covered area is the dues charge.

Notice that in the boss-dominated union, though the demand price of labor is above the supply price if the union is successful, no part of the difference goes to covered employees by virtue of their being covered employees. Thus in the presence of the boss-dominated union there will be no queuing up of persons eager to become covered employees in order to receive wages higher than in alternative employments.

Now consider the 'employee-dominated' union. In such a union, employment in the covered area is the necessary and sufficient condition for receiving the monopoly gains (dues) that in the boss-dominated union go to the bosses. (In the employee-dominated union, the union officers may be viewed simply as employees of the union receiving a competitive wage for the monopolizing services they perform.) The employee-dominated union, unlike the boss-dominated union, will face a queueing up of persons eager for covered employment in order to partake of the monopoly gains and *must* have procedures for deciding which of these persons will be admitted to employment. Furthermore, the employee-monopolizers must have arrangements insuring that the employees who benefit from the monopolizing pay 'dues' covering the costs (per unit of employment), HG, of monopolizing. In addition, if within the covered area some employment opportunities offer greater monopoly gains than others, there must be rules for deciding who is to get the plums.

The list of rules and procedures for solving these problems in the variety in which they appear in the real world is a very long one, including much of what are often viewed as 'bad' or 'monopolistic' practices: the closed or union shop, union hiring halls, state or local licensing, 'proficiency' examinations, seniority rules, many of the so-called 'make-work,' 'share-work,' and 'featherbedding' practices, and nepotistic and discriminatory rules specifying the race, sex, religion, kinship, etc., of those eligible for union membership.

The boss-dominated union uses price rationing methods, the employee-dominated union non-price rationing methods, to decide who is to be employed in the monopolized field. In general, price rationing is much the simpler of the two systems and offers greater opportunities for capitalizing the monopoly gains. It is reasonable to expect, therefore, that the members of the employee-dominated union at any given time would try to find ways of substituting price rationing for non-price rationing. Thus I would expect the members who play key roles in the rationing process to establish rules, *de facto* if not *de jure*, giving preferences in admission to the union to friends and relatives, and permitting the members to receive gifts in kind if not in money from applicants for membership in the union. Indeed, why should the transformation of an employee-dominated union into a boss-dominated union stop before it is complete?

The rationale for unionism in the eyes of the public is that it protects either the interests of labor or the health and safety of the public. The wage gains brought about by a successful boss-dominated union, however, do not go to covered employees. Furthermore, the public tends generally to be somewhat intolerant toward too handsome rewards for the protectors of its health and safety. The more closely a union comes to resemble the successful boss-dominated union, the more likely it is to be viewed as a 'racketeering' union and to be harassed by Congressional investigations, district attorneys, and disgruntled union members. Thus I would expect that, typically, monopoly unions would use *both* price rationing and non-price rationing methods.

The total of the dues, fees, taxes, and assessments per unit of employment levied by a union on covered employees cannot overestimate[3] but may underestimate the wage impact (HF in Fig. 3.3) of a monopoly union. If unions generally were the boss-dominated, price rationing variety, I would expect union dues, broadly measured, to be a first-rate guide to the differences in relative wage impact of different unions and of a given union over time. The greater the reliance a union places on non-price rationing methods, however, the greater the extent to which that union's dues underestimate its wage effect.

Fortunately, the amount of this bias can be at least crudely estimated from empirical data. The more a given union relies on non-price rationing, the larger the ratio of unaccepted to accepted applicants for membership in the union. Data on union dues together with data on this ratio, therefore, may provide quite good indexes of relative wage impact.

On the other hand, the non-price rationing rules and procedures will tend to be used both by unions that are trying to be monopolists but not succeeding very well and by quite successful monopoly unions. Hence they will have little usefulness as indicators of the relative wage effects of unionism. [. . .]

NOTES

1. Chicago, 1957.
2. In Fig. 3.3 marginal costs NP are positive at all levels of employment. This is not necessary, however; both marginal costs and marginal revenue may be negative at some levels of employment and even may be equal where both are negative. Thus the monopoly equilibrium point, F, may be one at which the demand curve is inelastic.

   Notice also that if monopolizing costs rise rapidly enough as wages are increased above Op, the average cost curve AP may lie entirely above the demand curve. Thus monopolizing may fail to occur even in situations in which the demand curve is not highly elastic in the neighborhood of the point P.
3. This assumes a conclusion reached earlier: that competitive unions generally will charge negligible dues.

3.3 The Theory of Wage Bargaining*

1. INTRODUCTION: INTENTION

The 'theory of wages' is dealt with at some length in the textbooks, although the relevance of this theory to the real world is, it must be admitted, purely tangential. Usually we are treated first to a full-dress exposition of the marginal productivity theory of distribution erected on the stern assumptions of perfect competition. In due course the analysis is developed to take account of imperfect competition, first in the product market, then in the labour market, and finally taken together: this also at length. Here analysis normally breaks off. The fact that in the real world the commonest relationship between employers and employed approximates to that of bilateral monopoly is reserved for mention, if it is mentioned at all, among the footnotes. Whenever a more ambitious treatment is essayed, we are likely to find analysis soon abandoned in the sands of conglomerate description.[1]

*From R. O. Hieser, 'Wage Determination with Bilateral Monopoly in the Labour Market: a theoretical treatment', *Economic Record*, Vol. 46, 1970.

It is the purpose of this paper to extend analysis into this area.[2] For simplicity, we shall assume that there is a situation of pure bilateral monopoly, with a pure monopolist seller of a single commodity on the one side, a trade union with unitary control over the labour supply on the other.

Our aim will not be a 'realistic' model in the sense of describing the factors which motivate or underwrite (in defence) employer or union, and certainly not what they say motivates them. Clearly, much on the surface and in the overt attitudes of the two parties will be purely rhetorical.[3] Rather, what we have to attempt is to distil from their confrontation situation the essence of the *economic* factors which underlies their respective postures. Once these are determined, much in the parties' actions and attitudes may be explained. In short, we seek an *explanation* of their behaviour, not merely a description of it. [...]

It would, of course, be untrue to say that analytical studies of the problem of bilateral monopoly in the labour market have not been undertaken before. Nevertheless, the literature of the subject is notoriously sparse, and even less convincing. Broadly speaking, there appear to be two main consensi.

In the first place, there are those who argue that the situation is fundamentally indeterminate, with the implication of ever-present possibility of deadlock. At least in the Anglo-Saxon tradition, Edgeworth appears to be the progenitor of this position. He concluded that: 'Contract without competition is indeterminate.'[4] According to Shackle this answer 'absolved economists from trying to explain how in bilateral monopoly a price is ever fixed.'[5] Certainly, Edgeworth was followed by Marshall and Pigou.[6]

Generally speaking, those who argue indeterminacy must hold that other than a purely economic calculus is required to define an 'equilibrium'. Appeal must be had to extra-economic considerations such as psychological propensities, custom, and perhaps Christian togetherness to provide the inertia requisite to stability.[7] This may well be the stuff for Moral Rearmament; but it hardly constitutes a foundation for economic analysis.[8]

One of the chief difficulties of the basic-indeterminacy school is that in the real world the general experience is, in fact, achievement of comparatively stable, determinate positions; and it is hard to believe that these positions are underpinned only by incidental, non-maximizing factors or, worse, derive from pure hit and miss. Deadlock, except in the very shortest term, is infrequent, so much so that when it does occur it is news — strike or lockout news.

Again, it seems to me that this first school of thought is too much influenced by the theory and practice of bilateral monopoly as it is seen to function in the commodity market. The labour market differs from the commodity market in two important respects.

First, in the exchange of commodities, buyer and seller stand in a direct antithetical relationship. Their interests are equal and opposite: the seller's gain is the buyer's loss, and vice versa. But in the labour market this is not altogether so. Indeed, there is a significant area within which a monopoly buyer of labour and the seller of labour have a common interest, namely in extracting the largest divisible surplus from the consumer.

Secondly, commodities are generally mobile in space and, to lesser degree, in time. Deadlock in one market may be countered by transfer to a different market. However, this alternative is not normally applicable in the labour market. Also, it is clear that labour cannot be held over as stocks. Nor is it possible for an employer who has a large fixed capital commitment to a particular place and time to liquidate his position readily. In the not very long run, deadlock will not be acceptable to either side.

The fact is that deadlock involves both sides in *costs* of an order quite different from a commodity market. (Unused·labour is lost completely; unsold commodities lose only their carrying costs.) In this matter, as in the exploitation of consumers, labour and capital have a *joint* interest; and these two common factors, it is suggested, lend a greater degree of determinateness and stability to the wage settlement than one might expect from a look at analogous situations in commodity markets.

The second school of thought, which includes the Marxists incidentally, would assert a (determinate) wage outcome representing a balance struck by the relative bargaining powers of the two parties.

The 'bargaining' power' thesis has a commonsense appeal; and it clearly reflects something significant about the real world. The difficulty with this theory is that, until we are offered an independent measure of bargaining power, the thesis is analytically meaningless. Indeed, it often seems that bargaining power is taken as something given in the situation, substantially exogenous, and therefore largely of non-economic content. Bargaining power is made to depend on such factors as the common loyalty of workers, the quality of union leadership, the enlightenment of management, and such like.

However, unless we do define an independent (economic) measure of bargaining power, the analysis becomes quite circular. 'High' wages become the result of 'strong' bargaining power on the part of the union, 'low' wages the result of 'weak' bargaining power. Contrariwise, 'strong' bargaining power is indicated by 'high' wages, 'weak' bargaining power by low' wages. Clearly, there is no explanation here. A break-out from this vicious circle is the primary purpose of this essay.

We have promised a highly abstract model, with the measurable, maximizing elements as its kernel. This does not imply that extra-economic (non-maximizing) factors — for example, corruption of union officials, security-preference of managements, even violence — do not, in certain circumstances, play an important role in the real world. However, what we seek is a common denominator, general to all bilateral confrontations between labour and capital: we seek an armature about which particular cases of the real world can be moulded.

Before launching into our model, it is first necessary to consider certain special conditions which face a trade union intent on maximization.

2. TRADE UNIONS AND MAXIMIZATION

Our approach leads us immediately to two, not unrelated, problems associated with maximization from a trade union point of view.

In the first place, maximization for a trade union, unlike maximization for the firm, is not a unique criterion. More accurately, certain difficulties attend the idea. A firm, when it maximizes its profits which are then distributed among partners or shareholders according to some predetermined formula, also automatically maximizes the incomes of its individual members. With a trade union, however, incomes accrue directly to individuals, not to the collective. An increase in wage rates may represent higher incomes for some workers, zero incomes for others.

The problem arises, of course, out of the reciprocal relationship between wage rates and employment. Although the strength of this relationship is commonly exaggerated, we must, and a trade union must, take account of it. There may be a clash, then, between maximizing wage rates and maximizing the wage bill (which is equivalent to maximizing the average wage rate of the [assumed] fixed membership of the union). However, divergence of the two criteria only occurs when the demand for labour becomes elastic, i.e., when a further increase in the wage rate will result in a reduction in total wages received. Up to this point, higher wage rates and higher wage bill move in consonance as far as maximization is concerned. We therefore treat this point as an upper limit to wage demands. This means in effect that, up to this limit, pressure to increase the wage rate also serves to maximize the total wage bill. Within this range, the union's objective is unambiguous.

The second way in which a trade union's position is different from that of the firm resides in the fact that, under ordinary circumstances, a trade union cannot pursue maximization by way of marginal adjustment. An employer may employ a few more men or a few less: a trade union cannot normally withdraw labour, except as a whole. It either accepts an offered rate of pay or it rejects it. If it accepts, it will supply all available labour at that price; if it rejects, it will supply no labour at all. (The idea of a continuous, upward-sloping curve for labour is, in general, quite unrealistic!)

In the last analysis, the final sanction of a trade union lies in its ability to exercise control over the *total* labour supply. Hence, in what follows, we shall consider the ordinary strike (withholding of the total labour supply) as the ultimate element of a trade union's bargaining power. In the last resort, when the chips are down, it will be the union's ability to sustain a total withdrawal of labour which will set the limit on its bargaining power.[9] Of course, it is not necessary that actual strike action be invoked it will be sufficient that the power be there and calculable.

This is not to say that a union cannot, within this limit, manoeuvre tactically, marginally, in order to bring pressure on an employer or to underline its ultimate power. For example, it may invoke lightning, disruptive strikes, apply overtime

bans, or it may restrict output by work-to-rule methods, and so on. Yet it remains basically true that total withdrawal of labour is the ultimate weapon; and
this is the assumption we make.[10]

A final preliminary point. We shall use the term 'wage' to embrace the
Marshallian notion of 'net advantages', that is, to include adjustment for
working hours, leave and sickness provisions, pension rights, work intensity,
and the like.

3. STATIC MODEL: BASIC ASSUMPTIONS

In establishing our static model, we make explicit two sets of assumptions.
There are first the substantive assumptions which provide a static framework
for this part of the analysis. There are also certain expository assumptions which
have a negligible effect upon the outcome of the argument but greatly facilitate
its presentation.

(a) *Substantive Assumptions*

1. The demand curve facing the monopolist is given.
2. The technical production function is given.
3. There is a wage at which qualified 'free' labour would offer; this we call
the *opportunity* wage. Looking at it the other way round, it is the next best
wage which members of our particular work force can command.
4. The trade union has a closed shop; and membership of the union is given.

(b) *Expository Assumptions*

1. The demand curve is linear over the relevant range; or what amounts to
the same thing, we take arc elasticity of demand as an approximation to point
elasticity over that range.
2. The prime cost curve is horizontal over the relevant interval, so that
average prime cost and marginal cost coincide over that interval. (This particular
assumption is introduced so that a common unit may be selected for both output and employment, thus enabling us to use a single output/employment axis
on the one diagram.)
3. Our monopolist is fully integrated, i.e., he produces all his own raw
materials, so that variable costs are simply wage costs. (It is always open to us
to deduct raw materials from both demand and cost curves, but this particular
assumption exempts us from that irksome arithmetic and the dual terminology
which would be involved.)

4. AREA OF THE BARGAIN

Having set down our assumptions, we are now in a position to delineate what
we shall call the *area of the bargain*. This will define the area within which the
ultimate bargain must lie, whatever the relative bargaining strengths of the two
parties.

We have a demand curve for the monopolist, *DD'*; and from this we may derive a marginal revenue curve, *DR*. Also, we have an initial cost curve, *CC'*, determined by the opportunity wage, W_0. We choose a unit of output representing the output per man in the selected accounting period — say, 1,000 mousetraps per man per week. Then, units of output and units of employment have a one-for-one correspondence along the *X*-axis. From Figure 3.4, it is clear that, without union intervention, the monopolist would maximize his position where $DR = CC'$, at *E*, with an output/employment of Q_0.

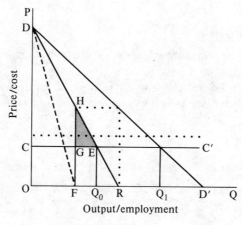

FIG. 3.4

At a glance it is obvious that any final bargain between the parties must lie within the triangle *DEC*. However, we may delimit this further. Draw *DF* such that $OF = FR$, and raise the perpendicular *FGH*. At the point *H* on *DR*, the elasticity of the marginal revenue curve, η, will be equal to unity. Any advance of the wage rate beyond the point *H* would diminish the total wage payout, and this would conflict with our maximizing assumptions. Hence, the area within which the wage bargain must fall is reduced to the triangle *HEG*.

Furthermore, any bargain struck within *HEG* may be extrapolated to the right to *HE*, since any such move to the right would benefit *both* parties. Therefor, in the end we have only to consider agreements along the segment *HE*.

Moreover, it may be shown that $\eta = \frac{1}{2}(\epsilon - 1)$, where ϵ is elasticity of demand. Then, when $\eta = 1$, at *H*, $\epsilon = 3$. Also, since

$$\frac{W}{P} = \frac{\epsilon - 1}{\epsilon} = \frac{2}{3}$$

we may state our first definitive result.

THEOREM I: In a static situation, irrespective of the degree of capitalization or of the comparative bargaining strengths of the two parties, the maximum wage bill cannot exceed two-thirds of value added.[11]

We must now look more closely at the relative bargaining power of the two parties. In substance, this relativity is to be found in the balancing of gains and losses by both sides in the stances of resistance or concession, respectively.[12]

5. WORKERS' ENDURANCE FUNCTION

If a union is acting as a simple maximizing unit, it must, if and when it resorts to strike action, balance the cost of such action (to its members) against the possible gains which may flow from that action. We begin with the question of cost.

(a) *Cost of Strike Action*

We take W as the prevailing wage rate and Q as the obtaining level of employment (= output).

Then, in Figure 3.5 we relate the loss of wages, L, to the duration of a strike, s. In the first instance, we should expect this to be a linear relationship, loss of

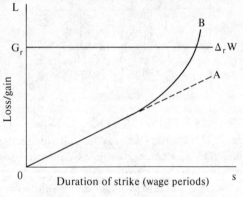

FIG. 3.5

wages being directly proportional to the length of the strike, as along OA. As a strike continues, however, the position of those involved must progressively worsen. Workers' savings dry up, strike funds tend to exhaustion, credit becomes increasingly difficult. All these factors may be best thought of as increasing the marginal utility of money, as workers' resources become more and more stretched. Hence, we may draw a curve OB describing workers' losses in real terms which we represent by

$$L = sQW + Q.U(s) \qquad (1)$$

where sQW is the loss in money terms and $Q.U(s)$ is a supplementary function representing the increasing marginal utility of that money loss as time proceeds. It is appropriate that we should make this function directly proportional with Q, since only those in employment will be affected by a stoppage of work. Then, $U(s)$ is an average-per-head function relating to those losing wages. After a certain point, one should expect OB to rise fairly sharply.

Now it is clear that there will be a whole family of OB curves, one corresponding to each particular wage, and it is unlikely that $U(s)$ will remain the same for all wage levels. It may increase or decrease as the wage level rises. For example, a higher wage may mean greater worker savings; or it may mean greater overheads such as rent or hire-purchase commitments. At any rate, strictly speaking we should re-write (1) as

$$L = sQW + Q.U(s, W). \tag{2}$$

Finally, it should be observed that $U(s, W)$ may be negative over a greater or lesser range: for instance (a) when, at a time of full employment, workers can take alternative jobs; or (b) when it may be anticipated that wages lost during a strike will be largely recouped by subsequent overtime.

(b) Gains from Wage Increase

Against these losses we must set off the potential gains. In general, of course, gains will not merely depend on the magnitude of any wage increase achieved. Account must be taken of any corresponding reduction in employment which may be associated with it. If G' represents net gains per wage-period, then[13]

$$G' = Q\Delta W - W\Delta Q$$

$$= Q\Delta W - Q\Delta W\left(\frac{W\Delta Q}{Q\Delta W}\right)$$

$$= Q\Delta W (1 - \eta) \tag{3}$$

where η is again the elasticity of the marginal revenue curve (assuming, as we do, that wage moves along the segment HE of Figure 3.4). It will be observed that, when η rises above 1, G' becomes negative, which is our argument of Section 4.

A wage increase represents a continuing sequence through time. Future gains must therefore be reduced to the present value if they are to be set off against current losses. The rate of discount applied will depend on a host of factors which will no doubt vary considerably from one situation to another. A similar difficulty arises in relation to the number of periods over which the sum is to be taken. (An analogous problem arises in deciding the number of periods through which profits should be projected when evaluating a business.) All that we can say is that the number of periods will depend on the overall length of time during which conditions are *expected* to remain static. We then write down total gains, G, accruing as the result of a given wage increase as

$$G = Q\Delta W(1 - \eta)V_m(j) \tag{4}$$

where $V_m(j)$ is the sum of unity over m periods, discounted at the rate j.

(c) Labour's Indifference Function

We are now in a position to equate workers' gains and losses, to give us a curve along which they will just break even. In other words, we will have an indifference curve the path of which may be taken as the locus of the union's sticking-points. The equation of this curve will be

$$sQW + Q.U(s, W) = Q \varDelta W(1 - \eta)V_m(j)$$

that is,
$$\varDelta W = \frac{sW + U(s, W)}{(1 - \eta)V_m(j)}. \tag{5}$$

Geometrically, this result may be reached by superimposing the G_r corresponding to each $\varDelta_r W$ on the ordinate of Figure 3.5 and reading off the points of intersection with OB.

Since $V_m(j)$ is a given constant in a particular situation, the curve described in (5) will, for a given W (and hence η) have the same general shape as OB of Figure 3.5. There will of course be a separate indifference curve in respect of each wage. As the wage (and η) increase, the curve moves to the left, with the slope rising (see Figure 3.6).

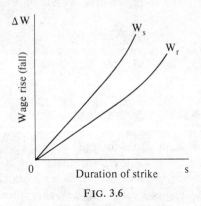

FIG. 3.6

In view of the fact that $\eta = \frac{1}{2}(\epsilon - 1)$, we may write (5) alternatively as
$$\varDelta W = \frac{sW + U(s, W)}{\frac{1}{2}(3 - \epsilon)V_m(j)}. \tag{6}$$

6. EMPLOYER'S RESISTANCE FUNCTION

On his side, the monopolist must match the loss of profits incurred by resistance (i.e., by involvement in a strike) against the extended loss of profits which would result from conceding various wage increases.

(a) *Loss of Profits from Strike*

At first sight, it might appear that the employer's loss from a strike, L_1, would be simply the profits lost during its currency, namely

$$sQ(P - W).$$

However, there will be some incidental losses to an employer associated with a strike which are likely to increase as the strike is extended. Two of these call for special attention.

First, an interruption of supplies to customers, or failure to meet contract deadlines, may involve the firm in substantial damage. The monopolist could even be faced with a permanent switch to substitutes. Generally, we may sum up the whole battery of possible injury of this kind as *loss of goodwill*. Secondly, a protracted strike may involve the firm in financial stringency, or liquidity crisis, as fixed expenditures are met while no revenue flows in.

Loss of goodwill and financial stress will clearly be increasing functions of the duration of the strike. We therefore add the supplementary function $Q.F(s, W)$ to represent these factors. Again, this function could turn out to be negative in the earlier stages of a strike since stocks may hold the line for some time. We have then

$$L_1 = sQ(P - W) + Q.F(s, W) \tag{7}$$

$$= sQW\left(\frac{P}{W} - 1\right) + Q.F(s, W)$$

$$= sQW\left(\frac{\epsilon}{\epsilon - 1} - 1\right) + Q.F(s, W)$$

$$= \frac{sQW}{\epsilon - 1} + Q.F(s, W). \tag{8}$$

(b) *Loss of Profits from Wage Increase*

The immediate loss of profit, L'_2, consequent on the granting of various wage increases is calculated in the Appendix:

$$L'_2 = Q \varDelta W.$$

This loss will of course be a continuing one, and we are again faced with the discounting of a future stream of payments. There is no reason to suppose that the 'telescopic faculty' of employers will be the same as that of workers. We therefore introduce $V_n(i)$ to represent the present value of a stream of unit payments over n periods, discounted at the rate i. Then we have

$$L_2 = Q \varDelta W.V_n(i). \tag{9}$$

(c) *Employer's Indifference Function*

Matching L_1 against L_2, we obtain an employer's break-even curve of the form

$$\frac{sQW}{\epsilon - 1} + Q.F(s, W) = Q\varDelta W.V_n(i)$$

that is,

$$W = \frac{1}{V_n(i)}\left[\frac{sW}{\epsilon - 1} + F(s, W)\right]. \tag{10}$$

7. 'PURE' CASE OF SIMPLE MONETARY GAINS AND LOSSES

To appreciate where we are going, it is worth pausing for a moment to investigate a very special situation. Let us assume that the 'telescopic faculties' of both parties are the same, i.e., that $V_m(j) = V_n(i)$; and let us also put aside for the moment the supplementary functions $U(s, W)$ and $F(S, W)$, i.e., assume that $U(s, W) = F(s, W) = 0$. We shall thus be concerned only with gains and losses in simple money terms.

Then, for a given wage (and hence given ϵ), both (6) and (10) become straight lines whose slopes are given by:

$$\frac{\partial(\varDelta W)}{\partial s} = \frac{W}{\frac{1}{2}(3 - \epsilon)} = \frac{W}{\epsilon - 1}. \tag{11}$$

These straight lines, OU (union indifference curve) and OE (employer resistance curve), are shown in Figure 3.7. It is clear that $1 < \epsilon < 3$; and as ϵ changes, OU

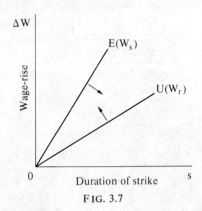

FIG. 3.7

and OE will change in the following manner: (i) as ϵ *increases* towards 3, the slope of OU will tend to that of the Y-axis, and the slope of OE will tend to $\frac{1}{2}W$; and (ii) as ϵ *falls* towards 1, the slope of OE will tend to that of the Y-axis, and the slope of OU will tend to W.

It will be seen then that the slopes of OU and OE move in opposite directions with changes in ϵ (and hence W). So long as OU lies to the right of OE, the union will always outlast the employer; and vice versa when *OE* lies to the right of *OU*. It becomes clear that pressure and counter-pressure from both sides will cease when *OU* coincides with *OE*, i.e., when

$$\tfrac{1}{2}(3 - \epsilon) = \epsilon - 1,$$

i.e., when
$$\epsilon = \frac{5}{3}.$$

THEOREM II: If there is no impediment to pursuit of a purely monetary maximum by both sides, and each side discounts the future at the same rate, then the break-even point between the two parties occurs when the elasticity of demand is 5/3.

8. STATIC EQUILIBRIUM

Our discussion in Section 7 gives us the clue to the conditions for equilibrium in the general case, i.e., when *OU* and *OE* may be presumed to be simple monotonic increasing functions but are not straight lines. In addition, it should be recognized explicitly that ϵ moves in the same direction as *W*. The slopes of the two functions move in opposite direction, because ϵ is in the one instance added and in the other subtracted. (Throughout we have followed the usual convention of taking ϵ itself in the positive sense.) As the wage (and ϵ) increases, *OU* moves to the left; *OE* moves to the right.

So long as *OU* is anywhere to the right of *OE*, the union can exert pressure for and (on our maximizing assumptions) secure a wage rise. This process will continue to the point where *OU* no longer stands to the right of *OE* at any point, i.e., to the point of tangency between the two curves (Figure 3.8). At this

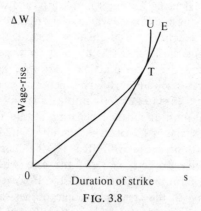

FIG. 3.8

point, union bargaining power in relation to employer's resistance will be exhausted. Of course, the progression to tangency need not be made in one jump but may occur as a succession of steps towards the final equilibrium.

The point of equilibrium occurs when the ordinates of OU and OE are equal, and their slopes are also equal. If we put $V_m(j)/V_n(i) = v$,[14] our conditions for static equilibrium are:

$$\frac{sW + U(s, W)}{\frac{1}{2}(3 - \epsilon)v} = \frac{sW}{\epsilon - 1} + F(s, W) \tag{12}$$

and

$$\frac{W + U(s, W)}{\frac{1}{2}(3 - \epsilon)v} = \frac{W}{\epsilon - 1} + F_s(s, W) \tag{13}$$

It is clear that, once the shapes of U and F are known, we may eliminate s and then solve for W, since v is given in the situation. In summary, we may write

$$W = \phi(\epsilon, v, U, F) \tag{14}$$

where v, U and F are given parameters of the situation and W varies with ϵ.

The dependence of W upon ϵ is complex. In the first place, elasticity of demand will determine the price which the monopolist can charge. Then, by virtue of the relationship $(P - W)/P = 1/\epsilon$, the proportion of wages as part of total revenue will vary directly with ϵ. Finally, the value of ϵ will determine, at one remove, the reciprocity of wage rise and disemployment.

A few further observations on this static solution are in order. First, the reason why an equilibrium may be achieved with OE to the right of OU, but not vice versa, is that the employer is balancing *two losses*, one against the other. He will never want to allow a higher W or an increase in the duration of a strike, since he will incur further losses on either account. He is *pushed* to the point T (Figure 3.8); he will not want to go beyond it of his own accord. On the other hand, the union is balancing a *gain* against a *loss*; and will be in a position to realize some gain so long as OU is anywhere to the right of OE.

Secondly, it will not have passed unnoticed that neither the given membership of the union nor the level of the opportunity wage figures as an explicit factor in determining the wage outcome. However, both have an indirect influence. In the first case, although some men may be rendered unemployed and thenceforth cease to enter directly into calculation, the magnitude of this unemployed element must affect the 'solidarity' of total union membership and hence influence the shape of U. Likewise, the differential between the attained wage and the opportunity wage will affect (a) the pressure for entry into the industry from outside workers, and (b) the ease with which disemployed members will drop out of the particular industry. However, these two considerations properly belong to the area of dynamics rather than to a static model. What the opportunity wage does do in a static situation is to put a floor under the wage which must be paid by the monopolist: it sets a limit to his monopsonistic power.

Finally, it would be unrealistic to make no mention of a basic factor which we eliminated by virtue of our maximizing assumptions. When we undertook to treat the union as a maximizing entity, we implicitly assumed that it could always act in a cohesive way. This clearly presupposes a high degree of unity between members of the union. The *de facto* degree of unity within a union will obviously have a significant influence on the shape of *OU*.

9. DYNAMIC FACTORS

When we consider bilateral wage determination as a dynamic process, we must allow ϵ, v, U and F to vary with time. Formally, the path of the dynamic system will be traced by the simultaneous equations:

$$\frac{sW + U(s, W, t)}{\frac{1}{2}[3 - \epsilon(t)]v(t)} = \frac{sW}{\epsilon(t) - 1} + F(s, W, t) \tag{15}$$

$$\frac{W + U(s, W, t)}{\frac{1}{2}[3 - \epsilon(t)]v(t)} = \frac{W}{\epsilon(t) - 1} + F(s, W, t). \tag{16}$$

We shall now need to know how ϵ, v, U and F behave over time, t.

At one time or another, it has been argued that an increase of demand (say) will increase the elasticity of demand, will decrease it, or will *ceteris paribus* result in an iso-elastic shift of the demand curve. It would require an article in itself to investigate this question. First, the passage of time and increase in demand may result in the development of substitutes which would have the effect of increasing elasticity of demand facing the monopolist. Also, such an increase may pave the way for new entrants (actual or potential) into the field, and this again would tend to increase the value of elasticity of demand. On the other hand, an increase in demand may serve to entrench further the monopolist, when economies of scale are running strongly. Decrease in demand over time would, of course, tend in the opposite direction. Secondly, in so far as an increase in demand is accompanied by a general, all-round increase in *per capita* incomes, this may make buyers less 'choosy' and thereby diminish elasticity of demand.

Little can be said, *a priori*, about the behaviour of v over time. In general, it is probable that the union has a greater 'telescopic range' than its individual members. As unions become better organized and more businesslike, and their members become better informed generally (with time), it is likely that their 'telescopic faculty' will increase in range in relation to that of employers. In other words, v might be expected to rise. In so far as increase of demand, growth, and a measure of inflation go hand in hand, this would tend to fore-shorten the 'telescopic faculty' of both parties, but more especially that of workers who mostly live in the short period. Of course, the wage varies directly with $v = V_m(j)/V_n(i)$, and anything that tends to increase this ratio tends to increase the wage.

How should we expect U and F to behave over time? In the first place, U

will depend largely on the general level of prosperity obtaining at a particular time. As we have observed, in times of high employment it is sometimes possible for striking workers to take other (lesser paid) jobs for the duration of the strike. Thus U may be rendered negative. Also in times of prosperity workers' reserves are likely to be high; so too are their fixed commitments. In times of recession, these factors should work in the opposite direction. As far as secular change over time is concerned, it is an open question whether higher real incomes increase the staying-power of workers or render them 'soft' to hardship such as is involved in strike action.

How then will F behave over the course of time? This will depend to a large extent on the nature of the commodity sold by the monopolist. Goodwill is a very fickle mistress. The maintenance of goodwill will be much more important for some commodities than for others. The more basic or essential the commodity, the less is its continued demand likely to depend on uninterrupted supply; by the same token, the more are the ripples of disruption likely to spread beyond the particular strike-bound industry. The preservation of goodwill by uninterrupted supply is probably most important in service and less essential trades. Also the matter of goodwill probably looms larger in a buyers' market than in a sellers'.

In the long run, a monopolist no doubt builds stature and financial reserves (often hidden) which make him better able to meet a strike, except when engaged in a secularly declining industry. However, if his reserves are invested in outside securities, any loss involved in liquidation of such securities would have to be added to the cost of a strike. Again, during a slump or credit squeeze, with money tight all round, the monopolist might find himself in acute financial stress which would not encourage him to face a protracted strike. On the other hand, there would probably be a build-up of stocks in these circumstances and this would cushion the impact of a strike. All in all, the firm is normally in a stronger position during slump or tight conditions than are the workers. In the long run, the shapes of U and F will largely depend on the progress of each party in organization, efficiency and education; and also in the building of reserves in the case of the union and its members, and in the build-up of stocks and financial reserves in the case of the firm.

Finally, we must look at our backroom variables — those ruled out explicitly by our assumptions of a static model. These must be let out of their static boxes. In the first place, demand will change (over time). We have already discussed tentatively how change in the conditions of demand affects elasticity. Increase of demand, as such, and also as part of a general, all-round increase, must be a factor favourable to union pressure. On the one hand, there will be a tendency on the part of the monopolist to hold onto workers, especially skilled workers, beyond the limit of strict profitability against anticipated future expansion. Further, an increase in demand may allow the rate of increase in union membership to be kept lagged behind the rate of increase in the demand for labour. In the final analysis, the union's unity and power will depend on its ability to eliminate or minimize disemployment of its members as it presses for higher wages. To a large extent this ability will reside in the degree of union control over entry of workers into the particular industry. This control reaches its highest expression in the closed-shop. With control over entry but not over exit, an increasing demand must always work in the union's favour and a decreasing demand against it.

The question of the ratio of labour supply to labour demand pervades all others. For example, technical change will affect the union *directly* in two ways. First, if the innovation is labour-saving, there is the likelihood of unemployment for some union members. The union will attempt to close entry and to allow normal wastage to take up the slack of unemployment so created. Secondly, it may be that the innovation only becomes profitable with an increase in scale, which will necessitate a reduction in price to *expand* the firm's sales. This expansion of demand would usually favour the union since it will probably also expand the demand for labour, always assuming that the union has some control over recruitment into the industry. Lower costs (higher productivity) in themselves do not necessarily benefit the workers.

One facet of technical change is that going on outside the particular industry with which we are concerned. Innovation and increased productivity in the competitive sectors will tend to raise the opportunity wage and thus relieve the pressure on entry into our particular industry. In so far as increased productivity in outside industries manifests itself in lower prices, the real wage of the monopolist's work force will also increase.

On the subject of changes in union membership, we have said nearly all that need be said. However, there is one aspect on which it is worth remarking. To a certain extent the union will have an ambivalent interest. In so far as it attempts to maximize the wage bill with a minimum of unemployment of members, it will want to do its utmost to restrict entry and minimize membership. On the other hand, it is natural for a union – at least from the point of view of union officials – to expand membership, the ordinary and common proclivity for empire-building. In practice this conflict is often plain to see.

10. CONCLUSION

The foregoing treatment does not purport to be definitive. If some windows have been opened onto an unilluminated subject, the author will be well content.

APPENDIX
Loss of Profit Per Period from Wage Rise ΔW

Old profit: $Q(P - W)$. (1a)

New profit: $[Q - \Delta Q][(P - \Delta P) - (W + \Delta W)]$. (2a)

Then, the loss of profit per period, L'_2, is given by (1a) minus (2a):

$$L'_2 = Q\varDelta W - Q\varDelta P + \varDelta Q(P - W) \qquad (3a)$$

$$= Q\varDelta W - Q\varDelta P + P\varDelta Q\left(\frac{P-W}{P}\right).$$

$$= Q\varDelta W - Q\varDelta P + \frac{P\varDelta Q}{\epsilon}$$

since $\dfrac{P-W}{P}$ is the reciprocal of elasticity of demand. Further,

$$L'_2 = Q\varDelta W - Q\varDelta P + \frac{P\varDelta Q}{Q\varDelta P} \cdot \frac{Q\varDelta P}{\epsilon}$$

$$= Q\varDelta W - Q\varDelta P + Q\varDelta P$$

$$= Q\varDelta W. \qquad (4a)$$

This simple result (loss = quantity of employment/output × wage rise conceded) is somewhat surprising, since there are three distinct components entering into its determination: (a) *loss* from increase in wage bill; (b) *loss* from reduction in output; and (c) *gain* from increase in price.

As this result is unexpected, it will not be out of order if we demonstrate it geometrically. We have to show that

$$Q\varDelta P = \varDelta Q(P - W)$$

thereby cancelling these out in (3a), leaving us with the first term only, $Q\varDelta W$.

In Figure 3.9. draw the horizontal AB, representing the actual wage, with W assigned to the point where AB intersects the marginal revenue curve, DR.

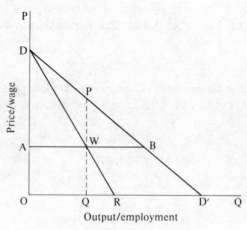

FIG. 3.9

We have

$$\frac{P-W}{WB} = \frac{\Delta P}{\Delta Q}$$

But

$$AW = Q = WB, \text{ since } OR = RD';$$

and therefore

$$\frac{P-W}{Q} = \frac{\Delta P}{\Delta Q}$$

that is,

$$Q\Delta P = \Delta Q(P - W)$$

which was to be shown.

NOTES

1. 'I fear when the economic theorist turns to the general problem of wage determination and labor economics, his voice becomes muted and his speech halting.' P. A. Samuleson, 'Economic Theory and Wages', *Collected Scientific Papers of Paul A. Samuelson* (M.I.T. Press, Cambridge, Mass., 1966), Vol. II, p. 1557.
2. If we need any justification for the abstract, theoretical content of this paper, we may again appeal to Samuelson: 'In my view disappointingly little has yet come from theorists in this field' (ibid., p. 1569).
3. 'The practical man of labor affairs has always acted by instinct, and to justify his behavior he has shopped around to choose the most suitable economic rationalizations' (ibid., p. 1557).
4. F. Y. Edgeworth, *Mathematical Psychics* (Kegan Paul, London, 1881), p. 20.
5. G. L. S. Shackle, 'The Nature of the Bargaining Process', in J. T. Dunlop (ed.), *The Theory of Wage Determination* (Macmillan, London, 1957), p. 298.
6. Cf. Pigou: 'Where, however, wage rates are settled, not by the action of free competition, but by bargaining between a workmen's association on one side and an employers' association on the other, the rate of wage is no longer determinate at a single point. There is, on the contrary, a *range of indeterminateness*' (Pigou's italics). *The Economics of Welfare.* Fourth edition (Macmillan, London, 1938), p. 452.
7. Jevons has it: 'Such a transaction [viz. in bilateral monopoly] must be settled upon other than strictly economic grounds.' *The Theory of Political Economy*, quoted by Edgeworth, op. cit., p. 30.
8. In this connection, Joan Robinson has, as so often, gone to the heart of the matter: 'It is this assumption [of maximization] that makes the analysis of value possible. If individuals act in an erratic way only statistical methods will serve to discover the laws of economics, and if individuals act in a predictable way, but from a large number of complicated motives, the economist must resign his task to the psychologist. It is the assumption that any individual, in his economic life, will never undertake an action that adds more to his losses than to his gains, and will always undertake an action which adds more to his gains than to his losses, which makes the analysis of value possible.' *The Economics of Imperfect Competition* (Macmillan, London, 1933), p. 6.
9. Clausewitz (or was it Bismarck?) said that war is merely the continuation of politics by other methods. Strike is war, and may be considered to be the continuation of negotiation by other methods. In this sense, it is the limit.
10. Cf. Hicks: 'The weapon by which Trade Unions endeavour to secure more favourable terms for their members than competition would give is the strike: the concerted withdrawal of considerable bodies of men from employment.' *The Theory of Wages* (Macmillan, London, 1932), p. 140.
11. By virtue of our integration assumption, in this context price = value added.
12. Cf. Hicks: 'When a Trade Union demands an advance in wages, or resists a reduction,

it sets before the employer an alternative: either he must pay higher wages than he would have paid on his own initiative (and this generally means a prolonged reduction in profits) or on the other hand he must endure the direct loss which will probably follow from a stoppage of work. . . . one alternative will generally bring him less loss than the other. If resistance appears less costly than concession, he will resist; if concession seems cheaper, he will meet the Union's claims' (op. cit., pp. 140-1). Unfortunately, Hicks scarcely progresses beyond this point.

13. In similar calculations throughout, we ignore quantities of the second order of smallness, in this case $\varDelta Q \varDelta W$.

14. One would normally expect the 'telescopic facuity' of the firm to range further than that of the workers, in which case we would have $0 < v < 1$.

3.4 The Incidence of Collective Bargaining*

I

A few years ago I tried to work out some ideas on 'The Incidence of Collective Bargaining' before the American Economic Association.[1] The results satisfied neither my critics nor myself, and I confess inconsistencies between my earlier paper and my present opinion.

Some of the peculiar difficulties of the subject may be clarified by reference to the theory of tax incidence, which is our model here. There is a perennial dispute in tax incidence theory as to whether one should or should not take account of the way the tax receipts are spent. There is another perennial dispute as to whether one should compare the post-tax situation with the situation which would have existed without any tax at all, or with the situation which would have existed had some other tax, such as a proportional income tax, been used to raise the same revenue.

Analogous methodological problems give us pause in discussing the incidence of collective bargaining. Should we confine ourselves to the incidence of collective bargaining narrowly construed? Or should we take into account the incidence of the political and other activities,[2] including pressure on the monetary authorities, which unions may undertake in aid of their bargaining positions? I take the first and more restrictive position, which seems to be necessary for analytical precision. But on the other hand, the political activities of unions are interwoven so inextricably with their collective bargaining that to ignore the political side makes our results unverifiable.[3]

Let me digress to illustrate what is worrying me. It may be that one important effect of collective bargaining by some unions is to price labor out of certain occupations, and to lower wage rates indirectly wherever the displaced workers go. In such a case its incidence would be on workers down-graded or disemployed. But at the same time, suppose that the political activities of the same unions have been directed at increasing employment opportunities for their members, so that the net result of all union activities taken together has been to

*From M. Bronfenbrenner, 'The Incidence of Collective Bargaining Once More', *Southern Economic Journal*, Vol. 24, April 1958.

down-grade and disemploy nobody — rather the reverse. For analytical purposes I separate the two effects, and talk of the incidence of collective bargaining on down-graded and disemployed workers — who may be invisible! This unhappy situation becomes less happy when we realize that the collective bargaining policies of unions might be quite different were their political pressures less effective.

II

So much by way of overture or prelude. There seem to be six main theories of incidence in the economic literature, which can be sub-divided into two groups of three theories each. The first group of theories maintains that incidence exists. These theories maintain, that is to say, that union members make gains at some other group's expense as a result of collective bargaining. The second group of theories maintains that incidence does not exist. These theories maintain, that is to say, either that union members make no gains as a result of collective bargaining that they could not have made in the free market, or else that their gains come out of increased rates of economic activity and growth rather than out of the incomes of anyone else.

1. The 'redistribution' theory. Collective bargaining redistributes income in favor of 'laborers' and against 'capitalists' — meaning receivers of rent and interest as well as receivers of profits in the strict sense. The incidence of collective bargaining is then on the capitalist class.

2. The 'reallocation' theory, which is perhaps more entitled than any other to be called 'orthodox.' The labor share of privately produced national income stays more or less constant — a kind of statistical wages fund — while collective bargaining distributes further this more or less constant share. Members of the most aggressively organized trades and industries get more. Their increases spread 'sympathetically' to a number of related trades, industries, and localities, by raising their supply schedules. At the same time, these increases reduce employment opportunities, displace workers into other labor markets, and hold wage rates down in these other markets. Sometimes the displacement is into unemployment or involuntary entrepreneurship of the peanut-stand variety, if organization is sufficiently broad. More frequently it is into some less aggressively organized type of labor. Part of the incidence of collective bargaining is on these displaced workers regardless of what finally happens to them.

The remainder of the incidence, by this same theory, is on that particular sub-class of consumers who consume most heavily those goods and services whose production costs and selling prices have been raised by wage increases, and who consume least heavily those goods and services whose production costs and selling prices have been pushed down by the displacement. These are however not 'consumers' as a whole. Another sub-class of consumers may very well be net gainers in consequence of collective bargaining, and we shall ignore in the discussion which follows any effects of relative price changes on 'consumers' as such.

3. The 'inflationary' theory. The main effect of collective bargaining is to force up money wages and prices. Its incidence is on fixed income receivers whose incomes lag behind the inflationary movement.

Passing to the theories which deny any incidence of collective bargaining, we have:

4. The 'illusion' theory. Collective bargaining gives the members of established unions[4] no more on the average than they could have expected through the competitive labor market as it operates on the wages of comparable unorganized workers.

5. The 'productivity' theory. Collective bargaining increases the rate of economic growth, in the first place, by 'shocking' employers into increasing their efficiency and introducing innovations of many kinds. At the same time it insures workers against wage cuts and unemployment when their productivity rises, and increases worker cooperation with technical progress. A differentially higher rate of growth results overall. Out of the differential it has been possible to increase the pay of organized workers without injury to any other group.

6. The 'consumption' theory. This is an extension of the redistribution theory which stresses longer-run effects. Collective bargaining redistributes income from the rich to the poor, which raises purchasing power, which in turn permits full consumption and full production, and leaves even capitalists no worse off in the long run than they would have been without it.

Speaking ideologically for a moment, the redistribution, productivity, and consumption theories are usually presented as pro-union in their implications. The reallocation, inflation, and illusion theories, differing widely among themselves, share a certain anti-union favor, although many illusion theorists maintain pro-union policy positions on sociological or political grounds.

The six theories are overlapping rather than mutually exclusive, and it is common to find writers holding more than one. Pro-union writers often combine redistribution and consumption theories, and often add productivity theories as well. Anti-union writers often combine reallocation and inflation theories, and speak of 'unemployment and inflation' as consequences of union power.

III

The literature on the incidence of collective bargaining is not one of which we can be proud as professional economists. Some writers present their views as matters of common notoriety, without rebutting or even mentioning the views of others. There is a certain amount of question-begging, and otherwise playing fast and loose with the evidence. (For example, when union wages rise faster than non-union ones within some industry, this is taken to show that collective bargaining has raised them. But when the opposite is the case, this allegedly proves that collective bargaining raises non-union wages as well.) I have also seen the fact of economic growth — the fact that all major groups have enjoyed rising real incomes since 1900 — used as evidence that collective bargaining has had no incidence.

Advocates of redistribution theories, and of the consumption theories often built upon them, assume that the share of manual or production workers in private national income has risen as a consequence of collective bargaining, or if they can isolate no rise, they assume that it would have fallen without collective bargaining because the overall capital–labor ratio has risen. Neither of these propositions is tenable without supporting evidence, and the little evidence I have seen points in opposite directions.[5] Nor have proponents of productivity theories, to the best of my knowledge, investigated by crafts or industries the empirical relations between union strength and the growth of productivity. We still do not know the comparative importance of union encouragement to efficiency in the use of machines and raw-material and union encouragement to 'feather-bedding' in the use of direct man-power.[6]

A final criticism of the literature is a certain tendency to generalize, to erect universal theories of incidence, based on one or a few specific episodes in recent economic history. The reallocation theorists of the 1920s and the 1930s in the United States and Great Britain seem to have been thinking about 1920–22 or 1929–33, when union wage rates were maintained while other wage rates fell, and when employment shifted (for whatever reason) largely away from sectors of union strength to sectors of union weakness. The American under-employment inflation of 1936–37, followed by the downturn of 1937–38, may have been uniquely important in providing supporting evidence for writers combining misallocation with inflation theories.[7] The even more unusual circumstances of 1945–48 in the United States, when an inflation burst forth into the daylight after four years of wartime suppression, saw the emergence and development of the illusion theory. Currently (1955–57) it is the inflation theory which is fashionable, mainly because of the effects of wage increases on industrial costs – despite the occasional use of collective bargaining as a screen for increased profit margins and the matching of union wage increases in many weakly organized trades (such as teaching) where shortages have been recognized.

IV

I take an eclectic position, trying harder to escape logical than temporal inconsistency. My view is that different theories (or combinations of theories) apply in good times than in bad, and different theories under easy money than under tight. We must, moverover, deal with continua, not dichotomies, especially since some crafts, industries, and areas are generally enjoying prosperity at the same time that others are suffering depression and still others are in an intermediate state.

When a craft, industry, or locality is enjoying prosperity, with money easy but prices temporarily stable, the major effect of collective bargaining is to get inflation under way from the cost side. Wage increases over and above productivity increases, and above wage increases obtainable under competition, can be secured and passed on (or magnified) in price increases. The money supply expands, or its velocity of circulation is allowed to increase without offset, so that the increased wages and prices cause no credit stringency. (The increased wages and prices are not only *financed*, but *underwritten* or *validated*, by easy money.)[8] When times are good but money is tight, any appreciable rise in prices in a strongly organized sector of the economy is accompanied or followed by a stringency of credit, with unfavorable effects on wages, prices, output, and employment generally. This is a reallocation effect, from whose consequences the original price- and wage-raising sectors are often insulated by their particular situations of prosperity. Thus a wage and price rise in autos or steel may lead through tight money to wage cuts or unemployment in textiles or construction – but *not* in autos and steel, the original 'culprits.'

When a craft, industry, or locality is suffering hard times, the major incidence of collective bargaining seems to be the reallocation one, which might alternatively be called anti-deflationary. Money wages are held at the levels of the last prosperity; or rather, they are nearly as likely to rise as to fall. Employment falls off in terms of hours, and usually also in terms of men. The unemployed go elsewhere; new entrants enter elsewhere; wages are often forced down elsewhere. The resulting displacement may be upward, as when coal miners from Kentucky become auto workers in Detroit. More commonly, if hard times are general, displacement will be downward, involving more unemployment of old skills than development of new ones. Accompanying the displacement and reallocation are assorted reactions favorable and unfavorable to particular classes of consumers, as relative prices follow the relative wage movements.

Monetary policy makes little difference here; easy money in depressions has been compared often and aptly to 'pushing on a string.' Fiscal policy, especially government spending, is more significant. The special phenomenon of unemployment (or under-employment) inflation often results when, as under the New Deal in 1936-37, collective bargaining diverts expansionary fiscal policy to wage rates rather than employment.

With an important limitation, in conclusion, one may concur with Sumner Slichter[9] as to the inflationary bias in our collective bargaining arrangements, if not in his recommendation to accept the resulting inflation gracefully. The limitation is to good times with temporary price stability. If times are bad or money is tight, collective bargaining reallocates labor and changes relative prices rather than inflating the general price level – except insofar as it generates unemployment inflation from expansionary fiscal policy during depressions. And at other extreme, when inflation gets under way for other reasons than collective bargaining, as it did in the American 1945-48 and 1950-51, bargained labor markets often escalate and inflate no faster than competitive ones, if the excess demand for labor at prevailing wage rates is at all general.[10]

In both good and bad times, but primarily the latter, collective bargaining probably also induces a slight redistribution of income in favor of wages and against profits. The evidence which has convinced me of this underlying movement was developed by H. M. Levinson,[11] but I shall not reproduce his statistical tabulations here. For those unfamiliar with his work, let me say only that he has broken down the private sector of the American economy into one group of industries where unionism or the threat of unionism are important and another group where neither unionism nor its threat is of much immediate significance. (The first or union group includes manufacturing, mining, construction, transportation, and public utilities. The second or non-union group includes agriculture, trade, finance, and services.) Levinson's figures indicate that in the union group the generation since 1929 has seen a shift from property income (rent and interest) to *wages*, whereas in the non-union group the shift has been from property income to *profits*, including both dividends and entrepreneurial income. I am impressed in each case by the *intra-industry* shifts only, computed after changes in the relative importance of different industries have been eliminated statistically.[12] The differences between the union and non-union groups are slight, and may not be statistically significant; they may also be sensitive to the particular choices of initial and terminal dates. But with these hesitancies and reservations, Levinson's hesitant and reserved conclusion seems acceptable, that a small amount of redistribution results from the collective bargaining process. (There is also supporting evidence from Great Britain and Western Europe.[13]) It is, however, probably unwise to go further and suggest any kind of consumption theory of incidence, or rather of non-incidence, on the basis of differences so small as those Levinson has isolated.

In summary, then, my eclectic theory of the incidence of collective bargaining is an inflationary theory for an easy-money prosperity, or for a depression with a carelessly expansionist fiscal policy, an illusion theory once inflation is under way, and a reallocation theory for most other circumstances. A redistributionist strain underlies the entire process, but on a scale too small to produce significant consumption effects or otherwise to influence the course of prosperity or depression. The illusion theory also warns us usefully at all times against exaggerating the quantitative significance of the other patterns of incidence.[14] The evidence for and against the productivity theory still awaits detailed examination.

V

Thus far nothing has been said of Lloyd Reynolds' *Evolution of Wage Structure*,[15] perhaps the decade's most significant contribution to the literature of the incidence of collective bargaining. This omission has been neither accidental nor disrespectful. Reynolds' conclusions do not fit neatly into our classification of incidence theories. He and his collaborators have asked different questions, and turned the whole discussion in a different direction.

Given the imperfections of actual non-union labor markets, Reynolds inquires whether collective bargaining has shifted wage structures closer to or further from the 'competitive norm' than they would otherwise have been. This competitive norm is thought of as devoid not only of collective bargaining but also of employer monopsony, worker ignorance and immobility, and also 'non-competing groups' of privileged workers. Reynolds concludes in general, and with reservations, that the countervailing power of unions, exercised through collective bargaining, has brought actual wage structures closer to the competitive pattern than they previously were.

It does not seem impossible to translate Reynolds' conclusions into my own terms, although my translation lacks Reynolds' approval. We may say, for example, that the redistributive effect of collective bargaining represents mainly the countervailing of monopsonistic exploitation and a movement toward the competitive norm. We may also suggest that many who suffer from reallocation or inflation effects are white-collar folk who have traditionally formed a closed group with respect to recruitment from the ranks of manual workers, so that these effects, too, may be presented as competitive rather than the reverse.

Translation in the opposite direction is more difficult, but it serves to point up both my agreements and my disagreements with Reynolds' position. We may for translation purposes employ the hackneyed expression 'labor aristocracy', subdividing it further into an old aristocracy and a new one, corresponding respectively to the elites of craft and of industrial unionism, and then proceed.

The old labor aristocracy consisted of members of the skilled trades, which old-style collective bargaining established as non-competing groups, often with monopoly power as against their small employers. On balance this kind of collective bargaining, with the incidence patterns we have ascribed to it, was probably an anti-competitive force despite its anti-monopsony aspects.

Reynolds bases his argument, however, mainly on the new labor aristocracy. This includes workers of all degrees of skill, but fortunate enough to work for large firms with substantial monopoly power and profits on the selling sides of their several markets, and therefore substantial ability to pay wage increases. Here collective bargaining as carried on mainly by industrial unions has had complex consequences. It has counteracted the monopsony power of these employers in hiring labor — clearly a competitive effect, which Reynolds stresses, and probably a redistributive one as regards incidence in the sense of the present discussion. But at the same time collective bargaining has raised these employers' costs, justified if not forced increases in their selling prices, and given their workers some share in what would otherwise have been their monopoly profits.

Should we call this a movement towards competition in general? From the viewpoint of the functional income distribution, it might appear so. Collective bargaining raises the labor share, and retards the shift to profits which Mrs. Robinson and others foresee as the ultimate end of a 'world of monopolies'.[16] But I have my doubts, which spring from the inflation and reallocation theories of incidence. There seem to be elements of collusion or conspiracy against consumers of particular products and fixed-income groups in general, elements of labor support for monopolistic restrictions, elements of cultivation of monopoly profits as pools for wage increases to strategic groups of organized workers — 'palace slaves,' Lenin would have called them.[17] These are reflected in the inflation and reallocation patterns of incidence of collective bargaining as has been said, and it is by no means certain that the injured parties are confined to the monopsonists or the non-competing groups of yester-years. Do they not include family farmers and agricultural workers, unskilled employees in domestic and service trades, widows and orphans, pensioners and annuitants, racial and religious minorities? Inflation and reallocation, like the biblical rain, fall alike on the just and the unjust. Reynolds' theory has conjured up for the just an umbrella that the good Lord may thus far have neglected to provide.

NOTES

1. M. Bronfenbrenner, 'The Incidence of Collective Bargaining,' American Economic Association, *Proceedings* (1954), pp. 293–307.
2. As an apt example of these 'other' activities we may cite the recent role of the United Mine Workers in assisting in the organization of the American Coal Shipping Company to increase the world demand for American coal. (For this illustration I am indebted to my colleague, Charles P. Larrowe.)
3. Many writers accordingly discuss all trade union activities simultaneously, a practice defended most explicitly by Clark Kerr ('Labor's Income Share and the Labor Movement,' in George W. Taylor and Frank C. Pierson (ed.), *New Concepts in Wage Determination*), 'The term "trade unionism," instead of "collective bargaining," is used deliberately. Unions can and do affect actions of both employers and governments, and some of both kinds of action have potential or actual consequences for distributive shares. To explore the impact of unionism in only the economic sphere and not also in the political sphere is to tell but half the tale.' (New York: McGraw-Hill, 1957, p. 266.)
4. An upward fillip to wage rates as the immediate consequence of organization is recognized quite generally, and may be attributed to the overcoming of labor monopsony. By 'established' unions we mean unions for whose members this short-run fillip has already come and gone.
5. For a useful summary, see Kerr, *op. cit.*, pp. 279–294. For the United States in particular, we quote from p. 281: 'Over the past century [including both periods of union strength and weakness] labor's share has risen primarily as employed persons have become a more important component in our population. In other words, employees are not comparatively better off as individuals; there are, however, many more of them.'
6. Here again, the relevant literature has been reviewed by Kerr, 'Productivity and Labour Relations,' *Reprint 96* of the University of California Institute of Industrial Relations (1957). The results are most inconclusive.
7. The standard presentations of this viewpoint are probably H. C. Simons, *Economic Policy for a Free Society* (Chicago: University of Chicago Press, 1948), ch. 6 (originally published 1944); C. E. Lindblom, *Unions and Capitalism* (New Haven: Yale University Press, 1949), ch. 11; and Fritz Machlup, *Political Economy of Monopoly* (Baltimore: Johns Hopkins University Press, 1952), ch. 9–10.
8. A clear distinction should be, but usually is not, made between that degree of monetary ease which finances a wage increase in the first instance, and that further degree of monetary ease which underwrites or validates it by providing higher money purchasing power at higher money prices. In an earlier essay' 'A Contribution to the Aggregative Theory of Wages,' *Journal of Political Economy* (1956), pp. 459–469, assuming the first and lesser degree of monetary ease, I arrived at essentially classical

inverse relations between wage rates and employment. In the present passage, assuming the second and greater degree of monetary ease, I suppose the Keynesian independence between wage rates and aggregate employment, my concern being concentrated on inflationary consequences. It would be easy to go to super-Keynesian direct relations between wage rates and employment under this degree of monetary ease, if the initial position were one of less than full employment.

9. Sumner H. Slichter, 'Do the Wage-Fixing Arrangements in the American Labor Market Have an Inflationary Bias?' American Economic Association, *Proceedings* (1954), pp. 342–346.

10. Compare particularly Albert Rees, 'the Economic Impact of Collective Bargaining in the Steel and Coal Industries During the Postwar Period,' Industrial Relations Research Association, *Proceedings* (1950), pp. 203–210.

11. For the period 1929–1947, see H. M. Levinson, *Unionism, Wage Trends, and Income Distribution, 1914–1947* (Ann Arbor: University of Michigan Press, 1951), esp. Table 25, p. 106. The results are extended through 1952 in Levinson, 'Collective Bargaining and Income Distribution,' American Economic Association, *Proceedings* (1954), pp. 308–316, esp. Table 1, p. 309. For further extension (through 1954) of some of Levinson's results see Kerr, 'Labor's Income Share,' *op. cit.*, esp. Table 2, p. 285.

12. Kerr, in criticizing Levinson's study (and other studies with similar results) does not distinguish between *intra-industry* and *total* share shifts (ibid., pp. 284 f.). The force of his criticism, and of other criticisms along the same line, is thereby reduced substantially.

13. E. H. Phelps Brown and P. E. Hart, 'The Share of Wages in National Income,' *Economic Journal*, June 1952, esp. pp. 276 f. and Phelps Brown, 'The Long-Term Movement of Real Wages' in John T. Dunlop (ed.), *Theory of Wage Determination* (London: Macmillan, 1957), pp. 48–65. Phelps Brown stresses the conventional element in profit margins, which can be squeezed by the coincidence of a 'hard' labor market (aggressive collective bargaining) and a 'soft' product market (generally depressed conditions and/or aggressive price competition). For additional consideration of the American results, see William Fellner, *Competition Among the Few* (New York: Knopf, 1949), pp. 317–321; Sumner H. Slichter, *Economics of Collective Bargaining* (Berkeley: University of California Press, 1950), pp. 36–38; George J. Stigler, *Theory of Price* (Revised edition; New York: Macmillan, 1952), p. 259.

14. Thus for example Milton Friedman suggests 15–20 per cent as the probable limit of upward wage distortion and 4 per cent as the probable limit of downward wage distortion in connection with what we call the reallocation theory. Friedman, 'Significance of Labor Unions for Economic Policy,' in D. McC. Wright (ed.), *The Impact of the Union* (New York: Harcourt Brace, 1951), p. 216.

15. Lloyd G. Reynolds and Cynthia Taft, *The Evolution of Wage Structure* (New Haven: Yale University Press, 1955), esp. ch. 7, 13. (See also Reynolds, 'The Impact of Collective Bargaining on the Wage Structure in the United States' in Dunlop, *op. cit.*, pp. 194–221 for a more condensed and less positive presentation of the same point of view.) Reynolds has also contributed to the discussion along less unconventional lines in his 'General Level of Wages,' in Taylor and Pierson (*op. cit.*). Here he traces in some detail the routes by which money wage increases may increase the labor share, in accordance with what we have called the redistribution theory of incidence (pp. 253 f.). He also sets himself against the inflationary theory in a manner justified when monetary authorities do not allow tight money policy to be influenced by the results of collective bargaining (pp. 243 f., 249 f.).

16. Although stated most explicitly by Mrs. Robinson in *Economics of Imperfect Competition* (London: Macmillan, 1933), Book X, the notion of a trend toward monopoly correlated with a reduction of the distributive share of labor dates back to Marx and beyond. Among the spate of turn-of-the-century 'Distribution' books it is found most clearly in John R. Commons, *Distribution of Wealth* (New York: Macmillan, 1893), pp. 101–107, 198–200, 229–237, 246–248, ch. 6. It underlies the aggregative wage theory of Michal Kalecki, 'The Distribution of the National Income,' reprinted in William Fellner and B. F. Haley, (ed.), *Readings in the Theory of Income Distribution* (Philadelphia and Toronto: Blakiston, 1946), selection 11. For a critical survey of this

literature, beginning with Mrs. Robinson, see Dean A. Worcester, Jr., 'Monopoly and Income Distribution,' *Western Economic Association, Proceedings* (1956), pp. 36–41.
17. The writer has expressed these doubts previously at somewhat greater length. See M. Bronfenbrenner, 'Wages in Excess of Marginal Revenue Productivity,' *Southern Economic Journal*, January 1950, pp. 307–309. Similar doubts were likewise not unknown to the founding fathers of labor economics. Compare e.g. the discussion of 'Capital and labor hunting together, their prey being the people who needed cheap housing' in John R. Commons, *Economics of Collective Action* (New York: Macmillan, 1950), pp. 31 ff. But as Kerr reminds us, collusive agreements between monopolistic employers and their favored employees antedated powerful trade unions, his wry comment ('Labor's Income Share,' *op. cit.*, p. 272) being: 'It is very difficult to keep the employers indefinitely from giving away their profits in part to their employees, in one way or another.

3.5 The Effects of Collective Agreements*

The purpose of this paper is to investigate, at the simplest level, the hypothesis that variations in the extent of the coverage of trade union negotiated collective agreements between occupations are a source of variation in the structure of relative occupational earnings. In addition, an attempt is made to estimate the mean value of any differential in the earnings of those whose pay is subject, directly or indirectly, to the terms of a collective agreement and those whose pay is not. If these appear to be limited objectives, it should be borne in mind that no such study has ever been undertaken for the U.K. and no such study, on anything approaching a global basis, has ever been undertaken anywhere else to our knowledge. The stimulus for this study was the publication of a unique series of data which, *inter alia*, indicates the percentage of workers in each occupation whose wages were subject to a collective agreement in 1973. The data are obtained in the 1973 New Earnings Survey undertaken by the Department of Employment and are published in the *DE Gazette*, February, 1974.

INTRODUCTION

The traditional method of estimating the influence of trade unions on relative wages has been to regress the percentage of the labour force in each industry who are trade union members on the wage level of each industry. A good deal of work of this kind has been undertaken in the U.S.A. but very little in the U.K. In the U.S.A. a few studies have also been carried out on inter-occupational wages but these have been limited virtually to case studies. Since no data on the occupational distribution of trade union membership has ever been available in the U.K. no such work has been done. (For an excellent and thorough discussion of the literature the reader should consult Lewis (1963) or, in more compact form, Lewis (1971).)

In Section I of this paper we describe the new data which has become available

*From C. Mulvey and J. I. Foster, 'Occupational Earnings in the U.K. and the Effects of Collective Agreements', *The Manchester School*, 1976, No. 3, September.

and formulate a test of our hypothesis. In Section II we present and interpret
our empirical findings and draw conclusions.

SECTION I

The Hypothesis

The hypothesis to be tested in this paper is entirely straightforward – that
variations in the occupational coverage of collective agreements influence the
relative structure of occupational earnings. Underlying this hypothesis is
another, which is implicit but which we cannot directly test, and it is that any
relationship between the coverage of collective agreements and relative earnings
is indicative of the influence of trade union activity on the structure of occupational earnings. We cannot test this implicit hypothesis directly because we have
no testable hypothesis as to the determinants of either the extent of coverage
of collective agreements or of the determinants of the earnings differential
between those whose pay is covered by a collective agreement and those whose
pay is not. In particular we see no reason to suppose that collective agreement
coverage and the size of the earnings differential are related to each other and
our empirical work supports the view that the two are unrelated. It is well
to be clear as much about what we are *not* hypothesising or intending to investigate as with what we *are* hypothesising and investigating.

The Collective Agreement Data (CA)

Since this paper derives much of its novelty from new data which measure
the extent of collective agreement coverage by occupation it is sensible to describe that data now. The Department of Employment (DE) have, since 1968,
carried out the New Earnings Survey (NES) which has as its main purpose to obtain detailed information on earnings, their components and distribution, and
classified by sex, age, industry and occupation. The method of surveying is by
questionnaire to employers. The sample size is approximately 180,000. The
survey is undertaken annually and in certain years particular pieces of additional
information are requested. In 1973 the survey asked employers to state which
of the following four classes the sample employees' earnings were subject to
directly or indirectly: (i) a national collective agreement, (ii) a national agreement plus a supplementary agreement, (iii) a local agreement only, or (iv) no
collective agreement. These data are expressed as percentages of the sample
and are broken down by occupation, sex, industry etc. Some features of the
particular quality of these data are:
(a) it is the only directly observed occupational data on the coverage of collec-
    tive agreements that we are aware of;
(b) the survey sample is very large so that occupational sub-samples (for adult
    males) are quite large enough for statistical reliability;
(c) the data were collected in the fifth annual survey, and therefore after
    its main teething-troubles were over and are therefore likely to be

reliable; and

(d) the questionnaire is simple and unambiguous and therefore likely to yield accurate data.

The NES data have a special quality in an analysis of the relative wage effects of trade union activity. Trade union membership data, even if they were available, which they are not on an occupational basis, are normally used to measure the coverage of the union wage in empirical estimates of trade union relative wage effects. (See for example Lewis (1963), Pencavel (1974).) However, it is well known that such data may not capture the full effect of trade union wage gains since non-union employees often benefit from the union rate for a job irrespective of whether the recipient is in the union or not and other employers may match the union rate in response to threats of unionisation. (See Pencavel (1974) on this question and observe the difficulties it imposes on his analysis.) *The NES data have the quality that they directly measure the extent of coverage of the union rate.*[1]

A broad indication of the difference in magnitude between the coverage of the CA data and trade union membership data can be given by noting that in manufacturing industry about 80 per cent of the full-time adult manual labour force were covered by a collective agrement whereas only about 55 per cent are estimated to be trade union members. (This latter estimate is taken from Bain's estimates for 1964 and reproduced in Pencavel (1974), Table A, p. 207.) Hence we have something like 25 per cent of the manual workforce in manufacturing being paid the union rate but not being union members.

The 'Coverage Differential'

Because the data on collective agreement coverage refer to *all* of those in receipt of the union negotiated wage the estimated earnings differential, corresponding to the more usual union/non-union differential, may be expected to be considerably greater than estimates of the conventional differential. This will be so to the extent that our measure captures 'spillovers' from the union to non-union sector. This, in fact, is one of the great advantages of the CA data. The literature on estimates of the union/non-union differential is quite explicit in pointing out that studies using trade union membership data will fail to capture spillover effects and understate the 'true' differential as a result (see Lewis (1963)). Rosen (1969) has attempted to come to grips with this problem but with limited success. To indicate that our concept of the earnings differential is different from the conventionally estimated concept, and to indicate how it is estimated, we shall call it the 'coverage differential'.

Agreement Coverage and the Coverage Differential

It is now necessary to consider the relationship between NES data on the coverage of collective agreements and the coverage differential. Let the proportion of workers in occupation i covered by a collective agreement (CA) be α_i. We assume that α_i is greater than the proportion of the labour force in occupation i who are members of trade unions. The geometrically weighted mean wage rate in occupation i is therefore:

$$lnW_i = (1 - \alpha_i)lnW_{ni} + \alpha_i lnW_{ui} \qquad (1)$$

where W_i, W_{ni} and W_{ui} are the mean wage, mean non-union wage and mean union wage respectively. Call the coverage differential λ_i, so that:

$$lnW_{ui} = lnW_{ni} + ln(1 + \lambda_i). \qquad (2)$$

Substituting (2) into (1) gives:

$$lnW_i = lnW_{ni} + \alpha_i ln(1 + \lambda_i). \qquad (3)$$

As it stands equation (3) is a simple identity which, by construction, must always hold. We may observe W_i and α_i from the data in the NES but lnW_{ni} and λ_i are unobservable. The simplest and most direct approach to achieving the objective of this paper is to estimate equation (3) in order to obtain an estimate of $\bar{\lambda}$ by replacing lnW_{ni} with a vector of its hypothesised observable determining variables and by observing W_i and α_i. Hence, in estimation, let $lnW_{ni} = lnW_{ni}(X_i, Z_i) + \epsilon_i$ where X_i is a vector of the long-run, and Z_i a vector of the short-run, determinants of the male non-union wage. ϵ_i is a stochastic disturbance term. Now let $ln(1 + \lambda_i)\alpha_i = \alpha_i ln(1 + \bar{\lambda}) + \epsilon_i'$, where $\bar{\lambda}$ is the mean coverage differential and ϵ_i' is a stochastic disturbance term. Equation (3) may now be rewritten:

$$lnW_i = lnW_{ni}(X_i, Z_i) + \alpha_i ln(1 + \bar{\lambda}) + \epsilon_i'' \qquad (4)$$

where $\epsilon_i'' = \epsilon_i + \epsilon_i'$. ($\alpha$ is hereafter relabled 'CA' for convenience).

The Non-Union Wage

We proceed to define the non-union mean wage in occupation i as follows:

$$lnW_{ni} = lnW_{ni}(X_i, Z_i) + \epsilon_i \qquad (5)$$

where X_i is a vector of the mean human capital investments of the members of occupation i, and Z_i is a vector of other characteristics of occupation i which may influence the mean wage.

Human Capital Investments and the Non-Union Wage

The theory of human capital has received so much attention in the literature in recent years that it would be superfluous to discuss it here. Suffice it to say that that theory postulates that differences in the earnings of different individuals comprise in part a return on investments made in education and training. Since *occupations* are probably the closest labour market classification of homogeneity in respect of human capital requirements, the theory would lead us to expect an association between mean occupational investments in human capital and mean occupational earnings. (See Parnes (1964).) The theory of human capital is obviously more complex than this. For practical purposes, however, it is pointless to elaborate on the theory since the limitations imposed by the data oblige us to test only the crude proposition set out above in an approximate way. (Useful surveys of the literature on the theory of human capital are Bowman (1966) and Blaug (1965).)

In order to approximate the mean investments in human capital associated with an occupation we require some information about schooling, training and post-school education. It is well known that in the U.K. such data are sparse. We offer the following three proxies of the vector of mean human capital investments of the members of an occupation:

(a) the percentage of the occupational labour force whose formal education continued after the age of 15 (SC);

(b) a scale of dummy variables intended to measure the years of training or apprenticeship normally associated with an occupation — the scale is based on the *Classification of Occupations (1970)* and allocates a value of 0 to those occupations classed as unskilled, a value of 0.5 to those classed as semi-skilled and a value of 5 to those classified as skilled (manual and non-manual) (SK);

(c) the percentage of Qualified Manpower recorded for the occupational group to which the occupation belongs in the GRO 1966 classification (QM).

Conceptually these proxies seem reasonable. The main pitfall to be avoided in selecting proxies for the purposes of this kind of study is to ensure that the investments in human capital for which proxies are selected represent investments which are not directly made by the employer. Otherwise, the rate of return on investments in human capital would not show up in the private pre-tax earnings of individuals. However, since almost all education and training in the U.K. is either partially state-financed or not employer-specific, the proxies chosen are theoretically admissible. The quality of the proxies is obviously far from perfect but is the best we can do given the data limitations.

Other Occupational Characteristics and the Non-Union Wage

While an occupation may be reasonably homogeneous with respect to the human capital investments of its members it may be heterogeneous in respect of certain other factors. For example, an occupation may be heterogeneous in respect of industry, location, sector etc. Lack of data make it impossible to take account of such factors but it is prudent to acknowledge their existence in a study of this kind. One of the characteristics which one would expect to affect the structure of relative occupational wages is the short-run pressure of demand.

It is very difficult to find a proxy variable which can be expected to capture the short-run influence of labour demand on the occupational wages structure. We therefore selected two variables which, while far from ideal, seemed capable of approximating both the broad pattern of demand change between occupations and the recent structure of occupational excess demands.

The variables designed to proxy changes in occupational labour demands is the proportional change in employment in each occupation between 1961 and

1971, (ΔE). This variable depends on at least two assumptions which are somewhat heroic. These are that the short-run elasticity of labour supply is less than perfectly elastic for each occupation and that short-run supply elasticities are about the same for each occupation. This proxy is a rather crude one but has been used with some success by Weiss (1966) in an inter-industry wage study.

The variable designed to reflect the structure of occupational excess demands is the ratio of unemployment to vacancies in each occupation observed one year before the wage data (U/V). Clearly this variable cannot reflect the cumulative shaping of the wage structure which has occurred in response to past structures of excess demands. However, the data suggest that there has been a tendency for a measure of stability in the structure of excess demands between occupations (as measured by U/V) over the last five years. The inevitable heroic assumption underlying this variable is that the reaction functions of each occupation should be similar, an assumption also made by both Arrow and Capron (1959) and Lipsey (1960).

The Dependent Variable

The dependent variable is the mean gross weekly earnings of full-time adult males in each occupation. This variable was chosen on the grounds that:
(a) both from the point of view of the individual worker and the trade union the most tangible final concept of 'wages' is the weekly gross wage;
(b) trade unions have a substantial degree of control over hours worked and the hours/hourly earnings settlement is often simultaneous – this is particularly important in the case of the present study since the CA data contain all local and supplementary agreements;
(c) other measures of wages suffer from various difficulties; straight time rates are inappropriate because they ignore supplementary and local agreements; and average hourly earnings take no account of the supply of hours, which may be simultaneously determined with pay by the collective agreement. Metcalf *et al.* (1974) lend support to the assumption that the supply of hours is influenced by trade unions.

The Sample of Occupations

Ninety-nine occupations were selected for the analysis. The criterion of selection was that the occupation should appear in both the NES earnings and CA data series. Six occupations which met this criterion proved unusable because they could not be traced in other important data series even on the rather *ad hoc* basis which had to be applied to secure estimates of some data for certain occupations. Occupational data are not easy to collect for the kind of study we are undertaking. By far the most serious difficulty is the different sets of occupational titles attached to different data series. Improvisation is usually possible but this must affect the quality of the data used and where no basis for improvisation exists the observation must simply be dropped. None of this reflects on the quality of the CA data. The data gathering process was based on a totally reliable series of matched earnings and CA data and these are of the highest quality as a result. The ninety-nine occupation sample obviously includes a number of occupations in the professional and managerial groups which are little affected by collective agreements. Therefore, in order to investigate the earnings differential for the 'manual' type of occupations which are more extensively covered by the terms of collective agreements, we arbitrarily constructed a second sample by excluding all occupations in occupational groups *I-V*. This gave us a sample of eighty-three occupations and we report the results of our analysis of this sample as well as for the whole sample.

The Estimating Equation

The equation to be estimated is:

$$lnW_i = \theta_0 + ln(1 + \bar{\lambda})CA_i + \theta_1SK_i + \theta_2SC_i + \theta_3QM_i + \theta_4\Delta E_i + \theta_5U/V_i$$

with prior sign hypotheses $ln(1 + \bar{\lambda}), \theta_1 \ldots \theta_4 > 0$ and $\theta_5 < 0$.

SECTION II

The Empirical Results

Selected regression equations for both the All-occupations and 'Manual' occupations samples are set out in Table 3.1.

In terms of the main objective of this paper the first point to note about the empirical results in Table 3.1 is that the estimated coefficient on *CA* in all the regressions fitted is highly significant and correctly signed. The hypothesis that trade unions affect occupational wage differentials through the coverage of collective agreements is strongly supported. However it is quite evident that, as expected, the *CA* variable is distinctly less power in the equations for Sample 1 than in those for Sample 2. The coefficient on *CA* is also generally and significantly smaller in the Sample 1 equations. The *CA* variable also has the virtue of being uncorrelated with any of the other independent variables in the equation. We shall defer interpretation of the coefficient on *CA* to the conclusions.

The second point to note is that our human capital variables all perform well in one or other of the regression equations for Sample 1 but that *SC*, while significant, performs distinctly less well for Sample 2 and *QM* is both incorrectly signed and insignificant in the latter sample. In Sample 1 there are problems of multicollinearity involving the three human capital variables and also ΔE. In particular *SC* and *QM* are highly correlated with each other ($r = 0.86$) since almost all qualified manpower continued formal education after the age of 15. Of the two, *SC* is more satisfactory on general theoretical grounds since it is a more broadly based variable which has relevance to investments in education throughout the occupations in the sample, but, since *QM* is critical in distinguishing the human capital characteristics of the professional and managerial occupations from the manual ones, we require to retain both in order to interpret the coefficient on *CA*. However, *QM* clearly has little relevance to the

Table 3.1

Selected OLS Regression Equations for All-Occupations and Manual Occupations in the U.K. 1973.
Dependent variable is the log of Mean Gross Weekly Earnings of Full-time Adult Males.
(t-values in parenthesis)

Equation No. Sample 1 (N = 99)	Constant	CA	SK	SC	QM	ΔE	U/V	R²	F
1.1	3.35 (47.36)	0.27 (3.34)	0.024 (3.92)	0.016 (1.68)	0.20 (1.76)	0.04 (0.09)	−0.0032 (1.77)	0.55	19.03
1.2	3.35 (47.90)	0.27 (3.35)	0.024 (93.96)	0.016 (1.77)	0.20 (1.77)		−0.0032 (1.78)	0.55	23.08
1.3	3.30 (50.44)	0.32 (4.26)	0.022 (3.66)	0.030 (6.59)			−0.0036 (1.97)	0.54	27.45
1.4	3.26 (51.59)	0.32 (4.30)	0.022 (3.66)	0.031 (6.93)				0.52	34.26
1.5	3.38 (56.86)	0.20 (2.82)	0.028 (4.77)		0.40 (7.02)			0.52	34.84
1.6	3.28 (48.92)	0.39 (4.98)		0.037 (8.35)				0.45	39.58
1.7	3.43 (53.23)	0.25 (3.22)			0.47 (7.62)			0.41	33.36

Sample 2 (N = 83)

2.1	3.23 (38.89)	0.40 (4.60)	0.021 (3.42)	0.031 (2.34)	−0.30 (0.20)	−0.08 (1.37)	−0.003 (1.57)	0.42	9.16
2.2	3.19 (40.02)	0.41 (4.68)	0.022 (3.62)	0.030 (2.25)	0.25 (0.17)	−0.09 (1.64)		0.40	10.31
2.3	3.27 (41.63)	0.37 (4.38)	0.020 (3.29)	0.024 (1.94)	−0.62 (0.42)		−0.003 (1.81)	0.41	10.50
2.4	3.23 (41.83)	0.40 (4.69)	0.022 (3.80)	0.030 (2.44)		−0.08 (1.43)	−0.003 (1.57)	0.42	11.13
2.5	3.23 (44.27)	0.38 (4.43)	0.021 (3.74)	0.021 (1.92)			−0.003 (1.86)	0.41	14.15
2.6	3.31 (53.29)	0.31 (3.93)	0.025 (4.38)					0.35	21.67
2.7	3.22 (40.93)	0.47 (5.37)		0.032 (2.85)				0.27	14.81

$t_{0.05} = 1.99$

Definition of variables:

CA = Proportion of each adult male occupational labour force whose wages are subject to a 'collective agreement'.

SK = Skill dummy variable in which occupations classified as 'unskilled' = 0, 'semi-skilled' = 0.5, and 'skilled' = 5.0.

QM = Proportion of 'Qualified Manpower' in each occupational labour force.

SC = % of occupational labour force whose formal education continued after the age of 15.

ΔE = Proportionate change in employment in each occupation between 1961 and 1971.

U/V = Ratio of unemployment to vacancies for each occupation in April 1972.

occupations in Sample 2. The correlation between SK and SC is not very strong ($r = 0.32$), presumably because the skills of most manual occupations can be acquired by apprenticeship and training with little or no formal education beyond the age of 15. Hence SK and SC are distinct in the types of investment in human capital which they measure, although there is some degree of overlap, and they are therefore admissible jointly on both theoretical and statistical grounds.

QM and SC are both quite closely correlated with ΔE, the employment change variable, ($r = 0.55$ and $r = 0.63$) but only for Sample 1. This evidently reflects the fact that the sixteen high wage professional and managerial occupations in Sample 1, with only two exceptions, experienced very substantial employment growth in the period 1961–71 while a substantial majority of the occupations in Sample 2 experienced declines in employment. This is very much what one would expect given the rapid growth of the non-utility service industries and the decline of manufacturing and primary industry employment. ΔE is however never significant in either sample and enters all the equations in Sample 2 with an unexpected sign. ΔE may therefore be neglected.

The other short-run demand proxy, U/V is never quite significant at the 5 per cent level although it is almost so in several cases and is also correctly signed. Unexpectedly, because one expects recorded unemployment and vacancy data for professional and managerial occupations to be less accurate than for manual ones, the U/V variable is as well determined in Sample 1 as it is in Sample 2.

Before we proceed, a statistical point requires to be noted. There is reason to suppose that the coefficient on CA may be biased upwards in many of the equations. This is because the estimate of lnW_{ni} may be low due to our inability to specify an equation with a complete and accurate vector of its determining variables. This is a familiar problem in this type of study and requires us to be ultra-cautious in interpreting the value of the estimated coefficient. (See Lewis 1963.)

CONCLUSIONS

The principal conclusions of the analysis are already clear. Variations in the extent of the occupational coverage of collective agreements are closely associated with variations in occupational earnings. Since the rate of pay prescribed by a collective agreement is influenced by trade union activity then we must be observing an association between trade union activity and relative earnings. While we can say little about the nature or direction of causation as a result of the analysis in this paper, the hypothesis that it is trade unions which affect relative wages appeals to commonsense and can easily be rationalised by economic theory. We are aware of only two assertions to the contrary, Pencavel (1971) and Reder (1965). Curiously enough it is Pencavel himself, in a later paper (1974), who most firmly reasserts the hypothesis that unions affect wages.

In particular his empirical results for the U.K., using instrumental variable (INV) estimates, strongly support that hypothesis.

There is nothing in this paper which sheds any light on the determinants of either the coverage of collective agreements or the size of the union/non-union differential. These are topics which we intend to investigate in further work.

An interesting by-product of the analysis is the extent to which crude proxy variables for investments in human capital assert themselves as significant determinants of occupational earnings. In itself this is an important result for the U.K. and points to the potential for more sophisticated and detailed analysis in an area of research in which the U.K. literature is fairly sparse. Lastly, the influence of the level or changes in the level of labour demand did not in practice emerge as important determinants of the occupational earnings structure. This may well reflect, however, more on the quality of the proxies used than on the validity of the hypothesis.

Interpreting the coefficient on the *CA* variable is a particularly hazardous exercise. The estimated coefficient is, in the nature of such an analysis, only an approximate figure. Accordingly, estimates of the coverage union/non-union earnings differential based on that figure must be very approximate indeed and treated with due caution. However, it would be unduly cautious not to attempt point estimates of the differential so long as these warnings are borne in mind.

The relative percentage wage effect of trade unions is $\exp(\lambda) - 1$. Hence for Sample 1 we have a range of estimates of the relative earnings effect of unions of from 22 per cent to 48 per cent. There are two reasons to prefer the lower end of this range. First, in view of the possibility of coefficient bias mentioned earlier it is prudent, over such a broad range of estimates, to prefer the low estimates. Second, it is clear that the variable *QM* affects the magnitude of the coefficient on *CA* quite markedly. The reason for this is clearly that in certain occupations which are highly paid, contain a high proportion of qualified manpower and are extensively covered by collective agreements, *QM* plays an important role in determining lnW_{ni}. When *QM* is removed its explanatory power is transferred to *CA* and inflates the coefficient accordingly. (The occupations concerned are mainly in the teaching profession.) In order to avoid attributing to *CA* an effect properly due to *QM* we must therefore confine ourselves to coefficients on *CA* estimates with *QM* in the equation. This policy narrows the range of estimates to 22 per cent to 31 per cent. Taking both points together, prudence suggests that for Sample 1 the broad order of magnitude of the effect of trade unions on relative earnings is about 22 per cent.

The estimated effect of trade unions on relative earnings for Sample 2 ranges from 36 per cent to 60 per cent. Again the range is broad and, as expected, higher for this sample than for the other. Much the same criteria as were applied to Sample 1 are relevant to Sample 2 except that it is the *SK* variable which most affects the size of the coefficient on *CA*. Not unexpectedly, the educational variable *SC* evidently does not pick up the effects of the *SK* variable when the latter is removed from the equation – once again it is *CA* which benefits. Adopting the same policy as for Sample 1, we suggest the low estimate of 36 per cent as the most plausible for Sample 2.

While these estimates of the coverage differential are relatively high compared with the finding of the only other study of this kind for the U.K., Pencavel (1974), we are satisfied that they are realistic. Pencavel (1974) estimated a conventional union/non-union differential for 29 industry orders for 1964 of 0–10 per cent. In principle there ought to be no difference in the estimated differential whether based on an occupational or industrial sample so long as the samples cover the same workforce. In practice Sample 1 in this study is more broadly based than that of Pencaval's since it includes non-manual occupations whereas Pencavel's was restricted, in effect, to manual workers. Sample 2 on the other hand is much more like that employed by Pencavel but, because we were forced to be selective, is by no means identical. Hence if we are to make comparisons with Pencavel's estimate of the union/non-union differential the most appropriate comparison is between the 10 per cent estimate of Pencavel and our estimate of 36 per cent. At first sight the disparity between the estimates is considerable and requires some explanation. However it should be noted that by comparison with estimates of the conventional union/non-union differential made for the U.S.A., the estimate of 36 per cent is by no means outrageous. Lewis's survey of U.S. studies (Lewis, 1963), shows that the range of estimates prior to 1962 was 0–25 per cent and since then Throop (1968) has estimated a 30 per cent differential for 1960. Allowing both for the conceptual differences between the 'coverage differential' estimated in this paper and the orthodox differential estimated in most U.S. studies and for the fact that the differential is affected in magnitude by the business cycle, our estimate is perfectly credible. (See Mulvey, 1976.)

Returning to the discrepancy between Pencavel's estimate of 10 per cent and ours of 36 per cent, there are three points to be taken note of. First, we must re-emphasise the conceptual differences involved in estimating the 'coverage differential' and the orthodox differential. The mean value of Pencavel's union density variable is about 55 per cent. The mean value of union wage coverage in our analysis is about 80 per cent. Hence we are taking account of about 25 per cent of the labour force who are not union members but who are paid the union rate and who are treated as though they were paid the non-union wage in Pencavel's analysis. This must have a very substantial effect on the magnitude of the estimated differential. Second, Pencavel's estimate was made for 1964 whereas ours is made for 1974. It is well known that the union/non-union differential varies in an inverse way with the level of economic activity. (See Lewis, 1963.) The year 1964 was a year of high and rising economic activity (measured by the unemployment rate) in the U.K. whereas the year 1973 was preceded by six consecutive years of decline in the level of economic activity. Further, one has the distinct impression that trade union activity was more intense in the years 1968–73 than in any other period in the recent past and this could have had the effect of increasing the relative wage effect of trade unions. (See Wiles (1973) on the latter topic. Although he talks in terms of trade unions and wage *inflation* his observations are still relevant.) Third, we can conduct a crude credibility check on the estimated differential of 36 per cent. The mean of the *CA* series for our sample is about 80 per cent. The NES publish data on the distribution of earnings for the same sample for which we have estimated the differential of 36 per cent. The mean earnings of the lower quartile of the sample – the nearest class size to the percentage not covered by a collective agreement – were £28.60 gross per week. A differential of 36 per cent is approximately equal to a mean money differential of about £12 per week and that implies a mean non-union wage of around £28.40 per week. While there is no evidence of any kind to indicate that the 20 per cent of our sample who were not covered by a collective agreement were contained within the lower 25 per cent of the earnings distribution, there must be a presumption that, if there exists a positive union/non-union differential at all, the two groups will tend to contain the same broad membership. However, the reader is left to judge for himself whether or not our estimate of the differential is credible in the light of the facts presented above.

Finally, then, we may say that our findings indicate that the influence of trade unions on the relative structure of earnings in the U.K. is considerably greater than has hitherto been supposed. The magnitude of the differential itself, even though our estimates are only very approximate, appears to be considerably in excess of previous estimates. Equally important, however, is the fact that the union rate of pay determines the earnings of a quarter of the male labour force who are not trade union members. Via these two routes the effects of trade union activity appear to have had a major impact on the structure of relative earnings and this raises the question of the degree to which resource allocation has been affected by trade union activity. In particular it would be of great interest to know how the U.K. compares with other countries in respect of the relative wage effect of unions, the resultant allocative effects and the general consequence for the performance of the economy. At first sight it does appear as though the U.K. has experienced a greater union relative wage effect than the U.S.A. but direct comparisons of estimated union/non-union differentials cannot be made since there are both conceptual and practical differences in arriving at the estimates. However it may prove possible in future work to attempt some such comparisons. [. . .]

NOTE

1. A point of clarification is required here in respect of workers who are covered by Wages Councils and are also included in the CA estimates. According to the Donovan Commission about four million workers come within the scope of Wages Councils and Agricultural Wages Boards (Donovan, 1968). However, Donovan estimates that of these, two and

a half million workers are in catering, retail distribution and hairdressing. None of these is included in our sample of occupations. Further, four of our occupations are in agriculture, which accounts for almost half a million workers covered by Agricultural Wages Boards, but, as Donovan points out, in agriculture there is an effective system of voluntary collective bargaining over and above the minima set by the Wages Boards (Donovan, 1968, p. 66). For the rest, we can only identify four other occupations in our sample which are covered by Wages Councils — one in clothing and three in road haulage. In each of these cases some measure of voluntary collective bargaining co-exists with the Wages Council (Donovan, 1968, p. 59). Hence, so far as our sample of occupations is concerned, the CA data are a very high quality series in measuring the occupational distribution of the coverage of collective agreements.

REFERENCES

Arrow, K. J. and Capron, W. M., 'Dynamic Shortages and Price Rises — the Engineer-Scientist Case', *Quarterly Journal of Economics*, Vol. 73, 1959.

Blaug, M., 'The Rate of Return on Investment in Education in Great Britain', *The Manchester School*, Vol. 33, 1965.

Bowman, M. J., 'The Human Investment Revolution in Economic Thought', *Sociology of Education*, Vol. 39, 1966.

Donovan Commission, *Report of the Royal Commission on Trade Unions and Employers' Associations 1965-1968*, London, H.M.S.O., Cmnd. 3623.

Lewis, H. G., *Unionism and Relative Wages in the United States*, Chicago, Chicago U.P., 1963.

Lewis, H. G., 'Unionism and Relative Wages in the United States' in Burton *et al.* (eds.), *Readings in Labour Market Analysis*, Holt, Rinehart and Winston, 1971.

Lipsey, R. G., 'The Relation between Unemployment and the Rate of Change of Money Wage Rates in the United Kingdom, 1862-1957: A Further Analysis', *Economica*, February, 1960.

Metcalf, D., Nickell, S., and Richardson, R., 'The Structure of Hours and Earnings in British Manufacturing Industry', mimeo, 1974.

Mulvey, C., 'Collective Agreements and Relative Earnings in U.K. Manufacturing in 1973', *Economica*, 1976.

Parnes, H. S., 'Relation of Occupation to Educational Qualification' in H. S. Parnes (ed.), *Planning Education for Economic and Social Development*, Paris, O.E.C.D., 1964.

Pencavel, J., 'The Demand for Union Services: an Exercise', *Industrial and Labour Relations Review*, No. 24, 1971.

Pencavel, J., 'Relative Wages and Trade Unions in the United Kingdom', *Economica*, May, 1974.

Reder, M., 'Unions and Wages: the Problems of Measurement', *Journal of Political Economy*, Vol. 73, 1965.

Rosen, S., 'Trade Union Power, Threat Effects and the Extent of Organization', *Review of Economic Studies*, Vol. 36, 1969.

Throop, A. W., 'The Union/Non-Union Wage Differential and Cost-Push Inflation', *American Economic Review*, March, 1968.

Weiss, L., 'Concentration and Labor Earnings', *American Economic Review*, March, 1966.

Wiles, P., 'Cost Inflation and the State of Economic Theory', *Economic Journal*, June, 1973.

3.6 Unions and Relative Wages*

[...]

1. METHODOLOGY

The methodology for estimating the impact of unions on relative wages and the conceptual problems involved in such estimates are set out in Lewis[1] and in more simplified form in Pencavel, and Mulvey.[2] Each analysis proceeds from a simple identity. The logarithm of the geometric average wage, W, may be thought of as a geometric weighted average of the logarithm of the geometric average union wage, W^u, and the logarithm of the geometric average non-union wage, W^n, so that

$$W = W^n(1 - T) + W^u T$$
$$= W^n + (W^u - W^n)T$$
$$= W^n + DT$$

where T is the fraction of workers who are union members or who are covered by collective agreements and $D = \ln(1 + M)$ is the logarithm of unity plus the proportionate union/non-union wage differential. W and T are obtained from published data. W^n is replaced by a vector of variables which determine it (e.g. skill, experience, age) and M is then estimated from regression analysis. It is M we are interested in here — the proportionate union/non-union wage differential (or mark-up) for otherwise homogeneous labour.[3]

Log of earnings is normally used as the dependent variable because proportionate differentials have more intuitive appeal and because if we wish to make comparisons of M over time or over local labour markets or across skill groups, the proportionate mark-up makes more sense than the absolute mark-up (in £ or pence) which is calculated if the dependent variable is not entered in logs. Further, if the data used to estimate M is from industry average wages and if the distribution of wages within each industry is log normal then log earnings is more 'representative' than earnings not in logs.

M can be estimated using two types of data in three different combinations. First, cross-section data on average unionisation level, average pay, average skill mix etc., by industry or occupation or local labour market can be used. Second, the data can refer to individuals. Third, a mixture of individual and industry/ occupation averages can be used. In this last case the observations are individuals but because the researcher does not know whether the individual is a union member or is union covered or not, the extent of unionisation in the individual's industry or occupation is used to calculate M. While these latter studies overcome the problem of the simultaneous determination of union membership and wage levels, they suffer from an omitted variable problem.

*From David Metcalf, 'Unions, Incomes Policy and Relative Wages in Britain', *British Journal of Industrial Relations*, Vol. 15, July 1977.

It is important to interpret M correctly. Where the data refer to individuals and it is known whether or not a person is unionised/covered, the interpretation is straightforward: the individual who is a union member/covered receives a proportionate wage differential of M per cent as compared with an otherwise identical person who is not a union member/covered. Unfortunately this type of calculation has not been made for Britain because of data problems. Data which indicate whether a person is a union member/covered (e.g. raw 1973 *New Earnings Survey* (N.E.S.) data on coverage of collective agreements) do not simultaneously give personal characteristics such as age, skill and experience. Data which are good on personal characteristics (e.g. the annual General Household Survey) do not indicate whether an individual is a union member/covered or not.

In the studies discussed below the unionisation variable usually refers to union coverage by industry. This causes a problem in interpreting M which is sometimes neglected. M may be interpreted in two similar ways. We may say that the average wage in an industry which is 100 per cent covered is, *ceteris paribus*, M per cent greater than an industry 0 per cent covered. Alternatively, a worker in the 100 per cent covered industry earns M per cent more, *ceteris paribus*, than a worker in the 0 per cent covered industry. The problem is that we seldom observe an industry with no coverage or with complete collective agreement coverage. Alternatively, therefore, one may say that the wage in an industry with 90 per cent coverage is M/2 per cent greater, *ceteris paribus*, than that in an industry with 40 per cent coverage. Even this may, however, be incorrect because the union coverage–wage relationship is likely to be non-linear.[4]

Finally, W^u/W^n must *not* be interpreted as the wage of union workers relative to the wage these workers would have received in the *absence* of unionism. It is this point that makes any calculation of the distortions imposed by unions on resources allocation extremely hazardous.

It must be emphasised that the estimates of M do not rest on any model of 'union power'. They are obtained solely by manipulating an identity and estimating a regression of earnings on unionisation and other variables. The *reason* union members/covered earn more than similar people who are not members covered has not been investigated in these studies. We return to this below.

Coverage data are preferable to membership data for estimating the impact of unions on the structure of relative wages. Estimates of M from membership data cannot properly control for wage spillovers between union members and those non-union members who are nevertheless covered by a collective agreement. For example, in the manufacturing industry in 1973 about 80 per cent of the full-time adult manual labour force were covered by a collective agreement but only about 55 per cent were union members.[5] Thus at least one-quarter of the manual work force in manufacturing is paid at the union rate despite not being a union member. The studies discussed below mainly use the Department of Employment's 1973 N.E.S. data on union coverage to estimate M. Coverage has been used rather than membership to estimate M not only because coverage data are preferable to membership data but also because it is notoriously difficult to calculate union membership across industries or occupations.[6] It is not sensible to make comparisons of M estimated from N.E.S. data with M estimated from union membership data because coverage and membership measure different things. Thus these 1973 estimates of M for Britain cannot be *directly* compared with estimates of M for the U.S.,[7] although it is true that coverage and membership overlap more closely in the U.S. than they do in Britain, or with Pencavel's estimate for Britain referring to 1964 which used membership data.[8]

2. RESULTS

The results of some recent studies which have calculated M using the 1973 N.E.S. data on coverage of collective agreements are presented in Table 3.2. This indicates the author, the year for which M is calculated, the observations used (industry or occupation or individual data), the definition of the earnings variable, the definition of the coverage variable, the other explanatory variables included in the regression equation, and the estimate of M.

In view of the problems of interpretation discussed above and other statistical problems elaborated later, the results of the various studies must be treated with caution. They are interesting but are only a tentative first step to estimating the impact of unions on relative wages in Britain. Nevertheless it seems clear that union coverage was associated with a positive M in Britain in the early 1970s. The results imply that, *ceteris paribus*, the average hourly wage in an industry whose labour force is completely covered by a collective agreement is around 25 per cent to 35 per cent greater than the average wage in a completely uncovered industry, and the corresponding weekly earnings differential is even larger. This accords with popular views on 'militancy' and 'union power', but the bald evidence in Table 3.2 must be both extended and qualified to get a fuller picture of impact of unions on relative wages.

Both Mulvey and Foster[9] who use data for occupations and Stewart[10] who uses data on individuals estimate M for weekly earnings. Their estimates of M lie between 22 per cent and 47 per cent. Stewart's estimate refers to manual workers only. When Mulvey and Foster recalculate M for manual occupations only (83 observations) their estimate is 36 per cent to 60 per cent, which brackets that of Stewart. However, M should be estimated from hourly pay data, not data on weekly earnings. It is hourly earnings which indicate the opportunity set (income and leisure) facing the individual: weekly earnings comprise the choice of hours given the opportunity set and the opportunity set itself. Weekly earnings cannot therefore be said to measure the effect of unions on the welfare of the individual. Further, from the firm's point of view, it is hourly earnings which determine its production costs: weekly earnings reflect the firm's choice between men and hours and do not measure the underlying labour costs. It has been tentatively estimated that, *ceteris paribus*, (i.e. at a

Table 3.2

Impact of Unions on Relative Wages

Author	Year	Observations	Definition of dependent variable	Definition of union variable	Other explanatory variables	M(%)
Mulvey (1976)	1973	77 M.L.H. manufacturing industries	F.T. adult male manual hourly earnings	% of F.T. adult male manual covered by collective agreement	Skill mix, concentration ratio, plant size, change in employment, output per man, % female	26–35
Mulvey and Foster (1976)	1973	99 occupation groups	F.T. adult male gross weekly earnings	% of F.T. adult male covered by collective agreement	Education years, education qualification, skill mix, employment change, unemployment/vacancy ratio	22–31
Nickell (1977)	1972	121 M.L.H. manufacturing industries	F.T. adult male/female manual hourly earnings	% of F.T. adult male/female manual covered by collective agreement	Skill mix, location, change in employment, index of concentration, age mix, plant size, conurbation, shift work, payment by results	19–26 (female) 18–21 (male)
Stewart (1976)	1971	2082 individuals	Male manual F.T. manufacturing employees aged under 65, weekly earnings	% male manual workers covered (2-digit industry corresponding to the individual)	Education qualifications, labour force experience, service with present employer, qualified apprentice or not, currently apprenticed or not, skill, concentration ratio, plant size, change in (employ. hours)	40–47

given hourly wage) unionised male workers supply two hours less per week than non-union workers.[11] Thus the estimates of Mulvey and Foster and Stewart *understate* the true M because labour supply effects of unions are mixed in with wage effects.[12]

In the 1960s industrial relations specialists, and others, became concerned at the apparently haphazard nature of local bargaining which was often super-imposed on official bargaining and which, it was claimed, contributed to strike activity and inflation. For example, the Donovan Report[13] suggested that many sectors of British industry had two systems of collective bargaining with in-formal workplace bargaining between shop stewards and plant management existing simultaneously with formal company or industry-wide bargaining, and the Commission expressed their distaste of the informal element.[14] It is interest-ing therefore to examine estimates of M by type of agreement. We are fortunate because the 1973 N.E.S. gives details of people covered by (i) national and sup-plementary agreements; (ii) national agreements only; (iii) company, district or local agreements only; and (iv) no collective agreement.

Each of the studies cited in Table 3.2, except Mulvey and Foster, give details of M by type of agreement. The results for males are tolerably consistent among the different studies. For example, using the same basic data described in Table 3.2, Mulvey calculates the union relative wage effect by type of agreement.[15]

	M(%)
national agreement only	0
national plus supplementary	41–46
district, local, company only	46–48

Thus in manufacturing industry those covered by a national agreement only do not gain relative to those not covered by a collective agreement, while those covered by district, local and company agreements have a wage advantage of over 40 per cent irrespective of whether or not they are also covered by a national agreement. Stewart confirms that the same pattern holds in non-manufacturing: those subject to local agreements have a substantially higher M than those only covered by national agreements.[16] Pencavel found a similar result using 1964 earnings data and union membership information.[17] (We cannot compare the absolute magnitude of Pencavel's findings with those in Table 3.2 because he used membership not coverage data, but we can compare the structure of relative magnitudes of M for local and national agreements derived from the different unionisation measures).

A problem of interpretation occurs when we consider these supplementary agreements. It appears that people covered by supplementary district, local or company agreements receive a higher M than those covered by national agreements only. However, many of the supplementary agreements have a national flavour. The industrial relations literature is rich in descriptions of institutional mechanisms whereby local bargains struck in one plant are transmitted to plants of the same firm in other areas or to plants of different firms.[18] Thus, even where the coverage is said to be 'supplementary district, local or company agreements', such agreements may have national dimensions. This accords with economic theory: a relatively high M is likely to be associated with an inelastic rather than elastic demand for labour. If a plant or local agreement gets transmitted to other plants in the industry making the same product the labour costs will rise by a similar amount in all plants causing the demand for labour in any one plant to be more secure than it otherwise would be (although industry demand for labour may fall if the relative product price is forced up by the higher labour costs).

Nickell has calculated M separately for males and females.[19] He finds that in 1972 union [coverage] raised female wages by around 19-26 per cent compared with non-union female wages, while the corresponding figure for males is between 18-21 per cent. The lower bound of the reported ranges occurs when average establishment size is included in the regression equations used to estimate M. This leads us to prefer the upper estimates because it is likely that the average establishment size is picking up an effect on wage levels which should more properly be associated with unionisation because it is easier (i.e. cheaper) to unionise large establishments. Nickell also presents results which distinguish M by type of collective agreement. Women in manufacturing who are covered by local agreements only (12 per cent of the female sample) have an M of 45-49 per cent, almost twice that estimated for males. Similarly women covered by national agreements only (29 per cent of the female sample) extract a premium of 20-23 per cent, again nearly double the male premium.

Nickell's results enable us to calculate the effect of union coverage on male-female wage differentials. This impact depends on (i) the respective number of males and females covered by collective agreements, and (ii) the respective M for males and females. Some 84 per cent of manual males in manufacturing are covered while only 75 per cent of females are covered. The impact of unions on the sex differential may thus be inferred from the following data:

$$\text{women } (.75 \times 1.26) + (.25 \times 1.00) = 1.190$$
$$\text{men } \quad (.84 \times 1.21) + (.16 \times 1.00) = 1.176$$

It appears that in 1972 unions narrowed the sex differential by over 1 percentage point.[20]

3. PROBLEMS AND SPECULATION

A number of unresolved statistical problems surround the estimates discussed above. These include the interrelated problems of simultaneous determination of the extent of unionisation and earnings levels, and variables omitted from the regression analysis which biases upwards the estimated M. Another more easily resolvable problem concerns the level of aggregation of the data. The estimates using data on industrial orders (2-digit industries) are different from those which use data on minimum list headings (3-digit industries).

Studies which use solely industry or occupation data or solely individual data calculate M inaccurately if levels of unionisation and levels of earnings are simultaneously determined.[21] If high levels of unionisation are partly 'explained' by high earnings, M will be biased upwards unless this feedback is allowed for. As yet no studies in Britain have explored this possibility and therefore we do not know whether or not M is biased and, if so, by how much. However, the results of Stewart[22] suggest this particular (narrow) problem may not be too important. Stewart calculates M from individual data on earnings and industry average data on unionisation. While the individual's earnings may influence his decision to become a union member his particular decision cannot influence the extent of union coverage in his 2-digit industry: it is one decision among thousands or millions. As Stewart's estimates of M are among the highest (and are underestimates of M for hourly wages for reasons discussed above), this suggests the M's calculated by other studies are not overstated much on the narrow grounds of simultaneity between earnings and unionisation.

It seems probable, however, that the M's presented in Table 3.2 are overstated for another reason. It is extremely difficult to control fully for inter-industry or inter-individual differences in labour quality. Thus unionisation may be 'credited' with an effect on wages which is really attributable to differences in labour quality. For example studies which use industry data attempt to control for labour quality by including inter-industry differences in skill-mix as an explanatory variable in the regression equation. As the skill-mix is itself partially determined by bargaining, it is not clear that this satisfactorily controls for quality.

This labour quality point is probably important in explaining the reason why the M estimated for local agreements is so high. Firms which operate company-wide bargaining (e.g. I.C.I., Ford) tend to have high quality labour and operate a high-wage–low turnover policy.[23] As it is not possible to control adequately for labour quality and labour turnover, unionisation is picking up (in part at least) a wage effect for which it is not responsible. This would be worth investigating further and would throw light on the so-called dual labour market hypothesis. In particular it suggests a reason why all employees do not clamour to get covered by a local agreement given such a favourable relative wage effect: some firms (in the secondary labour market?) operate non-union, low wage, low quality, high turnover strategies, while other firms (in the primary labour market?) use the reverse strategy (Pencavel and Nickell have both developed these ideas formally).[24] It is also possible that non-unionised small establishments tend to have more relaxed worker–employer relations than larger unionised establishments, and that some individuals take a lower money wage to work in the former plants. Thus some part of the premium received by the union members may represent a compensating wage-differential for the more rigorous industrial relations regime in which they work. Because it is not possible to easily allow for these non-monetary factors, the union–non-union comparison based only on pecuniary earnings may overstate the theoretically desirable differential, which relates to both psychic and pecuniary earnings.

Another reason why the estimates of M for local agreements are relatively high concerns piece work. Pencavel speculated that the reason union members covered by local agreements have a higher M than those covered only by national agreements was because 'domestic bargaining is especially prevalent in industries where payments-by-results schemes afford unions greater bargaining influence on hourly earnings'.[25] This idea has not yet been analysed – the test requires that an interaction variable between unionisation and payments-by-results schemes be included in wage equations – but it is interesting to note that neither Sawyer[26] nor Shorey[27] found the proportion of workers covered by payments-by-results schemes important in explaining the structure of industrial wages.

Thus employees and firms are heterogeneous but the available statistics are unable to control for this. A survey which collected data simultaneously on the characteristics of the individual and his household and the characteristics of the firm in which he works would enable us to circumvent many of these problems.[28] Alternatively (and more cheaply) merely adding a question on union membership/coverage to the General Household Survey would provide much of the required information.

This speculation concerning the role of differences among firms in their labour market strategies in determining the estimated union–non-union differential must not be pushed too far. Some tentative evidence suggests that M in the 1970s is double what it was in the 1960s.[29] If the main reason for the observed M was uncontrolled–for labour quality differences, it is unlikely M would increase so much in such a short period. Thus incomplete control for inter-industry and inter-firm differences in labour quality is probably one reason why the union–non-union differential is estimated to be relatively big, but it is by no means the whole story: there is some union impact on wages as well.

It is possible that after controlling properly for labour quality, M will be found to be small. A typical interpretation of this is that unions do raise relative wages but that, in turn, firms hire better quality labour and the wage per efficiency unit is nearly constant across firms.[30] This may be true as far as it goes, but it should be remembered that the initial union relative wage effect nevertheless led to distortions in the mix of employment quality across different industries and occupations.

The problem of omitted variables is not just confined to labour quality and labour turnover. In his regression equations for non-manufacturing industry Stewart finds that the 6 per cent of individuals covered by local agreements only benefit from an M of well over 6 per cent of individuals covered by local agreements only benefit from an M of well over 100 per cent.[31] As he points out, his earnings data are weekly rather than hourly, and these people are concentrated in the transport sector. Thus the estimated M is biased upwards because he did not control for factors such as long hours, shift work, and unsocial hours.

Another reason for caution before inferring too much from estimates of M is that such estimates are not unresponsive to the level of aggregation of the data. For example, Mulvey uses data on 77 M.L.H. (3-digit) manufacturing industries to arrive at a union relative wage effect of 26–35 per cent.[32] When he made a similar calculation using data on 16 S.I.C. orders (2-digit industries) the corresponding estimate was over 50 per cent.

4. EXTENSIONS

Work on the relative wage effect of unions in Britain might proceed in two directions. First, estimates of M of the type reported in Table 3.2 need to be firmed up. It is important to control adequately for labour quality and to provide more estimates of M for particular groups (e.g. men and women and blacks and whites) and over time. This will enable economists to say something sensible about the impact of unions on income inequality and on money wage inflation. Ideally such studies should use individual data [. . .]. Second, it is important to ask *why* those covered by collective agreements enjoy such an apparent wage advantage over similar people not so covered. This is a more difficult task than the first: it involves setting out a model of union wage policy and requires a detailed knowledge of the system of collective bargaining. As economists (and others) have been singularly lax in testing models of union wage policy and, in the main, are not much interested in institutional bargaining arrangements, it is unlikely that much progress will be made on the second task in the near future. [. . .]

NOTES

1. H. G. Lewis, *Unionism and Relative Wages in the U.S.*, Chicago University Press, 1963, Chapter 2.
2. J. Pencavel, 'Relative Wages and Trade Unions in the U.K.', *Economica*, May 1974, and C. Mulvey, 'Collective Agreements and Relative Earnings in U.K. Manufacturing Industry in 1973', *Economica*, November 1976.
3. The identity holds where W^n and W^u are both expressed either as arithmetic means or as logs of geometric means. When using data on industry average wages to calculate M (rather than micro-data) a problem occurs. In general arithmetic means are seldom used to calculate M because it is believed that proportionate differentials (i.e. in percentage terms) make more sense than absolute differentials. Unfortunately no data exist on the geometric mean wage in each industry. Thus when M is estimated in proportionate terms, the log of the (published) arithmetic mean wage is used in the calculation in place of the log of the (unavailable) geometric mean wage. This causes a minor bias in the result: Mark Stewart has worked out that if the distribution of earnings within industry is log normal, and if union coverage is negatively related to inequality in earnings, then M calculated from using the logs of the arithmetic mean instead of the log of the geometric mean is an underestimate of true M.
4. A. Rees, *The Economics of Work and Pay*, Harper and Row, New York, 1973, Chapter 10.

5. C. Mulvey and J. Foster, 'Occupational Earnings in the U.K. and the Effects of Collective Agreements', *Manchester School*, September 1976.
6. Even union coverage data may not be error-free. Just as there are well-known problems of compliance with minimum wages set by Wages Councils, so an employer may report in response to the D.E.'s enquiries that his firm does pay union wage scales when in fact it does not. This misreporting might occur if, for example, paying non-union workers at less than the union rates invites either social opprobium or investigation under the schedule in the Employment Protection Act which relates to firms which pay below 'normal' wages in their local labour market.
7. G. E. Johnson, 'Economic Analysis of Trade Unionism', *American Economic Review*, Vol. LXV, No. 2, May 1975 and O. Ashenfelter, 'Union Relative Wage Effects: New Evidence and a Survey of Their Implications for Wage Inflation', Princeton University, Industrial Relations Section, Working Paper 89, June 1976 (mimeo).
8. J. Pencavel, op. cit.
9. C. Mulvey and J. Foster, op. cit.
10. M. Stewart, 'Determinants of Earnings: Estimates from the General Household Survey', Centre for the Economics of Education, London School of Economics, 1976 (mimeo).
11. D. Metcalf, S. Nickell, and R. Richardson, 'The Structure of Hours and Earnings in British Manufacturing Industry', *Oxford Economic Papers*, Vol. 28, No. 2, July 1976.
12. The relationship between union coverage and hours of work by industry is complex. Thomson, *et al.*, (this Journal) show that covered groups tend to secure pay differentials over uncovered groups via higher overtime, incentive and shift premia and that actual weekly hours worked are similar for covered and uncovered groups. However, their data do not control for other factors which also affect hours such as skill and age.
13. *Report of the Royal Commission on Trade Unions and Employers' Associations*, 1965–1968, Cmnd 3623, H.M.S.O., London 1968.
14. Industry-wide bargaining is bargaining between national trade unions and employers' associations; company-wide bargaining is between national trade unions and a company and agreements apply to all the plants of that company; plant-wide bargaining refers to bargaining at the level of the whole establishment; workplace bargaining is between shop stewards and plant management. It should be noted that an 'industry' in the industrial relations sense differs from the economic notion of an industry. The industry in industrial relations refers to a collective bargaining unit and may be wider or narrower than an industry as defined in the Standard Industrial Classification. For example, the engineering industry in industrial relations covers at least five industrial orders, namely mechanical engineering, instrument engineering, electrical engineering, vehicles, and parts of metal goods.
15. C. Mulvey, op. cit.
16. M. Stewart, 'Determinants of Earnings: Estimates from the General Household Survey', Centre for the Economics of Education, London School of Economics, 1976 (mimeo).
17. J. Pencavel, op. cit.
18. See, for example, S. Lerner, J. Cable and S. Gupta, *Workshop Wage Determination*, Pergamon Press, Oxford, 1969.
19. S. Nickell, 'Trade Unions and the Position of Women in the Industrial Wage Structure', *British Journal of Industrial Relations*, July 1977.
20. This calculation assumes implicitly that the extent of unionisation is not a determinant of W^n, or alternatively, that if unionisation raises or reduces W^n, it does so uniformly for men and for women. These general equilibrium effects of unionisation have not been investigated in the British empirical literature.
21. Compare M. Reder, 'Unions and Wages: The Problem of Measurement', *Journal of Political Economy*, Vol. 73, 1964.
22. M. Stewart, op. cit.
23. Compare for example, O. Ashenfelter and G. E. Johnson, 'Unionism, Relative Wages and Labor Quality in U.S. Manufacturing Industry', *International Economic Review*, Vol. 13, No. 3, October 1972.
24. See J. Pencavel, 'Wages, Specific Training and Labour Turnover in U.S. Manufacturing Industries', *International Economic Review*, Vol. 13, February 1972, and S. Nickell, 'Wage Structures and Quit Rates', *International Economic Review*, Vol. 17, No. 1,

February 1976.
25. J. Pencavel, op. cit.
26. M. Sawyer, 'The Earnings of Manual Workers: A Cross Section Analysis', *Scottish Journal of Political Economy*, Vol. XX, No. 2, June 1973.
27. J. Shorey, 'Wage Differentials by Plant Size', University College, Cardiff (mimeo).
28. Compare G. E. Johnson, op. cit.
29. See R. Layard, D. Metcalf and S. Nickell, 'The Union Coverage–Non-Union Coverage Wage Differential', Centre for the Economics of Education, London School of Economics, 1976 (mimeo).
30. L. Weiss, 'Concentration and Labour Earnings', *American Economic Review*, March 1966.
31. M. Stewart, op. cit.
32. C. Mulvey, op. cit.

4. The Structure of Earnings

Introductory Note

In April 1977 the median gross weekly earnings of male manual workers in Great Britain were £68·20, but the dispersion around that figure was considerable.[1] One in ten workers earned less than £48·10, while one in ten achieved gross earnings of £98·50 or more. What was required of a worker that he might feature in the top end of the distribution? Finding a job in a well-paid occupation would have been a good start: whereas 'face-trained coal-miners' averaged £84·90 per week, general farmworkers managed a meagre £51·60. Working in a well-paid industry would do no harm: in 'coal and petroleum products' (mainly oil-refining) earnings averaged £86·10 for 44.7 hours per week, while agriculture brought up the rear with £56·30 for 47.0 hours. Finally, much depends on geography. Within Great Britain (that is, excluding Northern Ireland) it will surprise few to learn that the lowest median earnings were found in South-West England (£65·40).[2] Among the highest-paying regions, Greater London was beaten into second place by South Yorkshire (£75·90 as against £75·50). London, though, had the greatest concentration of extremely well-paid manual workers in the country, for one in ten grossed over £134·80 (all figures from Department of Employment, 1977). The causes of these disparities in pay remain as hotly disputed as the closely related question of their justice. (Remember, too, that inequality is much greater when women, and non-manual workers of both sexes, are taken into account.) The readings in this section provide a sample from the conflicting, incomplete, and inevitably inconclusive literature on earnings differentials.

If all labour markets were in perfectly competitive long-run equilibrium, and if all labour were homogeneous, there would be complete equality not of pay but of the 'net advantages' in all jobs. Money earnings would vary, but only to the extent required to compensate workers for differences in hours worked, in the degree of discomfort, monotony, and danger incurred in their work, and in the other non-pecuniary attributes of their jobs. Non-pecuniary advantages and disadvantages apart, there would be no reason for any dispersion in levels of pay. In general, then, wage differentials result either from market imperfections or from the heterogeneity of labour. Controversy has accordingly centred on the nature and significance of imperfections in the labour market on the one hand, and on the origins and importance of differences in the quality of labour on the other.

There are, broadly, two ways in which empirical evidence can be brought to bear upon these questions. The first, and more traditional, method of approach is to study the determinants of differences in pay between *groups* of workers, classified by occupation, by industry, or by region. The second, and more modern, perspective takes as its starting-point the *individual* worker, and attempts to explain earnings in terms of the individual's personal attributes and the characteristics of his or her employer. This second approach has been possible only since the invention of computers, with their ability to process vast quantities of data. It is not available for use in the analysis of changes in the wage structure over long periods. Nor has the individual earnings function approach been widely employed in Britain, where the law forbids the collection of income data in the census, and household surveys of labour market relevance are still in their infancy.

If research techniques differ, there may be at least a common theoretical foundation. The most general neoclassical framework for the analysis of pay structure combines marginal productivity theory with the economic analysis of the use of time, in an attempt to demonstrate the crucial role of human investment in determining individual earnings (and, by implication, the differences in average pay levels between groups of workers who differ in their ownership of human capital). Becker (Reading 4.1) provides an exceptionally clear statement of the argument. Individuals invest in human capital up to the point where its marginal rate of return equals the marginal cost. On the assumption that the consumption benefits of learning are negligible, the returns on any human investment equal its net contribution to the individual's earning capacity, which in turn (given a perfect labour market) is equal to the induced increase in his or her marginal product.

The downward-sloping *shape* of the individual's demand curve for human capital reflects Becker's belief that 'diminishing returns' apply to investments in education and training, while its *position* depends on the innate abilities of the individual in question (the more able I am, the greater the results when I devote a given amount of time and money to enhancing my productive capacity). The corresponding supply curve reflects the availability of finance for human investments. It slopes upwards, because the marginal cost of borrowing (or of abstaining from present consumption) is likely to increase as more and more investment is undertaken. Its position will depend on the individual's wealth and credit status.

For each individual the intersection of the demand and supply curves gives the optimum stock of human capital and the rate of return upon it, and hence the 'human capital component' of the individual's earnings (which, unless 'raw, uneducated ability' is especially important, is likely to dominate *total* earnings). The inequality in this component of earnings will depend both on the slopes of the curves and on the dispersion in their positions. Becker has much more to say about the latter, and points in particular to two extreme cases. The first is complete equality of opportunity, where all individuals have the same supply curve:

here earnings differentials result only from differences in innate abilities (Figure 4.3). The second is complete equality of abilities, where pay dispersion depends only on differences in access to finance (Figure 4.2). In general both sources of inequality will operate (Figure 4.4). Since innate abilities are by definition not amenable to change, it follows that unacceptable inequalities in pay can be attacked only by increasing the equality of opportunity – increasing, that is, the access of disadvantaged individuals and groups to channels of finance, through grants and subsidized loans for human investments.

Human capital theorists thus conclude that educational policy, rather than direct intervention in the labour market, is the most efficient means of reducing pay differentials. The labour market, indeed, enters the analysis only indirectly, by determining the marginal productivity conditions behind the demand curves for human capital. Skills are acquired *prior* to entry into the labour market, and the distribution of jobs is supposed to be perfectly malleable, depending on the distribution of human capital endowments (and thus on the distribution of skills) produced by the education system. There are serious logical problems with such models (see Oulton, 1974). Equally fundamental is the empirical evidence that differences in formal education account for only a small part of the variance in individual earnings, no more than 7 per cent on Mincer's (1974) reckoning. Mincer found job experience to be a much more important force than schooling in contributing to inequalities in pay, and interpreted his findings as evidence that most relevant skills are employer-specific and acquired informally, 'on-the-job'. Although Mincer himself concludes that the critical importance of experience variables is fully consistent with (a broadened version of) human capital theory, it is easy to see that other interpretations are possible.

One alternative is outlined by Thurow in Reading 4.2. He agrees with Mincer that most economically relevant skills are obtained on the job, after formal education has ceased. This takes place inside the firm, through formal training and informal learning-by-doing, as emphasized by internal labour market theorists (above, pp. 107–117). The distribution of *skills* within the firm is malleable, that is, subject to its own control. The distribution of *jobs*, however, is largely determined by technology, for fluctuations in relative wages have very little effect on job design (Piore, 1968). On this interpretation it is access to training opportunities which governs an individual's earnings, and education has no direct effect on pay. It may have an indirect effect if schooling influences one's place in the 'labour queue', that is, one's ability to gain access to the internal labour markets where training may be obtained. If true, this poses a serious challenge to human capital theory: education, if it produces anything at all, produces *credentials*, not marketable skills, and there is no reason to be surprised at the relatively weak relationship between schooling and earnings (see also Blaug, 1976). Reading 4.2 is in effect a brief and provisional summary of Thurow's later (1976) book, which contains a much longer and more convincing analysis of the relevant empirical evidence. Similar ideas have, as we shall see, influenced the recent theories of dual and segmented labour markets (below, pp. 320–48).

Thurow is concerned with the distribution of individual incomes from employment. Human capital theory has also been used to explain the pattern of group earnings differentials, by occupation, industry, and region. It should be noted right at the start that these categories are in no sense mutually exclusive. High-wage regions, for example, tend to be those with an exceptional proportion of workers employed in relatively well-paid industries and/or occupations, while high-wage industries will often be found to be concentrated in prosperous regions and to offer jobs in predominantly well-paid occupations. These inter-relations are often not easy to unravel, and the direction of causation is rarely obvious. Is South Yorkshire so prosperous because of its mining industry or, less plausibly (?), are miners relatively well-paid because they tend to live in high-wage regions? Are 'face-trained coal-miners' at the top of the manual wage-earners' ladder because they work in the coal industry, or is the prosperity of this occupation an independent factor pushing up the average for the industry as a whole? Readings 4.3–4.5 shed some light on these questions, but many shadowy recesses remain.

In Reading 4.3 Phelps Brown gives a kaleidoscopic account of differentials by occupation over several centuries for a number of countries. His data suggest that the human capital interpretation cannot be completely wrong, unless the twentieth-century narrowing of occupational wage differentials and the simultaneous expansion of mass education are entirely coincidental. Human capital theorists have less cause for satisfaction with the evidence concerning the timing of shifts in differentials (abruptly discontinuous, while the trend towards equality of opportunity has been slow and gradual); with their general failure to react in the expected fashion to cyclical fluctuations in economic activity; and with the continued importance in wage determination of custom and social norms. Too much should not perhaps be made of these anomalies, for it can be argued that occupational boundaries are inevitably too fluid for much economic significance to be attached to the average differences in pay between them.[3]

The hierarchy of wages by industry continues to fascinate labour economists. In Reading 4.4 Reder surveys the findings of an earlier generation of researchers, whose work in the late 1940s and the 1950s is now more appreciated than ever (see Reading 4.8), and presents a useful account of the theoretical importance of their work from an explicitly neoclassical viewpoint. According to the neo-classical 'competitive hypothesis', long-run equilibrium differentials in pay between industries will exist only if there are differences in the skill-composition of their respective labour forces. This is a simple human capital theory of inter-industry wage differentials in the long run. In the short run it is recognized that there will be a further source of inequality: because the short-run supply of labour to the industry is less than perfectly elastic, expanding industries will need, *ceteris paribus*, to pay higher wages than stagnant or contracting industries, so that they can bid labour away from the latter. There are no other reasons, from a neoclassical perspective, for inter-industry wage differences. If such differentials persist, over and above those resulting from differences in the skill-mix, then this implies that labour markets are not perfectly competitive, even in the long run. Reder's assessment of the empirical evidence is that any barriers to competition in the labour market are of relatively little long-run significance. There is now sufficient information as to the effects of unions to cast doubt on this conclusion (see Readings 3.5 and 3.6). As we shall shortly see, the theory of labour market segmentation poses an even more radical challenge to the 'competitive hypothesis'.

The forces responsible for differences in average earnings between regions are no less contentious. For Britain even empirical work is scanty, the most detailed study covering the period 1870–1914 (Hunt, 1973). The celebrated and apparently very persistent North–South differential in the United States has given rise to a substantial literature (see Perlman, 1969). Bradfield's trenchant criticism of the various explanations of the North–South differential is contained in Reading 4.5. Frequently encountered elements in such explanations include the immobility of labour, and regional differences in the capital–labour ratio, trade union power, and the level of technology. The immobility of labour, Bradfield argues, can be regarded as a necessary condition for a long-run wage differential between regions. It is not, however, a sufficient condition: if capital is sufficiently mobile the differential in earnings will be eroded, although workers are most reluctant to migrate. Regional variations in the capital–labour ratio also require that capital be immobile. Equally, if firms are able to migrate to poorly organized areas, it is unlikely that geographical differences in trade union power will long survive. But, Bradfield complains, the immobility of capital is itself never explained. No reliance can be placed upon regional distinctions in industrial- and skill-mixes, for these too are endogenous rather than exogenous variables. In the specific case of the North–South differential it seems that deeply entrenched racial discrimination and low educational levels are the primary factors involved (Scully, 1969), but the theory of regional wage differentials in general remains unsatisfactory.

There is one further source of inequality in pay to which considerable attention has been paid, and which is independent of the patterns of differentials considered so far. This is the dispersion of earnings within the local labour market, for workers of the same occupation, in the same industry, in the same locality. That such dispersion is considerable is not disputed, but interpretations differ. Kerr, in Reading 4.6, sees wage dispersion in local labour markets as the inevitable outcome of the 'balkanization' of labour markets which results from specific training and internal promotion practices within the internal labour market, the essence of which is the erection of barriers to labour mobility (see above pp. 107–117). At the extreme this process has been described as giving rise to a 'new industrial feudalism' (Ross, 1958), the implication being that firms need pay equal wages no more than feudal manors.

Addison (Reading 4.7) provides a framework of analysis which is much more in tune with mainstream neoclassical theory. He too observes that occupational titles may conceal more, in terms of the skill of the labour force, than they reveal. Following Stigler (Reading 1.3), he suggests that employers may regard the payment of relatively high wages as an acceptable substitute for intensive and costly labour market search operations. This implies that wage differentials are consistent with cost-minimization on the part of employers, so that unit labour costs may be equalized in the local labour market despite the wide variation in earnings.

We may recall at this point that, for the strict human capital theorist, earnings should depend only on the nature of the *skills* supplied by the individual worker, and not on the *job* in which they are performed. The firm, industry, and region of employment should be irrelevant to the size of the worker's pay-packet, at least in long-run equilibrium; and even the individual's occupation is relevant only to the extent that it serves as a proxy for his or her human capital endowments. The specific characteristics of individual firms (or 'establishment variables'), which Addison allows to play such a major role in determining earnings within the local labour market, are difficult to fit into a human capital framework. They may be more easily accommodated by Thurow's analysis, as a reflection of some of the more important influences upon the distribution of jobs. A little conceptual boldness leads directly to a theory of polarized or *dual* labour markets, according to which there are two markets in which labour may be sold, not one (or one thousand). Large, oligopolistic, capital-intensive, high-technology, strongly unionized firms offer 'good jobs', which combine relatively high wages at all points on the job ladder with favourable opportunities for progression up the ladder by means of internal training and promotion. Small, labour-intensive enterprises operating with backward techniques in fiercely competitive and largely non-unionized markets offer only 'bad jobs', with low wages and little or no prospect of advancement.[4]

A model of this type is developed by Wachtel and Betsey (Reading 4.8), who conclude that human capital theory, while not entirely disgraced, tells only part of the story. The individual's human capital endowments do affect his or her earnings, but only in conjunction with the opportunity to use them under favourable, rather than unfavourable, circumstances. *Ceteris paribus*, earnings are much higher in 'good jobs' in the 'core economy' (as it is termed by Bluestone, 1970) or the 'primary labour market' (Doeringer and Piore, 1971), than in the 'periphery' (Bluestone) or 'secondary labour market' (Doeringer and Piore). To the extent that industries may be allocated neatly to one or other of the two sectors, this provides an alternative perspective from which to criticize the 'competitive hypothesis' concerning inter-industry wage differentials.

The practical implications of labour market dualism are striking. Without an increase in the number of good jobs in the core or primary market, an extension of educational opportunities will be wasted. Its beneficiaries will either be trapped in bad jobs in the secondary market (periphery) where their education is of little use, or they will avoid such a fate by displacing incumbents of good jobs who will themselves be forced into the secondary market. Only direct intervention in the market mechanism offers the prospect of a significant reduction in inequality. The policy proposals of the dualists are therefore socialistic (or at least social-democratic) rather than liberal, which helps to explain why their ideas have not been well received in and around Chicago. Increases in statutory minimum wage levels, for example, seem more likely to benefit than to penalize the poor if viewed in a dualistic context. Secondary labour markets tend to display high rates of labour turnover, since internal labour markets are largely absent. Hence any reduction in employment resulting from an increase in the minimum wage will be spread fairly evenly across the whole, unstable, labour force, rather than concentrated on an unfortunate and permanently unemployed minority. Under these circumstances, as Allan King demonstrates in Reading 4.9, the conditions which must be satisfied for such a policy to benefit low-paid workers are much less stringent than neoclassical analyses suggest.

Dualism was developed largely as a result of the failure of human capital theory, and of policy programmes based upon it, in ghetto labour markets in large United States cities in the 1960s. The extent to which it may be generalized in time and space is still an open question. One initial attempt to apply similar reasoning to Britain (Bosanquet and Doeringer, 1973) was less than fully convincing, though in the narrower context of inner-city labour markets dual models may perform more successfully (see A. Friedman, 1978). Cain (Reading 4.10) summarizes the neoclassical counter-attack, which stands its ground on some points (notably, and successfully, as regards the suitability of 'bad workers' for 'good jobs'), while making a series of deft tactical retreats on others.[5] (In a much longer critique, Wachter (1974) concedes rather less.) Perspective may perhaps be gained by seeing dualism as a reaction against the single-minded neoclassicism of the earlier human capital theorists. In these terms, a reading of Cain's article suggests that dualism has not been a complete failure. Few would now argue, to return to the starting-point of this section, that inequalities in pay can be explained without detailed reference to the structure of labour markets.

NOTES

1. For female manual workers the corresponding figure was £43·70; for non-manual males, £88·90; and for non-manual female workers, £53·80.
2. More surprise may be occasioned by the information that the Scots (£72·50) and the Welsh (£72·20) earn more on average than the English (£71·30).
3. If internal labour markets have become progressively more important, and skills increasingly more specific to individual employers, one would expect occupations to become increasingly ill-defined. This tendency was being noted half a century ago (see the reference to Rowe's work in Reading 4.3, pp. 268–71). It may explain why, although average pay differentials between occupations have undoubtedly narrowed, the dispersion of *individual* earnings has altered only a little over the last century (Thatcher, 1968).

4. The historical origins of dual labour markets remain largely unexplored, though some radical economists trace their emergence to the growth of the giant corporation towards the end of the last century (Gordon, 1972; see also Stone, 1974). Some dualists, though by no means all, have been attracted by the analogies with the models of dualism in industrial organization proposed by Averitt (1967) and Galbraith (1973).
5. Reading 4.10 summarizes the much longer paper published subsequently as Cain (1976).

REFERENCES

Averitt, R. T. (1968) *The Dual Economy: the dynamics of American industry structure*, New York, Norton.
Blaug, M. (1976) 'The Empirical Status of Human Capital Theory: a slightly jaundiced survey', *Journal of Economic Literature*, 14, pp. 827–55.
Bluestone, B. (1970) 'The Tripartite Economy: labor markets and the working poor', *Poverty and Human Resources*, 5, pp. 15–35.
Bosanquet, N. and Doeringer, P. B. (1973) 'Is There a Dual Labour Market in Great Britain?', *Economic Journal*, 83, pp. 421–35.
Cain, G. C. (1976) 'The Challenge of Segmented Labor Market Theories to Orthodox Theory: a survey', *Journal of Economic Literature*, 14, pp. 1215–57.
Department of Employment (1977) *Department of Employment Gazette*, October.
Doeringer, P. B. and Piore, M. J. (1971) *Internal Labor Markets and Manpower Analysis*, Lexington, Mass., D. C. Heath.
Friedman, A. L. (1978) *Industry and Labour: class struggles at work and monopoly capitalism*, London, Macmillan.
Galbraith, J. K. (1973) *Economics and the Public Purpose*, Boston, Houghton Mifflin.
Gordon, D. M. (1972) *Theories of Poverty and Underemployment*, Lexington, Mass., D. C. Heath.
Hunt, E. H. (1973) *Regional Wage Variations in Britain, 1850–1914*, Oxford, Clarendon Press.
Mincer, J. (1974) *Schooling, Experience and Earnings*, New York, Columbia University Press.
Oulton, N. (1974) 'The Distribution of Education and the Distribution of Income', *Economica*, 41, pp. 387–402.
Perlman, R. (1969) *Labor Theory*, New York, Wiley.
Piore, M. J. (1968) 'The Impact of the Labor Market Upon the Design and Selection of Productive Techniques Within the Manufacturing Plant', *Quarterly Journal of Economics*, 82, pp. 602–20.
Ross, A. M. (1958) 'Do We Have a New Industrial Feudalism?', *American Economic Review*, 48, pp. 903–20.
Scully, G. W. (1969) 'Interstate Wage Differentials: a cross-section analysis', *American Economic Review*, 59, pp. 757–73.
Stone, K. (1974) 'The Origins of Job Structures in the Steel Industry', *Review of Radical Political Economics*, 6, pp. 113–73.
Thatcher, A. R. (1968) 'The Distribution of Earnings of Employees in Great Britain', *Journal of the Royal Statistical Society*, 131, pp. 133–70.
Thurow, L. C. (1976) *Generating Inequality*, London, Macmillan.
Wachter, M. L. (1974) 'Primary and Secondary Labor Markets: a critique of the dual approach', *Brookings Papers in Economic Analysis*, pp. 637–80.

4.1 Human Capital and the Personal Distribution of Income*

[. . .]

This model implies that the total amount invested in human capital differs among persons because of differences in either demand or supply conditions: those with higher demand or lower supply curves invest more than others. There is some evidence that in the United States, persons with urban employment or high IQ and grades tend to invest more in formal education than those with rural employment or low IQ and grades partly because the former receive higher rates of return.[1] If the model is empirically correct as assumed in the remainder of the essay, the sizable observed differences in education,[2] on-the-job training, and other kinds of human capital, would suggest sizable differences in either one or both sets of curves. [. . .]

A. 'EGALITARIAN' APPROACH

Instead of starting immediately with variations in both supply and demand conditions, I first treat a couple of important special cases. One of them assumes that demand conditions are the same for everyone, and that the only cause of inequality is differences in supply conditions. This can be considered an approximate representation of the 'egalitarian' approach to the distributions of investments in human capital and earnings, which assumes that everyone more or less has the same capacity to benefit from investment in human capital. Investment and earnings differ because of differences in the environment; in luck, family wealth, subsidies, etc., which give some the opportunity to invest more than others. Eliminating environmental differences would eliminate these differences in opportunities, and thereby eliminate the important differences in earnings and investments.

Adam Smith took this view in his *The Wealth of Nations* when he said 'The difference between the most dissimilar characters, between a philosopher and a common street porter, for example, seems to arise not so much from nature, as from habit, custom, and education.'[3] Currently, many persons in the United States argue that most persons are intrinsically equally capable of benefiting from a college education; only poverty, ignorance and prejudice prevent some from acquiring one.

Generally, the most important cause of differences in opportunities is differences in the availability of funds.[4] These in turn are derived from the same segmentation in the capital market which implies that cheaper funds are rationed, and that supply curves of funds are positively inclined even to individual investors. For a variety of reasons cheaper funds are more accessible to some persons than to others, and the former then have more favorable supply condi-

*From Gary S. Becker, *Human Capital and the Personal Distribution of Income; an analytical approach*, Woytinsky Lecture No. 1 (Institute of Public Administration and Department of Economics, the University of Michigan, Ann Arbor, Michigan, 1967).

tions. Some may live in areas providing liberal government and other subsidies to investment in human capital, or receive special scholarships because of luck, or political contacts. Others may be born into wealthy families, have generous parents, borrow on favorable terms or, willingly forgo consumption while investing. For all these reasons and more, supply curves of funds could differ considerably, and figure 4.1 shows a few that differ in level or elasticity. [. . .]

If supply conditions alone varied, the equilibrium positions of different persons would be given by the intersections of the common demand curve with the different supply curves; the points p_1, p_2, p_3, and p_4 in Figure 4.2 represent a few such positions. Full knowledge of these positions, of the marginal rate of

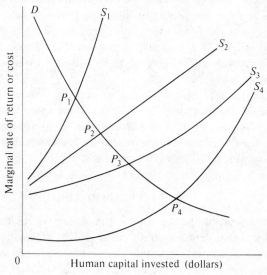

FIG. 4.1

return associated with each amount of capital investment, would permit the common demand curve to be 'identified.' Moreover, the marginal rates could themselves be 'identified' from the earnings received by persons with different capital investments.[5]

Persons with favorable supply conditions would invest relatively large amounts in themselves: the equilibrium positions in Figure 4.1 are further to the right, the lower the supply curves are. The distribution of the total capital invested obviously would be more unequal and skewed, the more unequal and skewed was the distribution of supply curves.

If the labor force period was long, earnings would be related to the amount of capital invested by

$$E = \bar{r}C, \tag{1}$$

where E is earnings, C the total capital invested, and $\bar{r}$ the average rate of return on C. The distribution of E clearly depends on the distribution of C; indeed, if the demand curve for capital was completely elastic, r̄ would be the same for everyone, and the distributions of earnings and investments would be identical except for a difference in units (r̄) that depended on the aggregate supply of and demand for human capital. Since it is shown above that C is more unequally distributed and skewed the more unequal and skewed is the distribution of supply curves, the same applies to the distribution of E.

As we have seen the demand curve for capital investment is usually negatively inclined rather than infinitely elastic primarily because human capital is embodied in investors. E will, therefore, usually be more equally distributed than C because a given percentage change in C will change E by a smaller percentage since r̄ will decline as C increases and increase as C declines. Moreover, both E and C will be more unequally distributed and skewed the more elastic the demand curve is; for the greater the latter, the more that persons with favorable supply conditions would be encouraged to invest still more by a higher r̄; and the more that those with unfavorable supply conditions would be encouraged to invest still less by a lower r̄.

Similarly, an increase in the elasticities of supply curves that held constant their locations at the average value of C would also increase the inequality and skewness in E and C. For persons with unfavorable supply conditions would be encouraged to cut back their investments at the same time that those with favorable conditions were encouraged to expand theirs. [. . .]

B. 'ELITE' APPROACH

At the other end of the spectrum is the assumption that supply conditions are identical and that demand conditions alone vary among persons. This can be considered an approximate representation of the 'elite' approach to the distributions of investment in human capital and earnings, which assumes that everyone more or less has effectively equal opportunities. Actual investments and earnings differ primarily because of differences in the capacity to benefit from investment in human capital: some persons are abler and form an elite. In spite of the position taken by Smith and Hume, educational policy in England and some other parts of Europe has been predicated on a version of the elite view:

> There is a tendency of long historical standing in English educational thought (it is not nearly so visible in some other countries) to concentrate too much on the interests of the abler persons in any group that is being considered and to forget about the rest.[6]

Just as opportunities have been measured primarily by supply curves, so capacities are measured primarily by demand curves.[7] For a given (dollar) amount invested, persons with higher demand curves receive higher rates of return than others; or looked at differently, they have to invest more than others to lower the marginal rate to a given level. Since all human capital is assumed to be identical, demand curves can be higher only if more units of capital are produced by a given expenditure. It is natural to say that persons who produce more human capital from a given expenditure have more capacity or 'ability.'[8]

Since a higher demand curve means greater earnings from a given investment, in effect, ability is being measured indirectly; namely by the earnings received when the investment in human capital is held constant.[9] This approach is an appealing compromise between definitions of ability in terms of scores on IQ, personality, or motivation tests without regard to the effect on earnings, and definitions in terms of earnings without regard to opportunities.[10] The former pay excessive attention to form and not enough to results, while the latter hopelessly confound 'nature' and 'nurture,' or ability and environment. Our approach directly relates ability to results and at the same time recognizes the impact that environment has on results.[11]

If demand curves alone varied, the capital investments and marginal rates of return of different persons would be found at the intersections of the different demand curves with the common supply curve. In Figure 4.2 there clearly is a positive relation between the height of a demand curve, the amount of capital invested and the marginal rate. Knowledge of the latter two quantities for many different persons would permit an 'identification' of the common supply curve, just as such information earlier permitted an 'identification' of a common demand curve.

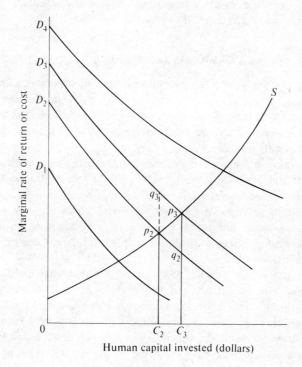

FIG. 4.2

An important difference, however, is that the marginal rates themselves could not now be 'identified' from information on the earnings and investments of different persons alone. In Figure 4.2 the marginal rate of return to investing OC_3 rather than OC_2 would be proportional to the area $p_2C_2C_3q_2$ for persons with the demand D_2 and to the larger area $q_3C_2C_3p_3$ for those with D_3. If a marginal rate was simply estimated from the difference in earnings between persons investing OC_2 and OC_3, the estimate would be proportional to $D_2p_2C_2C_3p_3D_3$, which clearly greatly exceeds both true rates. To arrive at correct estimates, either the earnings of persons investing OC_2 would be adjusted upward by the area $D_3D_2p_2q_3$, or the earnings of those investing OC_3 adjusted downward by the area $D_3D_2q_2p_3$.[12] Note, incidentally, that those arguing that most of the differences in earnings between persons at different levels of education or training result from differences in ability are essentially assuming a common supply curve and steeply inclined demand curves.

Earnings and capital investments are clearly more unequally distributed and skewed the more unequally distributed and skewed are demand curves. The same kind of arguments as those used in the previous section should make it apparent that both distributions are also more unequal and skewed, the greater the elasticities of the supply and demand curves. If the supply curve was positively inclined, the average rate of return would tend to be greater, the larger the amount invested. Therefore, earnings would tend to be more unequally distributed and skewed than investments. [...]

C. A COMPARISON OF THESE APPROACHES

Before moving on to the general case that incorporates variations in both supply and demand conditions, it is illuminating to contrast the more important implications of these special cases. For under the guise of the 'egalitarian' and 'elite' approaches, they are frequently explicitly advanced and are still more widely implicitly assumed.

The 'egalitarian' approach implies that the marginal rate of return is lower, the larger the amount invested in human capital, while the 'elite' approach implies the opposite relation. Marginal rates of return appear[13] to decline in the United States as years of schooling increase, which supports the 'egalitarian' approach. However, in Canada, a country in many economic respects quite similar to the United States, estimated marginal rates do not decline consistently as schooling increases.[14]

The inequality in earnings tends to be less than that in supply conditions in the 'egalitarian' approach, and greater than that in demand conditions in the 'elite' approach because the former implies a negative, and the latter a positive, correlation between rates of return and amounts invested. Put differently and perhaps more interestingly, to understand the observed inequality in earnings, the 'egalitarian' approach has to presume greater inequality in opportunities than the 'elite' one has to presume about capacities. Inequality in earnings is a more serious problem to the former, therefore, in the sense that a given observed amount implies greater underlying 'inequities' or 'non-competing groups'[15] than it does to the latter.

For a similar reason, the positive skewness in earnings is probably less than that in opportunities under the 'egalitarian' approach and greater than that in capacities under the 'elite' approach. Indeed, as pointed out in the last section, it is shown in the Mathematical Appendix using the assumptions of constant and identical elasticities of demand, and a constant elasticity of supply, that a symmetrical distribution of capacities *necessarily** results in a positively skewed distribution of earnings. Therefore, an age-old problem of economists, of how to reconcile a skewed distribution of income with a presumed symmetrical normal distribution of abilities,[16] turns out to be no problem at all.[17] In the 'egalitarian' approach, on the other hand, observed skewness is more difficult to explain because it implies still greater skewness in the distribution of opportunities, a skewness that may be associated with a skewed distribution of gifts and inheritance, etc.[18]

D. A MORE GENERAL APPROACH

If either all demand or all supply curves were identical, the supply and demand curves of persons investing the same amount would also be identical if different demand or different supply curves did not touch in the relevant region. This, in turn, means that all persons investing the same amount would have identical earnings. Yet if the amount invested is measured by years of schooling, there is abundant evidence of considerable variability in the earnings of persons with the same investment.[19] Possibly improved measures of investment or the introduction of transitory earnings would eliminate most of the variability; I suspect, however, that a significant portion would remain. If so, neither special case – that is neither variations in demand nor in supply curves alone – is sufficient, although one set of curves might vary much more than the other.

If both supply and demand curves varied, different persons could invest the same amount, and yet some could earn more than others because they had higher demand (*and* supply) curves; in Figure 4.3, the same amount would be be invested by persons with D_3 and S_1, D_2 and S_2, and D_1 and S_3. As this example indicates, knowledge of the various equilibrium marginal rates of return and investments would no longer be sufficient to identify either a supply or a demand curve because the equilibrium positions would be on different curves. Moreover, again the marginal rates themselves could not be identified from information on earnings and investments alone because persons with different investments would generally have different demand curves.

The distributions of earnings and investments would partly depend on the same parameters already discussed: both would be more unequal and skewed, the greater the elasticities of supply and demand curves, and the more unequal

[*Not reprinted here – Ed.]

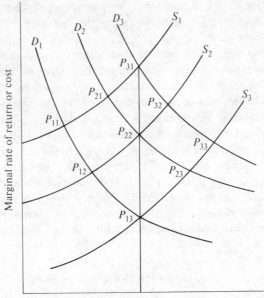

FIG. 4.3

and skewed their distributions. The distributions of earnings and investments also depend, however, on a new parameter: namely, the correlation between different curves.

There are several reasons why supply conditions do not vary independently of demand conditions. Abler persons are more likely to receive public and private scholarships, and thus have their supply curves shifted downward. Or children from higher income families probably, on the average, are more intelligent and receive greater psychic benefits from human capital. On the other hand, private and public 'wars' on poverty can significantly lower the supply curves of some poor persons. Since the first two considerations have, unquestionably, been stronger than the third, it is reasonable to presume a positive[20] correlation between supply and demand conditions, perhaps a sizable one.

If supply and demand curves were uncorrelated, one might have the equilibrium positions given by p_{31}, p_{32}, and p_{33} in Figure 4.3; if they were negatively correlated by p_{31}, p_{22}, and p_{13}, while if they were positively correlated by p_{11}, p_{22}, and p_{33}. The figure clearly shows that a positive correlation increases the inequality in both investments and earnings; it also increases skewness by increasing the earnings and investments of persons who would have relatively high earnings and investments anyway.

An impression of a negative correlation between supply and demand conditions – that is, between opportunities and capacities – is sometimes obtained from persons investing the same amount. As the curves D_3 and S_1, D_2 and S_2, and

D_1 and S_3 in Figure 4.3 clearly show, however, the supply and demand curves of persons investing the same amount *must* be negatively correlated, regardless of the true overall correlation between them. Valid evidence of this latter correlation is provided by information on the amount of variation in earnings 'explained' (in the analysis of variance sense) by the variation in investments. For example, if the correlation between supply and demand curves was perfect and positive, *all* the variation in earnings would be 'explained' by investments. Moreover, the smaller the algebraic value of this correlation, the less the variation in earnings is 'explained' by investments, and the more that earnings vary among persons making the same investment.

E. THE EFFECTS OF AGE

A common method of explaining the rise in the inequality of earnings with age is to introduce random influences and let their effects partly accumulate over time.[21] An alternative method suggested by our analysis is to introduce earnings during the investment period. It has already been stressed that investing in human capital takes time primarily because an investor's own time is an important input into the investment process. Persons who invest relatively little tend also to cease investing at relatively early ages; for example, drop-outs from elementary school generally cease investing before college graduates do. If, therefore, persons with higher demand or lower supply curves tend to have longer investment periods as well as larger investments,[22] the accrued earnings (i.e., the area under demand curves) of persons with high earnings would increase for longer periods than would those of others. The effect would be greater inequality in the distribution of accrued earnings at older ages as long as an appreciable number of persons are still investing. In other words, inequality could rise with age because it ' takes abler persons and those with favorable opportunities longer to reach their full earning power.

Measured earnings differ, however, from accrued earnings during investment periods partly because the income and capital accounts are confounded: measured are derived from accrued earnings only after some investment costs are deducted. Since the amounts deducted are large and variable, measured earnings during investment periods may be only weakly positively or even negatively correlated with earnings afterwards.[23] The effect of mixing earnings and investment costs on the inequality in earnings is less clear-cut: on the one hand, inequality is decreased because high earners invest larger amounts and for longer periods, on the other hand, the inequality is increased by the variation among persons in the amounts deducted. [...]

F. HETEROGENEOUS HUMAN CAPITAL

A major assumption has been that all human capital is homogeneous, an assumption that conflicts with obvious qualitative differences in types of education, on-the-job training, informal learning, etc., in the same way that the frequently used assumption of homogeneous physical capital conflicts with myriad observed differences in plant, equipment, etc. The advantage of these assumptions is that by sweeping away qualitative detail, detail that, incidentally, has received excessive attention in the literature on human capital, one can concentrate on more fundamental relationships.

For those unable to accept, even tentatively, an assumption of homogeneous human capital, let me hasten to stress that different kinds can rather easily be incorporated into the analysis. For example, with two kinds of capital, each person would have two sets of demand and supply curves, and in equilibrium, marginal benefits and financing costs would be equal for each set. The distribution of earnings would still depend in the same way on the distributions and elasticities of the supply and demand curves. The only significant new parameters introduced are those giving the correlations between the different supply and also between the different demand curves for the two kinds of capital. These correlations measure the extent to which people are relatively able or have access to funds on relatively favorable terms for both kinds. These correlations are presumably positive, but by no means perfect, because both ability and access to funds carry over to some extent, but not perfectly, from one kind of capital to another. It should be intuitively clear that positive correlations tend to make both earnings and investments more unequally distributed and skewed, for then persons who invest much (or little) in and earn much (or little) from one kind of capital also tend to invest and earn much (or little) from the other. [. . .]

NOTES

1. See [Gary S. Becker], *Human Capital*, [Columbia University Press, New York, 1964], pp. 79–104.
2. For example, the standard deviation of years of schooling exceeds three years in more countries.
3. E. Cannan, ed. (Random House, Modern Library, 1937), p. 15. Cannan remarks that Smith was following David Hume who said 'consider how nearly equal all men are in their bodily force, and even in their mental powers and faculties, ere cultivated by education' (quoted ibid.).
4. Of course, it is not the only cause; for example, discrimination and nepotism are often important, and yet usually affect the benefits from rather than the financial costs of investing in human capital.
5. Using the assumption that white males have the same demand curve for formal education, G. Hanoch first estimated the marginal rates of return to education from earning differentials between persons at different education levels, and then 'identified' their common demand curve. See his *Personal Earnings and Investment in Schooling* (unpublished Ph.D. dissertation, University of Chicago, 1965), chapter II.
6. *Fifteen to Eighteen*, a report of the Central Advisory Council for Education, Geoffrey Crowther, Chairman, 1959, p. 87. In addition, many formal models of income distribution developed by economists are largely based on an underlying distribution of abilities. See for example, A. D. Roy, 'The Distribution of Earnings and of Individual

Output,' *Economic Journal*, LX (1950), pp. 489–505, and B. Mandelbrot, 'Paretian Distributions and Income Maximization,' *Quarterly Journal of Economics*, LXXVI (1962), pp. 57–85.

7. Let me repeat, however, that some differences in opportunities, such as those resulting from discrimination and nepotism, affect demand curves. Similarly some differences in capacities affect supply curves.

8. The ith and j^{th} persons have the functions

$$h_i = f_i (R_i, T_i, B_i)$$
$$h_j = f_j (R_j, T_j, B_j).$$

The ith person has more ability if $f_i > f_j$ when R and T, the inputs of market resources and own time respectively, are held constant. If sometimes $f_i > f_j$ and sometimes $f_j > f_i$, there is no unique ranking of their abilities.

Note, however, that since demand curves incorporate psychic benefits and costs from human capital as well as monetary ones, i could have a higher demand curve than j, and thus be considered to have more capacity, simply because he receives more psychic benefits than j does.

9. Note the similar definition by R. H. Tawney, 'In so far as the individuals between whom comparison is made belong to a homogeneous group, whose members have equal opportunities of health and education, of entering remunerative occupations, and of obtaining access to profitable financial knowledge, it is plausible, no doubt, if all questions of chance and fortune are excluded to treat the varying positions which they ultimately occupy as the expression of differences in their personal qualities.' (*Equality*, Capricorn Books Edition, [New York], 1961, p. 121.) Aside from chance, Tawney mainly stresses the importance of holding constant health, education, and financial knowledge, which are simply different kinds of human capital.

10. For a review of these definitions in the context of analyzing income distributions, see H. Staehle, 'Ability, Wages, and Income,' *The Review of Economics and Statistics*, XXV (1943), pp. 77–87.

11. I have not tried to explain why some people are 'abler' than others; this might ultimately be traced back to differences in numerous basic ability 'factors.' For a model of this kind, see Mandelbrot, op. cit.

12. Some adjustments along these lines to estimated rates of return on formal education can be found in *Human Capital*, op. cit., pp. 79–86.

13. I say 'appear' because these rates have not been fully corrected for differences in the average level of 'ability' at different education levels; such a correction might eliminate the apparent decline (see Hanoch, op. cit., or *Human Capital*, op. cit., pp. 126–127).

14. See J. R. Podoluk, *Earnings and Education* (Dominion Bureau of Statistics, 1965).

Note that since different years of schooling are not perfect substitutes, the pattern of rates are also affected by the relative demand for and supply of different years. Thus the relatively small number of college-educated persons in Canada might explain the relatively high rates of return to college education there.

15. The interpretation of income inequality in terms of non-competing groups was popular among nineteenth and early twentieth century writers. For a review, see H. Dalton, *Some Aspects of the Inequality of Incomes in Modern Communities* (G. Routledge & Sons [London], 1920), Part II. 'Groups' may be non-competing either because of differences in opportunities, as assumed in the 'egalitarian' approach, or because of differences in capacities, as assumed in the 'elite' approach.

16. For example, A. C. Pigou said 'Now, on the face of things, we should expect that, if as there is reason to think, people's capacities are distributed on a plan of this kind [i.e., according to a symmetrical normal distribution], their incomes will be distributed in the same way. Why is not this expectation realized?' *The Economics of Welfare*, 4th edition (Macmillan, [London], 1950), p. 650. See also P. A. Samuelson, *Economics*, 6th edition (McGraw-Hill [New York], 1964), pp. 120–21.

17. It is not possible, however, to reconcile extremely large skewness in earnings with a symmetrical distribution of capacities.

18. Pigou's principal answer to the question he sets out in the footnotes above is largely

based on a presumed skewed distribution of inheritances, which affects, among other things, the distribution of investments in training (ibid., pp. 651–54). Or Allyn Young said, 'The Worst thing in the present situation is undoubtedly the extreme skewness of the income frequency curve . . . reflecting as it undoubtedly does the presence of a high degree of inequality in the distribution of opportunity.' 'Do the Statistics of the Concentration of Wealth in the United States Mean What they are Commonly Assumed to Mean?' *Journal of the American Statistical Association*, XV (1917), pp. 481–2. One should point out, however, that even 'a high degree of inequality in the distribution of opportunity' is not sufficient to produce skewness in earnings, and that skewed distribution of opportunities is necessary, at least in the 'egalitarian' approach.

19. For example, the coefficient of variation in the incomes of white males aged 35–44 in 1949 was 0.60 for high school graduates and 0.75 for college graduates (see *Human Capital*, op. cit., Table 8). Or in 1959, years of schooling explained less than 20 per cent of the variance in the earnings of white males aged 25–64 in both the South and Non-South. See Gary S. Becker and Barry R. Chiswick, 'Education and the Distribution of Earnings,' *American Economic Review*, LVI (1966), p. 366.

20. By 'positive' is meant that more favorable demand conditions are associated with more favorable supply conditions.

21. See, for example, J. Aitchison and J. A. C. Brown, *The Lognormal Distribution* (Cambridge University Press, 1957), pp. 108–111.

22. They necessary have larger investments if supply and demand curves are not negatively correlated.

23. For one piece of evidence indicating virtually no correlation, see J. Mincer, 'On-the-Job Training: Costs, Returns, and Some Implications,' *Journal of Political Economy*, LXX (Special Supplement, October, 1962), p. 53.

4.2 Education and Economic Equality*

However much they may differ on other matters, the left, the center, and the right all affirm the central importance of education as a means of solving our social problems, especially poverty. To be sure, they see the education system in starkly contrasting terms. The left argues that the inferior education of the poor and of the minorities reflects a discriminatory effort to prevent them from competing with better-educated groups, to force them into menial, low-income jobs. The right argues that the poor are poor because they have failed to work hard and get the education which is open to them. Moderates usually subscribe to some mixture of these arguments: the poor are poor because they have gotten bad educations, partly as a result of inadequately funded and therefore inferior school systems, but partly also as a result of sociological factors (e.g., disrupted families) that prevent poor children from absorbing the education that is available. Yet despite these differences, people at all points of the political spectrum agree that, if they were running the country, education policy would be the cornerstone of their effort to improve the condition of the poor and the minorities: if the poor or the minorities were better educated, they could get better jobs and higher income. This idea has had a profound influence on public policy in the last decade.

This acceptance of the efficacy of education is itself derived from a belief in the standard economic theory of the labor market. According to this theory,

*From Lester C. Thurow, 'Education and Economic Equality', *The Public Interest*, Vol. 35, Summer 1972.

the labor market exists to match labor demand with labor supply. At any given time, the pattern of matching and mismatching gives off various signals. Businesses are 'told' to raise wages or redesign jobs in skill-shortage sectors, or to lower wages in skill-surplus sectors; individuals are 'told' to acquire skills in high-wage sectors and are discouraged from seeking skills and jobs in sectors where wages are low and skills are in surplus. Each skill market is 'cleared,' in the short run, by increases or reductions in wages, and by a combination of wage changes, skill changes, and production-technique changes over the long run. The result, according to the theory, is that each person in the labor market is paid at the level of his marginal productivity. If he adds $3,000 to total economic output, he is paid $3,000; if he adds $8,000, he is paid $8,000.

This theory posits *wage competition* as the driving force of the labor market. It assumes that people come into the labor market with a definite, pre-existing set of skills (or lack of skills), and that they then compete against one another on the basis of wages. According to this theory, education is crucial because it creates the skills which people bring into the market. This implies that any increase in the educational level of low-income workers will have three powerful — and beneficial — effects. First, an educational program that transforms a low-skill person into a high-skill person raises his productivity and therefore his earnings. Second, it reduces the total supply of low-skill workers, which leads in turn to an increase in *their* wages. Third, it increases the supply of high-skill workers, and this lowers their wages. The net result is that total output rises (because of the increase in productivity among formerly uneducated workers), the distribution of earnings becomes more equal, and each individual is still rewarded according to merit. What could be more ideal?

Empirical studies seemingly have confirmed this theory. The economic literature on 'human capital' is full of articles that estimate the economic rate of return for different levels of education; while the results differ slightly depending on the data and methods used, most studies find a rate of return on higher education slightly above 10 per cent per year for white males. This rate of return, as it happens, is approximately the same as that of investments in 'physical capital' (e.g., new machines). From these findings, two conclusions seem to follow. First, educational investment produces just as much additional output as physical investments in plant and capital; and second, education is a powerful tool for altering the distribution of income in society. Such calculations are in common use in discussions of public education policy, and they form a major justification for heavy public investment in education.

Yet, despite this seeming confirmation, there is reason to doubt the validity of this view of the labor market and the importance of the economic role it assigns to education. As we shall see, a large body of evidence indicates that the American labor market is characterized less by wage competition than by *job competition*. That is to say, instead of people looking for jobs, there are jobs looking for people — for 'suitable' people. In a labor market based on job competition, the function of education is not to confer skill and therefore increased productivity and higher wages on the worker; it is rather to certify his 'train-ability' and to confer upon him a certain status by virtue of this certification. Jobs and higher incomes are then distributed on the basis of this certified status. To the extent that job ecompetition rather than wage competition prevails in the American economy, our long-standing beliefs about both the economic benefits of education and the efficacy of education as a social policy which makes for greater equality may have to be altered.

DEFECTS OF THE 'WAGE COMPETITION' THEORY

While it is possible to raise a number of theoretical objectsion against the 'human capital' calculations which seem to confirm the wage competition theory, it is more instructive to see if in our actual post-war experience, existing educational programs have had the effects that the wage competition theory would predict. In fact, there are a number of important discrepancies. The first arises from the fact that, in the real world, the distributions of education and IQ are more equal than the distribution of income, as Figure 4.4 indicates. The usual explanation for this disparity is that income is disproportionately affected by the *combination* of education and intelligence. This would explain the wider

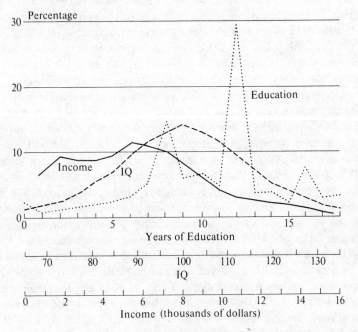

FIG. 4.4. Distribution of Income, Education, and Intelligence (IQ) of Males Twenty-five Years of Age and Over in 1965.

dispersion of income than of education or intelligence — but it cannot explain the markedly different *shapes* of the distributions. Clearly, other factors are at work.

A second discrepancy is revealed by the fact that, while the distribution of education has moved in the direction of greater equality over the post-war period, the distribution of income has not. In 1950, the bottom fifth of the white male population had 8.6 per cent of the total number of years of education, while the top fifth had 31.1 per cent (See Table 4.1). By 1970, the share of the bottom fifth had risen to 10.7 per cent and that of the top fifth had dropped to 29.3 per cent. According to the wage competition theory, this should have led to a more equal distribution of earnings, whereas in fact the distribution of income among white males has become more *un*equal, as Table 4.2 indicates.

Table 4.1

Distribution of Education Among Adult White Males

| | Percentage Share of Years of Educational Attainment | |
	1950	1970
Lowest Fifth	8.6	10.7
Second Fifth	16.4	16.4
Middle Fifth	19.0	21.3
Fourth Fifth	24.9	22.3
Highest Fifth	31.1	29.3

Table 4.2

Distribution of Income Among Adult White Males

| | Percentage Share of Total Money Income | |
	1949	1969
Lowest Fifth	3.2	2.6
Second Fifth	10.9	9.4
Middle Fifth	17.5	16.7
Fourth Fifth	23.7	25.0
Highest Fifth	44.8	46.3

From 1949 to 1969, the share of total income going to the lowest fifth has dropped from 3.2 per cent to 2.6 per cent while the share going to the highest fifth rose from 44.8 per cent to 46.3 per cent. Empirically, education has not been having the equalizing impact that the rate-of-return calculations would have led one to expect.

Black/white income gaps reveal the same discrepancies. From 1952 to 1968, the mean education of black male workers rose from 67 per cent to 87 per cent of that of white male workers — yet median wage and salary incomes rose only from 58 per cent to 66 per cent. Most of this increase, moreover, can be traced to black emigration from the South, with its lower relative incomes for blacks.

As a result, education does not seem to have equalized black and white incomes in the manner that the rate-of-return calculations would indicate.

Similarly, a more rapid rate of growth of education should have led to a more rapid growth of the economy. In the early 1950's, the college-educated labor force was growing at a rate of 3 per cent per year. In the late 1960's, it was growing at a 6 per cent rate. Yet there does not seem to be any evidence that the rate of growth of productivity of the economy as a whole has accelerated correspondingly. If anything, the opposite has happened. Productivity today may be increasing more slowly than its historic rate of growth of 2.9 per cent per year.

Moreover, the entire theory assumes a labor market where wage competition is the most important short-run method for equilibrating the supplies and demands for different types of labor. Yet the real world reveals very sluggish wage adjustments in most sectors of the economy. Not only is there considerable variance in wages for different individuals with the same skills; there is also little tendency for the existence of unemployment to lower wages. There may be many unemployed airline pilots or engineers today, but their joblessness does not lead to lower wages for those lucky enough to remain employed. In fact, wage competition simply is not the all-pervasive force that economic theory supposes it to be.

Perhaps the most devastating problem with the simple wage competition view is that it cannot explain the existence of unemployment. When the demand for labor falls, wages are supposed to fall until enough jobs have been generated to keep everyone fully employed at the new lower wages. Yet the real world is full of unemployed workers whose presence does not seem to have led to falling wages for those who are employed.

The absence of wage competition is also indicated by employers' lack of interest in relative wage differentials when designing new plants. In the several cases investigated by Piore and Doeringer, plant designers typically did not take account of (or even know) the relative prices of different types of labor when designing new plants. They could not economize on expensive skills since they did not know which skills were expensive and which cheap. They simply used an average wage rate in making their calculations.

Now there are plausible *ad hoc* explanations for all of these aberrant observations — but the necessity for so many *ad hoc* explanations is itself suspicious. Our experience with large investments in higher education entitles us to have doubts about the value of education as a means of altering the distribution of income. In the post-war years, this experience has not been encouraging. Large investments have been made. What little has happened to the post-war distribution of adult white male incomes has been contrary to expectation. Before further investments are made for such purposes, we should first get clear on why past investments have not had the expected and desired results.

THE 'JOB COMPETITION' MODEL

Govermental education and training policies have not had the predicted impact because they have ignored the 'job competition' elements in the labor market. In a labor market based on job competition, an individual's income is determined by (a) his relative position in the labor queue and (b) the distribution of job opportunities in the economy. Wages are based on the characteristics of the job, and workers are distributed across job opportunities on the basis of their relative position in the labor queue. The most preferred workers get the best (highest-income) jobs. According to this model, labor skills do not exist in the labor market; on the contrary, most actual job skills are acquired informally through on-the-job training *after* a worker finds an entry job and a position on the associated promotional ladder.

As a matter of fact, such a training process is clearly observable in the American economy. A survey of how American workers acquired their actual job skills found that only 40 per cent were using skills that they had acquired in formal training programs or in specialized education – and, of these, most reported that some of the skills they were currently using had been acquired through informal on-the-job training. The remaining 60 per cent acquired all of their job skills through such informal on-the-job training. More than two thirds of the college graduates reported that they had acquired job skills through such informal processes. When asked to list the form of training that had been most helpful in acquiring their current job skills, only 12 per cent listed formal training and specialized education.

Thus the labor market is primarily a market, not for matching the demands for and supplies of different job skills, but for matching trainable individuals with training ladders. *Because most skills are acquired on the job, it is the demand for job skills which creates the supply of job skills.* The operative problem in a job competition economy is to pick and train workers to generate the desired productivity with the least investment in training costs. For new workers and for entry-level jobs, it is the 'background characteristics' of the workers that form the basis of selection. Those workers whose backgrounds promise the lowest training costs will be hired. For workers with previous job experience, existing job skills (including skills like reliability and punctuality) are relevant to the selection process to the extent that they might lead to lower training costs.

In such a system, depending as it does on informal on-the-job transmission of knowledge and skills, the absence of direct wage competition and the restriction of any job competition to entry-level jobs are absolutely necessary. If workers feel that they are training a potential wage or job competitor every time they show another worker how to do their job, they have every incentive to stop giving such informal training. Each man, under the circumstances, would try to build his own little monopoly by hoarding skills and information and by resisting any technical improvements that would reduce the number of job opportunities in his occupation. But in a training system where no one is trained unless a job is available (which is what on-the-job training means), where strong seniority provisions exist, and where there is no danger of some competitor bidding down your wages, employees can freely transmit information to new workers and more readily accept new techniques. If anyone is made redundant by such techniques, it will be a clearly defined minority — new workers.

In a labor market governed by job competition, employers rank workers on a continuum from the best potential worker (trainee) to the worst potential worker (trainee) on the basis of estimated potential training costs. (Such costs certainly include the costs of inculcating norms of industrial discipline and good work habits.) But because employers rarely have direct and unambiguous evidence of the specific training costs for specific workers, they end up ranking workers according to their background characteristics — age, sex, educational attainment, previous skills, performance on psychological tests, etc. Each of these is used as an indirect measure of the costs necessary to produce some standard of work performance.

Entirely subjective and arbitrary elements may also affect the labor queue. If employers discriminate against blacks, blacks will find themselves lower in the labor market queue than their training costs would warrant. To some extent, the smaller the actual differences in training costs, the more such subjective preferences can determine the final ordering. If every individual had identical training costs, blacks could be placed at the bottom of the labor queue with no loss in efficiency.

The national labor queue depends upon the distribution of these background characteristics and upon employers' ranking of different background characteristics. While no two workers may be exactly alike, the costs of discovering small differences are so large that individuals are ranked on a finite number of background characteristics. This means that there are a finite number of rankings in the labor queue and that many individuals have identical rankings.

Jobs and their coresponding training ladders are distributed to individuals in order of their rank, working from those at the top of the queue down to those at the bottom. The best jobs go to the best workers and the worst jobs to the worst workers. Given a need for untrained labor, some workers at the bottom of the queue will receive little or no training on their jobs. In periods of labor scarcity, training will extent farther and farther down the queue as employers are forced to train more costly workers to fill job vacanacies. In periods of labor surplus, it is those at the bottom of the labor queue who will be unemployed.

To the extent that education and formal training are an important background characteristic used for screening individuals, alterations in the distribution of education can have an important impact on the shape of the labor queue. This queue can be skinnier at the top, at the bottom, or in the middle. The relevant empirical question is the weight that is attached to education in screening, relative to the weight that is attached to other factors. Although this obviously differs from job to job, educational screening tests are in fact ubiquitous. But although education can affect the shape of the labor queue, this does not necessarily mean that it can change the actual distribution of income. This is a function, not only of the labor queue, but also of the distribution of job opportunities. An equal group of laborers (with respect to potential training costs) might be distributed across a relatively unequal distribution of job opportunities. After receiving the resultant on-the-job training, the initially equal workers would have unequal productivities since they would now have unequal skills. As a result, the distribution of incomes is determined by the distribution of job opportunities and not by the distribution of the labor queue, which only determines the order of access — and the distribution of access — to job opportunities.

THE DISTRIBUTION OF JOB OPPORTUNITIES

The shape of the job distribution (and hence of the income distribution) across which individual laborers will be spread is governed by three sets of factors: (1) the character of technical progress, which generates certain kinds of jobs in certain proportions; (2) the sociology of wage determination — trade unions, traditions of wage differentials, etc.; and (3) the distribution of training costs between employees and employers, which will influence the wage that is associated with each job. The interaction among these factors is exceedingly complicated — and little studied.[1] The outcome of such studies would tell us with some assurance where exactly the American economy is to be located on a continuum between a wage competition economy and a job competition economy. Let me point out, however, that observed changes over the post-war period are in accordance with a job competition model.

If, at the beginning of the post-war period, an observer had been told that the composition of the adult white male labor force was going to change from 47 per cent with a grade school education, 38 per cent with a high school education, and 15 per cent with a college education, to 20 per cent with a grade school education, 51 per cent with a high school education, and 28 per cent with a college education (the actual 1949 to 1969 changes), expectations about the distribution of income would have been very different depending upon whether the observer subscribed to a job competition model or a wage competition model. Assuming there were no offsetting changes on the demand side of the market, the observer subscribing to a wage competition model of the economy would have predicted a substantial equalization of earnings. But the observer subscribing to the job competition model would have predicted something quite different. He would have expected an equalization of income within the most preferred group (college-educated workers), a rise in its incomes relative to other groups, and a decrease relative to the national average. He would have reasoned as follows. As the most preferred group expanded, it would filter down the job distribution into lower-paying jobs. This would lead to a fall in wages relative to the national average. As it moved into a denser portion of the national job (income) distribution, it would, however, experience within-group equalization of income. By taking what had previously been the best high school jobs, college incomes would rise relative to high school incomes.

Such a prediction would have been correct. The proportion of college incomes going to the poorest 25 per cent of white male college-educated workers rose from 6.3 to 9.0 per cent from 1949 to 1969, while the proportion going to the richest 25 per cent fell from 53.9 per cent to 46.0 per cent. While the median income of college-educated workers was rising from 198 per cent to 254 per cent of the median for grade-school-educated workers and from 124 per cent to 137 per cent of the median for high-school-educated workers, it was falling from 148 per cent to 144 per cent of the national median.

As the least preferred group (those with a grade school education) contracted in size, a job competition observer would have expected it to be moving out of the denser regions of the income distribution and becoming more and more concentrated on the lower tail of the income distribution. Given the shape of the lower tail of the American income distribution, such a movement would have led to falling relative incomes and increasing income equality. In fact, the incomes of grade school laborers have fallen from 50 per cent to 39 per cent of college incomes and from 63 per cent to 54 per cent of high school incomes. The income going to the poorest 25 per cent of all grade school laborers has risen from 2.9 per cent to 6.6 per cent of the group's total, and the income going to the richest 25 per cent has fallen from 53.5 per cent to 49.4 per cent.

Predictions of the position of the middle group (the high-school-educated) would have depended upon an analysis of the relative densities of the income distribution at its margin with the college-educated and the grade-school-educated. Since the American income distribution is denser on the margin with the grade-school-educated than on the margin with the college-educated, an expansion in the size of the middle group should have led to more within-group equality, an income rise relative to the grade-school-educated, and an income fall relative to the college-educated. In fact, the proportion of income going to the poorest 25 per cent of all the high-school-educated has risen from 8.2 per cent to 10.2 per cent, while the proportion going to the highest 25 per cent has fallen from 46.0 per cent to 41.6 per cent. High school incomes have risen relative to grade school incomes (from 160 per cent to 185 per cent) and fallen relative to college incomes (from 81 per cent to 73 per cent).

An alternative method for viewing the same changes is to look at the probablity each of these educational groups has of holding a job at different levels in the American job hierarchy. The increasing economic segregation based on education can be seen in Table 4.3, where each cell has been adjusted for changes in the proportions of those with college, high school, and grade school educations. (The table is constructed so that each cell would have the number 1.000 if incomes were randomly drawn with respect to education.) In 1949, a college graduate was six times as likely to hold a job in the top tenth of jobs as a grade school graduate, but by 1969 he was 15 times as likely to hold a job in

Table 4.3

Normalized Probabilities (Adult White Males)[1]

Quality of Jobs (Determined by Income of Total Males with Income, 25 yrs & Older)	Per Cent of Total Males in Each Job Class, in 1950 & 1970, by Educational Attainment (Divided by Per Cent of Total Males with that Educational Attainment that Year)					
	Elementary		High School		College	
	(1950)	(1970)	(1950)	(1970)	(1950)	(1970)
10% Best jobs — 1950: $5,239.3 & up 1970: $15,000 & up	.436	.1714	1.066	.648	2.715	2.549
2nd Best 10% — 1950: $4,028.84-$5,239.2 1970: $12,506.26-$14,999	.599	.3535	1.337	1.130	1.523	1.468
3rd 10% — 1950: $3,519.7-$4,028.83 1970: $10,012.9-$12,506.25	.772	.3535	1.354	1.130	.940	1.468
4th 10% — 1950: $3,025.2-$3,519.6 1970: $8,752-$10,012.8	.776	.621	1.354	1.248	.927	.960
5th 10% — 1950: $2,553.6-$3,025.1 1970: $7,573.9-$8,751	.952	.692	1.221	1.251	.649	.881
6th 10% — 1950: $2,101-$2,553.5 1970: $6,449.6-$7,573.8	1.079	.871	1.069	1.238	.5695	.704
7th 10% — 1950: $1,530-$2,100 1970: $5,148.3-$6,449.5	1.193	1.128	.910	1.148	.5629	.586
8th 10% — 1950: $706-$1,529 1970: $3,576.6-$5,148.2	1.328	1.564	.708	.933	.5827	.500
9th 10% — 1950: $270.6-$705 1970: $2,008.2-$3,576.5	1.500	1.960	.527	.712	.4304	.468
10% Worst Jobs — 1950: $0-$270.5 1970: $0-$2008.1	1.458	2.303	.564	.552	.4768	.3818

[1] Figures for 1950 — Money Income in 1949, Population in 1950; 1970 — Money Income in 1969, Population in 1970.

262   *The Structure of Earnings*

the top tenth. Conversely, the probability of a grade school graduate holding a job in the lowest tenth has risen from three to six times that of a college graduate. Similarly, probabilities of holding the best job have risen for college graduates relative to high school graduates (from 2.5 to 4 times those of high school graduates), while there has been a rise in relative probabilities of holding the worst jobs for high school graduates (from 1.2 to 1.5 times those of college graduates). Extrapolation of these trends for another 20 years would lead to a world where income was almost perfectly segregated according to education.

Although the job competition model seems to 'post-cast' accurately what happened to the American distribution of income in the post-war period, post-casting is not a definitive test, and there are other possible explanations for what happened in the post-war period. One explanation would be that increasing technical progress has simply made education more necessary for acquiring income-producing skills. Training costs differentials have risen, and this could explain the increasing economic segregation based on education. Another explanation would be that higher education has become more meritocratic in the post-war period (i.e., it is becoming more perfectly correlated with other income-producing factors), which would create the appearance of more economic segregation based on education. Still another explanation would be that the American economy has become more of a 'credential society,' in which education is used as a cheap (or defensible) screening device even though it is not very closely related to training costs.

ECONOMIC IMPLICATIONS

While education has many non-economic benefits, its strictly economic benefits may be of three types. First, education directly increases the productivity of a country's labor force and indirectly increases the productivity of its physical capital. The result is more output and a higher real living standard. Second, by altering the distribution of individual productivities, education can led to changes in the distribution of earned income between rich and poor. It can help the poor to catch up with the rich. Third, education can lead to economic mobility. Black earnings may catch up with white earnings, and the children of low-productivity parents need not themselves be low-productivity individuals. It is important to recognize, however, that each of these three impacts is merely possible. They may or may not occur. Whether they do or do not is an empirical question.

Even on the wage competition view of the labor market, education can be expanded to the point where it no longer increases a country's productivity. Nevertheless, large observed earnings differentials between the high-school-educated and the college-educated (after standardization for other factors such as IQ) have been taken as evidence to substantiate the fact that there are actual gains to be made. But if there is a substantial element of job competition in the economy, education's impact on individual productivity cannot be determined simply with rate-of-return calculations based on normalized income differentials. The exact impact on productivity of an alteration in the distribution of education depends upon a set of factors beyond the scope of this essay, but large observed income differentials could persist after the productivity impact of education was exhausted. An increasing supply of the college-educated would lead them to accept jobs farther down the job opportunities distribution. In the process, they would take the best high school jobs and thus bring down average high school incomes. This would preserve the observed wage differential between college and high school labor, but the differential would not indicate potential productivity gains or opportunities to equalize incomes between rich and poor.

There is, then, a need to be much more agnostic about the productivity impacts of education than public rhetoric would indicate to be our present inclination. In the wage competition view of education, additional education for someone with more education than I can never hurt my prospects. If anything, it must raise my potential earnings. From the job competition point of view, however, education may become a defensive necessity. As the supply of educated labor increases, individuals find that they must improve their educational level simply to defend their current income positions. If they don't, others will, and they will find their current job no longer open to them. Education becomes a good investment, not because it would raise people's incomes above what they would have been if no one had increased his education, but rather because it raises their income above what it will be if others acquire an education and they do not. *In effect, education becomes a defensive expenditure necessary to protect one's 'market share.'* The larger the class of educated labor and the more rapidly it grows, the more such defensive expenditures become imperative. Interestingly, many students currently object to the defensive aspects of acquiring a college education. This complaint makes no sense from a wage competition point of view, but it makes good sense from a job competition point of view.

While the current public policy emphasis on on-the-job training programs seems to fit in with the job competition view of the world, on-the-job training programs can have an impact only if they really lead to the training of a different class of workers than would ordinarily have been trained through the job market. Unfortunately, many government training programs have simply led to the training of the groups that would have been trained in any case; the only operative difference is that government foots the training bills.

Based on a wage competition view of the labor market government programs to equalize incomes and to raise the productivity of low-income individuals have been almost entirely devoted to changing the labor characteristics that an individual brings into the labor market. This is done in spite of the fact that individual labor characteristics typically do not explain more than half of the observed income differences between black and white, rich and poor, or male and female. Thus the emphasis has been entirely on changing the supplies of different types of workers rather than the demands for different types of workers.

In addition to being uncalled for by economic theory, this emphasis on altering labor supplies is at variance with our own history. To find a period of increasing income equality it is necessary to go back to the Great Depression and World War II. From 1929 to 1941 the share of total income going to the bottom 40 per cent of the population rose from 12.5 per cent to 13.6 per cent, while the share of income going to the top 5 per cent fell from 30.0 per cent to 24.0 per cent and the share of income going to the top 20 per cent fell from 54.4 per cent to 48.8 per cent. From 1941 to 1947 the share going to the bottom 40 per cent rose to 16.0 per cent, while the share going to the top 5 per cent fell to 20.9 per cent and the share going to the top 20 per cent fell to 46.0 per cent. In both cases alterations in the demand side, rather than the supply side, of the market seem to have provided the mechanism for equalizing incomes.

In the Great Depression an economic collapse was the mechanism for changes. Individual fortunes were lost, firms collapsed, and a wage structure emerged that was noticeably more equal than before the collapse. While interesting, the deliberate collapsing of an economy in order to equalize the distribution of income is not a policy that commends itself.

The World War II period is more interesting from this vantage point. As a result of an overwhelming consensus that the economic burdens of the war should be shared equally, the federal government undertook two major actions. First, it instituted a very progressive income tax (more progressive than the current federal income tax) that converted a regressive tax system into a mildly progressive tax system. Second, it used a combination of wage controls and labor controls to equalize market wages. This was accompanied by a conscious policy of restructuring jobs to reduce skill requirements and to make use of the existing skills of the labor force. To some extent, old skill differences were simply cloaked with a new set of relative wages and, to some extent, skill differentials were actually collapsed. Together the two factors led to an equalization of market incomes that was not dissipated after the war ended.

To some extent the wage policies of World War II were a deliberate — and successful — attempt to change the sociology of what constitutes 'fair' wage differentials. As a result of the war, our judgments as to what constituted fair differentials changed, and this was reflected in wage patterns. As a consequence of the widespread consensus that wage differentials should be reduced, it was possible to make a deliberate attempt to reduce wage differentials. After they had been embedded in the labor market for a number of years, these new differentials came to be regarded as the 'just' differentials and stuck after the egalitarian pressures of World War II disappeared.

From this experience, I would suggest that any time a consensus emerges on the need for more equality, it can be at least partly achieved by making a frontal attack on wage differentials. Elaborate educational programs are not necessary. Without such a consensus, I would suggest, massive educational investments are apt to be wasted. They simply will not bring about the desired equalization.

In addition to a frontal attack on wage differentials, programs to alter the

demands for different types of employees would include research and development efforts to alter the skill-mix generated by technical progress; guaranteed
government jobs; fiscal and monetary policies designed to create labor shortages;
public wage scales designed to pressure low-wage employers; and incentives to
encourage private employers to compress their wage differentials. If quick results
are desired, quotas must seriously be considered since they are the only technique for quickly altering the types of laborers demanded.

In any case, I would argue that our reliance on education as the ultimate
public policy for curing all problems, economic and social, is unwarranted at
best and in all probability ineffective.

NOTE

1. Further discussion of this matter may be found in Lester C. Thurow, 'The American
Distribution of Income: A Structural Problem,' Committee Print, U.S. Congress Joint
Economic Committee, 1972.

4.3 Changes in Skill Differentials*
[. . .]

Despite the heading for this section, we have to look first at a case of the differential for skill not changing at all from end to end of 500 years, and varying
little from time to time in between. The pay of the craftsman and labourer in
building can be traced fairly continuously in Southern England from about 1300
to the present day (Phelps Brown & Hopkins 1955). In the fourteenth century
the two rates stood in a varying relation with one another, but by 1412, at the
end of the doubling of the craftsman's rate that followed the Black Death,
they settled in the ratio of 3 to 2 — namely 6*d.* a day for the craftsman and
4*d.* for the labourer. In the 1890s the rates in the same series were 7½*d.* an hour
for the craftsman, 5*d.* for the labourer; in 1914 in central London they were
10½*d.* and 7*d.*: still 3 to 2. Fig. 4.5 is drawn on a ratio scale, so that the vertical
distance between its two curves measures the ratio of the one rate of pay to the
other, and it shows that in all the settled periods between 1412 and 1914 that
ratio was never far from 3 to 2.

At any one time we might see the craftsman's and the labourer's rate as each
being set by the supply of and demand for its own kind of labour, and the differential between them would then be only an arithmetic by-product and not an
object of policy. But when we see one and the same differential reasserting
itself over five centuries and it takes the simple form of 'half as much again', we
are bound to suppose that men kept it in their minds as a rule of thumb which
they accepted as fair and reasonable if only because it was so customary.

*From Henry Phelps Brown, *The Inequality of Pay* (Oxford University Press, 1977).

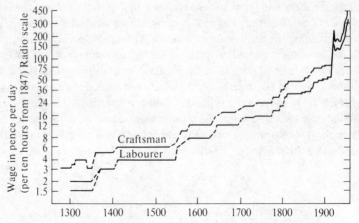

FIG. 4.5 Wages of building craftsman and labourer in Southern England, 1264–1954. Source: Phelps Brown & Hopkins (1955).

Yet custom could have maintained that rule only in the absence of other pressures, be these from market forces, governments, or combinations of masters and men. We shall see that it ceased to hold in England from 1914 onwards, and from what we know about some other localities in the earlier centuries it was evidently not inherent in the nature of building. In Vienna it did prevail through much of the sixteenth and eighteenth centuries. Augsburg did arrive at it eventually, but only for the mortar-mixer, whose rate seems to have been higher than the labourer's, and rose during the sixteenth century to make the ratio 4 to 3 or less, a ratio maintained for some 140 years until 3 to 2 was attained in 1713. In Valencia likewise the craftsman rose less than the labourer in the sixteenth century, until by 1589 the ratio was only 6 to 5. These relative rises of the rate for the unskilled in Augsburg and Valencia occurred in a century when population in Europe was rising rapidly, and we should have expected increasing numbers to have forced down the relative rate of the unskilled. But the rise in population enforced a general and drastic fall in the standard of living of the manual worker (Phelps Brown & Hopkins 1959), and when standards of living are being reduced, the real wages of workers who are not far above the subsistence minimum to start with can be reduced only in less proportion than those of the higher-paid. That may account for what happened in Augsburg and Valencia, but in Southern England it was different. Here, though by the 1600s the real wages of building workers had been brought down to 40 per cent or less of what they had been a hundred years before (Phelps Brown & Hopkins 1956), the craftsman was still getting half as much again as the labourer — 12 pence a day to the labourer's 8 pence. The reason may well be that the standard of living from which the descent had begun was substantially higher in England.

Evidently there was nothing universal in the appeal of the rule of thumb; and that it did prevail in some places for so long may well owe much to the exceptional technical stability of building – down to quite recent times, the workers in 'the industry that capitalism forgot' were performing the same processes with the same tools and materials as their predecessors of many centuries before, and there can have been little change in the relative number of craftsmen and labourers required. Where technical change impinges, it affects the differential for skill along with other differentials. The initial effect of industrialization has been to raise the pay of the skilled manual worker relatively to that of the unskilled. Towards the end of the eighteenth century in Great Britain, 'it would seem that the difference in pay between skilled and unskilled increased. The notion, widely prevalent, that machine production reduced the need for skill, receives no support from the evidence available. . . .' (Ashton 1955, p. 234). Men skilled in the new processes – the fitters, for example, who could build and maintain the new steam engines – were in great demand, and employers sought to entice them away from other firms by the offer of higher pay. At the same time the growth of population, and the movement of rural workers into industry, made it unnecessary to bid up the rate for unskilled labour except where industry was growing in a remote locality; where such remoteness was combined with operations demanding a high proportion of unskilled labour, in canals and railways, it did bring high relative pay to the navvy. In the American mainland colonies in the eighteenth century, rapid growth went with a higher differential for the craftsman than obtained in England at the time: instead of the English differential of 'half as much again', the carpenters and bricklayers in the province of New York were paid more than twice as much as the labourers (Smith 1776, I. viii).

The effect of population growth in widening the differential for skill is apparent on a comparison of that differential in the south and the north of the U.S.A. in recent years. Birth-rates in the south have been high; there has been much migration from the countryside into the towns of the region and much migration to other regions. But a 'relative labour surplus' has remained, 'largely at unskilled and semi-skilled level; it has exerted, despite migration, heavy and continuous pressure on job opportunities within the region'. This, Douty infers (1968, p. 76), explains why the differentials between north and south 'tend to vary inversely by occupational skill level'. He goes on to cite Heer (1930, p. 35) as finding the difference between wages in the South and in the rest of the country in the 1920s to be at its greatest for common labour and 'to become progressively less with each advance in grade of skill. In the case of one or two highly skilled occupations it disappears entirely.' This effect is not marked in 'industries in which differences in grades of skill are slight and in which advancement from one occupation to another is comparatively easy. It is strikingly evident, however, in industries in which there are broad differences in skill between various occupational groups and in which passage from one group to another is difficult.'

In recent years the countries in the early stages of industrialization generally show much wider differentials for manual skills than are found in the developed countries. In eight Latin American countries and three Caribbean countries, for instance, the pay of skilled workers in the metal industries and metal mining in 1965 was from 75 to 100 per cent above the unskilled rate; the corresponding margin in the United States was only about 40 per cent (International Metal Workers Federation 1965).

Yet it has also been observed that the differentials in the developing countries are narrowing rapidly (Gunter 1964; Turner 1965). A major factor is minimum wage legislation. Of the narrowness of the differential for skill in many African countries Taira (1966) observed 'This is because legal minimum wages are relatively high in these countries and are raised from time to time irrespective of the underlying economic conditions.' Brazil shows the effect on differentials of changing policy towards the minimum wage. Of the 1950s Fischlowitz (1959) remarked that despite shortages of skilled workers and a surplus of unskilled, the differential for skill had not been widening. 'Exactly the opposite tendency prevails — towards an extreme uniformity of wage rates which certainly discourages any great effort to acquire higher vocational skills. . . . This may be atrributed primarily to the levelling effect of public intervention in wage matters and paticularly to the minimum wage.' But in 1964–67 the minimum wage was indexed to the projected rate of inflation which the actual rise of prices exceeded, so that its real value was reduced by 20 per cent, and in 1968–70 it was barely constant, whereas by 1970 real salaries in industry stood 10 per cent above their 1964 level (Fishlow 1972).

In the second half of the nineteenth century more figures of the differential for manual skill became available for the first time. A number of them are set out in Table 4.4. These allow of two general statements. First, the ratio of the skilled wage to the unskilled generally lay on or between the building trades' typical ratio of 3 to 2 and the ratio of 19 to 10 more typical of the shipwrights, the patternmakers, and the compositors. In fact, nearly half the entries in this particular table lie between 150 and 169, and nearly four-fifths of them between 150 and 189. Only the German miner's ratio lies mostly below 150. The British railway engine driver stands out as receiving virtually twice the wage of the goods porter. Second, no series shows a rising or falling trend. From one date to the next there is a good deal of movement, some of it abrupt, especially in the U.S. series from the Aldrich Report, each of which is drawn from only one or two firms; but from end to end the movement is small.

That differentials in British engineering changed as they did through these years was noted by Rowe (1928, c. V.) as calling for an explanation. He described the revolution in engineering methods that came about at this time, and noted that though it left unchanged the relative skills required of many grades, it did bring about great changes in the two most extensive grades, those of fitter and turner. In the 1890s, he wrote, 'one could speak of a large and fairly homogeneous group of skilled men as fitters, but this grade has now become spread out into a large number of grades of specialists, with marked differences in degrees of skill and craftsmanship. On the average if one can be struck, the

Table 4.4

The Differential for Manual Skill, 1860–1910

Germany, U.K., and U.S.A. at dates from 1860 to 1910:
ratio of wages of skilled manual worker to those of his helper or of a labourer

U.S.A.   A: Aldrich Report, 1893.
             B: Bulletin 18 of the Dept. of Labor, 1898.
             M: McCormick Works, Chicago.

		1860	1870	1875	1880	1885	1890	1895	1900	1904	1907	1910
Germany												
Building			144[1]	147	152	165	160	157	156	155	143	137
Cotton spinning			164[1]	159	166	200	189	195	180	184	178	170
Mining, Dortmund					123	127	141	137	156	143	154	138
U.K.												
Building					157	157	153	149	150	153	154	153
Shipbuilding					185	185	196	189	192	189		
Engineering					167	167	170	167	172	167	196	
Railways[2]						198[3]						
U.S.A.												
Building	A	159	171		141		179					
	B[4]		170	168	178	185	189					
Blacksmiths	A	161	187		154		160					
	B		157	163	177	163	167					
Machinists	A	153	194		173		174					
	B		154	153	166	158	162					
Ironmoulders	A	151	165		155		157					
	B		175	155	168	159	163					
Patternmakers	A	119	182		161		189					
	B		176	184	194	182	193					
	M						163	150	156	173	180	173
Boilermakers	B		144	147	166	157	160					
Compositors	B		177	183	199	187	185					

[1] 1871.
[2] Engine drivers/goods porters.
[3] 1886.
[4] Weighted average of 4 building crafts/labourers in manufacturing.

Sources: Germany: Bry (1960), Table A.14. *U.K.:* Knowles and Robertson (1951). *U.S.A.:* A & B, Long (1960), Tables 45 and A.4; M, Ozanne (1968), Chart D-1.

modern fitter is undoubtedly far less skilled than his predecessors. The turner also is probably less skilled, and one might expect to find the rate for turners, and the rate, or rates, for fitters falling away during the last thirty years from the rates' for other skilled men. But actually a single rate for the fitter was maintained, and in the 1920s it was still about the same as the smith's rate; the turner's rate did show some tendency to fall relatively to the smith's, but not by any significant amount. Nor was there much change anywhere else in the structure. 'For practical purposes, it may be said that there was no disturbance in the structure of differential rates during this period of nearly thirty years' down to 1914.

Rowe gave two reasons for this. One was the predominance of the fitters and turners in the Amalgamated Society of Engineers, which in turn dominated the trade union side of the industry.

It was not to the interest of the turners that the fitters should disintegrate into a series of groups with varying wage rates, for the example would strike too near home, quite apart from the probable loss of organized bargaining power. Equally it was not to the interest of the fitters that the turners should abandon their equality of status with the other skilled grades, for that would have completely compromised the fitters' position, which was in reality even less tenable than that of the turners.

But trade union policy might not have prevailed against the shifts in the supply of and demand for particular grades that were coming about at the time, had it not had the support of custom. This was the second reason.

Table 4.5

The Differential for Manual Skill, 1900–61

Five countries at dates from 1900 to 1961:
ratio of wage rate of skilled manual labour to that of unskilled.

	U.S.A.		Canada		Australia	U.K.		France		Germany
	(a)	(b)	(c)	(d)	(e)	(f)	(g)	(h)	(j)	(k)
1900						150		145		155
1907	184	205	209[5]	190[5]		154		133[12]		143
1912–14	198		201[6]	188[6]	136[10]	150[11]	171[10]	119[13]		
1920–2	169	175[1]	229[7]	165[7]	126	127	133	108[4]		
1928–30	178	180[2]	235[8]	171[8]	124	134	140	103	144	127
1938–40	170	165[3]			128	130	132	107	138	124
1945–7	148	155	207[9]		126[9]	126	125	119	117	143
1951–3	137	137[4]	203	120	116	116	116	128[15]	145	
1959–61	127		161	134	125	113			153[16]	

(a) Building trades journeymen and labourer, union hourly rate.
(b) Skilled worker's and common labourer's rates.
(c) First two entries, bricklayer's and building labourer's rate, average of rates in 7 cities; 1920–2 onwards, bricklayer's and mason's rate, building labourers, Toronto.
(d) First two entries, machinist, car cleaner, railways; 190–2 onwards, machinists, maintenance, and labourer, in motor vehicles, parts and accessories, Ontario.
(e) 20 skilled, 20 unskilled occupations, Melbourne.
(f) Craftsmen, labourers, building.
(g) Fitters, labourers, engineering.
(h) Masons, navvies, Paris.
(j) Fitters, labourers, time workers in metal industries, Paris.
(k) Building.

[1] 1918–19.   [5] 1906.   [9] 1947.   [13] 1911.
[2] 1930–32.   [6] 1913.   [10] 1914.   [14] 1921.
[3] 1937–40.   [7] 1923–29.   [11] 1913–14.   [15] 1951–52.
[4] 1952–53.   [8] 1930–33.   [12] 1906.   [16] 1960–61.

Sources: Canada, entries for 1907 and 1912–14, Peitchinis (1965), Table 17.3. *Australia*, first 4 entries, Oxnam (1950); last 3 entries, Hancock (1969), Charts II and V. *Germany*, Bry (1960), Table A.14. *All other entries*, O.E.C.D. (1965), Table 6.

One cannot help being struck by a sense of the artificiality of the wage structure within any one industry, if not throughout industry as a whole, and in respect of the engineering industry, it is difficult to suppose that the influence of consciously directed trade union policy would have been at all considerable if it had not been reinforced by the domination of custom, not only in the minds of the wage-earners, but also to some extent in the mental attitude of their employers.

If the fragmentary evidence allows us any generalization about the differential for manual skill down to 1914, then, is that it did not change much; but since 1914 in a number of occupations and countries it has certainly contracted. In the U.S.A., for instance, skilled workers generally were paid more than twice as much as common labourers in 1907, and less than 40 per cent more in the early 1950s. In the U.K. the fitter in engineering was paid about 70 per cent more than the labourer in 1914, and less than 20 per cent more in the early 1950s. These and other movements are shown for six countries in Table 4.5 and Fig. 4.6. But a glance at Fig. 4.6 is enough to restrict generalization. The differential fell through both World Wars in building in Canada, U.K., and U.S.A., in engineering in the U.K., and in the series already cited for skilled workers and labourers generally in the U.S.A. Building in Germany shows a fall through the

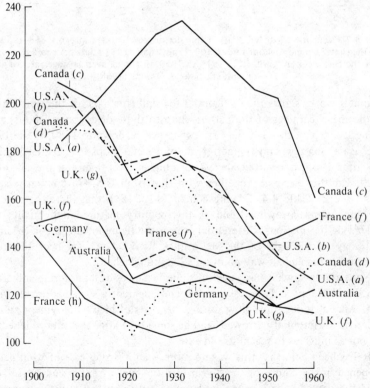

FIG. 4.6 Ratio of skilled to unskilled wage rate in six countries, 1900–60. (Rubrics and detail in Table 4.5)

First World War. But by 1926 the building craftsman's differential in Canada was much higher than before the war; the change in the general differential in Australia after 1921 was inconsiderable; and in France the building and engineering differentials were both higher after the Second World War than before.

A further warning against assuming a general tendency of the differential for manual skill to narrow since 1914 is provided by the remarkable study by Ozanne (1968) of a century of wages in the McCormick (International Harvester) works in Chicago. Fig. 4.7, which is reproduced by permission from

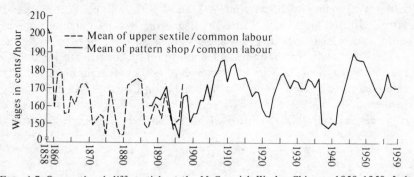

FIG. 4.7 Occupational differentials at the McCormick Works, Chicago, 1858–1959. Index is skilled rate/common labour rate × 100. From 1858 to 1914 data are based on wage rates as of the first week in April, from 1915 to 1959 on annual average wage rates of a sample of workers. Source: Ozanne (1968)

Ozanne's work, shows the differential for skill (for most of the time, the ratio of the mean earnings of the pattern shop to those of common labour) as on a falling trend only through the first twenty years, down to 1880. In the 1900s it rose again, sharply; and thereafter, despite steep drops in the First World War and after 1935, it reverted always to a higher level than ever prevailed before 1900. On this evidence, together with that from U.S. Government wage surveys cited in Table 4.4, Ozanne concludes (p. 154) 'that there has never been any long-term narrowing trend as this country matured industrially. Ober's 1907 wide occupational differential [this is the figure in U.S.A. col. (b) in Table 4.5] may, in the light of the McCormick Works data, have been the top of a wave rather than a half-way point on a long-run decline.'

None the less, what happened in some instances at least during and after the two World Wars stands out as a major and apparently sustained break with the past. Annual series show how during the years of high employment and rising prices the differential narrowed, and at some time after the wars widened again, but not so much as to regain its old extent.

It has been held that this was no more than a strong case of what generally happened in the course of the 8-year business cycle. We can see how, as activity rises, the demand for labour may be expected to extend in greater proportion for the less skilled than for the more skilled (Reder 1955). Firms will supply themselves with more workers in the higher grades by advancing some of their existing employees from lower grades. As the demand for labour subsequently contracts, an opposite process, of 'bumping' downwards, will set in. Fluctuations in demand are thus concentrated upon the lower grades, whose rates of pay will consequently vary more than those of the higher grades. This seems the more likely to have come about where, as was often the case, the pay of the higher grades was more regulated by collective agreements than that of the unskilled, so that it rose less promptly when demand rose, and was more resistant to cuts when demand fell. Silvestre (1971) has found that for purposes of wage movements the French economy since 1945 has had two sectors, one in which wages have been relatively high, output has been concentrated in a small number of firms, and employees have been highly unionized, and another which has been the opposite of the first in all three respects. In the first sector, the level of activity as evidenced inversely by unemployment has had no influence on wage movements, at least in the short run, but in the other sector the two have been closely associated — wage movements have depended on 'the state of competition in the labour market'.

So there are processes or institutions, both in the 'internal labour market' of the firm and in the labour market external to it, that seem likely to have made the differential for skill rise and fall inversely with the level of activity. But have they actually operated widely enough, and have they had sufficient possession of the field to the exclusion of other factors, to bring the supposed effect about? Outside the war years, this effect seems to have been expected rather than observed. We lack annual series of the differential for skill over a sequence of cycles, except in one case where the expected effect certainly did not appear. In the instructive study already referred to of the McCormick works in Chicago, Ozanne (1968, p. 152) reports that so far from widening differentials, 'recessions at McCormick's compressed differentials in 1858, 1873-79, and 1893-1894. In 1884, 1920-1921, and 1929-1933, wage cuts were strictly proportional and thus had no effect on differentials.' When compression occurred it was due to the resistance of common labour to any cut whatever. Thus a cut applied to common labour in 1884 in the same proportion as to the skilled workers led to a violent strike: 'the memory of this was so strong that in the recession beginning in 1893 all cuts of the first three years completely exempted common labour, despite skilled labour cuts in 1893 and 1894' (Ozanne 1968, p. 152). Again, in a wide survey of differentials in U.S. industries through 1914-46, Bell (1951) found that 'the conventional model of the occupational wage structure narrowing and widening during expansion and depression period, respectively, is, at best, a rough approximation, with the period 1929-33 . . . an exception to this general tendency'. The furniture, rubber, and leather industries did conform with the model. In agricultural implements, foundries, and railroads differentials remained little changed. Differentials in the other industries surveyed showed no consistent cyclical pattern. In the great recession of 1929-32, '. . . none of the 16 industries surveyed by the Bureau of Labor Statistics experienced a definite widening of occupational differentials', and in a number of them these differentials were contracted – as in McCormick long before, through the low-paid being spared. For the U.K., on a review of the evidence from 1880 to 1950, Knowles and Robertson (1951) found that 'fluctuations in employment (below the level of "full employment") do not seem to have influenced the fluctuations of skill differentials very much.' Brown and Sisson (1975, p. 26) report that the unemployment rate in Coventry, England, rose from 0.8 per cent in 1964 to 4.8 per cent in 1971, then fell back to 2.45 per cent in 1973. In the local engineering industry over the same 9 years there was a progressive reduction in the spread of the earnings of the 14 occupational groups, and a steady rise in the ratio of the labourers' earnings to those of skilled production workers.

Thus what economists have seen as likely to occur in the course of the cycle, through supply and demand, a certain type of managerial policy, and the greater unionization of the skilled workers, does in fact seem to have occurred only exceptionally. For the most part it did not occur because the administration or negotiation of wage changes was directed by other principles or pressures, especially the felt inequity of cuts to the low-paid and their resistance to them even when not unionized.

The contraction of the differential for manual skill through the two World Wars stands out as an effect specific to those periods. The reasons that may be given for it with some confidence only amplify those already suggested as operative in the rising phase of the 8-year cycle. In addition, the enforced reduction of consumption in wartime brought into play the same factor as we have seen narrowing differentials in cyclical depressions: when wartime scarcities manifested themselves in a rising cost of living, the public control of money wages eased the impact on the lower-paid by granting the same absolute cost of living allowance to them as to the higher-paid. If a public agency or private employer felt unable to give less than a certain amount to the low-paid, the total cost would be less if the rise were extended to other employees as an equal absolute and not an equal percentage rise. For a time, at least, the higher-paid might feel that their differential was safeguarded if it was unchanged as a sum of money. Meanwhile the balance of supply and demand was tending to raise the relative pay of the less skilled. The more skilled were drawn on less for military service; in the munitions industries, where the demand for the more skilled workers extended, the supply was raised by upgrading or training persons formerly excluded, or the work was broken down so that parts of it at least could be done by less skilled persons. Generally, resistance to the crossing of occupational boundaries was reduced, and women in particular were admitted to jobs that they used to be kept out of or thought incapable of doing. As vacancies in the more skilled occupations were filled by drawing the less skilled upwards, the extension of the demand for labour of all kinds, and the competition of employers, became concentrated upon the less skilled, at the same time as they were being removed in greater proportion to the armed forces. Thus supply and demand worked in the same way as the sense of equity in wage administration.

In the United Kingdom at least, a third factor may have had some effect before the end of the First World War: the number of trade unionists doubled in the course of the war, largely through the recruitment of the less skilled, whose inerests might then be expected to do more to shape trade union policy (Turner 1952). Douty (1953) has pointed to the effects in the U.S.A. during the Second World War of the then recent extension of trade unionism: the new industrial unions contained a numerical preponderance of the lower-paid, and were still preoccupied with gaining recognition and negotiating rises 'across the board', to the exclusion of concern for differentials. But that industrial unionism was not a necessary condition for the narrowing the differential for manual skill appears from this differential also having narrowed in building with its long tradition of craft unionism.

If these were the reasons for the contraction of the differential for manual skill during the two World Wars, how can we account for the three cases displayed in Fig. 4.6, where there was no such contraction? We can suggest answers at least for two of them. The comparative absence of change in the Australian differential from 1921 onwards has been attributed to the working of the system of public regulation of wages by conciliation and arbitration, in the states and the Commonwealth: the arbitrators were explicitly concerned with the differential, and generally accepted the claim that it should be maintained percentage-wise (Oxnam 1950; Hancock 1969). That the differential in France was wider after the Second World War than before it may be attributed to the adoption at the end of the war of the Parodi scale, which gave the three grades of skilled worker 40, 55, and 70 per cent more than common labour (Daubigny 1969).

After the wars, when controls were removed, and some of the shifts in supply and demand were reversed, the same processes and pressures as narrowed the skill differential during the war now worked to reopen it. In the cases we are discussing, however, after neither war did it return to its former size. A major change thus seems to have been brought about within the wage structure concerned.

These and other findings have led to a general recognition of a contraction of the differential for skill as a common feature of the developed economies since 1914. A number of reasons have been put forward to show how it arose naturally out of the course of their development. But before we take up these reasons we must pause on the question of fact. Two qualifications are necessary. First, the contraction of the differential was by no means general. If we look back at Table 2.19,* we see that though contraction predominated, none of the three differentials there — those of the machine compositor, the iron moulder, and the carpenter — contracted in all eleven countries between 1938 and 1972, and in seven countries at least one differential actually widened. If the reasons given for contraction were a sufficient cause of it in some cases, why were they not in others? The second qualification concerns Great Britain. Here at least it has been found that though the differentials of particular occupations certainly

[*Not reprinted here – Ed.]

have contracted, those between the broad classes of skilled, semi-skilled, and unskilled manual workers have changed extraordinarily little. Thus Routh (1965), Table 46) took the median earnings of men in each of three occupational classes —

(a) foremen, inspectors and supervisors, and skilled manual workers;
(b) semi-skilled manual workers;
(c) unskilled manual workers —

in six industries, in 1906 and 1960. On the average of the six, the ratio of (b) and (a) was 75.7 in 1906, and 73.3 in 1960; that of (c) to (a) was 61.9 in both years.

At first sight this looks like a conflict of evidence. In fact there need be no conflict, for where we find contraction we are following one occupation through, but where there is no contraction we are dealing with groups of occupations that are composed variously from time to time. Within the group of skilled occupations, while some of the old-established ones are losing ground new ones arise to command higher pay: in building, for instance, the traditional crafts may now be earning less than the new, non-craft occupations of steel erector, bar bender and fixer, and tower crane operator. Various economic and social forces tend to raise the relative pay of the unskilled, but meanwhile semi-skilled jobs are expanding relatively to the labourers'; and the relative pay of those who remain in the latter does not rise. We are confronted not with a change in the balance of supply and demand for different grades of skill, so much as a switch of demand from old forms of skill to new. Perlman (1969, p. 85) has suggested that switches of this kind have operated in the U.S.A. in recent years to delay or reduce the contraction of differentials that social development has been tending to bring about, in the same way as they operate to raise differentials in the early stages of industrialization. 'It can be argued that mechanization does not require relatively more skilled than unskilled labor than characterized the prior pre industrial labor mix. But because of the difficulty of transferring pre industrial skills into those required by mechanized industry . . . temporary shortage of skilled labor appears. This argument created problems in labor supply similar to those facing a developing country.'

We must not build too much on Routh's finding. Differentials did generally narrow within four of his six industries, and that they widened in the other two just enough to offset this may be only coincidental. Ober (1948), working with groups of the skilled, semi-skilled, and unskilled which, like Routh's, were variously composed from time to time, found a reduction of the differential for skill in the U.S.A. from 105 per cent in 1907 to 55 per cent in 1945-7. But evidently we have to allow for the presence, alongside the forces tending to narrow differentials, of others tending to widen them or set up new ones. The former are partly economic, but largely social, and affect the supply of labour to different occupations; the latter are technical, and create a demand for labour in new specializations.

The economic and social forces in the U.S.A. have been discussed by Muntz (1955) and Keat (1960). The sharp reduction from the First World War onwards of the immigration of predominantly unskilled and often illiterate workers reduced the rate of growth of the unqualified labour force. This opened job opportunities for Negroes as the general level of employment rose through the Second World War and after; the migration of Negroes from south to north was linked with a reduction in the wage differential between black and white manual workers. Meanwhile the approval of equal absolute rises by the National War Labor Board was an immediate cause of the narrowing of proportional differentials during the Second World War; and after the war the Fair Labor Standards Act with its minimum wage exerted an upward pressure on the lowest rates of pay. But the most pervasive and powerful force was the extension of education. The percentage of boys and girls of high school age who were actually at school was only 7 in 1889-90; by 1952-53 it had reached 77. This numerical expansion went with a shift from academic towards vocational education within the high schools.

That expansion of education has found its counterpart, if not on the same scale, still sufficiently to mark a 'silent social revolution' (Lowndes 1937) in most Western countries. Among manual workers a chief consequence has been the passing of the old dichotomy of craftsman and labourer, and the rise of the semi-skilled. Few workers remain who are unskilled in the old sense of that term. By upbringing and education most manual workers now are capable of learning to perform a variety of operations requiring understanding as well dexterity, and some of these operations are more complex, and involve no less problem-solving, than the traditional crafts. John Stuart Mill (1848, II. xiv. 2) remarked on the beginnings of this change from stratification to gradation in the England of his own day:

So complete, indeed, has hitherto been the separation, so strongly marked the line of demarcation, between the different grades of labourers, as to be almost equivalent to an hereditary distinction of caste. . . . The changes, however, now so rapidly taking place in usages and ideas, are undermining all these distinctions; the habits or disabilities which chained people to their hereditary condition are fast wearing away, and every class is exposed to increased and increasing competition from at least the class immediately below it. The general relaxation of barriers, and the increased facilities of education which already are, and will be in much greater degree, brought within the reach of all, tend to produce, among many excellent effects, one which is the reverse; they tend to bring down the wages of skilled labour.

This last sentence gives us pause. Why did the tendency that Mill thought he saw so clearly in 1848 take so little effect down to 1914, despite the great extension of education meanwhile? Two answers may be put forward. The first would accept that the pressure from the side of supply was indeed building up as Mill supposed, but its expected effect on relative wages was obstructed by the power of the craft unions and by sheer custom, until the great shake up of these things in the First World War. The second answer, which does not exclude the first, points out that there will have been shifts in demand as well as supply, and suggests that the increased supply of those capable of more skilled manual work was at least balanced by the extension of demand for them. Economists have differed in their assessment of the effects of technical change on the differential for manual skill. Some have seen such change as tending to reduce the differential. 'There are indications that many skilled occupations are becoming less skilled, arduous, and responsible with the improvement of mechanical equipment and working conditions. . . . At the other end of the ladder there are fewer and fewer jobs which are entirely unskilled. Labourers now work with an increasing amount of mechanical equipment, which both lends some element of skill to their work and raises their productivity' (Reynolds & Taft 1956, p. 357). Without calling those observations in question we can also accept Perlman's observations cited above concerning the switch of demand from old forms of skill to new. We have no measure of changes on the side of demand as we have in part at least of those on the side of supply; but the hypothesis of switches within the demand for skill, and of a sufficient extension of it in the aggregate to balance the extensions of the potential supply, does provide an answer to the main question posed by the actual course of events, namely why differentials among manual workers have not contracted more generally and unmistakably than they have done.

Among the factors mentioned as having brought about the contraction in the margin for manual skill in the U.S.A. during and after the Second World War was the enactment, in the Fair Labor Standards Act, of a minimum wage of wide coverage. We also noted the powerful effect ascribed to minimum wage legislation in Brazil. A number of other countries, developing or developed, have been enforcing a national minimum, or have taken statutory action to raise wages of particular groups of the low-paid. Have these measures tended to raise the pay of the unskilled generally relatively to that of the skilled? The British National Board for Prices and Incomes (1971, para. 124(2) and Appx. G), on a survey of the experience of other countries, found that they had not. 'No false hopes', it reported, 'should be attached to a national minimum wage. It does not offer an easy and direct way to effect a permanent improvement in the relative position of the low-paid; experience suggests that it does this only temporarily. . . . Because of the tendency of differentials to reassert themselves, the raising of national minimum wage levels in the wrong circumstances could be a dangerous source of cost inflation.' The finding that differentials tend to reassert themselves rests on U.S. experience. In a study of the effects of the raising of the U.S. minimum rate, Douty (1960) found that in Southern saw-milling the differentials of two skilled occupations over the unskilled rate declined in 1950, following the introduction of the $0.75 minimum in January of that year, but were restored partially by 1953 and completely by 1955. They fell again in 1956 when the minimum rate was raised to $1.00, but the next year, the last for which data were available at the time of report, they had recovered somewhat. It appears that minimum wage regulation is effective in raising the relative pay of isolated persons or groups, or of categories of labour like women or juveniles whose pay is hardly part of a common scale for different grades of labour, but that it is not effective save temporarily in raising the relative pay of the lowest grades within such a scale. [. . .]

REFERENCES

Ashton, T. S. (1955) *An Economic History of England: the 18th century* (London).

Bell, Philip W. (1951) 'Cyclical variations and trend in occupational wage differentials in American industry since 1914', *Review of Economics and Statistics*, 33, 4, Nov. 1951, 329-37.

Brown, W. and Sisson, K. (1975) 'The use of comparisons in workplace wage determination', *British Journal of Industrial Relations*, 13, 1, Mar. 1975, 25-53.

Bry, G. (1960) *Wages in Germany 1871-1945* (National Bureau of Economic Research, N.Y., and Princeton U.P.).

Daubigny, J. P. (1969) 'Actualité du système "Parodi" dans les comportements salariaux des entreprises', *Revue Économique*, 22, 3, May 1969, 497-514.

Douty, H. M. (1953) 'Union Impact on wage structures', *Proceedings of the Sixth Annual Meeting, Industrial Relations Research Association, Dec. 28-30, 1953*, 61-76.

—— (1960) 'Some Effects of the $1.00 Minimum Wage in the United States', *Economica*, 27, 106, May 1960, 137-47.

—— (1968) 'Wage differentials: forces and counterforces', *Monthly Labor Review*, 91, 3, Mar. 1968, 74-81.

Fischlowitz, E. (1959) 'Manpower problems in Brazil', *International Labour Review*, 79, 4, Apr. 1959, 398-417.

Fishlow, A. (1972) 'Brazilian size distribution of income', *American Economic Review, Papers and Proceedings*, 62, 2, May 1972, 391-402.

Gunter, H. (1964) 'Changes in occupational wage differentials', *International Labour Review*, 99, 2, Feb. 1964, 136-55.

Hancock, K. (1969) 'The wages of the workers', *Journal of Industrial Relations* (Sydney), 11, 1, Mar. 1969, 17-38.

Heer, C. (1930) *Income and Wages in the South* (Univ. of South Carolina Press).

International Metal Workers' Federation (1965) *Wages and Working Conditions in the Steel Industries of the Free World* (U.S.A.).

Keat, P. G. (1960) 'Long-run changes in occupational wage structure, 1900-1956', *Journal of Political Economy*, 68, 6, 584-600.

Knowles, K. G. J. C. and Robertson, D. J. (1951) 'Differences between the wages of skilled and unskilled workers, 1880-1950', *Bulletin of the Oxford University Institute of Statistics*, 13, 4, Apr. 1951, 109-27.

Long, C. D. (1960) *Wages and Earnings in the United States 1860-1890* (National Bureau of Economic Research, N.Y., and Princeton U.P.).

Lowndes, G. A. N. (1937) *The Silent Social Revolution* (London).

Mill, J. S. (1848) *Principles of Political Economy* (1st edn., London).

Muntz, E. E. (1955) 'The decline in wage differentials based on skill in the United States', *International Labour Review*, 71, 6, June 1955, 575-92.

National Board for Prices and Incomes (1971), *General Problems of Low Pay*, Report No. 169 (H.M.S.O., London, Cmnd. 4648, Apr. 1971).

Ober, H. (1948) 'Occupational Wage Differentials, 1907-1947', *Monthly Labor Review*, 67, 8, Aug. 1948, 127-34.

O.E.C.D. (1965) *Wages and Labour Mobility: a study of the relation between changes in wage differentials and the pattern of employment* (Organisation for Economic Co-operation and Development, Paris).

Oxnam, D. W. (1950) 'The relation of unskilled to skilled wage rates in Australia', *Economic Record*, 26, 50, June 1950, 112-18.

Ozanne, R. 91968) *Wages in Practice and Theory: McCormick and International Harvester 1860-1960* (Univ. of Wisconsin).

Peitchinis, S. G. (1965) *The Economics of Labour: Employment and Wages in Canada* (Toronto).

Perlman, R. (1969) *Labor Theory* (N.Y.).

Phelps Brown, E. H. and Hopkins, S. V. (1955) 'Seven centuries of building wages', *Economica*, 22, 87, Aug. 1955, 195–206.

—— (1956) 'Seven centuries of the prices of consumables, compared with builders' wage-rates', *Economica*, 23, 92, Nov. 1956, 296–314.

—— (1959) 'Builders' wage rates, prices and population: some further evidence', *Economica*, 26, 101, Feb. 1959, 18–38.

Reder, N. W. (1955) 'The theory of occupational wage differentials', *American Economic Review*, 45, 5, Dec. 1955, 833–52.

Reynolds, L. G. and Taft, C. H. (1956) *The Evolution of Wage Structure* (Yale U.P.).

Routh, Guy (1965) *Occupation and Pay in Great Britain 1906–60* (Cambridge U.P.).

Rowe, J. W. F. (1928) *Wages in Practice and Theory* (London).

Silvestre, J.-J. (1971) 'La dynamique des salaires nominaux en France', *Revue Économique*, 22, 3, May 1971, 430–49.

Smith, Adam (1776) *The Wealth of Nations* (London).

Taira, K. (1966) 'Wage differentials in developing countries: a survey of findings', *International Labour Review*, 93, 3, Mar. 1966, 281–301.

Turner, H. A. (1952) 'Trade unions, differentials and the levelling of wages', *Manchester School*, 20, 3, Sept. 1952, 227–82.

—— (1965) *Wage Trends, Wage Policies, and Collective Bargaining: the Problems for Underdeveloped Countries* (University of Cambridge, Dept. of Applied Economics, Occasional Paper 6).

4.4 Inter-Industry Wage Differentials*
[. . .]

LONG RUN

Most discussions of interindustry wage differentials proceed without much explicit consideration of economic theory. The literature abounds in *ad hoc* hypotheses, some of which are consistent with neoclassical price theory but many of which are not. However, these various hypotheses are usually treated as being equally plausible, *a priori*; consistency with the implications of price theory has counted for very little in appraising the merits of a theory. Our attitude is somewhat different; we believe that if a theory is inconsistent with the implications of price theory it is cause for concern, and that an explanation is in order. Consequently it will be helpful if we begin our discussion by spelling out what is implied by price theory for interindustrial differentials.

In the long run, under competitive conditions,[1] any industry will pay the same price for a given grade of labor as any other industry hiring in the same location. This remark must be qualified for differences in the nonpecuniary attractions of different industries and locations, but let us abstract from these at first. Therefore, in the long run, real wage differentials among industries will

*From Melvin W. Reder, 'Wage Differentials: theory and measurement', in National Bureau of Economic Research, *Aspects of Labor Economics* (Princeton: Princeton University Press, 1962).

reflect differences in the skill mix. Money wage differences among locations, for given skill, should be no greater than can be rationalized by differences in living costs.

This means that there should be no association of industry wage levels either with the amount of labor employed or with the amount of capital employed (total or per worker) except insofar as either of these quantities is correlated with the skill mix. This absence of association between industry wage level and quantity of labor utilized is an important distinguishing characteristic between long- and short-run situations (see Appendix).* In the short run, the greater the increase in employment over the recent past, the more likely is an industry to encounter rising wages because of short-run inelasticities of labor supply; hence the theory implies a positive association of increase in labor quantity used and wage increase in short periods, but not in long periods. Moreover, it seems reasonable to suppose that it will be more likely that skilled labor will become relatively scarce[2] to an expanding industry than nonskilled. Therefore, in the short run, skill differentials should be positively associated with changes in employment.[3]

That is, we interpret price theory as saying that in the long run each industry's wage level will, *ceteris paribus*, vary in the same direction as its skill and locational mix (see below) and, in particular, will not be related to changes in the quantities of labor or capital employed. Now if *ceteris* were exactly *paribus*, and our sample were large enough, the correlation coefficient (among industries) between long-run changes in wage levels and those in (any) factor quantity would be exactly zero. But our samples are limited and *ceteris* is never exactly *paribus*; hence the theory will be considered 'not inconsistent with the evidence' if the above mentioned correlation coefficients are approximately zero. Inconsistency with the evidence will emerge if *ceteris* is insufficiently *paribus* in the sense that forces affecting long-run relative wage changes are significantly correlated with long-run relative changes in factor quantities.[4]

Now, how do these inferences square with available evidence? One body of evidence is presented by Fabricant[5] in a study of average growth rates of real hourly wages, labor employed, and capital utilized in 33 industries from 1899 to 1953.[6] Let us suppose that in a period of 54 years the long-run forces that affect the relative levels of industries' wages make changes sufficiently large to permit us to treat differences between 1899 and 1953 as reflecting mainly these forces and, only to a minor degree, random and short-run forces.[7] That is, the differences between 1899 and 1953 are assumed to be explicable on the hypothesis that they are, save for random disturbances, positions of comparative statics. If so, there should be no association between either the relative growth in the quantity of labor utilized, or the relative growth in the stock of capital employed in a given industry, and the relative growth in wages (measured by average hourly earnings) in that industry. The rank correlation coefficients

[*Not reprinted here – Ed.]

between (a) wages and labor employed and (b) wages and tangible capital owned,[8] with each industry taken as a single observation, are +.21 between wages and labor quantity and +.29 between wages and capital quantity. The standard error of the rank correlation coefficient with 33 observations is .17, and hence neither coefficient is statistically significant at the 5 per cent level.[9]

These findings are compatible with the competitive hypothesis.[10] Indeed, the fact that both of the correlation coefficients are positive, as well as small, is what might be expected because of the tendency for rapidly growing industries to locate (as of 1953) in relatively high-wage urban centers. There is, moreover, further evidence that is also favorable to the competitive hypothesis.

(1) Contrary to much of the recent literature, there was only a slight correlation between productivity[11] and average hourly labor compensation among 33 industry groups during the period 1899-1953. The rank correlation during that period was +.24 (insignificant at the 5 per cent level); in various shorter periods the coefficient was appreciably higher.[12] Confirming this is the fact that during 1899-1947, among 80 manufacturing industries, the rank correlation coefficient between output per man-hour and average hourly labor compensation was 0.26 – not quite significant at 5 per cent; during individual decades of that period, the coefficient was invariably higher than this.[13]

It would be possible to hide behind the insignificance of the above coefficients and say that the competitive hypothesis is not disconfirmed. However, it seems more plausible to suppose that the two coefficients (noted above) together indicate the operation of some rather weak force systematically correlating average hourly labor compensation and productivity. One explanation of this that would not be incompatible with the competitive hypothesis is that there is a tendency for industries with a greater than average increase in productivity to experience a greater than average 'improvement' in skill mix[14] and, therefore, to have a greater than average increase in hourly labor compensation. Though not directly testable, this explanation seems to have considerable plausibility. Another possibility consistent with the competitive hypothesis is that increases in productivity are weakly associated with a tendency toward urbanization and higher wages. Last, but not least, in the short run a positive correlation between relative wages and employment is to be expected (see below). This coefficient may approach zero in the long run, but it may remain positive and finite for a very long time – long enough to generate (at least) some of the positive coefficients reported in this section.[15] Obviously, failing empirical tests of these and rival hypotheses, there is room for doubt and debate.

(2) Another finding consistent with the competitive hypothesis is that the ratio of capital compensation per unit of capital service is only slightly correlated with changes in average hourly labor compensation among 33 industries in the period 1929-53; the rank correlation coefficient was only +.12.[16] The competitive hypothesis implies that this coefficient be zero. Though the coefficient is insignificant at the 5 per cent level, we are inclined to take its positive sign seriously and rationalize it as follows: in industries with a higher

than average rate of increase in productivity, there is a slight tendency for both labor and capital 'quality' to increase more than the average.[17] A further finding that tends to support this conclusion is the very slight positive correlation (+.05) between (1) factor compensation (of both labor and capital) per unit of input, and (2) productivity among 33 industries in 1899–1953.

Contrasted with these slight positive correlations is the very substantial negative rank correlation coefficient, during 1899–1953, between unit prices of output and factor productivity, −.55, which is significant at 5 per cent.[18] The sign of this coefficient is what the competitive hypothesis would lead one to expect. Combined with the other findings cited it bears out the view that, as between industries, the relative gains of factor productivity are passed on to buyers and none accrue to the factors employed.

(3) Still a third finding that bears upon the competitive hypothesis is the behavior of the interindustrial wage structure itself. We have seen that there has been a secular decline in skill differentials in the economy as a whole. What has been said of skill differentials also applies to geographical differentials.

We also know that the ranking of industries with respect to their level of earnings per worker is quite stable over long periods of time. That is, the rank correlation of an industry's position in the industrial wage hierarchy in one year (or period) with another very distant in time is 'quite high.' For example, Cullen[19] found a rank correlation coefficient of +.66 for 76 manufacturing industries between ranks of per-worker annual earnings in 1899 and 1950. In Kendrick's data, the rank correlation between average hourly earnings in 1899–1909 and 1948–53 was +.46.[20] Slichter found a coefficient of rank correlation of +.7289 between the average hourly earnings of male unskilled labor among 20 manufacturing industries in 1923 and 1946.[21]

Because of the secular decline in skill margins and in regional differentials, the competitive hypothesis implies that there would have been a secular decrease in interindustry relative wage dispersion if the skills and geographical mix had remained more or less unchanged.[22] The evidence that there has been a secular decrease in interindustry relative wage dispersion is far from conclusive; and Cullen's scepticism of this evidence as proof of secularly[23] reduced dispersion seems fully warranted.[24] It is possible that further investigation will show that dispersion has indeed been reduced. But if it does not, certain more or less alternative inferences may be drawn: (1) despite the general decline in skill margins, the relative wage premiums that must be paid by industries that are expanding their labor forces rapidly were as great in the late 1940's as at the turn of the century;[25] (2) there was an increasing dispersion in the 'richness' of industrial skill mixes[26] which offset the reduced skill margins; (3) there were offsetting inter-industry changes in skill mixes, locational mixes, etc.; and (4) the competitive hypothesis is wrong. These inferences are not mutually exclusive, and they could all be true to a degree; however, none of the first three has yet been tested, though it is far from impossible to do so.

We have already presented some evidence which tends to reject (4); i.e., which tends to support the competitive hypothesis. And there is some further evidence to the same effect: both Cullen and Woytinsky find evidence of diminishing secular dispersion of interindustrial earning among the particular industries that happened to be at the upper and lower extremes of the distribution in a particular year.[27] This means that, although the over-all interindustry dispersion among a collection of industries may not have diminished appreciably over time, the spread among the group of industries that happened to be paying very high and very low wages in a given base year (e.g., 1899 or 1929) diminished. In other words, the particular industries that are toward the high and low extremes in the interindustrial earnings hierarchy in a given year tended to regress toward the mean with the passage of time.

This is what the competitive hypothesis implies will happen; for, in any given year, part of the interindustry dispersion of wages is due to disequilibrium of industries expanding and contracting employment more than the average, and this source of interindustry wage dispersion is reduced over time by the operation of the price system. The competitive hypothesis implies nothing concerning the long-term trend in interindustrial wage dispersion among a particular group of industries as a whole, except that it should depend solely upon variations in skill and locational differentials and random disturbances.

One further hypothesis, not strictly of a long-run variety, should be mentioned. The rise of an economy from a less- to a more-full utilization of its labor force (including its reserves) may cause a reduction in interindustry differentials, as happened when the economy emerged from the depression of the 1930's to the full employment of the 1940's.[28] Such behavior would follow from the narrowing of skill differentials during such periods. Whether this limited experience can be generalized to a proposition relating level of employment, or growth rate in labor demand, to the interindustry dispersion of wage rates is not clear. However, it is a possibility.

Several other hypotheses concerning the long-run equilibrium industrial structure of wage rates have been advanced by Slichter:[29]

(1) 'The average hourly earnings of male unskilled labor (U) tend to be high where the average hourly earnings of male semiskilled and skilled labor (S) are high.' Slichter found, in 1939, a rank correlation coefficient of +.7098 (among 20 manufacturing industries) between U and S. If this correlation is interpreted as resulting from a tendency for industries using relatively expensive types of skilled labor also to use expensive types of nonskilled, then it is compatible with the competitive hypothesis. Slichter accepts this interpretation in part,[30] but also contends that the correlation is partly due to company wage policy, which presumably is independent of market forces; on this point, see below. It should be noted that it is also possible that Slichter's observation reflects short-period and not long-period forces; i.e., expanding industries are more likely than others to encounter increasing supply prices (as a function of rate of increase of employment) for all kinds of labor.[31]

(2) 'The hourly earnings of male common labor (M) have some (not pro-

nounced) tendency to be low where the percentage of women (W) among wage earners is high.' The coefficient of rank correlation between M and W in 1939 (for 19 manufacturing industries) was +.4491, and in 1929, +.5224.[32] This, as Slichter (in effect) argues, may well reflect the operation of the competitive mechanism; i.e., women are hired mainly in low-wage industries and men, in order to compete with them, must accept less than the average male wage. That is, the correlation is presumed to reflect competition for similar jobs, and not osmosis. If this explanation is correct, then the industries where women are mostly highly concentrated should be those in which the unfavored (by the market) males, e.g., Negroes, are also concentrated; and this seems to be the case.[33]

(3) Slichter also found substantial rank correlation between net income after taxes, as a percentage of sales, π, and average hourly earnings both of unskilled and of skilled and semiskilled workers.[34] Slichter interpreted π as an index of profitability. Accepting this interpretation, we could easily rationalize the observed rank correlations as short-period phenomena resulting from the short-run association between increased labor demand and profitability. However, Slichter, like many other writers, contends that this phenomenon 'reinforces the view that wages, within a considerable range, reflect managerial discretion, and that where managements are barely breaking even, they tend to keep wages down.[35] This interpretation is incompatible with the competitive hypothesis.

We believe that the importance of this possibility can easily be exaggerated. Nonetheless, the field work on our study of interfirm wage differentials has confirmed the oft-expressed view that large and profitable firms will often ignore local labor market situations by over-paying on certain jobs in certain areas in order to avoid undesired intercompany differentials. Such firms also manifest a desire to be toward the top of any labor market in which they hire, both for reasons of prestige and quality selection.

To be sure, there is a tendency for out-of-line wages to be corrected 'as soon as the opportunity presents itself,' but it is also true that large firms are more dilatory about correcting overpayment (e.g., red circle rates) than correcting underpayment. This, together with a preference for selective recruitment policies, creates an upward bias in wage level relative to the market as of any given moment. Thus, we would be inclined to agree that large and profitable firms do tend to pay more at any one time than could be explained by the competitive hypothesis. However, this cannot explain *movements* in relative wages; at most, it can explain relative wage levels as of a given moment.

These remarks pertain directly to individual firms, and not to entire industries. Their relation to the industrial wage structure results from the fact that in some industries the percentage of workers employed in large firms is greater than in others. Industries concentrating relatively large fractions of their labor forces in large firms should tend to exhibit relatively high concentration ratios;[36] hence there might well be an association between high concentration ratios and high wages at a *given moment of time*.

However, this is no reason to suppose there would be an association between *changes* in relative industrial wage levels over time and the index of concentration as of a given moment, as some writers have argued.[37] These writers contend that the index of concentration is a rough (inverse) indicator of the relative degree of competitiveness of an industry;[38] and that noncompetitive industries tend to raise wages more than others. But, since it is not alleged that the indexes of concentration for different industries have changed during the relevant time period, it cannot be permanent differences in industry structure that are responsible for differential wage behavior; it must be differential *changes* in industry behavior. That is, what must be explained are differential changes in the willingness or ability or both of highly concentrated industries (relative to others) to grant wage increases; to our knowledge this has never been attempted. It should also be noted that to relate *levels* of concentration with *increases* (in favor of concentrated industries) in wages implies a secular increase in wage dispersion which is grossly inconsistent with known facts.

Because the hypothesis that interindustrial differences in degree of monopoly are an important factor in explaining the interindustrial differences in wage behavior has had wide currency, and is obviously a rival to the competitive hypothesis, we have attempted one rather simple test of it. We have taken Nutter's data on the relative extent of monopoly in 1899 and 1937 by major industry groups,[39] and correlated the change in the rankings between those dates with the change in the rankings of wages paid by those groups.[40] The correlation coefficient of these rank changes was −.05, indicating a slight (negligible) tendency for a decrease in monopoly to accompany an increase in wages − inconsistent with the hypothesis.[41]

(4) Slichter alleges a strong inverse association between hourly earnings of unskilled labor and the ratio of payrolls to sales. He explains this by saying: 'Managements naturally are more concerned about the rates which they pay for labor when payrolls are large in relation to the receipts of the enterprise than when payrolls are small.'[42] One (slightly astonishing) implication of this is that vertical disintegration, per se, leads to high wages. But, leaving this aside, let us concede that, in the absence of competition, a low ratio does make it easier for a benevolent employer or an aggressive union to raise wages than otherwise. However, before accepting this as an important determinant of industrial wage differences, we would urge consideration of the following alternative: high ratios of payrolls to sales are more likely to be found in industries that specialize in fabricating operations, and are associated with low wages because the likelihood of such specialization is greater where the fabrication can be performed by low-wage labor.

But at the very most, the above relation obtains only at a given instant. It provides no warrant for a long-run interpretation of Dunlop's contention that 'wage and salary rates would be expected to increase most . . . where labor costs are a small percentage of total costs.[43] So far as we are aware this contention has never been substantiated *for the long run*.

(5) One determinant of an industry's place in the interindustry wage hierarchy at a given moment is the relative richness of its skill mix. For 1950, we ranked industries by richness of skill mix and correlated this with rank in the interindustry wage hierarchy; the rank correlation coefficient was +.612.[44] This cross-sectional relationship reflects departures from long-run equilibrium, crudeness of industrial classifications, etc. Nonetheless it indicates a substantial degree of relation between the two sets of rankings.

SHORT RUN

Let us begin our discussion of the short-run behavior of the interindustry wage structure by considering the relation of its variations to those in employment. The competitive hypothesis explains such variations as due to wages rising in industries where employment is shrinking because of labor immobility. In the short run, *differential* changes in skill mix are assumed to be uncorrelated with differential changes in employment.[45]

There have been a number of studies of the relation of variations in the interindustry wage structure to changes in employment. Unfortunately, not all of their findings are mutually consistent. For example, Garbarino[46] found a rank correlation coefficient of +.48 between percentage changes in hourly earnings and employment (for 34 manufacturing industries) in 1923-40; Ross and Goldner found that in three of four periods studied there was a strong positive association of percentage increases in hourly earnings and percentage increases in employment.[47] Ostry found that in Canada there had been an appreciable correlation between percentage changes in hourly earnings and in employment; among 36 industries, the correlation coefficient in 1945-49 was +.44; in 1949-56, +.56.[48]

Moreover, Hansen and Rehn, in a study of wage differentials from 1947 to 1954 among eight industries in Sweden,[49] found substantial interindustry correlation between wage drift[50] and excess demand[51] for labor, which is consistent with the hypothesis that short-run wage differentials result mainly from differing rates of increase in labor demand. They found virtually no correlation of wage drift with gains in average man-hour productivity, but were unable to use Swedish profit data for interindustry analyses.

But the data do not all point to one conclusion: Slichter found among 20 industries, during 1923-39, a coefficient of rank correlation (between percentage changes in hourly earnings and percentage changes in employment) of only +.2812.[52] Eisemann found that in 1939-47, percentage increases in manufacturing wages were negatively correlated with percentage increases in employment; however, the absolute increase in average hourly earnings was positively correlated with percentage increases in employment.[53] Levinson[54] has found that in 4 of the 11 year-to-year changes between 1947 and 1958 there was a negative correlation among 19 manufacturing industries between percentage changes in straight-time hourly earnings and percentage changes in production worker employment. He also found a negative partial correlation coefficient between this pair of variables for 1947–53 and a negligible positive one (+.0046) for 1953–58.[55]

Bowen[56] computed correlation coefficients between percentage changes in average hourly earnings, *w*, and percentage changes in employment, *e*, during six subperiods of the interval 1947–59. These various coefficients reflect the association between *w* and *e* among 20 two-digit manufacturing industries. Bowen computed both simple and partial correlation coefficients. The partial coefficients between *w* and *e* held constant some or all of the following: (1) average level of profits in the industry; (2) the concentration ratio (in 1954); and (3) the percentage of the production workers unionized (in 1958). All possible first and second order partial correlation coefficients between *w* and *e* (holding constant the other variables, both singly and in pairs) are presented. The coefficients show a positive correlation between *w* and *e* in the three subperiods when unemployment was relatively low,[57] and this relation is generally stronger in the partial than in the simple coefficients. In the three subperiods in which unemployment was relatively high, the coefficients showed a different pattern: in two of these three subperiods the simple coefficients were negative; in one of them all of the partials were negative; and in another, half of them were negative.

Thus Bowen's findings (on this point) tend to support the competitive hypothesis for periods of 'low unemployment,' but not for those of higher unemployment. That the relation between *w* and *e* should be stronger in periods of low unemployment is in the spirit of the competitive hypothesis (though not its letter);[58] i.e., in periods of low unemployment, short-run elasticities of labor supply to industries are likely to be smaller, and differential increases in employment therefore more likely to produce differential wage changes. But if Bowen's findings are accepted, then the competitive hypothesis is uninformative, if not invalid, as an explanation of short-run wage movements in the presence of 'appreciable'[59] unemployment.

In short the evidence does not give unqualified support to the view that short-run variations in labor demand are a major cause of variation in straight-time hourly earnings. Some of the contrary evidence can be 'explained away.' The adverse findings of Ross and Goldner for 1942–46 and of Eisemann for 1939–47 may well be due to the fact that the war industries which expanded most rapidly were the very ones where dilution of the skill mix was greatest. However, it is harder to explain away the findings of Levinson, Conrad, and especially Bowen. Let us now turn to alternative explanations.

PROFITS, CONCENTRATION, AND RELATED VARIABLES

Levinson suggests that relative industry wage levels have varied either with (industry levels of) current profits or with profits lagged one year.[60] He measures profits as return on stockholders' equity both before or after taxes. This alleged relation is not, of itself, inconsistent with the competitive hypothesis, for the level of current profits would be expected to be associated with recent increases in employment. However, Levinson computes partial correlation coefficients between percentage wage changes, w, and percentage increases in employment, e (average profit level, P, constant), for 1947-53 and 1953-58 and also between w and P (e constant) for the same interval. In 1947-53, the coefficient between w and e was negative, while that between w and P was positive; in 1953-58, the latter coefficient substantially exceeded the former though both were positive.[61]

These findings were similar to those of Bowen, who finds a consistent positive correlation (among 20 manufacturing industries) between percentage change in average hourly earnings and percentage change in average level of profits.[62] This positive relation is found in the simple correlation coefficients in all of Bowen's subperiods; it is also found among the partial coefficients (save for three small negative ones). [...]

To argue that movements in relative wage levels are strongly correlated with levels of relative profits or changes in relative product prices is not to contradict the competitive hypothesis, per se. For both of the aforementioned independent variables may be correlated with variations in the level of employment and reflect only the influence of this variable on relative wage levels. Moreover, industries with high current profits might well be industries in process of an unusually marked tendency to be hiring workers to operate new processes or to work in newly developing high-wage areas, or both. Either or both of these tendencies could create (upward) labor market pressure on wage rates despite a tendency for over-all employment to decline. None of the studies to which reference has been made has attempted to control against these possibilities.

PRODUCTIVITY

Some writers have found that the increase in average hourly earnings was greater in industries where the increase in physical production per man-hour was greater; e.g., Dunlop[63] and Garbarino.[64] Barring a correlation of skill mix and/or location with productivity, such a relationship is incompatible with the competitive hypothesis in the long run; whether it is compatible in the short run depends upon whether increases in man-hour productivity are positively correlated with increases in employment via correlation with the *value* of labor's marginal physical product.

The alleged factual relation between man-hour productivity and wages has itself been disputed by Levinson,[65] Meyers and Bowlby,[66] and Perlman.[67] These authors, especially the last, rightly stress the importance of product price movements in determining the relative average value productivity of labor in different industries. Despite the dispute about whether the various correlation coefficients are significant, and which periods should be studied, it seems that the coefficients are usually positive,[68] which suggests the existence of a positive short-run association, but one which is disturbed by extraneous factors whose intensity varies from one period to another.

How one is to interpret this association is another matter. Garbarino found that in Dunlop's data (where the correlation between increases in man-hour productivity and wages was strong), the coefficient of rank correlation between increases in employment and in man-hour productivity was only +.08.[69] Obviously this militates against the short-run competitive hypothesis that there is a positive association between changes in hourly earnings and changes in man-hour productivity, because of an empirical association of the latter with rising output and employment. Another possible explanation, of pertinence in the long run as well as the short, is that industries in which man-hour productivity increases most are those in which the skill mix is likely to improve most. Yet another possible explanation of this phenomenon posits the existence of a link between wage increases and rises in productivity via profits and ability to pay, à la Slichter, Levinson, et al. But there is no good reason, either in theory or fact, for accepting any of these hypotheses.[70]

UNIONS

Our discussion of interindustry wage differentials has obviously left out unions; the omission is intentional. The main reason for exclusion is the failure of previous research to obtain very satisfactory results in relating them either to the levels or movements in interindustry wage differentials. The well-known conclusion of Douglas and of Ross and Goldner[71] that new unionism is associated with differential percentage wage gains to an industry, but long-established unionism is not, was about as far as anyone had been able to go before the work reported on by H. G. Lewis.[72] We shall not attempt to appraise this work here but only note its relevance to our discussion.

One possibility of detecting the influence of unionism is to analyze the association among industries between wage changes and profit levels, holding employment changes constant. If unionism is effective in making wages higher than they would have been in its absence, this should be reflected in a forced sharing of profits[73] which should be, in the short run, over and above the influence of labor market conditions. That is, the positive partial association between wage changes and profit levels should increase with the strength of unionism — however measured. Of course, the influence of extraneous factors such as changes in skill and locational mix must be somehow taken into account.

CONCLUSION

This paper's point of departure is that relative wage levels, both by skill and industry, behave more or less as though they were market prices reflecting predominantly the interplay of changing tastes, techniques, and resources — the competitive hypothesis. The implications of this hypothesis, however, are not so simple as they might seem because tastes, techniques, and resources interact in peculiar and complicated ways. Moreover, the basic hypothesis has required amendment to allow for the effect of changes in minimum wage laws, etc., for secular rural-urban migration, and for the gradual broadening of educational opportunities.

The competitive hypothesis is at its best, both in explaining skill margins and interindustry differentials, when it is used to explain variations over long periods of time. It can hardly be said to be firmly established as an explanation of wage phenomena even for long periods; but it has at least survived (reasonably well) the tests to which it has so far been put.

For the short run the competitive hypothesis does not appear very reliable. There are a number of findings concerning interindustry differentials which simply are not consistent with its short-run implication that relative industry wage rates vary in the same direction as relative changes in employment, in any given short-time interval. We are not without alternative short-run hypotheses; but these either break down during one time interval or another, or still are in a primitive state of formulation and testing. [. . .]

NOTES

1. We shall assume, except when the contrary is specifically stated, that competitive conditions exist.
2. That is, it will take longer to train workers with skills peculiar to the industry than unspecialized workers and hence, for a time, their elasticity of supply will be less.
3. This is analogous to Clark Kerr's contention that, 'The lesser the degree and the greater the rate of industrialization, the wider will be the occupational differentials and the greater the premiums for skill.' (See 'Wage Relationships – the Comparative Impact of Market and Power Forces,' in J. T. Dunlop, (ed.), *The Theory of Wage Determination* [MacMillan, London, 1957], p. 187, especially no. 2.)
4. Now a word about the nonpecuniary attraction of different industries. It is hard to believe – though imaginable – that industries *as such* have differing degrees of nonpecuniary attractiveness to labor force members. Most of the apparent nonpecuniary differences among industries would seem to boil down to differences in the relative attractiveness of different locations and of the specific jobs offered. For example, we submit that a job as bookkeeper in the New York office of a coal mining firm is no less attractive than a similar job in the same location in an electronics firm. However, coal mining will offer proportionately more jobs in mining towns, and underground, than (say) electronics manufacturing and therefore might well face a higher *pecuniary* supply price for its labor.

   It would not be correct, conceptually, to identify unskilled jobs with unattractive ones, but historically there has been a strong positive association. In general, as industries have shifted away from unskilled labor they have also improved working conditions and reduced nonpecuniary disutilities. And since it is obviously very difficult to measure or indicate the relative nonpecuniary attractiveness of different industries, we have assumed that the *rank* of the various industries with respect to nonpecuniary utilities varies with the percentage of its workers employed in unskilled jobs. Clearly, this is a rough approximation which must later be improved upon.
5. S. Fabricant, *Basic Facts on Productivity Change*, New York, NBER, Occasional Paper 63, 1959, especially pp. 29–37.
6. These data are presented in extended form in J. W. Kendrick, *Productivity Trends in the United States*, Princeton for NBER, 1961.
7. See Methodological Appendix. [Not reprinted here – Ed.]

8. Perforce, we use the Kendrick-Fabricant definitions of labor, capital, and output. The data used are contained in Table B, pp. 46–47, of Fabricant, *Basic Facts*. 'Wages,' 'labor,' and 'capital' mean here percentage change in each of these variables between 1899 and 1953.

9. It might be contended that, because we have two coefficients differing from zero, and with the same sign, the two coefficients together differ significantly from zero (to which theory implies they are both equal). However, output, capital and labor are all highly correlated so that we cannot suppose the two coefficients to be independent, and combining the tests is therefore extremely difficult.

10. By 'competitive hypothesis,' I mean the hypothesis that prices and quantities behave as though they were in long-run equilibrium under conditions of pure competition. When we speak of the short-run competitive hypothesis we mean the same hypothesis except for the modifications introduced by the substitution of Marshallian short-run equilibrium for long run.

11. 'Productivity' is total productivity as defined by Kendrick; i.e., output per unit of input of both labor and capital. However, output per unit of labor input is highly correlated with total productivity (rank correlation coefficient among 33 industry groups is +0.94) and, as Kendrick says, 'thus analysis of productivity change based on output-per-man-hour measures should give results comparable to analyses based on total factor productivity' (p. 155). Therefore, we shall consider Kendrick's results, where 'total productivity' is interchangeable with man-hour productivity.

The competitive hypothesis implies that there will be no correlation *in the long run* between (average) productivity and wages. That is, industries in which average productivity grows relatively to others will show an increasing ratio of average to marginal (labor) productivity because all industries must pay the same for given grades of labor *in the long run*. This, of course, is not true in the short run.

12. Kendrick, *Productivity Trends*, Table 55, p. 198.

13. Ibid.

14. That is, a greater than average increase in the percentage of high-earning and presumably skilled workers employed. 'Skill mix' is defined more precisely below.

15. The point was raised in discussion by both M. J. Bailey and H. G. Lewis.

16. Kendrick, *Productivity Trends*, Table 55.

17. By 'capital quality,' I refer to the intangible (and unmeasured) inputs that add to the nonlabor income of an enterprise, but are not included in its measured capital stock. Included in these would be entrepreneurial skill and investment in research and development. In this connection, Kendrick reports (Ch. VI, p. 183) a rank correlation coefficient of +.68 between research and development expenditures, as a per cent of sales in 1953, and the average annual rate of change in total factor productivity in 1948–53.

18. Kendrick, *Productivity Trends*, Table 57.

19. D. E. Cullen, 'The Inter-industry Wage Structure, 1899–1950,' *American Economic Review*, June 1956, pp. 353–69, especially Table II, p. 359.

20. Kendrick, *Productivity Trends*, computed from Table 54.

21. S. H. Slichter, 'Notes on the Structure of Wages,' *Review of Economics and Statistics*, Feb. 1950, pp. 80–91, especially p. 88 and Table 7.

22. Kerr ('Wage Relationships,' pp. 189–191) argues this very strongly, though without indicating the crucial role of the competitive hypothesis.

23. The very marked and undisputed declines since the late 1930's are irrelevant for long-run analysis, as it seems clear that at that time these differentials were abnormally large.

24. Cullen, 'The Inter-industry Wage Structure,' p. 361. Further evidence to the same general effect is provided by correlating the percentage wage change between 1899 and 1953 (from Kendrick's data) with the index of 'richness of skill mix' by industry, in 1950 (see n. 28). If the relative richness of skill mix of the various industries had been unchanged over time, the percentage wage increase should have been the smaller, the richer the skill mix, because of the secular decline in skill margins. However, the rank correlation coefficient was only −.086 (between richness of skill mix in 1950 and percentage change in wages between 1899 and 1953). The sign is in accord with the hypothesis of no change in relative skill mix, but far too small to be taken seriously.

25. That is, the industries that are 'very high' wage payers in any given year include a disproportionate number of those expanding rapidly, and therefore trying to increase their total labor force; the converse applies to those industries that are 'very low' wage payers. Industries at either end of the ranking include a disproportionate fraction of those in temporary disequilibrium. Naturally, those industries need not be the same ones in 1899 and 1950.

26. By 'richness of the skill mix,' I refer to the relative numbers of skilled, semi-skilled, and unskilled workers employed. An industry's skill mix is richer, the greater the fraction of the first, and the smaller the fraction of the last in the work force.

    We can measure the richness of the skill mix of different industries in 1950 from the Statistics of *Occupation by Industry* which, so far as we are aware, has not been published for any other Census. The measure of the richness of an industry's skill mix is defined as the following weighted average:

$$R_i = \frac{\sum\limits_{j=1}^{n} a_{ji}W_j}{E_i} \text{(males)} + \frac{\sum\limits_{j=1}^{n} a_{ji}W_j}{E_i} \text{(females)}.$$

    This weighted average refers to the ith industry; W_j is the median annual earnings of persons in the j occupation throughout the economy; a_{ji} is the number of persons of given sex employed in the ith industry, and the ith occupation; and E_i is the number of persons employed in the ith industry. R_i is a weighted average of the nation-wide median occupational earnings of the employees in the ith industry with the fraction of the ith industry employment in the various age-sex classes serving as weights.

    Sex, as well as occupation, is treated as a determinant of skill mix because women, even in the same occupational category and industry, tend to be paid less than men (for whatever reason). It would have been better to have corrected our weights for degree of unemployment, but we were unable to do so. The richness of skill mix in 1950 was rank correlated with median industrial annual earnings in 1949 by a coefficient of +.613.

27. Cullen ('Inter-industry Wage,' Table III, p. 361) found a reduction between 1899 and 1947–50 of 8–12 per cent in the difference between the median annual earnings in industries in the upper and lower quartiles of the distribution of 84 manufacturing industries, in 1899. W. S. Woytinsky (*Employment and Wages in the United States*, New York, Twentieth Century Fund, 1953, Chap. 39, pp. 460–462 and, 507–509) found a tendency for low-wage industries in 1929 to have climbed relatively to high-wage industries by 1950.

    Cullen (pp. 364–365) notes that most of the narrowing in dispersion in his data occurred before 1921. This, of course, would suggest that the short-run disturbances had been washed out before that date. The interpretation of Cullen's findings is different from (and possibly inconsistent with) his own.

28. This has been stressed in two studies of English data: P. Haddy and N. A. Tolles, 'British and American Changes in Inter-industry Wage Structure under Full Employment,' *Review of Economics and Statistics*, Nov. 1957, pp. 408–414; and P. Haddy and M. E. Currell, British Inter-Industrial Earnings Differentials, 1924–1955,' *Economic Journal*, Mar. 1958, pp. 104–111. This tendency also appears in Cullen's data ('Inter-industry Wage') for World War II; however, it does not appear during World War I.

29. Slichter, 'Notes on the Structure of Wages.' Slichter does not distinguish carefully between long- and short-run relations; consequently, the interpretation placed on his findings is entirely our own.

30. Ibid., p. 84.

31. This possibility would seem less likely in 1939, to which Slichter's data refer, than in the 1920's, 1940's, or 1950's. It is also possible that the correlation reflects the common effect of locational factors.

32. Industries are ranked in inverse order of male common labor earnings.

33. The rank correlation coefficient between percentage of women and percentage of Negroes (among males) employed (from 1950 Census data) for 14 industries was +.386; when finance and agriculture are excluded, the coefficient is raised to +.662.

However, the osmosis hypothesis requires further investigation.

34. Slichter, 'Notes on the Structure of Wages,' p. 88.
35. Ibid., see also p. 90.
36. As measured by (say) the percentage of the industry's employment concentrated in the four or eight largest firms.
37. For example, H. M. Levinson, 'Post-war Movement in Prices and Wages in Manufacturing Industries,' *Study Paper No. 4*, Joint Economic Committee, Congress of the United States, 1960, pp. 2–5 and 21; also J. W. Garbarino, 'A Theory of Inter-industry Wage Structure,' *Quarterly Journal of Economics*, May 1950, pp. 282–305, especially pp. 299–300.
38. This is highly debatable but, for the sake of argument, let us concede it.
39. G. W. Nutter, *The Extent of Enterprise Monopoly in the United States, 1899–1939*, University of Chicago Press, 1951, Tables 10 and 11.
40. The wage figures were obtained as follows: 1953 (annual average) hourly wages were extrapolated back to 1899 by means of Kendrick's data, and ranks were obtained; these were compared with the ranks of median annual earnings per worker in 1939 as reported in the 1940 Census (see H. P. Miller, 'Changes in the Industrial Wage Distribution of Wages in the United States, 1939–1949,' *An Appraisal of the 1950 Census Income Data*, Studies in Income and Wealth, Vol. 23, Princeton for NBER, 1958, Table B-2). It is assumed that the 1937 and 1939 rankings would be virtually the same.
41. David Schwartzman ('Monopoly and Wages,' *Canadian Journal of Economics and Political Science*, Aug. 1960, pp. 428–38) reaches a similar conclusion on the basis of comparing United States and Canadian industries with varying concentration ratios.
42. Slichter, 'Notes on the Structure of Wages,' p. 87.
43. J. T. Dunlop, 'Productivity and the Wage Structure,' *Income, Employment and Public Policy, Essays in Honor of A. H. Hansen*,' New York, Norton, 1948, p. 360. In fairness to Dunlop, it should be noted that he has not indicated whether he intended this relationship as long or short run. The short-run version is discussed below.
44. This coefficient was computed from an analysis of 14 major industry groups.
45. See Appendix [Not reprinted here – Ed.]
46. Garbarino, 'Theory of Inter-industry Wage Structure,' p. 304.
47. A. M. Ross and W. Goldner, 'Forces Affecting the Inter-industry Wage Structure,' *Quarterly Journal of Economics*, May 1950, pp. 254–281, especially Table VI, and pp. 272–276. The four periods studied were 1933–38, 1938–42, 1942–46, and 1933–46; the deviant period was the wartime interval 1942–46. The authors present no correlations but merely place industries into four quartiles in accordance with the percentage increase in employment.
    F. C. Pierson (*Community Wage Patterns*, University of California Press, 1953, Chap. VI) also finds a positive rank correlation between average hourly earnings and employment for manufacturing industries among several cities between 1929 and 1939, but not during the war period, 1940–48.
48. S. W. Ostry, 'Inter-industry Earnings Differentials in Canada, 1945–1956,' *Industrial and Labor Relations Review*, Apr. 1959, pp. 335–352, especially pp. 341–343.
49. B. Hansen and Gosta Rehn, 'On Wage-Drift: A Problem of Money-Wage Dynamics,' *Twenty-five Economic Essays in Honour of Erik Lindahl*, Stockholm, 1956, pp. 87–133, especially pp. 105–106 and 128–133.
50. That is, wage increase in excess of what was implied in collective bargaining agreements.
51. That is, unfilled vacancies minus unemployment.
52. Slichter ('Notes on the Structure of Wages,' p. 90) argues very explicitly that the relation between hourly earnings and profits is due to wage policy and not labor-market pressure. He found a small *negative* coefficient of rank correlation between changes in employment and changes in average hourly earnings in 1923–39 for *unskilled* workers (as contrasted to the positive coefficient for all workers). Somehow, this argument is not very impressive. (1) As argued above, one would expect the supply of unskilled workers to a given industry to be more elastic in the short run than that of semiskilled and skilled. (2) Slichter's period is almost identical with that of Garbarino ('Theory of Inter-industry Wage Structure'), who found evidence of a stronger relationship than Slichter, and with better data.

53. Doris M. Eisemann, 'Inter-Industry Wage Changes, 1939–1947,' *Review of Economics and Statistics*, Nov. 1956, p. 446.
54. Levinson, 'Post-war Movements,' Table 1, p. 3.
55. Ibid., Table 2, p. 4. A. H. Conrad ('The Share of Wages and Salaries in Manufacturing Incomes, 1947–1956,' *Study Paper No. 9*, Joint Economic Committee of Congress, Washington, 1959) obtained similar results on *Census of Manufactures* data for all 61 three-digit industries, for the period 1949–56.
56. W. G. Bowen, *The Wage-Price Issue: A Theoretical Analysis*, Princeton University Press, 1960, pp. 59–66 and Table E-1 pp, 134–135.
57. The subperiods of low unemployment are characterized by an unemployment percentage (of the civilian labor force) that was 'generally below 4.3.' The subperiods of light unemployment are those where the unemployment percentage was always above 4.3. Bowen, pp. 24–29.
58. The letter of the competitive hypothesis makes no provision for unemployment as a variable in supply or demand functions.
59. Using Bowen's 4.3 per cent as a criterion for distinguishing years of appreciable unemployment from others, 33 of the first 58 years of this century were years of 'appreciable unemployment.' Even if we exclude the 11 years, 1930–40, 22 out of 47 years showed appreciable unemployment. (These figures are Stanley Lebergott's as quoted by Bowen in Appendix A, pp. 99–101.)
60. Levinson, 'Post-war Movement,' pp. 2–7.
61. Levinson, 'Post-war Movement,' Table 2, p. 4.
62. Bowen, *Wage-Price Issue*, pp. 67–69 and 134–135.
63. Dunlop, 'Productivity and the Wage Structure.'
64. Garbarino, 'Theory of Inter-industry Wage Structure,' pp. 298–300.
65. 'Post-war Movement,' Table 1, p. 3.
66. F. Meyers and R. L. Bowlby, 'The Inter-industry Wage Structure and Productivity,' *Industrial and Labor Relations Review*, Oct. 1953, pp. 93–102.
67. R. Perlman, 'Value Productivity and the Inter-industry Wage Structure,' *Industrial and Labor Relations Review*, Oct. 1956, pp. 26–39.
68. But not always: Meyers and Bowlby turned up some negative coefficients ('Inter-industry Wage Structure,' p. 98) and so did Levinson.
69. 'Theory of Inter-industry Wage Structure,' p. 285.
70. In a recent paper, L. Johansen ('A Note on the Theory of Inter-industrial Wage Differentials,' *Review of Economic Studies*, Feb. 1958, pp. 109–113) concludes that 'we may expect not changes in wage differentials, but wage differentials themselves to be correlated with the changes in productivity.' This result, however, refers only to differentials that reflect labor market disequilibrium; i.e., his results depend on labor market disequilibrium embodied in his equation (4) on p. 110. For the short run, his conclusion is identical in empirical content with the conventional Marshallian one, where productivity is reflected in a parameter of the industry labor demand fraction.
71. P. H. Douglas, *Real Wages in the United States*, Houghton Mifflin, Boston and New York, 1930, p. 564; Ross and Goldner, 'Forces Affecting,' p. 267.
72. [See H. G. Lewis, 'The Effects of Unions on Industrial Wage Differentials', pp. 319–41 of National Bureau of Economic Research, *Aspects of Labor Economics*, Princeton University Press, 1962: Ed.]
73. To test our hypothesis, it is necessary that unions be not 'too strong'; i.e., unions must compel relatively more profitable firms to *share* their 'excess profits' with wage earners (but not obliterate them), so that there are still greater than average profits to be observed. It is conceivable – though not likely – that unions could be so effective in raising wages that all potential supernormal profits were transferred to wages, completely obscuring the hypothesized relation.

4.5 Regional Wage Differentials*

There is a tendency to explain interregional wage differentials by emphasizing a particular regional difference or imperfection (barrier) in a single market. For instance, Scully [5, p. 237], cites studies by Hanna, Fuchs and Perlman, Segal, Gallaway, and Borts which explain the North–South wage differential by either industry mix, degree and strength of unionization, or labor immobility. Scully, and later Batra and Scully [1], attempt to improve on these earlier studies by extending the analysis to include labor productivity (human capital), variations in capital/labor ratios, and regional variations in technology. Unfortunately, like the earlier studies, they employ a partial equilibrium analysis and they do not add significantly to our ability to explain stable wage differentials.

This article uses a complete industry model, not just the production function, to specify the types of imperfections which may occur in various markets. In doing so, we demonstrate that the capital/labor ratio is a function of these imperfections and as such cannot be used to explain wage differentials in a given industry. We also show that regional variations in industry mix, technology, prices (so that real wages are equated), or degree of unionization are not satisfactory explanations for the continuance of money wage differentials.

We start from the basic point that labor immobility is a necessary, but not sufficient, condition for wage differentials. Labor immobility must be coupled with imperfections in at least one other market in order to generate an equilibrium wage differential between two regions. Finally, these imperfections are used to explain differences in industrial mix, union strength, and production techniques.

1. THE MODEL

Our model is applicable to either the individual firm or to a regional industry and will be treated from the latter point of view. The production function is, therefore, the aggregate production function, assumed to be homogeneous of degree one. To prevent one firm from expanding to take over the entire industry of a region, there is an implicit assumption of a restriction to firm size so that competition prevails, at least within a region. Factor markets are also assumed to be competitive. The regional price of physical capital and the rate of interest are tied, but not necessarily equal, to their respective national prices, as is the price of the industry's product. Each region is assumed to be too small to affect the price in the national markets for capital or the final product. Hence, we assume competitive conditions within a region but permit barriers to product and factor flows between regions. In effect, the model applies to an industry in a peripheral region, relying on a central region or national markets for financial and real capital and for the bulk of its product market.

*From Michael Bradfield, 'Necessary and Sufficient Conditions to Explain Equilibrium Regional Wage Differentials', *Journal of Regional Science*, Vol. 16, No. 2, 1976.

As shown below, the flows of real and financial capital determine the equilibrium capital labor ratio, given the production function, product prices, efficiency levels of inputs, and the significance of barriers to capital flows. The wage rate is therefore determined and the quantity of labor forthcoming at that wage is determined by the supply of labor. The quantity of labor and the equilibrium capital/labor ratio determine the equilibrium stock of capital so that regional output level is determined.

The apparent immobility of labor is attributed to the economic and psychological barriers to labor flows out of the region. While there is some wage that is so low, relative to wages in other regions or in other industries within the region, that labor would move, it is assumed that the wage determined by the model is above this minimum. If this were not the case, the industry could not exist as it would be unable to hire any labor at the wage determined by capital flows. Thus, although there are wage differentials generated by the model, they are not large enough to encourage major labor flows.

The production function for an industry in a region is assumed to be the standard Cobb–Douglas form

$$X = P_x A Q^\alpha N^{1-\alpha} \tag{1}$$

where X is the value added by the industry,

P_x is the price received by the firm per unit of output,

A is the neutral efficiency coefficient for the industry,

$Q = CK$, where C is the efficiency coefficient of physical capital, K, and

$N = BL$, where B is the efficiency coefficient of physical (manhours) labor, L.

The value of the neutral efficiency coefficient, A, may be a function of agglomeration economies, the quality of entrepreneurship or the price and quality of other inputs not directly specified in the production function, such as resource prices or social overhead capital. The value of the capital efficiency coefficient, C, may be a function of the age of the capital stock, or of climate and institutions (such as pollution control requirements) which affect the functioning of capital. The labor efficiency coefficient, B, is a measure of the human capital component of hourly labor and may reflect labor's work attitudes in addition to its education, skills, health, and demographic composition. The efficiency coefficients are assumed to be exogenous.

From our assumptions, we can write

$$P_x = \gamma_1 \bar{P}_{xn} \tag{2}$$

$$r = \gamma_2 \bar{r}_n \tag{3}$$

$$P_K = \gamma_3 \bar{P}_{Kn} \tag{4}$$

where r is the rate of interest and P_K is the price of physical capital. The γ's represent the relationship between the regional variable and its national counterpart, and the subscript n denotes the national variable. These relationships are assumed fixed because transportation costs between regions, and lender behavior patterns, change slowly over time. The size of the γ's indicate the cost of the transportation and other barriers to capital and product flow, and would include the effects of any government capital subsidies or other interventions. An upward sloping labor supply curve is also assumed

$$L = f(W) \tag{5}$$

with $dL/dW > 0$. Given the assumptions of the model, the equilibrium condition for the use of capital is that the cost of capital equals its marginal product

$$rP_K = \partial X/\partial K = \alpha P_x AC^\alpha K^{\alpha-1}(BL)^{1-\alpha} \tag{6}$$

or

$$rP_K = \alpha P_x AC^\alpha B^{1-\alpha} k^{\alpha-1} \tag{7}$$

where

$$k \equiv K/L \tag{8}$$

i.e., k is the observed or physical capital/labor ratio. From Equation (7) we can write the equilibrium K/L ratio as

$$k = [rP_K/\alpha P_x AC^\alpha B^{1-\alpha}]^{[1/(\alpha-1)]}. \tag{9}$$

It is clear from Equation (9) that the physical capital/labor ratio, k, is a function of variables in the capital and product markets, as well as of the neutral, capital-biased, and labor-biased efficiency levels. Hence, regional variations in the capital/labor ratio are a function of variations in some or all of these underlying variables which affect the equilibrium in the capital market.

Equilibrium in the labor market requires that

$$W = \partial X/\partial L = (1-\alpha)P_x A(CK)^\alpha B^{1-\alpha} L^{-\alpha} \tag{10}$$
$$= (1-\alpha)P_x AC^\alpha B^{1-\alpha} k^\alpha.$$

Assuming that two regions, i and j, use the same production functions, we can find the determinants of the wage relative, $W_{ij}(=W_i/W_j)$, from Equation (10)

$$W_{ij} = P_{xij}A_{ij}C_{ij}{}^\alpha B_{ij}{}^{1-\alpha} k_{ij}{}^\alpha \tag{11}$$

where the subscript ij denotes a regional relative.

It is very tempting to 'explain' regional variations in wages as deriving from regional differences in prices, efficiency levels, and the capital/labor ratio. However, if we substitute from Equation (9) for k in Equation (11) we get

$$W_{ij} = [P_{xij}A_{ij}]^{[1/(1-\alpha)]} [r_{ij}P_{xij}]^{[\alpha/(\alpha-1)]} C_{ij}{}^{[\alpha/(1-\alpha)]} B_{ij}. \tag{12}$$

A comparison of Equations (11) and (12) shows that capital/labor ratio differences do not explain regional wage differences but are merely indicators of the existence of regional differences in underlying variables. Some of these differences are explicit in Equation (11); some implicit (capital costs), entering through the physical capital labor ratio. Even those variables which are explicit in Equation (11) are not totally accounted for in that equation, since they too affect the physical capital/labor ratio. It is only in Equation (12) that the full impact of all variables can be seen. Thus, using the capital/labor ratio as an explanatory variable may well bury real explanatory variables, such as the differential cost of capital.

For instance, if the only difference between regions is in the efficiency of labor, Equations (11) and (12) would become

$$W_{ij} = B_{ij}^{1-\alpha} k_{ij}^{\alpha} \tag{13}$$

and

$$W_{ij} = B_{ij} \tag{14}$$

respectively. If Equation (13) were used as the basis for a regression analysis, one would conclude that differences in labor efficiency and the capital/labor ratio were the source of the interregional wage differential. Equation (14) shows that the correct explanation lies with labor efficiency only. By not considering the factors which affect the capital/labor ratio, we are led to incomplete conclusions. This error is compounded when there are imperfections in a number of markets, such as in the cost of real and financial capital and in the price received for the product.

It may appear that Equation (14) shows that stable wage differentials are possible even though there are regional differences in the labor market only. This is only true because the wage differential reflects payments to different types of labor, to labor of different efficiency levels. Equation (14) shows that, if there are no barriers to capital and product flows, wage differences are equal to labor efficiency differences and there would be no wage differentials between regions for labor of a given efficiency level.

Batra and Scully [1, p. 378] claim that 'with interregionally invariant production functions the wage rate in the North can only be higher if the rate of return on capital is lower in the North.' This is only true if the sole market imperfection one anticipates is in the flow of financial capital.[1] If we do not assume away other imperfections, then Equation (12) clearly shows that stable wage differentials are possible because of regional differences in product price, the cost of physical capital, or efficiency levels, even though we assume that the rate of return on capital is equalized. Since we are trying to explain the source of wage differentials, it is not productive to assume away a number of possible and probable factors.

2. VARIATIONS IN UNIONIZATION

We have shown that the wage differential between regions may be the result of differences in a number of variables. However, it is not yet explicit why these differences cannot all occur in the labor market and still be capable of generating an equilibrium wage differential. In Equation (12), the only explicit labor market condition determining the wage relative is labor's efficiency. Of course, the fact that there is an equilibrium wage differential implies that labor lacks the mobility to move to the high wage zone and bring about wage convergence. Even with labor immobility, if there were no regional barriers for other input and factor flows, we would have a model similar to that of Borts [2] and we would obtain his result — long-run wage equality. If we wish to say that imperfections in the labor market, such as regional differences in the degree of unionization, are to be the basis of wage differentials, then it is necessary that they affect the independent variables or that they introduce new variables into the model.

What the model implies is that union ability to drive wages up is determined by normal market forces. If strong unions in one region drive the differential up beyond that determined by Equation (12), then capital will flow out of the high wage region, into the low. Thus the industry will expand in the low wage region, increasing the demand for labor there and bidding wages up. This process may be accelerated by growing union strength, perhaps made possible by the increasing demand for labor. Thus wages and union strength may well move together, because both may be related to market conditions. In the long run, union demands must be related to market conditions, i.e., to the independent variables in the model.

Of course, a strong union could successfully negotiate higher wages if its actions could, at the same time, affect one or more of the hitherto independent variables. A model of worker behavior which assumed that workers' attitudes and efficiency levels are a function of their economic security and working conditions could lead to the prediction that workers would become more efficient with the higher wages and better working conditions negotiated by a strong union. If this were actually the case, then wage increases might be matched by productivity increases so that unit costs need not rise. On the other hand, if one assumes that the stick is more important than the carrot in motivating workers, the presence of a strong union might lower labor productivity. Thus there could be an inverse relationship between increasing wages and efficiency levels. This would harm rather than help the competitive position of the firm in the more highly organized region, giving the firm still greater incentive to move to the less organized, lower wage region.

Union militancy and the concomitant wage increases may lead to higher labor efficiency because of management action. Faced by wages higher than those prevailing in other regions, management may be more selective in its hiring practices. If new workers are above the previous average efficiency level, then the labor efficiency level is raised, and the competitive disadvantage of the higher wage may be partially offset. However, the impact of such changes in the composition of the labor force is likely to be marginal and insufficient to offset any significant wage differentials.

The wage demands of a strong union may lead to management action which affect some of the other independent variables of the model. Management may be forced to find ways of raising the price of the product, to bargain harder for lower capital costs, to seek tax and other concessions from government, or to raise the level of capital's efficiency. However, this implies that management was not maximizing profits before the development of union strength. It also raises the question of why management does not engage in the same activities in the low wage region. Increased management vigilance may be a short-run response to rising wages. The long-run response would be to move to the low wage region. Nonetheless, the changes in the independent variables may be an indication of management weakness, not necessarily in its labor negotiations, but in its other functions.

Union strength and the security it provides the work force may explain labor immobility, and therefore provide a rationale for the necessary condition for regional wage differentials. However, unless union strength affects one or more of the independent variables in the model, it is not a sufficient condition for equilibrium wage differentials, since unions cannot, in the long run, generate wage differentials any greater than those that are consistent with the underlying market conditions. If a union consistently pushes the wage differential beyond that determined to market forces, we would expect the market to react by shifting capital and employment out of the high wage region. This would either mitigate union demands or lead to the eventual end of that industry in that region.

3. INDUSTRY MIX

Equation (12) shows the range of factors which will affect wage levels and regional wage differentials. It specifies what the wage relative must be for an industry to operate in both regions, given the barriers which generate different cost levels and product prices in the two regions. If we assume that region i has a small advantage in each factor, we can calculate what the wage differential would have to be for interregional equilibrium, given the parameters of the production function. Assume a production technology such that $\alpha = {}^2/_3$. If region i's advantage over region j is five percent for each independent variable, Equation (12) becomes

$$
\begin{aligned}
W_{ij} &= [(1.05)(1.05)]^{[1/(1-2/3)]} [1/(1.05)(1.05)]^{[2/3/(2/3-1)]} \times \\
&\quad \times (1.05)^{[2/3/(1-2/3)]}(1.05) \\
&= (1.05)^{13} \\
&= 1.89.
\end{aligned}
\tag{15}
$$

This implies that firms can and will, in equilibrium, pay their labor 89 percent more in i than in j, given the advantages of region i over j. If the wage differential is less than this, it would be to the firms' advantage to move to i, the high wage region. If sufficient growth occurs in i, relative to j, the wages in i will eventually be forced up to generate the equilibrium 89 percent wage differential. After that point, firms will be indifferent to locating in i or j.

If on the other hand, we assume an industry with a more labor intensive technology, e.g., with an α of ½, the equilibrium wage relative would be

$$W_{ij} = (1.05)^8 = 1.48. \tag{16}$$

Thus, interregional equilibrium in the more labor-intensive industry requires that wages be only 48 percent higher in i in order to offset the region's other advantages.

We can now see why labor supply and demand conditions will affect the industry mixes of regions. At any given time, there is an average efficiency of labor in each region and various other influences on its attractiveness, as well as an existing supply and demand for labor. These conditions generate a wage level in each region and a firm will be attracted to one region or another depending on the size of the interregional wage relative. With a given wage relative the firms attracted to the low wage region will be those whose labor intensity is sufficiently high that the labor savings will at least offset the disadvantages of the low wage region. Thus, there will be some industries for which the low wage region is attractive, given the differential, and some industries for which it is not. We would therefore expect the low wage region to be attracting relatively labor-intensive (low-wage) industries while the high wage region attracts relatively capital-intensive industries. Thus the wage level determines the industry mix in each region, given the wage level in other regions. At a later stage in a region's history, we might be tempted to attribute the wage differential to the industry mix, but the causal relationship may, in fact, be just the opposite.

Using this model, it is possible to explain why high wage regions may also be high growth regions. Borts [2, p. 375] predicts that, ceteris paribus, low wage regions should be high growth regions. The model used here shows that relative rates of growth may be reversed when there are a number of differences between regions. While it may appear that this growth in the high wage region is due to demand for its products, it may also be that a product which could be produced in either region will be produced in the high wage region because of its underlying advantages which are responsible for the high wage differential. Thus, the regional differences which generate wage differentials may also generate growth differentials.

This can be taken even further by assuming that growth industries tend to be capital-intensive industries. If this be the case, growth may favor the high wage region, at least until the wage differential is large enough to make the low wage region equally attractive. If institutional factors (government policy, industry-wide bargaining) prevent this widening of the wage gap, growth will favor the high wage region, unless the underlying disadvantages of the low wage region are offset or removed.

4. TECHNOLOGY DIFFERENCES

We have assumed that the same production function is used in two different regions for any particular industry. Batra and Scully [1, p. 386] believe 'the assumption of regional equality of the rates of return on capital and regionally different production functions are more realistic assumptions. We find that only with these assumptions is the wage differential consistent with long-run static and dynamic equilibrium.' This is an extremely strong conclusion, given the lack of evidence to show that there may not be differences in neutral or biased efficiency levels or in product prices. Until Batra and Scully can show that prices do not tend to vary with wages, and that wage levels do not vary with the other underlying variables, their conclusion is, at best, tenuous.

From the point of view of production theory, the conclusion that differences in production functions are the cause of wage differentials is unsatisfactory. Batra and Scully must explain why technology is not transferable. If one production function allows the producer in region i to pay a higher wage than is paid in region j where a different production technique is used, then would not the producer in region i be better off to take his technology to j, pay the prevailing wage, and make greater profits than the existing producers in region j who use the 'less efficient' technology? If this be the case, the expansion of the industry in j, and concomitant increased demand for labor, should drive up wages in j. This process would continue until wages are equalized and all producers are using the superior technology.

Thus differences in production functions are not compatible with stable wage differentials unless one assumes that technology is not easily transferable, perhaps because the 'superior' technology requires superior entrepreneurs. In this case, one would have to argue that the quality of entrepreneurship varied regionally and that entrepreneurs lack mobility. As an alternative, it might be assumed that there is immobility in the product market so that the superior entrepreneur is unable to move from the high wage region to the low wage region and sell his product back in the high wage region. In any case, if differences in production functions exist, they are like differences in capital/labor ratios, and require an explanation.

5. REAL WAGES VS. MONEY WAGES

Coelho and Ghali [4] indicate that regional price variations offset regional money wage differentials, so that real wages tend to be the same and therefore policy makers need not concern themselves with equating or diminishing differentials in money wages. Chernick [3] comes to the reverse conclusion for Canada – that wage levels and price levels tend to be inversely related, so that money wage differentials underestimate differences in real welfare. Thus, Coelho and Ghali's results may be specific to the U.S. and are not necessarily the result of causal links between wages and prices.

The basic behavioral effect of equal real wages is to provide another rationale for labor immobility. If the return to labor is equal in real terms in all regions, then labor has no incentive to move even though its money wage in a region may be lower than that available elsewhere. However, this does not explain why capital does not flow to take advantage of the cheaper labor. After all, the capitalist is concerned with maximizing profits and therefore, ceteris paribus, with minimizing costs. The capitalist is conscious of the relative money cost of his labor supply, not its relative welfare, in different regions. If labor is cheaper in one region relative to another, the capitalist should, ceteris paribus, make his investment in the cheap labor region.

Of course, the existence of regional price differentials means that we cannot automatically make the ceteris paribus assumption. Perhaps the low wage does not attract enough capital to equalize wages because the output of the less expensive labor will sell at a lower price. This is not entirely convincing because not all products are sold on the local market. One would therefore expect an inflow of firms which produce for the national markets. This inflow would drive up wages until any gap which remained would be necessary to offset the disadvantages of the low wage region, such as the extra transportation costs from the low wage region to primary markets. There is no reason to expect this wage differential to be equal to cost-of-living differentials also, as Coelho and Ghali claim to be the case.

6. CONCLUSIONS

The model developed in this paper shows that wage differentials for labor of a given quality require both labor immobility and imperfections in at least one other market for the differentials to be stable. With conventional market assumptions, the capital/labor ratio and the wage rate are both functions of the same variables, so that the capital/labor ratio cannot be used to explain regional wage differentials. The model also indicates the chicken and egg nature of the industry mix justification of regional wage differentials. Thus the model used here is useful in clarifying some of the issues surrounding regional wage differentials. It is still a can of worms, but by shaking it differently, the model makes it easier to tell heads from tails.

NOTE

1. From Equation (9), if there are barriers or differences only in the financial capital market, Equation (11) can be written

$$W_i/W_j = (k_i/k_j)^\alpha = (r_i/r_j)^{[\alpha/(\alpha-1)]}.$$

If $W_i/W_j > 1$, then $(k_i/k_j)^\alpha > 1$, and $(r_i/r_j)^{[\alpha/(\alpha-1)]} > 1$, and therefore $r_i/r_j < 1$, since $\alpha < 1$.

REFERENCES

1. Batra, R. and G. W. Scully. 'Technical Progress, Economic Growth, and the North-South Wage Differential,' *Journal of Regional Science*, 12 (1972), 375–386.
2. Borts, G. H. 'The Equalization of Returns and Regional Economic Growth,' *American Economic Review*, 50 (1960), 319–347.
3. Chernick, S. E. 'Interregional Disparities in Income,' Economic Council of Canada, Staff Study 14, 1966.
4. Coelho, P. R. P. and M. A. Ghali. 'The End of the North-South Wage Differential,' *American Economic Review*, 61 (1970), 932–937.
5. Scully, G. W. 'The North-South Manufacturing Wage Differential, 1869–1919,' *Journal of Regional Science*, 11 (1971), 235–252.

4.6 The Balkanization of Labour Markets*
[. . .]

INSTITUTIONAL LABOR MARKETS IN OPERATION

Ports of Entry — Not all jobs are open at all times to all bidders except in the structureless market. Even in the absence of institutional rules, most employers consider a job not open for bid so long as the incumbent fills it satisfactorily; and employers generally prefer to promote from within to canvassing the outside market. Institutional rules, however, set sharper boundaries between the 'internal' and 'external' markets and define more precisely the points of entrance.[1] In the craft case, the internal market is the area covered by the jurisdiction of the local union, and in the industrial case it is the individual plant. The port of entry in the former instance is the union office, and union membership (achieved through apprenticeship, transfer, or application) provides access to all the jobs on the inside. In the latter case, there are usually several ports of entry (each reached through company personnel office) — common labor for production workers, lower clerical occupations for the white-collar workers, and junior posts for sales and executive personnel, among others — although if qualified candidates are not available almost any job on an *ad hoc* basis may be opened to outsiders.[2] The external market is the totality of the labor force outside this one market or submarket, or at least that part of it which potentially might like to gain entry.

Thus the internal market has points of contact with the external market rather than interconnections all along the line-up of jobs. Workers inside the market, though they may compete with each other in a limited way, are not in direct competition with persons outside. Outside workers compete directly with each other, not with the inside workers, to gain admittance.

At these ports of entry, the individuals are selected who may enter. Employers have their hiring preferences which are usually dominant when

*From Clark Kerr, 'The Balkanization of Labor Markets' in E. Wight Bakke (ed.) *Labor Mobility and Economic Opportunity* (Cambridge: MIT Press, 1954).

it comes to hiring into the plant, although unions can and do affect these prefer-ences; and the unions have theirs[3] which determine who gains access to the craft, although employers can and do affect them also.

The process of selection is also the process of rejection. Decisions are made in favor of certain individuals but at the same time against others. The individuals and groups which control these ports of entry greatly affect the distribution of opportunities in economic society. The rules that they follow determine how equitably opportunity is spread and the characteristics for which men are re-warded and for which they are penalized. The controlling individuals and groups may and do choose between prospective efficiency and prospective social accept-ability. Since labor resources are being distributed, as well as individual opportunities, the comparative emphasis on efficiency and on acceptability affects the productivity of the economic system. When men fail to find jobs, it may be because there are not enough jobs to go around, or because they do not know about the jobs which do exist or do not think such jobs fit their expecta-tions, or because they do not meet the specifications set by employers and unions. In the last case, as the specifications become more formal and cover more jobs, determination of the specifications becomes of increasing concern to persons in the external market who are universally unrepresented in the councils which set the specifications. For society to remain free and open, many ports of entry should exist and the immigration barriers should not hold outside the able and the willing.

Impact on Movement – One can only surmise how institutional rules affect latent mobility (the willingness and ability to move with given incentives),[4] but actual movement is, in totality, probably reduced.[5] Whether the average union member moves less often than the nonunion member, he certainly moves in a somewhat different direction following the formal channels set by the insti-tutional rules. The craft worker moves horizontally in the craft area (Fig. 4.8*a*), and the industrial worker vertically in the seniority area (Fig. 4.8*b*). Interoccupa-tional movement is reduced for the former and employer-to-employer movement

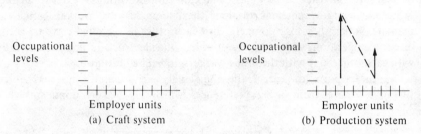

Occupational levels

Employer units

(a) Craft system

Occupational levels

Employer units

(b) Production system

FIG. 4.8

for the latter. Thus they are both captives, albeit ones who surrendered voluntarily or even enthusiastically, of the rules which guide their working careers. Job rights protect but they also confine. Reduction of insecurity also brings reduction of independence.

Both craft and industrial workers probably have their geographical movements restricted, although some craft systems (such as specialized construction or typographical) force or permit great change of physical location, and some employers require reassignment from one location to another as the price of continued employment. Movement from industry to industry in the craft case may be greatly increased (maintenance workers) or greatly reduced (longshore workers); but in the industrial case it is always restricted. Change of employment status from employed to unemployed and back again is reduced in both cases, since both systems are designed to yield greater employment security; and changes from participation in the labor force to non-participation and back again are also minimized since both types of arrangements usually require a high degree of attachment to the work force if rights are to be preserved.[6]

Institutional rules affect the movement of unprotected workers also. Some jobs are never open to them, and others only under certain conditions. Also the fewer people who leave their jobs because they do not wish to forfeit their security, the fewer other people can leave theirs for there are fewer places to which they may go. The production worker is particularly affected. If he loses employment in one seniority area (he is discharged or the plant closes, for example), he must drop to the bottom of the list in the next area to which he gains admission (see Fig. 4.8*b*); or he may, of course, never get back into a seniority area (the case of the production worker who becomes a janitor). The more secure are the 'ins,' the greater the penalty for being an 'out.'

Competition among workers is reduced. The internal and external markets are joined only at restricted points; and within the internal market, craft jobs are likely to be fairly standardized and industrial jobs filled in accordance with seniority, so that workers are not actively contesting with each other for preference. Beyond this, the distribution of work opportunities by the craft union and the rehiring rights of the industrial contract tend to hold unemployed workers in a pool attached to the craft or plant and thus keep them from competing for jobs so actively elsewhere.[7]

All societies are stratified to a degree, although the degrees vary enormously, and a key element in any society is the character and the intensity of stratification. For our purposes here we shall designate three systems of organization: the 'open,' the 'guild,' and the 'manorial.' The pre-Cairnes classical version of the labor market was of the truly open type — all workers competed for all jobs all of the time. The guild system stratifies the labor force horizontally. Walter Galenson has described such a 'closed labor market' under the control of craft unions as it operates in Denmark.[8] The manorial system places its emphasis not on skill but on attachment to the place of work and thus on vertical stratification. The industrial worker may demonstrate (albeit for somewhat different reasons) the same perpetual adherence to the plant as the serf did to the soil of the estate, although he does have opportunities for upward movement unknown to the serf.

The institutional rules we have been discussing move the labor force farther away from the open system of the classical economists which never, however, was as open as they thought it was or hoped it might be. But as it moves toward the guild and manorial systems, which will predominate? For they follow quite different principles of societal organization. The conflict in the United States evidences itself in the conflict between craft and industrial unions over the representation of skilled workers in industrial plants, in the effort of skilled workers in such plants to have their own job families and seniority lists, in the insistence of craft workers that their wages follow the market rather than the dictates of a job evaluation plan dedicated to internal consistency. In Denmark, the guild system is dominant; in Germany, with all the paternalistic devices of large employers and the life-long attachment of the worker to his plant, the manorial system, and this is one source of the union insistence on codirection at the plant level.

The stratification of the labor force affects the worker as citizen. Is he a free-roving mobile person ranging widely horizontally and vertically and probably having a middle-class outlook,[9] is he a carpenter, or is he a UAW-GM man? How he is located economically will affect his view of society and his personal identification with society and its constituent groups, and thus his political behavior.

Institutional Rules and Wage Setting — 'Potential mobility,' Hicks noted, 'is the ultimate sanction for the interrelation of wage rates.'[10] Other sanctions do exist and many times are the more important, but the less the potential mobility of workers the less the economic pressures that relate wage rates to each other. Institutional rules, to the extent that they reduce mobility, also lessen the economic pressures. As we have seen, some internal markets are quite isolated from their external markets by the working of these rules, and the interrelatedness of wage rates may be traced more to political, ethical, or operational than to labor market considerations. How do the rules we have been discussing impinge on the wage-setting process?

Extensive discussions with craft union leaders and the employers dealing with them in the San Francisco Bay area indicate that these unions do not generally use their control over the supply of labor to force up wage rates. They employ it rather to adjust supply to demand once the wage has been fixed.[11] If the supply falls too far short of demand, the employers are encouraged to introduce machinery or look to another craft for workers or even to non-union men. If the supply is too great, some union members are unemployed. This is politically uncomfortable for the union leaders and may require the members to undertake some work-sharing device. Further, employers may point to this unemployed group at the next wage negotiations and the members may be less willing to support wage demands with an effective strike threat. All in all, it is better to adjust supply to demand as closely as possible. This is done by controlling the flow of new members and by issuing work permits.

In neo-classical wage theory, supply (which is assumed to be relatively fixed in the short run) and demand are the independent variables which simultaneously determine the wage and the volume of employment. The standard craft market process runs instead along these lines: (1) the wage is set by collective bargaining in response to many considerations (including economic ones) and usually for a one-year duration; (2) demand which changes constantly determines the amount of employment at the fixed rate; and (3) supply is constantly adjusted by the union to keep close contact with the changing volume of jobs offered by the employers.[12] Control over supply is used more to preserve the integrity of the wage rate rather than to create it.[13] The wage rate determines supply more than supply the wage rate. Demand itself is subject to some control (foremen are limited in the work they may perform; one man may handle only so many machines; certain work must be reserved for a certain craft, and so forth). Demand, the wage rate, and supply all respond to more or less control by the bargaining institutions.

The production case is a different one. Industrial unions cannot control the supply of workers. Their attention is turned rather to stabilizing the demand for labor so that all workers with seniority rights may have assured employment, for example, by introducing the guaranteed wage or heavy dismissal bonuses.[14] These devices have no appeal to the craft unions. But, for the industrial union, the supply of workers with seniority rights is fixed, and this makes it more conscious of the impact of fluctuating demand. Institutional rules have two further wage results. Since seniority ties workers to the plant, the industrial union must be more concerned with the effect of a negotiated wage rate on employment. Were it not for seniority rules, wage rates probably could not have deteriorated comparatively so greatly for telegraph and railroad employees during the past quarter of a century. The seniority tie to the industry has reduced the minimum price which would hold the workers in the industry. Industrial unions, also, are more willing than are craft unions to make exceptions to the common rate to meet the necessities of the individual company and its employees. Further, institutional rules by reducing the contact points with the external markets encourage formal or informal job evaluation plans as a means of setting rates acceptable in the internal market.

Under both systems of rules, wage rates are less effective in allocating labor (just as the movement of labor is less potent in setting wage rates) than they are in less structured labor markets. [. . .]

NOTES

1. Labor markets are of two broad types: (1) the structureless and (2) the structured. In the structureless market, there is no attachment except the wage between the

worker and the employer. No worker has any claim on any job and no employer has any hold on any man. Structure enters the market when different treatment is accorded to the 'ins' and to the 'outs.' In the structured market there always exist (1) the internal market and (2) the external market. The internal market may be the plant or the craft group, and preferment within it may be based on prejudice or merit or equality of opportunity or seniority or some combination of these. The external market consists of clusters of workers actively or passively available for new jobs lying within some meaningful geographical and occupational boundaries, and of the port or ports of entry which are open or are potentially open to them. It may happen that some markets have only one port of entry, but this can hardly be the standard case as Bloom and Northrup, and Reynolds, state [Gordon F. Bloom and Herbert R. Northrup, *Economics of Labor and Industrial Relations*, Blakiston, Philadelphia, 1950, p. 265; Lloyd G. Reynolds, *The Structure of Labor Markets*, Harper, New York, 1951, p. 42]. They may be right where certain large manufacturing plants are involved, but more commonly such a cluster of workers will face several ports of entry. The extreme cases would be (a) one worker facing one port of entry and (b) large numbers of workers facing a large number of ports of entry. The more structured the market, the more precise will be the rules on allocation of opportunity within the internal market and the fewer will be the ports of entry and the more rigid will be the requirements for admission. Institutional rules do not usually introduce structure into a market – it often arises from the individual preferences of workers and employers – but they uniformly add to it.

2. Thus there are more ports of entry in a period of prosperity than in a period of depression.

3. For a discussion of union preferences, see Clyde Summers, 'Admission Policies of Labor Unions,' *Quarterly Journal of Economics* (November 1946).

4. For the distinction between 'mobility' and 'movement' see Clark Kerr, *Migration to the Seattle Labor Market Area, 1940–1942* (Seattle: University of Washington Press, 1941), p. 151: 'Relatively immobile groups may move in large volume, and potentially mobile groups may remain stationary depending on the circumstances they face.'

5. See Lloyd G. Reynolds and Joseph Shister, *Job Horizons* (New York: Harper, 1949), p. 48; and Reynolds, *The Structure of Labor Markets*, op. cit., pp. 55, 148, and 255. See also statement in Joseph Shister, 'Labor Mobility: Some Institutional Aspects,' *Proceedings of the Third Annual Meeting, Industrial Relations Research Association, 1950* (Madison, Wis.: 1951), pp. 42–59: 'Union policies reduce the amount of voluntary mobility, on net balance.' Other evidence, however, is exactly to the contrary. Lipset and Gordon conclude: 'Union members appear to be more mobile both area- and job-wise than do non-unionists . . .' Seymour M. Lipset and Joan Gordon, 'Mobility and Trade Union Membership,' in Reinhard Bendix and Seymour M. Lipset, editors, *Class, Status and Power* (Glencoe: The Free Press, 1953), p. 498. The two statements are, I think, reconcilable. Reynolds and Shister drew their own conclusions from the New Haven labor market survey and Lipset and Gordon from the Oakland study. New Haven is a manufacturing town and most unionists there are probably covered by seniority rules which tie them to the individual plant. Oakland is a community of small shops and a distributive center, and most unionists are probably subject to craft rules which permit or even encourage them to move from employer to employer. The two studies come to opposite conclusions because they are based on observations of two contrasting situations. To be fully useful in determining the effect of unionism on mobility, two questions should have been asked in both studies: (1) Did the worker belong to a craft or an industrial union? and (2) How does each type of movement (see the following footnote) relate to union status? For certainly union membership affects both the number and the nature of the moves differently for the industrial unionist and for the craft unionist.

6. Movement of workers is of six types: (1) one occupation to another, (2) one employer to another, (3) one industry to another, (4) one area to another, (5) between employment and unemployment, and (6) into and out of the labor force. (A single move may, of course, combine several of these changes.) Craft rules generally reduce (1), (5), and (6) and usually also (3) and (4), but greatly increase (2); industrial rules generally reduce (2), (3), (5), and (6), and usually also (4), but increase (1).

7. The craft and industrial systems react quite differently to the impact of large-scale unemployment. The former is more likely to resort to some form of work-sharing and the latter to layoffs in order of seniority; the former responds to the claims of equal opportunity, the latter to a diminishing scale of property rights in the job.
8. Walter Galenson, *The Danish System of Labor Relations* (Cambridge: Harvard University Press, 1952), pp. 195–200. See also remarks by Gladys Palmer on European labor markets in a paper presented to the Industrial Relations Research Association, May 1952.
9. Lipset and Gordon, op. cit.
10. J. R. Hicks, *The Theory of Wages* (London:Macmillan, 1935), p. 79.
11. 'The jobs must be rationed among the seekers for jobs. And this is the important economic function the so-called restrictive practices play.' Milton Friedman, 'Some Comments on the Significance of Labor Unions for Economic Policy,' in David McCord Wright (ed.), *The Impact of the Union* [Harcourt, Brace and Co., New York, 1951], p. 213.
12. The supply curve may be shown as a straight line which stops at or shortly before the volume of jobs normally expected at the fixed wage rate. If demand moves to the right temporarily, the supply line can be temporarily extended by the issuance of work permits, which can be cancelled if it moves again back toward the left.
13. This sets the craft groups apart from certain professional groups. These professional groups do not control the wage (the fee) and so they influence it by control of supply.
14. Once the wage has been set, the craft union tries to adjust supply to demand; the industrial union, demand to supply.

4.7 The Local Labour Market: a Neoclassical View*

Competitive labour market theory predicts that within a local labour market there will be a tendency for labour of the same quality to obtain parity of earnings irrespective of the employment location. More strictly, the theory posits the equalisation of net advantages through time for homogeneous labour inputs. No plant may, according to the theory, set wages and other conditions of employment independent of the behaviour of its competitors. Wage levels within the market are, then, subject to the equalising forces of competition. Consequently, any differentials enjoyed by one plant over another for a well defined homogeneous labour input must either be transient or reflect efficiency unit (labour supply) differences. In the absence of labour quality differences, then, wage differentials would be a short run phenomenon to be explained by differences in final product demand and productivity variations against a background of short run inelasticity of labour supply. Such disequilibrating forces should, in the long run, tend to be counterbalanced by actual or potential mobility within the labour market which would restore wage equality.

The neo-classical doctrine of wages and labour mobility has immediate attraction in that it succeeds in fusing mobility and wage determination into a single problem. In the case of *mobility*, the wage structure is a major determinant of movement among occupations, firms and areas. In the case of *wage structure*, then this is shaped by actual and potential mobility of labour. To quote Reynolds: 'One moves around in a closed circle of predictable relationships and

*From John T. Addison, 'On the Interpretation of Labour Market Earnings Dispersion: a comment', *International Journal of Social Economics*, Vol. 2, No. 1, 1975.

results [1]'. Unfortunately the theory poses distinct measurement problems. After all, the substance of the competitive theory is that there exist supply and demand schedules (and equilibria) which can range freely through time. Thus, given appropriate shifts in the functions, an analysis of relative changes in wages and employment based on a comparison of two positions of equilibrium may describe positive or negative or even zero association between the variables. Accordingly, almost any development of the wage and employment structure may be interpreted, after the event, as being consistent with the theory. The controversy surrounding the interpretation of intra-occupational wage dispersion directly reflects the severely restricted predictive content of the theory and the concomitant absence of agreement on critical test procedures. Moreover, as Crossley [2] has observed, since the theory may be given operational content only by the addition of further assumptions — such as that which postulates short run supply functions to be fixed but less elastic than in the longer term — there is the more general methodological complication that the failure of a derived empirical hypothesis does not thereby render the theory, as such, invalid.

Given these difficulties and the associated problems of temporal specification it is perhaps not surprising that a degree of controversy should surround the interpretation of wage differentials; particularly when empirical studies have consistently demonstrated the existence of a wide spread in occupational earnings levels as between plants in the same local labour market [3]. Although differences in detail do emerge according to the precise dispersion measure adopted, this conclusion may be generalised for the market, occupational group and time horizon [4].

We propose to review and comment upon these findings according to whether the earnings dispersion identified is respectively either of short term (even static) or longer term form.

SHORT RUN WAGE DIFFERENTIALS

A *range theory of indeterminacy* was posited by Lester [5] on the basis of the wide starting rate and average hourly earnings dispersion he observed within, inter alia, a New Jersey sub-market in 1951. Lester interpreted the continuing existence of sizeable differences in local wage scales as the outcome of institutional rules. These included: collusive activity between employers in the form of anti-pirating agreements; the application of seniority rules in filling job vacancies which discriminated in favour of employees against non-employees by restricting ports of entry to the bottom of the wage scale; the use of informal sources of information concerning potential recruits; and the cessation of benefit plan eligibility which accompanied termination of the employment contract. Such rules acted to impede the free operation of the market and were reinforced by a random and impulsive mobility process. Consequently, individual establishments were held to possess considerable discretion in fixing wage rates within a generous range, depending on their recourse to internal labour market structuring. Such strategies would also accord the plant a position of long run stability within the market spectrum of wages.

Similar evidence of local labour market wage diversity was reported by Robinson [6] in a series of analyses relating to the British (engineering industry) experience. Robinson considered the *going rate* to be an almost mythical concept. The spread of average earnings for occupations identified within the studies was typically in the order of 50% and, moreover, there was almost the same magnitude of diversity in wage increases over a two year span whether measured in absolute or percentage terms. His interpretation of these findings was that economic forces or market pressures did not in fact exert inescapable influences which firms had to yield to or perish. Firms were presented, in reality, with a wide variety of economic reactions on wages. If, indeed, economic forces operated within the local labour market setting they did so in much diluted form and were so open to distortion that other factors predominated. Firms were viewed, nevertheless, as being subject to the constraints of imperfect knowledge, reinforced by a variety of institutional pressures.

Thus, both Lester and Robinson allege that wage determination theory must take cognisance of impeditive factors that can only be understood by reference to an appropriate (and specific) historical and institutional framework.

What, one might ask, is that status of such influential studies [7]? In particular, does the evidence of wide intra-occupational earnings dispersion conflict wth the implications of competitive labour market theory? The short answer is that the above studies, even in their most favourable interpretation [8], leave that theory more or less intact. A basic problem with these and other studies is that they make no real attempt to assess differences in worker efficiency; that they impute economic arbitrariness to institutional factors; and, most damning of all, that they fail to provide an alternative theory of the wage determination/ dispersion process. Against this, recent theoretical developments and applied work have yielded more than a measure of support for the neo-classical model of the operation of labour markets.

Human capital theory has shown that where there is *specific training* firms and employees will normally share both the costs of and returns to that training [9]. However, their relative shares may vary greatly between firms – depending on the relationship between quit rates and wages, lay-offs and profits, attitudes towards risk, the cost of funds and desires for liquidity – with obvious implications for wage level diversity. This would appear to be extremely important in semi-skilled occupational areas where there are also considerable technical differences among firms in the needs and scope for specific training. Again, we would expect starting rates to be functionally related to the expected duration of employment and the potential for vertical mobility within the organisation. Considerations such as these received scant attention from institutionalists in their formulation of internal labour market operation.

Again, since the theory posits an equalisation of efficiency unit earnings there is an obligation to assess the contribution of labour quality differences to differential wage levels. Weiss [10] has indicated that quality differences are important in explaining personal wage differentials, such that the familiar positive association between product market concentration and earnings appears insignificant once personal characteristics are introduced. In supportive vein, Rees and Schultz [11] find positive association between wage levels and various proxies for worker efficiency (namely, previous work experience, seniority and schooling), and Metcalf [12] reports that wage dispersion within the academic labour market is substantially reduced after correction for labour heterogeneity.

Significantly, the critics of the competitive theory have made no real attempt to evaluate the costs of search associated with the employment contract. There is very real evidence to suggest that wage costs and search costs (together with training costs) are substitutes [13]. As Stigler has observed: 'Wage rates and skilled search are substitutes for the employer: the more efficiently he detects workers of superior quality the less he need pay for such quality [14]'. Schultz [15] provides some direct evidence that employers in the Boston area increased their 'buying effort' by advertising and more careful employment interviewing as a partial substitute for increases in wage rates. The extent of search/wage substitutability may then be said to reflect the efficiency of labour market information systems. The more closely differences in search costs offset differences in wage costs the more perfect the market information system, since if workers were unable to wage-discriminate the highest paying firm would have to search as much as would low-wage employers. Implicitly, search and quality become substitutes if wages are held constant. Ullman [16] tests the relationships between wages and search costs (together with training costs) for a random sample of Chicago *employers* employing key-punch operators and typists. Overall, the results of his regression analysis — which explains between 43 and 58% of wage variance — give strong support to the hypothesis that wage and search methods are indeed substitutes. High wage employers apparently search less, and have less recourse to market intermediaries, than do lower wage plants. Ullman's study points to the importance of informal labour market contacts for job seekers, and indicates that such information channels are not necessarily abstract from an economic point of view once the uncertainties and screening costs attaching to the creation of an employment contract are recognised.

Protagonists of the competitive theory, we conclude, have been able to parry the early empirical challenge to orthodoxy by refining their theoretical base and in turn conducting empirical tests that have at least explained some of the variance in wage levels observed within labour markets. Since the antagonists have offered little hypothesis testing but have, rather, concentrated on letting the facts of wide earnings dispersion speak for themselves the hide of orthodox theory may be said to have been hardly dented. Nevertheless, we submit that there is a need to modify the theory to take account of such institutional and historical factors as are observed within these essentially static studies which have as yet no firm economic explanation. In particular, traditional theory must attempt to explain the significance of *establishment variables* in inter-plant occupational earnings dispersion. MacKay *et al.* [17] have shown fairly convincingly that the plant, *per se*, rather than occupational group may be the more important factor in determining an individual's earnings level or rate of increase in earnings. Moreover, a number of studies have exhibited evidence of a direct and significant association between wage level and plant size [18]. Differences, then, in the efficiency of the establishment as a whole rather than, more narrowly, of the labour force require explanation.

The findings of the institutional/historical school do provide a stimulating framework of ideas but fail to offer anything approaching a rigorous theory. Until such a theory is developed their findings run the risk of being labelled 'ad hoc hypotheses (yielding) untestable explanations of unique events [19].'

CHANGES IN WAGE DISPERSION THROUGH TIME

The obvious implication of the preceding section is that the existing dispersion of wage levels may be given an equilibrium interpretation — earnings level diversity otherwise might have easily been interpreted as the result of incomplete clearing of labour markets, namely as a disequilibrium phenomenon. This being so, it would be not unreasonable to suggest that the rate of change in earnings through time would show greater uniformity than would wage levels at any point in time. Empirical support for this view is provided by Knowles and Robinson [20] who indicate that, although not all firms' earnings move in the same direction at the same time, over longer periods the different movements are more similar than short-run changes would suggest; that is, much of the short period deviation from the average rate of increase tends not to be sustained over the long run. Moreover, there is some suggestion that the existing industrial wages structure — in terms of wage differentials — tends to vary much less in the short run than might otherwise be expected. Crossley has argued that collective bargaining may have established wages that are reasonably close to long run labour supply prices. Empirically, the amount of change in the (industrial) wages structure which occurs in the short run does not appear to be significantly greater than over the long run and, even in the short run, modest wage changes seem to be able to bring about major shifts in the distribution of employment. The key to Crossley's argument is his introduction of uncertainty into the static model of perfect competition. In the static model, with perfectly elastic fixed long run supply functions but relatively inelastic short run functions, wages would oscillate with demand shifts about their long run equilibrium levels, thereby frustrating the expectations of those who moved in response to short run wage changes. There might thus be 'scope for institutional developments which can damp down the scale of change without impairing the efficiency of the market [21]'. Clearly once a market is accustomed to small changes, via the agency of collective bargaining, labour supply elasticity is greater for a given wage change than it would be in the absence of collective bargaining, because 'the job chooser has more confidence that the wage being offered, or one close to it, will be maintained over the long run [22]'.

The above interpretation may provide a solution to the vexed problem of whether or not the pattern of closely similar wage movements among firms/ industries constitutes a denial of the competitive hypothesis. The problem is, however, compounded by the difficulty of testing the uncertainty hypothesis — it is simply not possible to isolate real labour markets that are free of institutional rules governing relativities. Moreover, the explanation of the existing wage structure in terms of a spectrum of long run supply prices co-exists rather uncomfortably with the empirical observation that long run conditions in the product market are directly associated with wage level. Here, the importance of trade union *impact effects* — given widely different elasticities of product demand — cannot be ignored [23].

The pattern of similar earnings movements as between industries and firms through time has occasioned a controversial debate over the respective roles of economic and power forces in the determination of wages. The institutionalist approach stresses the relevance of equitable or coercive comparisons in the wage determination process. The terminology used to describe this process has varied considerably — spillover, key bargains, wage leadership, pattern wage adjustment, limitation, demonstration effect and diffusion. The basic notion underlying what we will term the *spillover hypothesis* is that wage movements in the ith sector not only reflect traditional market forces in that sector but also wage movements in some jth sector. The wage relationship between the ith and jth sectors is derived from a political influence theory which suggests that traditional economic variables are, at the very least, supplemented by additional spillover variables if a complete explanation of wage movements is to be obtained.

Maher [24] argues that one major criterion is established for wage change within basic industries in the US, namely changes in the wages of workers in 'comparable' employments. This was held to be the result of four factors characterising such basic industries: their input–output nexus; their similar internal technological and economic constitution that produces similar responses to external change; their geographical concentration and the concentration of workers into a few large national unions; and the similarity of unions involved and their competition for representation of similar workers causing a common type of response to bargaining stimuli [25].

Maher's study bears a superficial resemblance to the earlier analyses of Ross [26] and Dunlop [27] with their respective *orbits of coercive comparison* and *wage contour* constructs. He differs from Ross in seeing only one pattern in basic industry and from Dunlop in denying the relevance of varying market and technological positions.

Maher argued that the 'striking similarity' of inter-industry wages increases over 1946–57 constituted a denial of the competitive hypothesis or, more strictly, of the (short-run) productivity forces specified by the competitive model. We do not propose here to comment directly upon statistical questions, such as whether Maher's data represented only a portion of the true wage distribution, except to note that there appears little or no justification for taking sides on the relative size of earnings dispersion (see Appendix). More fundamentally, the predictions of similar wage increases as between industries is consistent with both the competitive and institutional explanations of wage determination. Again, it must be emphasised that the competition model of wage determination predicts that wages will move in like fashion in different sectors of the labour market as a result of intersectoral supply shifts in response to changes in relative net advantages of various occupations.

The institutional hypothesis is itself strictly not testable because the key- or spillover-group concept cannot be precisely defined. Moreover, the essentially ad hoc hypotheses of the institutionalists are not strong enough to derive alternative predictions which would enable us to discriminate between the competing theories.

The competitive theory has been shown not only to possess resiliency but also to possess a degree of predictive power. Yet the theory by itself does not seem sufficiently informative for most particular applications. If the principal weakness of the spillover theory is its inability to specify unambiguously the spillover domain, then it must be said that a similar difficulty confronts the competitive theory, namely the specification of the alternative wage domain [28]. Where the two domains overlap there is clearly a serious identification problem. A positive relationship between wage changes in one sector and those in a spillover sector will be unambiguous evidence of a spillover mechanism only where the spillover variable cannot be interpreted as a labour supply variable. The process of aggregation might well intensify this problem.

A NON-CONCLUSION

The magnitude of inter-industry/inter-firm wage level or wage change dispersion has been claimed to refute the predictions of the competitive hypothesis. In purely statistical terms, dispersion analysis, *per se*, is likely to be a fruitless exercise yielding at best ambiguous results. Perhaps the most useful approach would be to conduct disaggregative labour market studies designed to test whether similar wage increases are brought about through the agency of labour supply shifts or the coercive actions of union pressure. A prerequisite of such analysis is, however, the development of a rigorous theoretical basis of the institutional process.

APPENDIX

A comparison of wage variances is an inappropriate method of gauging the relative strength of market and power forces in the wage determination process. Statistically, the market model may imply either a greater or a lesser variance of wage changes than does the spillover model. To illustrate this point it is sufficient to indicate that the presence of a pure market mechanism provides no grounds for favouring an *a priori* expectation concerning sample variance. A similar result follows from the formulation of a mixed spillover-market mechanism, although this is not presented here.

Under the competitive hypothesis, wage changes within a particular firm will reflect variations in underlying labour demand and supply conditions. The demand by the fth firm for any factor of production is a function of the prices of all other inputs, technology and the appropriate variables of the final demand schedule. The supply to the fth firm is a function of the wage rate in that firm and the alternative wage rates for comparable (in efficiency unit terms) labour offered by other firms. Given equilibrium, a reduced form equation relating the equilibrium wage rate and exogenous demand and supply variables may be obtained which, in the region of equilibrium may be expressed as,

$$W_f^* = \alpha_0 + \alpha_1 L_f + \alpha_2 W_f^x + u_f;$$

where W_f^* is the equilibrium percentage change in the wage rate paid by the fth firm,

L_f is the percentage change in a labour demand shift variable,

W_f^x is the percentage change in alternative, comparable skill, wages,

u_f is a random error term.

Assuming that the explanatory variables are uncorrelated with the error term, the sample variance of W^* where $S_{h w^x}$ is a covariance and all other S^2 terms are variances is,

$$S_{w*}^2 = \alpha_1^2 S_l^2 + 2\alpha_1\alpha_2 S_{h w^x}^2 + \alpha_2^2 S_{w^x}^2 + S_u^2.$$

Clearly, the sample variance of W^* will depend upon both the variance of the error term (which summarises omitted factors and random disturbances in the structural equations) and the sample variance of the independent variables. Where each firm in the sample experiences similar demand and supply shifts over the period in question, the only source of variance will be that of the residual error term. This may be either large or small. If inter-firm demand and supply characteristics differ markedly this divergence will impart a further source of variation to the sample W^*s. Either way, the theory does not specify that the variance of the error term (S_u^2) will be small; that is, the theory implies nothing about the variance of inter-firm wage changes.

In the long run the elasticity of labour supply to the fth firm will be infinite. Wages in the fth firm will move only in response to labour supply price changes (captured by the variable W_f^x). Changes in demand will only influence the level of employment. Thus,

$$W_f^* = W_f^x + v_f.$$

The sample variance of W^* will be

$$S_{w*}^2 = S_{w^x}^2 + S_v^2.$$

Given constant inter-firm skill mix utilisation through time, the sample variance of W^* is simply the sample variance of the residual error term (S_v^2). Again, the sample variance of wage changes may be either 'large' or 'small'.

It has been shown that the implications of the traditional competitive theory for inter-firm wage change dispersion are such that there is no basis for favouring an *a priori* expectation concerning the sample variance of wage changes. Consequently, it is concluded that comparisons of variances of wage changes are likely to be ambiguous test procedures in assessing the relative merits of market and power forces in the wage dispersion process.

REFERENCES

1. Reynolds, L. G., *The Structure of Labour Markets*, New York: Harper, 1951, p. 207.
2. Crossley, J. R., 'Collective Bargaining, Wage Structure and the Labour Market in the United Kingdom', in Hugh-Jones, E. M. (ed.), *Wage Structure in Theory and Practice*, Amsterdam: North Holland, 1966, p. 216.
3. See, *inter alia*: Lester, R. A., 'A Range Theory of Wage Differentials', *Industrial and Labor Relations Review*, July 1952, 5(4), 483-500; Knowles, K. G. J. C., and Robinson, D., 'Wage Movements in Coventry', *Bulletin of the Oxford University Institute of Economics and Statistics*, February 1969, 31(1), 1-21; Buckley, J. E., 'Intra-Occupational Wage Dispersion in Metropolitan Areas 1967-68', *Monthly Labor Review*, September 1969, pp. 24-9; Robinson, D., 'External and Internal Labour Markets' in Robinson, D. *Local Labour Markets and Wage Structures*, London: Gower Press, 1970.
4. The proviso being that earnings dispersion may well be less for higher skilled occupations. See for example: Douty, H. M., 'Sources of Occupational Wage and Salary Rate Dispersion within Labor Markets', *Industrial and Labor Relations Review*, October 1961, 15(1), 67-74.
5. Lester, R. A., op. cit.
6. Robinson, D., 'Myths of the Local Labour Market', *Personnel*, December 1967, 1(1), 36-9; *Wage Drift, Fringe Benefits and Manpower Distribution*, Paris: OECD, 1968.
7. The influence of the 'indeterminacy approach' arises because of its intuitively appealing policy prescription content. For a dissenting view see: Addison, J. T., 'Productivity Bargaining: The Externalities Question', *Scottish Journal of Political Economy*, June 1974, 21(2), 123-142.
8. That is, assuming an accurate identification of discrete labour markets and the existence of a positive association between non-pecuniary benefits and earnings levels. See, respectively: Goldner, W., 'Spatial and Locational Aspects of Metropolitan Labor Markets', *American Economic Review*, March 1955, 45(1), 113-128; Reynolds, L. G., op. cit., pp. 202-3.
9. See: Becker, G. S., *Human Capital*, New York: National Bureau of Economic Research, 1964, pp. 7-36.
10. Weiss, L. W., 'Concentration and Labor Earnings', *American Economic Review*, March 1966, 56(1), 96-117.
11. Rees, A. and Schultz, G. P., *Workers and Wages in an Urban Labor Market*, Chicago: University of Chicago Press, 1970.
12. Metcalf, D., 'Pay Dispersion, Information and Returns to Search in a Professional Labour Market', *Review of Economic Studies*, October 1973, 40(4) No. 124, 491-505.
13. See: Ullman, J. C., 'Inter-Firm Differences in the Cost of Search for Clerical Workers', *Journal of Business*, April 1968, 41(2), 153-165.
14. Stigler, G. J., 'Information in the Labour Market', *Journal of Political Economy*, October 1962, Part II, 70(5), p. 102. [Reprinted here as Reading 1.3 – Ed.]

320 The Structure of Earnings

15. Schultz, G. P., 'A Non-Union Market for White Collar Labor' in *Aspects of Labor Economics*, New York: National Bureau of Economic Research, 1962.
16. Ullman, J. C., op. cit., pp. 158–63.
17. MacKay, D. I., *et al., Labour Markets under Different Employment Conditions*, University of Glasgow Social and Economic Studies 22, London: George Allen and Unwin, 1971, pp. 123–8.
18. See: Lester, R. A., 'Pay Differentials by Size of Establishment', *Industrial Relations*, October 1967, 7, 57–67.
19. See: Crossley, J. R., *The Present Pay Structure: Theory and Evidence*, Mimeo, 1972, p. 3.
20. Knowles, K. G. J. C. and Robinson, D., op. cit., p. 9.
21. Crossley, J. R. in Hugh-Jones, E. M. (ed.). *Wage Structure in Theory and Practice*, op. cit., p. 228.
22. Ibid., p. 228.
23. One can, nevertheless, argue that such differentials, achieved under initial *impact effects*, persist through time and thereby acquire acceptability and hence constitute viable supply prices. Empirical support for this view is provided by the stability of the industrial wages structure and the (arguably) powerful allocative role played by that structure.
24. Maher, J. E., 'The Wage Pattern in the United States', *Industrial and Labor Relations Review*, October 1961, 15(1), 3–20.
25. A similar approach is followed by Eckstein and Wilson, who refer to these industries having similar institutional background for wage setting as the *key-group*. They demonstrate that such industries have also experienced similar wage movements in the short run. Key wages, in association with specific industry variables, also provided statistically significant explanations of wage changes in non-key industries for 8 of the 11 industry sample. See: Eckstein, O., and Wilson, T. A., 'The Determination of Wages in American Industry', *Quarterly Journal of Economics*, August 1962, 76(3), 379–414.
26. Ross, A. M., *Trade Union Wage Policy*, Berkeley: University of California Press, 1948.
27. Dunlop, J. T., 'The Task of Contemporary Wage Theory' in Taylor, G. W., and Pierson, F. C. (eds.), *New Concepts in Wage Determination*, New York: McGraw-Hill, 1957.
28. See: McGuire, T. W., and Rapping, L. A., 'The Role of Market Variables and Key Bargains in the Manufacturing Wage Determination Process', *Journal of Political Economy*, September/October 1968, 76(5), 1015–36.

4.8 Employment at Low Wages*

People are poor because the rate of wages paid by the industries of the United States will not permit them to be anything but poor.
(Scott Nearing, *Poverty and Riches. A Study of the Industrial Regime* (Philadelphia: The John C. Winston Company, 1916), p. 190.)

In our society work is invariably prescribed as the path out of poverty. However, for a significant proportion of the poor this remedy falls on deaf ears, since they *work* but are *poor*. The working poor earn their poverty! Perhaps this segment of the poor has been neglected precisely because its existence belies our belief that work is the panacea for all social ills.[1]

The focus of this study is the individual full-time wage earner and the forces affecting his/her wage income. In particular, we are interested in evaluating the relative importance of the individual characteristics of workers and the structure of the labor market in which they work. The first section contains a review of

*From Howard M. Wachtel and Charles Betsey, 'Employment at Low Wages', *Review of Economics and Statistics*, Vol. 54, May 1972.

the theory of individual wage determination in preparation for the exposition of the model of wage determination (section II). In section III we present the empirical results of the investigation, and in section IV we evaluate public policy as it has been applied to the poor and the low-wage worker in our society.

I THEORY OF INDIVIDUAL WAGE DETERMINATION

Since World War II, two separate schools of thought pertaining to the labor market have developed. One dominated during the 1950's, followed by a competing view of labor markets during the 1960's, with little attention given to any possible synthesis of these differing analyses of the labor market.

In the 1950's, with public attention directed towards the economic power of trade unions and concentrated industries, labor market analysis was focused upon the demand side of the market. This became translated into operational terms via the specification of several characteristics of industries and labor markets as determinants of wages among fairly aggregated categories of labor markets. For example, the studies of Levinson, Segal, Ross, and others specified varations in profits, industrial concentration, labor union membership, rates of change in productivity, and employment as determinants of wage differentials among industries.[2] The *structure* of an industry was analyzed for its impact upon the wages of workers in those industries. For future reference in this paper, analyses of this type will be referred to as *structural analyses*, and the hypotheses flowing therefrom, *structural hypotheses*.

In the 1960's, with public attention diverted from problems of the interaction of unions and corporations toward low income concerns, labor market analysis become directed towards what can be construed as supply considerations. This was translated into operational terms with analyses of the 'human capital' an individual brings to the labor market.[3] Of primary concern were the determinants of human capital, although some attention has also been directed toward the effect of human capital upon an individual's opportunity in the labor market. The focus was the individual – his/her inherent productivity. For convenience we shall refer to the hypothesis of this analyses as *personal characteristic hypothesis*. Since both supply and demand considerations may be important, it may be wise to reconsider the two rather separate views of the labor market to see if a possibility for synthesis exists.

Consider first, only one industry (therefore, homogeneous with respect to its structural characteristics) employing individuals with varying amounts of human capital. Such a labor market, with only two classes of human capital, is represented in Figure 4.9. Given a homogeneous demand for labor, individuals earn different wages and are employed in different amounts as a unique function of variations in their human capital – formal education, on-the-job training, innate skills, etc.

In the neoclassical analysis of the labor supply decision in the household, workers supply their labor according to the labor supply equation:

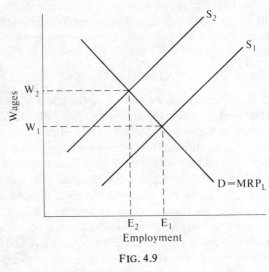

FIG. 4.9

$$S = a \pm bw.$$

Neoclassical theory concerned itself almost exclusively with the relationship between the changes in wages and changes in labor supplied by the household, or in terms of the above equation, the slope coefficient, b. In so doing, labor was assumed to be either of homogeneous 'quality,' or alternatively, labor was aggregated into efficiency units. In short, the choice was made to abstract from differences in human capital among the labor force, or, in terms of the above equation, the shift coefficient, a, was ignored. The emphasis is reversed in this study: the slope coefficient, embodying household income-leisure decisions is to be ignored, and attention will be directed towards the shift coefficient. The shift coefficient can be taken to represent the individual's reservation price which is a function of the individual's stock of human capital.

However, the difficulty with this model is that it ignores the possible important effects on individual wages of differing industrial structures identified in the research of the 1950's. Figure 4.10 depicts a model of the labor market with one homogeneous labor supply function and two segmented industries with differin labor demand functions. The shift parameter, c, in the demand function ($D = c + dw$) captures the differing structures of industries in terms of their technology, profit rates, product market concentration, effective tax rates, government contracts, and degree of unionization. The view of the labor market embodied in Figure 4.10 has been receiving increasing attention in recent years, particularly in the works of Doeringer, Piore, and Bluestone.[4]

In sum, there are two possible ways to analyze the labor market. The one posits demand fixed and examines variations in human capital as the determinant

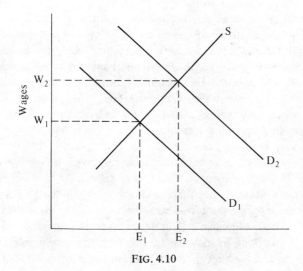

FIG. 4.10

of wages. It is a short theoretical step to a synthesis of the two models, but complex econometric problems arise when estimation is attempted. We return to this later.

Bluestone has suggested a theoretical synthesis in a model of *bilateral labor market segmentation.*[5] In this model, depicted in Figure 4.11, segmentation exists on both sides of the market, a condition in the labor market which is quite consistent with the dual labor market theories noted above.[6] The structure of different industries is indicated by I_1, I_2, and I_3. Variations in the human capital

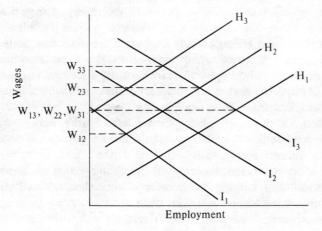

FIG. 4.11

among individuals is represented by the curves H_1, H_2, and H_3, where H_3 indicates a larger stock of human capital than H_2 or H_1. The curves attain their position on the graph due to the higher reservation price associated with individuals possessing more human capital and the fewer numbers of individuals possessing the larger stocks of human capital. Now the problem of wage determination for the individual assumes more complexity but hopefully greater realism. Thus, an individual with a substantial amount of human capital, represented by H_3, will be earning a wage of W_{13}, working in industry I_1. The individual receives a maximum wage, in this example, of W_{33} if he works in industry I_2. Thus, wages vary across industries for individuals with identical human capital depending upon the structure of those industries. On the other hand, wages will vary within a given industry depending on the differing amounts of human capital of its employees. Individuals employed in I_3 will earn anywhere from W_{33} to W_{31} depending upon their human capital.

A final implication is that individuals with low amounts of human capital will, under certain circumstances, earn the same as (or more than) individuals with larger amounts of human capital. In this example, an individual with human capital of H_3, working in industry I_1, will earn the same amount (W_{31}) as the individual with less human capital (H_1) working in industry I_3 (W_{13}). This occurs because of the balkanization of labor markets and the important barriers to mobility that can persist in labor markets over long periods of time. These barriers can arise because of direct discrimination in the labor market (by sex and race), trade union barriers to entry, high financial cost and risk involved in geographical mobility, insufficient labor market information, artificial educational barriers to job entry, and so on.[7]

II A TESTABLE MODEL OF WAGE DETERMINATION

The objective of this section is to develop a model of individual wage determination which both faithfully adheres to the theory of wage determination outlined above and accomplishes the essential purpose of decomposing the supply and demand effects on individual wage determination. Stated formally, the basic hypothesis to be tested posits wages as a function of both personal characteristics (loosely supply-type variables) and structural variables (demand-type variables).[8] The goal of the empirical exercise is to subject to verification a model which illuminates these relationships.

Translating a theory of individual wage determination into a testable model poses some difficult multicollinearity problems. We observe individuals working in certain industries and occupations, and at the same time these individuals embody different levels of human capital. To some extent the attributes of individuals and their status in the labor force are collinear. To mitigate some of the problems of multicollinearity, we employed a two-step regression procedure.

Let us consider, first, the problem of testing for the presence of the effect of structural variables upon an individual's wage. To accomplish this, we must first eliminate the effects of the personal characteristic variables upon the individual wage and then test for the effect of structural variables upon a new wage variable with the personal characteristic effects removed. In operational terms this means first performing a regression with wages specified as a function of personal characteristic variables, then calculating an adjusted wage variable with the personal characteristic effects removed. At this point, it is then possible to test for the effects of structural variables. Translating this process into a series of equations yields:

$$W = a + b_1 EX + b_2 R + b_3 A + b_4 S + b_5 E + b_6 M + u_1 \qquad (1)$$

where
$$
\begin{aligned}
W &= \text{Wages,}\\
EX &= \text{Years in present job,}\\
R &= \text{Race,}\\
A &= \text{Age,}\\
S &= \text{Sex,}\\
E &= \text{Years of education,}\\
M &= \text{Marital status,}\\
u &= \text{Residuals,}
\end{aligned}
$$

$$u_1 = c + d_1 O - I + d_2 RG + d_3 C + d_4 UM, \qquad (2)$$

where
$$
\begin{aligned}
O - I &= \text{Occupation and industry in which the individual is employed,}\\
RG &= \text{Region of employment,}\\
C &= \text{City size,}\\
UM &= \text{Union membership status of the individual.}
\end{aligned}
$$

This set of equations can be used to examine the effects of the structural variables ($O - I$, RG, C, and UM) after eliminating the effects of the personal characteristic variables (EX, R, A, S, E, and M) on the wage. It should be noted that this method places a very stringent test on the structural hypothesis.

The process can then be reversed to test for the effect of personal characteristic variables upon the wage after eliminating the effects of the structural variables. The following equations operationalize this test

$$W = e + f_1 O - I + f_2 RG + f_3 C + f_4 UM + u_2 \qquad (3)$$

$$u_2 = g + h_1 EX + h_2 R + h_3 A + h_4 S + h_5 E + h_6 M. \qquad (4)$$

Equation (3) measures the variance in wages among individuals associated with the structure of their employment environment (demand-type variables), and equation (4) analyzes the impact of personal characteristic variables after the structural effects have been eliminated.[9]

III TESTING THE MODEL

The data used in the empirical sections come from the 1967 Survey of Consumer Finances conducted by the Institute for Social Research of the University of Michigan.[10] They used a multistage area probability sample to select a group of representative dwelling units for the continental United States. The empirical research was confined to full-time, full-year workers, defined as individuals working at least 40 weeks during 1967 and working an average of at least 30 hours per week. The year 1967 was chosen because employment levels were high. The study was also confined to the following occupations: laborers, service workers, craftsmen, operatives and kindred workers, and foremen. This yielded 1023 individuals, with mean annual wage earnings of $6223, or an annual income close to the Bureau of Labor Statistics *lower* 'Moderate But Adequate Standard of Living' for that year.[11] The variance in wages is substantial enough to learn something about low wage workers in the economy. Some 14 per cent of the sample are 'working poor' — individuals employed full-time with earnings below the Social Security Administration's poverty level.

All the variables in the analysis are categorical, and for each variable a dummy specification is used. The dependent variable (wages) is stated in terms of annual earnings. The independent variables in the analysis are categorical, and for each a dummy specification is used. The industry-occupation variable was constructed by assigning each individual a dummy specification simultaneously for his/ her occupation and industry.[12]

The results for equation (1) are contained in Table 4.6. Wage earnings, measured by annual earnings from wages, are specified as a function of the

Table 4.6
Wage Earnings and Personal Characteristics[a]

Explanatory Variable	Relative Importance (beta coefficient)
Education	.294[b]
Years in Present Job	.274[b]
Race	.239[b]
Sex	.142[b]
Age	.142[b]
Marital Status	.130[b]
$N = 1023$	Multiple $R^2 = .34$

[a]Equation (1).
[b]Significant at the .01 probability level.

several personal characteristics discussed in the previous section. All of the variables are significant at the 99 per cent confidence level. The R^2 is quite high for this type of micro analysis. The beta coefficient — the regression coefficient standardized about the mean — permits the ranking of variables in terms of their 'explanatory' importance. There appear to be two constellations of personal characteristics. Education, years in present job, and race are the most important variables. There is a discrete change to a second constellation of variables, consisting of sex, age, and marital status.[13]

The results for the regression corresponding to equation (2) are contained in Table 4.7. The regression specifies a wage variable with the effects of personal characteristics eliminated; this imposes a very severe test upon the structural hypothesis. It is no doubt true that in the initial regression (Table 4.6) some of the variance in wages is absorbed which is not directly related to personal characteristics but is due to the multicollinearity between the personal and structural variables.

The results contained in Table 4.7 indicate that the structural hypothesis has been able to withstand this severe test. Apparently, there is a substantial portion of the variance in wage earnings that can be explained by industry structure

Table 4.7
Residual Wage Earnings and Structural Characteristics[a]

Explanatory Variable	Relative Importance (beta coefficient)
Occupation-industry	.421[b]
Region of Employment	.247[b]
City Size	.206[b]
Union Status	.092[b]
$N = 1023$	Multiple $R^2 = .28$

[a]Equation (2).
[b]Significant at the .01 probability level.

after the effects of personal characteristics have been eliminated. The R^2 of 0.28 is not too much lower than the R^2 obtained in the earlier regression, confirming our contention of the multicollinearity between structural and personal characteristic variables. This implies that, first, there is a substantial amount of unexplained variance in wage earnings that survives after the personal characteristic effects have been specified; and second, that part of this variance can be accounted for by the structural variables. All of the variables are significant, lending additional confidence to this interpretation. Of the four structural variables, occupation–industry is the most important. The relatively low beta coefficient for union status may be due to the intercorrelation between that variable and occupation-industry.

The next step in the analysis involves reversing the process and performing a regression, first, with wage earnings as a function of the structural variables and then performing a regression with a wage variable, adjusted for the effects of the structural characteristics, as a function of personal characteristics. These results, corresponding to equations (3) and (4) are contained in Tables 4.8 and 4.9. As one would expect, the size of the R^2's are now reversed; the structural characteristics have a higher R^2, implying that not all of the multicollinearity has been removed even in this careful empirical testing procedure. The one new interesting result worth noting occurs in Table 4.9, where there is some

Table 4.8
Wage Earnings and Structural Characteristics[a]

Explanatory Variable	Relative Importance (beta coefficient)
Occupation-industry	.408[b]
Region	.285[b]
Union Status	.201[b]
City Size	.141[b]

$N = 1023$	Multiple $R^2 = .35$

[a]Equation (3).
[b]Significant at the .01 probability level.

Table 4.9
Residual Wage Earnings and Personal Characteristics[a]

Explanatory Variable	Relative Importance (beta coefficient)
Race	.261[b]
Education	.258[b]
Years in Present Job	.177[b]
Marital Status	.126[b]
Sex	.110[b]
Age	.072[c]

$N = 1023$	Multiple $R^2 = .25$

[a]Equation (3).
[b]Significant at the .01 probability level.
[c]Not significant.

rearrangement of the rank order of explanatory variables. Race now replaces education as the most important variable, though great caution should be exercised in making too much of this result because of the remaining multi-collinearity and the sensitivity of the beta coefficient to such statistical problems. Most significantly, however, the industry-occupation dummy variable retains its primary importance even after the order of the regressions is reversed.[14]

In employing a two-step regression technique to mitigate the effects of multicollinearity, we have created the possibility of specification bias. If the relationships among the several structural and personal characteristic variables are positive, then the results (both regression coefficients and R^2) of the first step in each pair of regressions will be biased upwards. For this reason, the analysis was run in both directions to determine the seriousness of the specification bias. Since the analysis was sustained in both directions, we conclude that the specification bias is not so great as to render the results meaningless.[15]

The regression results yield additional information about the validity of the wage hypothesis under scrutiny. In the computer procedure each category of

Table 4.10

The Effect of Occupation-industry on Wage Earnings

Occupation-industry	Effect on:	
	Original Wages[a] (dollars)	'Residual' Wages[b] (dollars)
Personal Services		
Craftsmen	4729	5943
Operatives	4071	4896
Laborers	4559	4708
Manufacturing: Durables		
Craftsmen	7747	7044
Operatives	5481	6064
Laborers	5751	5775
Manufacturing: Nondurables[c]		
Craftsmen	7596	7196
Operatives	5461	5782
Laborers	5571	5886
Transportation, Communications and Public Utilities		
Craftsmen	7381	7149
Operatives	6930	6851
Laborers	6038	5043
Construction		
Craftsmen	7488	6839
Operatives	6199	6182
Laborers	6156	5838
Retail Trade		
Craftsmen	6530	6557
Operatives	5243	6302
Laborers	4858	6136
Wholesale Trade		
Craftsmen	6321	5807
Operatives	5375	5926
Laborers	5472	5834
Miscellaneous Services		
Craftsmen	7017	6890
Operatives	5429	5785
Laborers	4591	4748
Agriculture, Forestry, Mining		
Craftsmen	5943	7352
Operatives	6911	6710
Laborers	4178	5377

[a]Mean annual earnings: $6223. Equation (3).
[b]Equation (2).
[c]Includes printing and publishing.

every independent variable is given a dummy specification, and the regression coefficients can be used to calculate the mean values of each category of each independent variable after controlling for all other effects.[16] Furthermore, the second step in each of the two sections of the analysis provides information on the effect of one set of independent variables upon a 'residual' dependent variable. Thus, for example, we can compare the effects of differing levels of education upon the initial wage and upon a wage variable with structural effects eliminated.

In Table 4.10, the results for the effect of the occupation-industry variable are presented both for the 'original wage' and the 'residual wage' variable, corresponding to Table 4.8 (equation (3)) and Table 4.7 (equation (2)), respectively. For example, a 'typical' craftsman, employed in the manufacturing durables industry, will earn $7747, net only of the effect of the three other structural variables on this individual's wage — specifically, union status, region of employment, and city size. However, this does not take into account the effect of personal characteristics upon the wage of that individual. This is done in the column ' "Residual" Wages.'

Two general observations emerge from the analysis. First, there is a substantial variation in wage earnings across industry categories, after the effects of personal characteristics have been eliminated. Individuals employed as laborers, with the same personal characteristics (education, years on job, age, race, etc.), earn from $4708 to $6136 depending upon the industry in which they are employed, after adjusting for the effect of personal characteristics on the wage. This observation lends additional support to the structural hypothesis.

The variation in wage earnings across personal characteristic variables is revealed in Tables 4.11 and 4.12, which present the results for the two most important personal characteristic variables — education and years-in-present-job. The most important observation to note from Tables 4.11 and 4.12 is that the variation in wages within both education and years-in-present-job categories is substantially reduced after eliminating the effects of structural variables upon the individual's wage earnings. The narrowing occurs at both extremes — low and high levels of education and experience. The most consistent and important

Table 4.11

The Effect of Education on Wage Earnings

Education (years)	Effect on:	
	Original Wages[a] (dollars)	Residual Wages[b] (dollars)
0–5	4429	4854
6–8	5433	5829
9–11	6154	6152
12	6460	6443
College, no degree	7446	6963
College, bachelor's degree	7197	6493

[a]Mean annual earnings: $6223. Equation (1).
[b]Equation (4).

Table 4.12

The Effect of Years in Present Job on Wage Earnings

Years in Present Job (years)	Effect on:	
	Original Wages[a] (dollars)	Residual Wages[b] (dollars)
1	4899	5867
2–3	5663	5985
4–5	5911	6195
6–7	6116	5814
8–9	6345	6196
10–14	6552	6228
15–24	6873	6574
25 or more	7353	6579

[a]Mean annual earnings: $6223. Equation (1).
[b]Equation (4).

result of this investigation is the confirmation of the hypothesis that structural characteristics are important in the determination of individual earnings. Of the four structural characteristics tested in this study, the industry and occupation in which the individual is employed stands out clearly as the most important, no matter what test is applied.[17]

IV IMPLICATIONS FOR LOW-WAGE EMPLOYMENT

Two themes have dominated the ideology and attitudes towards the poor in western countries since the industrial revolution. First, being poor is the result of some individual failure; and second, the state of individual poverty is due to the absence of work, caused either by individual laziness or the absence of jobs.[18] Since the New Deal and the postwar Employment Act, public policy has been concerned almost exclusively with providing jobs but not with the quality or wage levels of jobs. George Schultz stated this proposition most cogently when he testified as Secretary of Labor on the Nixon Family Assistance Plan:[19]

I hasten to add that the labor market itself must be recognized as a constraint . . . It is a fact that our economy has a lot of jobs that pay low wages. We are not going to be remaking the economy in this program. We can only put people in the jobs that exist . . . we will have to thread our way between our goals of providing good jobs – . . . and the realities of the kinds of jobs that are available.

The human capital concerns of the 1960's, translated into programmatic terms in training and education legislation, are based on the premise that workers have made inadequate investment in themselves. The cause of this investment failure has been traced either to simple irrationalities on the part of the investors or discrimination in educational markets. This approach is not too far removed from the nineteenth-century view of poverty in which the poor were blamed for their own condition.[20]

Public policy and its supporting research has focused almost exclusively on the problem of the *acquisition of human capital* — the level and distribution of education and training and the way in which human capital is produced. But the problem of low income does not end there; along with the process of acquisition of human capital, there is a question of *how this human capital is used in the labor market.* A clue to the reason for the ambiguous results of training programs is to be found in this distinction. Perhaps human capital has been augmented somewhat by these programs, but is it put to different uses in the labor market? If not — if the individual is removed from one structural environment only to be placed back in the same structural environment — then we should not be surprised by the absence of any significant improvement in the worker's earning ability. To understand how human capital is used requires an analysis of the labor market, a task undertaken in this paper.

The evidence developed in this paper raises several important issues for public policy. Recently, 2.9 million poor family heads worked full time.[21] For these people the problem is not simply providing jobs in an aggregate Keynesian sense, but in providing decent jobs at adequate wage levels. Moreover, structural conditions in the labor market tend to exert a substantial influence upon wage levels. This study has identified the importance of these structural variables. A laborer in personal services, or in transportation, communication and public utilities will receive low earnings, independent of the personal characteristics of the worker. As long as public policy focuses exclusively on the characteristics of individuals, and not as well on the structure of the economic environment in which the individual works, we can continue to anticipate the same disappointing results that public policy has produced in the last decade.

In this paper a theory of the labor market was developed, which integrated both supply and demand considerations into a model of bilateral labor market segmentation. The data and method used to test for the validity of the model supported the existence of bilateral labor market segmentation, in which the structure of labor demand and personal characteristics determined individual wage earnings.

NOTES

1. In contrast to the relatively abundant literature on other aspects of poverty, the material on wage poverty is quite sparse. See Bluestone (1968), Cummings (1965), Perrella (1967), Orshansky (1968), Dawn Day Wachtel (1967), Delehanty and Evans, U.S. Department of Commerce (1969), Sinfield and Twine (1968), Doeringer (1968), Harrison (1971), and Lecht (1970).
2. Levinson (1960), pp. 1–22, Segal (1961), and Ross and Goldner (1950).
3. Thurow (1970) and (1969), chap. V; and Mincer (1970).
4. Piore (1969) and Doeringer (1968) refer to their model as a *dual labor market*; Bluestone (1970) uses the term, *tripartite economy*. F. W. Taussig first suggested such models in his theory of 'non-competing groups.'

5. Bluestone (1970), pp. 21–24. The version used in this paper departs slightly from the one employed by Bluestone.
6. To be more precise, we would require a third dimension to Figure 4.11 to indicate that the horizontal axis is stated in efficiency units when the 'human capital' functions are held fixed and demand is permitted to vary.
7. Bluestone (1970), p. 23.
8. The actual specification of the model imposes a broad interpretation on 'supply' and 'demand' type variables. This is the reason for substituting the nomenclature: 'personal characteristic' and 'structural' type variables.
9. This statistical procedure has been used effectively to differentiate between the effects of individual characteristics and school characteristics on student development. See Astin (1968) and Creager (mimeo).
10. Katona (1968), chaps. 14 and 16.
11. U.S. Department of Labor (1969).
12. These categories are contained in Table 4.10.
13. Small differences in the sizes of the beta coefficient within each constellation should be interpreted gingerly due to the imperfect nature of the beta statistic. See Andrews (1967), chap. 6.
14. A regression was run in which all of the variables were entered – both personal characteristic and structural variables. Industry-occupation, years in present job, and region (in that order) were most important. Education was ninth (out of ten variables) in importance.
15. Goldberger (1964), p. 196.
16. Andrews (1967), chap. 3.
17. Roughly similar conclusions are reached by Rees and Schultz (1970), especially chap. 12.
18. A good treatment of poverty in history appears in Coll (1969) and Bremner (1967).
19. Schultz (1969), p. 16.
20. Theories of poverty in their historical and contemporary context are examined in Wachtel (1971).
21. U.S. Department of Commerce (1969).

REFERENCES

Andrews, F., Morgan, J., and Sonquist, J. *Multiple Classification Analysis* (Ann Arbor: Institute for Social Research), 1967.
Astin, A., 'Undergraduate Achievement and Institutional "Excellence," ' *Science*, 1961 (Aug. 1968), 661–8.
Bluestone, B., 'Low Wage Industries and the Working Poor,' *Poverty and Human Resource Abstracts*, 3 (Mar.–Apr. 1968), 1–14.
—— 'The Tripartite Economy: Labor Markets and the Working Poor,' *Poverty and Human Resources* (July–Aug. 1970), 15–35.
Bremner, R. H., *From the Depths: The Discovery of Poverty in the United States* (New York: The New York University Press, 1967).
Coll, B. D., *Perspectives in Public Welfare: A History* (Washington: U.S. Government Printing Office, 1969).
Craeger, J. A., 'Academic Achievement and Institutional Environments: Comparison of Two Research Strategies' (mimeo).
Cummings, L. D., 'The Employed Poor: Their Characteristics and Occupations.' *Monthly Labor Review*, 88 (July 1965), 828–41.
Delehanty, G. E. and Evans, R., 'Low-Wage Employment: An Inventory and an Assessment' (mimeo).
Doeringer, P. B., 'Manpower Programs for Ghetto Labor Markets,' *Proceedings of the Industrial Relations Research Association* (1968).

Goldberger, A. S., *Econometric Theory* (New York: John Wiley & Son, 1964).

Harrison, B., 'Education and Underemployment in the Urban Ghetto,' in David M. Gordon (ed.), *Problems in Political Economy: An Urban Perspective* (Lexington, Mass.: D. C. Heath, 1971).

Katona, G., Morgan, J., Schmiedeskamp, J., and Sonquist, J., *1967 Survey of Consumer Finances* (Ann Arbor: Survey Research Center, 1968).

Lecht, L., *Poor Persons in the Labor Force: A Universe of Need* (Washington: National Planning Association, 1970).

Leftwich, R. H., 'Personal Income and Marginal Productivity,' in David M. Gordon (ed.), *Problems in Political Economy: An Urban Perspective* (Lexington, Mass.: D. C. Heath, 1971), 79–85.

Levinson, H. M., *Postwar Movement of Wages and Prices in Manufacturing Industries.* Study Paper no. 21, Joint Economic Committee Study of Employment, Growth, and Price Levels. (Washington: U.S. Government Printing Office, 1960).

Mincer, J., 'The Distribution of Labor Incomes: A Survey with Special Reference to the Human Capital Approach,' *Journal of Economic Literature* VIII (Mar. 1970), 1–26.

Orshansky, M., 'More About the Poor in 1964,' *Social Security Bulletin*, 29 (May 1966), 3–38.

—— 'The Shape of Poverty in 1966,' *Social Security Bulletin*, 31 (Mar. 1968), 2–32.

Perrella, V. C., 'Low Earners and Their Incomes,' *Monthly Labor Review*, 90 (May 1967), 35–40.

Piore, M. J., Cassel, F., and Ginsberg, W. (eds.), 'On-the Job Training in the Dual Labor Market,' in A. Weber, *Public-Private Manpower Policies* (Madison: Industrial Relations Research Association, 1969).

Rees, A. and Schultz, G. P., *Workers and Wages in an Urban Labor Market* (Chicago: University Press, 1970).

Ross, A. M. and Goldner, W., 'Forces Affecting the Interindustry Wage Structure,' *Quarterly Journal of Economics* (May 1950), 254–281.

Segal, M., 'Unionism and Wage Movements,' *Southern Economic Journal*, XXVIII (Oct. 1961), 174–181.

Schultz, G., 'Statement of George Schultz, Secretary of Labor, Before Committee on Ways and Means, on the Family Assistance Act of 1969' (mimeo, 1969).

Sinfield, A. and Twine, F., 'The Low-Paid: The Employment Market and Social Policy' (mimeo, 1968).

Thurow, L., *Investment in Human Capital* (Belmont, Mass.: Wadsworth Publishing Company, 1970).

—— *Poverty and Discrimination* (Washington: The Brookings Institution, 1969).

U.S. Department of Commerce, Bureau of the Census, *Current Population Reports*, Series P-60, no. 78, 1969.

—— 'Year-Round Workers with Low Earnings in 1966,' *Current Population Reports*, no. 58 (Apr. 4, 1969).

U.S. Department of Labor, Bureau of Labor Statistics, *Three Standards of Living for an Urban Family of Four Persons.* Bulletin no. 1570–1575, 1969.

Wachtel, D. D., *The Working Poor* (Ann Arbor: Institute of Labor and Industrial Relations, 1967).

Wachtel, H. M., 'Looking at Poverty from a Radical Perspective,' *Review of Radical Political Economics*, III (Summer, 1971), 1–19.

4.9 Minimum Wages and the Secondary Labor Market*

1. INTRODUCTION

There has recently emerged in the literature of labor economics a theory of dual labor markets [1; 2]. While the boundaries between markets are not sharply drawn, researchers have been able to distinguish the salient characteristics of low wage or secondary labor markets from those of the more familiar mainstream or primary, labor markets. Of these characteristics, two are perhaps most noteworthy. First, observers have been struck by the fluidity with which workers move between employment and unemployment, and enter and leave the labor force. The casualness of these markets has been attributed both to the socioeconomic characteristics of the work force and the nature of the product markets facing employers in these markets, e.g., demand schedules with large stochastic components. Second, during any market period, workers appear to be allocated among jobs almost randomly; variables such as experience and years of education, which are good predictors of earnings and employment status in the primary labor market, do poorly in secondary labor markets.[1] This paper develops the implications of these secondary labor market characteristics for the analysis of a policy issue of recurring social concern — the desirability of minimum wage legislation.

As the minimum wage issue is usually analyzed, the legislated increase in wages above the prevailing level is seen to reduce employment in covered low wage labor markets, provided the elasticity of demand for this type of labor is (absolutely) greater than zero. While the higher wage benefits those who retain their jobs, it is likely to be detrimental to those who are displaced and to those in uncovered employment.[2] Thus, the effects of the minimum wage are dichotomous, and to condone the legislation implies a willingness to sacrifice the welfare of members of one group for the benefit of those in another, perhaps smaller, group.[3]

A rethinking of the issues involved in the controversy seems desirable, for despite a large literature on the subject and an apparent consensus within the profession, economists have failed to persuade policy makers or the public of the harm wrought by the legislation. Unfortunately, economists have too often reacted to this communications failure much as the traveler abroad who, in an effort to have his English understood by the non-English-speaking natives, simply talks louder. The present paper suggests that by ignoring labor turnover, apparently an important characteristic of a certain class of labor markets, the traditional analysis has led to an unduly pessimistic view of the effects of minimum wage laws.

*From Allan G. King, 'Minimum Wages and the Secondary Labor Market', *Southern Economic Journal*, Vol. 41, October 1974.

II. THE MODEL

The issue is analyzed from the perspective of the group most directly affected by the legislation — low income workers; economy-wide (allocative) effects are ignored.

The concept of the market period is fundamental to this discussion. It is defined as the length of time during which work commitments are honored. In the academic labor market, the market period may be thought of as lasting one year; in the market that once characterized longshoring, recontracting occurred daily. Throughout this paper, secondary labor markets will be defined as those labor markets characterized by short market periods.[4]

With these definitions in mind, consider a labor market where the minimum wage W per year and the unemployment rate U prevail. The assumption that the probability of being employed in each period is a random occurrence, independent of previous experience, implies that an individual's yearly earnings (Y) have an expected value, $E(Y)$, equal to $W(1 - U)$. During the course of a year, some individuals will average out with greater earnings, others with less; if the market period averages $1/n$th of a year, the variance in yearly earnings is given by:

$$\text{Var}\,(Y) = W^2(1 - U)U/n, \tag{1}$$

on the simplifying assumption that employment follows the binomial probability law.[5]

In the most casual labor markets, n may be quite large. The more frequently jobs turn over, the more is the 'average' experience descriptive of the experiences of each worker; i.e., the variance in earnings approaches zero, making it meaningless to distinguish between those who benefit and those who are harmed by the legislation. This is not to say that the dispersion in earnings should be ignored; rather, it indicates that there is a second dimension to the analysis. This may be incorporated into the model by adopting the perspective of an individual who perceives changes in both his mean level of earnings and the dispersion in outcomes around the mean as a result of the proposed minimum wage.

Viewed in this light, the minimum wage issue can be analyzed as a problem in risk-bearing. Accordingly, a judgment regarding the merits of the current wage level relative to any proposed increase in minimum wages must be based on a comparison of the associated probability distributions of earnings. In most labor markets, if unemployment effects accompany the increased minimum wage, the standard deviation of earnings will increase [see equation (1)]. Since it is usually assumed that individuals are risk averse, i.e., they are willing to incur greater risk (empirically identified with the variance or standard deviation in earnings) only in conjunction with a higher expected income, workers in this market will benefit only if expected earnings increase as well. This requires that the percentage increase in the wage rate exceed the percentage decline in the employment ratio, i.e., the elasticity of demand for the affected labor force groups must be less than one (assuming, initially, a constant labor force). This property is a necessary condition for an increase in wages to benefit members of the target group.[6]

Let us attempt to obtain a sufficient condition. When the demand for labor is inelastic, an increase in the minimum wage will increase both expected earnings and its standard deviation. To make welfare comparisons under these circumstances requires that one have some *a priori* basis for judging whether the increase in expected earnings is sufficient to compensate an individual for the greater risk with which he is now saddled. Tsiang [11] has argued that indifference curves drawn in the mean-standard deviation plane should generally not exceed a slope of unity.[7] Consequently, if the increase in expected earnings (E) resulting from a higher minimum wage exceeds the increase in the standard deviation of average earnings (σ), one can conclude that an improvement in the welfare of those directly affected by the legislation will result. Using this criterion we will derive an upper bound for the elasticity of demand for labor which will represent a sufficient condition for a welfare gain.

Tsiang's criterion, $dE > d\sigma$, may be rewritten as

$$\dot{E}/\dot{\sigma} > \sigma/E^8 \tag{2}$$

i.e., the ratio of the rates of increase in the mean to the standard deviation must exceed the coefficient of variation. Write the left hand side of the inequality as

$$\frac{\dot{E}}{\dot{\sigma}} = \frac{\dot{W} + (1 - \dot{U})}{\dot{W} + 1/2[(1 - \dot{U}) + \dot{U}]} \tag{3}$$

and note that $\dot{U} = -(1 - \dot{u})(1 - u)/u)$, and that the elasticity of demand for labor (ϵ) is given by $(1 - \dot{U})/\dot{W}$. Substituting these relations into (3) enables us to express the sufficient condition as

$$\frac{1 + \epsilon}{1 + \epsilon[1 - (1/2U)]} > \frac{\sigma}{E}. \tag{4}$$

The coefficient of variation can be expressed in terms of the rate of unemployment and the length of the market period:

$$\frac{\sigma}{E} = \frac{\sqrt{(1 - U)U/n}}{1 - U}. \tag{5}$$

Thus the restriction on the demand elasticity can be derived from knowledge of only the unemployment rate and the length of the market period.

Unemployment statistics are now quite disaggregated, and data for the labor force group of interest to the analyst should generally be available. Estimating the length of the market period is more difficult; however, Perry [10] has recently estimated the average number of spells of unemployment per year experienced by members of various demographic groups at given levels of aggregate unemployment. These estimates may be used to obtain a conservative estimate of n by reasoning as follows. If during any market period an individual has a probability U of being unemployed, then the average number of periods of unemployment (N) experienced by individuals in a given group is

$$N = Un. \qquad (6)$$

If it is assumed that the number of periods of unemployment is equal to the number of spells of unemployment, clearly understating the former since consecutive periods of unemployment count as a single spell, then Perry's estimate can be used to approximate N. Since the level of unemployment is known, an estimate of n, and hence the coefficient of variation, can now be obtained.

As an illustration, consider the effect on teenagers of increasing the minimum wage at a time when the national unemployment rate is 5 percent. Perry estimates that this level of aggregate unemployment is associated with an average of 1.82 and 1.94 spells of unemployment per year for males and females aged 16-19. In January of 1973, an aggregate unemployment rate of 5 percent was associated with unemployment rates of 13.4 and 15.4 percent for these groups. Substituting these figures into equation (6) indicates there are approximately 14 market periods a year for boys, and 13 market periods a year for girls.

Using the unemployment rates noted above and the derived values of n, we can calculate the coefficient of variation for each demographic group and thus obtain the restrictions on the elasticities of demand from equation (4). The coefficients of variation are .10 for boys and .13 for girls. These statistics imply that sufficient conditions for an improvement in the economic welfare of members of each group are that the elasticity of demand for teenage males and females be less than .71 and .67 in absolute value.

In a recent paper Katz [7] reports estimates of the elasticity of demand for teenage workers of .62 for males and .61 for females. Both estimates satisfy the conditions we have obtained and indicate that a *small* increase in the minimum wage will improve the welfare of these groups. It should be noted, however, that the demand elasticities Katz obtains for non-white teenagers of both sexes are very much greater, failing to satisfy even the necessary condition of inelasticity and indicating that these groups will be harmed by an increase in the minimum wage. Classifying labor markets along industrial lines, Zucker [12] reports that demand elasticities of less than one are characteristic of non-durable manufacturing, while the demand for labor is greater than one in the manufacture of durable goods. Undoubtedly a regional breakdown of the labor force would point to other labor markets with high demand elasticities.

III. CONCLUSION

This paper proposes a reformulation of the issues involved in the minimum wage controversy in light of what are generally regarded as important characteristics of low wage labor markets. The usual dichotomy drawn between the welfare of those who remain employed and those who become displaced was argued to be invalid because of the homogenizing effect of casual labour markets.

Because of the random nature of hiring, the evaluation of the effects of a minimum wage must be treated as a mean-standard deviation problem, the standard deviation being smaller the higher the turnover rate. In that context, the requirement of a perfectly inelastic demand schedule for labor for no one to be made worse off by an increased minimum wage is seen as too stringent; in labor markets characterized by short market periods admissible demand elasticities may approach unity.

A further implication is that the spillover effect of minimum wages on the welfare of those in uncovered labor markets should be in the *same* direction as the direct effect. This occurs because an improvement in the welfare of those in covered employment should attract individuals away from uncovered markets, thereby increasing wages in the uncovered labor market. In the event the minimum wage increase diminishes the welfare of those directly affected, an influx of workers into uncovered unemployment should occur, resulting in a wage reduction in that market.[9] There is also a presumption that the elasticity of demand for labor will be smaller, the broader is the coverage of the minimum wage law. Consequently, when proposals to increase the minimum wage are accompanied by plans to extend coverage, as they so frequently are, the relevance of the experience gained with previous minimum wage increases may be questionable.

Because the judgment of a welfare gain or loss must ultimately be made with reference to the values of the affected individuals, an implication of the analysis is that these persons should have a direct input into the legislative debate and their recommendations should be accorded serious consideration.

NOTES

1. The studies that form the basis for these generalizations are summarized in Gordon [2, 43–53]; also, see Hall [4].
2. For the analysis of an exceptional case in which minimum wages benefit those in both the covered and uncovered sectors see Johnson [6].
3. For example, see the introductory remarks by Moore [9, 897].
4. In the subsequent discussion it will be assumed that the market period is an institutional characteristic of the labor market under discussion. Most importantly, it is assumed that the length of the market period is independent of the minimum wage. Exception may be taken to this assumption, for Kosters and Welch [8] maintain that high turnover (marginality) results from such laws. Their argument is based on the assertion that marginality is caused by the wage rigidity associated with the legislated minimum. On the other hand, a referee has noted that if a minimum wage leads to an excess supply of labor to covered firms this would enable those firms to upgrade the quality of their labor force through selective discharges and more efficient screening. This, in turn, might be expected to lead to a reduction in the turnover rate. For a discussion of the origins of high-turnover labor markets that is largely independent of the minimum wage issue see Doeringer and Piore [1] and Gordon, Edwards, and Reich [3].
5. The specifications appropriate to the 'traditional' analysis of minimum wages may be obtained by setting n equal to one. That is, the traditional model regards an individual's

assignment to employment and unemployment as being permanent throughout the period of analysis.

6. It has been shown that in evaluating risky prospects the efficiency frontier cannot generally be represented in terms of the mean and standard deviation; however, the assumption of high turnover in the labor markets under discussion makes the central limit theorem applicable. Since the mean-standard deviation criterion is appropriate to the normal distribution, the necessary condition we obtain is of greater validity the higher the rate of turnover.

7. Tsiang's result derives from a Taylor expansion of a utility function which is general in nature and the assumption that the marginal utility of income is non-negative; it is most applicable where σ/E is small, a condition which should be satisfied by equation (5) below.

8. Dots denote percentage changes.

9. Indeed, Jacob Mincer has suggested that the workers' evaluation of the effects of minimum wage laws can be evaluated, *ex post*, by observing the labor supply effects.

REFERENCES

1. Doeringer, P. B. and Piore, M. J., *Internal Labor Markets and Manpower Analysis*, Lexington, Massachusetts: D. C. Heath Co., 1971.

2. Gordon, D. M. *Theories of Poverty and Underemployment.* Lexington, Massachusetts: D. C. Heath and Co., 1972.

3. Gordon, D. M., Edwards, R. C., and Reich, M., 'Labor Market Segmentation in American Capitalism.' Paper presented at the Conference on Labor Market Segmentation, Harvard University, March 1973. Mimeo.

4. Hall, R. E., 'Why Is the Unemployment Rate So High at Full Employment?' *Brookings Papers on Economic Activity*, 3: 1970, 369–402.

5. Harrison, B., 'Education and Underemployment in the Urban Ghetto.' *American Economic Review*, December 1972, 796–812.

6. Johnson, H. G., 'Minimum Wage Laws: A General Equilibrium Analysis.' *Canadian Journal of Economics*, November 1969, 599–603.

7. Katz, A., 'Teenage Employment Effects of State Minimum Wages.' *Journal of Human Resources*, Spring 1973, 250–256.

8. Kosters, M. and F. Welch, 'The Effects of Minimum Wages on the Distribution of Changes in Aggregate Employment.' *American Economic Review*, June 1972, 323–332.

9. Moore, T. G., 'The Effect of Minimum Wages on Teenage Unemployment Rates.' *Journal of Political Economy*, July/August 1971, 892–902.

10. Perry, G. L., 'Unemployment Flows in the U.S. Labor Market.' *Brookings Papers on Economic Activity*, 2: 1972, 245–278.

11. Tsiang, S. C., 'The Rationale of the Mean-Standard Deviation Analysis, Skewness Preference, and the Demand for Money.' *American Economic Review*, June 1972, 354–371.

12. Zucker, A., 'Minimum Wages and the Demand for Low Wage Labor.' *Quarterly Journal of Economics*, May 1973, 267–277.

4.10 Dual Labor Market Theories: a Neoclassical Assessment*

Ideally, a paper that attempts to evaluate a challenge to established theory should accomplish the following objectives:

1. Present the theoretical substance of the challenging theory, which is here called the dual and radical theories, and indicate how it differs from the existing theory, which I will refer to as neoclassical or orthodox theory;

2. Point out the empirical implications of the new theories and explain their differences with the existing theory;

3. Assess the empirical basis for discriminating between the competing hypotheses or, if this is lacking, provide the theoretical or evidential counterarguments of the neoclassical response to the dual and radical challenge; and, finally,

4. Spell out the policy implications of the competing theories.

Meeting these objectives is an impossible task for a short paper. The space constraint is compounded by the fact that in my judgment the dual and radical theories are too varied, incomplete, and amorphous to present concisely. The strategy I adopt to describe these theories in the longer paper consists of, first, discussing their linkages to historical criticisms of classical and neoclassical theory; second, developing their empirical challenges to orthodox theory. Only the second part is emphasized below.

To establish the context of the challenge, let us begin with the observation of Leo Rogin (p. 13) that: 'new systems (of economic doctrines) first emerge in the guise of arguments in the context of social reform.' The dual and radical (or *D-R*, for short) theories began to emerge in the 1960's when the movement for social reform mainly involved the war on poverty and the drive for full participation in the economy by minority groups, including women. Dissatisfaction with the pace and progress of reform in these areas and dissatisfaction with the conventional analysis of the problems and their remedies have led to arguments within the economics profession, especially on the part of the younger labor economists.

Let me simply assert, without defending the proposition [. . .] that the neoclassical school does dominate the profession today, even within labor economics where, as I mention below, it was not dominant during the 1940's and 1950's. I will also assert that neoclassical theory means, in general: (1) the theory of the demand for labor contained in the marginal productivity theory and the associated research on production functions; and (2) the theory of labor supply consisting mainly of models involving the labor/leisure choice and human capital investments.

Theory, however, operates on at least two levels. As a framework for analysis, neoclassical theory implies a set of methods and techniques — for example, marginal analysis of behavioral relations in which income and prices are key

*From Glen G. Cain, 'The Challenge of Dual and Radical Theories of the Labor Market to Orthodox Theory', *American Economic Review*, Vol. 65, May 1975.

variables. Second, as a body of substantive behavioral propositions, neoclassical theory implies a large number of qualitative predictions and quantitative estimates of parameters about behavioral relationships. The dual and radical critics attack both the methodology and the collection of predictions and substantive hypotheses. Those attacks inevitably spill over into policy disputes.

I. A CLASSIFICATION OF ISSUES RAISED IN THE DUAL AND RADICAL LITERATURE

Out of this background we can discern three types of issues raised in the *D–R* literature: first, criticisms of the outcomes and processes taking place in the labor market; second, a rejection of the existing theories and methods that have purported to explain the operations of the labor market; and third, a call for new and more radical policies.

A. *Empirical Generalizations*

It is useful to distinguish between two types of facts which contribute to controversy. The first are those that indicate some sort of hardship or distress, such as high levels of unemployment and poverty. The facts about these problems may not be in dispute. The second type of descriptive empirical findings consists of unresolved and inadequately treated problems, which may or may not concern matters of hardship. The empirical challenges raised by the *D–R* spokesmen usually concern the overlap — empirical anomalies about pressing social problems. I will list eight problem areas, some of which have sub-topics.

1. As noted above, the most important problem motivating the *D–R* economists was the persistence of poverty in conjunction with the affluence of society and the scope of governmental efforts to eradicate poverty. This problem is too broad, however, and we must turn to its more particular aspects, listed below as items 2 through 7.

2. One such problem is the failure of education and training programs which, according to the *D–R* critics, demonstrate a failure of the human capital models and call into question the conventional acceptance of a causal connection between formal education and labor productivity. I comment on the alleged failure of social action programs below. Concerning the general education-productivity relation, my judgment is that its empirical support is shakiest regarding the intensive margin of education investment — that is, the effect of more educational resources, holding years of schooling constant. There is, I believe, ample empirical support for a payoff at the extensive margin — that is, positive returns to more years of schooling. The orthodox interpretation of this empirical relation is, however, called into question by the next point.

3. Employers used educational and training indicators merely as screening devices — either to discriminate on grounds other than productivity, or to serve as a proxy for potential productivity that is not directly related to what was actually learned in the educational institution. The latter purpose, it should be

noted, redefines the investment nature of education as 'information'; it does not deny that any investment takes place. However, a denial of either the real productivity of education or of the potency of the informational content of educational attainments does challenge the orthodox assumptions about rational behavior and/or about the degree of competitiveness in the economy.

4. The income distribution remains as unequal now as it did twenty years ago, in spite of the decrease in the variance of educational attainments in the adult population.

5. A collection of problems concern the large and persistent differentials in earnings between white and black males and between males and females. These challenge neoclassical models of discrimination which predict a withering away of the differential under conditions of competition. Several more specific empirical puzzles in connection with labor market discrimination may be listed: the decline in black male labor-force participation rates relative to white males in recent years; the near-constant ratio of black-to-white earnings from 1950 to 1966 or so; the long-standing empirical relation showing a decline in the ratio of black-to-white male income with higher educational attainment; the flat wage-earnings profile of black males and all females relative to white males as revealed by cross-section surveys; and, finally, the stagnant trend in earnings and occupational attainments of women relative to men during recent years. Associated with this trend is the slower growth in female educational attainment compared with men from 1940 to 1973, despite the sharp increase in labor-force participation of women during this period.

6. The roles of monopolies, unions, and other sources of protected labor markets have been a long-standing problem area. The *D–R* spokesmen imply that these are so pervasive as to make untenable the empirical work of orthodox labor economists, which usually assumes competition.

7. Another area is the role of psychological variables measuring the attitudes and motivations of workers. Conventional economists have customarily viewed tastes for work as exogenous and as one of the (unexplored) causal variables explaining employment, earnings, and occupational achievements. The challenge of the *D–R* theories lies in their claim that tastes are endogenous and a result of one's labor market achievements.

8. Alienation among American workers is the final listed problem. If we assume as true the disputed contention that alienation and dissatisfaction among *U.S.* workers are widespread and increasing, the challenge to orthodox theory may be stated as follows: why has the market not responded to the workers' tastes and preferences either by a redesign of jobs and up-grading of working conditions or simply by appropriate wage rate compensations?

The foregoing list of empirical generalizations about outcomes and operations of the labor market covers, I believe, the main bill of particulars in the *D–R* indictment. Let us now comment briefly on their theories of how the labor market operates.

B. *Alternative Theories*

In the absence of any single, well-articulated theory in the dual and radical literature, I will mention three versions that veer progressively further from orthodox theory.

Perhaps closest to the orthodox is Lester C. Thurow's job competition theory, which is contrasted with the orthodox wage competition theory (Thurow, and Thurow and R. E. B. Lucas). Its main elements are: (1) the number and type of job slots are technologically determined; (2) the workers' skills (i.e., human capital) and wage offers are nearly irrelevant in determining the number and type of job positions actually filled; (3) queues of workers for jobs offered at fixed wages constitute the supply of labor, and the employer's assessment of the workers' trainability and adaptability determines which workers are hired; and (4) fluctuations in macro policies will lead to changes in the demand for labor and thus to changes in the lengths of the queues. The theory emphasizes the within-firm (or internal) labor market as the locus of decisions about allocations, promotions, and on-the-job training — all of which are relatively insulated from the external labor market. In many respects this theory is similar to the dual market theory.

The dual labor market theory of Peter B. Doeringer and Michael J. Piore depicts a labor market divided into primary and secondary markets. The former contains the jobs in large or profitable firms and the unionized jobs. These jobs are higher paying, offer promotion possibilities, better working conditions, and greater stability. The secondary labor market contains the low-paying jobs which are held by workers who are discriminated against and who have unstable working patterns. The discussion of this duality tends to be merely descriptive, and perhaps descriptive only of polar cases. Many of the theoretical ideas are similar to the job competition theory; namely, the demand-determined allocation of jobs and the downgrading of human capital characteristics as determinants of wage levels. In addition, considerable attention is given to the role of employer discrimination. Also, the worker's attitudes, motivations, and work habits are viewed as mutually reinforcing determinants of a worker's assignment (and confinement) to the primary or secondary sector of the labor market.

The third version of a labor market theory is referred to variously as radical, segmented, and stratified theory (see David M. Gordon). It expresses a more explicit critique of capitalism, acknowledges its ties to Marxian dialectical analysis, and emphasizes class conflicts. The dual labor market idea is sometimes expressed in terms of an analogy with an underdeveloped economy or even with a colony which is exploited by the primary economy. Radical theories are also similar to dual market theories in drawing upon sociological analyses of the determination of workers' and employers' attitudes, preferences, and motivations.

The expositions of these theories are stronger in their criticisms of neoclassical theory than they are in advancing a coherent replacement. Criticism of classical and neoclassical theory has a long and, in many instances, a distinguished history, so casting the *D-R* writings in this mold can be complimentary. To the extent that the issues raised have appeared before (even though in different terms) and remain unresolved, the challenge is all the more compelling. On the other hand, if the issues have been satisfactorily answered before, the challenge is less compelling. In either case an historical perspective can be informative.

Space limitations prohibit this development, but mention should be made of the similarities of the dual and segmented market theories to the Mill-Cairnes theory of noncompeting groups and to several ideas of the neoinstitutionalist group of labor economists who dominated their field in the 1940's and 1950's. Of this latter group, John Dunlop had written of internal labor markets, and Clark Kerr had advanced the idea of labor market segmentation in his famous article about the 'balkanization' of labor markets.

C. *Policy Implications of the D-R Theories*

One set of policies advocated in the *D-R* literature concentrates on the labor market; another deals with the larger issues of power relationships and nonlabor market institutions in society. The first set of policies is most clearly distinguished by a focus on the demand side of the labor market. Specifically, public employment, wage subsidy, and antidiscrimination programs are stressed. Intervention on the supply side of the market, particularly the human capital investment programs of education, training, and job search assistance, is de-emphasized if not rejected.

A second set of policies advocated by the radical economists is less specific. These include prelabor market conditioning of the consciousness of people, perhaps calling for a reorganization of schools and other community institutions. They may also advocate that workers gain a more dominant role in governing their work — thereby combating alienation and partly achieving a general realignment of political power.

II. THE MODERN NEOCLASSICAL RESPONSE TO THE D-R CHALLENGES

Again, space limitations prohibit much more than a listing of comments. I have divided these into a methodological theoretical section and an empirical theoretical section.

A. *Methodological and Theoretical Issues*

The defense of neoclassical research includes the following points: (1) adherence to the view that positive economic analysis is separable from normative analysis and, in particular, a denial that neoclassical models presume a regime of harmony rather than conflict among various economic groups in society; (2) belief in the utility of building models which assume either that tastes and institutions are fixed and/or that these variables may be omitted from the model without biasing the estimated economic parameters, such as price and income effects; and (3) finally, a denial that neoclassical theories of wages and employment rest solely, as *D–R* spokesmen often claim, on the marginal productivity theory.

B. *Empirical and Theoretical Issues*

What follows is a listing of five topics which provide an arena for debate. My main message is that more empirical evidence is needed, but that the *D–R* position is generally weaker than the neoclassical position on a priori grounds.

1. Two questions arise about the *occupational structure*. Does a static snapshot reveal a duality, and if so, what metric of occupational status produces this bimodality?[1] Another question concerns occupational mobility. Over time, are workers with a definable premarket characteristic confined to one segment of the occupational spectrum? There is little evidence on this question.

2. The neoclassical theories of *discrimination* have developed along three lines; competitive models which predict a long-run disappearance of wage (or job) discrimination; noncompetitive theories, which are downplayed on grounds that monopoly and monopsony are not empirically important; and competitive-statistical models, which in my opinion place too much of a burden on informational unreliability to rationalize the extent of discrimination that we observe. In their empirical work, neoclassical economists have stressed prelabor market sources of the disadvantages for both blacks and women, thus attempting to reduce the burden of explaining market discrimination. These approaches, taken in total and despite their defects, appear more persuasive to me than the *D–R* models of exploitation, employer strategies of dividing and conquering their work force, or self-perpetuating and vicious circle theories.

3. Two points may be made in response to the *D–R* emphasis on *unemployment and job instability*. One is that if the human capital models explain individual workers' low wages, then they are in principle capable of explaining other undesirable forms of job rewards, such as instability. Second, a more direct analysis of job instability is addressed in the job search literature of neoclassical economists, which also attempts to reconcile macro and micro theories of unemployment. This effort is just beginning, however, and there are some theoretical and empirical gaps. (See James Tobin.)

4. The question that separates the *D–R* from the neoclassical views of the issue of *wage rigidities and protected labor markets* is almost entirely one of the empirical frequency, duration, and importance of these market imperfections. The neoclassical economists have, in fact, used these ideas in studying underdeveloped economies and in analyzing minimum wage laws and the effects of unions on wages and employment in the *U.S.* economy.

5. The alleged *failure of training and educational programs* raises the messy problem of evaluating the evaluations of social action programs. I question whether a simple verdict of failure or success is justified. There is, however, one technical point about the statistical estimation of human capital models which has led to a misinterpretation by the *D–R* spokesmen. The allegation that human

capital variables have small or zero effects on earnings of the lower strata of workers is often based on regression models in which the dependent variable is effectively truncated — consisting of predominantly low values. However, the regression coefficients of independent variables like years of schooling or training are clearly biased toward zero in these truncated regressions, so the pessimistic findings are partly artifactual.

III. CONCLUSION

My brief summary judgment of the *D–R* challenge is that it does not begin to offer a theory of the labor market that can replace neoclassical theory, despite our various degrees of dissatisfaction with the empirical corpus of that theory. The *D–R*'s theoretical and methodological criticisms of the neoclassical theory are not substantial and are often misguided; nevertheless, a tradition of criticism of orthodox economics is sustained and this is healthy. Neoclassical research can become terribly inbred and out of touch with policymakers or practical users of economic predictions. This danger is particularly acute because the standards for empirical verification are so weak.

The *D–R*'s theoretical contributions, which amount to modifications and additions to orthodox theory, are: (1) the ideas of the endogenous determination of attitudinal variables among workers; and (2) the institutional dimensions of internal labor markets — which enrich our understanding of the economics of bureaucratic organizations.

In the areas of empirical research and policy prescriptions, the dual and radical school represents an important voice. Although their research suffers, in my opinion, because it is not anchored to as tight and consistent a theory as neoclassical theory, this fault is compensated by their new ideas and their discovery of empirical anomalies in the orthodox paradigm.

NOTE

1. Occupational segmentation associated with sex and race groups is treated separately below under the topic of discrimination. Presumably, the segmentation of teenagers and the aged could be set aside as well, since there is no puzzle about their occupational differences compared with prime age workers.

REFERENCES

P. B. Doeringer and M. J. Piore, *Internal Labor Markets and Manpower Analysis*, Lexington, 1971.
J. Dunlop, 'The Task of Contemporary Wage Theory,' in G. W. Taylor and F. C. Pierson, eds., *New Concepts in Wage Discrimination*, New York, 1957.

D. M. Gordon, *Theories of Poverty and Underemployment*, Lexington, 1972.

C. Kerr, 'The Balkanization of Labor Markets,' in E. W. Bakke et al., *Labor Mobility and Economic Opportunity*, New York, 1954, 92–110.

L. Rogin, *The Meaning and Validity of Economic Theory*, New York, 1956.

L. C. Thurow, 'Education and Income,' *The Public Interest*, Summer 1972, 66–81. [Reading 4.2 above – Ed.]

—— and R. E. B. Lucas, 'The American Distribution of Income: A Structural Problem,' committee print, U.S. Congress, Joint Econ. Comm., Mar. 17, 1972.

J. Tobin, 'Inflation and Unemployment', *Amer. Econ. Rev.*, Mar. 1972, 62, 1–18.

5. The Macroeconomics of The Labour Market

Introductory Note

IN the early 1960s there was, at least in Britain, substantial agreement among economists concerning the macro-economics of the labour market. Unemployment, it was believed, resulted either from deficiencies in aggregate demand or from frictions and structural imbalances within individual labour markets. Involuntary or 'Keynesian' unemployment would respond to appropriate demand management policies, and since 1945 it had in fact very largely been eliminated in this way. In the absence of direct intervention in the operation of particular markets, however, 'non-demand deficient' unemployment constituted an irreducible minimum below which the total unemployment rate could not be lowered without a significant inflationary cost. There was, in fact, a fairly stable and empirically verified trade-off relationship between unemployment and wage inflation, known after its discoverer as the Phillips curve (Phillips, 1958). According to one reputable authority, if the unemployment rate were allowed to rise to about 2¼ or 2½ per cent this would give rise to an annual rate of increase in money wages of some 3 per cent. Given the trend rate of productivity growth, and constancy in the relative shares of labour and property incomes in total output (itself assumed to be a fact of economic life), such a rate of *wage* inflation would be consistent with a stable *price* level. Direct controls over wages would be unnecessary if unemployment were maintained at the appropriate level, and useless if it were not (Paish, 1964). There were those who dissented from this view. Some argued that full employment, free collective bargaining, and a stable price level were mutually inconsistent goals, only two of which could be enjoyed simultaneously. Others suggested that some form of incomes policy represented an effective anti-inflationary alternative to higher unemployment. Most of the critics, though, shared much of the theoretical framework of the majority school, from which they were separated only by shades of emphasis.

By the end of the 1970s this framework of ideas lay in ruins, and with it the post-Keynesian theoretical consensus. In part this must be counted as the inevitable product of events. By 1979 the unemployment rate in Britain was almost *three times* as great as the 'non-inflationary' level prescribed by Paish, while the rate of wage inflation (though lower than it had recently been) remained in double figures, vastly in excess of the productivity growth rate. Far from remaining constant, relative income shares had begun to oscillate wildly. Other advanced capitalist countries had undergone a similar experience. At the same time, theoretical analysis had polarized. A minority held that economic theory was in part irrelevant to the explanation of these events; that greater 'trade union pushfulness' had determined the increased rate of wage inflation, only weakly influenced by labour market conditions; and that nothing short of permanent wage controls could curb inflation. The course of relative income shares, according to this line of thought, was heavily dependent on union power and its exercise (Wiles, 1973). The opposing view led to the old conclusion, that incomes policies were ineffective and unnecessary, but by what appeared to be a quite different route. The new monetarist majority argued that wage inflation resulted from excess demand in the labour market, and thereby from excessive monetary expansion. Trade unions were merely a transmission belt for inflationary forces which were generated elsewhere, and the downward-sloping Phillips curve was a purely transitory phenomenon which offered no stable 'menu for policy choice'. In equilibrium the 'natural rate' of unemployment reflected the (voluntary) job search decisions of individuals, rather than Keynesian forces of deficient aggregate demand. The relative shares of wages and profits could be explained without reference to unions, by the traditional marginal productivity theory of distribution (Friedman, 1975).

As this controversy is an international one, it is fitting that the readings in this section have a transatlantic flavour, seasoned by the addition of an antipodean contribution. In Reading 5.1 Lloyd Ulman sets forth a rather restrained version of the minority view of wage inflation. Low unemployment encourages strike action, boosting union wage demands and weakening employer resistance to them, so that wage settlements are higher than they would be if unemployment were higher. Given (once again) productivity growth and relative shares,[1] the rate of price inflation will also be higher. A successful incomes policy blunts union aggression, stiffens employers' resolve, reduces settlements, and shifts the (otherwise stable) Phillips curve towards the origin, improving the nature of the trade-off between unemployment and inflation. Whether this argument may legitimately be described as a 'conservative' one need not concern us. Something very similar to it has exerted great influence over governments of all colours in many countries. It has proved less persuasive among economists. For one thing, its empirical status is questionable. Although the association between strike activity and unemployment is quite well established,[2] the bargaining relationship which mediated between union aggression and union success and forms the heart of quadrant II of Figure 5.1 in Reading 5.1 has not been modelled successfully — not, that is, in testable form (see Reading 3.3). A *direct* relationship between strike activity and wage inflation has been reported (Godfrey and Taylor, 1973), but the causality involved is in doubt. In most bargaining models strikes result from *mistakes*, and it is entirely plausible that an increase in strike activity means nothing more than a reaction to inflationary forces, imperfectly perceived and understood by the parties to the negotiations, which have quite different origins (Parkin, 1974).

This interpretation is suggested by the neoclassical analysis presented by

Phelps in Reading 5.2. Phelps claims to have 'found it instructive to picture the economy as a group of islands between which information flows are costly' (Reading 5.2, p. 363). Wages are set by atomistic competition rather than bilateral monopoly, but it is an ill-informed competition. Workers must row from island to island in their quest for wage information, and it is the need to spend time searching for better jobs which accounts for the existence of unemployment (which is therefore voluntary rather than Keynesian in nature).[3] *Unanticipated* inflation produces a temporary reduction in unemployment, as worker-oarsmen confuse a general increase in the wage level with an exceptionally favourable job offer specific to them, moor their boats, and go back to work. As more accurate information filters through, workers who had succumbed to such errors quit their jobs to resume search activities, and unemployment increases once more. (Where workers are unionized, strikes may *result* from conflicting views on the future course of prices and wages, but in no sense do strikes *cause* inflation.) In the long run, then, there is no trade-off between unemployment and inflation, and the long-run Phillips curve is a vertical line. This argument is derived directly from individual maximizing behaviour, and is justifiably seen by Phelps as part of the 'new microeconomics' of imperfect information. In effect there *is* no macroeconomics specific to the labour market, but only monetary theory. Phelps is thus applying to wages the Friedmanite maxim that inflation is 'always and everywhere a monetary phenomenon' (Reading 5.5, p. 387).

Turvey (Reading 5.3) is not convinced. For him inflation results from an excess of income claims over real national output, and can be stopped 'by abating claims or by depriving groups of the power to implement them' (Reading 5.3, p. 371); on both counts incomes policy may be an effective anti-inflationary device. Interestingly enough, this argument appears *not* to be necessarily inconsistent with the monetarist explanation advanced by Phelps and Friedman. 'Given that people are so stubborn about the amount they hold in the form of money' (Reading 5.5, p. 391), higher wage settlements must be financed by expansion of the money supply, or else real output will fall and unemployment increase. If trade unions' political influence is strong enough to ensure the maintenance of full employment, then 'union pushfulness' and monetary laxity complement each other, the latter being a by-product of the former (Machlup, 1960). That unions are 'so stubborn' about the income claims of their members may explain why monetary stringency in the later 1970s gave rise to greatly and permanently increased levels of unemployment, and why avowedly monetarist governments continue to act as if the long-run Phillips curve were downward-sloping.[4] On this argument, as on Turvey's, the monetarist objections to incomes policies are ill-founded, whatever the validity of the Quantity Theory. The main concern of Turvey's paper, however, is different. He asserts the necessity of price controls, along with wage restraint, as a part of any income policy. The regulation of prices has a direct effect on wage settlements, by inducing increased employer resistance to union claims. It also exerts an indirect influence by convincing workers that acceptance of wage controls will not result in a distributive shift towards property incomes.

The essential objection to price controls is simply stated. As Turvey's checklist (Reading 5.3, p. 377) makes clear, the regulation of prices must be based in large part on profit criteria. But in a capitalist economy profits constitute an essential signal, indicating the direction and scale of the shifts in resource allocation required in a changing world. State control of profits means, in effect, cutting off the 'invisible hand' at the wrist. In Reading 5.4 Whitehead grasps this nettle firmly. Price controls are both damaging and unnecessary, he suggests, while regulation of wages will not significantly impede the efficient allocation of labour. It is unnecessary to control prices, Whitehead asserts, because the relative shares of wages and profits are not influenced by the rate of change of money wages. Wage controls do not adversely affect the operation of the labour market, he believes: the structure of earnings is already remarkably rigid, and shifts in the allocation of labour between industries, regions, and occupations are instead induced by the availability of jobs. Shifts in wage differentials may be rendered difficult by the imposition of wage controls, but such shifts are neither necessary nor particularly desirable. This point of view contrasts sharply with that of Reading 5.5, where considerable concern is expressed at the inefficiency induced by 'suppressed inflation'. Friedman's case rests heavily on the alleged need for price as well as wage controls, and is noticeably weak on detailed and specific treatment of the labour market. It is likely, on the other hand, that Whitehead exaggerates the rigidity of the wage structure. Certainly it is doubtful whether wage controls would long survive without regulation of prices, if only for reasons of political feasibility.[5]

One reason for wage inflexibility is indicated by Rees in Reading 5.6. It may be deduced from the reactions of *employers* to an increase in labour demand, a question which (as Rees observes) is consistently underplayed in the expectations literature. Employers will be reluctant to raise wage levels instantaneously if significant adjustment costs are involved. But considerations of internal equity point to such costs being an important deterrent to rapid adjustments, since disturbances to the firm's internal wage structure upset morale and encourage opportunistic behaviour.[6] Wage rigidities, as Rees demonstrates, are sufficient to give a stable downward-sloping Phillips curve even in the long run. This conclusion is reinforced by his assessment of the nature of unemployment. Rees believes that Phelps and Friedman exaggerate the importance of search or 'frictional' unemployment, neglecting what he terms the 'structurally unemployed', who 'are involuntarily unemployed in the Keynesian sense — that they would prefer to take employment at slightly below the prevailing real wage rather than continue to remain unemployed' (Reading 5.6, p. 400). A rise in the demand for labour will lead to a *permanent* (rather than merely to a transient) decline in this type of unemployment, an outcome strengthened by the improvement in the average quality of the labour force which the extended access to on-the-job training brings about.

Empirical support for the concept of search unemployment comes from Maki and Spindler in Reading 5.7.[7] If job search is viewed as a human investment, its extent will depend on the returns and the costs associated with it. The costs consist largely of forgone earnings, which are offset to a greater or lesser degree by unemployment compensation and other social benefits. In 1966 there occurred a sharp increase in the ratio of benefits to earnings in Britain owing to the introduction of the Earnings Related Supplement (ERS) to unemployment compensation. This coincided with a significant upward shift in the unemployment rate relative to such indicators of demand pressure as job vacancies and capacity utilization. Maki and Spindler suggest that the higher level of unemployment was largely 'benefit-induced', that is, accounted for by the reduction in the costs of job search resulting from the introduction of ERS. One of the aims of ERS was to improve the allocation of labour by allowing the unemployed to search more intensively for jobs fully suited to their skills, and the resultant increase in the duration of unemployment would, *ceteris paribus*, also increase the unemployment rate. According to Maki and Spindler's estimates, this is precisely what happened. Note, however, their conclusion that by no means all of the growth in unemployment between 1967 and 1972 can be explained in these terms. Note also that their argument is again one-sided, giving no analysis of *dismissals* (as opposed to quits), and that subsequent and much larger increases in unemployment after 1972 are most unlikely to have been predominantly benefit-induced.

One problem with the theory of search unemployment is its apparent inconsistency with the observed structure of unemployment, and with the behaviour of the unemployed themselves. In the United States unemployment is disproportionately high among teenagers and members of ethnic minorities, who move frequently between employment and unemployment and whose erratic work histories and lack of disciplined commitment to the labour force are at odds with the characteristics expected of rational searchers for information.[8] Feldstein (1973) regards this simply as proof that 'the New Unemployment' is voluntary in nature, and should either be ignored or reduced (as Reading 5.7 implies) by cuts in unemployment benefits. The solutions proposed by Doeringer and Piore (Reading 5.8) are radically different. Basing their analysis on dual labour market theory (see Readings 4.8–4.10), Doeringer and Piore argue that job instability results from the insufficiency of 'good jobs' in the primary sector of the labour market, and the unattractiveness of the 'bad jobs' provided by the secondary sector. The remedy is to accompany a sustained increase in aggregate demand with systematic encouragement of the expansion of the primary sector at the expense of the secondary sector, together with vigorous anti-discrimination measures to ensure that the disadvantaged have fair access to primary jobs. More rather than less intervention in the labour market is called for. Growing interest in inner city problems in Britain suggests that this debate has a wider relevance, outside the United States.

We saw earlier that constancy in the relative shares of labour and property in national income featured in the analysis of incomes policy, either as an assumed empirical fact or as a policy prescription. One problem with this is the pronounced cyclical variability of relative shares. Corporate profits in particular are highly sensitive to economic fluctuations, and this can easily muddy the longer term picture (as Turvey notes in Reading 5.3, p. 372). Even in the long run, however, the case for constant shares is questionable. In Reading 5.9 Phelps Brown and Browne arrive, with evident reluctance, at a similar conclusion in their study of income distribution in four advanced capitalist countries (Britain, the United States, Germany, and Sweden) over the best part of a century. Their Table 5.4 indicates the wage–income ratio in all but Sweden to have been significantly higher in the 1950s than before 1914, and suggests that there are quite wide limits to the 'zones of stability' which constrained relative shares within each of the three periods studied.[9] A more recent study of the empirical literature for a number of countries concluded that 'labour's share shows more signs of increasing than of remaining constant in the long run. . . . The weight of the evidence clearly refutes the claim that labour's share is a constant' (King and Regan, 1976, p. 27).

Theoretical accounts of the level of (and changes in) relative income shares are very largely unconvincing. Phelps Brown and Browne propose a neoclassical theory of income distribution, which hinges on the application of the marginal productivity principle at the level of the whole economy. If there exists an aggregate production function which is homogeneous of degree one (that is, displays constant returns to scale), and if perfect competition prevails in all markets, then the exponents of the capital and labour terms of the function determine the relative shares of the two 'factors of production'. Specifically, when the production function is of the Cobb–Douglas form, then

$$Y = AL^{\alpha}K^{\beta} \qquad (1)$$

where Y is total output, L and K represent inputs of labour and capital into the entire economy, and A, α, and β are constants (with $\beta = 1 - \alpha$ if there are constant returns to scale). A little elementary calculus is sufficient to demonstrate that α and β are the income shares of labour and capital respectively.[10] Phelps Brown and Browne interpret the empirical evidence as proof that α is approximately 0.75 and β is about 0.25 in most Western countries. Now the relationship between the *share* of profits in total output and the *rate* of profit on capital employed is given by the identity

$$\frac{P}{Y} \equiv \frac{P}{K} \cdot \frac{K}{Y} \equiv r \cdot \text{ACOR} \qquad (2)$$

where P is total profits, r is the rate of profit, and ACOR stands for the average capital–output ratio. If, as Phelps Brown and Browne believe, the rate of profit is constrained at about 10 per cent by the reluctance of capitalists to invest at a rate of return lower than this figure, the capital–output ratio must settle down at around 2.5, so that the value of the total capital stock must be two-and-one-half times annual output.

These 'stylized facts' of macroeconomic life are extremely neat, but they cannot be taken as providing an empirical justification for the aggregate validity of marginal productivity theory. This is so for a number of reasons. In the first place, there are immense difficulties connected with aggregate production functions, both in theory (Harcourt, 1972) and at the econometric level (Fisher, 1971). Their use is now very largely discredited.[11] Secondly, the 'stylized facts' of Reading 5.9 can be interpreted in an entirely different way, as evidence that marginal productivity is quite irrelevant to the determination of relative shares. We can replace equation (2) by a slightly different identity:

$$\frac{P}{Y} \equiv \frac{P}{S} \cdot \frac{S}{Y}. \tag{3}$$

Here P/S is the inverse of the proportion of total profits which is saved (we assume that there is no saving out of labour incomes), and S/Y is the investment ratio, that is, the proportion of output devoted to accumulation. The share of profits, according to equation (3), is higher, the lower is the capitalists' propensity to save and the higher is the investment ratio. The more capitalists spend, the greater is their share of total output. This proposition, which is expounded in a slightly different form by Kalecki in Reading 5.10, has been termed the 'widow's cruse' theory of relative shares, after the biblical story of the widow whose jar of cooking oil was miraculously replenished each time she depleted it. Essentially Keynesian in spirit, its coherence remains a matter of dispute (see Samuelson and Modigliani, 1966 and Pasinetti, 1974).

Reading 5.10 is fascinating in the way in which Kalecki weaves together three strands of income distribution theory, all owing much to his earlier work, all inherently non-neoclassical, and all presented in a neo-Marxian three-sector framework. Of these strands one relies on the widow's cruse. The second has microeconomic roots of a sort, being derived from a consideration of firms' pricing behaviour in oligopoly. Profit margins, Kalecki argues, depend on the size of the the mark-ups applied to prime costs when prices are set, and these in turn are determined by the degree of competition in the relevant product markets. The third element in his argument brings in conditions in the labour market by allowing for the effects of collective bargaining in constraining mark-ups. Kalecki integrates this with the Keynesian strand by introducing something very similar to Bronfenbrenner's 'consumption effect' of a wage increase on aggregate demand (see Reading 3.4). If all this seems rather closer to the realities of a capitalist economy than Phelps Brown's perfectly competitive Cobb–Douglas world, it must be noted that none of the three lines of inquiry pursued by Kalecki has ever been put convincingly to the test, nor (even) is it clear how this might be done (King and Regan, 1976, chapters 5–7). Reading 5.10 does however remind us, not least in its title, that labour economics is concerned with conflict rather more than with harmony, and thus supplies a fitting note on which to end.

NOTES

1. Together these two factors determine the position of the RR curve in quadrant III of Ulman's Figure (5.1).
2. Not just for the United States: see, for Britain, Pencavel (1970) and for Australia, Bentley and Hughes (1970).
3. Attentive readers will have noticed a parallel with Stigler's analysis in Reading 1.3.
4. The 'natural rate' of unemployment is supposedly consistent with any constant rate of inflation (including zero). Unless the natural rate for Britain at the end of the 1970s was in excess of 6 per cent, the monetarist prescription should have been a reduction in unemployment, the decline coming about without any acceleration in inflation.
5. It is only fair to add that Whitehead has changed his position on this question, under the influence of the simultaneous wage explosion and profit squeeze in Australia in 1974–5.
6. Support for this argument may be found in the analyses of the internal labour market given by Doeringer and Piore (Reading 2.2) and Williamson (Reading 2.5), and in Thurow's criticism of the 'wage competition' model (Reading 4.2).
7. The taxonomy of unemployment proposed by Maki and Spindler (Reading 5.7, p. 408) is a little confusing. It is probably inadvisable to conflate frictional and structural unemployment, and there appears little justification for their treatment of 'induced' unemployment as a separate category. The substance of their argument is not affected by this criticism.
8. Similar observations regarding workers' behaviour formed an important part of the 'institutionalist' critique of neoclassical labour economics mounted in the 1950s (see, for example, Reynolds, 1951). The relevance of such evidence was denied on methodological grounds by many (for example, Rottenberg, 1956), as involving the illicit testing of 'assumptions' instead of the 'predictions' of neoclassical theory. The discussion of search unemployment in the text illustrates the vacuous nature of this methodological prescription, since a single proposition – 'Workers behave purposively and deliberately in the labour market' – may be interpreted *both* as an assumption (required to derive maximizing models of individual labour supply) *and* as a prediction (entailed by the theory of job search).
9. Periods one and two refer respectively to the pre-1914 and inter-war years; base years differ slightly for each country. Definitions of terms and sources of data are exhaustively specified in *A Century of Pay*. The 'wage–income ratio' has a rather wider usage. In general terms, it can be defined as $w/y \equiv W/Y \big/ n/N$, where W/Y is the share of wages (sometimes including salaries) in total output, and n/N is the proportion of employees in the total occupied population. The latter term has increased significantly over the last century almost everywhere, owing to the decline in peasant agriculture and in other forms of self-employment. This by itself tends to increase the size of W/Y, and the calculation of wage–income ratios is designed to correct for the distortion which would otherwise arise.
10. Applying the marginal productivity principle, in what is assumed to be a one-commodity universe, we have the wage rate

$$w = \frac{\partial Y}{\partial L} = \alpha A L^{\alpha-1} K^{\beta} = \alpha \frac{Y}{L},$$

so that the wage share in total output is $wL/Y = \alpha$. Similar reasoning shows that the profit share is equal to β.
11. Ironically Phelps Brown himself was one of the earliest critics of the employment of Cobb–Douglas production functions in this way (Phelps Brown, 1957).

REFERENCES

Bentley, P. and Hughes, B. (1970) 'Cyclical Influences on Strike Activity: the Australian record', *Australian Economic Papers*, 9, December, pp. 149–70.

Brown, E. H. Phelps (1957) 'The Meaning of the Fitted Cobb–Douglas Production Function', *Quarterly Journal of Economics*, Vol. 71, November, pp. 546-60.

Feldstein, M. (1973) 'The Economics of the New Unemployment', *The Public Interest*, 33, Fall.

Fisher, F. M. (1971) 'Aggregate Production Functions and the Explanation of Wages: a simulation experiment', *Review of Economics and Statistics*, 53, November, pp. 305-25.

Friedman, M. (1975) *Unemployment Versus Inflation?*, London, Institute of Economic Affairs.

Godfrey, L. and Taylor, J. (1973) 'Earnings Change in the United Kingdom 1954-70: excess labour supply, expected inflation and union influence', *Bulletin of the Oxford University Institute of Statistics*, 35, August, pp. 197-216.

Harcourt, G. C. (1972) *Some Cambridge Controversies in the Theory of Capital*, Cambridge University Press.

King, J. and Regan, P. (1976) *Relative Income Shares*, Basingstoke, Macmillan.

Machlup, F. (1960) 'Another View of Cost-Push and Demand-Pull Inflation', *Review of Economics and Statistics*, 42, May, pp. 125-39.

Paish, F. W. (1964) 'The Limits of Incomes Policies', in F. W. Paish and J. Hennessy (eds.), *Policy for Incomes?*, London, Institute of Economic Affairs.

Parkin, M. (1974) 'United Kingdom Inflation: the policy alternatives', *Westminster Bank Review*, May, pp. 1-15.

Pasinetti, L. L. (1974) *Growth and Income Distribution: essays in economic theory*, Cambridge University Press.

Pencavel, J. (1970) 'An investigation into Industrial Strike Activity in Britain', *Economica*, 37, August, pp. 239-56.

Phillips, A. W. (1958) 'The Relation Between Unemployment and the Rate of Change of Money Wage Rates in the United Kingdom, 1861-1957', *Economica*, 25, November, pp. 283-99.

Reynolds, L. G. (1951) *The Structure of Labor Markets*, New York, Harper.

Rottenberg, S. (1956) 'On Choice in Labor Markets', *Industrial and Labor Relations Review*, 9, January, pp. 183-99.

Samuelson, P. A. and Modigliani, F. (1966) 'The Pasinetti Paradox in Neoclassical and More General Models', *Review of Economic Studies*, 33, October, pp. 269-301.

Wiles, P. (1973) 'Cost-Inflation and Economic Theory', *Economic Journal*, 83, June, pp. 377-98.

5.1 Towards an Incomes Policy for Conservatives*

A country's effort to stabilize price and wage behavior may be viewed as a particular subset of (hopefully) compatible policy elements drawn from a wider collection of alternative and complementary policy elements. The latter may be classified with the aid of a price-wage push trade-off curve, as depicted in Figure 5.1. Just as the structuralists' Phillips curve is obtained by interposing the vacancy-unemployment relationship between the level of unemployment and the rate of change of money wages, so might a push Phillips curve be constructed utilizing an observed inverse relationship (the SS curve in Quadrant I) between the level of unemployment and strike activity (measured along the OT axis as time spent on strikes per member of the work force) — the muscle behind the push on wage costs. The latter is then related to the rate of change of money

*From Lloyd Ulman, 'Phase II in Context: towards an incomes policy for conservatives', in W. Galenson (ed.), *Incomes Policy: what can we learn from Europe?* (Ithaca: New York State School of Industrial and Labor Relations, Cornell University, 1973).

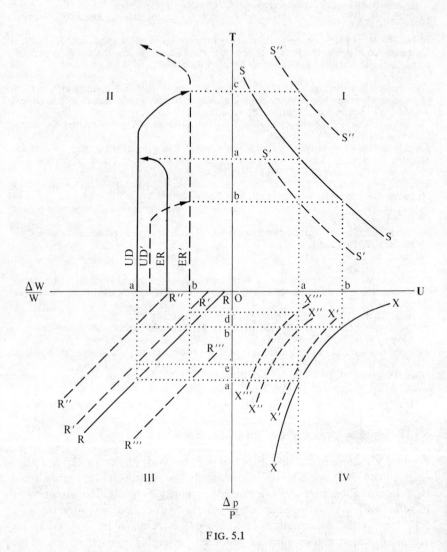

FIG. 5.1

wages by means of a family of modified Hicksian union demand (UD) and employer resistance (ER) functions. Two pairs are drawn in Quadrant II.[1] A further functional relationship between the rate of change of money wages and the rate of change in prices (the RR curve in Quadrant III) yields the full trade-off relationship, the curve XX in Quadrant IV.

Thus, the intersection of UD and ER in Quadrant II corresponds to given levels of strike activity and of unemployment and generates a given percentage increase of wages (through disputes settled on the unions' predeadlock terms)

and a given percentage increase in prices (through a given rate of increase in productivity depicted by the RR curve in Quadrant III). These levels of unemployment and strike activity and the corresponding rates of increase in money wages
and prices are all indicated by the distances Oa. At some higher level of
unemployment, Ob, increased employer resistance is depicted by ER′, reflecting
willingness to take longer strikes for lower settlements. Decreased union militancy in the face of greater employer resistance, however, depicted by UD′,
means that lower settlements (Ob) will be reached (more) on the employers'
terms and with a lower level of strike activity. Thus, a higher level of unemployment − a lower level of economic activity − results in lower rates of increase
in money wages and prices. (As one moves towards the origin along RR, the
ratio of money wage changes to associated price changes increases. Thus, at
higher levels of unemployment, money wages would rise relative to prices and
this rise in the rate of increase in real wage rates would contribute to a decline
in union militancy.)

In the short run unemployment and wages and prices may move in the same
direction for limited periods of time if the wages and prices respond more slowly
to changes in aggregate demand than does output and employment. In terms of
Figure 5.1 an example of such a loop about the presumptively stable Phillips
curve may be depicted as follows. As unemployment falls from Ob to Oa, the
levels of union militancy and/or employer resistance remain for a while at UD′
and ER′, respectively (implying a fall from SS to S′S′ in Quadrant I). As a result
the economy is moved off the long-run Phillips curve XX in the direction of
X″X″. But then if prices begin to move up ahead of wages (so that RR falls),
a movement downward from X″X″ is generated. Next, the rise in prices, together
with the cyclical increase in activity, tends to increase union militancy and to
reduce employer resistance so that wages tend to catch up with prices and to
force the latter upward (shifting R‴R‴ back to the position RR). This cost-push
phase of the inflationary process succeeds a demand-pull phase. At this stage the
authorities might intervene by deflating the economy, but once again wages and
prices lag behind employment so that all three might rise as union militancy and
employer resistance remain at levels UD and ER, appropriate to the lower rate
of unemployment. As a result wage and price increases at rate Oa are combined
with Ob unemployment, on a point to the right of XX (not shown). As UD and
ER move towards UD′ and ER′, however, the rate of wage-price inflation falls
at the higher rate of unemployment. Such short-term movements around the
presumed stable trade-off relationship frequently inspire experiments with
incomes policies. If the authorities are obliged to deflate, it would be nice if
they could eliminate movements below XX, characterized by simultaneously
rising unemployment and inflation. They would feel more confident in reflating
the economy if they could hold wage and price increases at levels hitherto
normally associated with excessively high levels of unemployment. In terms of
Figure 5.1, they wish to combine rates of inflation Ob with a rate of unemployment Oa. This implies an inward shift in the long-run Phillips curve, XX.

The trade-off curve in Quadrant IV may be shifted inwards by policies which are aimed at restraining wages directly and prices indirectly and/or by policies which are aimed at restraining prices directly and wages indirectly. The former, policies of direct wage restraint, originate in Quadrant II. They are supposed to shift the UD curve downwards by decreasing either the unions' propensity or their capacity to strike, in which case the S curve in Quadrant I is shifted inward to S'S', or they may be intended to shift the ER function increasing the employers' propensity or capacity to resist union demands, in which case the SS curve is shifted outwards to S"S". It is therefore assumed in Figure 5.1 that a combination of the low rates of wage and price increase Ob and the low rate of unemployment Oa is targeted by a policy of direct wage restraint, shifting the Phillips curve inward from XX to X"X".

The curve UD' might be taken to indicate a certain degree of effectiveness in reducing the average level of the union's propensity to push, in which case the unemployment and wage-price objectives could be reached at a level of strike activity (Ob), otherwise associated only with lower levels of economic activity. In this case SS is shifted inward to S'S'. (This, obviously, is not the only possibility. Complete success in persuading the unions to accept the Ob wage norm, while leaving their capacity to resist unimpaired, would result in shifting UD from the level Oa to Ob; in this case SS in Quadrant I would coincide with the abscissa OU.) At the other extreme if the rate of wage change is held down to Ob solely by inducing increased employer resistance, shifting ER to ER', strike activity would be raised to Oc rather than reduced, and the SS curve would be shifted out to S"S", depicting more time lost at any given level of employment.

Policies designed to restrain wages directly by lowering the unions' propensity to strike for excessive wage demands include official exhortation in the general interest, especially in the interest of the balance of payments or in the presumed interest of all sectors of the community in a reasonable degree of price stability, and incentives, such as special allowances for the lowest-paid groups and the adoption − or promised adoption − of social and economic policies favored by the trade union movement in question. Special penalty taxes levied on individual workers (for example, in the form of increased social security contributions) to recover all or part of negotiated wage increases in excess of wage increases allowable under the policy would also tend to lower the unions' propensity to strike by reducing the members' (after-tax) gains from striking. Policies designed to lower the unions' capacity to strike include the availability of legal sanctions in cases of violation of legally enforceable decisions by an administrative tribunal or by arbitrators. They might also include legislation designed to limit the behavior or alter the structure of trade unions. Policies to restrain wages by increasing the employers' propensity or capacity to resist unions could include official exhortation (for example, warning of the adverse consequences of appeasement) and the imposition of special tax increases levied on enterprises to penalize the granting of excessive wage increases.

Policies which impinge directly upon prices or upon productivity are depicted by an upward shift in the RR function in Quadrant III. An upward shift in RR connotes a rise in the wage-price ratio; the extreme (and unlikely) case, represented by a shift to R"R", would imply combining low rates of price increase (Ob) and of unemployment (Oa) with unchanged high rates of money wage increase (Oa). Policies which originate in Quadrant III, however, are designed as complements to rather than as substitutes for policies which originate in Quadrant II. Policies originating in Quadrant III include price controls, with or without subsidies, and productivity bargaining.

Direct price controls are supposed to stiffen employer resistance in order to avoid shrinkage of profit margins; they are also supposed to reduce union appetite for money-wage increases by protecting real wages. If price controls could shift UD to UD' and/or ER to ER', it would be possible to achieve a more favorable trade-off than a price change of Ob and an unemployment rate of Oa. This is depicted by the improved trade-off curve X'''X''', which is associated with a shift in RR to R'R', and permits a combination of Oa unemployment and Od price change.

If wage control is to be effective, price control may be necessary, not merely to shift RR outward but to prevent it from shifting downward (to R'''R'''). The latter could occur if discretionary price setters failed to respond to wage restraint by proportionately reducing their rates of price increase. Thus, if prices continued to rise at the rate Oa while the rate of wage increase is reduced to Ob, for example, profit margins would increase, XX would not be shifted inward, and labor's share in the distribution of income would be reduced at Oa unemployment.

If, on the other hand, effective price controls are not accompanied by equally effective wage restraint, subsidy may be required in order to maintain the unemployment target. The subsidy would be in proportion to the vertical distance between RR and, for instance, R'R'. In the latter case an unrestrained rate of wage increase Oa could be combined with a subsidized rate of price increase Oe on the trade-off curve X'X'.

In the case of productivity bargaining the upward displacement of RR would represent increased productivity due solely to union concessions (in principle), completely offsetting an associated rise in wages and thereby permitting a rise in the wage-change/price-change ratio without impairment of profit margins. To the extent that productivity bargaining contributes directly to price stability (for example, at rate of increase Oe), it should increase union acceptance of a policy of general wage restraint as well and thus make a further contribution to price stability (for example, in the amount of Oe–Od). [. . .]

NOTE

1. The Figure draws heavily on the work of Orley Ashenfelter and George Johnson ('Bargaining Theory, Trade Unions, and Industrial Strike Activity,' *American Economic*

Review, March 1969, pp. 35–49) and E. R. Livernash ('The Relation of Power to the Structure and Process of Collective Bargaining,' *Journal of Law and Economics*, October 1963, pp. 10–40, especially pp. 14–22). Ashenfelter and Johnson have contributed the inverse empirical relationship depicted by the SS curve in Quadrant I and the relationships (depicted in Quadrant II) between strike frequency and the rate of increase in the money wage rate rather than the money wage level (as in Hicks's model).

Quadrant II, on the other hand, follows the graphic approach of Hicks, utilizing the intersection of what he termed the employer's concession and union's resistance curves. This does not rule out acceptance of either an investment theory of employer strike behavior or of the *a priori* inflated expectations of the union membership, two important elements in the very valuable Ashenfelter and Johnson theory. The latter seems to assume that the firm is aware of the parameters of the union reaction curve, which the members themselves learn only from experience, and that, in consequence, the occurrence or duration of a strike is determined solely by the decision of the employer. For the present purpose the latter is not a comfortable conclusion. It does not unambiguously predict the inverse relationship between unemployment and strike activity which these authors established empirically. According to their argument the (capitalized) gains from striking vary inversely with both the magnitude of the wage increase which is minimally acceptable to the employees and the difference between that wage increase which would be acceptable to them without striking and the minimally acceptable increase. In times of increased unemployment it might be expected that both rates of increase would undergo reduction, but whether the employer's gain from taking a strike would be reduced depends on whether and to what extent the no-strike increase falls relative to the rock-bottom increase.

If the no-strike increase is sufficiently sticky relative to the product price, the gains to the employer from taking a strike could rise rather than fall in recession. Moreover, the costs associated with taking a strike could fall, for the latter include loss of market share during shutdowns (the probability of which diminishes when inventories rise relative to sales) and the costs of make-up production (which require less overtime work and less utilization of marginal plant and equipment) as well as fixed production costs. Thus, if the net present value of strike-taking does not decline while strike activity does decline, the latter would appear to reflect decreased union initiative.

This is reflected in the ER and UD functions in Quadrant II, which have been modified to conform to three observations by Livernash. The first is that 'once a strike starts, both sides become committed to the positions held prior to the strike.' Accordingly, the Hicksian smoothly downward-sloping union function and the initially rising employer function have been replaced with two curves, which are horizontal over the interval between the beginning of the strike and the immediate neighbourhood of collapse.

Livernash's second observation is that, in the case of the short strike, 'the settlement price remains at the terms set and held by the union,' while 'management frequently tends to win the long strike.' Finally, Livernash discerned both a rising trend in duration and a downward in time lost between the late 1940s and the early 1960s. Both phenomena may have also reflected the relatively high levels of unemployment rates which prevailed from the mid-fifties to the early sixties. Hence, in Quadrant II, the intersection of UD and ER represents generous settlements (on the unions' terms in this stylized version) resulting from a high incidence of strikes of short average duration during a period of low unemployment. The intersection of UD' and ER' represents lower settlements, on management's pre-strike terms, resulting from a lower incidence of strikes, possibly of longer average duration.

5.2 The New Microeconomics in Employment and Inflation Theory*
[. . .]

Labor economists have long noticed that, in a large complex economy, the labor market is beset by seriously incomplete information on the part of the worker and firm concerning current wage rates elsewhere in the economy; a certain amount of 'search unemployment' is therefore normal. [. . .] On a reasonable expectational hypothesis, the quantity of search unemployment and thus the level of employment will vary with aggregate demand through its effect on sampled money wage rates. Specifically, an increase of aggregate demand will reduce search unemployment by causing some searchers to mistake a *general* rise of money wage rates for the discovery of a high *relative* money wage offer, high enough that its acceptance is preferred to search for a higher one.

I have found it instructive to picture the economy as a group of islands between which information flows are costly. To learn the wage paid on an adjacent island, the worker must spend the day traveling to that island to sample its wage instead of spending the day at work. Imagine, only for simplicity, that total labor supply — the sum of employment and (search) unemployment — is a constant for every household, independent of real wage rates, expected real interest rates, and so on. Suppose also that labor is technically homogeneous in production functions and indifferent among the many heterogeneous jobs of producing a variety of products. Producers on each island are in pure competition in the labor market as well as in the interisland product markets. Each morning, on each island, workers 'shape up' for an auction that determines the market-clearing money wage and employment level. To start with, imagine a very stationary setup in which there is no taste change and no technical change, with constant population size.

Initially, wage rates are moving as has been expected, and it is believed that unsampled wage rates (on other islands) are equal to the sampled (own-island) one. The economy is thus in a kind of *non-Walrasian equilibrium* in which wage rates are correctly guessed. But they are never truly known as in the Walrasian world; a change of some island's wage would not be immediately learned. For simplicity of exposition, suppose that money wages have been expected to be stationary. The initial equilibrium is therefore one of steady wages and prices.

Now let aggregate demand fall. If the decline of derived demand for labor were understood to be general and uniform across islands, money wage rates (and with them prices) would fall so as to maintain employment and the real wage rate (provided that a new equilibrium exists). But suppose that workers on every island believe the fall of demand is at least partially island-specific, owing to their island's individual product mix. It is natural then to postulate that workers' expectations of money wage rates elsewhere (on other islands) will 'adapt' less than proportionally to the unforeseen fall of sampled money wage

•

*From E. S. Phelps, 'Introduction', in Phelps (ed.), *Microeconomic Foundations of Employment and Inflation Theory* (New York: Norton, 1970).

rates. To the extent that the island-specific component of the wage change is believed to be enduring enough to make a search for a better money wage rate seem worthwhile, the acceptance wage on each island will fall less than propor- tinally to product prices; some workers will refuse employment at the new (lower) market-clearing money wage rates, preferring to spend the time search- ing for a better relative money wage elsewhere. *Effective* labor supply thus shifts leftward at every real wage rate; real wage rates rise, and profit-maximizing output and employment fall. [. . .]

The faint shape of a Phillips curve relation between the steady unemployment rate and the rate of wage change appears even in the ultra-simple island model. If the government were to manipulate aggregate demand to keep the average money level constant at its new lower level, then the unemployed would be dis- appointed at finding money wage rates equally low elsewhere and would hence revise downward their expectations of the mean wage elsewhere relative to sampled wage rates; search would become less attractive and effective labor supply would shift rightward. To prevent the market-clearing employment rate from rising, therefore, the government would have to continue to reduce money wage rates by contracting aggregate demand − or by holding aggregate demand steady if the quantity of aggregate output demanded is independent of the price level. This action would be effective on the hypothesis that every unexpected decrease of sampled money wage rates produces a less-than-proportional decrease of expected money wage rates elsewhere. Some continuing decline of money wage rates (of the right magnitude) thus accompanies the maintenance of the specified volume of search unemployment.[2] The rate of decrease of money wage rates is clearly larger the greater is the shortfall of actual wage rates from expected wage rates. It is also true that the volume of search unemployment is larger the greater is this shortfall. Hence we deduce a Phillips-like relation between the steady level of unemployment and the algebraic rate of increase of money wage rates. In this relation, the expected long-run trend rate of money wage increase figures as a parameter. If workers look backward and see that money wage rates are steadily falling and adapt their expectations of the general wage trend accordingly, an ever-accelerating rate of decrease of wage rates will occur if the search unemployment level is maintained.

In the above story, every steady state of positive unemployment is one of dis- equilibrium in the sense that sampled wage rates are continually and systemati- cally different from (less than) what they were expected to be.[3] Equilibrium, in the non-Walrasian sense, denotes a state in which wage rates and other prices on average are found − over space and over time − to be what they were expected to be. Steady-state equilibrium in this sense occurs in the simplified island model only at zero unemployment. To escape this implication, it is necessary to intro- duce structural change, such as 'real' microeconomic product-demand shifts, relative-cost shifts, or population-shifts.[4] Then the islands where money wage rates are *above* the average money wage rates expected elsewhere will be numerous enough relative to the islands where wage rates are *below* expected wage rates elsewhere that the equilibrium steady unemployment rate will be positive. There will be enough job 'vacancies' — as defined by the quantity of labor that would be demanded at expected mean wage rates elsewhere minus actual employment where wage rates are 'high' — in relation to the quantity of search unemployment that equilibrium 'in the large' is possible, although individual searchers and nonsearchers may be disappointed or delighted.[5] In the model so extended, 'overemployment' is possible. It results when, starting from the equilibrium level of search unemployment, money wage rates are driven above average expected levels. Such unexpected wage rises induce some of the search unemployed to stop earlier, to accept employment at the sampled wage rates (and some employed to postpone search) — if, as hypothesized before, every unexpected wage increase produces a less-than-proportional increase of mean expected money wage rates elsewhere.[6]

Thus the island scenario suggests a wage-change equation in which the Phillips relation is one element. The rate of wage change is connected to the level of the unemployment rate, the rate of change of employment, and the expected trend rate of increase of wage rates — the latter entering the equation with a unitary coefficient. [. . .]

In the present author's paper,* the approach to the derivation of the momentary Phillips curve is somewhat similar. Start the economy in an equilibrium where the actual rate of mean wage change conforms to average expectations of the mean wage change. An increase of aggregate demand opens up more jobs; the unemployment rate declines as searchers find these openings and as firms succeed in their additional nonwage recruitment efforts [. . .]

If a steady state with a below-equilibrium level of unemployment is to be maintained, the job-vacancy rate must remain higher — otherwise, with workers harder to find, recruitment would be smaller; but recruitment cannot be smaller if unemployment is to remain lower, for at the lower unemployment rate the separation rate is at least as high, indeed the quit rate is higher. There is a negative steady-state relation, therefore, between the unemployment rate and the vacancy rate.

Although the greater willingness to hire and greater use of nonwage recruiting measures, such as help-wanted advertising, are the principal means by which aggregate unemployment is reduced, the individual firm regards its money wage rates as an important recruitment tool. When vacancies rise and unemployment falls, each firm will wish to raise its wage relative to its expectation of the general wage level over the near future, for such an increase of its relative wage wil assist it in its recruiting. But in the disequilibrium state under discussion, every firm raises its wage more than its expectation of the increase in the average wage elsewhere. Every firm must therefore come to be disappointed in the actual results from its *ex post* wage over the wage contract. Every firm will be disappointed in its recruiting performance because its relative wage turns out

[*'Money Wage Dynamics and Labor Market Equilibrium', pp. 124–66 of Phelps, ed., *The New Microeconomics.* . . . – Ed.]

to be less than intended. Firms adjust to this surprise by a further increase of money wage rates to 'catch up,' to attain the recruitment performance they had intended. Likewise, workers will have been disappointed with their relative wage over the past contract period and will demand such catch-up wage increases. The result is that there exists a steady-state constant rate of money wage increase (in excess of the expected rate of increase) corresponding to a steady unemployment rate below the equilibrium level. The rate of wage increase is shown to be greater the smaller the unemployment rate. (Of course, there may be requirements upon fiscal and monetary policy if, as money wage rates go up, the incentive upon firms to maintain employment is not to fall.)

It could be, incidentally, that the relation of the rate of change of money wage rates, on the one hand, to the vacancy and unemployment rates, on the other, is of the simple 'excess demand' form — where only the difference beween the latter two rates matters. Thus there is no conflict between 'excess demand' and the Phillips curve in theories of money wage change. The point is that vacancies jointly determine unemployment and thus excess demand and the rate of inflation — more precisely, the excess of the rate of money wage increase over the expected rate of money wage increase, all in steady states.

We have been talking about a momentary Phillips curve that corresponds to a particular expected rate of money wage increase. When the actual rate of wage increase steadily exceeds that expected rate, the steady-state unemployment rate is given by the momentary steady-state Phillips curve. When the actual rate of wage increase just equals the expected rate of wage increase, the corresponding point on the curve is, by definition, the equilibrium unemployment rate. Clearly, there can be a different equilibrium unemployment rate corresponding to every value of the expected rate of wage increase. Such an equilibrium locus will generally be steeper than the family of momentary Phillips curves; it could be negatively or positively sloped. It is argued, in the present author's paper, that, to a first approximation, the equilibrium unemployment rate is independent of the expected rate of wage increase; i.e., the equilibrium locus is vertical. The unique unemployment rate has been called the warranted rate (Phelps), the natural rate (Friedman), the normal rate (Harberger), and the full employment rate (Lerner). In that case, a fluctuationless 'anticipated inflation' would be associated with the same rate of unemployment as a fluctuationless regime of steady prices in which money wage rates are rising only as fast as productivity. Essentially, the argument for this proposition is that in a given real situation in terms of unemployment and vacancy rates, every worker will demand an additional point on his percentage wage increase, and each employer will want to pay an additional 1 percent increase in wages, for every one point addition to the expected percentage rate of money wage increase elsewhere in the economy. These formalisms take on significance if we introduce a behavioral hypothesis about the expected rate of wage increase, e.g., the adaptative-expectations hypothesis. Then the engineering of a faster growth of aggregate demand and hence a higher rate of inflation cannot achieve a lasting reduction of the unemployment rate below the natural rate — though it may bring enormous happiness in the transition. Several qualifications to all this are acknowledged and underlined in the present author's paper. [. . .]

Let us face now a question that we have so far skirted: What keeps the natural unemployment rate positive? Why is it realistic to suppose that any unemployment equilibrium tends to stay positive? It is clear we would not be able to achieve zero unemployment this year without having inflation well in excess of expectations. Everyone knows that in order to have nonpositive excess supplies in each and every submarket, it would unquestionably be necessary to have huge excess demands in some submarkets. There exist elegant static models to illustrate this. The mismatch of resources that exists this year is customarily attributed to some unevenness in shifts of demand functions and supply functions across industrial sectors and across geographical regions. The thought, presumably, is that it will take some time for workers to conclude that, this year at any rate, Nottingham is a bad scene for employment — if it has not always been that way. But it would be unlikely to find that unemployment was perennially well above average in rural areas simply because there was below-average growth in the demand for food compared to other products, above-average growth in productivity, and above-average growth of population. Such a pattern is not new in agriculture, so one presumes that the market ably 'discounts' it. The kind of unevenness that makes the natural unemployment rate positive is unsystematic, unforeseen unevenness. [. . .]

Yet uneven shifts, differential rates of change, are not entirely essential for positivity of equilibrium unemployment rates. In an imperfectly informed labor market, it seems likely that the typical new entrant into the labor force will want to look around for his best opportunity — or one better than that which first meets the eye. Only a few workers will be able to place themselves in jobs before becoming available for work. In that case, a positive birth rate by itself ensures that the natural unemployment rate is a positive number. And indeed we find that unemployment rates are greatest among the very young — those looking for their first job and probably those looking for a job preferable to their first one. [. . .] The other parameter which surely plays a role is the rate of productivity growth. It will be of some interest to touch briefly on the parameters affecting the natural unemployment rate that are easily alterable by public policy. But let us first complete the taxonomy of unemployment and corresponding models of wage dynamics.

In the models of search unemployment under discussion, the alternative to accepting a job is looking for another one. It is important to recognize another possibility: accepting leisure. The corresponding idleness might be called 'wait unemployment.' In any real-life situation, unemployment is likely to be an admixture of search and leisure (and some of the leisure may be spent in kinds of production, such as making one's own meals or making home repairs). [. . .]

The quantity of wait unemployment, like the amount of search unemployment, is not impervious to changes in aggregate demand. When an increase in aggregate demand increases the mean demand for the services of workers, most suppliers who happen to have been idle will respond to the increase in demand by accepting employment at their old standard rates. But as the unusual frequency of demands persists, suppliers will adaptively revise upward their expectations of mean demand and raise their standard wages accordingly. Hence, if employment were to be maintained at some level in excess of its equilibrium level — at the latter, the mean demand is being correctly estimated — there would be a succession of wage increases (in excess of the normal trend rate of increase that sellers believe to be appropriate to the secular growth of demand). The rate of wage increase is greater the larger the excess of employment over its equilibrium value. Thus a kind of momentary Phillips curve again emerges. [. . .]

It remains to point, with some pride, to [. . .] some concerns of public policy. Unemployment and inflation are matters of social as well as intellectual interest. On the other hand, it must be emphasized that the formulation of policy recommendations is beyond the scope of this book. In the main, the authors have been content with predictions of some of the effects of this or that government action, without offering any judgment as to the welfare basis for such a move or any estimate of its score in a cost-benefit test.

One of the policy arsenals, one that can do its bit even if it cannot alone bring total victory, is stocked with the weapons of money and taxes. In framing policy toward aggregate demand, the question inevitably arises as to whether a period of unexpected inflation and temporary overemployment would bring welfare gains in the interval. [. . .] Unemployment is productive. It would be as senselessly puritanical to wipe out unemployment as it would be to raise taxes in a deep depression. Today's unemployment is an investment in a better allocation of any given quantity of employed persons tomorrow; its opportunity cost, like that of any other investment, is present consumption. [. . .] They also serve who only stand and wait. But whether the natural rate of unemployment is 'just right' is difficult to say. The world of frictions, uncertainties, queues, and whatnot portrayed here is bound to be fraught with exernalities. Hence a small amount of overemployment, for example, might be Pareto-superior to the natural amount — neglecting the effects upon expectations of inflation and the ramifications of that for economic efficiency. The distributional consequences of a deviation from the natural rate must also be reckoned. [. . .]

NOTES

1. I assume that workers differ in age, and hence differ in their appraisal of the lifetime gain from a specified expectation of wage rate improvement, or that workers differ in the 'adaptability' of their wage expectations so that each island's effective labor-supply curve slopes upward.
2. A rigorous argument that the rate of wage decline is constant, at least asymptotically, would require more detailed specifications of the model.
3. If the expected long-run trend rate of money wage change is, say, 4 percent, a small

enough steady unemployment rate will be associated with rising money wage rates; but they will be rising at less than 4 per cent, so that the same average overestimate of wage rates elsewhere will exist and net disappointment will occur.

4. There is a lengthier discussion of the requirements *infra* in connection with the Archibald paper. [See G. C. Archibald, 'The Structure of Excess Demand for Labor', pp. 212–33 of E. S. Phelps (ed.), *The New Microeconomics in Employment and Inflation Theory*, New York, Norton, 1970: Ed.]

5. Unlike some models, in the kind of economy I have been sketching, wage rates will be high and *falling* where vacancies are defined to be present, while in sectors where wage rates are below expected wage rates elsewhere (the current loci of the unemployment), wage rates will be low and *rising*. These rates of change, I believe, need not characterize more thoroughly non-Walrasian markets where each firm is an island.

6. I should mention a weakness in the above search-unemployment model. A fall of aggregate demand may fail to produce the expectation of finding better relative money wage rates elsewhere and thus fail to increase search unemployment if workers observe that the cost of living has fallen in proportion to sampled money wage rates (or in greater porportion) insofar as they take those consumer prices to be some indication of general wage rates. (This suggests that price-level stickiness has a role to play in search unemployment.)

5.3 If We Had an Incomes Policy, Should We Have a Prices Policy Too?*

An incomes and/or prices policy would be desirable if it stopped inflation in such a way that the net effects on the distribution of income and wealth, the degree of employment of resources, and the efficiency of resource allocation, were, on balance, worth having. A non-inflationary economy with a just distribution, full employment, efficient resource allocation and no prices or incomes policy would be better still. Unfortuantely, we do not know how to secure such a happy state of affairs.

In this context the balance of payments only matters because meeting its exigencies may interfere with the things which are mentioned. In particular, if the domestic prices of foreign currencies are not free to rise when domestic inflation outpaces foreign inflation, the requirements of the balance of payments may necessitate widespread underemployment of resources. To avoid this, either exchange rates must be free to rise or domestic inflation must be prevented from outpacing foreign inflation. Hence from the point of view of allowing full employment, an exchange-rate policy necessitates an incomes and/or prices policy. The possibilities which are currently open to this country are thus:

(a) Full employment, no exchange-rate policy, optional incomes and/or prices policy;

(b) Full employment, exchange-rate policy, incomes and/or prices policy;

(c) Underemployment, exchange-rate policy, no incomes or prices policy.

If full employment were all that counted, distribution and resource allocation being of no interest, the first possibility should be chosen since it is easier than the second and better than the third.

*From R. Turvey, 'If We Had an Incomes Policy, Should We Have a Prices Policy Too?', in F. Blackaby (ed.), *An Incomes Policy for Britain: policy proposals and research needs* (London: Heinemann, 1972).

So if an incomes and/or prices policy is to be desirable it must either be because of some atavistic attachment to an exchange-rate policy or, more rationally, because of its effects on the distribution of income and wealth and on the efficiency of resource allocation. Inflation certainly does do damage in these respects. Wealth and income are redistributed to debtors from creditors; in particular it is old people who suffer. Money and prices are less useful when the standard of value is changing. So for those who do not particularly care whether or not we have an exchange-rate policy, there are two questions to be asked: what kind of an incomes and/or prices policy would stop inflation? and would its substitution for inflation worsen or improve the distribution of income and wealth and the efficiency of resource allocation?

A THEORY OF INFLATION AND ITS CURE

To answer the first question requires us to understand the cause of the present inflation. Here, I still find it illuminating to say that inflation is the process resulting from attempts to earn, buy or produce more than real national income, expenditure, or output.[1] At present it is the first of these three 'excesses' which counts, as there is currently more than enough unemployment of capacity and labour for extra output to be available in response to an increased demand for goods and for extra labour to be available if producers attempted to raise output. So our inflation is caused by a struggle between different groups to increase their shares of national income.

In the simple model of my paper, only two groups were considered. There were 'workers' who attempted to raise their real wages by pushing up money wages, and 'capitalists' who endeavoured to preserve or increase their real gross profit margins by raising prices as fast as, or even faster than their labour costs. This, like most such models of the inflationary process, was excessively simple in assuming solidarity within each of only two groups. But the fundamental idea holds just as well when there are many groups. If any group endeavours to earn more by pushing up the price of its goods or services, and if a significant number of other groups refuse to accept the resulting fall in their real earnings, seeking instead to maintain them by in turn pushing up the prices of the goods or services which they sell, then an inflationary process results. It will go on as long as there remain any groups who both regard their real earnings as inadequate and are able to push up their money earnings in an attempt to improve them.

This idea explains why we have inflation at a time of unemployment and excess capacity. Total real income could be raised by increased employment and higher capacity utilization. But this fact does not help any group to obtain a higher real income by its own actions; a trade union cannot increase the employment of its members and the firms in an industry cannot make their customers buy more. So the union can only demand higher pay and the firms can only charge higher prices if they are to do anything which is income-increasing.

A group's dissatisfaction with its real incomes can be absolute or relative. In the first case the group (either collectively or individually on the part of all its members) wants more in absolute terms, it seeks some given improvement in its standard of living. In the second case it seeks, say, to earn 10 per cent more per week than some other group. If this other group will accept only a 5 per cent differential, then leapfrogging results. Thus inflation can result either when the sum of independent demands for absolute real incomes exceeds the available total or when the pattern of related demands for relative real incomes is inconsistent. We can describe these two extreme cases as 'excess additive claims' and 'intransitive relative claims' respectively.

If all this is correct, inflation can be stopped by abating claims or by depriving groups of the power to implement them. With excess additive claims, but not with intransitive relative claims, it would also be stopped by an increase in the total real income available.

At present, more real income could be made available by reflating the economy, so we must ask whether this could be done in such a way as to meet excess additive claims and abolish or reduce the excess (it will obviously do nothing to cope with intransitive relative claims). The answer must depend upon whether there are any groups which are currently claiming more than they are getting; have the power to push up the prices of the goods or services which they provide; and could not be made to share in the increase in real income resulting from an increase in output or employment instead of pushing up these prices. The obvious beneficiaries from reflation are the unemployed, those on short time, and the recipients of profits. In fact the rise in their pre-tax incomes is the rise in total incomes less the increase in social security contributions and the decrease in unemployment and social security benefits. The rise in their post-tax incomes equals the rise in total incomes (GDP at factor cost) less the net gain of central government in respect of income tax and net social security receipts. So this net gain is the amount which can be distributed via tax cuts or increases in central government transfers to give other groups increases in real income. A ridiculously simple example will make the analysis clear. Suppose that reflation would raise GDP by £1,000 million at constant prices and that £200 million of this would accrue to central government. Then if enough of the £200 million can be distributed to meet the demands of those groups who are claiming more real income than they are getting and who are ready to push up pay and prices in order to achieve their claim, the inflation can be stopped.

Claims are not articulated in this way and many of them appear to be relative intransitive claims. Hence we can neither calculate how much the upward push on pay and prices would be checked nor assert that a complete cure is even conceivable. All the same, a well-managed once-and-for-all increase in employment and capacity utilization ought to make a big contribution towards stopping inflation. Subject to the point that all this might help, let us get back to the statement that inflation can be stopped by getting groups to abate their claims or by depriving groups of the power to implement them. An incomes policy would attempt the former and might also attempt the latter. My remit is to examine what additional contribution a prices policy might make.

ABATING INCOMES CLAIMS

One reason for having a prices policy is to make an incomes policy acceptable; it may be a necessary part of the bargain. This bargain can be explicit, or it may merely be judged necessary to secure the tacit acquiescence of people in general. In either case, the requirement that prices also be subjected to the policy stems from two sources.

The first is the desire of individual families to safeguard their own standard of living. If money income is to rise more slowly than before, it is obvious that consumer prices must do the same if one's standard of living is not suffer. Nobody will voluntarily accept an incomes policy which makes them worse off. This, of course, is justifiable; it should be possible to guarantee that nobody's standard of living will fall. A prices policy can form part of that guarantee, though the main effect might be achieved through reduction in indirect taxation.

The other source of the popular requirement that an incomes policy be complemented by a prices policy is an anti-profits attitude. Some people would resent a policy which caused or allowed increased profits while restricting their own wage or salary. Hence the price of their acquiescence in an incomes policy is a prices policy which is aimed at regulating profits. This demand is an awkward one. Fixed costs being important in many industries, an expansion of demand is likely to raise profits there more than proportionately if prices are not actually reduced. Furthermore, low profits and poor liquidity may be inhibiting capital expenditure so that there is a case in favour of a marked rise in profits.

Many of us dislike striking attitudes about the fairness or unfairness of profits. Equity to us is a matter of the income and wealth of individual families and these are affected by taxation as much as by the profit experience of large corporations. Hence we want to oppose the notion that a prices policy is necessary to secure fairness between wages and salaries on the one hand and profits on the other. Our moralizing relates to people and their circumstances not to accounting aggregates. We do want fairness, but we think of it in personal terms. Thus if a successful incomes policy led to expansion and this produced capital gains for industrial shareholders, we would want to make sure that such gains were justly and adequately taxed; we would not want to prevent industrial profits from increasing. But while I do not sympathize with the idea that a prices policy should aim to regulate aggregate profits, this need not exclude an attempt to squash particular unjustified profit-raising price increases. The primary justification of this is to help implement the guarantee that nobody would lose through the introduction of an incomes policy, but it may incidentally serve to meet popular objections to excessive profits. Furthermore, an effective competition policy will involve Monopolies Commission investigations of particular firms to see whether the *level* of their profits is too high. Here too, though the primary purpose is not in any way to stop high profits in general, it can also be described as an attack upon 'exploitative' profits.

The fairness argument is much better put in terms of dividends rather than profits. If wages and salaries are to be prevented from rising fast then, since they are another kind of income, dividends should receive the same treatment. In terms of resisting inflation, there is not much to this argument; dividends do not affect the price level in the same way that wages and salaries do. But in terms of fairness the argument seems irresistible. It may be countered that dividends ought to rise relative to wages and salaries when the economy revives because they are too low now. But this answer is itself based on a notion of fairness. Thus in either case fairness dictates one's view about how dividends should behave. And if one thinks that they would rise too fast under a successful wages and salaries policy, then a wages, salaries and dividends policy is desirable.

The trouble lies in laying down the criteria for a dividends policy. If dividends are kept down, business saving is kept up, and unless it is wasted, future profits are thereby increased. So lowering dividends now generates a pressure for higher dividends in the future which is quite unlike any relationship between the level of a wage or salary now and its level in the future. There are other difficulties. It has been possible to lay down rough and ready criteria for wages, such as that they may only rise by more than x per cent a year if there is a shortage of labour, a clear inequity or a respectable productivity agreement. It is difficult to think of any analogous criteria for dividends, and if they were simply confined to x per cent, while wage drift and the exceptions allowed average earnings to rise faster, the result might be an unfair decline in dividends relative to other incomes.

These are nasty problems and it is tempting to make loud noises about dividends without actually doing anything about them. But a policy which secures the consent of wage and salary earners by false pretences will not last very long, and we want a policy which will endure. So a dividend policy is probably necessary in order to see that justice is done while avoiding an anti-profits prices policy. The best rule I can think of is that the ratio of dividend to value-added should not be permitted to rise unless a particularly good case for an increase could be made out.

This suggestion will probably tempt the theorists into analysis of the resource-allocation effects of value-added maximization as compared with profit maximization. I had better stress therefore, that the proposal is part of a package whose ultimate aims are to stop the redistribution of real income away from those living on fixed incomes or savings, and to remove the balance of payments constraint upon running the economy at capacity. What has to be examined is thus the whole package. The gains from running the economy at full capacity without inflation are pretty large. Even quite a big price would be worth paying.

REDUCING THE POWER TO IMPLEMENT CLAIMS

Apart from the case for having a prices policy to make an incomes policy acceptable, there is the argument that a prices policy would help to make an incomes policy effective by reducing the power of groups to impose their claims for higher real incomes. Suppose, for example, the incomes policy frowned upon any pay increase which exceeded productivity, then a prices policy which frowned upon any increases in labour costs as an excuse for price increases would obviously complement and reinforce it. More generally whatever the incomes policy, a prices policy which 'disallowed' cost increases caused by pay increases not consistent with the ruling incomes policy would support that policy by giving employers an incentive to conform.

The difficulties in running a prices policy are not an absolute argument against it: what matters is whether the burden of running it would weigh more or less heavily than the consequent reduction in the burden of running the incomes policy which it supported. It is even conceivable that a really effective prices policy would make an incomes policy so easy as to be unnecessary. If no price whatsoever were allowed to rise by more than the c.i.f. value of its direct and indirect import content, to take an extreme case, any rise in labour cost per unit of output would involve an equal decrease in profit per unit of output. Employers would then have to choose between resisting pay increases in excess of productivity gains or going broke. This dilemma could be avoided while the real gains from utilizing spare capacity were being shared out, but once production reached capacity pay increases would be at the expense of profits and excessive pay increases would cause unemployment.

There are several objections to this scenario:

(a) developing scarcities would result in quality deterioration, unnecessary new products and under-the-counter transactions;
(b) wage changes would reflect only productivity changes so that occupations with low productivity growth might lose labour even when this was obviously the wrong thing to happen;
(c) alternatively, where pay rose faster than productivity, profits and perhaps employment would fall, with adverse effects upon investment.

In the short run these effects may be tolerable, so if such a policy was needed for less than a year to stop inflation permanently, it might be a good idea. But while our inflation is now beginning to feed on the expectations it generates, it is not *caused* by them. Even if a temporary prices policy succeeded in making people think that prices were not going to rise in the future, it would thus not stop the inflation. The cause of our inflation, I have argued, is that the sum of the real incomes being claimed by the inhabitants of the UK exceeds the real income that is there to be earned. A downward revision of price expectations will merely moderate claims expressed in monetary terms without removing this excess.

A short-run prices policy would thus slow inflation but not stop it, and a long-run policy is needed. But if it were sufficiently wide and firm to stop inflation all by itself, the adverse resource allocation effects and the unemployment it might cause would be intolerable. So it must complement any incomes policy, not replace it.

PRACTICAL POSSIBILITIES

In the light of the government's July measures, I now turn to examine the practical possibilities for a prices policy. One such possibility is evidently a pledge by 200 large firms to raise prices by no more than 5 per cent if real GDP expands by 4 per cent. Despite admiration for the CBI, I must point out that for Europeans, if not South Americans, 5 per cent a year is still inflation. Furthermore, the favourable effect upon profits of an increase in the degree of capacity utilization is a once-and-for-all gain. The readiness of the government to allow nationalized industries to stay within the 5 per cent ceiling amounts to a decision that one way in which government will 'give away' part of its gain from reflation is via negative indirect taxes on nationalized industries. This too is a once-and-for-all effect. The CBI initiative is thus a step in the right direction. Several further steps are needed, however, if we are to cure inflation permanently.

The opposite extreme from the CBI pledge, in terms of both the scope and status of a prices policy, would be the sort of price control system which we had during the war. In between these comes the sort of prices policy which we had a few years ago: notification of price increases on a very wide range of products; justification to, or negotiation with, government departments concerning many of them; thorough investigation by a separate agency of a very few of them. At most points in this continuum there are three categories of prices which present especial difficulties. They are market-determined prices, e.g. fresh cod; negotiated prices for once-off jobs, e.g. factory building; and prices fixed for new products.

Curiously enough, a voluntary self-operated prices policy encounters less difficulty with the last two categories than does an extremely controlled policy. A firm can very readily follow some rule in such cases, but it is nearly impossible for any outside agency to check its application. Anyone who doubts this should consider the example of a Sheffield engineering firm whose staff produce about one hundred quotations a day for actual or potential customers.

For price-competing industries, such as retailing and road haulage, there are good reasons for their omission (which is not the same as their exemption) from the scope of the prices policy. The first is that a prices policy is unnecessary because whatever it would prescribe will be secured by competition anyway. The second argument is that, except with the most extensive and draconian price control system, a prices policy is impracticable in such an industry. A multitude of firms of varying degrees of respectability, scattered across the country, is just not amenable to gentlemanly persuasion and casual inspection. But this is not to say that attempts by Trade Associations to justify and encourage general price increases should not be prohibited.

There is a third group of prices, those charged by firms who sell a large proportion of their output to a small number of powerful and well-informed buyers, where no prices policy seems necessary. Where such countervailing power exists, excessive profits ought to be rare. Such buyers as Tesco and Marks and Spencer can be relied on to tolerate no unnecessary price increases on the part of their suppliers, although this will not help the final purchaser unless the large buyers are themselves subject to competition. Perhaps there is enough competition at the retail level, combined with enough concentration in purchasing — about 62 per cent of total grocery turnover in 1969 was covered by only 300 buying points — for the case for a prices policy for food manufacturing to be somewhat weaker than for other large-firm industries.

Finally, while it may be good public relations to subject nationalized industries to the same prices policy as the private sector, it is unnecessary. Government can tell the nationalized industries how to behave.

What, then, are we left with as the appropriate field for any prices policy which falls short of wartime price control? The answer must be goods and services where a substantial part of output is provided by a few large firms; where countervailing power on the part of buyers is either not strong or itself unchecked; and where goods are not made to individual orders.

The emphasis is on products, not firms. However, once the list of candidate goods and services was settled, there are two good reasons for converting it into a list of firms. First, there is the purely administrative reason that it is firms which must be dealt with. Secondly, where a firm produces both products which are subject to a prices policy and products which are not, it is difficult or impossible to separate the costs and profits of the former.

Whether the firms voluntarily adopt a code of behaviour or are subject to some form of control, criteria will have to be promulgated as part of a prices policy. Here the CBI undertaking has the great merit of simplicity, but in the long run it will not serve, for two reasons: first, a ceiling on price increases does nothing to secure desirable price decreases; and secondly, a ceiling which is adequate to cover legitimate cost increases for all firms will be too high for some of them. Prices have a cost component and a profit component, so something must be said about both of them. Hence a code of behaviour which related to costs alone would not serve the purpose either. A requirement that price changes be limited to matching 'legitimate' cost changes implies that existing profits were acceptable. Conversely, a policy which concentrated entirely on profits would admit all cost increases as justifying price increases even if they reflected 'illegitimate' pay increases. Prices must behave so as to promise capacity-expanding investment a DCF rate of return sufficient to cover the cost of funds; penalize firms which grant 'illegitimate' pay increases; and give customers some share in the gains from increased efficiency (but not such a high share that the firm and its workers receive no reward). The first requirement and the *caveat* to the third stem from the resource-allocation function of prices. The second reflects the function of a prices policy in reinforcing an incomes policy. The third reflects its function in helping to make an incomes policy acceptable.

Under the last prices and incomes policy, the criteria sought to disallow price increases to cover cost increases which could be offset by increased efficiency, but it may be sensible to abandon this complication. If it is to be more than a pious declaration, its application demands an independent investigation of the efficiency of firms which seek to raise prices. Although I believe that NBPI work of this sort was valuable, it does involve interference which is resented by many firms and which could make them less willing to co-operate in a prices policy. Furthermore, greater efficiency is *generally* desirable, not only in firms which wish to raise their prices.

Price reductions could also be required when unit costs fall because of increased capacity utilization. It is tempting to require prices to fall when this happens, particularly if the policy is launched when capacity utilization is low. But its corollary is a rise in prices when demand falls, and the resulting anti-cyclical movement of prices does not help efficient resource allocation. In so far as stockbuilding reflects expectations about prices and availability, such price behaviour exacerbates cyclical production movements.

We are left, then, with:

(a) allowing price increases necessary to make new investment adequately remunerative where the desirability of the extra capacity can be convincingly argued;[2]

(b) allowing price increases to cover cost increases *excluding* 'illegitimate' pay increases or [cost increases] due to a decline in capacity utilization;

(c) requiring price decreases where new investment is unnecessarily remunerative;

(d) requiring price decreases when increased efficiency has reduced costs.

Clearly it is much more difficult to require price decreases than to control price increases. Increases are initiated by firms and can be observed; it is possible to require prior notification. But the search for potential price decreases demands more self-sacrifice by firms under a voluntary policy or more initiative by government under a compulsory one. The experience of the last prices and incomes policy was that it was almost impossible to spot potential price reductions. Hence if voluntary conformity is not enough, random sampling should be considered. A selection of firms would then be asked to explain why they had not reduced prices, without any presumption that they should have done so.

Even though efficiency investigations may be inadvisable, the application of the 'rules' would probably demand an element of compulsion. It is difficult to see that *all* large firms involved would *always* obey them over a long period. Even if they did, they would have to be seen to do so, so that investigation would be necessary to certify good behaviour and, in some cases, it might also be necessary to ensure good behaviour. Investigation would probably be best performed by an independent body for several reasons. Government departments can find that such a role interferes with the relationships they have developed with their client industries. An independent body could be headed by people known to be capable of understanding business problems, and such a body could recruit to its staff people who were not civil servants as well as having on secondment people who were. There could be an appeal to the government against such a body's decisions, and if it stuck to a well-defined task it would not be blamed for silly things done by government. It could use publicity to attack price increases better than a government department.

CONCLUSIONS

If we had an incomes policy, it should include a policy for dividends and we should have a prices policy too. This should neither be like wartime price control nor merely a temporary freeze; instead it should be an attempt to implement the 'rules' set out on page 377. Compulsion would probably be necessary and an independent agency would be preferable.

NOTES

1. See also R. Turvey, 'Some aspects of the theory of inflation in a closed economy', *Economic Journal*, vol. 61, September 1951, pp. 531–43.
2. The vagueness and difficulties of this are discussed at length in R. Turvey, 'Rates of return, pricing and the public interest', *Economic Journal*, vol. 81, September 1971, pp. 489–501.

5.4 Wages Policy and the Market Mechanism*

[. . .] Price controls would be a cumbersome and inefficient method of controlling cost inflation. Although a wages policy is not usually referred to as 'wage control' its object is to secure the complete or partial control of wages. Economists who favour a wages policy seldom recommend that the government directly controls wages but this is because they deem it undesirable or unacceptable to vest such general power in the government. Nevertheless what is being sought is control of wages in the public interest, albeit indirect control. It is therefore necessary to show why wage controls are superior to price controls. Clearly this superior attraction of wage controls must depend on a distinction beween the function of the price system in the market for goods and the market for labour.

*From D. W. Whitehead, *Stagflation and Wages Policy in Australia* (Camberwell, Victoria: Longman, 1973).

The efficient functioning of the market for goods depends on a considerable flexibility of relative prices. Movements in relative prices reflect changes in the pattern of demand and — more important — changes in relative costs. The movements in relative prices influence relative profits and thereby direct resources in response to consumer demands; at the same time they help to encourage the purchase of those commodities whose costs of production have fallen. Large movements in relative prices still occur during cost inflation: the relative changes occurring by different rates of increase in the prices of various commodities rather than by some prices rising and some falling. The rationale of wage control is that the market does not require a similar flexibility of relative wages. This view has two aspects. The first and most important depends on the interpretation of empirical studies of relative wages. These studies seem to show that in contemporary Western economies relative wages are inflexible and that this inflexibility has proved compatible with considerable structural changes within each economy. The second depends on arguments for believing that the relative wage structure should not change at all rapidly. These normative arguments obviously rest on a particular set of value judgments about the desirable function of wages. If the view can be sustained that relative wages are not, and perhaps should not be, flexible this clearly has important implications for the possibility of a wages policy. The practicability of comprehensive price controls founders on the need to supervise and adjust each individual price. In contrast a wages policy is able to be confined to influencing the general movement of wages without being much concerned with the elaborate machinery required to regulate particular wage rates.

The most comprehensive investigation of changes in relative wages and the functioning of the labour market was undertaken by an OECD 'expert group' and published — in three volumes — in 1965. The working party consisted of nine distinguished economists from nine countries and it both conducted its own enquiry and surveyed the existing literature. The study covered ten countries for periods up to fifteen years. The major conclusions are worth quoting at length.

In general, however, it is our main finding that there is no evidence of a strong systematic statistical relationship between changes in earnings among individual industries and variations in relative employment. This finding applies equally to the shorter and longer term relationships studied and to periods when unemployment was relatively low and/or falling, although it may be that there is some tendency for a higher relationship to be observed as countries move from periods of higher to lower unemployment. Moreover, in most instances where the data provide evidence of a statistically significant relationship, it is clear that the explanatory role of relative wages is overshadowed by the influence of other factors.

The most obvious interpretation of these findings is that changes in wages have not in practice played an important role in the allocation of labour between different employments. On this view, the movement of labour has been preponderantly wage-insensitive. Opposed to this is our everyday knowledge of employers sometimes raising wages to attract or retain labour, and the widely accepted view that changes in relative pay have an important and sometimes indispensable part to play in drawing labour towards expanding employments and diverting it from others. Neither view is uniquely imposed by our findings. The first view is evidently consistent with them. But so also is the second, because the same findings might be held to show that the wage mechanism is so sensitive and powerful that only slight and temporary variantions are required to effect substantial re-allocation of labour.

We have therefore tried to discriminate between the two views by considering our findings in conjunction with additional evidence. This has led us to believe that, with some important exceptions, it is the wage-insensitive explanation that applies, for the additional evidence strongly suggests that (i) the observed changes in the allocation of labour are often brought about by mechanisms other than changes in the wage structure, and (ii) the observed changes in the wage structure are often brought about by forces other than those that allocate labour.[1]

The Working Party's first report on *Policies for Price Stability*, OECD, Paris, 1963, notes that exceptions to the general guideline that earnings should rise in line with the national trend rate of productivity growth might be called for 'on the grounds that charges in relative wages have a function in re-allocating labour between different industries and occupations,' (paragraph 33). *The evidence in the Expert Group's report that labour deployment has on the whole been rather insensitive to changes in relative wages suggests that it would be easy to exaggerate the need for exceptions on these grounds.*[2]

A recent large-scale study by H. A. Turner and D. A. S. Jackson[3] points in the same direction. This examined the disaggregated data for 23 developed countries between 1956–65. It showed correlations in excess of 90 per cent for most developed economies between the relative earnings position of industries — not simply the rank order coefficient — in 1956 and 1965. Examples are U.S.A. 98 per cent, Canada 99 per cent, U.K. 95 per cent and France 97 per cent. In general, those countries operating some species of incomes policy were more likely to change relativities than the decentralized bargaining economies.[4]

It would seem that there are four major reasons for these empirical findings of the small role played by the variation in wage relativities in the allocation of labour and their apparent contradiction of the statements frequently made by firms that 'during the year wages had to be raised to attract or retain labour'. The background against which these explanations will be offered is that of a typical economy in which the general level of earnings is rising faster than productivity but in which profit margins are preserved intact by raising prices. The change in relativities therefore requires that in a particular firm or industry wages would have to rise faster than the general level of wages.

1 As Hancock suggests[5] if such a rise in relative wages were at the expense of profits it would be an extremely expensive way of attracting marginal workers. Thus a desire to attract an additional 10 per cent of workers by a rise in relative wages of 5 per cent (which would have to be paid to all workers) would only be justified if the extra workers are worth 55 per cent more than the previous going wage. It can be objected that the extra wages

can be paid for by raising prices but this is only profitable if prices were formerly set irrationally low and even then should still be weighed against the possibility of raising prices without expanding output. Consequently the attempt to attract labour would only be justified by a situation of sharply increasing returns or perhaps by the need to expand in order to shut out new entrants.

2 It is suggested in the OECD report that other mechanisms for allocating labour are usually adequate. Even where the labour force as a whole is not growing there will still be new entrants coming on to the labour market to match those who are retiring. The new entrants and also existing members of the work force will be attracted to expanding sectors because this is where the job opportunities exist (assuming no general excess demand for labour). They will be particularly attracted to the new sectors because it is here that the opportunities for promotion will be greatest. There is also scope for paying disguised higher wages by recruiting younger and less qualified workers. If this is carried too far it can lead to discontent among existing workers and pressure on their part for higher wages. However, in many circumstances employers can avert these difficulties by such devices as the creation of new categories of labour, making 'temporary' appointments and the like. Although such upgrading could undermine a wages policy if used on a large scale its moderate use by expanding industries is probably an acceptable lubricant.

3 On examination the statements attributed to firms concerning the need to raise wages in order to attract and retain workers usually mean that wages had to be raised at the same rate as elsewhere rather than at a higher rate: precisely the movement in each firm's wages that would occur as part of a general cost inflation. Some cases of 'new entrants' paying higher wages undoubtedly exist. However, in at least some cases the higher wages may be explained by factors which place them in a different category from normal differentials and reflect the inadequacy of classification of the work force. These include cases in which higher pay is made for work outside established urban areas and where differences in money wages do little more than compensate for differences in cost of living and social amenities. Also there are cases where for various reasons the new entrant is prepared to pay more for faster, more continuous and strike free work; these again are differences in money wages rather than real wages. Such cases could probably be accommodated within a wages policy.

4 In some cases an attempt may be made by employers to signal a shortage of labour by means of what is expected to be a rise in relative wages but the pressure for stable relativities from the Union side may be too difficult to break. In this case the original upward movement in wages will be matched elsewhere. What is usually called 'secondary drift' will emerge. This is, of course, a major part of the cost-inflation mechanism and the original upward movement in wages may be caused in any number of ways unconnected with

labour shortages, (e.g. by the interaction of 'time' and 'piece' rates, militant bargaining, and abnormal profits). Secondary drift spreads the original impetus towards higher wages to the economy as a whole as efforts are made to maintain relativities. Our snapshot statistical pictures record a mixture of primary and secondary drift which prevents correlations emerging – except by chance in particular periods. The occurrence of rapid secondary drift also prevents the relative wage mechanism playing an important allocative role. Earnings data is murky because of the presence of real and spurious overtime payments, real and spurious incentive and production payments, payments in kind, regional differences in the cost of living and social amenities, problems of worker classification and changes in the composition of the groups that are being compared. The explanatory variables are frequently even more murky. In studies that attempt to relate changes in relativities to changes in the relative demand for different groups there is no satisfactory measure of demand. Studies use the rate of growth of the work force – i.e. a demand *and* supply determined value – as a proxy for 'the need to attract labour'.

However, while acknowledging these difficulties in the way of investigation, the findings of empirical studies suggest that the most reasonable position to hold is that – in general – there is a small or zero association between relative wage changes and the allocation of labour. And, further, that this small association occurs because changes in wage relativities are unnecessary to allocate labour to most fast growing sectors.

The second ground for believing that a wages policy tribunal should not be concerned with frequent revisions of the wage structure does not depend on empirical evidence. Instead it flows from certain rather general views about the function of wages and the general relationship of the worker to society. This belief that relative wages ought in general to remain rather inflexible in no way precludes the possibility of moving to a more – or less – equal distribution of income. It does, however, reflect the belief that a wider approach through fiscal policy should be taken to questions of the distribution of income than can be achieved by tinkering with relative wages. Some qualifications to the desirability of preserving relativities are, however, noted below. In addition there would also be a need to review the general relationship of skilled and unskilled wages. Quite large changes in this relationship have taken place in the past but they have taken place at infrequent intervals. It seems clear that infrequent broad adjustments of this kind could be undertaken within the framework of a wages policy together with a review of such matters as male/female relativities.

The rather general equity grounds for preserving the contours of the earnings structure can be briefly stated. They are in an important sense an extension of the notion of job security provided by a full employment policy. At root the view depends on a contrast between the function of wages and profits in the market mechanism. In order to preserve economic efficiency relative profits need to fluctuate. This is part of the risk-taking function of the entrepreneur for which if he is successful he should be rewarded and if unsuccessful penalised.

On the other hand, the wage earner does not expect to share in the losses of un-succesful enterprises (and should not — save as a consumer — expect to share in their profits however large). He enters what is usually a life-time contract with society for a particular position in the earnings hierarchy. If his job disappears society should provide adequate compensation for him by retraining him on full pay for a comparable occupation. The cases where his relative earnings should change seem to fall into three main classes. The first is where the nature of the work has substantially changed: this may be because of changes in skill, respons-ibility, unpleasantness, risk or location. The second is where for reasons usually connected with weak bargaining a particular occupation seems substantially undervalued. Or, if earnings within an occupation fall under the general floor wage below which no one in the community should be expected to work. In both cases the institutions operating a wages policy should contain provisions for review.

The third case intermeshes with the earlier discussion of the role of a wages policy under conditions of sector excess demand and requires rather more dis-cussion. Let us imagine that the demand for the services of a particular occupa-tion increases sharply and that the supply curve is inelastic. What should occur?[6] In this case it seems likely that the unimpeded market mechanism *would* provide an increase in relative wages. Our standard analysis tells us that this would have two effects. First, to ration the scarce labour by making it more expensive and second to stimulate an increase in its supply. However, the increase in wages provided by the market mechanism would be likely to be excessive on three grounds:

(i) it would raise false expectations about the long-term worth of this type of labour

(ii) for this reason it would tend to generate an excess supply

(iii) an excessive rise in this sector might stimulate wage increases elsewhere.

Consequently a wages policy tribunal should approach such a situation in two ways. The increase in wages that it should recommend would be based on an estimate of the long-term elasticity of supply. However, in addition, it should move directly to stimulate supply by recommending the use of funds to increase the number training for the scarce occupation (e.g. the use of training bursaries etc.). In the short run it should act as a control on wages although no doubt practices such as up-grading would be used. Therefore in this case the critics would be correct in believing wages policy would preserve a disequilibrium situa-tion. The reason it would do so, however, is that in this situation the free market solution can be seen to be far from optimal.

One concern about the effect of a wages policy has been that it would distort and ossify the market mechanism. It was argued [above] that this fear is gound-less.[7] Even greater concern has been expressed about another possible effect of a wages policy. This is that wage restraint would change the distribution of income in favour of profits. The evidence for this prediction will be examined below. [. . .] Any sustained variations in the share of wages and profits would discredit a wages policy. The case that will be argued in the rest of this section is that 'constancy of shares' is irrelevant to the acceptance or non-acceptance of a wages policy *because in a closed economy the available evidence points to the conclusion that the relative shares of profits and wages are not influenced by the rate of growth of money wages.*

This is the conclusion of E. H. Phelps Brown in *Pay and Profits*[8] where he reflected upon and generalized the findings of the major study that he undertook (together with M. H. Browne) of the experience of France, Germany, Sweden, the U.K., and the U.S.A. between 1860–1960.[9] He cites, for example, the French experience in 1936–37 which is especially significant because it occurred at a time of heavy unemployment.

It is said that you cannot experiment in economics, but the Popular Front government of Leon Blum came near doing that in 1936–37, when within nine months of its return to office its own measures, and those of the trade unions it encouraged, raised the cost to the employer of an hour's work in French industry by some 60 per cent. The impact was great, but not greater than the power of French firms to absorb it, for before long the prices of industrial products had also risen by some 60 per cent and profit margins were restored.[10]

These findings are paralleled on a small scale using Australian data in a study that the present writer made (together with Malcolm Cockburn).[11] We found there was no relationship between the movement of money wages and fluctuations in the ratio of Company Income to Total Wages and Salaries. This was in spite of the extremely large variations in the annual change of minimum awards and average earnings. The largest three annual increases in minimum awards during the period were 22.6 per cent, 16.7 per cent, and 12.7 per cent, while the three smallest were 1.9 per cent, 2.0 per cent, and 2.2 per cent. Our finding was that the major causes of fluctuations in the ratio of Company Income to Total Wages and Salaries were changes in the level of activity as measured by changes in factory production and to a smaller degree changes in the value of imports. [. . .]

In brief therefore the drift occurred because of a quickening of the pace of economic advance in Australia between 1964 and 1971. This was marked by sustained high activity, an acceleration in the growth of the work force and a rise in the proportion of G.N.P. invested: all interrelated factors conducive to an increase in the ratio of profits to wages. Given these factors there seems no reason to look to the variations in the rate of growth of money wages as a causal factor. There will be inevitably be periods in which coincidental changes occur and this was one of them.

As far as this aspect of a wages policy is concerned it is sufficient to show that *in aggregate* the ratio of wages to profits is not influenced by the rate of change of money wages. The sectoral pattern of changing ratios that produces this constancy is not particularly relevant. Nevertheless it may be worthwhile to fill out the picture by commenting on the argument that 'a reduction in the growth of money wages will tend to produce a drift to profits because prices are sticky downwards'. This argument harks back to the kinked demand curve models of Hall and Hitch in the U.K. and Sweezy in the U.S.A. and seems to have more relevance to the analysis of price behaviour in the face of downward movements in demand rather than reductions in average cost. *Prima facie* it is likely that some price reduction takes place because overall profit-wage constancy is maintained in spite of the much wider spread of the rate of productivity change than dispersion of earnings. The existence of a close association between changes in relative prices and relative rates of growth of labour productivity was shown in the study of 28 U.K. industries over the period 1924–50 by W. E. G. Salter.[12] Similar results — including many examples of apparent price reductions — were obtained in an examination that the present writer made of 39 Australian Manufacturing Industries for the period 1953–54 to 1957–58.[13] One does not, of course, expect to find perfect correlation between the movement of relative prices and relative productivity growth, because rapid productivity growth industries are usually high investment industries. The pattern that emerges is much as one would expect: in the industries with rapid productivity growth relative prices fall somewhat more slowly than labour costs and in the slowly growing industries relative prices rise somewhat more slowly than labour costs: the one counterbalances the other with the pattern in itself seeming to have no particular relevance to the general level of prices. Both the Salter study and the Australian study use calculated 'average values' rather than quoted prices. However, another — neglected — English study by W. A. H. Godley and C. Gillion 'Pricing Behaviour in Manufacturing Industries'[14] used actual price quotations to show that outside engineering (which seems a special case) there is ample evidence in Britain of manufacturers reducing prices. Certanly there seems little reason why they should raise their profit margins because of industry-wide productivity growth as long as the degree of actual and potential competition does not change.[15] The alternative of paying higher relative wages does not seem to occur given the constancy of relative wages discussed above.

The foregoing argument suggests that a wages policy would operate without a drift to profits even unaccompanied by a more general incomes policy. This does not rule out the possibility that it may be a pre-condition of Union acceptance that a wages policy forms part of a general incomes policy. For this reason it may be important to try to devise a policy for profits. This is a difficult task because the efficient functioning of a capitalist system obviously depends on a wide variability of *relative* profits. So far we have limited ourselves to the economics of a wages policy and to refuting the objection that within a closed economy its operation would reduce labour's share relative to that of profits. [. . .]

NOTES

1. O.E.C.D., *Wages and Labour Mobility*, 1965, pp. 16–17.
2. Ibid., foreword by P. de Wolff, Chairman of the Group, p. 9.
3. 'On the Stability of Wage Differences and Productivity-based Wages Policies: An International Analysis', *British Journal of Industrial Relations*, April 1969.
4. In Australia the best study is by Hancock, 'Earnings Drift in Australia', *Journal of Industrial Relations*, July 1966, who found that there was some simple correlation between the growth of employment and relative earnings drift but that most of the explanatory power of this variable was absorbed when the growth of value added was included as an additional variable. Since Hancock presents correlations for more than one period it is possible to compare the value of his correlation coefficients. In the period 1948–49 to 1953–54 during which minimum awards were growing at over 12½ per cent *per annum*, the value of R^2 in the correlation of relative earnings drift with relative employment growth by industries was only 0.02. For the period 1953–54 to 1959–60 when minimum awards grew at only 3.3 per cent per annum the R^2 rose to 0.35. *Prima facie* this indicates that allocative forces may have been a stronger influence on drift in the period of wage restraint. However, the most plausible interpretation seems to be that in the first period minimum rates rose so rapidly that they significantly disturbed earnings relativities by devaluing overwards. Earnings drift, therefore, was brought about by an attempt to restore these relativities. We cannot tell whether changes in relative earnings were more or less responsive to the labour market in the first or second periods from this analysis of drift.
5. Ibid., p. 133.
6. The subsequent discussion has been strongly influenced by the analysis provided by J. R. Hicks, *Essays in World Economics*, Oxford, 1959, Supplementary Note A, pp. 247–50.
7. [See pp. 379–82 – Ed.]
8. Manchester University Press, 1968.
9. E. H. Phelps Brown and Margaret H. Browne, *A Century of Pay*, Macmillan, 1968.
10. *Pay and Profits*, op. cit., p. 17.
11. Whitehead, D. H. and Cockburn, M., 'Shares of National Income: Some Neglected Implications,' *Journal of Industrial Relations*, October 1963.
12. W. E. G. Salter, *Productivity and Technical Change*, Cambridge, 1960.
13. D. H. Whitehead, 'Price-cutting and Wages Policy', *Economic Record*, June 1963.
14. *National Institute Economic Review*, No. 33, August 1965. The article was first brought to my attention by my colleague, Professor F. Davidson.
15. In certain circumstances productivity growth may itself reduce the degree of competition. This will occur where the productivity growth is based on technical change which can be kept secret, patented or which raises the minimum profitable level of operation. It is assumed here that most technical change can be copied and that the 'scale of operations' effect is not biased towards a substantial increase in economies of scale.

5.5 What Price Guideposts?*

The student of inflation is tempted to rejoin, 'I've heard that one before,' to exhortations now emanating from Washington. Since the time of Diocletian, and very probably long before, the sovereign has repeatedly responded to generally rising prices in precisely the same way: by berating the 'profiteers,' calling on private persons to show social responsibility by holding down the prices at which they sell their products or their services, and trying, through legal prohibitions

*From Milton Friedman, 'What Price Guideposts?', in G. P. Schultz and R. Z. Aliber (eds.), *Guidelines, Informal Controls and the Market Place* (Chicago: Chicago University Press, 1966).

or other devices, to prevent individual prices from rising.[1] The result of such measures has always been the same: complete failure. Inflation has been stopped when and only when the quantity of money has been kept from rising too fast, and that cure has been effective whether or not the other measures were taken.

The first section of this paper explains why the attempts to hold down individual wages and prices have failed to stop inflation. Direct control of prices and wages does not eliminate inflationary pressure. It simply shifts the pressure elsewhere and suppresses some of its manifestations.

Inflation is always and everywhere a monetary phenomenon, resulting from and accompanied by a rise in the quantity of money relative to output. This generalization is not an arithmetical proposition or a truism, and it does not require a rigid relation between the rates of rise in prices and in the quantity of money. The precise rate at which prices rise for a given rate of rise in the quantity of money depends on such factors as past price behavior, current changes in the structure of labor and product markets, and fiscal policy. The monetary character of inflation, as the second section points out, is an empirical generalization backed by a wide range of evidence which suggests that substantial changes in the demand for money seldom occur except as a reaction to a sequence of events set in train by changes in the quantity of money. It follows that the only effective way to stop inflation is to restrain the rate of growth of the quantity of money.[2]

Given inflationary pressure, rises in recorded or quoted prices and wages can be suppressed to some extent. The less severe the inflationary pressure, and the more vigorous and effective the enforcement of price controls, the greater the extent to which the manifestations of inflation can be suppressed. As the third section points out, such suppressed inflation is far more harmful, both to efficiency and freedom, than open inflation, and the more effective the suppression, the greater the harm. It is highly desirable to avoid inflation but if, for whatever reason, that is not feasible, it is far better that inflation be open than that it be suppressed.

The final section of the paper asks what harm, if any, will be done by the guideposts. Even granted that compulsory price and wage controls cannot stop inflation and can do great harm, may not some measure of voluntary compliance by businessmen and union leaders ease the tasks of other instruments of policy and enable businessmen and union leaders to display their sense of social responsibility? In my opinion, the answer is clearly in the negative. Compliance with the guideposts is harmful because it encourages delay in taking effective measures to stem inflation, distorts production and distribution, and encourages restrictions on personal freedom.

Entirely aside from their strictly economic effects, guidelines threaten the consensus of shared values that is the moral basis of a free society. Compliance with them is urged in the name of social responsibility; yet, those who comply hurt both themselves and the community. Morally questionable behavior – the evading of requests from the highest officials, let alone the violation of legally imposed price and wage controls — is both privately and socially beneficial. That way lies disrespect for the law on the part of the public and pressure to use extra-legal powers on the part of officials. The price of guideposts is far too high for the return, which, at most, is the appearance of doing something about a real problem.

I. WHY DIRECT CONTROL OF PRICES AND WAGES DOES NOT ELIMINATE INFLATIONARY PRESSURE

An analogy is often drawn between direct control of wages and prices as a reaction to inflation and the breaking of a thermometer as a reaction to, say, an overheated room. This analogy has an element of validity. Prices are partly like thermometers in that they register heat but do not produce it; in both cases, preventing a measuring instrument from recording what is occurring does not prevent the occurrence. But the analogy is also misleading. Breaking the thermometer need have no further effect on the phenomenon being recorded; it simply adds to our ignorance. Controlling prices, insofar as it is successful, has very important effects. Prices are not only measuring instruments, they also play a vital role in the economic process itself.

A much closer analogy is a steam-heating furnace running full blast. Controlling the heat in one room by closing the radiators in that room simply makes other rooms still more overheated. Closing all radiators lets the pressure build up in the boiler and increases the danger that it will explode. Closing or opening individual radiators is a good way to adjust the relative amount of heat in different rooms; it is not a good way to correct for overfueling the furnace. Similarly, changes in individual prices are a good way to adjust to changes in the supply or demand of individual products; preventing individual prices from rising is not a good way to correct for a general tendency of prices to rise.

Suppose that there is such a general tendency, and suppose that some specific price (or set of prices), say, the price of steel, is prevented from rising. Holding down the price of steel does not make more steel available; on the contrary, given that other prices and costs are rising, it reduces the amount that producers can afford to spend in producing steel and is therefore likely to reduce the amount available from current production. Holding down the price of steel does not discourage buyers; on the contrary, it encourages consumption. If the suppressed price is effectively enforced and not evaded by any of the many channels that are available to ingenious sellers and buyers some potential buyers of steel must be frustrated — there is a rationing problem. Chance, favoritism, or bribery will have to decide which buyers succeed in getting the steel. Those who succeed pay less than they are willing to pay. They, instead of the steel producers, have the remainder to spend elsewhere. Those who fail will try to substitute other metals or products and so will divert their demand elsewhere; the excess pressure is shifted, not eliminated.

The situation is precisely the same on the labor market. If wages are tending to rise, suppressing a specific wage rise will mean that fewer workers are available for that type of employment and more are demanded. Again rationing is necessary. The workers employed have less income to spend, but this is just balanced by their employers having larger incomes. And the unsatisfied excess demand for labor is diverted to other workers.

But, it will be said, I have begged the question by *starting* with a general tendency for prices to rise. Can it not be that this general tendency is itself produced by rises in a limited number of prices and wages which in turn produce sympathetic rises in other prices and wages? In such a case, may not preventing the initial price and wage rises nip a wage-price or price-price spiral in the bud?

Despite its popularity, this cost-push theory of inflation has very limited applicability. Unless the cost-push produces a monetary expansion that would otherwise not have occurred, its effect will be limited to at most a temporary general price rise, accompanied by unemployment, and followed by a tendency toward declining prices elsewhere.

Suppose, for example, a strong (or stronger) cartel were formed in steel, and that it decided to raise the price well above the level that otherwise would have prevailed. The price rise would reduce the amount of steel people want to buy. Potential purchasers of steel would shift to substitute products, and no doubt the prices of such substitutes would tend to rise in sympathy. But there is now another effect. Steel producers would hire fewer workers and other resources. These would seek employment elsewhere, tending to drive down wages and prices in other industries. True, wages and prices might be sticky and decline only slowly, but that would only delay the downward adjustments and only at the expense of unemployment.[3]

A textbook example is provided by John L. Lewis and the United Mine Workers. Coal mining hourly earnings rose by '163 per cent from 1945 to 1960. Bituminous coal mining employment dropped from 284,000 to 168,000. By way of comparison, in the same period, manufacturing production hourly earnings rose . . . 122 per cent and manufacturing employment rose.'[4] High coal prices undoubtedly put upward pressure on the prices of oil and gas; but the high unemployment put downward pressure on other prices.

The only example I know of in United States history when such a cost-push was important even temporarily for any substantial part of the economy was from 1933 to 1937, when the NIRA, AAA, Wagner Labor Act, and associated growth of union strength unquestionably led to *increasing* market power of both inustry and labor and thereby produced upward pressure on a wide range of wages and prices. This cost-push did not account for the concomitant rapid growth in nominal income at the average rate of 14 per cent a year from 1933 to 1937. That reflected rather a rise in the quantity of money at the rate of 11 per cent a year. And the wage and cost-push had nothing to do with the rapid rise in the quantity of money. That reflected rather the flood of gold, initiated by the change in the United States price of gold in 1933 and 1934 and sustained by the reaction to Hitler's assumption of power in Germany.

The cost-push does explain why so large a part of the growth in nominal income was absorbed by prices. Despite unprecedented levels of unemployed resources, wholesale prices rose nearly 50 per cent from 1933 to 1937, and the cost of living rose by 13 per cent. Similarly, the wage cost-push helps to explain why unemployment was still so high in 1937, when monetary restriction was followed by another severe contraction. [. . .]

II. INFLATION IS A MONETARY PHENOMENON

Yet, the central fact is that inflation is always and everywhere a monetary phenomenon.[5] Historically, substantial changes in prices have always occurred together with substantial changes in the quantity of money relative to output. I know of no exception to this generalization, no occasion in the United States or elsewhere when prices have risen substantially without a substantial rise in the quantity of money relative to output or when the quantity of money has risen substantially relative to output without a substantial rise in prices. And there are numerous confirming examples. Indeed, I doubt that there is any other empirical generalization in economics for which there is as much organized evidence covering so wide a range of space and time. [. . .]

The fact that inflation results from changes in the quantity of money relative to output does not mean that there is a precise, rigid, mechanical relationship between the quantity of money and prices, which is why the weasel-word 'substantial' was sprinkled in my initial statement of the proposition. First, over short periods, the rate of change in the quantity of money can differ and sometimes by appreciable amounts from the rate of change in nominal income or prices because of other factors, including fiscal policy. Second, and more important, changes in the quantity of money do not make their effects felt immediately. It may be six months or a year or a year and a half before a change in the quantity of money appreciably affects nominal income or prices. Failure to allow for this difference in timing is a major reason for the misinterpretation of monetary experience. Third, and most important of all, there is a systematic and regular difference between changes in money and in prices in the course of an inflationary episode that is itself part of the very process by which monetary changes produce changes in prices.

The typical life history of an inflation is that the quantity of money per unit of output initially increases more rapidly than prices. During this period, the public does not anticipate price rises, interprets any price rise that occurs as temporary, and hence is willing to hold money balances of increased 'real' value (i.e., corresponding to a larger volume of goods and services) in the belief that prices will be lower in the future. If the quantity of money continues to increase faster than output, however, prices will continue to rise, and sooner or later the public will come to anticipate further price rises. It then wishes to reduce its money balances not only to their former real value but to an even smaller level. Cash has now become a costly way to hold assets, since its purchasing power is decreasing. People therefore try to reduce their cash balances. They cannot, as a whole, do so in nominal terms (i.e., in terms of dollars), because someone or other must hold the amount in existence. But the *attempt* to do so bids up prices, wages, and nominal incomes. The result is to reduce 'real' balances. During this stage, therefore, prices rise more rapidly than the quantity of money, and sometimes much more rapidly. If the rate of rise of the quantity of money stabilizes, no matter at how high a level, the rate of price rise will ultimately settle down also. The total price rise may bear very different relations to the rise in the quantity of money per unit of output depending on the size of the monetary expansion. In moderate inflations, as for example the rise in prices in the United States by a third from 1896 to 1913, prices and money may rise by about the same percentage. In really substantial inflations, such as have occurred in recent decades in many South American countries, the price rise will generally be several times the monetary rise; in hyperinflations, the price rise will be many times the monetary rise [. . .]

Why should money be so critical a factor in price level behavior? Why should it occupy such a central role in the process? The key to an answer is the difference, already referred to, between the *nominal* quantity of money, the quantity of money expressed in terms of dollars, and the *real* quantity of money, the quantity of money expressed in terms of the goods and services it will buy or the number of weeks of income it is equal to.

People seem to be extraordinarily stubborn about the real amount of money that they want to hold and are unwilling to hold a different amount, unless there is a strong incentive to do so. This is true over both time and space. [. . .]

Given that people are so stubborn about the amount they hold in the form of money, let us suppose that, for whatever reasons, the amount of money in a community is higher than people want to hold at the level of prices then prevailing. It does not for our purposes matter why, whether because the government has printed money to finance expenditures or because somebody has discovered a new gold mine or because banks have discovered how to create deposits. For whatever reason, people find that although on the average they would like to hold, let us say, the four weeks' income that they hold in the United States, they are actually holding, say, five weeks' income. What will happen? Here again it is essential to distinguish between the individual and the community. Each individual separately thinks he can get rid of his money and he is right. He can go out and spend it and thereby reduce his cash balances. But for the community as a whole the belief that cash balances can be reduced is an optical illusion. The only way I can reduce my cash balances in nominal terms is to induce somebody else to increase his. One man's expenditures are another man's receipts. People as a whole cannot spend more than they as a whole receive. In consequence, if everybody in the community tries to reduce the nominal amount of his cash balances, on the average nobody will do so. The amount of nominal balances is fixed by the nominal quantity of money in existence and no game of musical chairs can change it.

But people can and will try to reduce their cash balances and the process of trying has important effects. In the process of trying to spend more than they are receiving, people bid up the prices of all sorts of goods and services. Nominal incomes rise and real cash balances are indeed reduced, even though nominal balances, the number of dollars, are not affected. The rise in prices and incomes will bring cash balances from five weeks' income to four weeks' income. People will succeed in achieving their objective, but by raising prices and incomes rather than by reducing nominal balances. In the process, prices will have risen by about a fifth. This in a nutshell and somewhat oversimplified is the process whereby changes in the stock of money exert their influence on the price level. It is oversimplified because there is a tendency to overshoot, followed by successive readjustments converging on the final position, but this complication does not affect the essence of the adjustment process.

Emphasis on the key role of the quantity of money leaves open the question of what produced the changes in the quantity of money. Hence, if an analysis of inflation is to deal not only with the change in the quantity of money but with what brought it about, it will be a very pluralistic theory. Historically, the actual sources of monetary expansion have been very different at different times and in different places.

There is a widespread belief that inflation is somehow related to government deficits. This belief has a sound basis. The existence of deficits tempts governments to finance them by printing money (or the equivalent, creating deposits), hence deficits have often been the source of monetary expansion. But deficits per se are not necessarily a source of inflation. As already noted, the federal budget ran a surplus during 1919–20 when prices rose rapidly; similarly, there were extremely large surpluses immediately after World War II, when prices also rose rapidly. On the other side, the budget was in deficit during 1931–33, when prices fell sharply. Deficits can contribute to inflation by raising interest rates and so velocity; for the rest they are a source of inflation if and only if they are financed by printing money.

The same considerations apply to other alleged sources of inflation. Increasingly strong trade unions can be a source of inflation if by their actions they produce unemployment and if a government committed to full employment expands the quantity of money as part of a policy of eliminating unemployment. This particular chain of events has often been alleged but, as already noted, seldom observed in the United States. More generally, a full employment policy can be a source of inflation if it produces undue monetary expansion.

III. SUPPRESSED INFLATION IS WORSE THAN OPEN INFLATION

The distinction between inflation and deflation, important as it is, is less important than the distinction between open inflation, one in which prices are free to rise without governmental price controls, and suppressed inflation, one in which the government attempts to suppress the manifestations of the inflationary pressure by controlling prices, including prices not only of products but also of factor services (i.e., wage rates, rents, interest rates) and of foreign currencies (i.e., exchange rates).

Open inflation is harmful. It generally produces undesirable transfers of income and wealth, weakens the social fabric, and may distort the pattern of output. But if moderate, and especially if steady, it tends to become anticipated and its worst effects on the distribution of income are offset. It still does harm, but, *so long as prices are free to move*, the extremely flexible private enterprise system will adapt to it, take it in stride, and continue to operate efficiently. The main dangers from open inflation are twofold: first, the temptation to step up the rate of inflation as the economy adapts itself; second, and even more serious, the temptation to attempt cures, especially suppression, that are worse than the disease.

Suppressed inflation is a very different thing. Even a moderate inflation, if effectively suppressed over a wide range, can do untold damage to the economic system, require widespread government intervention into the details of economic activity, destroy a free enterprise system, and along with it, political freedom. The reason is that suppression prevents the price system from working. The government is driven to try to provide a substitute that is extremely inefficient. The usual outcome, pending a complete monetary reform, is an uneasy compromise between official tolerance of evasion of price controls and a collectivist economy. The greater the ingenuity of private individuals in evading the price controls and the greater the tolerance of officials in blinking at such evasions, the less the harm that is done; the more law-abiding the citizens, and the more rigid and effective the governmental enforcement machinery, the greater the harm. [. . .]

IV. WHAT HARM WILL BE DONE BY THE GUIDEPOSTS?

Even granted that legally imposed and vigorously enforced wage and price ceilings covering a wide range of the economy would do enormous harm, some may argue that the enunciation of guideposts, their approval by businessmen and labor leaders, and voluntary compliance with them, or even lip service to them, is a palliative that can do no harm and can temporarily help until more effective measures are taken. At the very least, it may be said, it will enable businessmen and labor leaders to display their sense of social responsibility.

This view seems to me mistaken. The guideposts do harm even when only lip service is paid to them, and the more extensive the compliance, the greater the harm.

In the first place, the guideposts confuse the issue and make correct policy less likely. If there is inflation or inflationary pressure, the governmental monetary (or, some would say, fiscal) authorities are responsible. It is they who must take corrective measures if the inflation is to be stopped. Naturally, the authorities want to shift the blame, so they castigate the rapacious businessman and the selfish labor leader. By approving guidelines, the businessman and the labor leader implicitly whitewash the government for its role and plead guilty to the charge. They thereby encourage the government to postpone taking the corrective measures that alone can succeed.

In the second place, whatever measure of actual compliance there is introduces just that much distortion into the allocation of resources and the distribution of output. To whatever extent the price system is displaced, some other system of organizing resources and rationing output must be adopted. As in the example of the controls on foreign loans by banks, one adverse effect is to foster private collusive arrangements, so that a measure undertaken to keep prices down leads to government support and encouragement of private monopolistic arrangements.

In the third place, 'voluntary' controls invite the use of extra-legal powers to produce compliance. And, in the modern world, such powers are ample. There is hardly a business concern that could not have great costs imposed on it by anti-trust investigations, tax inquiries, government boycott, or rigid enforcement of any of a myriad of laws, or on the other side of the ledger, that can see no potential benefits from government orders, guarantees of loans, or similar measures. Which of us as an individual could not be, at the very least, seriously inconvenienced by investigation of his income tax returns, no matter how faithfully and carefully prepared, or by the enforcement to the letter of laws we may not even know about? This threat casts a shadow well beyond any particular instance. In a dissenting opinion in a recent court case involving a 'stand-in' in a public library, Justice Black wrote, 'It should be remembered that if one group can take over libraries for one cause, other groups will assert the right to do it for causes which, while wholly legal, may not be so appealing to this court.' Precisely the same point applies here. If legal powers granted for other purposes can today be used for the 'good' purpose of holding down prices, tomorrow they can be used for other purposes that will seem equally 'good' to the men in power – such as simply keeping themselves in power. It is notable how sharp has been the decline in the number of businessmen willing to be quoted by name when they make adverse comments on government.

In the fourth place, compliance with voluntary controls imposes a severe conflict of responsibilities on businessmen and labor leaders. The corporate official is an agent of his stockholders; the labor leader, of the members of his union. He has a responsibility to promote their interests. He is now told that he must sacrifice their interests to some supposedly higher social responsibility. Even supposing that he can know what 'social responsibility' demands – say by simply accepting on that question the gospel according to the Council of Economic Advisers – to what extent is it proper for him to do so? If he is to become a civil servant in fact, will he long remain an employee of the stockholders or an agent of the workers in name? Will they not discharge him? Or, alternatively, will not the government exert authority over him in name as in fact?

V. CONCLUSION

Inflation being always and everywhere a monetary phenomenon, the responsibility for controlling it is governmental. Legally enforced price and wage ceilings do not eliminate inflationary pressure. At most they suppress it. And suppressed inflation is vastly more harmful than open inflation.

Guideposts and pleas for voluntary compliance are a halfway house whose only merit is that they can more readily be abandoned than legally imposed controls. They are not an alternative to other effective measures to stem inflation, but at most a smoke-screen to conceal the lack of action. Even if not complied with they do harm, and the more faithfully they are complied with, the more harm they do.

Nonetheless, we should not exaggerate either the problem or the harm that will be done by false cures. Prices will almost surely rise in coming months. We shall probably continue to experience inflationary pressure on the average over the coming years. The price rise, however, will be moderate. A major war aside, I cannot conceive that the monetary authorities will permit the quantity of money to rise at a rate that would produce inflation of more than, say, 3-to-10 per cent a year. Such inflation will be unfortunate, but if permitted to occur reasonably openly and freely, not disastrous. And, despite all the talk, prices and wages will be permitted to rise in one way or another. The guideposts will be more talked about than they will be voluntarily complied with or enforced by extra-legal pressure. Hypocrisy will enable effective evasion to be combined with self-congratulation. Debasing the coin of public and private morality is unfortunate, but in moderate doses not disastrous. The greatest harm will continue to be done by the measures taken to peg exchange rates. It is well to keep in mind Adam Smith's famous comment, 'There is much ruin in a nation,' but only to avoid overstating a good case, not to condone bad policy.

NOTES

1. In a market economy, prices of particular goods and services, including labor services, are always changing relatively to one another, some rising, others falling, some rising rapidly, others slowly, and so on. When rises predominate, in some sense which allows for the relative importance of the items whose prices are considered, there is inflation; when declines predominate, there is deflation. This definition is purposely vague because there is no unique way to measure the 'average' behavior of prices; different indexes often give different answers not only about the size of any price change, but even about its direction. These differences are sometimes very large and are important for many purposes. In the context of this paper, however, they are not. We shall restrict attention to cases in which the general tendency for prices to rise is so clear and widespread that it would be reflected in just about every broadly based index number.
2. As Robert Solow pointed out in his comments on this paper at the conference, the argument of the other sections of this paper (sections I, III, and IV) is almost entirely independent of my generalization about the central role of the quantity of money in the inflationary process. The words inflationary pressure can be interpreted to mean an

aggregate nominal demand in excess of the value of prior (or potential) output at prior prices. Whether this excess nominal demand reflects a change in the quantity of money, as I believe it generally does, or a change in velocity produced, for example, by changes in fiscal policy or investment demand, as others may believe, the analysis of the effects of price and wage guidelines or controls is precisely the same.

I am indebted to Mr. Solow for making this point explicit at the conference. [See Robert M. Solow, 'The Case Against the Case Against the Guideposts', and 'Comments', pp. 41–54 and 62–6 of George P. Schultz and Robert Z. Aliber (eds.), *Guidelines, Informal Controls and the Market Place*, Chicago University Press, 1966 – Ed.]

3. Note that even for such a temporary effect, it is not enough that there exist monopolies of business and labor; it is necessary that monopoly power increase, otherwise, relative prices will already have become adjusted.

4. Yale Brozen, 'Guide Lines and Wage Laws: How Should Wage Changes Be Determined?', unpublished paper, p. 8.

5. The word money is used in at least three different senses: (1) as in 'money balances' when the reference is to the pieces of paper we carry in our pocket or the credits to our account on the books of banks – this is the sense in which I shall use it; (2) as in 'making money' when the reference is not to a counterfeiter but to a recipient of income; and (3) as in 'money markets' when the reference is to 'loans' or 'credit,' paper claims that cover a vastly broader range of instruments than those we designate 'money' in the first sense. Confusion among these meanings underlies much misunderstanding about the role of money in economic affairs. In particular, confusion between the first and third has led to great overemphasis on the 'credit' effects of governmental monetary policy rather than the effects on the quantity of money. Hence, the statement that inflation is a monetary phenomenon is sometimes interpreted not as I do in the text but as indicating that inflation reflects changes in credit markets.

5.6 The Phillips Curve as a Menu for Policy Choice*

A major reason for the importance of Professor A. W. Phillips' article in 1958 on the rate of change of money wages in the United Kingdom[1] in the economic literature of the past decade is that it seems to offer the policy maker a menu of choices between employment and inflation. The dishes listed in the left-hand column of the menu are states of over-full, full or less than full employment; the column of prices on the right-hand side gives the cost in terms of inflation that must be paid for each.

Given the set of alternatives or trade-offs provided by the Phillips curve, the policy maker then chooses a position according to the weights he attaches to the evils of unemployment and inflation. In general the countries of Western Europe have chosen positions of low unemployment and rather continuous inflation, while the United States and Canada for most of the post-war period have chosen substantially higher levels of unemployment and lower rates of inflation. These choices no doubt reflect differences in the political acceptability of unemployment and inflation between the two areas.

Academic discussions of policy have attempted to clarify the weights that should be used, for example by arguing whether inflation, like unemployment, causes a reduction in output, or whether inflation hurts the poor more than the rich. But for most of the period since 1958 there has been little questioning

*From Albert Rees, 'The Phillips Curve as a Menu for Policy Choice', *Economica*, Vol. 37, May 1970.

of the basic argument underlying the Phillips curve. The technical literature has consisted largely of estimates of the Phillips curve for various countries and periods, with different investigators introducing supplemental variables or different functional forms and arguing their merits. More recently, however, a number of articles have been published questioning the underlying theory of the Phillips curve. The most important of these comprise the 'expectations' approach, whose strongest proponents have been Professors Phelps and Friedman.[2]

The authors of these articles argue with great conviction that the historical Phillips curve is not a menu for policy choice because it is traced out by relations between the level of unemployment and *unexpected* rates of inflation or deflation.[3] Once a position on the Phillips curve is chosen as a matter of policy, and adhered to firmly enough so that it comes to be expected, it is argued that the historical relation will no longer hold and the curve will shift. Indeed, in much of this literature the 'steady-state' Phillips curve corresponding to a condition in which expectations are not disappointed is said to be a vertical line at some 'natural' rate of unemployment. In the long run the policy maker has no choices at all in the unemployment dimension – at whatever rate of inflation he chooses, the rate of unemployment will be the same. He should therefore choose price stability, since it is desirable in its own right.

The argument just sketched is often stated quite briefly – sometimes in not many more words than I have used to state it here. It is regarded as self-evidently correct given only the assumption of rationality on the part of participants in the labour market. Rationality is equated for the most part with the absence of money illusion.

Because the expectations approach to the Phillips curve has such importance for policy formation, I believe that it deserves a more careful critical scrutiny than it has yet received. This is the task I propose to attempt here. The first of two basic propositions I shall try to establish is that even when all prices change in the same proportion and all wages also change in some larger uniform proportion, lags in the adjustment process are sufficient to generate a downward-sloping long-run Phillips curve, though one with a steeper slope than the historical Phillips curve. The second proposition is that when there are variations in relative wages and in relative prices there is an additional reason for expecting the long-run Phillips relation to have a negative slope.

I shall use the concept of equilibrium in the labour market to mean a condition in which there is no tendency for wages to be bid up by employers because they are having difficulty in filling vacancies.[4] This condition need not, and probably will not, involve equality between the number of unemployed and the number of unfilled vacancies. If the labour market is composed of a number of sub-markets by occupation or location, in each of which wages are rigid downward, an excess of vacancies over unemployed workers in any one sub-market will be sufficient to cause wages in that market to rise and hence to cause the average of all wages to rise. This may occur when in all sub-markets taken

together the number of unemployed substantially exceeds the number of unfilled vacancies. It is even possible for wages to rise in a given sub-market when
the number of unemployed exceeds the number of vacancies — quite apart
from any possibility of wages being pushed up by trade unions. This would only
require that employers regard some of the unemployed as unsuited to fill their
vacancies, so that they prefer to offer higher wages than to hire these unemployed at going wages.

The basic Phillips mechanism involves a rise in employment and a fall in
unemployment whenever there is an unacceptably high level of unfilled
vacancies, because employers relax hiring standards and accept workers who
would not previously have been employed. The fall in unemployment in these
circumstances permits us to use the unemployment rate as an index of the presence of excess demand where vacancy statistics are not available directly. The
Phillips mechanism also involves the notion that the adjustment of wages to
excess demand is not instantaneous, for if it were the excess demand would be
wiped out immediately and never be observed.

The increase in demand that causes employers to bid up wages could be
caused by technological change that increases the marginal product of labour, or
it could be generated by an increase in product prices (arising, say, from an inflationary monetary policy) rather than by an increase in productivity. For
Phillips, this would make no difference, since his basic argument is framed in
terms of money wages and the value of labour's product in current prices. Employers react to difficulty in filling vacancies by raising their money wage, since
it is the only wage parameter over which they have control. And they will do
this in response to forces which either raise the price of their products relative
to wages or lower the cost of production relative to prices, since either of these
forces makes it profitable to expand output and employment.

But it is precisely at this point that Phelps, Friedman and their followers part
company with Phillips. Friedman considers the failure to distinguish between
nominal wages and real wages to be a basic defect of Phillips' analysis.[5] The
stimulating effect of a rise in money demand, he argues, will be felt only so long
as it is unanticipated — once it is expected, it ceases to have a stimulating effect
unless it proceeds at an accelerating rate. At first reading, this argument seems
eminently sensible, but it is worthwhile to probe it more deeply. We may begin
by asking: 'Whose expectations are adjusted — the workers', the employers'
or those of both?' If the question were put this way to the authors of the literature on expectations, I would expect them to reply, 'Both'. Yet in what they
have written there is a curious stress on the behaviour of workers. Friedman
writes: 'Employees will start to reckon on rising prices of the things they buy
and to demand higher nominal wages for the future.'[6] Similar passages can be
found in most of the other articles in this vein, the exception being Phelps (in
his 1968 article).

In some cases, the emphasis on the supply response goes so far as to suggest
that the initial reduction in unemployment following the increase in money

demand resulted from the behaviour of workers rather than, as I have argued above, from the behaviour of employers. Workers could reduce unemployment in response to an increase in demand in one of two ways. First, some workers could drop out of the labour force; these could be some of the unemployed or they could be employed workers whose places would be taken by the unemployed. However, everything we know about the cyclical behaviour of the labour force argues that the effect of a rise in demand is to increase the labour force, not to decrease it.[7] Of course, the historical evidence on cyclical increases in the demand for labour does not involve reductions in the real wage, reductions which would occur if the increase in demand were generated solely by an increase in the price level, with a lag in the response of money wages. Even in this case, however, the effect of more job opportunities on inducing new entry would seem likely at the outset to swamp any withdrawals caused by the falling real wages of those already employed. The vast majority of the employed are not at the margin of indifference between market work and leisure, but would strongly prefer work to no work at real wages anywhere in the neighbourhood of those prevailing.

The second possible way of reducing unemployment from the supply side as a result of increased demand is that the unemployed could accept employment that they had previously refused to accept. This, indeed, is an argument that is made by the expectations school. The most explicit form of the argument is advanced by Phelps and attributed to Armen Alchian.[8] It begins with the idea that at any time there are workers looking for work who will accept an offer they believe to be better than the average of the offers they could reasonably expect to receive. It is argued that when the general level of wages rises, these workers mistake offers to them at the mean of the higher distribution of offers to workers of their ability for an unusually favourable sampling of offers from the original distribution. They hasten to accept, feeling that they are unlikely to draw a better offer by further search. This produces a temporary reduction in unemployment, or in the duration of search, which will be reversed when workers become aware of the change in general wage levels and again become as choosy as before with reference to the new, higher wage distribution.

This argument is tremendously ingenious, for which credit must be given. But it considers only frictional unemployment, or as it is called in the expectations literature, 'search unemployment'; and it neglects the probability that structural unemployment will form part of the lowest level of unemployment compatible with no change in the wage level. If wage stability requires that there be no excess demand in any sub-market, then wages will be stable only when there are substantial pockets of unemployment in certain industries and areas, greatly exceeding frictional levels. Similarly, there may be substantial pockets of unemployment among racial or ethnic minorities such as Negroes, Spanish Americans and American Indians in the United States, Algerians in France, or West Indians in the United Kingdom. When employers seek to expand output and employment, they cannot do so in the aggregate by hiring from groups already fully employed, and therefore structural unemployment diminishes. I assume that the structurally unemployed are involuntarily unemployed in the Keynesian sense — that they would prefer to take employment at or slightly below the prevailing real wage rather than continue to remain unemployed. In contrast, the assumption made about 'search unemployment' in the expectations literature is that it is essentially voluntary, since only those offers will be accepted that are believed to be above the mean of the current distribution of offers to a particular kind of worker, and other offers will be rejected in favour of longer search. As workers' expectations become more realistic with longer search, until they eventually accept job offers at prevailing rates, their place is taken by new job seekers whose initial expectations are on average unduly optimistic.

In my opinion, a decrease in structural rather than in frictional unemployment accounts for most of the reduction in unemployment that initially accompanies a rise in the demand for labour. For the frictional component of unemployment, there is an important offset to the effect mentioned by Phelps and Alchian. Increases in demand shorten the duration of frictional unemployment, perhaps in part for the reasons Alchian suggests. However, they also tend to raise the volume of frictional unemployment by increasing the quit rate. Professors Corry and Laidler have gone so far as to suggest that this second effect might dominate the first, creating a forward-sloping Phillips curve in which higher rates of increase in money wages are associated with higher unemployment.[9] Like the contrary view of Phelps and Alchian, this position seems to me greatly to over-emphasize the importance of the supply response and of frictional unemployment in the Phillips relation.

Further consideration of supply conditions suggests another reason for not expecting the decrease in unemployment to be fully reversed when wages catch up with prices.[10] When employers are forced to hire the long-term unemployed or members of disadvantaged minorities in order to fill vacancies, these workers will get on-the-job training in new skills. Some of them, previously discriminated against on the basis of employer judgements about groups, will prove to be unexpectedly competent, and will be kept on when real wages per man have returned to their original level. The average quality of the labour force will have gone up, and the fraction of the labour force worth employing at the old real wage will have increased as a result. This effect is most relevant when a period of full employment follows a period of slack demand. It would not continue to operate indefinitely during sustained full employment.

The final consideration on the supply side is the position of trade unions, and it is here that the expectations argument comes closest to being correct. In the short run, the rigidity of collective bargaining agreements will contribute to a lag of wages behind prices; but if inflationary expectations develop, unions will come to insist on compensation for price increases, and tighter labour markets will improve their bargaining power. In the interim, however, union/non-union wage differentials may be narrowed, with possible desirable effects on resource allocation.

It would be possible to generate a curve that looks like a Phillips curve without ever having excess demand in any market. One need only assume that trade unions push up the level of money wages faster when unemployment is low than when it is high, even though unemployment never gets low enough so that employers want to raise wages on their own initiative. The cost-push version of the Phillips mechanism is more relevant in economies such as Great Britain or Sweden, where the fraction of all employees in unions is very high, than it is in the United States. The relevance of the expectations argument to this model depends on the relative weights attached to price changes and to the level of unemployment by the two parties — their importance in determining the size of union demands and the aggressiveness of union action on the one hand, and in determining the vigour of employer resistance to union demands on the other.

There is, of course, substantial empirical evidence to support the proposition that price changes are a major independent factor in the wage-adjustment mechanism. Friedman quite correctly cites the significant positive coefficients on price-change terms in many wage-adjustment regressions as evidence that suppliers do take price changes into account. It should be noted, however, that these coefficients are almost uniformly signifcantly different from unity as well as from zero, which by the same token indicates that, historically, price changes have not been *fully* taken into account. How long it would take for the coefficient to reach unity under conditions of sustained moderate inflation is difficult to tell; it is not certain that it ever would. Whether full adjustment would ever take place depends not only on whether expectations are correct but also on the costs of adjustment.

One of the principal avenues of adjustment open to the trade union is an escalator clause or sliding scale that ties wages to the retail price index. The limited popularity of such clauses in both the United States and Great Britain after a rather long period of moderate inflation suggests that the cost of frequent adjustment is regarded as high. The alternative for the union, given correct expectations, is to build wage increases into long-term agreements without stipulating that they are intended to cover price increases.

In non-union markets, at least, the forces on the supply side do not seem capable on balance of causing a fall in unemployment in the presence of excess demand. But the situation on the demand side is quite different. It should be remembered that in the great majority of labour markets, employers take the initiative. The employer quotes the wage, which the job seeker accepts or rejects. The employer, except in the few cases where he hires through a union, sets hiring standards and modifies them as he finds necessary. If he has many vacancies and discovers that they are hard to fill, he will raise wages, relax hiring standards, or do both. Thus it is employer expectations that are crucial to the expectations theory.

The expectations argument on the demand side has been made by Phelps (in his 1968 article). Phelps argues that a firm experiencing difficulty in filling vacancies will want to raise its wages relatively to wages elsewhere. But if wages elsewhere are rising, it cannot raise its relative wages without taking the rise of other wages into account. The expected rate of wage increases elsewhere must therefore explicitly enter into the firm's own rate of wage increase. Employers as a group will be in equilibrium only when the expected rate of increase in wages equals the actual rate, for only then will employers of roughly equal numbers of workers be seeking to increase and to decrease their position in the relative wage structure. So long as a majority seek to raise their relative wages, the average money wage must rise. And so long as a majority are seeking to fill an abnormally large number of vacancies, hiring standards will be lowered and the number of unemployed will be reduced. However, Phelps concludes, by an argument too complicated to reproduce here, that all the solutions in which the actual and expected rates of wage changes are equal lie at the same unemployment rate. The argument seems to assume that the level of unemployment is determined by relative prices, including relative wages and the real rate of interest, all of which in the long run are not changed by inflation. In a world in which wage adjustments were costless, I would be prepared to accept much of this reasoning. But I question whether it holds even where substantial adjustment costs are present.

Except in hyper-inflations, employers generally seem to behave as though the costs of changing wages were very substantial. When faced with labour shortages, they frequently lower hiring standards, raise expenditures on recruitment, and contract-out work before raising wages. In part, this behaviour may represent a form of wage discrimination, since it is usually not possible for employers to pay higher money wages to new employees than to old ones doing the same work. In part it represents the expectation that the labour shortages will be temporary, while with money wages rigid downward a wage increase would be permanent. But there are also elements in the reluctance to raise money wages that come closer to being costs in the usual sense of the term. One of the most important of these is that every change in wages tends to raise questions of internal equity that can be very troublesome to solve. Even if it is decided to raise all wages uniformly, it must be decided whether this is to be by a uniform percentage or a uniform amount, and whether the increase is to extend all the way up the structure of wages and salaries or only part way. The problems are not unlike those faced by the United States Congress in separating problems of the level of the income tax from issues of tax reform.

Although we know very little about the exact nature of the costs of making wage changes, we can infer that they exist. Wages are, next to house rents, the stickiest general class of prices in the economy, seldom adjusted more frequently than once a year. This stickiness may be reinforced by unionism and collective bargaining, but it was present long before unions arrived. American evidence suggests that, except in the rather rapid inflations, upward wage adjustments are made less frequently by non-union employers than by union employers. In the presence of substantial adjustment costs, it seems possible for the labour market to be for long periods in a state of dynamic disequilibrium in which money wages are rising faster than average productivity, so that prices are rising, and in which unemployment is lower than it would be with prices stable. In other words, the stickiness of wages permits a negatively-sloped Phillips curve with correct expectations.

The argument here brings to mind the old controversy among economic historians about the lag of wages behind prices in inflations, except that it is in a context of rising productivity. In historical contexts, the argument was that in major inflations money wages failed to keep pace with prices so that profits rose and real wages fell. In the present context, the question becomes whether money wages lag behind the combined effects of productivity gains and inflation so as to create a continuous incentive for employers to employ more workers than they would employ without such a lag. Suppose that the rise in money wages is determined by the rise in productivity and the rise in the price level, but that it only adjusts to these determining variables with a lag that averages six months. Real wages will be lower than they would be with no lag, and umemployment will also be the lower. Or, viewed differently, real wages and unemployment will both be lower in the presence of inflation than with no inflation, since for any given length of lag the size of the wedge between real wages and the value of output in current prices will depend on how rapidly the value of output is rising. This will continue to be true unless the rate of inflation becomes so rapid that it pays the participants in the labour market to take measures to make the adjustment lag shorter than normal.

The situation just described is unlike that in which productivity is constant and prices are rising faster than wages. In our situation the trend of real wages is upwards even though real wages fall during each adjustment period. Workers are not likely to be much upset by this so long as each adjustment brings them to a higher level of real wages than they have enjoyed before.

One may ask whether the behaviour suggested here involves money illusion. As originally used by Keynes, the term 'money illusion' meant that workers would accept a cut in real wages caused by rising prices with stable money wages, where they would not have accepted an equal cut in real wages produced by stable prices and lower money wages. Of course, this does not mean that cuts in real wages produced by rising prices will be accepted no matter how prolonged and severe. Eventually such cuts in real wages would lead to strong reaction from workers and unions. But in the most general sense, any asymmetry in response to the two forms of wage cuts involves some degree of money illusion, and in this sense no observer of industrial relations can doubt that it is present.

By extension, it could be argued that a worker who, when prices are stable, receives increases on money wages at the rate of 3 per cent per annum is a victim of money illusion if, when prices rise at 2 per cent, he will accept money wages rising at 4 per cent. To concede that this behaviour may also be called money illusion is not to concede that it is so irrational that it could not occur. How is the worker to know his alternatives? He will only become aware of neglected opportunities when the faster rise of productivity than of real wages causes employers to want to expand employment and improve their wage offers. In short, the worker must eventually get real wages that rise in keeping with productivity not because he will insist on it as an individual, but because in a reasonably competitive labour market they will be offered to him, or because his trade union obtains them through collective bargaining.

Let us try to summarize the argument up to this point. If changing wage rates frequently involves costs both to employers and to unions, then the labour market will not be in a state of continuous equilibrium. A moderate inflation can, even if anticipated, produce a higher level of employment than price stability, and therefore the Phillips curve will have a negative slope to the left of a point corresponding to price stability. Where the expectation of rapid inflation becomes so strong as to overcome the costs of change moderate inflation tends to become hyper-inflation, and the Phillips curve becomes vertical. In contrast, Phelps would insist that the curve becomes vertical where the rate of change of prices is zero because wages and productivity are rising at equal rates. This point on most fitted Phillips curves lies so far to the right that it is unacceptable to policy makers.

Let us now drop the assumption that there are no changes in relative prices and relative wages. Where relative prices can change and there are downward price rigidities, there is a further important reason not yet mentioned why the rate of unemployment should be related to the rate of price change. We have all accepted the reasoning involved long ago with respect to relative wages. It used to be argued in the 1920s that the rate of change of average wages should be zero and that all productivity gains should be distributed through lower prices so that the retired would participate in them.[11] But this would require that all decreases in relative wages also be absolute decreases. Since a worker's money wage is an index of the esteem in which he is held, a reduction in it is a universal affront, and cuts in money wages for any reason have become extremely rare.[12] Stable average wages would make it almost impossible to reduce relative wages (or by the same token, to increase them!). The likely outcome is that attempts to increase relative wages would eventually raise the average; but if this was not permitted to occur, there would be an ever increasing volume of structural unemployment in declining industries and areas and ever-growing labour shortages in expanding markets.

It is also generally true that firms find it easier to raise product prices in response to excess demand or rising costs in particular product markets, and do so more promptly, than they find it to lower prices in response to deficient demand or reduced costs. This amounts to little more than saying that some product prices are administered rather than market determined, and that firms that administer prices are not continuously at a profit-maximizing position. But if the behaviour of price administrators is asymmetrical, the argument made above for a rising average wage level also applies to the average level of product prices. A gently rising price level will lubricate relative price changes, since to lower a relative price one need only hold the absolute price constant. This lubricating effect will help prevent the generation of excess unemployment in industries or areas where relative prices are too high.[13] The importance of this point is that the rise in the price level need not accelerate in order to affect unemployment. So long as the pricing behaviour of firms is asymmetrical for price cuts and price increases, moderate inflation generates higher output and employment than price stability, even when it is fully anticipated.

This brings me to my final comments on the expectations literature. It constantly asks us to choose between under-employment and hyper-inflation, arguing that any intermediate position is unstable and any reductions in unemployment achieved now by letting prices rise will be balanced by increases in unemployment to be suffered later. The examples chosen to illustrate this proposition are often drawn from the hyper-inflations of such Latin American countries as Brazil, and it is pointed out that these hyper-inflations have not lowered unemployment. The choice between the policies of post-war Brazil on the one hand and of the United States in the period of 1958–64 on the other is, indeed, a sorry one. Economic planners in Great Britain, Sweden or Japan faced with these alternatives would resign their portfolios or commit hari-kari. But fortunately the experience of developed Western countries outside North America does not suggest that the choices are so dismal. Most of these countries have been running their economies at full employment and moderate rates of inflation for more than two decades. The inflation, to be sure, produces some vexing problems, but it does not show the tendency to constant acceleration predicted by the expectations school.

Let me take care to emphasize that there must be some rate of inflation high enough so that, when prolonged, it begins to affect the behaviour of ordinary workers as well as that of sophisticated investors and thus begins to produce changes in customs and institutions of long standing. There is a danger that moderate inflation will become galloping inflation, and policy makers must guard carefully against approaching this point too closely. Yet I cannot draw from this the conclusion that the choice is between price stability and hyper-inflation, with stability the only possible long-run policy.

It is beyond the scope of this paper to discuss how policy makers should make the choice between unemployment and inflation. But the discussion here does imply that in a range of rates of inflation between, say, zero and 6 per cent, there is a choice to be made that could be reasonably stable over rather long periods. The long-run Phillips curve along which this choice must be made is steeper than the historical Phillips curve, which means that the cost in terms of inflation of maintaining low rates of unemployment for long periods is greater than the historical record suggests. But this does not dictate a policy of price stability — to agree that something is expensive is not necessarily to conclude that one should not purchase any of it.

The strongest policy conclusion I can draw from the expectations literature is that policy makers should not attempt to operate at a single point on the

Phillips curve (assuming very generously that they have the power to do so if they choose to). Rather, they should permit fluctuations in unemployment within a band, so that optimistic or inflationary expectations are from time to time disappointed, and those who bet against the currency sometimes lose. But it makes an enormous difference whether (in American terms) this band is from 3 per cent unemployment to 4.5 per cent, or whether it is from 4.5 to 6 per cent — a difference of hundreds of thousands of jobs and billions of dollars of real product.[14] Unless there is much clearer evidence than we have now that staying within the lower band will result in hyper-inflation, the gains from doing so, both economic and social, are far too great to be thrown away.

NOTES

1. A. W. Phillips, 'The Relation between Unemployment and the Rate of Change of Money Wage Rates in the United Kingdom, 1861-1957', *Economica*, vol. XXV (1958), pp. 283-99.
2. See especially E. S. Phelps, 'Money-Wage Dynamics and Labour Market Equilibrium', *Journal of Political Economy*, vol. 76 (1968), pp. 678-711; E. S. Phelps, 'The New Microeconomics in Inflation and Employment Theory', *American Economic Review*, vol. 59 (1969), pp. 147-58; and Milton Friedman, 'The Role of Monetary Policy', *American Economic Review*, vol. 58 (1968), pp. 1-17.
3. The original Phillips curve, of course, had the rate of change of money wages on the vertical axis and the rate of unemployment on the horizontal axis. However, the vertical axis is frequently transformed to a rate of change of the general price level by assuming some constant rate of growth in output per man-hour. Although the basis for this transformation is not as clear as it is often made to seem, to question it here would divert us from our main purposes. For a discussion of this issue and an analysis that does not assume that price changes are proportional to changes in unit labour cost, see Frank Brechling, 'The Trade-off between Inflation and Unemployment', *Journal of Political Economy*, vol. 76 (1968), pp. 712-36.
4. The definition distinguishes only between equilibrium and excess demand, and not between equilibrium and excess supply. Defining disequilibrium in the wage dimension for cases of excess supply is precluded by the downward rigidity of money wages.
5. Friedman, op. cit., p. 8.
6. Ibid., p. 10.
7. See William G. Bowen and T. Aldrich Finegan, *The Economics of Labour Force Participation*, Princeton, N.J., 1969, chs. 16 and 17 and the literature cited there.
8. Phelps, 'The New Microeconomics . . .', op. cit. The same position is taken by Axel Leijonhufvud in his comment on Brechling's paper, *Journal of Political Economy*, vol. 76 (1968), pp. 738-43.
9. Bernard Corry and David Laidler, 'The Phillips Relation – A Theoretical Explanation', *Economica*, vol. XXXIV (1967), pp. 189-97.
10. The argument of this paragraph was advanced briefly by Frank Brechling in his discussion of Phelps' 1969 paper, *American Economic Review*, vol. 59 (1969), p. 160.
11. The gain to the retired is in fact not clear, since a falling price level would be reflected at least in part in a lower rate of interest.
12. I do not interpret this in the way it is sometimes interpreted as indicating that 'workers are reluctant to offer their services at less than the prevailing rates when the demand for labour is low and unemployment is high'. Phillips, op. cit., p. 283. Rather, I would argue that *employed* workers will resist wage cuts and employers are unwilling to make them even when unemployed workers are eager to supply services for less than prevailing rates. See A. Rees, 'Wage Determination and Involuntary Unemployment', *Journal of Political Economy*, vol. 59 (1951), pp. 143-53.

13. I owe the argument of this paragraph to a conversation with Milton Friedman many years ago, but I do not know whether he would still agree with it.
14. Professor Harry Johnson has reminded me that not all of the difference in gross national product between periods of full and less than full employment is a difference in welfare, since the increased leisure has some value. However, in keeping with the argument above that most unemployment is involuntary, I would contend that the value of this leisure is a small part of the total change in product.

5.7 The Effect of Unemployment Compensation*

Starting in the fourth quarter of 1966, there was a substantial and apparently permanent increase in Great Britain's measured unemployment rate as well as a change in the relationships between that rate and other variables such as the vacancy rate and the rates of increase of wages, earnings, and prices.[1] These phenomena were noted by a number of researchers; various explanations were suggested and, in a few cases, investigated.[2] One of the most frequently suggested causal factors, perhaps due to its timing, was the introduction into Britain's unemployment compensation scheme of an extra 'Earnings Related Supplement' (ERS) which was first paid in October 1966.[3] Most recently it was suggested by Gujarati (March 1972) that the introduction of ERS along with the introduction of Redundancy Pay (RP) in 1965 were responsible for the change in behaviour between unemployment and vacancies; this was contested by Taylor (1972) who thought that the 'shake-out' of hoarded labour was a more significant explanation.[4]

Unfortunately, the effect of ERS on the unemployment rate has not been adequately investigated. [. . .]

Consequently, it is both reasonable and important to investigate the hypothesis that the increase in unemployment rates in Great Britain was to some extent induced by the increase in unemployment benefits. This paper uses the methodology developed by Grubel and Maki (1974) to provide empirical evidence for this hypothesis and to calculate 'adjusted' unemployment rates for the post-1966 period. The paper is organized into five remaining sections which briefly present the model, the variables and data, the empirical results, the analysis of those results, and the conclusions.

THE MODEL

The theoretical and empirical work of Grubel and Maki (1974, 1975) indicates that the traditional model of the causes of unemployment should be revised by including as one of the causes a rational, utility maximizing reaction to the existence of (or changes in) unemployment compensation. Such a revised model can be represented as:

*From Dennis Maki and Z. A. Spindler, 'The Effect of Unemployment Compensation on the Rate of Unemployment in Great Britain', *Oxford Economic Papers*, Vol. 27, November 1975.

$$U = f(FU, CU, SU, IU) \tag{1}$$

where U is the measured unemployment rate and FU, CU, SU, and IU are frictional-structural, cyclical, seasonal, and 'induced' unemployment, respectively.

The first three types of unemployment have been extensively analysed in the literature and need not be explained here. However, 'induced' unemployment — that is, induced by unemployment compensation — is still a relatively unfamiliar concept in the literature, albeit the possibility of this phenomenon was certainly not unknown to those who designed and maintain unemployment compensation schemes (which accounts for the inclusion of restrictive provisions such as waiting periods, job search, job acceptance, etc.) and it has been mentioned occasionally in British economic literature, most recently by Gujarati who entitled it 'artificial' unemployment.[5] Consequently, some of the main theoretical results from consumer choice or job search models will be briefly summarized.

Basically, changes in unemployment compensation tend to change the budget space facing an individual who may be eligible for such payments. These changes in the budget space will have both income and substitution effects on the labour-leisure decision and, if leisure is a normal good, will tend to lead to an increased consumption of leisure when the *ratio* of benefits to ordinary work income is increased.[6] This may take place by employed workers initiating their own 'unemployment' for some period of time or by unemployed workers extending their period of unemployment. Unemployment compensation may induce both employed and unemployed workers to use unemployment time to undertake job search activity as well as more leisure but both of these may be indistinguishable statistically from 'involuntary' unemployment.[7] Restrictions on unemployment compensation that are designed to reserve it for those persons who are really 'involuntarily' unemployed (such as waiting periods, quit rules, job search and acceptance rules) and higher costs of job search tend to reduce the extent of this 'induced' consumption of leisure and job search time. But since there are definite economic incentives to being identified as 'involuntarily' unemployed, it will be difficult to make these restrictions completely effective and job search costs may provide an effective deterrent mainly during times of severe depression and widespread unemployment.

Thus, it may be reasonable to expect that with any unemployment compensation system some induced unemployment will exist. Further, for any given state of restrictive provisions and job search costs, induced unemployment will be an increasing function of the ratio of benefits to income which is a measurable variable. Similarly, other forms of unemployment can be written as functions of measurable variables. Thus, for an econometric analysis of the effect on the total unemployment rate of the various types of unemployment, Equation 1 may be rewritten as:

$$U \text{ Rate} = f(\text{Ben/Inc, CycVar, StrucVar, SeasVar}) \tag{2}$$

where the unemployment rate (U Rate) is a function of the benefit–income ratio (Ben/Inc) and variables determining cyclical (CycVar), structural (StrucVar), and seasonal (SeasVar) unemployment.

The benefit–income ratio may not only affect the unemployment rate but it may also be affected by it. An obvious source of such a feedback effect is that during periods of high unemployment incomes may be lower due to lower demand for labour. If there exists substantial reverse causation, then empirical estimation of equation (2) will yield biased coefficients if ordinary least square (OLS) techniques are used, and it becomes desirable to specify an equation for the benefit–income ratio so that a consistent estimating technique may be employed. Obviously, variables which affect the benefit–income ratio are variables which affect the numerator and denominator differentially. A large number of variables affect incomes but do not directly affect benefits, but we investigated only two of these, and neither of them appears in our final estimation. The variables we tried were the price level and a productivity measure, under the rationale that incomes may be affected by these variables given the existence of escalator clauses or productivity-geared wage increases. Benefits are set by legislative action, and are thus the product of social preferences for providing relief to unemployment victims, as moulded by and expressed through the political process. Holen and Horowitz (1974) successfully utilized a variable which attempted to measure the sympathies of the members of the U.S. Congress in their benefit–income ratio equation, but their variable did not appear useful in a situation involving a parliamentary form of government. We assumed instead that social preferences on the question of aid to the unemployed change linearly through time, and introduced a dummy variable to account for an obvious discrete change in benefits. Thus our initial general form specification of an equation for the benefit–income ratio may be written in the following form:

$$\text{Ben/Inc} = g(\text{U Rate, ChangVar, RPI, O/PE}) \tag{3}$$

which shows the benefit–income ratio as a function of the unemployment rate (U Rate), variables for changes in social preferences (ChangVar), the retail price index (RPI) and output per person employed (O/PE).

Equations 2 and 3 represent the model in general form. Although Equation 2 (specifically, the role of Ben/Inc in that equation) is the most interesting for this study, Equation 3 is included in the model so that with two stage least squares estimation one source of simultaneous equation bias may be reduced.

THE VARIABLES AND DATA

A relevant series for the Ben/Inc variable is calculated by the Department of Health and Social Security. It is calculated for October of each year by dividing the standard rate of Unemployment Benefit plus Earnings Related Supplement plus Family Allowances by Average Weekly Earnings plus Family Allowances less tax and National Insurance Contributions. Basically, this is a ratio of net

unemployed income to net employed income. It is calculated for single persons
and married persons with zero to four children. As a matter of interest, the
ratios for a married person with two children are reported in Table 5.1. (Figures
for other categories are basically similar.) These figures show much year-to-year

Table 5.1
Benefit relative to net income: married, 2 children

Year (Oct.)	Ben/Inc.	Year (Oct.)	Ben/Inc.
1948	0.396	1961	0.443
1949	0.383	1962	0.430
1950	0.365	1963	0.474
1951	0.360	1964	0.446
1952	0.415	1965	0.493
1953	0.393	1966	0.686
1954	0.367	1967	0.732
1955	0.394	1968	0.728
1956	0.371	1969	0.710
1957	0.355	1970	0.727
1958	0.440	1971	0.776
1959	0.419	1972	0.737
1960	0.395		

variation, a substantial upward shift in 1966 (when the ERS was introduced),
and an upward trend. They were used for the Ben/Inc variable.

Date for other variables were taken from *British Labour Statistics: Historical
Abstract and Supplements.* [. . .]

THE EMPIRICAL RESULTS

Two stage least squares (2SLS) estimation for specific forms of Equations
2 and 3 yielded the following results with U Rate being the over-all unemployment rate and without RPI and O/PE (which proved to be insignificant) in the
second equation:

$$\text{Ln (U Rate)} = -1.129 + 1.197 \text{ Ben/Inc} - 11.615 \text{ Ln(RTTGNP)}$$
$$(-5.590) \quad (2.558) \qquad (-5.607)$$

$$-4.557 \text{ Ln(RTTGNP}_{-1}) + 0.00009067 \text{ ILSET,}$$
$$(-2.224) \qquad\qquad (2.458)$$

$$\bar{R}^2 = 0.907, \text{D.W.} = 1.258; \qquad (4)$$

$$\text{Ben/Inc} = 0.3135 + 0.02617 \text{ U Rate} + 0.2231 \text{ SHIFT}$$
$$(14.738) \quad (1.841) \qquad (10.919)$$

$$+ 0.005747 \text{ TIME,}$$
$$(3.267)$$

$$\bar{R}^2 = 0.975, \text{D.W.} = 1.998. \qquad (5)$$

The *t*-values are given in parentheses under the regression coefficients.[8] All coefficients have the expected signs and are significant at the 5 per cent level. The $\bar{R}^2$s and D.W.s are reasonable although it must be noted that these latter statistics do not have the same interpretation with the 2SLS estimating procedure as with the OLS procedure. It must also be noted that Equation 4 is in semi-log form which implies that the relationship between U Rate and Ben/Inc is a function of U Rate.[9] Further, the benefit income data used in Equation 4 was for married persons with two children; the results with data for single persons and married persons with no children were basically similar.[10] Experiments with other variables in both equations were performed, but these did not yield improved results; the results for the Ben/Inc variable turned out to be quite robust under these various specifications.[11]

Since there is an asymmetry in the treatment of men and women under Britain's unemployment compensation scheme[12] it might be argued that changes in Ben/Inc will have more influence on the male unemployment rate than on the over-all unemployment rate.[13] Accordingly 2SLS estimates of equations 2 and 3 with the U Rate being the male unemployment rate were performed and are as follows:

$$\text{Ln(U Rate) (Male)} = -2.030 + 1.303 \text{ Ben/Inc.} \tag{6}$$
$$(-9.708) \quad (3.193)$$

$$-12.216 \text{ Ln(RTTGNP)} - 4.557 \text{ Ln(RTTGNP.}_1)$$
$$(-6.615) \qquad\qquad (-2.929)$$

$$+ 0.0001793 \text{ ILSET,}$$
$$(4.898)$$

$$\bar{R}^2 = 0.965, \text{D.W.} = 1.620;$$

$$\text{Ben/Inc} = 0.3263 + 0.02390 \text{ U Rate (Male)} \tag{7}$$
$$(16.760) \quad (1.903)$$

$$+ 0.2192 \text{ SHIFT} + 0.004934 \text{ TIME,}$$
$$(10.180) \qquad\quad (2.442)$$

$$\bar{R}^2 = 0.974, \text{D.W.} = 1.849.$$

Again all coefficients have the expected signs and are significant at the 5 per cent level (all coefficients in the first equation are now significant at the 0.5 per cent level).[14] The *t*-values, $\bar{R}^2$, and D.W. statistics are uniformly higher for Equation 6 than for Equation 4; these statistics for Equation 7 are not substantially or uniformly different from those for Equation 5. As expected the coefficient for Ben/Inc is higher (with a higher *t*-value) in Equation 6 than in Equation 4.[15]

ANALYSIS OF RESULTS

The regression coefficients for the Ben/Inc terms from Equations 4 and 6 can be used to calculate the elasticities of the unemployment rates with respect to the benefit–income ratio; at the mean of Ben/Inc, this elasticity is equal to 0.62 and 0.68 for the over-all and male unemployment rates, respectively. These figures compare favourably with a similar elasticity calculated for Canada ($E_{Canada} = 0.69$) but they are much lower than that calculated from time series data for the United States ($E_{U.S.} = 1.5$) and a bit lower than that calculated from cross-section data for the U.S. ($E_{U.S.} = 0.80$).[16] They also appear to be higher than the elasticity for the U.K. implied by the work of MacKay and Reid (although in many respects their results are not directly comparable.[17]

The effect of the 1966 change in Britain's unemployment scheme can now be estimated. The most fundamental change at that time was the introduction of Earnings Related Supplements (ERS) and this had a substantial effect on subsequent benefit–income ratios. In the first two columns of Table 5.2, the benefit–income ratios for subsequent years are given without and with, respectively, the Earnings Related Supplements for those years. The next column gives the changes in the benefit–income ratios due to the Earnings Related Supplement. These figures, along with the regression coefficients for Ben/Inc and the actual unemployment rates, are used to calculate the changes in the unemployment rates that were induced by the Earnings Related Supplement which are presented in the fourth and seventh columns. Finally, the actual unemployment rates and the unemployment rates expected in the absence of Earnings Related Supplements are given in the fifth, eighth, sixth, and ninth columns, respectively.

The estimated effect of ERS shown in Table 5.2 is in essence based on an impact multiplier, and since any effect on the unemployment rate caused by ERS through the benefit/income ratio will further increase that ratio due to the feedback effect contained in the specification of equation (5), the reduced form multiplier is also of interest. Assuming that the SHIFT variable captures the effects of the introduction of ERS, we can calculate ∂U Rate$/\partial$ SHIFT, and evaluate this both as a 'first round' and reduced form effect. The impact multiplier is straightforwardly 0.2669 times the unemployment rate, or evaluated for illustrative purposes at an unemployment rate of 2.66 per cent (the mean of the unemployment rates in the period 1967–72), 0.71. The reduced form multiplier cannot be calculated directly because of the non-linearity of equation (4), but can be approximated to any desired degree of precision by iterative means. The reduced form multiplier corresponding to the impact multiplier of 0.71 given above is 0.79. The fact that the two multipliers are so nearly alike in value is due directly to the relatively small coefficient attached to the unemployment rate term in equation (5). Because of this small difference in multipliers and the computational difficulties associated with dealing with reduced form multipliers, we base ensuing discussing on the impact multiplier concept.

As can be seen from Table 5.2, the expected effects of Earnings Related

Table 5.2

Effects of ERS on over-all and male unemployment rates

Date	(1) B/I without ERS[a]	(2) B/I with ERS[a]	(3) ERS ΔB/I[a]	(4) ERS induced U Rate (Over-all)[c]	(5) Actual U Rate (Over-all)	(6) U Rate (over-all) without ERS induced U Rate[d]	(7) ERS induced U Rate (male)[e]	(8) Actual U Rate (male)	(9) U Rate (male) without ERS induced U Rate[f]
1967	0.518	0.732	0.214	0.49	2.19	1.70	0.64	2.63	1.99
1968	0.506	0.728	0.222	0.52	2.23	1.71	0.71	2.81	2.10
1969	0.476	0.710	0.234	0.55	2.26	1.71	0.75	2.87	2.12
1970	0.583	0.727	0.144	0.38	2.43	2.05	0.53	3.10	2.57
1971	0.518	0.776	0.258	0.90	3.40	2.50	1.24	4.36	3.12
1972	0.504	0.737	0.233	0.84	3.47	2.63	1.13	4.30	3.17
Means	0.518	0.735	0.218	0.61	2.66	2.05	0.84	3.35	2.51

[a]Source: Department of Health and Social Security.
[b]Equals Column 2 less Column 1.
[c]Equals Column 5 less Column 6.
[d]Equals the anti Ln of (Ln Column 5 less 1.197 × Column 3).
[e]Equals Column 8 less Column 9.
[f]Equals the anti Ln of (Ln Column 8 less 1.3026 × Column 3).

Supplement are quite substantial; on average the over-all and male unemployment rates were 30 per cent and 33 per cent higher, respectively, during this six-year period as a result of ERS. However, ERS does not account for the entire difference in experience with post-1966 unemployment rates compared with pre-1966 unemployment rates. Even after the adjustment for ERS effects, the average over-all and male unemployment rates during the 1967–72 period were 33 per cent and 54 per cent higher, respectively, than that for the 1960–5 period.

In the present model, the difference between average rates of unemployment for two periods can be explained by the difference between averages for the independent variables. These latter values were calculated for 1960–5 and 1967–72 periods and multiplied by the respective regression coefficients and an average unemployment rate. This yielded the amounts of the difference in average unemployment rates that were explained by differences in the average levels of independent variables; these are presented in the first and second columns of Table 5.3 for the over-all and male rates, respectively. The percentages of the total difference in average unemployment rates due to each variable are presented in the third and fourth columns for over-all and male rates, respectively.

Table 5.3
*Difference in average unemployment rates due to differences
in average values of independent variables,
1967–72 compared with 1960–5*

Variable	Differences in average unemployment rates		Per cent of total difference in average unemployment rates	
	Over-all	Male	Over-all	Male
Ben/INC$_{ERS}$	0.65	0.75	58	44
Ben/INC$_{W/O\ ERS}$	0.21	0.24	18	14
ILSET	0.52	1.09	46	63
RTTGNP	−0.25	−0.36	−22	−21
Total	1.13	1.72	100	100

These figures also show that the changes in the benefit–income ratio due to the introduction of Earnings Related Supplement were largely responsible for the change in unemployment experience (the Ben/Inc$_{ERS}$ variable accounting for 58 per cent and 44 per cent of this difference between the average over-all and male rates, respectively, for 1960–5 and 1967–72). However, even without ERS, the average benefit–income ratio was higher in the post-1966 period than in the pre-1966 period although the effect of this on the average unemployment rate was not as substantial as that of ERS (only 18 per cent and 14 per cent of the difference in average over-all and male U Rates, respectively, was explained by the Ben/Inc$_{W/O\ ERS}$ variable).

Another important factor in explaining the higher post-1966 unemployment rates appears to be the higher average value of the efficiency adjusted labour force index (ILSET accounts for 46 per cent and 63 per cent of the difference in average over-all and male U Rates, respectively). This in turn is mainly due to the higher average value for the efficiency index (Output per Person Employed) rather than for the labour force index (which actually decreased slightly on average). Thus, a large part of the different experience with the unemployment rate during the post-1966 period may be due to the greater rate of technical progress during that period and this appeared to have a greater effect on the male unemployment rate than the over-all rate.[18]

The final factor, the cyclical component (RTTGNP and RTTGNP.$_1$) was apparently responsible for post-1966 unemployment rates being somewhat lower than if pre-1966 cyclical experience had applied. This might be hailed as a small achievement for government stabilization policy, but in an open economy, such as that of the U.K., other factors may have been responsible. However, the latter is a question which is not the issue here.

CONCLUSION

Our initial hypothesis that the post-1966 increase in measured unemployment rates was to some extent induced by the increase in unemployment benefits has been supported by our empirical results; the hypothesized relationship was not only significant but also substantial. In addition, our results show that a large part of the post-1966 change in unemployment experience may be due to an increase in the rate of technical progress which has affected the efficiency of the existing labour force. However, of these two main results, the first is by far more important — not only in terms of the size of effect but also in terms of policy implications.

Perhaps the most clear and important policy implication is that the un-adjusted unemployment rate can not be used directly as an unambiguous target or indicator for macroeconomic policy. The usual post-Keynesian procedure has been to formulate one macroeconomic policy goal in terms of the rate of un-employment that represents 'full employment' and to recommend the manipu-lation of macroeconomic policy instruments in order to attain that rate. But if the 'full employment' unemployment rate is in part determined by other govern-ment policies or by structural characteristics of an economy which are not affected by macroeconomic policy instruments, changes in these policies or characteristics may induce the government to undertake 'incorrect' macro-economic policies (perhaps leading to more inflation and less of a reduction in unemployment than expected or desirable). In such a case, for example, govern-ment unemployment compensation policy and expenditure policy may be sub-stitutes with respect to changing the unemployment rate.[19] Obviously, if any un-employment rate is appropriate as an indicator or target for macroeconomic policy, it is a rate that has been adjusted for insurance induced unemployment (in much the same way as rates are currently adjusted for seasonal variation). Our results may serve as a first approximation for deriving an adjusted rate.

Another policy implication is that the costs of any new or proposed unemployment compensation scheme are likely to be under-estimated unless insurance-induced unemployment is taken into account. For example, while standard amounts of benefit per family unit for several types of units (single, married, and married with two children) went up by an average of 165 per cent between 1965 and 1971, actual total expenditure on unemployment benefits for Britain (excluding administration costs) went from £44,907,000 to £150,425,000 or up by 235 per cent. Expenditure excluding ERS payments went up by 179 per cent even though the standard benefit (excluding ERS) went up on average by only 48 per cent. Obviously, in order to improve the welfare of those persons unemployed for non-insurance-induced reasons, extra costs must be incurred to finance payments to insurance-induced unemployed persons. These extra costs are not necessarily without personal or social benefit. One of the implications of the previously described theory is that those who experience insurance-induced unemployment are more likely to have lower income levels than those who pay for the unemployment payments (since with a lower average income, the benefit–income ratios and, hence, induced unemployment will tend to be higher). Thus, there may be reason to believe that the marginal utility of income for the transfer recipients is higher than that for taxpayers. Such is the logic behind many tax-transfer schemes, so transfers for the insurance-induced unemployed need not be singled out for special criticism. Indeed such transfers may have several favourable effects. For example, another theoretical implication is that both voluntarily and involuntarily unemployed workers may be induced into undertaking greater search activity by higher benefit–income ratios. This in turn may lead to a better matching of workers to jobs and other improvements in labour market efficiency. However, as pointed out by Feldstein (1972), under certain conditions unemployment insurance may lead to greater seasonalization of employment in some industries, an inefficient expansion of these industries relative to other industries, and lower prices and wages for these industries that do not properly reflect private and social costs.

A further theoretical implication of our model is that restrictive provisions and administrative techniques that are designed to reduce insurance-induced unemployment may result in extra hardship for the non-insurance-induced unemployed, since in many cases the two types of unemployed persons will be indistinguishable because of the economic incentive of the former to appear to be the latter. Overly harsh administration may simply lower the social value of the unemployment compensation programme while raising administrative costs, yielding a net loss for society.[20] On the other hand, administration should attempt to eliminate the obvious cheaters, namely those who make fraudulent and multiple claims, since these tend to undermine the legitimacy of the tax-transfer system. A full solution to the problem of social control necessarily would involve an optimal level of administration, restrictions, insurance-induced as well as non-induced unemployment.

Clearly, such considerations indicate the need for more study of unemployment compensation as a tool of social policy. The present study represents only one step toward meeting this need.

NOTES

1. During the 1967–73 period the unemployment rate averaged 2.8 per cent v. 1.8 per cent for the equivalent length 1959–65 period and 'Phillips curve' type relationships which involved the unemployment rate seemed to change after the last quarter of 1966. See Bowers *et al.* (1970) for empirical investigations of pre- and post-1966 Phillips relationships.
2. For a comprehensive list of possible explanations see Bowers *et al.* (1970).
3. An ERS equal to one-third of weekly earnings between £9 and £30 (maximum of £7) was paid in addition to the normal flat rate benefit (which, in part, is related to the number of dependents). ERS payments last for twenty-six weeks and are not paid for six weeks if the potential recipient has quit voluntarily or was fired due to a misdemeanour.
4. As Gujarati has pointed out in his reply (Dec. 1972), Taylor's reasons for a 'shake-out' during the post-1966 period are not entirely convincing. An exception is that the introduction of the Redundancy Payments Act in 1965 may have induced employers to turn over labour more rapidly. It may be argued also that the ERS could have a similar effect since it would reduce pressure on employers to retain redundant workers. Thus, ERS and RP may have caused both Taylor's 'shake-out' and Gujarati's 'artificial' unemployment and thus be responsible for the change in unemployment rates as suggested by Gujarati. While Gujarati does not *directly* measure the effect of these factors on the employment rate, he suggests that it would be an interesting research project. Gujarati (Mar. 1972), p. 195.
5. Other short discussions can be found in Cairncross (1970), pp. 112–13 and MacKay and Reid (1972), pp. 1261–2.
6. Given the size, the restrictions, and the once-and-for-all nature of redundancy pay, it might be expected to have a slight income effect on the labour–leisure decision as it would mainly change the level of permanent income rather than the rate of the labour-leisure trade-off. Accordingly, empirical work by MacKay and Reid (1972) and by the present authors (results available on request) shows that the effect of redundancy payments on the unemployment rate is positive and relatively small but not statistically significant.
7. Of course, such an increase in time for leisure and for job search and a drawing of unemployment compensation payments would affect the unemployment tally and rate, since recipients must register as unemployed in order to receive unemployment benefits.
8. The OLS results are virtually identical to the 2SLS estimates. For those who may be interested, OLS yields:

$$Ln(U\ Rate) = -1.122 + 1.221\ Ben/Inc - 11.571\ RTTGNP - 4.604\ RTTGNP_{-1}$$
$$\qquad\quad (-5.692)\ (2.768) \qquad\quad (-5.636) \qquad\qquad (-2.272)$$

$$+\ 0.00008888\ ILSET, \qquad\qquad \bar{R}^2 = 0.925, D.W. = 1.272$$
$$(2.533)$$

$$Ben/Inc = 0.3156 + 0.02317\ U\ Rate + 0.2243\ SHIFT + 0.005932\ TIME$$
$$\qquad\quad (15.266)\ (1.861) \qquad\quad (11.101) \qquad\quad (3.479)$$

$$\bar{R}^2 = 0.979, D.W. = 2.049.$$

418 *The Macroeconomics of the Labour Market*

Since the coefficient of U Rate in the second equation is significantly different from zero at the 0.05 level, there is evidence that the OLS results are biased, and the TSLS results are preferred.

9. That is, from Equation 4,

$$\partial(\text{U Rate})/\partial(\text{Ben/Inc}) = 1.197 \text{ U Rate.}$$

This is consistent with the theoretical analysis of Grubel, Maki, and Sax (1975) 'which suggests that induced unemployment is drawn from the changed behavior of workers who are structurally or cyclically unemployed and that unemployment itself through its effect on the cost of job search influences the net incentives for the consumption of leisure created by benefits alone', p. 16.

10. Regression coefficients and *t*-values for Ben/Inc – Single and Ben/Inc – Married were 0.960 (2.159) and 1.036 (2.288), respectively. Other regression coefficients in Equation 1 were virtually identical. Only the coefficients of U Rate in Equation 5 were not significant at 5 per cent for both data sets.

11. Variables experimentally included in Equation 4 were time, per cent of labour force in 25–49 age group, labour force index (separately), output per person employed (separately), percentage changes in GNP index, and a redundancy payments index; variables experimentally included in Equation 5 were Retail Price index, Output per Person Employed and RPI × OPE. In most cases the coefficients of these variables were not significant. Since LFI and O/PE were colinear, it was decided to include them multiplicatively rather than separately in Equation 4 as this yielded improved results and had some theoretical justification. RPI and O/PE were also colinear in Equation 5 but in this case including RPI × OPE did not yield a significant coefficient.

12. Married women can be exempted from contributions to and, hence, benefits from the scheme. Figures from the *Supplement to British Labour Statistics: Historical Abstract* reveal that an extremely low percentage of unemployed married and single women receive ERS and that the percentage of unemployed married and single women that receive any benefit is lower than that for males.

13. It would be desirable to use the U Rate for only those who are fully eligible for unemployment compensation. However, a complete data series for such a variable was not available at the time of this study.

14. Again, the OLS results are virtually identical to the 2SLS estimates. OLS yields:

$$\text{Ln(U Rate) (Male)} = -2.058 + 1.224 \text{ Ben/Inc} - 12.352 \text{ RTTGNP}$$
$$(-10.081) \quad (3.153) \qquad\qquad (-6.742)$$

$$-5.264 \text{ RTTGNP}_{-1} + 0.0001859 \text{ ILSET}$$
$$(-2.873) \qquad\qquad (5.296)$$

$$\bar{R}^2 = 0.965, \text{D.W.} = 1.566$$

$$\text{Ben/Inc} = 0.3279 + 0.01750 \text{ U Rate (Male)} + 0.2231 \text{ SHIFT}$$
$$(17.076) \quad (1.648) \qquad\qquad (10.653)$$

$$+ 0.005584 \text{ TIME}$$
$$(2.956)$$

15. 2SLS estimation of the model using the female unemployment rate for U Rate revealed that the coefficient of Ben/Inc was insignificant at the 5 per cent level in that case.

16. See Grubel, Maki, and Sax (1975), p. 20 and Grubel and Maki (1974), p. 24.

17. MacKay and Reid investigate the relationship between *length* of unemployment after redundancy and unemployment benefits for a married man with two children using cross-section data from the 1966 to 1968 period. The regression coefficient for the unemployment benefit variable was 0.42; i.e. for a £1 change in unemployment benefit there would be a 0.42 week change in length of unemployment. Using the mean for the latter variable reported by MacKay and Reid and benefit–income ratios from our

data for the 1966–8 period, this implies an elasticity of weeks of unemployment with respect to the benefit income ratio ranging between 0.45 and 0.55 but this is not directly comparable with our elasticities. Further MacKay and Reid calculate that the introduction of the Earnings Related Supplement would increase total unemployment occurring from redundancy by about 12,000 men for 1968. Using figures from our data for total unemployment and Ben/Inc, this would indicate an elasticity for the unemployment rate with respect to Ben/Inc of approximately 0.07. However, this latter figure does not allow for those who may leave their jobs voluntarily.

18. This greater rate of technical progress might be observed in the graphs presented by Taylor (1972), pp. 1357–9, and, as he admits on p. 1356, may be an alternative to his labour-hoarding hypothesis. To distinguish between these hypotheses would require a more extensive microeconomic investigation.

19. However, these policies might be complementary with respect to influencing personal or social welfare. Even an adjusted unemployment rate might not be an unambiguous indicator of welfare since welfare may depend more directly on leisure and market and non-market income rather than on employment or unemployment *per se*.

20. However, the initial results of Holen and Horowitz (1974) indicate that certain increases in administrative effort may be very effective in lowering the unemployment rate in the United States.

REFERENCES

1. Bowers, J. K., Cheshire, P. C. and Webb, A. E., 'The change in the relationship between unemployment and earnings increases: a review of some possible explanations', *National Institute Economic Review*, No. 54, Nov. 1970, pp. 44–63.
2. Cairncross, A. K. (ed.), *Britain's Economic Prospects Reconsidered* (London, 1970).
3. Feldstein, M., 'Lowering the permanent rate of unemployment', Harvard Institute of Economic Research, Discussion Paper 259, Oct. 1972.
4. Grubel, H. G. and Maki, D., 'The effect of unemployment benefits on U.S. unemployment rates', Simon Fraser University, Department of Economics and Commerce Discussion Paper, Revised Dec. 1974.
5. —— —— and Sax, S., 'Real and induced unemployment in Canada', *Canadian Journal of Economics* (forthcoming), May 1975.
6. Gujarati, D., 'The behaviour of unemployment and unfilled vacancies', *Economic Journal*, Mar. 1972, pp. 195–204.
7. —— 'A reply to Mr. Taylor', *Economic Journal*, Dec. 1972, pp. 1365–8.
8. Holen, A. and Horowitz, S. A., 'Unemployment, unemployment insurance and the work test', Center for Naval Analyses Discussion Paper, Apr. 1974.
9. MacKay, D. I. and Reid, G. L., 'Redundancy, unemployment and manpower policy', *Economic Journal*, Dec. 1972, pp. 1256–72.
10. Parkin, M., 'Incomes policy: some further results on the determination of the rate of change of money wages', *Economica*, N.S. 37, Nov. 1970, pp. 386–401.
11. Taylor, J., 'The behaviour of unemployment and unfilled vacancies: Great Britain, 1958–1971. An alternative view', *Economic Journal*, Dec. 1972, pp. 1352–64.
12. Wallace, T. W., 'The effect of unemployment insurance on the measured unemployment rate', Queen's University, Institute for Economic Research, Discussion Paper, 1974.

5.8 Unemployment and the 'Dual Labor Market'*

Since the end of World War II, the United States has experienced persistently high unemployment. There have been 19 postwar years in which the unemployment rate exceeded four per cent; in 11 of those years it surpassed five per cent; in only four years did it fall below 3.5 per cent. This is a record far worse than that of any of the industrialized nations of Western Europe or Japan.

To explain this situation there were, until recent years, two divergent theories, the 'structuralist' and the Keynesian. The structuralists argued that its principal causes were technological displacement, shifting patterns of industrial production, foreign competition, and similar features which disrupted the matching of jobs and workers in the labor market. The Keynesians, on the other hand, were less concerned about labor market imbalances. They saw the labor market as a long 'queue': if the government's macroeconomic policies stimulated expansion, then eventually almost everybody in the line would be absorbed; where such policies were cautious and failed to keep pace with an increasingly productive labor force or the influx of workers into the market, unemployment would rise.

Both these interpretations saw unemployment as involuntary – i.e., individuals were actively seeking jobs and unable to find them – but their remedial policies differed. The structuralists argued for programs to correct imbalances through training and relocation – an approach that was embodied in manpower legislation in the 1960's. The Keynesians favored increasing demand through more aggressive monetary and fiscal policies.

Now the policy debate has been complicated by a third explanation, which disputes the *chronic* and *involuntary* character of unemployment, and argues that a significant portion of the unemployment in recent decades is both *temporary* and *voluntary*. This is the argument, for example, of Martin Feldstein in *The Public Interest* ('The Economics of the New Unemployment,' No. 33, Fall 1973). It holds that the measured level of unemployment exaggerates the degree of underlying imbalances in the labor market. In the case of youth, where the unemployment rates have been double or triple that of older workers, Feldstein argues that many young workers adopt a casual attitude to work, holding many jobs briefly, with spells of unemployment in between, and prefer this as a way of life. More generally, it is said that much of our unemployment does not reflect any Keynesian 'shortages' or structural skill imbalances, but results from the fact that many jobs are unattractive because of low pay or other undesirable characteristics; thus individuals choose an in-and-out pattern, combined with unemployment compensation, rather than stick to such jobs as steady work.

There is some evidence to support this view. In periods of both high and low unemployment, the duration of joblessness tends to be surprisingly short. More than half the unemployed are 'job searchers,' individuals who have just entered

*From Peter B. Doeringer and Michael J. Piore, 'Unemployment and the "Dual Labor Market" ', *The Public Interest*, Vol. 38, Winter 1975, pp. 66–79.

the labor market or have quit to change jobs. These 'voluntary' movements are especially common among women and young persons, the groups which have composed a growing fraction of the unemployed in recent years. Many of the unemployed, particularly among the relatively low-paid, can find work, but only in dead-end jobs. Much unemployment, therefore, seems to be 'voluntary,' in that jobs may be available but are undesirable; and this is why the overall rate is high and the turnover of the jobless is so large.

This view of unemployment has gained a variety of adherents. For economists, it has the attraction of newly discovered 'facts' that seem to contradict much of the conventional wisdom in the field. For policy makers, particularly those advocating free markets and fiscal conservatism, it challenges the interventionist thinking that guided employment and training policy in the 1960's. From such data, it is but a short step to argue that responsibility for unemployment should be shifted from the public sphere (where it rested in the 1960's) to individuals. The failure of workers to take jobs, not inadequate aggregate demand or ineffective manpower policies, becomes the root of unemployment. Where labor market policy is to be faulted is in its intrusion into the structure of employment incentives through welfare, unemployment compensation, and minimum wages. Given the new interpretation of unemployment, it is argued that the effort to reduce unemployment to a three or four per cent level by Keynesian or structuralist policies is misguided. In short, the unemployment problem may best be 'solved' by accepting more slack in the economy and by reducing some of our social welfare arrangements.

THE NATURE OF LABOR MARKETS

What is clear is that the 'conventional' explanations of unemployment, or more specifically, of the nature of labor markets in American society, are inadequate. Even though there is some agreement on the *facts* about 'voluntary' unemployment, there is certainly less agreement about the reasons for such unemployment, and still less about the policy consequences that would derive from such facts. Behind all this controversy is a major effort within economics to recast the old theories and find some better explanation for how individuals behave in the labor market. It is only by going to these theories, and the differences among them, that we can seek to understand the 'chronic' character of unemployment in the United States.

Within the terms of the current debate, there are three somewhat conflicting approaches to understanding the character of labor markets and the responses of individuals to them. These are: 1) human capital theories; 2) job search theories; and 3) dual labor market theories.

1. *Human capital.* The human capital perspective on the labor market is most commonly associated with economists at the University of Chicago, particularly Gary Becker. It takes as its model the rational economic man who acts to maximize his returns, and extends this to labor market decisions. The theory of

human capital treats unemployment as part of a concern with the determinants of earnings. Unemployment, like income, is thought to reflect differences among workers in ability, in levels of training and education, and in types of work experience. The latter two, it is argued, are to be understood in terms of 'invest-ment' decisions of time and money made by *individuals* (workers and sometimes their employers), to acquire skills necessary for different kinds of jobs and levels of pay. The unemployed are those whose abilities, skills, and productive capa-cities are insufficient to make it worthwhile for employers to hire them *at the prevailing market wages.*

2. *Job search.* This theory grows out of efforts to explain an observed trade-off between unemployment and rates of change in wages. The work done in this area, much of it by Charles Holt and his colleagues at the Urban Institute in Washington, emphasizes that unemployment is the outgrowth of a process of job search where workers have limited information, uncertainty, or faulty ex-pectations about the labor market. It assumes, for example, that people who first begin looking for jobs lack basic information about the labor market, and have higher expectations about pay than can be realized. As a result, workers may reject the jobs that they first encounter and continue searching. Gradually, this procedure enables them to make a more realistic evaluation of available jobs and to adjust their expectations accordingly. Eventually the search process re-sults in employment, or in withdrawal from the labor market; thus the emphasis is on the job hunt and its outcomes. In its extreme form, this theory would interpret all unemployment as 'frictional' – i.e., largely 'temporary' and always resolved in one way or another.

3. *Dual labor markets.* The third revision of the traditional views of unem-ployment – with which the authors of this article are strongly identified – derived from empirical study of the lower-paying labor markets. Much of this experience was gained in the civil rights activities and studies of anti-poverty programs in the 1960's, but the theories to which it leads are closely related to an earlier tradition of institutional labor economics associated with names such as John R. Commons, Selig Perlman, and John T. Dunlop.

The dual labor market approach postulates a labor market which is divided into *primary* and *secondary* sectors. The primary sector contains the better-paying, steady, and preferred jobs in the society. Those employed in this sector possess job security and advancement opportunities, established working condi-tions, and, whether unionized or not, employment relationships governed by a more or less explicit system of industrial jurisprudence. Work in the primary sector is associated with an *established position* in the economy. Workers here tend to identify with institutions: the company for which they work, their union, their craft, or other occupation. One who has lost a primary-sector job is unemployed in the involuntary, Keynesian sense. He has not chosen to go to look for another job, but has been laid off because of contractions in the economy or in his industry. He may accept less attractive work temporarily, but essentially he is waiting to regain the clearly identified position from which he has been displaced. Being 'unemployed' really means being out of one's accustomed place of work.

The secondary sector, by contrast, is marked by low-paying, unstable, and dead-end employment, with frequent lay-offs and discharges. Because second-ary sector jobs tend to be self-terminating, or are basically unattractive, they provide little incentive for workers to stick with them, and consequently have high voluntary turnover as well. Unemployment in the secondary sector thus is not associated with workers waiting around to regain an accustomed position, but is part of a shuttling process from one low-paying position to another.

What is important to note is that the kind of unemployment which public policy has recently focused upon (and which Feldstein has dealt with) is less the displacement of primary-sector workers than the unemployment concentrated among teenagers, women, and ethnic and racial minorities — those who tend to be employed in the secondary labor market.

SOCIAL PATTERNS AND INSTITUTIONAL FORCES

The human capital and job search theories both share a common tie to tradi-tional economic theory. They presume the existence of a fluid and competitive labor market shaped by economic motivation. Relative wages are assumed to be flexible, employers are believed willing and able to adjust their employment in response to changes in wages and productivity, and workers are assumed to make training and information investments easily in response to changes in relative wages. For both human capital and search theories, unemployment is the result of personal barriers to job access within this competitive market framework. In human capital theory, the main barrier is thought to stem from insufficient 'purchases' of education and training. In search theory, lack of information is the main barrier, and job hunt of the unemployed is interpreted as an investment process, i.e., gathering further information about the labor market. For both theories, investment by workers of time and money to secure higher future incomes is assumed to be the major way adjustment takes place in the labor market.

Within the economics profession there is a growing uneasiness with these assumptions — particularly the assumption that self-development or human investment decisions are made by individuals acting independently of one another, are motivated largely by economic gain, and are implemented through the market system. Yet economists do not find it easy to dismiss these assump-tions, for they do derive from the utilitarian theory of human behavior on which the models of neoclassical economics rest. While few economists have argued that such assumptions characterize the entire range of human behavior, there has been almost no attempt to define the limits within which they are realistic.

One could say that the nature of educational and informational barriers could equally explain the nature of dual labor markets. But the research on which the dual labor market hypothesis is based rejects that interpretation. Put most baldly, it argues that the character of dual labor markets is best explained by institutional and sociological, not economic variables (in the neoclassical sense) — that the problem of unemployment is rooted less in individual behavior than in the character of institutions and the social patterns that derive from them.

Let us take one important instance where the dual labor market theory stands in contrast to human capital theory. This is the argument, based on our empirical observation, that much skill training is not the outgrowth of economic decisions. A considerable portion of the training necessary for the preferred jobs in the primary sector takes place not in schools or in classes, but *on the job*, and is essentially a process of 'socialization' as this is understood in sociology. The acquisition of the skills to perform particular tasks — what, in other words, is normally thought of as being acquired through education or formal training — really depends on the new employee's acceptance by the established group of workers, who must show him what to do in order for learning to take place. Without such acceptance, and his conformity to their norms, the employee faces not only the psychological discouragement of being excluded from the group, but the failure to acquire the requisite skills — the 'learning of the ropes' of the job.

In effect, a key factor in obtaining 'primary-sector' skills and a job in the primary sector is 'social acceptability,' which cannot be 'bought' in the usual sense. This means that jobs and upward mobility in the primary sector are sensitive to such factors as *race, sex, and shared social beliefs*, which determine social acceptability within incumbent work groups.

Institutional factors also account for observed rigidity in the labor market. Wages often seem unresponsive to changes in the supply and demand for labor, not because of trade unions or governmental wage relations, but because the sociological character of the training process and of the demands for equity at the work place discourage the type of competition among workers upon which competitive pay adjustments are predicated. Similarly, the *job structure* within enterprises is relatively unresponsive to changes in wages or productivity, not because employers fail to make rational manning and equipment decisions, but because the economics of job design is dominated by other variables such as the degree of product standardization and the scale of production.

Thus the dual labor market hypothesis suggests that microeconomic theory needs to be recast on the basis of a very different set of assumptions from those which underlie much of contemporary economic thought. If reductions in unemployment are to occur through changes in job structure, through on-the-job training, or through adjustments in relative wage rates, then the *institutional* forces governing these variables must be explicitly considered. In a theoretical sense, it is this conflict about the very assumptions of contemporary economics that lies at the heart of the recurrent controversies over the interpretation of unemployment.

THEORY AND PUBLIC POLICY

Controversy over the theory of labor markets is of more than academic interest, for it entails differences about the policies necessary to reduce unemployment. Basically, both human capital and job search theories lead to policies directed at the supply side of the labor market and at the decisions of individual workers. These theories favor solutions that subsidize worker investments in training, that facilitate the realistic assessment of employment prospects, and that permit market forces to express (free of 'distortions') the economic incentives that are thought to govern worker investments in training, information, and job search. These theories do not inquire into the social factors affecting worker choice, nor do they concern themselves with understanding the determinants of training opportunities that are presumed to control such investments.

The policies suggested by Martin Feldstein in his article in *The Public Interest* illustrate the job search–human capital approach to reducing unemployment. The most novel of these are proposed changes in the application of minimum wage laws to youth and in the unemployment insurance system. The minimum wage, he argues, prevents youths from 'purchasing' training from employers by forbidding wage bargains that would allow youth to get training on the job, and some way must be found to get around this obstacle. Similarly, Feldstein argues that the large cushion of unemployment insurance both encourages an 'over-investment' in job search on the part of workers and reduces incentives for their employers to eliminate cyclical and seasonal fluctuations in jobs. He would correct these 'perverse effects' by imposing penalties upon individuals, through reduced compensation, as the frequency and duration of their unemployment increased.

Such proposals are open to question even within the theoretical framework in which they were conceived. The suspension of minimum wages for teenagers might mean simply the supplanting of adult women and minorities in the secondary-sector employment opportunities which these groups now share in common; the price of increased employment for youth, therefore, might be higher unemployment rates for women and minorities. The proposed changes in the unemployment system would penalize all the unemployed — those without control of their employment patterns as well as those with a substantial range of choice.

The dual labor market approach, however, questions these policy proposals on broader analytical grounds. The critique centers on two main issues: the origins of short-term unemployment in the secondary sector, and the importance of the structure of employment and training opportunities as a cause of unemployment.

The first point can be illustrated by the labor market behavior of high-unemployment groups, such as youth and ethnic minorities. It is often argued that young workers are interested only in short-term employment which will interfere minimally with school or leisure-time activities, yet will yield incomes capable of supporting these activities. Thus jobs in the secondary sector, with their tolerance of lateness, absenteeism, and high turnover, are particularly suited to such workers, and it is this combination of casual work attachment and irregular jobs that seems to explain a great deal about youth unemployment.

Yet virtually all young people in our society eventually decide to marry and settle down into permanent employment. The timing of such decisions and the shift to a stable life style is in large part a function of the availability of stable jobs. In periods of full employment, stable job attachment occurs earlier in working life as employers in the primary sector reach into the youth labor pool. And recent studies of youth, especially low-income youth, suggest that if more such primary-sector jobs were available, more youths would settle down, and settle down earlier.

There also seem to be important threshold effects. Most youths, particularly those from lower-class and working-class backgrounds, during their adolescence belong to relatively tight peer groups. Under favorable labor market circumstances, the members of the group marry and obtain permanent jobs at about the same time. The fact that the group makes the move together supports each individual in the transition to stable life styles and work routines. When the labor market is loose, however, and most people cannot find stable jobs, the group continues its adolescent pattern of behavior. The few individuals who do find steady jobs are forced either to abandon their friends, or to face a continual choice between the demands of their life style and those of their old associates. For many this conflict is resolved by abandoning stable employment.

The conflict is particularly acute for many minority youths, who have difficulty in forming the kinds of social bonds at work which might substitute for the adolescent bonds on the street. That problem, combined with the difficulty of finding a sufficient number of stable jobs to permit the street group as a whole to shift its routine, undoubtedly contributes to the relatively high rates of failure in employment among even those few youths who manage to find stable shelters in the labor market.

Processes of this kind make it difficult to evaluate youth unemployment by a simple economic measure. They also suggest that the historical spread between teenage and adult unemployment rates is not immutable, but is rooted in the sociological character of group life.

Like the employment difficulties of young people, those of ethnic and racial minorities are directly related to the socioeconomic structure. As far back as these markets can be traced, the low-paying job market in general, and that for minorities in particular, has to be understood in terms of migration. Historically there have always been secondary-sector jobs ('dirty work') which the native labor force has refused to accept. Thus migrants from less affluent rural areas, or immigrants from foreign countries, have been imported to fill them. These migrants usually conceive of their stay as temporary. Many immigrants intend to, and a great many actually do, return home within months. Or, if they stay, they accept these jobs as the 'price' of change and hope that their children will do better. And quite often, such jobs, unstable and dead-end though they may be, are still preferable to the conditions in the place which the migrant has left.

Out of the migration stream, however, there eventually grows a 'second generation' raised in the urban areas. This second generation shares the perspective of the native population and no longer accepts the kind of jobs which originally attracted its parents. But unlike the earlier white migrant groups that were assimilated into the good, primary-sector jobs, today's 'new' immigrants — largely black or Spanish-speaking — face continuing discrimination that largely confines them to the secondary sector.

The current black labor force is the offspring of a migratory stream from the rural agricultural South, initiated by the World War II and postwar boom. But the old migration is exhausted, and the changing unemployment and labor force participation rates among blacks in urban areas are a product of a gradual transition from 'first' generation migrants, to a new generation that is unable to move up to the kinds of jobs in the primary sector to which it aspires. The high unemployment rates in the minority labor force are less a result of unwillingness to work than of an inability to obtain jobs in the primary sector.

THE DISTRIBUTION OF JOBS

If this diagnosis of youth and minority unemployment is correct, then what is needed are two kinds of responses: 1) Public policies which end the discrimination that has closed primary-sector jobs to various groups of workers, and 2) policies which shift the distribution of jobs away from the secondary and into the primary sector.

The idea of discrimination is not neglected today in orthodox economic theory. But the orthodox view, as expressed in the work of Gary Becker, implies that discrimination operates in the market and is restrained by competitive forces. It can be eliminated by strengthening competition and by raising the cost of discriminatory behavior. This kind of analysis thus calls for 'economic,' not 'political' action. But the dual labor market hypothesis, by viewing hiring, training and promotion as social processes, suggests that race, sex, and ethnicity are central factors in determining who gains access to the primary sector, and suggests that the necessary corrective action lies in instruments like the Federal Contract Compliance program and Title VII of the Civil Rights Act of 1964. The political opposition to compliance programs such as affirmative action really seeks primarily to preserve the existing social character of job allocations, rather than to protect the efficiency of the market.

The means of shifting the distribution of jobs from the secondary to the primary sector are more difficult to develop. Market dualism is the result of a complex array of decisions that govern recruitment, hiring, training, subcontracting, technological change, and capital investment. These decisions are made by corporations, trade unions, and informal work groups and, when looked at individually, they seem to be dominated by unique circumstances — local labor market conditions, particular personalities and social attitudes, political considerations, and the varied objectives of trade unions. The complexity of these relationships between institutional policies and labor market structures almost defies rational analysis and has been largely ignored by economists in the United States, leaving the economic literature barren of clues to the specific origins of dualism.

But in Japan and Italy, two industrialized countries where dualism is a widespread theme in economic analysis, the labor market structure is seen as closely related both to differences in employment practices between large and small business enterprises and to the relative strength of trade unions. In these countries, the initial emergence of dualism can be traced to rigidities in labor utilization introduced by large firms and to strong work-place union organizations. Because large corporations can smooth out fluctuations in production through marketing efforts, inventory adjustments, and sub-contracting, their employment tends to be stable relative to smaller enterprises. Stability of employment and large size also favor union organization at the work-place, and union activity appears to foster further improvements in the employment security and economic advancement associated with the primary sector. The persistence of labor market duality as these countries industrialize can be traced, in part, to the failure of unionization to penetrate the secondary sector and to the tendency of government to subsidize indirectly the secondary sector through the exemption (*de facto* or *de jure*) of small businesses from various costs of social welfare legislation.

Some obvious parallels can be found in the United States. Large enterprises dominate the primary sector and, with some notable exceptions such as the garment industry, union activity has historically been concentrated in the primary sector.[1] Until quite recently, the smallest firms have received exemptions from the coverage of social welfare legislation, and in some states and localities government assistance has contributed to keeping secondary employment alive.

These limited examples of the sources of market duality imply that reform of the structure of labor markets must be undertaken in a wider policy context than is ordinarily considered. It must include policies of governing industrial structure, trade unions and collective bargaining, patterns of exemption from social welfare legislation, and the competitive position of small business, as well as manpower training and employment. Such widespread intervention, however, is outside the scope of labor market policy as it has traditionally been conceived and certainly exceeds our present capacity to manage labor market processes through public policy.

TRANSFORMING LABOR MARKETS

While major reorganization of the dual market structure through microeconomic policies seems beyond the reach of government action, there do remain important and largely untapped opportunities for inducing structural change through aggregate employment policy. To illustrate this point, consider the effect of expanding the demand for labor uniformly throughout the economy. In principle, adding workers to the primary sector would require employers to reduce hiring standards, to recruit from among previously rejected or excluded sources of labor, and to enlarge their training and upgrading activities – in short, the secondary sector would provide the major supply of new hires in the primary sector. The logic of this scenario would indicate that a policy of full employment, if pursued long enough and far enough, would either eliminate the secondary sector or, through competition for scarce labor, cause secondary sector jobs to conform more closely to those of the primary sector.

Unfortunately, however, full employment policy is too crude an instrument to insure that a tightening of the labor market would expand the primary sector significantly. In fact, employers and unions in the primary sector often seem to favor *temporary* solutions to tight job markets, solutions that do not provide the newly hired with the full career benefits of primary employment. Thus one finds companies in the primary sector relying on subcontracting and the use of temporary workers to avoid the costs and risks associated with giving primary market status to workers from the secondary sector.

As a result, the pressures for structural change that should accompany full employment often leave the dual labor market intact during periods of both high and low unemployment. Much of this preference for temporary solutions can be traced to the historical experience with 'stop-and-go' growth. Recessions reduce labor demand in the primary sector, but they do not provide corresponding relief in the costs of commitment to career employment. These costs, combined with aversion to uncertainty, and with race and sex issues that inevitably accompany the expansion of the primary sector, often lead to the avoidance of structural adjustments that might be irreversible.

In general, obligations of steady employment are accepted only when there is an expectation of a stable level of demand. In the factory, these are the jobs associated with relatively permanent production levels. In the craft union, this is the level that yields relatively continuous employment for permanent members. The unstable employment residual is left to the secondary sector. Any use of aggregate policy as an instrument of structural change, therefore, means that one has to establish a credible commitment to stable and continuous full employment.[2]

On the basis of these contrasting theories of the labor market, the efforts to transform labor markets can go in either of two directions. The human capital and search theories would seek either to make the labor market more flexible and competitive by reducing or offsetting the importance of market 'distortions' like minimum wages and 'transfer payments' that reduce work incentives or, when necessary, to subsidize the employment of those with labor market difficulties.

The alternative, suggested by the dual labor market analysis, is to focus on the importance of market institutions and the behavior of work force groups in the operation of the labor market. The search for policy instruments to redress labor market duality involves improved anti-discrimination activities, the reorganization of the secondary sector to stabilize and rationalize the utilization of man-power, and the exploration of institutional solutions to encourage the growth of primary-like employment in the secondary sector. Above all, the dualist approach stresses the primary role of full employment in encouraging the structural transformations required to reduce inequalities in employment and training opportunities. Full employment is necessary on the demand side to expand the primary labor market and to facilitate the absorption of hard-to-employ groups. And on the supply side of the labor market, this increase in primary opportunities should favorably affect the labor market commitment of many of the young and the disadvantaged.

NOTES

1. Despite serious competitive obstacles to improving employment conditions in the secondary sector, where unionization has taken hold in industries such as apparel, hospitals, longshoring, and building services, it has introduced benefits that resemble those in the primary sector.
2. For example, when the central authorities are committed to achieving a *sustained* unemployment rate of 3.5 per cent, an economic expansion leading to a four per cent unemployment rate will encourage employers to increase their volume of primary jobs. When the target is five per cent, however, a similar rate of expansion and level of unemployment will be perceived as a temporarily aberration of policy, and the expansion in jobs is more likely to occur in the secondary sector.

5.9 The course of distribution*
[. . .]

To trace the course of distribution distinctly we need more detail than we have been able to provide. It is true that because shares in the whole national product have depended much on the relative size of different sectors, and especially that of the sector of self-employment, we have confined our study to industry — that is, generally, to mining, manufacturing, transport, public utilities and construction. But even within industry alone, the division of the aggregate product depends on the relative sizes of the particular industries, as well as on changes in the share of pay and profit in the value added by any one of them. Industries differ widely in the amount of capital per worker, but not nearly so much in the rate of profit on capital: so changes in the relative sizes of different industries will raise or lower profits relatively to pay in industry as a whole. It is probable that differences in the proportionate composition of the aggregate

*From E. H. Phelps Brown and Margaret H. Browne, *A Century of Pay* (London: Macmillan, 1968).

industry of different countries account for some of the differences we have found between their wage/income ratios; and that, in any one country, changes in that composition account for some of the observed movements of the wage/income ratio over time. It seems unlikely, however, that they can account for so much movement as we find. This must also be due to changes in the rate of profit relatively to the pay per man that run through a number of industries at the same time. What account of the process of distribution does our evidence suggest?

It will be remembered that our materials have lent themselves to arrangement within the identity

$$s \equiv 1 - rk,$$

where s is the share of labour in the product, r is the rate of profit on capital, and k is the capital/output ratio. (We shall follow convenient precedent here in using 'labour' to comprise all employed, which in turn, within industry, we take as virtually equivalent to all occupied; and in denoting all earned incomes by 'wages'.) We have not directly estimated the share of labour, but can take the year to year movements of our wage/income ratio in industry as a sufficiently close indicator of the corresponding movements of the share of labour as here defined — the two will differ only to the extent that the proportion of wage-earners among all employed changes, and this will be small in the short run. We can therefore obtain a synoptic view of the course of distribution, by following the movements of the wage/income ratio in industry, the rate of profit, and the capital/output ratio. Unfortunately all three are available only for Germany, the U.K., and the U.S.A., and that only in the first two periods, for we have not been able to draw on continuous estimates of the capital stock throughout Period Three. Period Two, moreover, is too short, and within its limits too much affected by the great depression of the 1930s, to throw much light on distributive trends.

The purpose of Table 5.4 is to survey the prevailing levels of these three variables and the extent of their variability, by citing the lowest and highest values of each in each period. Because the annual series were moved about so sharply by the trade cycle in the first two periods, we have removed most of that fluctuation by taking a seven-year moving average, and it is the lowest and highest entries of this that we have taken. Period Three suffered fewer fluctuations and we cover only eleven years, so here we have taken simply the lowest and highest annual entries.

Table 5.4 reveals some differences between periods and countries. That the rates of profit lie in a zone that is altogether lower in Period Two than in Period One is due partly to the downward displacement of the early 1920s [. . .] but even more to the impact of the deep and protracted depression of the early 1930s. In Germany and the U.K. the wage/income ratio ruled higher in Period Three than ever before, and in the U.S.A. it remained around the high level reached under the New Deal, which likewise appears to have been without

Table 5.4

Five countries, three periods: Lowest and highest value of 7-year moving averages in Periods One and Two, and annual entries in Period Three, of the wage/income ratio in industry (in U.K. Period 2, in U.S.A. Periods 1 and 2 manufacturing only), and of the rate of profit and the capital/output ratio in the mainly industrial sector

	France	Germany	Sweden	U.K.	U.S.A.
Period One					
Span begins		1860[1]	1870	1870	1889
1. Wage/income ratio, %		62–67	51–67	63–73	59–71
2. Rate of profit, %		9.0–12.0[3]		11.5–14.7[4]	8.4–14.1[3]
3. Capital/output ratio		2.14–3.27		2.16–3.17	2.52–2.88
Period Two					
Span begins		1925	1920	1924	1921[2]
1. Wage/income ratio, %		62–64	56–62	68–71	68–80
2. Rate of profit, %		0.29–4.35[4]		9.2–11.7[3]	2.3–7.9[4]
3. Capital/output ratio		3.11–3.82		2.07–2.30	2.31–2.97
Period Three					
1950–1960					
1. Wage/income ratio, %	58–69	70–81	50–62	76–82	71–76

[1] Wage/income ratio, 1880   [2] Wage/income ratio, 1920
[3] Inferred rate   [4] Directly calculated rate

precedent; but there seems to have been no such shift in the zone containing the Swedish ratio. We have already [. . .] discussed the possible reasons for higher wage/income ratios appearing in Period Three; unfortunately we lack estimates of the associated levels of the rate of profit and the capital/output ratio. In all three Periods, the Swedish zone lay lower than the others.

But these differences apart, what Table 5.4 brings out is the extent to which each variable has lain within the same not very wide zone throughout a number of years and in more than one country. Through most of Periods One and Two, and in four countries, the wage/income ratio appears to have lain in the region of 60 to 70 per cent. Throughout the long span of Period One, the range of 8 to 15 per cent contains the variations of the rate of profit, after cyclical fluctuations have been removed, in all three countries for which we have estimates. The capital/output ratio, taking Periods One and Two and the three countries together, lay between extremes of 2.07 and 3.82; but the 3.82 is due to the catastrophic fall of output in Germany in 1931–1933, and if we except this the maximum becomes 3.27.

It appears, then, that each of the three variables remained for the most part within a determinate and limited zone of values that was common to different countries. The numerical values of these zones are familiar to us: we commonly expect, for instance, that the prevailing rate of profit, on capital bearing the risks of enterprise, will be the order of 10 per cent, and not 3 per cent, or 23. But what seems part of the natural order of things requires all the more to be accounted for. There is no immediately apparent reason why an economy should not be found in which pay of all kinds absorbed only half the product, the remainder accruing to capital as a rate of profit of 12½ per cent on a capital stock amounting to four times the output −

$$0.5 = 1 - (0.125 \times 4);$$

or in which the share of pay was nine-tenths, with a 5 per cent rate of profit and a capital/output ratio of two −

$$0.9 = 1 - (0.05 \times 2).$$

How can we account for the actual values being those we commonly find, such as

$$0.75 = 1 - (0.10 \times 2.5)?$$

We can offer an explanation in two stages. First, formally, we can draw on the findings of the mathematical economists who have built models of economies that are developing through the growth of the working population, the accumulation of capital, and technical progress (R. G. D. Allen, 1967).* Among these models the neoclassical have been designed so as to generate a behaviour over time which in three respects reproduces salient features of the actual course of western economies: the real rate of return per man-year rises in proportion to the output per man; the rate of profit is steady; the capital/output ratio is steady. This behaviour flows from assumptions built into the model, of which the chief again are three. First, there is a market for the factors of production labour and capital, in which the demand for each is derived from its marginal productivity, and the rate of return on each is brought into equality with the marginal productivity of the quantity employed. Second, production is carried on under technical conditions such that there are constant returns to scale, and technical progress affects the relation of inputs to output in certain defined ways. Third, a condition is formulated by which the amount of investment is determined: one such is that investment must equal the amount of savings made out of the income currently generated according to fixed propensities to save.

The macroeconomic theorist, then, shows us how the share of pay in the product, the rate of profit and the capital/output ratio will behave as we have seen them to have done in the western economies, if their factor markets, technical conditions and investment determination conform with the assumptions out of which his models are built. In this there is a great gain of understanding. True, we do not know that it is the mechanism of these models and these alone that can generate behaviour like that of the western economies, but we do see one intelligible way in which that behaviour could have been generated: we see

[*R. G. D. Allen, *Macroeconomic Theory*, London, Macmillan, 1967 − Ed.]

how our variables can have been kept within certain zones common to different countries, because the markets and techniques of those economies had certain basic traits in common.

Yet so far this is only in general terms: it shows us in what conditions, for instance, the rate of profit will lie within a certain zone, but for all we know this zone might as well be centred on 50 as on 10 per cent. In the second stage of explanation, however, the actual numerical values can be accounted for if it is the case that investible funds have generally been in elastic supply at prospective rates of profit not far removed from 10 per cent, and that enterprise has been persistent and pervasive in carrying investment into openings that held this prospect forth. In that case we can formulate a new equation to govern the flow of investment: instead of setting this equal to the flow of savings that arises when savings are a fixed proportion of income, we require it to be such as to adjust the stock of capital so that the marginal productivity of capital shall be equal to a rate of profit, say 10 per cent, which is given as a parameter of the system. The marginal productivity of capital being maintained at this rate, the capital/output ratio will also be determined numerically. Thus supposing the production function is of the Cobb–Douglas form and, with suitable choice of units can be written

$$Y = L^{0.75} C^{0.25} \tag{1}$$

then the marginal productivity of capital, held say at 10 per cent, will be a quarter of its average productivity, and this puts the capital/output ratio at 2½ –

$$\frac{\partial Y}{\partial C} = 0.25 \frac{Y}{C} = 0.1,$$

$$\frac{C}{Y} = 2.5. \tag{2}$$

The basic assumption here is of a stream of investible funds available at prospective rates of return lying within a zone around 10 per cent, and channelled by enterprise into expanding production at many points in the economy. This assumption is not merely heuristic, but is substantiated by a fact of experience. Save for France, the western economies had to find jobs for working populations that were growing at rates of from 10 to 15 per cent per decade: but they solved the problem – as the numbers seeking jobs grew, so did the number of jobs. There was cyclical unemployment, and much unemployment at all times among the unskilled; but over a span of fifty or sixty years in which the numbers needing jobs would double, the margin of unemployment did not widen. This can have been so only if new jobs were being opened as new hands were looking for them, if existing businesses were expanding and new ones starting up in so far as labour was available. There was no invisible hand to match applicants with vacancies place by place, and from one year to another the balance between them tilted now this way and now that. But in the aggregate the match was made. It has not been made in some of the poor countries whose population has been rising in recent years. That it was made in the western economies is best explained by the pervasive pressure of enterprise and investible funds in them towards the expansion of activity and the creation of employment.

So far, then, we account for the rate of profit, the capital/output ratio and the share of pay in the product all remaining within certain not very wide zones, as follows. At a prospective rate of profit in the region of 10 per cent the supply of investible funds has been so elastic that investment has adjusted the capital stock so as to keep its marginal productivity within the region of 10 per cent. This steadying of the rate of profit has gone on while the labour force has been growing and technique has been changing; but the form of the aggregate production function has ensured that the growth of the capital stock which in these changing circumstances will steady the rate of profit will also steady the capital/output ratio. Thereby and necessarily the share of pay in the product is steadied too. The outcome depends in part on the technical relations of inputs and output expressed by the aggregate production function, in part on the decisions made by economic agents. These decisions are of two kinds. There is first the decision to invest — a combination of the willingness to provide funds with the initiative of the entrepreneur in seizing or creating an opening for investment, wherever the prospective rate of return is not less than that which is generally looked for and at which the funds are available. Second, and no less necessary to the outcome, there are the decisions taken in the labour market, which similarly check any divergence between the marginal productivity of labour and the prevailing rate of pay. If it is the marginal productivity that for the moment is the higher, more workers may be employed so that the marginal productivity is reduced; and/or, to the extent that the supply of labour is inelastic, competition between employers will raise the rate of pay.

Evidently there is room here for some shifting of the zones from time to time, and for some wandering within them. The zones will shift if the technical conditions of production change, or if there is a change in the rate of profit that is sufficient to attract investible funds. There will be wanderings within the zones, and occasional excursions outside them, if the adjustments between marginal yields and the intakes or prices of factors are sluggish and lag behind the course of change, or on the other hand overshoot the mark; and if they respond only to big divergences.

Table 5.4 indicated the extent of the stability of the zones, but also — notably in the rate of profit in Period Two — the possibility of their shifting. What also of the wanderings in and around them? These are illustrated in Figure 5.2. The sharp fluctuations of the 8-year cycle have been largely eliminated here, in all but the most severe cycles, by the use of moving averages. The remaining movements are still marked. Three variables are shown, but because (if the wage/income ratio can be taken as varying closely with the share of pay in the product) they are locked into the identity $s \equiv 1 - rk$, only two of them are capable of independent movement. The most conspicuous feature is the inverse

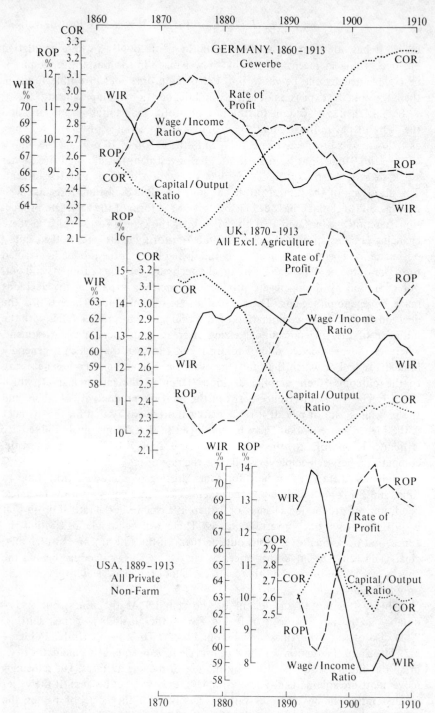

FIG. 5.2 Three countries, 1860–1913: (1) Wage/income ratio. (2) Capital/output ratio. (3) Rate of profit inferred from (1) and (2). 7-year moving averages.

movement of the rate of profit and the capital/output ratio in Germany and the U.K., a relationship which appears also in the U.S.A., though less strikingly, for here the movements of the capital/output ratio are smaller. This inverse relation can have a number of explanations.

The simplest would be that it arises from errors in the estimates of the capital stock. It is these estimates that are suspect rather than those of profits, partly because they are inherently more difficult and hazardous, partly because they stand largely on their own whereas the estimates of profits have to fit into those of pay and product. If the estimates of capital stock do have a steady bias upwards, we shall find − what Germany shows from the 1870s onwards − a rising capital/output ratio and a falling rate of profit; and if, conversely, their bias is downwards, that would account for the fall of the capital/output ratio and the rise of the rate of profit in the U.K. between the mid-70s and the mid-90s. But the extent of the error needed to make those movements appear when the capital/output ratio had actually been constant is improbably great. In Germany, for instance, our estimates (taking the values for single years) show the capital/output ratio as rising from 2.09 in 1874 to 3.32 in 1908, and the stock of capital itself as rising at an average annually compounded rate of 4.76 per cent. To keep the capital/output ratio constant the stock would have had to rise at no more than 3.39 per cent a year, and if this was the rate at which it actually did rise the estimates have overstated annual net investment by an average of 40 per cent. In the U.K. the extent of the error required to reconcile the apparent fall of the capital/output ratio from 3.21 in 1874 to 2:10 in 1895 with an actually constant ratio is even greater: the estimate of the capital stock shows it rising at less than one per cent a year, but if the capital/output ratio were actually constant the stock must have been rising at nearly 3 per cent a year. It is unlikely that the estimates are out so far as that. Part at least of the movements of Fig. 5.2 must be accepted as significant. They call for other explanations.

One such can be provided on the assumption of rigorous determination and close adjustment by the mechanism of the model. It is that progressive changes were taking place in the technical conditions of production expressed in the aggregate production function, and/or in the prospective rate of profit at which investible funds are readily forthcoming. It might be, for instance, that in Germany between 1874 and 1908 the course of technical change was raising the amount of capital required per unit of output, while it was lowering that amount in the U.K. between 1874 and 1895. But there seems little support for that in what we know of the two economies, and it is specially hard to see why the types of technical change their industries experienced at this time should have been opposite. The explanation by shifts in the supply of funds seems more probable. In Germany there was a willingness, conspicuous to contemporary observers, to invest in equipment and operate it at a lower rate of return than was looked for in the U.K., and this may have made it possible for the capital stock to be so expanded that its average and marginal productivities fell, and with the marginal the rate of return, without checking investment. In the U.K., on the other hand, where the market for funds was international, the higher rates of return offered overseas may have kept up the rate expected from investment at home and so reduced its amount. Between 1870 and 1900 capital per head failed to rise in U.K. industry, whereas in German industry it nearly doubled.

There remain some explanations that rest upon the possibility of the adjustment between marginal productivities and factor prices having been tolerant of divergences. Suppose, for instance, that a general rise in pay per man raises total pay, and this is compensated by an equal fall in profits. The total product, as valued at the sum of payments to factors, is unaffected, so that the capital/output ratio is unchanged, but the wage/income ratio goes up and the rate of profit down. The effects will be of the same kind if the increase in total pay is not offset, or is offset only partially, by a fall in profits: the total product at current prices will now be raised, but the capital stock valued at current prices will rise in the same proportion, and the capital/output ratio will remain unchanged, while again the wage/income ratio goes up and the rate of profit down. Another possibility with the same kind of outcome is that total profits are reduced without a compensating increase in total pay. To each of these possibilities there corresponds an opposite case in which it is profits that gain on pay: once again the capital/output ratio will be unchanged, but here it is the wage/income ratio that goes down and the rate of profit that rises.

We cannot hope simply by inspection of Fig. 5.2 to identify phases in which one or other of these various possibilities has predominated. The shifts we have just noticed that originate in factor shares may, and very probably will, have been taking place at the same time as those noticed earlier that originate in the technical conditions of production and the supply price of investible funds; and their influences may have offset or reinforced one another. But the most striking feature of Fig. 5.2 is the wide and opposite movements of the capital/output ratio and the rate of profit in Germany and the U.K. They go too far to be explained by lack of adjustment between marginal productivities and factor prices. We have seen that a possible explanation lies in the different conditions of the supply of investible funds in the two countries.

At the end of this discussion of variations we must remind ourselves that the shifts of the zones are less remarkable than their persistence over time and similarity between different economies, and that the wanderings of the variables are less remarkable than the narrowness of the zones that contain them. We are brought back to the neoclassical models of the growing economy as indications of what sort of technical conditions and human propensities may be doing the steadying in the actual world. Chief of these propensities for our present purpose seems to be the influx of enterprise and investible funds. [. . .]

5.10 Class Struggle and the Distribution of National Income*

1. Until fairly recently it was generally accepted that profits would decline *pro tanto* if wages were raised. Even though in the analysis of other phenomena Say's Law was not adhered to, at least not strictly, in this case the preservation of purchasing power was not put to doubt. The analysis of an increase or reduction in wage rates dealt with the physical consequences of this absolute shift from profit to wages or *vice versa*. In the case of rising wage rates the reconstruction of capital equipment in line with the higher spending on wage goods and lower outlays on investment and capitalists' consumption was emphasized. At the same time, there was assumed a tendency to higher unemployment as a result of substitution of capital for labour that has become more expensive.

Although quite a number of economists would argue in this fashion even today, the fallacy of this approach is widely recognized. It may be countered by various economists in somewhat different ways. My counterargument is based on the following assumptions: There is a closed economic system and a proportional rise of all wage rates. In a certain short period the annual wage bill increases as a result of the rise of wage rates by ΔW. The workers spend all their income immediately. The investments and capitalists' consumption are determined prior to the short period considered and are therefore not affected by the wage rise in this period.

If we subdivide the economy into three sectors producing (I) investment goods, (II) consumption goods for capitalists, and (III) wage goods — including the respective intermediate products —, it follows that employment in the first two sectors is not affected by the rise in wages. Thus, denoting the wage bills in these sectors measured in 'old' wage rates by W_1 and W_2 and the fraction by which wages are raised by α, we obtain for the increment in aggregate wages in sectors I and II $\alpha(W_1 + W_2)$. The profits in these two sectors decline *pro tanto* provided the prices of their products have not risen, which is assumed in the argument based on 'preservation of purchasing power'.

The position in sector III, however, is quite different because the workers immediately spend their additional proceeds. The increments of the wage bills in sectors I and II, equal to $\alpha(W_1 + W_2)$, must unavoidably cause profits in sector III to rise *pro tanto*, as the profits of this sector consist of the proceeds from the sale of the goods not consumed by the workers in sector III. Thus, the increments in the wage bills of these two sectors, $\alpha(W_1 + W_2)$, will cause an equal rise of profits in sector III. This may come about either through the rise in output in that sector or through a rise in the prices of its products. As a result total profits remain unaltered, the loss of sectors I and II of $\alpha(W_1 + W_2)$ being counterbalanced by an equal gain of sector III. It follows that no absolute shift from profits to wages occurs and the argument based on

*From Michal Kalecki, 'Class Struggle and the Distribution of National Income', *Kyklos*, Vol. 24, No. 1, 1971.

Say's Law would thus prove fallacious — at least in the short run.

This last qualification is essential. For it may be argued that the decline in the volume of investment and capitalists' consumption as a result of the wage increase would admittedly not come about immediately but would be delayed — possibly to the next short period. This would be true if the capitalists at least *decided* to cut their investments and consumption immediately after having agreed to wage increases. But even this is unlikely, for their decisions are based on current experience. This assumption according to the above will show that no loss in total profits occurs in the short period following the wage rise and that thus there will be no reason for a cut in investments and capitalists' consumption in the following period. If a decision for such a cut is not taken right away on the basis of the bare fact of the wage rise, it will not be taken at all. As a result, profits will not decrease in the next period either. The argument of a shift from profits to wages as a result of a wage rise based on Say's Law is therefore fallacious even if we consider all the ramifications of this event.

The same obviously applies to a wage cut: no increase in profits will occur either in the short period following it or subsequently.

2. So far we have assumed that prices of investment goods and consumption goods for capitalists remain unchanged when wages rise. This was in line with the theory of the shift from profits to wages to the extent of the wage increase. (The preceding section in a sense amounted to the *reductio ad absurdum* of this theory.) However, stable prices are unlikely in our case; they will rather rise under the impact of the wage increase (perhaps not in the short period following the wage rise but later on). But to discuss this question as well as other repercussions of a wage rise (or a wage cut) we want to know more about price formation in the system considered.

We shall first abstract from all semi-monopolistic and monopolistic factors, i.e. we shall assume the so-called 'perfect competition'. This is, however, a most unrealistic assumption not only for the present phase of capitalism but even for the so-called competitive capitalist economy of past centuries; surely this competition was always very imperfect in general. Perfect competition — when its real nature, that of a handy model, is forgotten — becomes a dangerous myth.

As follows from the argument in the preceding section, the volume of capitalists' investments and consumption is maintained in the short period following the wage rise and consequently thereafter. On the assumption of perfect competition and of supply curves sloping upwards at some point, the rise in wage rates must cause a proportional rise in prices at given levels of respective outputs (perhaps not in the first short period but later on). As a result profits in sectors I and II will rise in the same proportion as wages, i.e. $1 + \alpha$ times.

It is now easy to prove that the volume of production and consumption of wage goods remains also unaltered. Indeed, in such a case profits in sector III, similarly to those in the other two sectors, increase in proportion with the wage rise, i.e. $1 + \alpha$ times. As mentioned in section 1, profits in sector III are equal to the proceeds from sales of wage goods to the workers of the sectors I and II and therefore they must increase in the same proportion as the wages in these sectors, i.e. $1 + \alpha$ times. Should the volume of production and consumption of wage goods increase or decline, that could not be the case.

Hence, with perfect competition the volumes of production in all three sectors remain unchanged while their values increase each by $1 + \alpha$. The total wage bill and total profits increase therefore in the same proportion and the distribution of national income remains unaltered.

We have shown the fallacy of the theory based on Say's Law, which maintains that wage movements have a direct and full impact upon the distribution of national income, and arrive at the opposite statement that they have no influence upon this distribution at all. But such a conclusion is based on the untenable assumption of perfect competition. Only by dropping it and penetrating the world of imperfect competition and oligopolies are we able to draw any reasonable conclusion on the impact of bargaining for wages on the distribution of income.[1]

3. In fact, a major part of the economy may be plausibly represented by a model very different from perfect competition. Each firm in an industry sets the price p of its product by 'marking up' its direct cost u consisting of the average costs of wages plus raw materials in order to cover overheads and achieve profits. But this mark-up is dependent on 'competition', i.e. on the relation of the ensuing price p to the weighted average price of this product $\bar{p}$ for the industry as a whole. Or:

$$\frac{p-u}{u} = f\left(\frac{\bar{p}}{p}\right) \tag{1}$$

where f is an increasing function: the lower p is in relation to $\bar{p}$, the higher the mark-up will be fixed. From formula (1) we obtain:

$$p = u\left[1 + f\left(\frac{\bar{p}}{p}\right)\right]. \tag{2}$$

It should be noted that the function f may be different for various firms in an industry. It will reflect semi-monopolistic influences resulting from imperfect competition or oligopoly. The more intensive these factors are, the higher is $f(\bar{p}/p)$ corresponding to a given relation $\bar{p}/p$. Prices p will be in general different for various firms because of the differences in direct costs u and because of those in the function f.

The price system is determined. Indeed, with s firms in an industry there will be $s + 1$ price values to be determined, i.e. $p_1, p_2, \ldots, p_s, \bar{p}$, and as many equations: s equations of type (2) and one determining $\bar{p}$ in terms of $p_1, p_2, \ldots, p_s$.

If all direct costs u increase with given functions f by $1 + \alpha$, prices $p_1, p_2, \ldots, p_s$ will do so as well. Such a solution indeed satisfies (1) and (2) because u by assumption increases by $1 + \alpha$ and $\bar{p}/p$ remains unaltered. If, however, the direct cost u_k increases for one firm only (again with given functions f), it is easy to see that p_k increases in a lesser proportion because $\bar{p}$ will not rise in the same proportion as u_k.

4. Since prices p for a product are generally not equal, the above applies strictly to imperfect competition only or to differential oligopoly but not to non-differential oligopoly or monopoly. However, apart from basic raw materials produced frequently in conditions approaching perfect competition, most of the products do have differential prices. (Let us not forget that absolutely identical products with the same transport costs but different periods of delivery may have different prices.)

It seems therefore a fairly good approximation to an actual economy if we assume the model described above, while the sector of basic raw materials conforms in its price formation to the model of perfect competition.

Let us now imagine that in a closed system of this type wage rates in all industries increase in the same proportion, by $1 + \alpha$. It follows easily that all prices will also increase by $1 + \alpha$ *provided that the function f in industries to which they are relevant remains unchanged.* If these conditions are fulfilled, it follows that we shall reach the same conclusions as for a perfectly competitive economy described in section 2: a general increase in money wage rates in a closed economy will not change the distribution of national income. The same would apply to the case of decreasing money wage rates. However, we shall argue that the functions f do depend on the activity of the trade unions.

5. High mark-ups in existence will encourage strong trade unions to bargain for higher wages as they know that firms can afford to pay them. If their demands are met but the functions f are not changed, prices will also increase. This would lead to a new round of demand for higher wages and the process would go on with price levels constantly rising. But certainly an industry will not like such a process making its products more and more expensive and thus less competitive with products of other industries.[2] To sum up, the power of the trade unions restrains the mark-ups, i.e. it causes the values $f(\bar{p}/p)$ to be lower than they would be without their existence.

The power of the trade unions manifests itself in the scale of wage rises demanded and achieved. If an increase in bargaining capacity is demonstrated by spectacular achievements, there is a downward shift in functions $f(\bar{p}/p)$ and the mark-ups decline. A redistribution of national income from profits to wages will take place. But this redistribution is much smaller than it could be if prices were stable. The rise in wages is to a great extent shifted to consumers. 'Normal' wage increases will usually leave the functions f unaffected while otherwise mark-ups may tend to get higher because of the rise in the productivity of labour.

6. Let us imagine that a spectacular wage rise somewhat depresses the mark-ups so that a redistribution of national income from profits to wages occurs. From section 1 it follows that profits in sector III will increase in the same proportion as wage rates. However, as there is a redistribution of income from profits to wages as a result of the reduction of mark-ups in sector III, the wage

bill in sector III increases more than wage rates, i.e. there will be a rise in employment and output. Output and employment will stay unaltered in sectors I and II. In other words, the volume of investments and capitalists' consumption remains constant, while the workers' consumption will increase. Such an expansion of total output and employment will be feasible because our model of semi-monopolistic price fixing, as developed in section 3, presupposes the existence of excess capacities.

The money value of the wage bill will clearly increase more than wage rates. However, total profits will increase less than wage rates. Indeed, profits in sector III increase proportionately to wage rates, employment in sectors I and II remaining unaltered, but profits in the latter two sectors increase less than the wage rates as a result of the decline of mark-ups.[3]

If the power of the trade unions declined, the process described would be reversed. Employment and output in sectors I and II would remain unchanged, but in sector III they would decline. Or the volume of investment and capitalists' consumption would remain unchanged while the workers' consumption would fall. Total output and employment would thus decline. The value of the wage bill would fall more and the value of profits would fall less than wage rates.[4] Since the decline in mark-ups tends to increase aggregate output, this would cause a rise in the prices of basic raw materials, subject to conditions of perfect competition, in relation to wages. As a result the increase in output and employment would be somewhat restrained. In the same fashion this factor would somewhat restrain the decline of output and employment caused by the rise of the mark-ups. It follows from the above that a wage rise showing an increase in the power of the trade unions leads – contrary to the precepts of classical economics – to an increase in employment. Conversely, a fall in wages showing a weakening in their bargaining power leads to a decline in employment. The weakness of trade unions in a depression manifested in permitting wage cuts contributes to the deepening of unemployment rather than to relieving it.

7. It follows from the above that the class struggle as reflected in trade union bargaining may affect the distribution of national income but in a much more sophisticated fashion than expressed by the crude doctrine: when wages are raised, profits fall *pro tanto*. This doctrine proves to be entirely wrong. The shifts that occur are (a) connected with widespread imperfect competition and oligopoly in the capitalist system, and (b) contained in fairly narrow limits. However, the day-by-day bargaining process is an important co-determinant of the distribution of national income.

It should be noted that it is possible to devise other forms of class struggle than wage bargaining, which would affect the distribution of national income in a more direct way. Actions may, e.g., be taken for keeping down the cost of living. This may be achieved by price controls, which, however, may prove difficult to administer. But there exists an alternative: the subsidizing of prices of wage goods financed by a direct taxation of profits. Such an operation, by the way, will not affect aggregate net profits. The argument here is the same as in section 1 in the case of a wage increase. The same applies to the effect of price controls. If such measures cannot be carried out in parliament by political parties associated with trade unions, the power of the trade unions may be used to mobilise supporting strike movements. The classical day-by-day bargaining for wages is not the only way of influencing the distribution of national income to the advantage of the workers.

8. The redistribution of income from profits to wages as described in the last two sections is feasible only if excess capacity exists. Otherwise it is impossible to increase wages in relation to the prices of wage goods because prices are determined by demand, and the functions f become defunct. We return then to the position described in section 2 where the wage rise could not effect a redistribution of income.

Under these circumstances price control of wage goods will lead to scarcities of goods and haphazard distribution. Subsidizing prices of wage goods, too, can reduce prices only in the long run by stimulating investment in wage good industries.

It should be noted, however, that even contemporary capitalism, where deep depressions are avoided as a result of Government intervention, is generally still fairly remote from such a state of full utilization of resources. This is best shown by the fact that prices of finished goods are fixed on cost basis rather than determined by demand.

NOTES

1. We abstract here from the influence of the increase in the price level upon the rate of interest by assuming tacitly that the supply of money is elastic. Otherwise the higher demand for money would have increased the rate of interest which would affect adversely investments and consequently profits. Such an effect seems unlikely to be of any greater importance, especially because the changes in the bank rate are reflected in the long-term interest rate on a much reduced scale.
2. Despite the fact that for the sake of simplicity we assumed that all wage rates are raised simultaneously in the same proportion, we consider realistically that bargaining is proceeding by industries.
3. This, however, is subject to the following qualification. As a result of the increase of total output there will be an increase in prices of basic raw materials, *inter alia* of those used alike by sector I or II and sector III. This, although not very likely, may offset the influence of the decline in mark-ups in the sectors I and II upon the distribution of income between profits and wages. In any case, however, total profits will rise less than the total wage bill.
4. Subject to a qualification analogous to that stated in the preceding footnote.